A History
of the Catholic Church
in the United States

A History
of the Catholic Church
in the United States

Thomas T. McAvoy, C.S.C.

UNIVERSITY OF NOTRE DAME PRESS
NOTRE DAME   LONDON

Contents

On July 5, 1969, as this book was in the final stages of production, Thomas T. McAvoy, C.S.C., died suddenly in his office in the Archives at the University of Notre Dame. He was alone when death overtook him, working on a Saturday morning when the Archives were closed. But he was surrounded by books and papers familiar from a lifetime of usage, and he was immersed in the work he loved. Only a few days before had he completed the task of correcting the page proofs of this book. The popular history finished, he was already turning over in his mind what he would do next. At sixty-five he had slowed down a little on his doctor's advice, but he still had more than one book left in him. The thought that we shall never see them deepens our sorrow now. Those who knew Father McAvoy as a teacher, a colleague, a confrere in religion, or simply as a friend, have their private sorrow; but his death is also a serious loss to scholarship and to the Catholic Church in the United States.

But Father McAvoy never thought of himself as writing only for scholars. He wanted history to be of interest to the layman, the general reader. Whenever possible, he followed the narrative approach to win the reader's interest, always keeping in mind that he was telling a story. But it was facts that made the story true, that gave it weight. Hence his work was generously packed with circumstantial detail and sometimes interrupted for a statistical or factual review of the scene. The story of the past, like life itself, was complicated; it could not be shaped to preconceived theories, and it permitted few unambiguous conclusions. Despite his interpretive boldness and originality, Father McAvoy was therefore reluctant to deal in generalizations. He had the rare capacity to describe diverse historical personalities with sympathy and understanding. His preference was to tell their story, and let his readers draw whatever conclusions they wished after coming to know the men of the past and the problems they faced. This popular history embodies much that Father McAvoy knew, and exemplifies the method he liked best for sharing his knowledge. I hope its readers will glimpse the man behind its pages.

Philip Gleason
July 9, 1969

Introduction

The history of Roman Catholicism in the United States has resembled in many ways the history of the many peoples that form the American population. Just as all these peoples and races have formed the American people, so all these nationalities and peoples belonging to the Catholic Church have formed Roman Catholicism in the United States. There are differences, however, between these parallel entities. The dominant culture of the United States has been Anglo-American and in that sense predominantly Protestant. Although there have always been Catholics in the area now called the United States, at least since 1634, the American Catholic group has not been predominantly of English stock or traditions since the beginning of the nineteenth century. Yet American Catholicism as it has developed in this area has had to adapt itself to the Anglo-American cultural tradition without accepting also Protestantism in religion.

The cultural nucleus of American Catholicism has been the English Catholic group that settled first in Maryland and from there passed on in time to other parts of the country, chiefly to Pennsylvania and Kentucky at first and then to other areas. Roman Catholicism has been recognized as an American institution just insofar as it has been permeated by the spirit of this Anglo-American group, which was enlarged quickly by converts from Anglo-American Protestantism and from immigrants from

1

other cultures and their children who adopted permanently the American cultural traditions.

Religion is undoubtedly the most important element in a cultural tradition, yet the Anglo-American Catholics were above all faithful to their Catholicism while accepting the political, social, and economic elements in the American cultural tradition. Just as the population of the United States increased greatly by immigration as well as by the generation of children, so American Catholicism also increased but, since Great Britain continued to be a Protestant area, the Catholic immigrants from that area were comparatively few and the great increase in Catholics in the United States came chiefly through immigrants from non-English but Catholic areas of western Europe. There were at all times recognizable numbers of the immigrants from Great Britain and their descendants who were converted to Catholicism, and there were always non-English Catholics who seemed to adopt quickly the culture of their new country. Nevertheless by the fourth decade of the nineteenth century Roman Catholicism in the United States was predominantly a non-English minority of which the cultural leadership remained in the Anglo-American Catholic group and those who had adopted their traditions.

There is a further complication in this account of the growth of American Catholicism. Since the days of the English reformation the most important Catholic group in the English-speaking world—since Gaelic was spoken by only a minority of the Irish—were the Catholics of Ireland. In that English-speaking world wherever Catholicism survived, one could usually find at least some Irish Catholics upholding the standards of Catholicism. This was to be true of Catholicism in English America. Not only were there Irish Catholics in most of the port towns along the Atlantic coast, among them were soon found also priests of Irish nationality. Catholicism in English America would hardly have survived had it not been strengthened and supported by these Irish laymen and clergymen.

The Irish immigrant in the United States, even when he had been educated solely in the English language, was not an Englishman and had to accept a foreign cultural tradition while persevering in his Catholic faith. Since he usually spoke the language of America and accepted the American political and economic traditions, it was difficult for the Irishman to understand that he was not socially also an American except when he was forcefully reminded of the difference by his American neighbors of the English social tradition. It was quite patent that the social distinction was basically religious, but that did not make the distinction any less real and as a matter of fact the Irish—perhaps with justice—came to believe that the discrimination against them was solely religious.

A serious complication in the adoption of the Anglo-American traditions by these immigrant Irish arose out of the desperate circumstances under which they came to America. At best most of the Irish immigrants were poorer than the English immigrant, but the masses who came during and after the Great Famine of 1845–1846 were not only very poor, but to a high degree illiterate. It can scarcely be said that they brought with them much of their Irish cultural tradition besides their Catholic religion, which was their chief consolation in their desperate condition. There was no necessary connection between their poverty and ignorance on the one hand and their nationality or their religion on the other, but they did not possess the means of alleviating their poverty or ignorance, and thus the Irish Catholic ignorance and poverty were considered serious defects in the United States where the dominant Protestantism was Puritan in cast.

The middle period of American history is clouded over by the bitter struggle over slavery and other aspects of sectionalism; the middle period of American Catholicism is involved in the problem of the amalgamation of the Anglo-American nucleus with the overwhelming non-English Catholic immigrants who multiplied the number of Catholics in the country. Of these immigrants, the largest number were Irish. American Catholicism insofar at it had social position was still Anglo-American but in numbers it was an immigrant institution in which the leadership was dominantly Irish both in the hierarchy in the Church and in the politicians who rose to local leadership in civic life. The Anglo-American Catholics tended to partake in the problems of American social and political life, the Irish Catholics tended to fend for themselves, primarily in the political world of the large cities. There were no important differences in the religious life of the groups composing the Catholic minority in the middle period of American history in the nineteenth century—there was not even a notable discussion. The clergy spent themselves and their funds building churches, orphanages, and sometimes schools. There were never enough priests for all the settlements, and where Catholics were usually the most numerous they were also the most indigent.

After the Civil War as the new nationalism began to take shape —expressed notably in the celebration of the centennial of American Independence in 1876—the continued immigration of non-

English Catholics made difficult the organization of unified American Catholicism. Rome, while admiring the numerical growth of American Catholicism, was disturbed about the haphazard way in which it was growing and finally in 1884 insisted that the American hierarchy meet in the Third Plenary Council and adopt the Roman rules for government. But that did not solve the practical problem of how these hundreds of thousands of Catholics who spoke foreign tongues and knew little of American cultural traditions could be molded into a practical American Catholicism. Some, living in compact groups, insisted on retaining their foreign languages and traditions with their Catholicism; others resented being ruled by Catholics of other nationalities—particularly the Irish—since they saw the American bishop of such ancestry as really an Irishman. There developed a series of disagreements about foreign languages in the schools and churches, about the schools themselves, and about Americanization. These disagreements Rome suppressed but did not really solve, even on into the twentieth century.

In 1908 during the reorganization of the Roman curia, the Roman government of the Church in the United States was taken out of the hands of the Congregation of Propaganda Fide, a sign that American Catholicism had grown of age. But American Catholicism was a unity in name only, except for the accidental leadership of Cardinal James Gibbons, the only American Cardinal, holder of the first American see but forbidden to be a primate in the strict sense. An accidental circumstance of American entrance into World War I and the even more accidental circumstance of the need for some Catholic unity in the war created the National Catholic War Council in 1917. With papal benediction, that Council was succeeded by the National Catholic Welfare Council which expressed its grand concepts in a few pastorals before the divisive elements of the hierarchy silenced it and revived the old material and sectional divisions.

The American Catholicism that served particularly in World War II was a unity only in the war service. The traditional problem remained to be solved. Old nationalisms were indeed dying out, but the wounds from old battles were still apparent. Suddenly the spirit of Pope John XXIII, which revived all Roman Catholicism, gave new vigor to American Catholicism as well. There were already many movements seeking expression in American Catholicism before Pope John issued his call for the Council. The *aggiornamento* was more than a conciliar word. It signifies many things, many movements, which are affecting the very soul of American Catholicism.

To bring this story into a unity is the purpose of this volume. Some events must be overlooked to give perspective to the narrative, and some minor events may seem overemphasized because they are the manifestations of greater movements. Much of the earlier story has been told elsewhere in detail; there are fewer accounts of later movements. Undoubtedly the passage of time will give different evaluations of the recent decades; but there is no time like the present to see where we are and whence we have come to our present position.

Over the years the author has had many conversations and conferences with historians and researchers in American Catholicism who have undoubtedly added their knowledge and ideas to his. His students both in and outside of class have likewise helped clarify obscure events. Miss Mercedes Muenz, his associate archivist, has been particularly helpful. Professor Philip Gleason and Father Thomas Blantz have criticized parts of the manuscript. For these and many other contributions to the volume the author is deeply grateful.

CHAPTER ONE

Catholic Dissenters
Found a Colony

IN THE RELIGIOUS WORLD FOLLOWING
Vatican II, no one doubts that American Catholicism is part of the
universal Church. Whenever the American bishops, either individually or as a group, seem to be neglecting the prescriptions of
the Council, the more vocal portion of the Catholic press and
some portions of the general public are very critical of the delay
and nonconformance to the decrees. There is a new understanding
abroad in the country about the connection between Catholicism
in the United States and the Catholicism of Vatican II, but there
is not the same interest in the connection between historical American Catholicism and the general history of Roman Catholicism.
Many factors contribute to this failure to connect American Catholic history with general Catholic history. Undoubtedly, the most
important cause of confusion has been modern nationalism because
almost all American Catholic history has taken place since the rise
of the great Western European nationalities which have contended
for control of the Western world. To make the confusion worse
for the Church historian, in the past two centuries a new American nationalism has arisen in the English-speaking United States.
One can even make a further observation that, among the European immigrants, the resistance to acceptance of this American
nationality as an equal has been strongest among Roman Catholics. The chief reason for this resistance is the fact that the cultural
tradition of the United States is basically English and Protestant,

6

and the majority of American Catholics, whether they came from Ireland, Germany, Poland, the Slavonic areas, or from Italy, have been non-English.

The English world has been Protestant since the seventeenth century, and the American nationality for the most part has been described as Anglo-Saxon Protestant white. An American Catholicism does not fit easily into this pattern, because the majority of American Catholics have not been English. An American Catholicism is in that sense a contradiction in terms. In a sense, the condemnation by Pope Leo XIII of the so-called heresy of "Americanism" in 1899 was the high-water mark in this opposition of European Catholics to the acceptance of American Catholicism as a respected group. Consequently, to understand American Catholicism in the world after Vatican II, the religious observer must remember that, while there have been remarkable changes in American Catholicism, the body of American Catholics of Vatican II are the same forty or so millions who constituted American Catholicism before the Council and who have their roots in nineteenth-century American Catholicism.

American Catholicism begins in the seventeenth-century Maryland colony. In the seventeenth century, if one were to speak of Spanish America or New Spain, he would take for granted that the religious denomination of the newly settled lands would be Roman Catholic, whether they were in the heart of South America, in the island empire, or in the northern areas comprising Florida and New Spain or what is now Mexico. Likewise in speaking of the religion of New France, the religious denomination would also be Roman Catholic from the Gulf of Saint Lawrence through the Great Lakes and Mississippi valley to New Orleans. Those French who were not Roman Catholics settled generally in the English colonies. So likewise the colonists of the English colonies in the New World would naturally adhere to the English Church, generally Protestant, from Georgia to Maine. Yet, in speaking of the beginnings of Catholicism in the area now called the United States, one will find those beginnings in this Protestant English area, in Lord Baltimore's Maryland.

These English Protestant colonies generally offered no welcome to Catholics but there were English Catholics in the English colonies just as there remained a small minority of Catholics in England at the same time despite the general acceptance by the English people of Protestantism in the sixteenth and seventeenth centuries. For a brief time there was even this Catholic oasis in Maryland where Catholics enjoyed full religious liberty; but, for most of the time that is normally designated as the colonial period of the United States, Catholicism was proscribed and Catholics were merely tolerated, and that only in the colonies of Maryland and Pennsylvania. That is the reason that the history of Roman Catholicism in the United States has its origins in these two colonies and in the flowering of the Catholic minority there with its growth coming chiefly by immigration throughout the United States until it is now the largest single body of religious persons in the nation.

The minority position of Roman Catholics in the English-speaking world during the seventeenth century was primarily the result of the series of events sometimes called the Protestant Reformation in England by which most of the English Catholics, under the leadership of English kings and religious leaders, withdrew from Roman Catholicism. Except for their common rejection of Roman authority, English Protestants were much divided in their Protestant faith and at times the historian has difficulty distinguishing Anglicans from Puritans, Presbyterians from Independents, or recognizing other forms of English nonconformists. People who embraced nearly all these forms of English Protestantism migrated in some numbers to the English colonies in the New World before the American Revolution. Probably the most numerous, and, when there was a king, the dominant form of English Protestantism in the colonies was Anglicanism, whose adherents accepted the rule of the English bishops. More influential in what is now called New England were the Congregationalists, usually designated as Puritans. There were also great numbers of Presbyterians and other independents in the English colonies. Methodists in the eighteenth century could be considered within the Anglican Church for a while, but the Baptists were nonconformists. Farther to the left of these were the followers of George Fox, or the Friends, and undoubtedly there were a number who were to earn the name of deists by the decline of their Christian faith. Anglicanism was strongest in the southern states and in New York. Congregationalism was strongest in New England and wherever the New Englanders moved into New Jersey and New York. The Quakers were chiefly in Pennsylvania and New Jersey. The Presbyterians were strongest where the Scotch-Irish settled, especially in central and western Pennsylvania and in the Carolinas. The Baptists and Methodists grew in numbers among the middle and lower classes all along the coast. Thus, to study Catholicism in the English colonies in the seventeenth and eighteenth centuries, the historian has to turn from a majority who accepted the Protestant religious viewpoint to examine a small Catholic exception.

There were two motives impelling the English Catholics who sought to establish settlements in the New World.[1] Some hoped to find a refuge against persecution, and all hoped to achieve some measure of financial profit. In 1583, Sir George Peckham and Sir Thomas Gerard attempted the first English Catholic settlement. The project, under the direction of Sir Humphrey Gilbert, reached the coast of Maine but met disaster. Sir Humphrey Gilbert lost his life in the effort. A second attempt was made under Sir George Weymouth in 1605, but it did not achieve any settlement, although some explorers of the group skirted the coast of Maine. The first Catholic project which successfully established a Catholic colony in English America had the motive both of commercial success and the desire for religious toleration, although the man who planned the company, Sir George Calvert, did not live to see his colony established.

Sir George Calvert, born in 1582, was of noble family and had been educated at Oxford. He entered into the public service, eventually becoming a clerk in the Privy Council. In 1618, King James appointed him one of the Secretaries of State and gave him a grant of land in Ireland. Calvert had acquired early in his career an interest in America and had become a member of the Virginia Company in 1609. In 1620, he purchased from Sir William Vaughan his rights to the southern part of New Foundland and prepared to send there in 1621 a colony under the direction of Captain Edward Wynne. He sent out for a short time a colony called Ferryland, and, on receiving a favorable report from the colony, Calvert obtained from the King a charter on April 7, 1623, for the southeastern shore of New Foundland, which he named Avalon. Also Calvert had become a Roman Catholic in 1624. He first visited Avalon in 1627 and then returned there with forty new settlers and his wife in 1628. But the country was not suitable for his agricultural plans, and in 1629 he asked the King for a new charter for land in Virginia. However, when he visited Virginia with his wife he was not able to stay there because he could not take the oath of supremacy, which was contrary to his Catholic faith. Leaving his wife and some of his property in Virginia, Sir George Calvert, now Lord Baltimore, returned to England to seek a grant of his own. Although the details of the grant were settled by him, he died on April 15, 1632, two months before the

---

[1] For more detailed accounts of the beginnings in Maryland there are: John Gilmary Shea, *The Catholic Church in Colonial Days* (New York, 1886) pp. 17–43; J. Thomas Scharf, *History of Maryland,* 3 vol. (Baltimore, 1879) I, 24–81; Matthew Page Andrews, *The Founding of Maryland* (New York, 1933) pp. 1–66.

charter was actually granted to his son and heir, Cecilius Calvert, the second Lord Baltimore. As proprietor of the colony of Maryland, Calvert was granted over it the rights equal to that of the Palatine of Durham, a rich feudal barony in northern England. Although there was nothing in the charter that recognized Roman Catholicism, it is evident that George Calvert had intended to found a colony in which he and his fellow Catholics would enjoy religious liberty, and his son proceeded to carry out this interpretation of the grant. The new colony was named Maryland, land of Mary, in honor of Queen Henrietta Marie. It was a commercial venture set up in the manner of a feudal lordship.

But English Catholics did not rush to participate in Lord Baltimore's overseas venture. Some Catholics did not have the means; others hoped for the freedom in England, if not the restoration of Catholicism. Even Lord Baltimore, while planning freedom for Catholics in his colony, seemed content that all forms of English Christian belief should be tolerated in it. The seventeen gentlemen who joined in the enterprise were Catholics, but, of the more than two hundred laboring men, the majority were Protestants. Lord Baltimore asked the English Jesuit Superior, Father Richard Blount, to send some priests to the colony at their own expense and appointed his younger brother, Leonard Calvert, governor of the colony. There is some mystery about their leaving England on the two ships, the *Dove* and the *Ark* on November 22, 1633, because according to law, before leaving, they should have had to take the oath of allegiance with its elements against Roman Catholicism. Some say the Catholics boarded at the Isle of Wight. The ships visited Barbados on the way and then approached the coast of Virginia. Entering Chesapeake Bay and sailing up the Potomac River, the colonists landed at St. Clement's Island and offered their first Mass in thanksgiving on the feast of the Annunciation, March 25, 1634. This was a quiet beginning; they made a peace treaty with the Indians of the region, offering them gifts for the land and setting up, as soon as they could, a series of medieval baronies. The Jesuits, since they had come at their own expense, claimed the headrights of ordinary settlers and set up their own manor. Father Andrew White, who with Father Altham and Brother Thomas Gervase were the Jesuits of the colony, began immediately to instruct the Indians in the meaning of the Christian Faith.[2]

[2] Thomas Hughes, *History of the Society of Jesus in North America, Colonial and Federal*, Text (New York, 1908) I, 249–277. Scharf, note 1 above, pp. 52–81.

Besides the two brothers of Lord Baltimore, Leonard and George Calvert, the two Commissioners assigned by Cecil Calvert, Jerome Hawley and Thomas Cornwaleys, were Catholics as well as John Lewgar, the Secretary. The records are thus clear that the foundation of the Catholicity in the English colonies was the work of laymen. Cecil Calvert, the second Lord Baltimore, made clear in his instructions to his brother and the Commissioners that "they suffer no scandall nor offence to be given to any of the Protestants, whereby any just Complaint may hereafter be made to them, in Virginia or in England, and that for that end they Cause all Acts of Romane Catholique Religion to be done as privately as may be, and that they instruct all the Romane Catholiques to be silent upon all occasions of discourse concerning matters of Religion; and that the said Governor and Commissioners treat the Protestants with as much mildness and favor as Justice will permitt. . . ."[3] Later when the Jesuits began to accept grants of land from the converted Indians without the permission of the Governor and to claim the rights of the Church as they existed in Catholic countries, the Proprietor objected and appealed to the Sacred Congregation in Rome for other missionaries. But the Provincial of the Jesuits in England met with the Proprietor and agreed to make the Jesuits in the colony give up the Indian grants and abide by the laws of the colony. The Jesuits did obtain the lands or headrights to which, as settlers, they were entitled. This land was to be the chief support of the Church in Maryland during the colonial period.[4]

The Jesuit who was considered the representative of the clergy in the founding of Maryland was Father Andrew White, a learned priest already about fifty-five years old, who had taught theology in the colleges of Valladolid and Seville in Spain and had also spent several years in the mission in England. He and Father John Altham and Brother Thomas Gervase were soon joined by other Jesuits, but both Father Altham and Brother Thomas as well as Father Knolles, one of the newcomers, died within a few years after their arrival. The Jesuits were not permitted by the Governor at first to go among the Indians to live because the Governor was not sure that their lives would be safe among the natives. From St. Mary's, the first settlement, however, the Jesuits made brief trips to the Indian centers and began the conversion of the Indians, notably a chief and his wife. The first chapel of the colony

---

[3] Hughes, *Ibid.,* note 2 above, I, 260.
[4] Hughes, *Ibid.,* pp. 430–454. Andrews, note 1 above, pp. 162–172.

was set up by the Jesuits at St. Mary's, and regular services were held only there for some time. But at least by 1640, there were other Catholic congregations at the settlements of New Town and Port Tobacco, after the controversy between the Jesuits and the Proprietor had been settled. The land on which the chapel was erected was transferred to the Governor, and the Jesuits took title to their own lands and served both the Catholic English and the natives.

Of the Catholic laymen who helped Leonard and George Calvert establish the colony of Maryland, the chief, besides the Calverts, were Jerome Hawley and Thomas Cornwaleys, the Commissioners, and John Lewgar, the Secretary. The official list of founders of the colony mentions also Richard Gerard, Henry Wiseman, Edward and Frederick Wintour, Messrs. John Saunders, Edward Cranfield, Henry Greene, Nicholas Fairfax, John Baxter, Thomas Dorrell, John Medcalfe, William Saire, and Captain John Hill. The Jesuits were not listed. Other Catholics who figure in the early history of the colony include Cuthbert Fenwick, William Bretton, George Manners, John Mansell, Thomas Green, John Pile, Robert Clarke, John Price, and the members of the Brent family. Perhaps there is no clearer testimony of the fidelity of these pioneers than their fervent professions of faith in their last wills and testaments.

There was little of the lives of the Catholics in Maryland to distinguish them from their Protestant neighbors. In the setting up of the manors according to the feudal charters of the proprietorship, several manors were maintained by Catholics. This was important later because, being among the most respected citizens of the colony, they were preserved by the more cultivated of their Protestant friends from the grosser persecutions. These richer Catholics could likewise afford in their homes a place for religious services for the less fortunate Catholics of the neighborhood. The colonists had settled in a fertile region with mild temperatures which gave to the first Catholic leadership in English America a rural and agrarian quality. For want of a chronicler, we do not know the details of the religious life of the lay founders of the Church in English America, but their perseverance under trial and persecution earns for them a special place in the history of the Church in this country. However, Catholics were not to enjoy for long the toleration for which the colony was established and which had been proclaimed by its wise founders.

One who most persistently opposed the plans of the Calverts was William Claiborne of Virginia, who claimed title to Kent

Island along the Maryland coast in Chesapeake Bay, which Calvert regarded as part of Maryland. In England, Claiborne had even succeeded in preventing the granting of the charter for a while, and, after it was granted, he made claim to Kent Island, but the judges rejected his plea. Lord Baltimore, however, had invited him and other Puritans to join the Colony. When the Civil War broke out in England and the King was deposed, Claiborne, in 1645, with the aid of a pirate, Captain Richard Ingle, invaded the colony and pillaged the property of the Catholics, especially that of Commissioner Cornwaleys and of the Jesuits, whose records he burned. Claiborne and Ingle held the colony for two years until 1647, when Leonard Calvert with the aid of Cornwaleys and other Catholics drove them out. During the occupation by Claiborne, Fathers Andrew White and Thomas Copley were arrested and sent as prisoners to England for violating the laws against priests ordained abroad and coming to England. They pleaded that they had not come into the country but had been brought in as prisoners and obtained their release. During the invasion, two other Jesuits, Fathers Roger Rigbie and John Cooper, fled to Virginia, where they died shortly after. The Superior, Father Bernard Hartwell, was in Virginia at the time but also died before the colony was restored to the Calverts. Thus by 1647 there were no priests left in the colony. Leonard Calvert then appealed to the Jesuit Superior in England and Father Copley returned in January 1648 and was joined by Father Lawrence Starkey to take care of the Catholic colonists.

Before his death, Leonard Calvert had appointed Thomas Greene as temporary Governor. But his brother, Lord Baltimore, chose as the regular Governor William Stone, a Protestant, and gave him a set of instructions that were to be enacted into law. Among them were the principles that were to become the famous Maryland Religious Toleration Act of 1649. Actually, the law merely made legal the policies of toleration that Lord Baltimore had included in his instructions when the colony left England and that had been practiced except during the invasion of Claiborne and Ingle. The Act prohibited molesting anyone who professed to believe in Jesus Christ, either in his religion or in the free exercise thereof. Events in England were to show the necessity for the appointment of a friendly Protestant as Governor and the enactment of the principles of religious toleration. The Parliament of England, after beheading King Charles I, had forbidden the colonies to recognize his son as King Charles II. Stone, however, recognized Charles II. A fleet, sent to enforce the demands of Parliament, made Claiborne Governor of Virginia. At first Claiborne removed Stone as Governor, then reappointed him. When Claiborne heard that Lord Baltimore had refused to give up his Proprietorship of Maryland, he invaded Maryland and took over the government on July 22, 1654. He left Stone as Governor but enacted the English laws against Catholics. Governor Stone tried unsuccessfully to drive Claiborne out of the colony in 1655. Then in 1656, Parliament restored Baltimore to the Proprietorship, and he appointed Josias Fendall Governor. Fendall, however, was not loyal, and in the following years he plotted with another Puritan agitator, John Coode, against the Proprietor. When the Revolution of 1688 took place in England, these men rebelled against the existing Maryland government and took over the colony, sending their submission to King William and Queen Mary. The anti-Catholic laws were reenacted. Insofar as Maryland had ever been a refuge for Catholics in the English-speaking world, that refuge ceased to exist. The Catholics did not leave the colony, and only in Maryland during the colonial period were there to be Catholics of prominence and wealth who could act as leaders of their persecuted brethren.

A few years prior to the Revolution of 1688, under the governorship of Thomas Dongan, a Catholic, the New York colonial assembly passed a bill of rights on October 30, 1683, which allowed toleration to Catholics. Father Thomas Harvey, S.J., went to New York to attend the Governor, and there were plans for establishing a center of Jesuit activity in the colony for a brief period. Dongan was replaced as Governor in 1688, and the revolution of 1689 not only changed the government of the colony but brought about the repeal of the bill of rights and the end of the Catholic services, since Father Harvey fled to Virginia.

The efforts of these Catholic lay people to preserve their Faith had an additional handicap because they were dependent upon the Catholic minority in England to supply them with priests. In 1669, the papal representative at the English court, Abbate Claudio Agretti, wrote to Rome that there were only two priests to attend more than two thousand Catholics in the colony. These were Fathers William Pelham and Michael Forster. A helper, Father Peter Pelcan, came that year but was drowned a short time later. In 1672, a Franciscan, Father Thomas Massey, came and in 1674 Father John Pierron, a Jesuit from the French Maine missions, visited Maryland but did not remain. That same year two more Franciscans came, and in 1677 Father Michael Forster and Mr. Thomas Hothersall, Jesuits, founded a classical school at New

Town. But with the change in government the Catholics of Maryland returned to the status of the Catholic minority of Protestant England. A sheriffs' report on the status of Romish priests, brothers, and properties in 1698 reads as follows:

The Sheriff of Charles County:

Here are three Romish Priests, and one Lay Brother, vizt: Richd Hubbert Fryar, after the Order of St. Francis; Wm Hunter & Robt Brook, of the Order of the Jesuits; Wm Burley, Lay Brother; and the places of worship are, one Chapel, near Newport Town, about 40 feet feet long and about 20 feet wide, has been built above twenty years. Also another Chapel, at Major Wm Boroman's about 30 feet long and 20 wide, being within two miles of the aforesaid, and has been built about 16 or 18 years; also a place of worship commonly used at Priest Hubbert's own dwelling-house, about a mile and a half from the aforesaid Chapel, and another at M^r. Hunter's, living at Port Tobacco, a house fitting up for a Chapel near the dwelling-house of the said Hunter, which is the present place of meeting.

The Sheriff of St. Mary's County:

LIST OF ROMISH PRIESTS, &c.

M^r. John Hall, M^r. Nicholas Gewlick.
One Lay Brother at St. Inagoe's.

Chapels.

1 Brick Chapel at St. Mary's.
1 Wooden Chapel at M^r. Gewlick's Plantation.
1 Wooden Chapel at Clement's Town.
1 Wooden Chapel beyond Petuxant Road, near M^r. Hayward's.

The Sheriff of Talbot County:

No Romish Priest nor Lay Brother residing within the County; as to their places of worship, Clapboard house at Doncaster Town.

The Sheriff of Kent County:

No Popish Priest nor Lay Brother, nor public place of worship in this County; only 3 Papists, vizt:

Edm^d Mackdonall,
Tho. Collins,   } *Papists*.[5]
James Bruard,

In addition, while there were neither priest nor churches in Anne Arundel, Calvert, Baltimore, Prince George, and Dorchester Counties, there were private chapels.

Undoubtedly, there were scattered Catholics in the other colo-

---

[5] William Stevens Perry, D.D., ed., *Historical Collections Relating to the American Colonial Church*, 5 vol. (Hartford, 1870–1878) IV, 20–23.

nies, but only those in Virginia and Pennsylvania could hope to receive the ministrations of the priests in Maryland. Any isolated Catholics who landed in New York, in New England, or in the ports of the southern colonies could receive no priestly ministrations. The Toleration Act of 1689 enacted in England after the Revolution of 1688 gave toleration to all except Roman Catholics and is also a good measure of the position of the American Catholics under English rule at that time.

CHAPTER TWO

The Darkness before
the New Dawn

JUST AS IN WESTERN EUROPE AFTER THE Reformation the ruling power determined the religion of the nation, so in the colonies of those nations in the New World only one religion was tolerated. Roman Catholicism was the religion of the French, who settled along the shores of the Saint Lawrence, around the Great Lakes, and down the Mississippi valley, and of the Spanish, who remained in Florida and southwest of the French settlements on into Mexico and Central America. By the same reasoning, Roman Catholicism was despised and its adherents persecuted in the English colonies. The survival of even a small group of Roman Catholics in England and in the English colonies was remarkable after the Reformation era. Hatred of Catholicism had been aroused again in 1678 by the so-called Popish Plot of Titus Oates and by the renewal of opposition to Romanism in the Glorious Revolution of 1688–1689.

Some form of English Protestantism was the official religion of each of the English colonies. In New Hampshire, Massachusetts, and Connecticut, the Congregational or town church was the legal ecclesiastical establishment, to the support of which the taxpayers were obliged to contribute whether they were members of the congregation or not. In Rhode Island there was no establishment of any sort, but Roman Catholics were excluded. In New York, the Dutch Reformed Church as a legal establishment had fallen with the Dutch government in the colony at the time of the English

conquest, but Catholicism was not tolerated after the revolution
of 1689, and in 1693 the Anglican Church was established by law.
A somewhat similar situation existed in New Jersey, where the
Anglican Church was established by royal decree. In Pennsylvania
and Delaware, which were separated from one another in 1702,
there was no establishment, and some Catholics were to be found.
In Maryland, from 1692, and in the Carolinas, the Anglican
Church was the state church as it had been in Virginia from
the beginning.[1]

The difficulties which faced Catholics in England in the last
decades of the seventeenth century caused some of them to make
their way to Maryland, according to tradition, especially in the
years following the exposure of the so-called Popish Plot of Titus
Oates. Most of these settlers seemed to have belonged to the working classes and to have come as redemptioners, who worked out
the costs of their transportation to the New World. Among other
Catholics who found their way into Maryland and Pennsylvania
were Irish servants, against whom laws began to be enacted at the
end of the century. Likewise, the failure of James II to hold the
English throne was apparently not a surprise to all the English
Catholics. In the turmoil of the preceding decade, notably about
1681, the ancestors of several Maryland and Kentucky families of
today were among the redemptioners who came to Maryland.
There is some doubt that they and the other lower class Catholics
in Maryland would have been able to weather the storm of nearly
a century of religious oppression that followed the Revolution of
1688 if there had not been other Catholics among the wealthier
and gentleman-farmer class of the colonists. No history of these
Catholic families has yet been written. Nevertheless, among the
newcomers during the years immediately before that revolution
one name has figured importantly in the American Catholic history, that of Charles Carroll, whom the third Lord Baltimore,
Charles Calvert, sent with a writ appointing him the Attorney
General of the colony. On October 13, 1688, the twenty-eight-
year-old Carroll presented to the government of the colony the
commission making him Attorney General: "to prosecute and
defend all and all manner of suites and accons whatsoever any-
waies relateing to us or our Interest in the said Province," and
stating that he was to receive a salary of twelve thousand pounds

[1] James Truslow Adams, *Provincial Society, 1690–1763* (New York, 1927)
pp. 17–18.

of tobacco over and above "all manner of Fee Perquisites and advantages whatsoever. . . ."[2]

The accession of William and Mary eventually affected the position of Roman Catholics in the Maryland colony. By a strange coincidence the messenger that Lord Baltimore, after making his submission in England on February 27, 1689, sent to the colony to arrange the acceptance of King William and Queen Mary, died in Plymouth on the way to the colony. In the colony in the meantime there was excitement, and on August 25 Colonel Henry Jowles sent word to the Provincial Council in session at St. Mary's that three thousand Indians were at the head of the Patuxent River marching toward the interior settlement. The Council sent Colonel Digges with arms and Colonel Henry Darnall to Jowles to investigate. They reported that the rumors of Indian invasion were without foundation.[3] However, in the absence of any message of submission from Lord Baltimore, John Coode had formed an "Association in Arms" in April 1689. On July 16, Coode and Colonel Jowles with about seven hundred of the Associators assembled on the Potomac river to protect the Protestants against a rumored plot of the Papists and the Indians. They marched against St. Mary's. Colonel Digges with a hundred men attempted to defend the State House, but, being outnumbered, surrendered. Coode took possession of the State House and issued a statement defending his action and expressing submission to King William and Queen Mary.

Besides charging the government with excessive fees, seizures of Protestants in their homes, and failure to cooperate with the new sovereigns, the Associators' long declaration gave as their reasons for acting: "to preserve, vindicate and assert the sovereigne Dominion and right of King William and Queen Mary to this Province, to defend the Protestant religion among us and to protect and shelter the Inhabitants from all manner of violence, oppression and destruction. . . ."[4] The existing government surrendered at Mattapany where they had gone on August 1. Coode and the Associators drew up an address to King William and Queen Mary on August 3 and ordered the people to elect a new Assembly to replace the Papists and those who had acted against the new rulers. King William received the declarations of the new

[2] *Archives of Maryland,* VIII, 48.

[3] J. Thomas Scharf, *History of Maryland,* 3 vol. (Baltimore, 1879) I, 307–319.

[4] *Ibid.,* p. 314.

Assembly with its charges against Papists and especially against the Proprietor, and issued in August 1691 a commission to Lionel Copley as the First Royal Governor of Maryland. Copley arrived in Maryland early in 1692 and reorganized the colonial government.

The first act of the Assembly under Copley recognized the title of William and Mary. The next act made the Church of England the established church of the Province, dividing the colony into thirty-one parishes and imposing a tax of forty pounds upon each taxable person for the building of churches and the support of the Anglican clergy. This act was annulled and a more exact law enacted in 1702.[5] Copley died September 12, 1693, and Sir Thomas Lawrence, his former secretary, took office until the arrival in late July 1694 of the next governor, Francis Nicholson. Nicholson called the Assembly but had them meet not at St. Mary's but at Annapolis, then called Anne Arundel town. At this session the capital of the colony was removed to that place, obviously because St. Mary's was so Catholic and so much attached to the Proprietor. The decision took from St. Mary's its public buildings and its importance. Catholics, since they could not take the prescribed oath for voting or holding office, were in part disfranchised.

Catholics protested in vain, sending letters to the new monarchs, denying the stories about plottings between them and the Indians, and pledging their loyalty, but to no avail. The priests in the colony at that time seem to have been three Jesuits, Nicholas Gulick, William Hunter, and Francis Pennington, and a Franciscan, apparently Basil Hobart.[6] Charles Carroll protested so vehemently that he was put in jail. Allowed out of jail on bail, he renewed his protests and was again jailed, this time without bail. Eventually he was released and began his career as a lawyer. Carroll was a likeable young man of talent and a good lawyer. He did not lack clients, even among those who did not share his religious faith. When the capital was moved to Annapolis, he moved there also, and continued to look after the interests of the Proprietor, Lord Baltimore. He opened in Annapolis a store and imported from England his dry goods, which he sold at a great profit. An increasing acreage of farmland was granted to him by the Proprietor until finally he owned about sixty thousand acres. The money he made from these enterprises, he loaned out, also at a good inter-

---

[5] *Ibid.*, p. 343.
[6] John Gilmary Shea, *The Catholic Church in Colonial Days* (New York, 1886) p. 348.

est. Thus, Charles Carroll was reported to be among the richest men in the colony and maintained his freedom despite his sharp wit and ready tongue because of his attractive personality and his available wealth.[7]

Other Jesuits arrived from England to minister to the Catholics in the colony, and they were joined by Father Thomas Harvey, S.J., who had been forced out of New York. A census of Papists in 1696–1697 listed four chapels in St. Mary's county with two priests and one lay brother; in Charles County, four chapels with three priests and one lay brother, and one chapel in Talbot County. In 1697, when an epidemic broke out in the colony, the valiant services of the priests in caring for the sick drew attention and some conversions resulted. The Assembly felt called upon to threaten the priests with expulsion if they did not desist from their effort to convert the Protestants, and Father Hunter was silenced by special act.

In 1700 the Assembly passed a law requiring the use of the Book of Common Prayer in all religious assemblies but, since this was against the practices of the dissenting Protestants, the law was vetoed. In 1702, the toleration granted to Anglicans was extended to all Protestant dissenters. Catholics alone remained outside the law. In 1704 the Governor summoned Fathers William Hunter and Robert Brooke, Jesuits, to appear before him on September 11 on the charge of consecrating a chapel contrary to the laws. When they asked to be accompanied by Charles Carroll as their lawyer their request was turned down. The Fathers could justly answer that they had not consecrated the chapel, because that was an episcopal function. The priests were then released but warned that they would suffer severe penalties if they did not cease their activities.[8] The House of Delegates of the Assembly passed a resolution as a result of these actions praising the religious activity of the bigoted Governor John Seymour and suggesting the closing of the Catholic chapel at St. Mary's. In the meantime the same kind of laws against Catholics, especially against priests, had been enacted in Massachusetts and New York.

Charles Carroll, called the Attorney General, lived until 1720 and was survived by his second wife, Mary Darnall Carroll, and

---

[7] Some documents on the imprisonment of Charles Carroll are printed in vol. VIII of the *Maryland Archives*. Cf. also Kate Mason Rowland, *The Life of Charles Carroll of Carrollton, 1737–1832*, 2 vol. (New York, 1898) I, 5, 6, and Ellen Hart Smith, *Charles Carroll of Carrollton* (Cambridge, 1942) pp. 12–16.

[8] Shea, note 6 above, pp. 353–356.

four of their ten children. There were three sons, one of whom, Henry, died returning from his education in law at Gray's Inn in London. The second son bore the father's name and was eighteen at the death of his father; he had to give up his studies to manage the family affairs. The youngest son, Daniel, was able to complete his education. By reason of the wealth and social prestige of the founder of the Maryland Carrolls, his descendants were in a sense immune to the worst of the persecution from the Protestants, but that was not true of the ordinary Catholic colonists of Maryland.[9]

On October 3, 1704, the General Assembly under the direction of Governor Seymour, passed a law containing several anti-Catholic measures. By them, Catholic priests or bishops were forbidden to convert children or to perform any Catholic function, even privately, with a penalty for conviction of fifty pounds or six months in prison; for a second conviction, the penalty was to be deportation to England. Catholic children were called to take the oath of allegiance within six months after they attained their majority under the penalty of being incapable of taking lands by descent, with the nearest Protestant kin succeeding to the inheritance. Anyone sending his child abroad to be educated in the Catholic faith was to forfeit one hundred pounds, and Protestant children of Popish parents were not to be impelled to join the Papists. Even the non-Catholics found these laws objectionable and forced the Governor to reconvene the Assembly on December 9 and make inoperative for eighteen months the prohibition against Catholic services in a Catholic home. By an act of the Assembly of April 15, 1707, under the demand of Queen Anne, the Assembly revoked the Act of 1704 insofar as it concerned services in a private family. But in the same session of the Assembly, a law was passed against the introduction of Irish Catholic workers into the colony under penalty of a fine of twenty shillings. In 1717 the tax on Irish laborers was doubled, and within sixteen years twelve such prohibitions against the importing of Irish Catholic servants were passed. It was evident that Irish Catholics were selling themselves as servants to get to the colony.

In 1708 the General Assembly passed a law requiring the sheriffs of the various counties to take a census of Catholics. According to the returns from this census Catholics in Maryland numbered only 2,974 out of approximately 40,000. The largest group was in St. Mary's County, 1,238. Next were 709 in Charles County and 248 in Prince George County. There were 179 in Queen Anne County,

[9] Rowland, note 7 above, I, 9.

and 161 in Anne Arundell County. Other counties had: Baltimore, 53; Calvert, 28; Cecil, 49; Kent, 40; Talbot, 87; Dorchester, 79; and Somerset, 81. The priests listed were Fathers William Hunter, S.J., Superior; Robert Brooke, S.J.; William Wood, S.J.; George Thorold, S.J., and Thomas Mansell, S.J., who had come in 1700. There was no legal support for any of them, and the Catholic services could not be held publicly. Attached to the homes of the more prosperous Catholic landholders usually was a small building which contained a chapel for Mass and similar services.

A further blow to the Catholics of the colony came when Benedict Leonard Calvert, the fourth Lord Baltimore, gave up his Catholicism and became a Protestant in 1713. He did not long survive his apostasy, and his son, Charles Calvert, a child, succeeded him on April 5, 1715. Since the son was also a Protestant, the King, now George I, restored the Proprietorship to him, with the full rights of government. Because the Catholics celebrated the restoration of the proprietorship, the Protestants felt impelled to renew their demand that all who participated in the government of the colony must take the oaths of allegiance, which the Catholics could not take. This prohibition was renewed with vigor in 1718 and Catholics were subject at times to double taxation.

When Queen Anne died in 1714, Charles Carroll was in England as he was also when the third Lord Baltimore died the same year. He aided the widow as an attorney and returned to Maryland with a new commission from her son, the Protestant Lord Baltimore, to continue to look after the Proprietor's interests. This appointment was very annoying to the Protestant Governor, John Hart.

Later, the second Charles Carroll was as shrewd as his father in business and increased the family wealth, acquiring some reputation for harshness in his business dealings. He built himself a home at Annapolis and married a cousin, Elizabeth Brooke. They had but one child, Charles Carroll of Carrollton.

In the meantime on July 10, 1706, Father Mansell obtained four hundred fifty-eight acres a few miles southeast of the junction of the Great and Little Bohemian Rivers near the Pennsylvania border and added to it the St. Inigo tract given by James Heath, a Catholic Proprietor. This Bohemia Manor was to be a center for missions in Delaware, Pennsylvania, and the nearby regions of Maryland. In 1711 four Jesuits arrived from England, Peter Attwood, Francis Beaumont, Charles Brockholes, and Thomas Hodgson. In his instruction of September 12, 1712, Charles Calvert, the third Lord Baltimore, instructed Charles Carroll to pay yearly eight thousand pounds of tobacco to Mr.

Robert Brooke and his companions and one thousand pounds to Mr. James Haddock, the Franciscan. The Proprietor continued to support the missionaries until the apostasy of Benedict Leonard Calvert in 1713.

The conversions to Catholicism in the colony continued despite the persecution and despite the apostasy of a few others such as Charles Carroll, a cousin of the Proprietor's representative, and further legislation against Catholics was enacted by the Assembly. On April 26, 1715, an oath of allegiance to King George was required of all officials. This oath contained the declaration against the Pope. Another act of July 17, 1716, required four oaths of officials: of allegiance to King George, abhorring the Pope's right to depose sovereigns, abjuring King James II, and that the swearer did not believe in Transubstantiation. Further the law decreed that if any official attended a Catholic service he would forfeit his office.

Of the Roman Catholics in other colonies there are only surmises in most cases. Undoubtedly, there were some in nearly every port of entry but, without priestly ministrations or Catholic companionship, most of them lost the Faith. Both Virginia and Pennsylvania could be served by the priests from Maryland at times. Pennsylvania in its laws had extended toleration to all who believed in Christ, and Catholics who resented the anti-Catholic laws in Maryland went to that colony. According to one account, there was a Roman Catholic with Daniel Pastorius when he came to Pennsylvania in 1683. Also one of the original purchasers of land in the colony was a J. Gray, alias Tatham, a Catholic, who died in 1701. He was appointed Governor of East and West Jersey but he could not serve because of the oaths of office. A George Q. Nixon from County Wexford in Ireland came to the colony, but his children did not remain in the Church. Most of the French who came to the colony were Huguenots, but a Peter Dubuc, who died in 1693, apparently was a Catholic since he left goods to a Father Smith, one of the names used by the priests attending the Catholics in the colony. Some say that this Father Smith was Father Thomas Harvey.[10] The Jesuits of Maryland visiting in Pennsylvania made occasional converts, such as Lionel Britten in Philadelphia in 1707. There is no official record of their activities until Father Joseph Greaton began to attend Philadelphia in 1720. He remained there until 1729, a year in which Pennsylvania also passed a bill against the importation of popish servants. The first chapel in Philadel-

[10] Joseph L. J. Kirlin, *Catholicity in Philadelphia* (Philadelphia, 1909) pp. 14–17.

phia was not built until 1733. It was dedicated to St. Joseph.

In Maryland, the faithful Catholics continued their struggle against anti-Catholic pressure. In 1720 Father Haddock, the Franciscan, died. In 1722 the Jesuits obtained from Bishop Bonaventure Giffard, the Vicar Apostolic of the London District, an exemption from the observance of the Holy Days from May to September except Ascension, Whitmonday, Corpus Christi, and Assumption. At that time there were twelve Jesuit priests in Maryland and four "temporal coadjutors" who took care of the farm, now the only means of support for the missionaries. Father William Hunter died in 1723 and Father Mansell in 1724, but six new Jesuits arrived that year: Fathers John Bennett, James Whitgrave, Francis Floyd, Henry Whetenhall, Peter Davis, and James Case. When George II came to the throne, the Roman Catholics of Maryland sent a letter pledging their allegiance and congratulating the new monarch. They did the same to Charles Calvert, the fifth Lord Baltimore, when he came to the Proprietorship, even though he was not a Catholic.

In other colonies at this time, there are occasional evidences of Catholics in New York, and in 1741 a certain John Ury was tried on the charge of inciting a Negro riot and of being a priest. He was not permitted to defend himself and was hanged August 15, 1741, but it is evident that he was not a priest. In Pennsylvania there are evidences of a chapel near Nicetown, close to Philadelphia, in 1729, a gift of an Elizabeth McGawley. From 1730 to 1750 Father Greaton worked in and around Philadelphia and was succeeded by Father Robert Harding, who supervised the erection of St. Mary's Chapel. In 1741 two German Jesuits, Fathers Theodore Schneider and William Wapeler were sent to Philadelphia to care for the German immigrants. Father Schneider, in 1741, visited Catholics living near Frankfort and Germantown. Other Catholics were living near Conewago, where John Digges and some other Catholics settled in 1727. They were visited by Father Wapeler until he returned to Europe in 1748 and by Father Henry Neale, who succeeded him. Father Schneider visited Catholics in Germantown, Cedar Creek, Lebanon, North Wales, and New Furnace, and in 1743 Goshenhoppen, Haycock, Conewago, and Frankfort. He visited at times, also, Salem, New Jersey, although Catholics were banned by law in that colony. About this time Father Steinmeyer, called Ferdinand Farmer, began his mission to Lancaster in Pennsylvania.[11]

The lives of the Catholics in Maryland were frequently dis-

[11] Shea, note 6 above, pp. 386–394.

turbed by charges that they were planning to overthrow the Protestant government, and, when the English were engaged in the wars with the French, Catholics were regularly accused of conspiring with the French. They were not allowed to serve in the militia and were instead taxed doubly to pay for the expenses of the wars. Their lives were further complicated when Prince Edward in England raised a revolt against the King in 1745, although there was no trace of participation in the revolt in the colony. In 1751 when a bill was presented in the Upper House of the Maryland Assembly, "To Prevent the Growth of Popery," the Catholics sent a remonstrance to the Governor, Samuel Ogle, and to the Upper House, "The Humble Petition and Remonstrance of Charles Carroll in behalf of Himself and all the other Roman Catholics of the Province of Maryland." While appealing to the traditions of toleration under which the province had been established by the Calverts, Carroll pleaded: "That your petitioner was born in Maryland and has lived therein in a state of Manhood upwards of thirty years; that during that time he does not know nor has he heard that the Roman Catholics as a body have given any just grounds of complaint to the Government, or any one . . . in it but on the contrary have always behaved with as much decency and Regard to the laws of the Land as any people of any religious society whatsoever."[12] He said that the bill against Catholics had already passed the Lower House but that, as Catholics, they could not be present to protest. He further stated that Catholics have "constantly and quickly submitted to the civil power." The signers of the petition besides Carroll were W. Digges, H. Roger, Basil Waring, Dan'l Carroll, Clement Hill, Ignatius Digges, Henry Darnall, P. Mannor, Phil Darnall, and Henry Brooke.[13]

The remonstrance had little effect on the Lower House of the Assembly because that body tried to confiscate the Jesuit Properties in 1754. In August 1755, when reports were circulated about activities of Negroes and Catholics and about the unexplained absences of Roman Catholic priests from their homes, the Governor required the officials of the various counties to make a report of such activities. The charges were denied by officials of the counties of St. Mary's, Charles, Anne Arundel, Kent, and Chester (three males and eight females of little property), Worcester, Talbot, Frederick (none), Somerset, and Dorchester.[14] Later Gover-

[12] Document in the British Museum. Papers relating to New Hampshire, Rhode Island, Pennsylvania, Maryland, etc., 15489.

[13] Ibid.

[14] Report of Governor Sharpe, August 15, 1755, British Museum, as in note 12 above.

nor Horatio Sharpe defended the Catholics in the colony against charges reaching England. But Cecilius Calvert wrote to Sharpe on March 3, 1758, about Charles Carroll, ". . . As a Romanist he seems Jesuitical, Crafty & of Tergiversation subtil, tending agst the New Administrators who have been admitted by the Present Proprietor to have proved themselves by real service."[15] Charles Carroll himself, when he went to France in 1757 to visit his son at St. Omer's, approached King Louis with a proposal that he be granted property in Louisiana where he might enjoy religious peace. Of this, Governor Sharpe wrote to William Sharpe on July 6, 1757:

One Mr Charles Carroll who is at the Head of that Sect & is possessed of a Fortune of £30,000 or £40,000 Stg among us has taken a passage to England in a Vessel that lately sailed hence & will probably be in London before this can be dld [sic]. What his Views or Intentions are in taking such a Voyage at this time I know not. It has been said that he has Thoughts of leaving Maryland & carrying his Fortune to Europe. He has a Son about 22 years of Age now at Paris & if he should determine to spend the Remainder of His Life in Europe it is not improbable that he will take Up his Residence in some part of France as he seems by sending his Son to that Kingdom while he was very Young & by supporting him there since he has finished his Studies to prefer that Country. He is a sensible man, has read much & is well acquainted with the Constitution & Strength of these American Colonies. If he is inclined to give the Enemy any Intelligence about our American Affairs none is more capable, but indeed I do not conceive that he has any such Inclination. He was heretofore a bitter Enemy to the Lord Proprietary but having behaved with moderation since I came hither we were on good Terms till I incurred his Displeasure by assenting to an Act which I thought equitable & which you say appears to you in the same Light. since that time all Correspondence between us has been broken off. . . .[16]

In 1755 the English Government, engaged in constant warfare against the French, had decided to expel the French Catholics from Acadia, the area on the eastern coast of Canada taken from France in 1713. The expulsion of these Acadians was carried out with heartless cruelty. There were about seven thousand of them, of whom five hundred from Minas, Piziquid, and Cobequid and Rivière du Canard were sent to North Carolina, one thousand to Virginia, two thousand to Maryland. From Annapolis River, three hundred were sent to Philadelphia, two hundred to New York, three hundred to Connecticut, and two hundred to Boston. About five hundred escaped into the woods. In fact hundreds

[15] *Archives of Maryland*, XXXI, 500–501.
[16] *Archives of Maryland*, IX, 46.

came to Massachusetts, where they could not obtain the ministrations of their religion. Those who fled to New York also found themselves without priests. Only in Pennsylvania and Maryland did they find the ministrations of a priest. Although the officials in Maryland were unable to force the Protestants to receive these exiles, some in Baltimore were attended by Father John Ashton, and they set up a chapel in one of the houses there. Ashton was residing at the Carroll country home, Doughoregan. Some Acadians remained in Maryland, and some of these lost the Faith. Their fate in the other colonies varied although many of them made their way to the French Catholic colony of Louisiana, settling in what has been called Evangeline country after the heroine of Longfellow's poem. Acadians who came into the English colonies may have increased the number of the Catholic faithful in some settlements, but they added neither wealth nor prestige to the Catholic community in the English colonies.[17]

When the final war between England and France, the so-called Seven Years' War, broke out in 1754 and General Braddock was defeated at Fort Duquesne, some agitators aroused considerable feeling against Catholics, who were charged with being in league with the French and Spanish. Catholics could boast in reply that they had oversubscribed their share of the money raised for the defense of the frontier against the French and Indians. Yet the bill assessing taxes for the war imposed double taxes on Catholics. This was the bill that caused Charles Carroll to refuse to deal with Governor Sharpe. There were several other anti-Catholic measures introduced into the Lower House, and some of them passed but were rejected by the Upper House. Governor Sharpe, who had defended the loyalty of the Catholics, claimed that the Protestant clergy and others who were urging these laws sought to share in the properties of the Catholics. Father James Beadnall, S.J., was arrested for saying Mass in a private home and for attempting to convert a Quaker, but he was not proved guilty. A deserter from the French who claimed that he was a French spy and had carried on correspondence with a Catholic priest was proved in court to be lying. In Berks County, Pennsylvania, there was some clamor that Catholics in the colony would unite with the French against the colony. Lord Loudon, the Commander of the English forces, did make some inquiries about the number of Catholics in the colony. His report indicates that in and near Philadelphia there were 72 men and 78 women, Irish or English, and in Chester County, 18

[17] Shea, note 6 above, pp. 421–439.

men and 22 women under the care of Father Robert Harding. Father Theodore Schneider at Goshenhoppen had under his care 107 men and 121 women, all Germans, in and about Philadelphia and also in Berks and Chester Counties, apparently also Germans. Father Ferdinand Farmer at Lancaster had under his care 208 Irish and German men and 168 women in Lancaster, Berks, Chester, and Cumberland Counties. Father Manners at Conewago had in York County 89 men and 100 women, including Irish and Germans. There were churches at Goshenhoppen, St. Joseph's in Philadelphia, and in Lancaster. The colonial government required the Catholics to surrender within a month all their arms and ammunition. Those who would have been able to serve in the militia, from which they were excluded by their religion, had to pay a tax of twenty shillings.

On July 23, 1765, Father George Hunter, the Jesuit Superior, estimated that there were 10,000 Catholics in the two colonies of Maryland and Pennsylvania. The stations and missionaries he reported as follows: Assumption at St. Inigoes, 1 missionary; St. Xavier's at New Town, 3 missionaries; St. Ignatius at Port Tobacco, 3 missionaries; St. Francis Borgia at Whitemarsh, 2 missionaries; St. Joseph at Deer Creek, 1 missionary; St. Stanislaus at Frederick, 1 missionary; St. Mary at Queenstown or Tuckahoe, 1 missionary; St. Xavier at Bohemia, 1 missionary; St. Joseph at Philadelphia, 2 missionaries; St. Paul at Goshenhoppen, 1 missionary; St. John Nepomucene at Lancaster, 1 missionary; and St. Francis Regis at Conewago, 1 missionary. In Delaware there were 6 Catholic families at Dover who were attended once a month by a priest from Maryland.[18]

In 1750 Charles Carroll had purchased 12,000 acres on the Potomac and Monocacy Rivers and let it out in small farms. Many of the tenants were Catholics, such as the Darnalls, Abells, Paynes, Brooks, Jamesons, and Jarboes. These attended the mission center of St. Stanislaus at Frederick. There are no records of Catholics at this time in Virginia or New York, and there were no churches in New Jersey.

Because public chapels were not allowed, the more important landowners in Maryland built a chapel in a wing attached to their home in which the Catholics of the neighborhood would attend Mass and receive the ministrations of the priests. The Maryland Catholics were rural, many of them owning large manors with slaves, although there were also many Catholics among the tenants

---

[18] Shea, note 6 above, pp. 449–450.

of smaller farms. Catholic education had to be conducted in the home, although the Jesuits did maintain a kind of preparatory school at Bohemia Manor, which the sons of the wealthier Catholics attended. Among the youngsters at this school were Charles Carroll of Carrollton, and John Carroll, the future Bishop. For further schooling these youngsters were sent overseas to St. Omer's in Flanders. Charles Carroll, who called himself "of Carrollton," went from St. Omer's to various colleges in France and then to England for four years. He became enamored of a young lady in England but her father would not consent to the marriage. He returned to America in 1765 to find Maryland already engaged in tax disputes with the mother country that would eventually bring on the American Revolution.

As frequently happens when the public becomes deeply interested in a political discussion, the tendency toward religious bigotry suffered eclipse. No laws were repealed against Catholics, but there seems to have been a period of toleration once the Catholic enemy, France, had been disposed of in the Treaty of 1763. The Jesuits were able to visit the Catholics of the colony and in neighboring Pennsylvania. Their superior, Father George Hunter, rebuilt the house at Port Tobacco and lived there. At Frederick, Father John Williams had a chapel in his residence. At New Town, Father James Ashbey rebuilt the Church of St. Francis Xavier. These missions were, in general, supported by the income from the farms. At St. Xavier's in New Town, for example, the three missionaries had 1,500 acres with an income of 88 pounds; Assumption at St. Inigoes with one missionary had 2,000 acres with an income of 90 pounds. St. Ignatius at Port Tobacco with three missionaries had 4,400 acres with an income of 188 pounds; St. Francis Borgia at Whitemarsh with two missionaries had 3,500 acres with an income of 188 pounds; St. Joseph at Deer Creek with one missionary had 127 acres with an income of 24 pounds; St. Stanislaus of Frederick had three lots from which the missionary, Father John Williams, received no income but received instead 30 pounds from the Superior; St. Mary's at Queenstown or Tuckahoe had one missionary, Father Mosley, with 200 acres and an income of 18 pounds; and St. Francis Xavier at Bohemia on the eastern shore had 1500 acres and an income of 108 pounds. In Pennsylvania St. Mary's of Philadelphia was attended by Fathers Harding and Farmer. The latter also attended St. Joseph's. They received 45 pounds from the rent of property, 20 pounds from the Sir John James Fund, and 25 pounds from regular gifts. At St. Paul's in Goshenhoppen, Father John Baptist de Ritter had a farm of

500 acres which gave him an income of 45 pounds, and he received also 20 pounds from London. The mission of St. John Nepomucene at Lancaster had lots in town from which the income was 4 pounds, 5 shillings to which the missionary added also 20 pounds from London. Father Farmer visited New Jersey and perhaps New York.

This gives us some notion of the skeleton of the Catholic organization at this time. Each of the missionaries attended an area about 130 miles long by 35 miles wide. There were about 3,000 adult Catholics in Pennsylvania and about 10,000 adult Catholics in Maryland. There were 19 Jesuits listed in the missions at this time. Father John Walton succeeded Father William at Frederick, and Father Joseph Hathersty at Philadelphia died on May 8, 1771, at the age of 35. Father Robert Harding at Philadelphia died in September 1772 at the age of 70. In 1770 the Catholics at Baltimore decided to build a church. They purchased a lot 25 by 35 feet at Saratoga and Charles Streets for St. Peter's Church, but, because of a disagreement, the church was not opened for several years.

In 1763 when the Jesuits were withdrawn from the French missions, the withdrawal was almost a death sentence for the French Catholic missions in the Great Lakes and upper Mississippi valley; and the defeat of France in 1763 caused an even greater loss of Catholic missionaries in the areas. The suppression of the Jesuits by Pope Clement XIV by the decree *Dominus ac Redemptor* on July 21, 1773, was a similar blow to the English Catholic missions. On October 6, Bishop Richard Challoner of the London district sent the decree to the American Jesuits, requiring their written submission to it. In this case the missionaries did not leave the missions but continued to attend to the colonial Catholics. As a result of the suppression of the Society, the future of the missions looked very bleak. Challoner appointed the Superior, Father John Lewis, as his Vicar General. That did not make any provision, however, for future missionaries. Of the twenty priests who had signed the decree of suppression only one was as young as thirty, and several were over the age of sixty.

There are fewer accounts of the lay Catholics of Maryland during this period of toleration after the French and Indian wars. They were disfranchised and barred from office, but that was the usual situation for Catholics in the English-speaking world. The Catholic Carrolls were respected members of the community and correspondence shows that, socially, Charles Carroll of Carrollton was treated as an equal by non-Catholics, including George Washington, who dined at least once with Carroll when visiting in Maryland. Washington and Carroll were associated also in the project for deepening the Potomac River.

Charles Carroll of Carrollton married his own cousin, Mary Darnall, June 5, 1768. Since he was not a member of the colonial legislature, his participation in any controversy had to be through the newspapers. In 1773, when Daniel Dulany, a prominent lawyer, published under the name of "Antillon" a dialogue between First Citizen and Second Citizen defending the imposition of fees by the Governor, Charles Carroll answered him with a dialogue in which the fees were condemned. Carroll showed that, since these fees amounted to taxes and were imposed without the consent of the persons concerned, those who paid the fees were being taxed illegally. There were several exchanges. When Dulany brought in the question of religion, Carroll said of his fellow Catholics:

> They cannot, I know (ignorant as I am) enjoy any place of profit or trust, while they continue papists; but do these disabilities extend so far as to preclude them from thinking and writing on matters merely of a political nature? "Antillon" would make a most excellent inquisitor; he has some striking specimens of an arbitrary temper, the first requisite. He will not allow me freedom of thought or speech.[19]

It was generally conceded that Carroll had the better of the argument.

In this period of toleration, the lines of division in colonial Maryland were rather between the upper and lower classes than on the basis of religion. The clergy of the Anglican Church were not zealous and had incurred the disrespect of the people. The Catholic clergy, on the other hand, were noted for their zeal in visiting the people, particularly in time of sickness. There were some converts to Catholicism, but it seems that the Catholic minority, given toleration, were content to be a minority, even though disfranchised, in their Maryland world, just as the Catholics in England were tolerated by their English neighbors. The Maryland atmosphere was one in which Catholicism could maintain itself, especially since there were Catholics among them who were accepted among the upper classes. Of the number of Catholics, no one is certain. They were probably about one twelfth of the population of the colony.

[19] Kate Mason Rowland, *The Life of Charles Carroll of Carrollton, 1737–1832*, 2 vol. (New York, 1898) I, 127.

CHAPTER THREE

The Return of
Toleration 1774-1789

WITH THE END OF THE FRENCH AND IN-
dian wars in 1763 and the withdrawal of French power from
North America, the prospects for Catholicism in that area seemed
to depend mostly on the Spanish empire which then included
Louisiana and the southwestern areas. Spain had ceded Florida to
England in 1763, but few Catholics remained there despite the
English promise of toleration.[1] In that portion of the French
empire between the Appalachians and the Mississippi River, the
treaty of Paris in 1763 had guaranteed religious freedom to the
Catholic peoples, much to the distress of the New England Protestants. Although these Western regions were not part of the English colonies, as future parts of the United States they are of
interest to the historian of American Catholicism. They are of interest also because even at this time there remained in them traces
of the Catholicism that had been begun under the French and
Spanish missionaries. The future of Catholicism in the English-
speaking colonies depended, however, on the small minority in
the older English area of the east coast.

In Florida, the Catholics who remained after 1763 were joined
at New Smyrna by a colony of Minorcans brought over in 1768
and their pastor, Father Peter Camps. In 1783 England ceded East

[1] A very fine account of Catholicism in early Florida is Michael V. Gannon,
The Cross in the Sand, The Early Catholic Church in Florida, 1513–1870
(Gainesville, 1965).

Florida to Spain, and Spain claimed West Florida by right of con-
quest. Spanish priests again administered the territory. In the
Spanish regions of Louisiana there were a few priests, chiefly
Capuchins, who tried besides their own work to replace the
departed Jesuits. The area of the Floridas and Louisiana was
under the jurisdiction of the Spanish Bishop of Havana. In the
old French settlements and missions in the upper Mississippi and
Great Lakes areas, there were three former Jesuits (Sebastian
Meurin at Kaskaskia, Pierre Du Jaunay at Arbre Croche, and
Lefranc at Green Bay), two Recollects (Simplicius Bocquet at
Détroit and Luke Collet at Fort Chartres in the Illinois country),
and after 1768 Father Pierre Gibault at Kaskaskia and Vincennes.
Although by the treaty of Paris of 1763 the Catholics in this area
were to retain their religious liberty, few missionaries came during
this time from Quebec. There were small colonies of French
Catholics and half-breeds at Detroit, Green Bay, Kaskaskia, Prairie de Rocher, Vincennes, and Mackinac hoping for priestly ministrations. Many of the French from these outposts, however,
had crossed the Mississippi into upper Louisiana, which had been
ceded to Spain and was Catholic country.

The Catholics in the English colonies had their own problems.
Undoubtedly the suppression of the Jesuits had complicated the
task of the Vicar Apostolic of the London District, Bishop Richard Challoner, who had charge of the American continental missions. Now that Quebec had come under the British rule and there
would probably be exchanges between the former French territory
and the English colonies, the Bishop thought it quite desirable that the giving of Confirmation or any other episcopal function be supplied by the Bishop of Quebec, Jean Olivier Briand.
But the Catholics of the English colonies, chiefly in Maryland and
Pennsylvania, did not welcome such a change.

On the contrary, they were fearful of what would happen if
such episcopal ministrations were tried among the Anglo-Americans who were so opposed to bishops. Some of the Catholic laymen
of Maryland had even sent to Bishop Challoner in 1765 a petition
to Rome that there would not be any bishop appointed for the
English colonies because of this opposition to bishops.[2] The toleration of Roman Catholics in the colonies of Maryland and
Pennsylvania at this time consisted chiefly in allowing priests to
function publicly and in some cases to build churches.

[2] Peter Guilday, *Life and Times of John Carroll, Archbishop of Baltimore
(1735–1815)*, 2 vol. (New York, 1922) I, 153–155.

The chapels in Maryland from which the former Jesuits and other priests worked were usually in the Jesuit manors or in an attached wing of the Jesuits' residences, if there were not similar chapels in the houses of important plantation owners. Father John Mattingly in his report of 1773 described the work of the missionaries when they visited such a station: from early morning until eleven o'clock they heard confessions; then they said Mass, at which they gave Communion and closed the services with a sermon. They also visited the sick and dying. A few churches had, indeed, been built in Pennsylvania such as the one at Lancaster and the church of St. Joseph in Philadelphia. There was also a colony of Scottish Catholics from Glengarry that had come over with an Irish chaplain, Father John McKenna, to the lands of Sir William Johnson near the present city of Albany, New York, in 1773; but when the Revolutionary War began both priest and colony in 1776 retreated to Canada.[3] This Father McKenna later returned to the area for a time as a chaplain to the troops of General St. Leger attacking Fort Stanwix. But this loyalist Catholic colony and its chaplain were exceptional among the Catholics in the English colonies, if they could be considered English. Of the Catholics in the English colonies during the American Revolution, very little can be said about their Catholicism. Most of the arguments that preceded the Declaration of Independence were not religious but political and economic. Some Catholics did feel that there was greater hope for toleration in the independence of the colonies, but others, who knew the narrow prejudices of their American Protestant neighbors against Catholicism, had little hope that life with them would be any better than under English rule. This bigotry was manifested in the reaction of some leading Americans to the Quebec Act of June 22, 1774, which had recognized the Catholic Church in the captured French territories of Canada. In New England John and Samuel Adams found this toleration of Catholics a cause for revolt and there were similar feelings expressed in Virginia and other parts of the colonies. These patriots did not show any respect for the Catholics of Maryland. Of the German Catholics in Pennsylvania, there is little record that they participated much in the discussions about independence or engaged in warlike activities. Of the Irish there

[3] Thomas F. O'Connor, "Catholicism in the Fort Stanwix Country (1776–1786)" in *American Catholic Historical Society Records*, LX, 82. Also Richard K. MacMaster, S.J., "Parish in Arms: a Study of Father John MacKenna [*sic*] and the Mohawk Valley Loyalists, 1773–1778," *Historical Records and Studies* (New York) XLV, 107–125.

is considerable record that most of them, having little affection for England, did not find it too difficult to align themselves with the Americans.

While there was an outline of ecclesiastical authority in the colonies through the former Jesuit Superior, Father John Lewis, who had been named Vicar General by Bishop Challoner, the Catholic Church as an organization did not exist in the colonies. There was no Catholic press, and Catholics were really forbidden by law to congregate in public. Therefore, one can only speak of Catholics in the Revolutionary era, not of the Catholic Church, and, of course, the most prominent Catholic was Charles Carroll of Carrollton, who deserved the description given by Governor Seymour of his father as "the head of that sect" because of his influence among the Catholics of the colony. His cousin, Father John Carroll, was a member of the suppressed Society of Jesus, who had returned to Maryland in 1774. While John Carroll did not join the Select Body of the Clergy formed by the ex-Jesuits, he did submit to the rule of Father Lewis, the Vicar General. He began to serve the Catholics in the region around the home of his mother in Rock Creek, Maryland, where he soon built St. John's Church as the center of his ministrations.

The influence of the religious clauses of the Quebec Act on the minds of the colonists was various. To the Protestant majority, the establishment of Catholicism on their western frontier was a serious evil, although not as harmful as the cutting off of the western lands for their trade in the same act. The famous Suffolk Resolves said in Article 10:

That the late act of Parliament for establishing the Roman Catholic Religion and the French laws in that extensive country, now called Canada, is dangerous in an extreme degree to the Protestant religion and to the civil rights and liberties of all Americans; and, therefore, as men and Protestant Christians, we are indispensably obliged to take all proper measures for our security.[4]

These sentiments about the Quebec Act were also included in the Appeal to the English People and the Appeal to the King issued by the Continental Congress in October 1776. While this religious factor was hardly a primary cause for revolt, it was used by some Protestant Americans, such as Samuel Adams and Alexander Hamilton, to arouse the colonists to revolt. Alexander Hamilton in his *Full Vindication of the Measures of Congress* wrote:

[4] Guilday, note 2 above, p. 76.

The affair of Canada is still worse. The Romish faith is made the established religion of the land and his Majesty is placed as the head of it. The free exercise of the Protestant faith depended upon the pleasure of the Governor and Council. . . . They may as well establish Popery in New York and the other colonies as they did in Canada. They had no more right to do it there than here. Your lives, your property, your religion, are all at stake.[5]

The grant of toleration to the French Canadians, on the other hand, was a primary factor, under the advice of Bishop Briand of Quebec, in the French Canadians' refusal to join the revolt.

Since Catholics could not be officials in the colonies, it is noteworthy that Charles Carroll of Carrollton was present with the Maryland Delegation at the meeting of the First Continental Congress in Philadelphia in 1774. Back in Anne Arundell County, he was named a member of the Committee to enforce the nonimportation agreements of the Congress. His next appointment was to the City and County Committee of Correspondence, and when the leaders of the colony met he became a member of the Provincial Committee of Correspondence. The next year when a convention was called to determine the fate of the colony, Carroll was among the nine representatives from Anne Arundell County. When the Convention appointed a Committee of Safety, Carroll, along with the other Charles Carroll (who was not a Catholic), was appointed with fourteen others. Charles Carroll of Carrollton as a member of the Committee of Safety was also very active in preparing ammunition and arms for the defense of the colony. Soon he was called upon to render another service to the Revolutionary cause.[6]

Despite the early victories of Crown Point and Fort Ticonderoga, the invasions of Canada by Benedict Arnold and Montgomery had failed, and the American rebels then tried to win peacefully the cooperation of the French Canadians. For this purpose the Continental Congress appointed a committee of three, two of whom were members of the Congress (Samuel Chase and Benjamin Franklin) and Charles Carroll of Carrollton, a fellow townsman of Chase. Carroll was not a member of the Congress because he was the leader of the Catholics. It was also suggested the Charles Carroll try to "prevail on Mr. John Carroll to accompany the Committee to Canada." The commission to Canada failed in its purpose. That there was any real desire on the part of

---

[5] *Ibid.*, p. 78.

[6] The fuller account of Carroll's activities is found in Kate Mason Rowland, *The Life of Charles Carroll of Carrollton, 1737–1832*, 2 vol. (New York, 1898) I, 132–135.

the Canadians to join in the revolt is hardly probable, because of their recollections of the bitterness of the New Englanders towards Catholicism in the recent French and Indian wars. The chief factor, however, in the refusal to join in the Revolution was undoubtedly Bishop Olivier Briand, who appreciated not only the hostility of the Puritans but more the advantages of the toleration that the English government had given in the Quebec Act. He forbade his clergy to receive Father John Carroll. Father Pierre Floquet, a former Jesuit, received Carroll in his house at Montreal and permitted him to say Mass there. Later he was suspended for his actions by Bishop Briand. When Carroll tried to speak of the new toleration of the English Americans he was confronted with Father McKenna who testified to the English intolerance. The military invasion of Canada had failed as well as these efforts of the Commissioners, and Canada remained safely an English possession. The Commission, which had left Philadelphia on April 2, 1776, returned there June 11. This acquaintance between Father Carroll and Benjamin Franklin had an important effect on the later career of Carroll and the Church in the United States.[7]

Father John Carroll was perhaps the only Catholic clergyman to participate in the Revolution. Most of the priests apparently assumed that they were not to take sides and restricted their activities to serving any Catholics who came under their ministrations. Of the Catholic laymen, it seems that most in Maryland followed the lead of the Carrolls, the Darnalls, and the Brents and supported the rebellion. There is no listing of them based upon religion, and even the attempt of some to claim all names of Irish vintage is not reliable. When the Maryland Convention adopted a resolution calling for independence from England, the resolution was attributed to Charles Carroll of Carrollton, and because of this he was elected a Maryland representative in the Continental Congress on July 4. He joined the Congress on July 18, and on August 2 the Declaration of Independence, which had been passed on July 4, was solemnly signed. Charles Carroll of Carrollton signed for Maryland.

In Philadelphia some non-Catholic members of the Continental Congress were able to witness the fervor of Catholic worship in what might be called a typical Irish Catholic community. Apparently George Washington and John Adams were the witnesses of the service in Philadelphia described by John Adams to his wife, Abigail, on October 9, 1774:

[7] Guilday, note 2 above, I, 92–105.

. . . I heard a good, short moral essay upon the duty of parents to their children, founded in justice and charity, to take care of their interests, temporal and spiritual. This afternoon's entertainment was to me most awful and affecting; the poor wretches fingering their beads, chanting Latin, not a word of which they understood; their Pater Nosters and Ave Marias; their holy water; their crossing themselves perpetually; their bowing and kneeling and genuflecting before the altar. The dress of the priest was rich with lace. His pulpit was velvet and gold. The altarpiece was very rich, little images and crucifixes about, wax-candles lighted up. . . .[8]

The wealth of detail might indicate that he had witnessed these ceremonies before. The loyalties of the Catholics in Pennsylvania depended upon their personal political interests, not on their religious affiliation. Among the Catholics in Philadelphia who distinguished themselves on the American side were Commodore John Barry, sometimes called the Father of the American Navy, Thomas Fitzsimons, later, a signer of the Constitution, Stephen Moylan, the Master Muster-General of Washington's troops, George Meade, Captain John Walsh, Captain Roger Kean, and Emmanuel Holmes, all members of St. Mary's parish. When the British General Howe arrived in Philadelphia, he suggested the raising of a regiment of Roman Catholic Volunteers. It was placed under the command of Lieutenant Colonel Alfred Clifton, an English Catholic, also of St. Mary's parish, and, when evacuated, it was listed as "The Roman Catholic Battalion" consisting of 180 men. The names on the roster of Clifton's Regiment besides the Lieutenant Colonel are given as Major John Lynch, Captains Keneth McCulloch, Mathias Hanley, Martin McEvoy, Nicholas Wuregan, John McKinnon, Lieutenants Peter Eck, John Connell, Edward Holland, James Hanrahan, Ebenezer Wilson, John O'Neill, Ensigns John Grashune, Arthur Bailie, Thomas Quinn, and Edward Gadwin. Father Farmer was listed as Chaplain and John Holland as Quartermaster, but there is no record that Father Farmer ever acted as Chaplain. A Catholic historian found the following names among the Tories of Philadelphia: Reynolds, the looking-glass maker; Bernard Fearis, a vendor; Dennis Dougherty, a shopkeeper; Joseph Griswold; and John Bray, a schoolmaster. There were others. Of the Catholic Tories

[8] Charles Francis Adams, ed., *Familiar Letters of John Adams and His Wife, Abigail, During the Revolution* (New York, 1876) pp. 45–46. Apparently these were October devotions.

not attended by Catholic priests, we have no way of knowing.[9]

After King Louis XVI announced the Treaty of Alliance with the United States, the arrival of the French troops and navy brought another Catholic influence into the city and country. Already General Charles Ducoudray and twenty-nine officers from France had arrived in May 1777 to join Washington's army, and General Lafayette came in May the same year. Other Catholics who enlisted in the American cause were Baron Frederick William Steuben of Prussia and Thaddeus Kosciuszko and Count Casimer Pulaski from Poland. Members of the Continental Congress attended the burial services for General Ducoudray, who had drowned in an accident, which were held in St. Mary's Church on September 18, 1777. On July 4, 1779, the President and members of Congress attended a *Te Deum* service in St. Mary's in honor of the third anniversary of the Declaration of Independence at the invitation of M. Gerard, the French Minister. The address on the occasion given by Abbé Seraphin Bandol, the Chaplain to the French Minister, was later published. Again the officials of the American government went at the invitation of the new French Minister, Chevalier De Luzerne, to St. Mary's on May 8, 1780, to attend memorial services for the Spanish agent, Don Juan de Miralles. There were some strange accounts printed about the role of a catafalque in the services. Finally at the news from Yorktown of the English surrender, the French Minister arranged a Mass of Thanksgiving on Sunday, November 4, 1781, at which members of Congress were present. In the wake of the peace, Father Robert Molyneux with the other trustees, Patrick Byrne, James Gallagher, and John Rudolph bought a house and ground on February 17, 1781, for a parish school. Later, when Washington visited Philadelphia in December 1783 to surrender his command, Father Ferdinand Farmer's name led those of the Philadelphia citizens who addressed to him a message of congratulations and thanks. Father Farmer, whose family name was also Steinmeyer, was listed as a trustee of the University of Pennsylvania.

Just how many Catholics participated in the American Revolution will probably never be ascertained. Colonel John Fitzgerald, Washington's aide-de-camp, was a Catholic, and so were Colonel Francis Vigo, Joseph Cauffmann, and Timothy Murphy. It is presumed that the French soldiers who served in the war were all

[9] The most scholarly account of Catholics in the Revolution is Charles H. Metzger, S.J., *Catholics and the American Revolution* (Chicago, 1962); on the Tories, pp. 237–266.

Catholic. Attempts to determine how many Catholics were represented by the Irish names on the Revolutionary army registers are
fruitless because many Scotch-Irish, mostly Presbyterians, had
adopted Irish names. Of the chaplains of the French Army, we
have the names of only a few. Other French clergy who served
in the missions during the war include Father Huet de la Valinière
in Philadelphia, Father Francis Louis Chartier de Lotbinière
(chaplain of two American legions raised in Canada), and Pierre
Gibault. Of Gibault we know most because, in cooperation with
George Rogers Clarke, he helped in the surrender of the French
of Vincennes to the American forces on February 25, 1779. Subsequently Bishop Briand manifested displeasure at Gibault's
action, and Gibault, receiving no aid from the United States,
crossed the Mississippi to Spanish Louisiana.

Father Charles Metzger, S.J., the chief historian of Catholics in
the Revolution, found no fewer than thirteen Catholics on the
General Committee of St. Mary's County, Maryland: William
Neale, Athanasius Ford, Maffey Leigh, Edward Fenwick, Henry
Carroll, Nicholas Sewell, John Fenwick, John Greenwell of Igna-
tius, Ignatius Combs, William Jenkins, Jr., Enoch Fenwick,
Ignatius Taylor, and Nicholas L. Sewell. Two Catholic members
of Maryland's Committee of Correspondence were Ford and Jere-
miah Jordan. In the regiments formed from the counties where
Catholics were numerous, Metzger noted among the soldiers
Catholics such as Ignatius Douglass; Clement, Edward, and John
Edelen; Ignatius Boon; John Neale; Joseph Mattingly; and Fran-
cis and William Baggott. There were many other names whose
Catholicity is probable, many of whom carried the first name
Ignatius, and especially prominent were the family names of
Boarman, Fenwick, and Spalding.

An important factor in the toleration of Catholics during the
period of the American Revolution was the alliance with France,
then recognized as a Catholic country, and her ally Spain, also
Catholic. This was made public when General Washington in 1775
forbade the public celebration of Pope Day, November 5, the
anniversary of the infamous Gunpowder Plot, on which it was
customary to burn the Pope in effigy. Washington gave as his reason not only the need of unity in the States but also the desire not
to offend their prospective ally, the French Canadians. Nevertheless, in the new constitutions drawn up by the rebelling colonies,
there was no deliberate toleration of Catholics. In the constitutions of New Hampshire, Massachusetts, New York, New Jersey,
North Carolina, and South Carolina, the acceptance of Protestant-

ism for office holding was presumed. Virginia led the way in enacting statutes providing for religious freedom, and penal laws against Catholics were abolished in Pennsylvania, Delaware, and Maryland. In Rhode Island and Connecticut, as in Massachusetts, Congregationalism was virtually established as the state religion.

Wartime alliances always create strange situations in which countries that disagree unite against a common enemy. So the toleration and even acceptance of Catholics which arose during the American Revolution was really a temporary arrangement in a group of American states that were Protestant by a tradition of two centuries. French Canada did not join in the revolt. French and Spanish forces had retired from America except where they held the regions of Louisiana and Florida. The Catholic minority of the United States, which had begun to form, consisted of a few thousand English with some Irish and German immigrants. These Catholics were numerous only in Maryland and Pennsylvania. Orestes Brownson writing of this period later rightly said that, for the majority of Americans at this time, Catholicism in the English-speaking world was practically dead. American leaders discussed the future of the American colonies only in terms of English Protestantism, including its somewhat deistic and more liberal departures. Another important development in English Protestantism in America was the permeation of the Puritan spirit that combined a harsh external morality with a kind of autonomy of conscience. This Puritan spirit rejected any real dictation by clergymen or hierarchy. The brief period of the theocracies in some of the Puritan regions and the civic rule of ministers had ended long before the Revolution. With the decline in the power of the ministers, the state had become the only real moral power capable of laying down laws and governing public behavior. The Protestant groups might disagree with each other on details of public worship, but in general this moral atmosphere of the country was English Protestant and Puritan, despite a tendency toward deism and free thought among the political leaders of the states. In the minds of most of the English-Americans, all modern culture and civilization in the English-speaking world (and that was the best world to them) supposed the supremacy of this Protestantism.[10]

In contrast to the Protestant majority, the Catholics in English America during and at the end of the American Revolution were represented by only a few upper-class families in Maryland, by some ordinary people in Maryland and Pennsylvania, by workers

[10] Cf. Winthrop Hudson, *Religion in America* (New York, 1965) pp. 94–105.

on small farms in Pennsylvania, and by French mechanics and laboring men in Philadelphia and other port towns. It is doubtful that even the leaders of this small minority felt in 1783 that Catholicism, numbering scarcely one percent of the population, having no hierarchy, no institutions of education, would ever amount to much more than it did at that time in the England from which their leaders had come. There was, indeed, one great difference, these American English had already achieved legal freedom in Maryland, Pennsylvania, Virginia, and Delaware and would soon have it confirmed in the new national Constitution. Nevertheless, Catholicism in America received acceptance socially only where these English and older Irish families in the country advanced and only where they lived. The centers of political and cultural activity, on the other hand, were already beginning to be in the towns where there were few wealthy Catholics of social standing. The Catholic leadership, mostly in Maryland, was agrarian and Southern during the first decades of Catholic freedom.

The Catholic clergy of this minority, in general, did not have any social position worth mentioning. Father John Carroll, who had returned in 1774, was rather the exception because he belonged to the Carrolls who had recognition in Maryland. The ordinary missionary in rural Maryland, or the German priest in Pennsylvania, abstained from expressing opinion about the Revolution because they were not part of the social or political organization of their neighborhood. In this sense the reorganization of these few missionaries after the suppression of the Society of Jesus in 1773 had no great public significance. To the Jesuit priests themselves, this suppression was a serious blow because they were devoted to their community. They accepted the suppression obediently but with a hope that it would be revoked. To protect themselves, since they intended to remain in their missionary work, they resolved to incorporate their property, which was the chief support of the missions. The plans for incorporation, however, did not affect their position as missionaries in the Catholic organization in the colonies, where they were subject to Father John Lewis as superior.

Official Catholicism in the English-speaking world had suffered much buffeting since the appointment of the first English post-Reformation bishops. In general, the English overseas missions, such as Maryland, had been subject to the Vicar Apostolic of the London District, and there are records of the granting of faculties by these Vicars Apostolic to the Jesuits in the regimes of Bishops Giffard, Petre, and Challoner. When some religious communities claimed an exemption from this rule because of the limited character of these Vicars, Pope Benedict XIV on May 30, 1753, had made obligatory the submission of the religious to these Vicars Apostolic. Challoner, the last Vicar to try to administer the English colonies in America, had endeavored to have Confirmation given in the English colonies by the Canadian bishops since Canada was now under English rule, but the Maryland and Pennsylvania priests did not agree to that solution. In the meantime, also, two hundred fifty-six Catholic laymen of Maryland, including Charles Carroll, Ignatius Digges, and Henry Darnall, had sent a petition to Rome through Challoner in 1765 against the appointment of a Vicar Apostolic for Maryland because they thought it would increase the danger of a renewal of persecution. When Challoner died in 1781 his successor, Bishop James Talbot, refused to grant faculties to two American priests, Fathers John Boone and Henry Pile, who were coming back to the missions. Father John Lewis, however, continued to act as Talbot's Vicar General.

Writing to his friend Father Charles Plowden, formerly an English member of the Jesuits, Father John Carroll pointed out that the priests needed some better form of government.[11] Father Lewis was well respected, but apparently he was not capable of sharp decisions. Carroll explained to his friend that there were no checks and balances and no way to enforce needed ecclesiastical discipline. At this time, while attending to his own district near Rock Creek, Father Carroll worked out a plan of organization for the former Jesuits which he submitted in 1782 to their consideration. He had not accepted any claim on the property of the Jesuits in Maryland since he had not been with them before the suppression, but he was equal to them under the superiorship of Father Lewis. The reaction of the former Jesuits to his plan is not clear, probably those whom he wanted to place under direction may have had some objection to it. Nevertheless, on June 27, 1783, at the request of Father Lewis, six deputies of the ex-Jesuits assembled at Whitemarsh, halfway between Georgetown and Annapolis, to draw up a form of government. Carroll's plan was not actually adopted until October 11, 1784. At the June 27 meeting, the clergy were divided into three districts, Northern, Southern, and Middle, and each district was to meet and choose two delegates to a General Chapter. The General Chapter was held at Whitemarsh on November 6, 1783. At the November Chapter, they

[11] Guilday, *Carroll,* Chapter XII, "Church Administrations During the War (1775–1784)." See note 2 above.

appointed a committee of five, Lewis, Diderick, Matthews, Walton, and Carroll, to draw up a petition to Rome to have Father John Lewis appointed as their superior with necessary episcopal powers, especially for Confirmation and blessing, although they did not want a bishop appointed to rule over them. Fearing that this petition had not been drawn up properly, a second Committee of which John Carroll was also a member drew up another petition which was sent through a friend in Rome. In the meantime at the November 1783 Chapter, they accepted a plan of government based essentially on the plan proposed by Carroll. It consisted of three parts: (1) a form of government in nineteen articles, (2) a set of rules for the particular form of government for the Body of the Clergy in six articles, and (3) regulations respecting the management of the plantation in eight articles. They drew up also a formula of promise to be taken by the members of the Select Body of the Clergy. This Plan became for all purposes the governing constitution for the ex-Jesuits until they were reestablished in 1806. In the meantime other forces were at work deciding on the future of this group because the Catholics in Maryland and Pennsylvania were members of the Church Universal, and the Sacred Congregation of the Propaganda had the responsibility for governing the existing organization and for providing for the Church in this missionary region.[12]

When the peace treaty between England and the colonies was being arranged, Cardinal Leonardo Antonelli, the Prefect of the Propaganda, through the Nuncio in Paris, Archbishop Doria Pamphili, suggested that a clause be inserted in the treaty guaranteeing religious freedom. Count de Vergennes, the French Minister, assured the papal Nuncio that Article VIII of the treaty did guarantee this freedom. Antonelli also suggested to Pamphili that the King of France be asked to take an interest in the affairs of the Catholics in the new nation. There should be appointed there a religious superior, probably a Vicar Apostolic with episcopal powers. If a suitable American subject were not found for this appointment, one should be chosen from another country. If the missionaries chosen were French, the Holy Father was sure that the French King would grant them aid.

Archbishop Pamphili consulted Count de Vergennes, who assured him that the treaty took care of the religious peace, that he was sure there would be no objection to the appointment of a

---

[12] Guilday and Shea insist on a French plot, but this is discounted in Jules Baisnée, *France and the Establishment of the American Hierarchy, The Myth of French Interference, 1782–1784* (Baltimore, 1934).

vicar apostolic, and that he would consult Benjamin Franklin, the American plenipotentiary, to make sure. Franklin assured him that the Congress would not be interested in the appointment since it concerned solely spiritual matters, and Congress did not act on such affairs. Franklin, however, did receive assurances from the Congress of its lack of concern on this matter. Franklin further suggested that the four Benedictine colleges in France for the training of English clergy be abandoned and the funds derived from their sale be used for setting up a college for training American clergy. This proposal about the four colleges, however, was not acceptable to the French government. In the meantime Franklin, asked to suggest a suitable person for the Superiorship, mentioned his friend, Father John Carroll, with whom he had traveled to Canada in 1776. As a result of this exchange, Cardinal Antonelli sent to Father Carroll on June 9, 1784, a letter appointing Father Carroll "Prefect Apostolic and Superior of the missions in the provinces of the New Republic of the United States of North America" and requesting information about the status of the church in the United States. In the meantime the Nuncio at Paris had also sent a letter to Luzerne, the representative of the French government in the United States, asking him to have the senior priest in the United States supply him with information about the conditions of the Church in the United States. The questions asked in these two letters were almost identical, one about the missionaries, especially those who might be appointed to the office of Vicar Apostolic and their number as well as the number of Catholics in the United States, especially Maryland and Pennsylvania, and, second, whether there were any schools in which prospective seminarians could learn the Latin language and their humanities before going to France or Rome for theological studies.

Father Carroll received the news of his appointment from four sources: from Father John Thorpe, an ex-Jesuit friend in Rome on August 20; from Father Plowden on September 17–18 to whom he had written in protest against French interference in the appointment of a religious superior; from Francois de Barbé-Marbois, the French agent, on November 7–8, whom Pamphili had notified; and finally on November 26 when he received the official notice from Cardinal Antonelli. Carroll, Plowden, and some historians have seen in the activities of Archbishop Pamphili a plot by the French to control the nascent American Church. But there is no reason to see anything more sinister in the appointment than the watchfulness of the Holy See for the interests of the Catholics in the new republic who were now cut off from dependence on the English Vicar Apostolic. The suggestion of Carroll by Benjamin Franklin was a natural action, since he had come to know Father Carroll and undoubtedly felt that his appointment would be for the best interests of the new nation. But the appointment created a few problems for Father Carroll and his associates in the select Body of the Clergy, who had written to Rome asking that Father John Lewis be appointed the religious superior.

Although the dates of the reorganization of the Church in the United States and those of the reorganization of the civil government almost coincide in many instances, some would like to make a comparison between the formation of the national government in the United States and the development of the Catholic organization. In many other points, however, there are differences. One difference arises in the roles played by the chief personages, George Washington and John Carroll, before 1781. While Washington played such an important part in winning the war, John Carroll was acting as the pastor of St. John's in Rock Creek, Maryland, with the exception of his accompanying the Commissioners to Canada in 1776. Also, in the reorganization among the clergy in Maryland, John Carroll began to wield something like authority without any real power. It is extremely doubtful that he had any expectation of being appointed superior when he signed the petition with the other members of the committee requesting not only that Lewis be superior but that they be permitted to elect their own superior hereafter. Prompted by his feeling about the suppression of the Jesuits, he did want to prevent an appointment arising from the plans of someone outside the group. It is doubtful that they had any fear that John Thayer, a converted Congregational minister, would be appointed. Thayer, received into the Church on May 25, 1783, had asked Franklin if he could return as a priest to the United States. The fear that the Maryland Jesuits had of an outsider, if it existed, was rather that a Frenchman would be appointed.

There is a portrait of Father John Carroll by Gilbert Stuart. He seems to have been a man of moderate height with the rounded features of a genial parish priest and lacking the gaunt look of an ascetic or the persistent scholar. He did not belong to the wealthier Carroll family, but his branch of the family could afford to send him to Bohemia Manor and abroad for his higher education before he joined the Jesuits. His experience with the Church politics that led to the suppression of the Jesuits had made him a bit wary of European interference in American affairs, and his association with Samuel Chase and Benjamin

Franklin gave him a high appreciation of the tolerance of his fellow-American non-Catholics. Writing to his friend, Father Plowden, on February 28, 1779, Carroll may have been too optimistic:

> . . . You enquire how Congress intend to treat the Cath. in this country. To this I must answer you that Congress have no authority or jurisdiction relative to the internal government or concerns of the particular states of the union: these are all settled by the Constitution & laws of the states themselves. I am glad however to inform you that the fullest & largest system of toleration is adopted in almost all the American states; public protection and encouragement are extended alike to all denominations & R.C. are members of Congress, assemblies & hold civil & military posts as well as others. For the sake of your & many other families I am heartily glad to see the same policy beginning to be adopted in Engl[d] and Irel[d]. and I cannot help thinking that you are indebted to America for this piece of service. I hope it will soon be extended as far with you as with us. . . .[13]

The Carrolls and the wealthier Catholics of Maryland were treated as social equals of the other planters of Maryland, and Father Carroll's optimism probably had that foundation. There were parts of Maryland and the hinterlands of most of the other states where Catholics were feared if not hated as some kind of ogre bent upon creating a dark popish tyranny over Protestants. Nevertheless, the mind of the Catholics enjoying legal freedom for the first time in generations was that they wanted to work their future out among themselves without foreign interference. It is noteworthy that the plan for government of the Select Body of the Clergy was not ratified until October 11, 1784, after Carroll had been named Prefect Apostolic, just as the Articles of Confederation of the United States was ratified only in 1781, almost after the Revolution was over. Each turned out to be a temporary solution of the problem of government. This parallel between the years 1783–1789 in American political history and the 1784– 1789 period in the history of the Church in the United States has its chief value in placing the two stories in chronological relation, but one government dealt with the two million inhabitants of the new country and the other with scarcely twenty thousand Catholics.

Carroll was inclined at first to refuse the appointment as Prefect Apostolic since he had not been seeking it; but his friends persuaded him that he should accept it. He then sent to Cardinal

---

[13] Jesuit Archives, Woodstock, Maryland.

Antonelli through Father Thorpe the statement that had been requested on the condition of Catholicism in the American colonies. Meanwhile the Chapter that had adopted the form of government for the Select Body resolved also that they did not want a bishop, that any bishop appointed should not share in their estates, and that a committee composed of three priests should send a memorial to Rome against the appointment of a bishop. The prime mover in the last point was Father Bernard Diderick.

Carroll had been engaged during the year 1784 in a controversy with Father Charles Wharton, a native of Maryland and a former Jesuit who left the Church after returning to America from England. Wharton had published in Philadelphia the *Letter to the Roman Catholics of the City of Worcester* in which he described his gradual turning from Catholicism to Protestantism. Because of the high tone of Wharton's pamphlet and the way it was accepted in Maryland and Pennsylvania, Carroll felt that it should be answered. In his answering *Address to the Roman Catholics of the United States of America* Carroll defended the Catholic doctrines attacked by Wharton. The pamphlet was twice the length of Wharton's. Later in a further discussion of some of the ideas he had expressed in answering Wharton, Carroll exchanged letters with Father Joseph Berington of England, who also had published an answer to Wharton, in which Carroll expressed a strong personal feeling against the retention of Latin as the language of worship instead of using the vernacular.

Carroll had scarcely finished his answer to Wharton, when he began to carry out the instructions of Cardinal Antonelli. In the first place, as instructed by Antonelli, he announced the jubilee of 1775–1776, which was to be preached in the United States from November 28, 1784, to November 28, 1785. Carroll's letter of announcement was dated January 12, 1785. In the meantime, Antonelli had corrected the limitation in faculties in the appointment and had given Carroll the power of confirming and of giving priestly faculties to his associates. By an error, the first document had not given him power to give faculties to priests other than his associates.

Carroll wrote on February 17, 1785, to Father Thorpe in Rome exposing his situation regarding the appointment and indicating in outline what he was writing to Cardinal Antonelli. Carroll's official letter in Latin was dated February 27, 1785. In this letter he acknowledged the documents sent by the Cardinal and expressed his unworthiness of the honor. He indicated that with the attainment of independence by the United States Catholics had achieved full toleration only in Maryland, Pennsylvania, Delaware, and Virginia although they were not molested in any part of the country. Nevertheless, since the Congress had forbidden the acceptance of any gift or title from a foreign power, there was some fear about the reception that might be accorded the appointment of a bishop who could be subject to foreign jurisdiction. Since, however, the Protestants had claimed the right to appoint a bishop there might be no objection to a Catholic bishop, and the Fathers would suggest, if there was to be a bishop among them, it would be better if he be chosen by the priests who have labored so long in this part of the vineyard. Carroll spoke of similar difficulties in choosing and sending two students to study at the Propaganda as suggested by Antonelli in his letter. He asked also for fuller faculties than he had been given so that he could appoint other priests to care for those Catholics living in other parts of the country. Carroll promised to send later the statement of the condition of the Church in the United States, requested by Antonelli.[14]

That report on the condition of the Church was dated March 1, 1785.[15] In it Carroll estimated the number of Catholics in Maryland to be about 15,800 of whom 9,000 were over 12 years of age, 3,000 were children, and 3,000 were Negro slaves. In Pennsylvania there were at least 7,000 among whom were a few slaves. In Virginia there were not more than 200, who were visited by priests four or five times a year. There were many Catholics in other states, but he did not know how many and they were without religious services. Carroll understood that there were about 1,500 Catholics in New York and that there was there a Franciscan to whom he could not give faculties because of the limitations of his letter of appointment. There were many Catholics in the western areas near the Mississippi, but he did not know the number. There was a German Carmelite there but Carroll did not know much about him. This area had formerly been cared for by the Bishop of Quebec.

In Maryland, Carroll noted that a few of the more prominent and richer families had retained the Faith from the beginnings of the colony. They were all planters, as were those of Pennsylvania with the exception of merchants and mechanics in Philadelphia. As to the piety of the Catholics, Carroll said that it was quite good but that there was a want of fervor among many who heard the word of God only once a month or every two months.

[14] Given in English and Latin by Guilday, note 2 above, pp. 208–219.
[15] Ibid., pp. 223–227.

Even that fervor was wanting among the new immigrants who were coming into the states, especially in the commercial towns. He noted, among other evils, the unavoidable intercourse with non-Catholics, a free intercourse between the sexes, a fondness for dances and amusements, and the reading of love stories brought over from Europe. He mentioned also a neglect of instruction of children and slaves in their religion.

Of the priests in the mission, he said there were nineteen in Maryland and five in Pennsylvania but that two were over seventy years of age and three others very near that age. Others were in bad health, and one he hesitated to use because of his previous conduct. The others were zealous and worked hard. They were maintained chiefly from the estates of the clergy and the liberality of Catholics. There was no real ecclesiastical property. There were one college in Philadelphia and two in Maryland to which Catholics might be admitted. They further hoped that from these they would get some who would study for the priesthood. For that purpose they planned to establish a seminary. He asked other faculties for witnessing marriages and celebrating Mass in the afternoon. His lack of power to appoint other priests to the mission was an unintentional error and was corrected by a letter from Cardinal Antonelli on July 23, 1785. Father Carroll meanwhile had begun to exercise his new authority.

Church history tends to concentrate on clergymen, but in the history of the Church in the United States the laity generally have preceded the clergyman in most localities so that the problem of the Church in this country has always been to gather into congregations the scattered flock that was already there and to build for them churches, meeting halls, and, where possible, schools. This process began with this nucleus of Catholic pioneers in Maryland and Pennsylvania. Of the Catholics in the other colonies besides those visited occasionally in Virginia, Delaware, and New Jersey or nearby areas, we learn only if they persisted in the Faith until regular missionaries came to them. On March 27, 1785, François de Barbé-Marbois, the French Chargé d'Affaires, estimated for his superior that the number of Catholics in New England was six hundred. He may have included in this number the Catholic Indians of Maine, but he probably meant the French who stayed in the country after the return of the French troops and navy to France and the Irish who were arriving at nearly every Atlantic seaport. The French consul at Boston[16] reported among the

---

[16] Robert H. Lord, John E. Sexton, and Edward T. Harrington, *History of the Archdiocese of Boston*, 3 vol. (New York, 1944) I, 347–372.

Catholics, Beaury de Bellerive, a planter from Santo Domingo, some officers of the French consulate who had also become merchants, others who were engaged in importing goods, some distillers, and some bakers. Thousands with Irish names had arrived in the recent immigrations to Boston, but there was no way of knowing whether they were Catholics or whether they persisted in the Faith unless they were found in the first congregations set up by the later missionaries. There was a Mrs. George Lobb (whose maiden name was Mary Connell), a blacksmith named John Magner, merchants by the names of Francis Mulligan, Daniel Haley, Mullens, Joshua Farrington, Joseph Harrington, Patrick and John Duggan, Patrick Campbell (a blacksmith), and Elizabeth Larkin. Other Irish who later became members of Father John Thayer's congregation include the Corbetts, Butlers, Callahans, Cavanaughs, Cottrils, Dohertys, Driscolls, Dowayers, Doyles, Fitzgeralds, Flinns, Hamiltons, Jacksons, Kennys, Longs, Lynches, O'Briens, O'Donnells, Reillys, Ryans, Sullivans, Tobins, Torpys, Walshes, Wards, and Whites, whose names persist through the 1790 list of Catholics. Irish names like these could probably be found at every port of entry along the coast, such as Salem, Newport, New York, Philadelphia, Baltimore, Norfolk, Charleston, Savannah, and the like. Along with these immigrant laymen, there were some immigrant priests on whom Father Carroll would have to depend if these wandering Catholics were to receive the Sacraments. Some were former chaplains of the French fleet, some were zealous missionaries from Ireland, and some were not so zealous. Some came from French Canada. The most likely places to establish new congregations were the ports of entry where the immigrants gathered and where a French or Spanish consul or minister could contribute to the support of a church or chapel.

Father Carroll had expressed his optimism about the liberty and the future prosperity of the Church to Father Plowden, but his fear about accepting a bishop showed that this English-speaking Catholic group, enjoying liberty for the first time since the Reformation, was not certain what they would be allowed to do. Catholics could legally acknowledge themselves as Catholics and hope to erect churches and perhaps schools. The process of changing the Catholic group from a missionary organization in a country of persecution to a free church with full Catholic church government was a process of education and training that would take years. All the civil institutions of the country were impregnated with Protestant traditions. Most of the civil offices were held by Protestants. Most of the states had Protestant religious qualifications for office. The Puritanical sabbath and Puritanical prohibitions were in force. Although Catholics might worship God in freedom if they were to earn a livelihood and become part of the nation socially, they had to accept the dominant Protestant culture as a fact. As Carroll noted in his report, it was hard to accept this dominance without also accepting Protestant morality, especially in marriage, or without accepting, for want of Catholic instruction, the Protestant faith. Only in Maryland and Pennsylvania did some Catholics have economic and social parity with their non-Catholic neighbors. Although these respected Catholics were generally English, they included some Irish and Germans who had been long enough in the country to acquire some property. Catholics as a group were not wealthy and had scarcely ceased to be proscribed politically. Father Carroll and his fellow missionaries could do little for the economic and social welfare of the Catholic people, but those problems were the concern of laymen. The priests were devoted to the religious life and to the formation of those institutions which were regarded as essential to the proper functioning of the Church. To return to the parallel between Carroll and Washington, unlike Washington, Father Carroll had to act as superior before he had a functioning organization but, like Washington, he manifested real executive ability in organizing a group of missions into a diocese.

Given the rugged means of communication in 1785, Father Carroll could not spare the time to go over the mountains and down the Ohio to visit the scattered French missions in the west where Gibault was working or to Kentucky where a band of Maryland Catholics had gone that same year. After giving Confirmation in the Maryland mission, he started toward the north on September 22, 1785, going first to Philadelphia, where he gave Confirmation at St. Mary's in October and at the other Pennsylvania missions. The missions there were in charge of zealous missionaries, the chief of whom was Father Ferdinand Farmer who was reaching the end of his missionary career. With Farmer, was Father Huet de la Valinière, who attended the French, and Father Thomas Hassett who looked after the Spanish. From Philadelphia, Carroll went to New York, where he found a congregation cared for by Father Maurice Whelan, a Capuchin. The twenty-two Catholics there had signed a petition asking him to help erect a church. Among these were the French consul, Hector St. Nolin Crèvecoeur; Dennis McReady; Michael Burke, M.D.; Cornelius Buchanan; José Roiz Sylva, and Andrew Morris.[17] Father Whelan

---

[17] Leo Raymond Ryan, *Old St. Peter's, The Mother Church of Catholic New York, 1785–1935* (New York, 1935) pp. 42–43.

had served as a chaplain in the French navy in eighteen engage-
ments. Taken prisoner, he was for a time imprisoned at Jamaica
in the Bahamas. When he was released, he came to New York and
felt constrained by charity to stay and attend the neglected Catholics, mostly Irish, in that port town. Father Farmer asked Carroll
to give him faculties but, because of the error in Carroll's letter
of appointment, Carroll could not give him faculties. At Carroll's
suggestion, Whelan applied directly to Propaganda for faculties.
Father Whelan estimated Catholics in New York at two hundred,
and Carroll, considering the circumstances, presumed permission
to give him faculties so that the neglected Catholics could make
their Easter confessions. Father Farmer had been shocked to find
Whelan exercising faculties before they had been formally granted
but attributed Whelan's action to ignorance of canon law since he
had found Whelan properly submissive to authority. Carroll did
not change anything in New York, where a group of Catholics,
a Frenchman, a Portuguese, and two Irishmen, had incorporated
themselves as the Catholic trustees in the City of New York and
secured a lot on Barclay street on which to build a chapel.

But Carroll had scarcely returned to Rock Creek in December
when he learned that trouble had developed in New York when
a second Irish priest, Father Andrew Nugent, also a Capuchin, had
arrived. Father Nugent was a better preacher, an important qualification for a minister in Protestant America, and soon attracted
the admiration of the trustees of the chapel. Father Huet de la
Valinière had been sent by Father Farmer to attend some Canadian Catholics who were living in New York, and he sent word
back to Farmer of the division of the congregation between the
two Capuchins. The trustees took the side of Father Nugent, cut
off the salary of Father Whelan, and threatened to go to law to get
rid of him. Father Carroll wrote a letter to each of the priests
asking them to make peace and a third letter to the trustees condemning their assumption of authority they did not have. He
acknowledged that he had received two letters from the trustees
on the matter, as well as letters from the two priests. He charged
the trustees with not abiding by the articles he had set down for
them during his visit and of claiming the right they did not have
of choosing the parish priest. Further, he told them he understood
that two members of the congregation had seized the collection
and retained it without authorization. He denied the trustees
authority to appoint a parish priest, and further denied that there
were properly any parishes in this country yet. He protested their
threat of going into the courts. He said that he could not remove

Whelan without cause and proposed instead to make the two Capuchins joint chaplains, since they were not really parish priests. In the meantime Father Whelan, becoming disgusted with the controversy, had sent his resignation to Father Farmer and gone to a village above Albany to visit his brother, a physician who lived there. Father Farmer then appointed La Valinière as pastor, but La Valinière decided to resume his wanderings. Carroll gave faculties to Nugent, but already by April 1786 the trustees and Nugent were quarreling about his salary.

Carroll made another visit of his prefecture during the summer of 1786. On November 4, 1786, there was a solemn dedication of St. Peter's Church in New York for the construction of which the trustees had received $1,000 from the Spanish minister, Diego de Gardoqui. The dedication was held on the feast day of the Spanish King, Charles III. Present besides Father Nugent and the trustees, were the chaplains of the French and Spanish embassies, with Gardoqui in the sanctuary. Carroll was not able to be present. Meanwhile, Father Farmer had died on August 17, 1786, and, when the quarrel between Nugent and the trustees broke out again the next year, Carroll had to go himself in October to New York to settle the affair. This time Father Carroll appointed in place of Nugent, whom he now learned had been suspended before leaving Ireland, Father William O'Brien, O.P., who was then serving in Philadelphia. When Carroll appeared at St. Peter's Church the following Sunday, Nugent appeared also and warned the people not to support Carroll. Faced with the physical opposition of the Nugent faction, Carroll and the obedient portion of the congregation went to Gardoqui's residence for Sunday Mass, while Nugent said Mass at St. Peter's despite his suspension. Carroll appealed in a letter for the support of the faithful Catholics but the next Sunday Nugent and his followers again refused to permit him to say Mass, and he again went to Gardoqui's chapel. Carroll left New York, and the trustees went to court and ousted Nugent. Father O'Brien then took charge of the congregation.

The next fall, 1788, Boston Catholics were pleased when Father Claude Florent Bouchard de La Poterie,[18] a former chaplain with the French army, came to Boston. On December 24, Carroll gave him faculties. La Poterie announced his appointment with a florid pastoral letter calling himself "vice-prefect and Apostolic Missionary." Public Mass was said for the first time in Boston

---

[18] The best account of La Poterie is in Lord, Sexton, and Harrington, I, 375–411. See note 16 above.

November 2, 1788, and a former Huguenot church was purchased and dedicated as the Church of the Holy Cross. The congregation of one hundred and twenty were French and Irish. The faithful seemed to be skeptical about La Poterie and his boasting. When he appealed to France through the French consul for vestments and sacred vessels, the Archbishop of Paris sent them but also sent word that La Poterie had been suspended previously in Paris for unbecoming conduct. Hearing of these matters, Carroll sent his faithful Dominican, William O'Brien, to Boston. On receiving O'Brien's report of the doings of La Poterie, Carroll suspended La Poterie on May 20, 1789. Some signs indicate that La Poterie was mentally unbalanced. Before he finally left America he published, in 1789, an attack on the Church under the title, *The Resurrection of Laurent Ricci; or a True and Exact History of the Jesuits*. At the same time another French priest had appeared in Boston. He was Father Louis Rousselet, another suspended French priest, who also came with letters of recommendation. When Carroll obtained information about the man's previous suspension he took away his faculties.

Before he died, Father Farmer had written to Father Laurence Graess'l, a young Bavarian priest, asking him to come to Philadelphia to help care for the German Catholics. He arrived in October 1787. That same month two other German priests, John Charles and Peter Heilbron, brothers and Capuchins, came uninvited to Philadelphia. Carroll had appointed Father Graess'l pastor of St. Mary's, but, when he left the city to care for other German Catholics, Carroll appointed in his place Fathers Robert Molyneux and Francis Beeston. Molyneux was old and in bad health and soon retired to Bohemia, leaving Beeston as pastor. At this time, the German Catholics of St. Mary's under the leadership of Adam Premir decided that they should have a church in which their ancestral language would be spoken. Premir became the chairman of a committee which purchased in February 1788 a lot where Holy Trinity Church now stands, at that time outside the city limits. Premir notified Carroll of their plans, but Carroll, while praising their zeal, did not approve of the action of the committee nor did Molyneux or Beeston. Beeston protested even Carroll's recognition of the trustees' action with a letter. Carroll certainly did not approve the choice by the trustees of Father John Charles Heilbron as pastor. The Germans, when Carroll did not approve, went into a schism in 1796, which lasted until 1802.

In the West, Carroll had sent Father Huet de la Valinière and the Carmelite, Father Paul de Saint Pierre, to the Illinois missions.

They found there already Father Pierre Gibault, who had aided George Rogers Clarke in the capture of Vincennes. Gibault's cooperation with the Americans in the Revolution had made him unwelcome in Canada. Bishop Hubert of Quebec, meanwhile, wrote to Carroll that his predecessor had administered the western territory formerly but, now that the lands of the Illinois country had been transferred to the United States by the peace treaty of 1783, he would yield the administration to Carroll. Further, he expressed some unwillingness to take back Father Gibault to Quebec. Bishop Hubert did retain the care of Detroit, which was still under the English flag.

Carroll moved his center of operations in 1786 from Rock Creek to Baltimore, where St. Peter's Church was then open for services. Also, in 1788 he received a copy of a pamphlet by the Reverend Patrick Smyth, an Irish priest, who had just returned from Maryland. In the book, Smyth accused the Jesuits under Carroll of operating a novitiate secretly, of planning the restoration of the suppressed Society, and of keeping all the good missions for the ex-Jesuits. He told his readers also of a decline in the missions and charged the former Jesuits of various misdeeds, including mistreatment of their slaves. Carroll prepared a first draft of a long answer but, when Archbishop John Troy of Dublin assured Carroll that he should not answer it, he did not publish his answer. The Smyth pamphlet caused some inquiries when Cardinal Antonelli received a copy of it, but the Cardinal was quickly reassured by Carroll's friends. But, in this and other difficulties, Father John Carroll could see now that he needed broader powers to handle his responsibilities as Superior.

When the ex-Jesuits met for the Second General Chapter on November 13, 1786, there were three major problems facing them: the incorporation of the Select Body of the Clergy; the question of receiving a bishop; and the growing need for a Catholic college. On the first point, a committee was appointed consisting of Fathers Carroll, Walton, Matthews, Ashton, Leonard Neale, and Jenkins to study whether it was expedient and safe to incorporate the estates. They reported in favor of incorporation and the act of incorporation was passed by the Select Body six years later. Secondly, the resolution about the election of a bishop said that the form of government of the Church is properly episcopal, that only a diocesan bishop was adequate to the task, that the representatives of the clergy in the country were the proper ones to choose such a bishop, and that a memorial should be drawn up by a committee consisting of the Prefect Apostolic and two other

Fathers, Robert Molyneux and John Ashton, and sent to the Pope asking for the carrying out of these provisions. Over the signature of Father Charles Sewall as secretary, a letter explaining their actions on the appointment of a bishop was sent to all the members of the Select Body. Father Diderick, Father Leonard Neale, and Father James Walton opposed the appointment of a bishop. Carroll and those who supported the decision issued an answer to their objections. Eventually, however, the decision of the Second Chapter was approved and on March 12, 1788, the committee of Carroll, Molyneux, and Ashton sent their *Memorial* asking for the appointment of a bishop. The *Memorial* stated that since Cardinal Antonelli in his letter of July 23, 1785, had announced the intention of the Holy See to appoint a bishop as Vicar Apostolic as soon as the time was suitable, they wished to state that now was the proper time, because, as in the example of the quarrel in New York, those who were causing difficulties did so because of the lack of episcopal authority in the country. To attain the desirable purpose they suggested that there be appointed a bishop directly subject to the Holy See and that for the first time, at least, his choice be allowed to the priests who had been exercising faculties there. After this first time, the Holy Father would, after due consultations, decide how future bishops would be chosen.

The letter was sent with the official mail of the Spanish embassy in New York. In the meantime, the Sacred Congregation had been gradually coming to the decision to appoint a bishop to the United States. Acting on the appeal of the clergy on June 23, 1788, the Sacred Congregation approved the request that the bishop be chosen for the first time by the clergy exercising jurisdiction in the United States. These clergy were also to decide upon the see site and whether the title would come from that see or be titular. The Pope, Pius VI, approved of these decisions on July 6, 1788, and Antonelli sent his letter announcing the decision on July 12, 1788. In a letter Carroll, Molyneux, and Ashton announced the papal decision on March 25, 1789. The fathers assembled at Whitemarsh and chose Baltimore for the see and Father John Carroll as bishop. The Pope confirmed the choice on September 14, 1789. The brief appointing John Carroll as Bishop of Baltimore, *Ex hac apostolicae,* was issued November 6, 1789.

While Father John Carroll was experiencing the need of regular episcopal government in the Church in the United States, the representatives of the various states had assembled in Philadelphia in May 1787 and produced the Constitution of the United States. There was no question that the spirit of the old Congress was one of toleration as was shown in the message it had sent to Benjamin Franklin refusing to pass on the choice of a Catholic bishop and in the freedom clause of the Northwest Ordinance of 1787. This spirit pervaded the new Constitution also, which directly forbade religious qualifications for office in the sixth article. The absence of a bill of rights guaranteeing fundamental liberties seemed to presume liberty, but this absence was soon remedied by the first ten amendments. In the Constitutional Convention itself, Charles Carroll, although elected a delegate, did not serve, but the brother of Father John Carroll, Daniel Carroll, and Thomas Fitzsimons, a Catholic from Pennsylvania, were present and signed the final document.

When the election of the President under the new Constitution was held, George Washington was elected unanimously, and took office in April 1789. Many religious bodies saluted the President, among them the Roman Catholics late in 1789. The signers of this document were, besides the Bishop-elect John Carroll, Charles Carroll, Daniel Carroll of Maryland, Dominick Lynch of New York, and Thomas Fitzsimons of Pennsylvania. The letter contained a brief apology for its lateness, because the signers lived in widely distant places and some time was required to make the necessary exchanges between them. The writers expressed pleasure at the unanimous election of Washington, especially because of his service in war and peace which had guaranteed peace and prosperity. As his election guaranteed the continuance of this peace and prosperity, they hoped that they would share in them with their fellow citizens "equal rights of citizenship, as the price of our blood as spilt under your eyes, and of our common exertions for her defence, under your auspicious conduct—rights rendered more dear to us by the remembrance of former hardships."[19]

In his answer dated March 12, 1790, Washington noted that the delay in their letter had given the writers a chance to see already the prosperity obtained by the new government. He expected America to become one of the foremost nations in justice and liberality. ". . . And I presume that your fellow-citizens will not forget the patriotic part which you took in the accomplishment of their Revolution and the establishment of their Government: or the important assistance which they received from a nation in which the Roman Catholic faith is professed."[20]

The parallel between the formation of the Catholic organiza-

[19] Guilday, note 2 above, pp. 365–366.
[20] *Ibid.*, p. 366.

tion in the United States and the formation of the new government under the Constitution can be pushed too far, since the institutions are quite dissimilar. But there are some qualities and actions of John Carroll and George Washington that are alike, and the chief of these are their executive abilities and their high purposes.

CHAPTER FOUR

John Carroll,
Bishop and Archbishop

ALTHOUGH FATHER JOHN CARROLL HAD heard from unofficial sources that he had been elected the first Bishop of Baltimore, he did not receive the official letter of appointment until some time in April 1790. In the meantime he had already made up his mind that he would go to England to receive consecration. Cardinal Antonelli had suggested that he go to Quebec, and Archbishop Troy had invited him to Dublin. Carroll had to be polite in insisting on going to England, and there are a few documents that indicate that he intended all the implications of his choice. The Carroll family itself was Irish, and there is nothing to indicate that the Bishop-Elect did not feel proud of his ancestry. But the new country was English in its traditions, and its culture was basically Anglo-Saxon. If Roman Catholicism was to rise higher in influence and social importance in the new English-speaking nation, that elevation would come about through its participation in the English-American traditions and culture. The unwillingness of the former Jesuits to accept a foreign bishop and their desire to choose their own bishop indicate a certain desire to remain within this English tradition.

It is probably true that these former Jesuits did not argue, as some have argued since, that the basic English traditions of political freedom date back to the Catholic England of the Middle Ages, but there seemed to be a determination among them that Catholicism in the United States would be preserved and would grow not as an Irish or a French or German invasion but as an institution fully Catholic yet fully acceptable to the Anglo-American cultural traditions. Carroll had other more personal considerations in the choice of the place of consecration. Going to England would permit him to visit his close friend, Father Charles Plowden, one who had even more pointed opinions about the undesirability of a Latin bishop. More positively, he was accepting the invitation of English friends, Mr. and Mrs. Thomas Weld. Weld, whose friendship with Carroll dated to Carroll's visits in England, had taken advantage of the easing of the persecution of Roman Catholics to build a small chapel on his Lulworth estate in 1786. This chapel, apparently the first Catholic church built in England since the Reformation, was a fitting place for the consecration, on August 15, 1790, of the first bishop enjoying full liberty in the English-speaking world. The consecrating prelate was Bishop Charles Walmesley, Bishop of Rama and Vicar Apostolic of the Western district. The ceremony took place during a solemn Mass celebrated by Bishop Walmesley, and the prelates were attended by Fathers Plowden and James Porter as assistants. Also present were Father C. Forrester, a missionary, and Father Thomas Stanley. The sermon was preached by Father Plowden, who alluded to the recent separation of the United States from England and added:

. . . the earliest and most precious fruit of it [the American Revolution] has been the extension of the kingdom of Christ, the propagation of the Catholic religion, which heretofore fettered by restraining laws, is now enlarged from bondage, and is left at liberty to exert the full energy of divine truth.[1]

Bishop Carroll had some business to take care of in England but declined the invitation of his old friends, Lord Arundell of Wardour, Weld, and others to prolong his stay. Informed that the Sulpician Fathers in Paris, now under duress because of the French Revolution, were desirous of having him visit them about their coming to America to found a seminary, he, nevertheless, declined to go to the continent and Father Nagot, the Assistant Superior of St. Sulpice, came to England to see him. Bishop Carroll did at this time exchange letters with Cardinal Antonelli. While in England, he wrote also, on September 27, 1790, to Pope Pius VI thanking him for choosing him to be a bishop and declaring his unworthiness of so great an office. At the same time he

[1] Peter Guilday, *Life and Times of John Carroll, Archbishop of Baltimore (1735-1815)*, 2 vol. (New York, 1922) I, 377-379.

promised the Pope that he "would never at any time, fail in obedience and docility to the Holy See. . . ."[2] He left England on October 8 on what was a very rough journey lasting until December 7, when he arrived at Baltimore. Returning with him on the ship was Dr. James Madison, the newly consecrated first Bishop of the Protestant Episcopal Church in Virginia, who had also been a fellow passenger on the trip to England.

When the Catholics of Baltimore learned that the Bishop was arriving, a considerable number went to meet him on the wharf and escorted him to his residence, the rectory of St. Peter's alongside his procathedral. The following Sunday a large crowd, including some non-Catholics, assembled at the church desirous to see a bishop. He was met at the door of the church by five priests who escorted him to the sanctuary where he knelt during the *Te Deum* and then took his throne to receive the obeisance of the clergy and some of the laity. This was followed by a pontifical Mass in which he gave his solemn benediction and proclaimed the papal indulgences he had been given for those present. He also gave his first sermon as Bishop. In the sermon, describing the office to which he had been chosen, he indicated also in a long litany all the tasks that had been placed upon his shoulders generally from exhorting and guiding his flock to building up a new portion of Christ's Church from its foundation. He mentioned particularly the need to establish religious education for the Catholic youth, especially for the training of priests, and his obligation to care for those Catholics who lived in distant areas. He placed the diocese under the patronage of Our Lady and urged his flock to have special devotion to her. Except for the high social position of the Carroll family, it is doubtful that the arrival of a Roman Catholic bishop was of any general interest in the new United States. The events of national importance were taking place in the temporary capital of the United States, Philadelphia.

Before Bishop Carroll left England he was faced with two competing projects from Europe, based partly on European ignorance of America and partly on the irresponsibility of some Americans. One project was the establishment of a bishopric among the Oneida Indians in upper New York. There had appeared in Paris an agent of the Oneidas, Jean de la Mahotière, who presented to the Apostolic Nuncio, Archbishop Antonio Dugnani, four documents. The gist of the documents was that having become entirely Catholic the Oneidas, as the leaders of the six Indian nations,

[2] *Ibid.*, p. 380.

wished to have their chaplain, Father John Louis Victor Le Ton-
nelier de Coulonges, made their bishop. Since he had aided them
in their conversion, they had adopted him as one of their own. If
the petition was granted, six Capuchins were to accompany de la
Mahotière back to the bishopric. Dugnani apparently did not
know what to do about the matter, but, feeling that the agent
was sincere, he sent the documents on to Cardinal Antonelli.
Antonelli noted that there was no awareness in the document of
the appointment of Carroll as Bishop, although one of the letters
did speak of the new church in New York. He asked the agent to
determine whether the mission was in the territory of the Bishop
of Quebec or that of the new Bishop of Baltimore. When it was
made clear that the Indians were in the Diocese of Baltimore,
they were asked to direct their petition to Bishop Carroll, who
eventually sent a priest to minister to them, and the proposed
Oneida episcopate was dropped.

The other project arose from a land speculation of the Scioto
Company which tried to sell in France over three million acres of
land alongside the land granted by the government to the Ohio
Company formed under the Reverend Manasseh Cutler. The
French Company of the Scioto sold out to a "Company of the
24." This company, in turn, sold a large number of tracts of land
to French people, mostly of the middle class who did not care for
the Revolutionary rule and thought of starting anew in the New
World. The Frenchmen first asked that M. Duboisnantier of Saint
Roch be named bishop to have charge of the spiritual welfare of
the Scioto settlement. Duboisnantier did not come with the first
group of settlers, but a Benedictine monk of Saint Maur's monastery, Dom Pierre Joseph Didier, did. The Company then asked
the Papal Nuncio, Dugnani, that Father Didier be made the
Bishop of the colony. The Nuntio pointed out to Didier that
there was now a bishop of the United States at Baltimore, but
Didier indicated that the distance of Scioto from Baltimore was
so great that the colony should have its own bishop.

Dugnani wrote to Cardinal Antonelli on March 22, 1790, and
again on March 29 about the project indicating that several other
priests would also go with the proposed bishop. Cardinal Antonelli
yielded but made Didier not Bishop or Vicar Apostolic but Vicar
General in spiritual matters for seven years provided that his
jurisdiction did not conflict with that of Bishop Carroll and that
he obtain the Bishop's approval. The colonists left for America
before Carroll had left for England for his consecration. Cardinal Antonelli seemed to be uncertain whether the colony was

under the dominion of the United States, and therefore under the jurisdiction of Bishop Carroll, but he had notified Carroll of the departure of the colony while Carroll was in England. Writing from England on September 27, Carroll informed Antonelli that the Scioto colony was within the territory of the United States. When Dom Didier arrived at the Scioto colony near the present Marietta, Ohio, he discovered this and returned east to Baltimore and submitted to Bishop Carroll before continuing his ministrations to the French colonists. The colony was a failure, partly because of the lack of necessary equipment and the fear of Indians and partly because of a general insecurity. Many of these Frenchmen later settled in many parts of the country, the greater number continuing down the Ohio to Missouri, and Dom Didier went with them. He spent the last five years of his life in St. Louis, dying on September 2, 1799. Only a small group of the French remained in Gallipolis, the proposed Episcopal See, and eventually the colony itself dwindled into insignificance.

A third problem requiring the immediate attention of the newly consecrated Bishop was the mission in Boston. When Carroll arrived in England he was faced with the pamphlet of La Poterie, *The Resurrection of Laurent Ricci* and was warned to his disgust by Cardinal Antonelli to appoint other than Jesuits to the missions. At that time Carroll thought Father Rousselet was a good priest. Also, in this connection, Father John Thayer, the convert Congregationalist minister who had spent two years on the mission in London, had toward the end of 1789 set out for the United States, going first to New York and then to Boston, arriving there on January 4, 1790. Within a few days after his arrival, he wrote to Carroll asking for the "superiorship of the New England States." He complained of the effects of La Poterie's spendings and of the excessive religious services of Rousselet. Telling of his experiences in Boston some time later, Thayer said that at first large crowds came to hear him, mostly out of curiosity. He had instructed a few in Catholicism but most of the Boston people were indifferent to his doctrine. Rousselet, in the meantime, had not only held extra long services but had exchanged services with a Protestant minister.

Bishop Carroll had now received word of Rousselet's previous suspension and suspended him again. At Thayer's request, the Bishop went also to Boston to reconcile the differences between the French, who sided with Rousselet, and the Irish in the city. Writing to Father Plowden he spoke of the great civilities rendered him in Boston by people who formerly "would have crossed to the opposite side of the street, rather than meet a Roman Catholic. . . ."[3] He added his regrets that he did not have a more suitable priest than the antagonizing Thayer to attend the mission. Of Thayer he added that "not a little of the uncompromising Puritan spirit clings to him to the end." Later the Bishop wrote to Governor John Hancock, thanking Hancock for his courtesies during his visit to Boston. When the Bishop heard a report that Father Thayer had said that he would refuse to leave Boston even if asked by the Bishop, Carroll wrote to him about that and received a denial by Thayer. But Carroll was relieved when he could send in 1792 a more congenial priest to Boston in the person of Father Francis Matignon, a delicately spiritual Frenchman. In the meantime, the chief work of the new bishop was the organization of the new diocese.

The Bishop retained, at first, the three districts established by the General Chapter of the Select Body of the Clergy. The northern district included Pennsylvania, Delaware, New Jersey, New York, and New England. The other districts remained the same, and as soon as possible he sent another Vicar General, besides Dom Didier at Scioto, Father Michael Levadoux, to the Illinois country. There were churches at Baltimore, Philadelphia, New York City, Boston, Charleston, St. Inigoes, New Town, Newport, Port Tobacco, Rock Creek, Annapolis, Whitemarsh, Bohemia, Tuckahoe, Deer Creek, Frederick, and Hagerstown in Maryland, Lancaster, Conewago, Goshenhoppen, Elizabethtown, York, Reading, Carlisle, and Greensburg in Pennsylvania, Coffee Run in Delaware, and Vincennes, Kaskaskia, Cahokia, Prairie du Rocher in the Mississippi Valley. Detroit, Raisin River, Mackinac, and Fort Miami were still under British rule and were cared for by the Bishop of Quebec. The Catholics were clustered mostly in Maryland and Pennsylvania with small congregations in the other port towns along the Atlantic coast and in the French villages in the Illinois country.[4] They constituted less than one percent of the population of the country.

On October 27, 1791, Bishop John Carroll sent out an invitation to the priests of the Diocese to assemble on November 7 for a diocesan synod. He was aware of the wide extent of his diocese and was thinking of asking Rome for an immediate division; but he told his friend, Father Plowden, that first "a uniform discipline" needed to be established in all parts. He added to this letter

---

[3] Letters of Carroll to Plowden, June 11, 1791, Woodstock Archives.
[4] Cf. Guilday, note 1 above, II, 386–387.

another sentence that shows that this founder of the American Church was aware of the cultural lineage of America: "But we have no European metropolis, and our clergy soon will be neither Europeans nor have European connexions. There will be the danger of a propension to a schismatical separation from the centre of unity."[5] Carroll sensed then the contradictory cultural movements of Roman Catholicism in an English-American Protestant milieu.

On November 7, the clergy assembled at the Bishop's residence, and the priests in cassock and surplice preceded the Bishop in pontifical vestments with mitre and crosier to the procathedral for Pontifical Mass at ten o'clock.[6] The Bishop opened the Synod with a sermon explaining the purposes of the Synod. Fathers Leonard Neale and William Elling were appointed Promotors of the Synod and Father Francis Beeston was named Secretary. Among those present at the opening were Father James Pellentz, the Vicar General of the Diocese; Father Robert Molyneux, the Vicar General of the Southern District; Father Francis Nagot, S.S., President of St. Mary's Seminary; Father Robert Plunkett, President of Georgetown College; and Fathers Louis de Lavau, James Frambach, John Ashton, Henry Pile, Stanislaus Cerfoumont, Laurence Graess'l, Anthony Garnier, Leonard Neale, Charles Sewall, Sylvester Boarman, James Van Huffel, Joseph Eden, and John Tessier. Fathers John Bolton and John Thayer arrived on November 10. These men were to lay the foundations for the discipline of Catholicism in the United States. At the first regular session, that afternoon, the Synod decreed about Baptism that converts and those baptized by non-Catholic nurses should receive conditional rebaptism, that baptisms should be registered, and that ceremonies were not to be supplied in the cases of converts previously baptized; and that Confirmation should be given after the age of reason when the child had ability to make a confession. On November 8 the Synod adopted rules on the Holy Eucharist: that in the services there should be nothing unbefitting the Sacrifice; that the collection should be taken up after the reading of the Gospel, and that the collection was to be divided threefold, for the support of the priest, for the poor, and for the needs of the church—with the precaution that the offering was not to be too

[5] Letter of John Carroll to Charles Plowden, October 27, 1791, Woodstock Archives. Cf. Guilday, note 1 above, II, 428.

[6] Guilday, note 1 above, Chapter XXIII, "The First National Synod," II, 419–446. A manuscript copy of the synod decrees is in the University of Notre Dame Archives.

great or so small as to render the service vile; that the priest should wear the cassock under the vestments for Mass, and the cassock and surplice for other liturgical ceremonies; and that there should be preparation of the children before the the First Communion, and that the First Communicant should have the use of reason.

On November 9 the other Sacraments were taken up. Regarding Penance, it was stipulated that it was necessary, in order to ensure validity, that the priest have faculties and approbation; that the priest who acted as confessor without faculties would be suspended; and that priests were not to go from their own congregation to others to hear confessions. Extreme Unction was to be given also to children if they were capable of sin.

On the question of Marriage, the Synod showed a special awareness of the problems of Catholics in America. To prove freedom to marry, the banns were to be announced on three occasions, and those about to be married must prove adequate knowledge of their religion. In this matter slaves were to show knowledge according to their ability. Catholics were to avoid mixed marriages. In the first place, Catholics should be warned of the danger of such marriages and urged to avoid them. If the couple insisted, the priest could proceed if there was no danger of perversion, but the non-Catholic party must agree not to place any obstacles to the Catholic's observation of his religious duties or the Catholic education of the children. However, the pastor was to consider the dangers of his refusal to perform the ceremony, and to avoid greater evils he could marry them. Such marriages were not to be blessed.

At the fifth session on November 10, the Synod decided the order of services on Sundays and Feasts where possible: the Litany of the Blessed Virgin, the Asperges, and High Mass. In the Mass there should be prayers for the Republic, a reading of the Gospel in the vernacular, followed by the announcements of marriage banns and the like and a sermon. In the afternoon there should be Vespers and Benediction with the Blessed Sacrament with a hymn in between. After Mass the whole congregation was to recite the *Pater, Ave, Credo,* and acts of faith, hope, and charity in the vernacular. The Synod decided also that the Blessed Virgin was to be patroness of the American church under the title, Our Lady of the Assumption, and the patronal feast was to be the Sunday within the octave of that feast. Because of problems about manual labor on Sunday, the local pastor was to decide on the rules concerning such work to be observed in each congregation.

As to the problems of the clergy themselves, the clerical black was prescribed, and women residing in the presbyteries were to be of high morals and over forty years of age. However, to provide for the living of the clergy, the laity must contribute, and failure to support the priest would be sinful. For those who failed to receive the sacraments at Eastertime, Christian burial was to be denied, but only if the condition was longstanding and there was contumacy and depravity—if possible, the Bishop should be consulted before imposing the penalty.

At the close of the Synod, Father John Ashton gave a long sermon in which he outlined the practices expected of the good priest and the reasons for doing them. The pastoral of the Synod was published by Bishop Carroll on May 28, 1792. In it he stressed the need of Catholic education, especially of seminaries, and the obligation of the people to contribute to the support of the schools and seminaries and of the priests. He left to their local priests the instructions on other matters. In the meantime in 1792, he defined the lenten regulations and also wrote an instruction for the faithful on the Sacrament of Marriage. In that he insisted that those who had married contrary to the laws of the Church would have to submit to the Church's law and admit their fault.

Before the priests of the Synod separated, Bishop Carroll discussed with them the need for a coadjutor who could assume the office of Bishop in case of his death or incapacity, since the difficulty of communication to Rome and back might cause unusual delay in the episcopal succession. The Bishop preferred a division of the Diocese to having an ordinary Coadjutor Bishop. This matter and the acts of the Synod were contained in a report to the Sacred Congregation by Bishop Carroll on April 23, 1792. The Sacred Congregation insisted that two equal bishops might be a source of division and asked instead that Bishop Carroll with the advice of his priests choose someone to be his coadjutor.

While the naming of Carroll as Bishop constituted the American Diocese, this Synod is in reality the real formation of American Catholicism, the fusion of Catholic principles with American circumstances. A hundred years later this fusion would be still under debate because, from western Europe, Catholics have brought to the United States many pious customs and local traditions which the faithful consider part of the Faith but which clash with the Anglo-American religious traditions.

By 1792 two essential institutions of Catholic life, a college and a seminary, had been started. The Select Body of the Clergy, as former Jesuits, were very desirous of establishing some kind of

institution for higher education and had even outlined its form
and determined to raise the funds for it in the Second General
Chapter of November 13–22, 1786. Father Carroll had told Cardinal Antonelli of these plans in his letter of January 12, 1787,
and a short time later he suggested to Father Plowden that he
would make the proper rector of the new college. Land for the
college had been given on the banks of the Potomac, and some
English friend gave money for it. There was some opposition by
those former Jesuits who foresaw the reestablishment of the Society and wanted to wait for that event, but Carroll insisted that
the suppressed Society had no rights to the college at that time.
The plans for the college were submitted to Cardinal Antonelli
and received approval of the Cardinal, who suggested Father
Robert Plunkett for its president for want of other men he
would have preferred. At first there was only one student, and it
was symbolic of the purposes of the foundation that this student,
William Gaston, was later United States Senator and Judge of
the Supreme Court of North Carolina.[7]

The other educational institution needed was an ecclesiastical
seminary.[8] Fortunately for Bishop Carroll, France was in the
throes of the Revolution when he went to England for his consecration as Bishop. At the suggestion of Archbishop Dugnani, the
Nuncio in Paris, Father Jacques-André Emery, the Superior of the
Seminary of St. Sulpice in Paris, invited Carroll to Paris to discuss
the establishment of a Sulpician seminary in Baltimore. Bishop
Carroll was anxious to return to his Diocese and did not wish to
cross the Channel. Instead, Father Francis Nagot came from
France to England to visit him. As Carroll notified Cardinal
Antonelli on September 27, 1790, the Sulpicians agreed to come
the next summer to open the seminary and to help in the missions.
The first party of ten, including five seminarians, sailed from
Saint Malo on April 8, 1791, and arrived in Baltimore on July 10.
They secured a house on the site where the Paca Street seminary
stands and opened the seminary October 3, 1791. When the first
retreat began on December 10, two of the seminarians had left.
There were only five seminarians during the first two years, two
in 1794, and none from 1795 to 1797. The first seminarian ordained to the priesthood was Stephen Theodore Badin, who came
as a cleric. After ordination to the priesthood, he was sent to

[7] John M. Daley, S.J., *Georgetown University: Origin and Early Years*
(Washington, D.C., 1957) p. 63.

[8] Guilday, *Carroll*, note 1 above, Chapter XXV, "The Coming of Saint Sulpice," II, 463–477.

Georgetown for some further study in English and then to the Kentucky mission.

In 1791 Father John Dubois, a Sulpician from Paris, arrived in Virginia with a letter from General Lafayette to James Monroe and spent some time in the state. The next year two additional bands of Sulpicians arrived in Baltimore. On March 29, Fathers John Baptist Chicoisneau, John David, and Benedict Joseph Flaget came with two seminarians, M. Barret and Stephen Theodore Badin, and on June 24, Fathers Ambrose Maréchal, Gabriel Richard, and Francis Ciquard arrived. Father Louis William Valentin DuBourg came in 1794 and joined the Sulpicians in 1795. In 1792 came the Russian Prince, Demetrius Gallitzin, who was ordained in 1795. The first American seminarian to be ordained was Father William Matthews in 1800. There were not many students available for these experienced teachers, but the accident that brought them to the United States gave Bishop Carroll several zealous missionaries for his neglected missions for the next few years. As the teachers in the first American seminary these Sulpicians, more than any other group, formed the character of the American priest. They brought with them the spirit of the reformed clergy of France, inclined to sternness in public conduct, to close observance of Church discipline, and to total devotion to the sacramental services. They carried with them the ideal of clerical training demanded by the Council of Trent. St. Mary's was chartered by Maryland as a University and did conduct a college for a while, but the traditional American seminary is not part of a university. By coincidence the American Protestant seminary movement dates from this period also.

While Bishop-Elect Carroll was on his way to England to be consecrated, there arrived in New York on July 2, 1790, four Carmelite nuns with their confessor, Father Charles Neale. These nuns were of American origin who had joined a convent of the English Carmelites at Hoogstraet, Belgium. The Superioress of the Convent, Mother Bernardine of St. Joseph (Ann Matthews) was from Charles County, Maryland. Two of her companions were Sister Mary Aloysia (Ann Theresa Matthews) and Sister Mary Eleanor (Susanna Matthews). The fourth was Sister Clare Joseph Dickinson, an Englishwoman. They went from New York to Norfolk and then to Port Tobacco, Maryland, to establish their convent. When Bishop Carroll had begun to organize his vast Diocese, he noted the lack of any school for young ladies, and he wrote to Cardinal Antonelli for permission for these contemplatives to be dispensed from the severity of their rule so that they could undertake the instruction of young ladies. The Cardinal consented because of the great need, but the Sisters decided not to give up their rule and their special vocation. Also, three Poor Clares from France came to Maryland in 1792 and tried to establish a house of their community at Frederick. They were Mother Mary de la Marche, Abbess of St. Clare, Mother Céleste de la Rochefoucault, and Mother St. Luc, and they were accompanied by a lay brother. They met with little success, and when the Abbess died in 1805 the others returned to Europe.

The losses and gains of Catholicism during the 1790s in the United States are hard to measure. In Boston Father Thayer had interrupted his newspaper and pulpit controversies to attend the Synod of 1791. When he returned in the spring he resumed the controversies despite the fact that Bishop Carroll had expressed displeasure about them. He did make some converts, but he did not promote friendly attitudes toward the Church among the Protestant clergy and civic leaders of Boston. In October 1792 he departed for the south, going to Norfolk. On August 20, 1792, Father Francis Matignon, a French theologian, arrived in Boston from Baltimore bringing with him Father Francis Ciquard, also a French émigré, who was on his way to the Indians of Maine. Although Father Matignon was only thirty-eight years old, he was already a professor of theology at the College of Navarre and, from all accounts, a learned gentleman and in manners the opposite of controversial Father Thayer. For a short time there were four priests in Boston. Rousselet, who had been attending the Indians, was there for a short time until Matignon persuaded him to depart; Thayer had not yet left for Norfolk. Soon Ciquard left for the Indian missions, and Matignon carried on the work of reconciling the French who had been disturbed by Rousselet and attending to the other Catholics.

At this time there occurred a kind of French Revolution in Santo Domingo and many of the French families that fled the terror came to Baltimore and Philadelphia. Whether they brought with them to Philadelphia the plague of yellow fever is not certain, but in the spring and summer of 1793, the disease began to spread and within the limitations of medical science of the day there seemed to be no effective way to check the epidemic.[9] Well people in the city began to fear any public meeting or any possible contact with afflicted people. Sometimes corpses were unburied

<hr/>

[9] Joseph L.J. Kirlin, *Catholicity in Philadelphia* (Philadelphia, 1909) pp. 138–150.

for several days. Some thought the air could be purified by fires or by firing of guns, and personal preventives of all kinds were used. Father Thomas Keating was one of the early victims in March. Father Christopher Keating survived an attack, but Father Laurence Graess'l, the young German priest whose career seemed so promising and who had been named Coadjutor of Bishop Carroll, died in October. Father Francis Anthony Fleming, also of Saint Mary's, was another victim of the plague. There were 251 burials in St. Mary's graveyard besides 30 in the German portion of the same cemetery and 34 in the Holy Trinity graveyard. The fidelity of the priests to their flock was noted by Matthew Carey in his history of the epidemic. To replace Father Graess'l Bishop Carroll appointed Father Leonard Neale as pastor of St. Mary's on December 21, 1793, and the Bishop also requested from Rome his appointment as Coadjutor. Father Neale, a former Jesuit, had served in England and Demara after the suppression, and his health was impaired by the latter service. His bulls as Coadjutor were dated April 17, 1795, but the first two sets were lost in transit.

Other clerical recruits that came from France at this time were Fathers John Moranville, Donatien Olivier, and Jean Rivet in 1794; Fathers M.J.C. Fournier and John Lefevere Cheverus in 1796; and Anthony Salmon in 1798. Very important arrivals in 1795 were Father Matthew Carr from the Augustinian Monastery in Dublin and Father Michael Ennis, who planned to join the Augustinians. Father John Rosseter, O.S.A., had arrived earlier and was living in Wilmington. They were authorized by Rome on May 27, 1797, to found the Augustinian Province of Our Lady of Good Counsel. In 1797 Father Matthew O'Brien, O.P., established a church for the Catholics at Albany, New York, who had previously been attended by Father Whelan after he had left New York City.

In 1796 Father John Goetz arrived in Philadelphia and at the suggestion of Father Leonard Neale was admitted to the Diocese by the Trustees at Holy Trinity and was elected an assistant to Father Heilbron at Holy Trinity. Goetz was unwilling to be only an assistant and insisted on being copastor. When he was refused that title, Goetz joined with the Trustees and demanded on October 8 that Father Heilbron leave the pastorship. Heilbron refused but retired to St. Joseph's with the faithful members of the congregation. Goetz was elected pastor by the Trustees and was joined by another errant priest, Father William Elling. On February 22, 1797, Bishop Carroll wrote a pastoral to the Trustees of Holy

Trinity condemning their actions, but they would not yield. The trustees then quarrelled with Goetz, who resigned. Nevertheless they voted his ouster and elected Elling pastor and invited Father Caesarius Reuter, a German schismatic from Baltimore, to join them. Eventually Father Elling submitted, and then the Trustees submitted to Bishop Carroll on January 29, 1802. The other priest, Caesarius Reuter, had been for a short time in Baltimore where he had urged the Germans to set up a separate church. Reuter later went to Rome to complain of Bishop Carroll's treatment of the German Catholics. He returned in 1799 and took charge of the completed German church, St. John's Church, and when he was not recognized by Carroll he took the congregation into schism.

In 1801 Father Michael Egan of the Irish Reformed Franciscans at St. Isidore's in Rome was invited by the Catholics of Lancaster, Pennsylvania, to be their pastor, and in 1803 he asked the Holy See for permission to establish a province of his community. The permission was granted, but others of the community did not come.

The characteristics of the Catholic Church in America were beginning to develop, and the elements of change and the problems of growth were to create further trouble. The Roman Catholics in the United States were beginning to enjoy freedom, the first granted Catholics in the English-speaking world since the Reformation. The freedom was legal with the exception of a few state laws that had not yet been erased. But maintenance of a church organization without the aid of the state was something new in the Western world, not fully acceptable to either the Catholic minority or the Protestant majority, even when the church building and the clergy could be supported by the members of the congregation. No matter how dedicated the Church was to spiritual work, it was a material, physical, human organization also and had to face the problems of material, physical, and human existence. Somehow the notion was accepted that the United States was a Protestant country in which the small Catholic groups had full legal freedom. The Select Body of the Clergy had anticipated part of the problem by incorporating their estates to support their activities. The new Diocese had to find a way to protect its property under laws that would not recognize an "establishment of religion." The natural way, especially since the members of the Church usually existed in the port towns before the clergyman arrived, was to have the laity incorporate themselves by chosen agents, sometimes called trustees. The other way of incorporation was to have the clergyman hold the property, but to hold it in such a way that he could not defect with the property or give it away through inheritance. Sometimes the laity, when they were the trustees given authority by law, tried to dictate also the choice of the priests. In some instances they even received cooperation from clergymen with whom they formed schismatic congregations when the Bishop refused to accept their choices.

The other major problem of the Catholic minority in the United States at this time arose from the growth by immigration of the body of the faithful. With the exception of the Maryland colony, it can be said generally that the faithful arrived before the clergy in the expansion of Catholicism in America. The result was that Roman Catholicism in any area tended to take on the quality of the faithful whether it was rich or poor or whether it was English, as in the beginning, or later Irish, German, or French. The English-Americans were handicapped by the fact that England had not been Catholic for centuries and had a kind of defeatist attitude in defending the civil privileges of Catholics. The Irish Catholics generally were used to English laws and customs, but they were in rebellion against them particularly where they interfered with religious freedom. The Germans and French and other nationalities when they were numerous enough to have their own congregations tended to want the kind of Catholic life they had enjoyed in the fatherland. The Church organization, while it existed chiefly to administer the Sacraments, had to have property and buildings in which to hold religious services and the instruments of worship. To resolve all these elements into a manageable whole was the problem of the chief priest, Bishop Carroll.

Bishop Carroll did not always find a solution to these difficulties, but as the administrator and guide of the Roman Catholicism during these first years, he did remarkably well. He was of Irish ancestry, but seemed to ally himself chiefly with the English Catholics in cultural tradition and in his respect for Anglo-Saxon legal traditions. Socially he was accepted by his Protestant Anglo-American neighbors, and in this way with the other English Catholics he could establish a tradition of American Catholicism. He was to have troubles, some of which he could not solve. The history of the Church in America is in reality the story of the efforts of Carroll and his successors during the next hundred and fifty years, at least, trying to find the proper solutions. There were few dogmatic problems involved in these early years, and few important moral crises to endure. The problems of the Church were chiefly social and legal. Had all the Catholics been on the social level of the Carrolls and the Brents the acceptance of Catholics socially might have been easy, but the Catholics coming into most of the port towns in 1795–1800 were mostly Irish peasants without property and education, often illiterate and without any skills. The legal problems of the Bishop were to come to a head in the problem of trusteeism and there were implications in the trustee squabble about other facets of American Catholic life. American Protestantism was going through a period of revival noted for emotional experiences on the frontier and the establishment of seminaries as centers of orthodoxy in the east. Roman Catholics had little in common with the Protestant experiences.

To care for the neglected missions, Bishop Carroll used immediately the clerical refugees from the French Revolution. He sent Fathers Gabriel Richard and Michael Levadoux to Kaskaskia and Benedict Flaget to Vincennes in 1792, changed Levadoux to Detroit in 1796 and Jean Dilhet in 1798, and changed Stephen Badin to Kentucky in 1793, where he was joined by Michael Fournier in 1797. He assigned John Cheverus and Francis Matignon to Boston and New England. When Father Flaget was recalled to teach in the college planned in Havana in 1795, Carroll sent Father Jean Rivet of Limoges to Vincennes to replace him. Garnier was assigned to care for St. Patrick's congregation in Baltimore. Jean Tessier became for a while a missionary to the Negroes of the region. Maréchal was sent to St. Mary's County and later was assigned to teach at Georgetown College. DuBourg was made President of Georgetown in 1796, and Gallitzin was sent to Loretto in Pennsylvania. Ciquard continued among the Micmacs in Maine only a short time and then went to Canada. Father Cheverus went to Massachusetts to replace Father Ciquard. At Matignon's request he returned to Boston and took care of Newburyport and Plymouth. Besides the Maine missions they reported 249 Catholics in 1798 in New England, 210 in Boston, 15 in Plymouth, 21 in Newburyport, and 3 in Salem. Cheverus visited the Penobscot in 1798. In 1797 Matignon and Cheverus were joined by Father John Ambrose Songé. In January 1800, when Cheverus married a couple in Newcastle, a writ was issued against him on the charge that he could not perform the ceremony because he was not a minister in Maine. The case was never really tried, but Father Cheverus became the pastor of Newcastle where he stayed usually with the Edward Kavanaugh family. The efforts to build a church in Boston were delayed mostly because of a want of funds, since the Irish were mostly among the poorer classes.[10]

[10] Lord, Sexton, and Harrington, *History of the Archdiocese of Boston*, 3 vol. (New York, 1944) I, 478–587. Annabelle Melville, *Jean Lefebvre de Cheverus, 1768–1836* (Milwaukee, 1958) pp. 63–99.

In New York City, Father William O'Brien, O.P., continued his zealous efforts but was taxed almost beyond his strength when the yellow fever ravaged the city in 1795 and 1798. In 1792 a petition signed by 121 Catholics of New York asked the trustees of St. Peter's to get an assistant for Father O'Brien. He sent the petition to Carroll. They suggested that Carroll appoint Father Thayer, but the Bishop would not consent. At first Father Michael Burke, O.P., returned from Mexico to help him, but he was drowned in February 1800. Then Father Augustine McMahon, O.P., came but died apparently of yellow fever. At the request of the trustees, Father Matthew O'Brien, O.P., who was being transferred from Albany to Natchez was permitted to come to New York.[11] It was during Father O'Brien's pastorate in New York that Elizabeth Ann Bayley Seton, the widow of William Magee Seton, after years of study and prayer, entered the Church on March 14, 1805. Her family joined her. Later in 1808 she went to Baltimore to open a school for girls and in 1808 she founded with Father DuBourg the Sisters of St. Joseph and moved in 1809 to Saint Joseph's at Emmitsburg. In 1810 the community became the Sisters of Charity.

In Philadelphia Father Matthew Carr, the Augustinian, decided to build a church dedicated to St. Augustine and announced a public solicitation. With the money he received, he purchased a lot on June 11, 1796, on Fourth Street below Vine. While the church was being built, he and Father John Rosseter, who had joined him and Father Michael Ennis, lived at St. Mary's with Father Neale. During the yellow fever epidemic of 1798, however, Father Ennis died.

In 1797 a Miss Alice Lalor from Queens County, Ireland, came to Philadelphia and with two companions opened an academy for girls. Father Neale took great interest in the project. However, in 1799 Bishop Carroll transferred his Coadjutor-elect, Father Neale, to the Presidency of Georgetown College, and Miss Lalor followed him to Georgetown where, after some training with the Poor Clares, she participated in the establishment of the Visitation Order in this country. In Philadelphia in the meantime there were many recent immigrants from Ireland and France who were quite distressed by the passage of the Alien and Sedition Acts. On February 10, 1799, under the leadership of Samuel Cummings, some Catholics attempted to hold a meeting at St. Mary's to pro-

[11] Leo Raymond Ryan, *Old St. Peter's, The Mother Church of Catholic New York, 1785–1935* (New York, 1935) Chapter V, "Pastorate of Reverend William O'Brien, O.P. (1787–1807)," pp. 61–93.

test against the Acts. Other members of the congregation, however, objected, and the quarrel and physical disturbance caused
several of the members of the Church to be brought into court.
In 1799 the yellow fever broke out again in the city, and this time
Father John Burke who had arrived in 1797 from Ireland was
among the victims.

The church of St. Augustine in Philadelphia was finally completed and dedicated on June 7, 1801. On April 12, 1803, the
Trustees of St. Mary's elected Father Michael Egan, O.S.F., and
he was appointed Pastor of St. Mary's by Bishop Carroll. Bound-
aries between the two parishes of St. Augustine and St. Mary
were then set up.[12] In western Pennsylvania Father Theodore
Brouwers bought an estate in Westmoreland County in 1789 for
religious purposes, but he died in 1790. A Father Francis Fromm,
a wandering German priest, tried to take possession of the property fraudulently, but the Catholics of the area won possession
through the courts, and Father Lawrence Phelan was sent by
Bishop Carroll to take charge. Eventually, this became the seat
of St. Vincent's Archabbey.

In Baltimore Bishop Carroll was deeply moved by the death of
George Washington on December 14, 1799. He wrote a pastoral
letter on December 29 in which he asked the pastors to have some
observance of respect for the deceased on Washington's birthday,
February 22. Passages from the eulogy (now in the Cathedral
Archives) of Bishop Carroll were carried in the newspapers. He
begged pardon of the "departed Spirit of the first of Heroes" for
the cold accents of his praise compared to that given by those
more capable. He outlined in glowing terms the career of the
departed General, noting that he did not resort to war until other
means had been exhausted, adding:

For his country's safety, he often had braved death, when clad in
her most terrific form; he had familiarized himself with her aspect; at
her approaching to cut the thread of his life, he beheld her with constancy and serenity; and with his breath, as we may believe from knowing the ruling passion of his soul he called to heaven to save his
country, and recommended it to the continual protection of that Providence, which he so reverently adored.

In Philadelphia the eulogy on the occasion was given in St. Mary's
Church by Father Carr.

South of Baltimore there were some Catholics in Alexandria,
Virginia. Father Thayer was there for a while but did not remain

---

[12] Kirlin, note 9 above, pp. 130–172.

long and Father Francis Neale attended the mission from Georgetown. Hearing of Catholics in Charleston, South Carolina, Bishop
Carroll sent there Father Simon Felix Gallagher, an Irish priest,
who came recommended from Archbishop Troy of Dublin.
Father Gallagher was a good speaker but was also intemperate,
and Bishop Carroll soon sent Father John Ryan, O.P., to replace
him. Father Gallagher appealed to Rome against the action.
Bishop Carroll then changed Father Le Mercier who had been
serving in Georgia to Charleston, but the trustees rejected him.
Carroll then appointed Father Joseph Pierre Picot de Clorivière
in 1812. In Augusta, Georgia, the Catholics were attended from
time to time by refugee priests from Santo Domingo until Bishop
Carroll sent Father Robert Browne, O.S.A., in 1810 to Augusta.

The Catholic settlements in Nelson County, Kentucky, consisted
mostly of descendants of the early Maryland settlers. The largest
groups began to move to Kentucky about 1787 and for a while
they had the attention of Father Maurice Whelan, the Capuchin
who had worked in New York. The first church, Holy Cross, was
built in the settlements on Pottinger's Creek by Father William De
Rohan. Father Stephen Badin was sent by Bishop Carroll in 1795,
and, while he had the aid of a few priests for the first decade, by
1803 he was again the only priest in the Kentucky missions attending the six Catholic congregations. In 1805 the Kentucky missions
received the stern missionary, Father Charles Nerinckx, the group
of Trappists led by Father Urbain Guillet, and the English
Dominicans led by American-born Father Edward Fenwick.[13]

Although Father Leonard Neale had been elected Coadjutor to
Bishop Carroll in 1795, because of the disturbed conditions in
Europe, the bulls or the duplicates did not reach Carroll. Finally
the third set arrived in the summer of 1800. Then the ceremony
of consecration originally planned for September was postponed
until the eve of the feast of the Immaculate Conception, Decem-
ber 7, because of the yellow fever epidemic. Father Nagot of the
Seminary and Father Beeston acted as assistants. Bishop Leonard
Neale continued as President of Georgetown and as Vicar General.
He visited also some missions in Maryland and Virginia.

In 1803 the Church of the Holy Cross had been completed in
Boston and Bishop Carroll, at the invitation of Father Matignon,
journeyed there to officiate at the dedication on September 29.
After his return to Baltimore, he officiated at the wedding of
Elizabeth Patterson to Jerome Bonaparte on December 24, 1803.

[13] Ben. J. Webb, *The Centenary of Catholicity in Kentucky* (Louisville,
1884) is an imperfect, but the only Kentuckywide, study of Catholicism.

Newly arrived European priests were assigned to growing missions: John Dubois to Frederick, Nicholas Zocchi to Taneytown, Benjamin Duhamel to Hagerstown, William Pasquet to Bohemia on the Eastern Shore, Sebastian Durosier to St. Mary's, Thomas Monely to St. Joseph's, Germain Bitouzey to Whitemarsh. Michael Lacy was at Norfolk and Portsmouth and Jouly at Alexandria. Anthony Caffrey attended St. Patrick's in Washington, D. C., until 1805 when he was succeeded by William Matthews, the first American priest ordained in the country. In 1804 Edward Dominic Fenwick, an American-born member of the English Dominicans, applied to Rome for permission to found an American Province. Before receiving an answer Fenwick (with the Dominicans, Thomas Wilson, William Raymond Tuite, and Robert Angier) went to Baltimore. Bishop Carroll directed them to Kentucky where Fenwick bought a farm near Springfield in 1806. Rome gave permission for the establishment of the Province on March 11, 1805, and a novitiate was begun in 1809. Wilson became Provincial Superior.

When the Jesuits had been suppressed in England, France, and Spain, Catherine of Russia did not permit the bull of suppression to be served in White Russia, and the Society continued to exist there.[14] English ex-Jesuits pleaded with the Holy Father to be allowed to become members of this surviving province. Finally in 1801 Pope Pius VII formally acknowledged the existence of the Society in Russia and on May 27, 1803, the English ex-Jesuits obtained oral permission to aggregate to the Russian Province. There was some difficulty in getting the oral permission ratified formally. The American ex-Jesuits were watching these events carefully because they were determined to reestablish the Society in the United States. In a meeting in 1788 they had even resolved to ask for restoration at the first opportunity. Finally on August 30, 1802, seven former Jesuits wrote to the American Bishops Carroll and Neale asking permission to affiliate with the Russian Province. The Bishop wrote to Gabriel Gruber, the Jesuit General in Russia, asking whether the Pope had allowed an establishment of the Society outside Russia and the conditions for such an establishment. Gruber wrote on March 12, 1804, justifying the aggregation of the Americans to the Russian Province and prescribing the formula for the former Jesuits' reentry. When this answer was received, Carroll appointed Molyneux as Superior of the restored

[14] Cf. Guilday, *Carroll*, note 1 above, Chapter XXVIII, "The Restoration of the Society of Jesus in the United States," II, 524–566.

Society of Jesuits in the United States on June 21, 1805. Molyneux lived only until 1808, but in the meantime John Bolton and Sylvester Boarman joined the community, and the Jesuit Superior sent Adam Britt, John Henry, Francis Malevé, Anthony Kohlmann, and Peter Epinette from Europe. Charles Neale was appointed Novice Master at the Novitiate opened at Georgetown. Later there was friction between the Bishop and the successor to Molyneux, Charles Neale, about the manner in which the members of the restored Society were being moved about, but the restoration was a promise of good things for the struggling Diocese, particularly as Georgetown College passed immediately to the control of the Society. On August 7, 1814, the Society was restored throughout the world by the bull, *Sollicitudo omnium ecclesiarum,* which arrived in Baltimore four months later.

When Bishop Carroll was consecrated Bishop, he had objected to the oath usually taken by the bishops, which contained a promise to seek out and oppose heretics, as not suitable for the United States. In 1794 the Sacred Congregation of Propaganda allowed the American bishops to take the oath taken by the bishops of Ireland, which omitted the irritating promise. The next question in Bishop Carroll's mind to be taken up with Rome was the division of the Diocese. This he had suggested in the Synod of 1791, but then Rome had refused. In 1805 Carroll learned from the Propaganda that Rome was now willing to consider the division of the Diocese. He wrote in answer to this news, suggesting four dioceses at least: one diocese in New England with the See at Boston; one See at New York for New York and East Jersey; and one See at Philadelphia with jurisdiction over Pennsylvania, Delaware, and West Jersey; and one See somewhere in Kentucky with jurisdiction over Kentucky and Tennessee. A fifth might soon be established for the territory beyond the Ohio River. At the same time, Carroll would retain Maryland and all south of that state including Georgia. For Boston, although he preferred Matignon, who asked not to be considered, he suggested Cheverus; for Philadelphia, Michael Egan, O.F.M.; for Kentucky, Carroll recommended one of four, Badin, Charles Nerinckx, Benedict Joseph Flaget, or Thomas Wilson, O.P., who had come with Edward Dominic Fenwick to establish the Dominicans in Kentucky. Carroll did not recommend anyone for New York, and for that See the Office of Propaganda recommended three Irish Dominicans of Rome, Luke Concanen, John Connolly, and Joachim Cowan. On April 18, 1808, Pope Pius VII established the four Sees with Cheverus in Boston, Concanen in New York, Egan in Philadelphia, and Flaget in Bardstown, Kentucky. In another brief, Baltimore was made a metropolitain see with the other four Sees as suffragans. Also in 1805, Rome had asked Carroll to take over the administration of Louisiana which had been purchased by the United States from France in 1803. While Louisiana was under the Spanish regime, Cyril de Barcelona had been Vicar General from 1772 to 1781 and then Auxiliary Bishop of Santiago with residence in New Orleans in 1781. In 1793 Louisiana and the two Floridas were made into a separate diocese and on April 25, 1793, Louis Peñalver y Cardenas was made Bishop. He arrived in New Orleans on July 17, 1795, and remained until 1801. The Diocese was administered by Vicars General from then until October 1, 1805, when it was turned over to the administration of Bishop Carroll. The chief of these Vicars General was Patrick Walsh, one of the several Irish priests recruited from the Spanish colleges for the Spanish missions. Walsh died in 1806. Father Antonio de Sedella, a Capuchin, conducted a schism in New Orleans in defiance of the Vicars General.

Bishop Concanen was consecrated Bishop of New York in Rome on April 24, 1808, but could not travel because of the blockade of Italy. Concanen, who had been ill when appointed, had recovered sufficiently to be consecrated in Rome, but died in Naples on June 19, 1810, while waiting for passage to America during the embargo. In the meantime duplicates of the appointment had been forwarded through Paris and came to the United States with Bishop-Elect Flaget, who had gone to France for a visit. Bishop Carroll proceeded to the consecration of the three other appointees in the procathedral in Baltimore, Bishop Egan on October 28, 1810; Bishop Cheverus on November 1; and Bishop Flaget on November 4. Before leaving Baltimore, the three Bishops joined with their Metropolitan in a pastoral letter of November 15, 1810, and formulated a set of important regulations dated November 19, 1810, which were to be followed until they could meet two years later for a formal council.

In the formal statement, the four prelates agreed that strange or unknown priests were not to be allowed to exercise priestly functions unless they could exhibit authentic proofs of their bishop's permission; the Sacrament of Baptism was to be conferred only in church; marriages were recommended to be performed in church; pastors were urged to try to discourage among the faithful attachments to entertainments and diversions of a kind dangerous to morality; and they agreed not to admit to the Sacraments members of the Freemasons. They drew up also a more formal set of regulations: on the calling of councils and synods, episcopal visitations, and choice of bishops; on the status of priests and their dress; on the adoption of the Douay version of the Scriptures; on the preservation of sacramental records; on rubrics; and on the official attitude toward Freemasonry.[15] On November 15, 1810, the bishops signed also a long protest against the imprisonment of Pope Pius VII.

After the meeting of the bishops, Bishops Cheverus and Egan visited Mt. Saint Mary's at Emmitsburg and especially Mother Seton at Saint Joseph's on their way to Philadelphia. Bishop Flaget did not have sufficient funds to pay his way to Bardstown and delayed his departure until May 1811. Father Anthony Kohlmann remained as the administrator of the See of New York. The Church in the United States was entering a new phase with one archbishop, three bishops, one vacant see, about seventy priests, of whom thirteen were west of the Allegheny Mountains. Just as the country was passing through troublous times because of the war between England and France, the expansion into the west and also into Louisiana, the beginning of friction over slavery and the tariff, and the traces of sectionalism, the young Church with its several bishops, dioceses, and priests had serious problems brought about by the sudden growth in membership and the conflict of nationalities.

The external relations of the new ecclesiastical province were complicated by the imprisonment of the Pope, by efforts of Irish and French ecclesiastics to interfere in the government of the new province, and by the embargo that eventually led to the War of 1812. In the United States the romantic notion of full religious freedom was fading with the rise of political and economic quarrels among the people. The toleration exhibited by the Deists like Jefferson was replaced by a narrower denominationalism during the revival of Protestantism after the turn of the century. Revived Protestantism produced a flood of religious pamphlets, established Sunday Schools for working children, set up many new theological seminaries, and instigated anti-Catholic activity as a stimulus to religious fervor. American Catholics insisted in turn on their patriotism to their country and joined in prayers for peace before the War. The tone of Catholic expression was conservative with a fear of the excesses of the French Revolution, and there was a vague feeling among Catholics and non-Catholics alike

[15] Guilday, note 1 above, pp. 591–593. The Latin document is printed in *Concilia Provincilia, Baltimore, 1829–1849*, editio altera (Baltimore, 1851) pp. 25–28.

that there was a natural opposition between Roman Catholicism and democracy.

When the news came to Philadelphia that Michael Egan was to be the first Bishop of Philadelphia, Bishop Carroll wrote to the Trustees of St. Mary's and Holy Trinity on October 20, 1808, telling them the news and suggesting that they arrange for his support as bishop. The Trustees of St. Augustine's Church were also consulted by the trustees of the other two churches, and together they allotted the new Bishop $800 a year. In addition the Trustees of St. Mary's offered $500 a year (the whole collection) and a further sum of $1,600 for the support of the Bishop and his two clerical associates. One of these additional priests was Father William Vincent Harold, an eloquent and learned Dominican of Irish origin who had been stationed in Lisbon.[16] Hearing of the new bishops, he had come to New York to serve Bishop Concanen, but, finding that that Bishop had not arrived, he went on to Philadelphia. The Trustees there welcomed him and, after he had preached, elected him copastor. The Trustees decided also to enlarge St. Mary's in preparation for the new bishop. The free school attached to St. Mary's was also enlarged. Finally in August 1810, Egan received his bulls and was consecrated in Baltimore on October 28. Later when Bishop Egan and Father Harold had returned to Philadelphia, Father Harold told the Trustees that the funds allotted to him for his salary were not sufficient and threatened to resign. A compromise was reached on December 16 to go into effect on January 1, 1811. The newly enlarged cathedral was opened on January 6 for the installation of the new bishop. The list of pewholders showed people who were predominantly Irish but included names apparently English, French, and Spanish.

On March 16, 1811, Bishop Egan wrote to Archbishop Carroll that Father James Harold, the uncle of Father William, had arrived in Philadelphia on his way back from the penal colony in Australia. He was welcomed by the nephew and was elected by the trustees as copastor to replace Father John Rosseter whose health was failing. In April, Father James Harold was elected as one of the three priest trustees, according to the charter, with Bishop Egan and Father William Harold. The trustees were having a hard time paying the debt on the church.

Bishop Egan began his visitation of his Diocese in August 1811, going to Pittsburgh, Conewago, and Lancaster, confirming 1,460

[16] Guilday, *Carroll*, note 1 above, Chapter XXXII, "The Suffragan Sees: III. Philadelphia (1793–1815)," II, 644–685.

persons, but suffering much from the heat. Meanwhile the collections for the church were not sufficient to pay the debt, and the priests were not paid their salary. On August 22, 1812, the priest trustees called a meeting of the pewholders for August 24 to demand their salaries. The letter, written in harsh words by Father James Harold, complained of the trustees and their treatment of the priests. The meeting raised $1,000 for the clergy but was marked by violence. The trustees answered Father James Harold's letter in their own "Appeal," which listed the increases in the priests' salaries in the foregoing years. When many of the congregation began to go to church at Holy Trinity, the Bishop forbade them. The Harolds in their public defense of the Bishop really hoped to win the people and isolate the Bishop so that Father William would be elected Bishop Egan's coadjutor. Finally on Sunday, February 21, 1813, the Harolds publicly announced their resignation, expecting the people to support them and prevent their departure. To their surprise the Bishop accepted their resignations and refused to reconsider. Fathers Patrick Kenny and Matthew O'Brien were appointed to succeed them. The Harolds appealed to Archbishop Carroll, who asked Bishop Egan to reconsider, but Egan refused. The Harolds then managed the election of the trustees so that their followers were in the majority. At the meeting of the new board, Bishop Egan's salary was reduced to $800. The Bishop and Father Kenny retired from the meeting. Nevertheless, Bishop Egan refused to reinstate the Harolds, and they returned to Ireland. However, the antibishopites won the election of trustees again in April 1814, and the Bishop, worn out by the struggle, died on July 22, 1814. Archbishop Carroll appointed Father Louis DeBarth, who had been appointed Vicar General by Bishop Egan a day or so before his death, as Administrator.

In New York Father Anthony Kohlmann, S.J., was assisted by Father Benedict Fenwick, S.J., and four scholastics, with whom he founded the New York Literary Institute, which was suppressed, however, in 1813. He estimated that there were about 15,000 Catholics in New York at that time. Fathers Kohlmann and Fenwick persuaded the trustees of St. Peter's to purchase ground for a new church which was begun on June 8, 1809. The imprisonment of Pope Pius VII by Napoleon interfered with correspondence between Archbishop Carroll and the Pope about the successor of Bishop Concanen after the latter's death in Naples. Father John Connolly, O.P., from the same San Clemente's Monastery in Rome from which Bishop Concanen had come, was appointed to succeed Bishop Concanen. Consecrated in Rome on November 6,

1814, Bishop Connolly arrived in New York on November 24, 1815.

Bishop Cheverus arrived in Boston on December 20, 1810, and formally entered the Cathedral on December 22. His clergy consisted of Father James Romagné, who worked among the Indians of Maine, and the aging Father Matignon. In June he visited the Catholics of Newcastle and Damariscotta in Maine and on September 8, 1811, he gave Confirmation to the Indians. This rather small dignified and cultured French clergyman was respected by the better class of New England Yankees, although few of them were converted to the Catholic faith. At this time the embargo and the preliminaries of the War of 1812 had thrown many of the poor Irish out of work. Even the Kavanaugh and Cottril families suffered and had to withdraw their sons from Mt. Saint Mary's. When news arrived on June 3, 1814, that Pope Pius VII had been released from Fontainebleau, the Bishop had a solemn *Te Deum* sung and preached of his joy in the Boston cathedral. When Father Matthew O'Brien came to Boston to stay, Bishop Cheverus sent him as Pastor to Salem. Father O'Brien died, however, on a trip to Baltimore, October 20, 1815.

Father Benedict Joseph Flaget had tried to refuse the appointment to Bardstown and, in the interim from his appointment to his consecration, he went to France where he was told by his friends to accept the appointment. But he had no funds after his consecration on November 4, 1810, to make the trip to his new See. The following May, however, (with Father John David; a Canadian priest, Father Savine; and a subdeacon, Guy Ignatius Chabrat) he set out for the West, meeting Father Edward Fenwick and his fellow Dominicans at Pittsburgh. They went down the Ohio in a flatboat arriving at Louisville thirteen days later. He was installed by Father Badin in the little church at Bardstown, June 9, 1811. His clergy were Fathers Badin, Nerinckx, and O'Flynn, four Dominicans, and the Sulpician Father, John David. Father Chabrat was ordained at Christmas. Father David had been permitted to come to Bardstown to establish a seminary on a farm called St. Thomas. The next year, 1812, Father Nerinckx founded the Sisters of Loretto and Father David the Sisters of Charity of Nazareth. Hearing no news of a postponement of the Council, Flaget returned by way of Ohio to Baltimore for it, arriving on November 3, 1812. He set out again for Bardstown on April 22, 1813. On April 10, 1815, he sent a detailed report of his diocese to Propaganda. In it, he reported that Kentucky had ten priests, six subdeacons, four students in minor orders, and six admitted to tonsure. Four of the priests and five of the subdeacons were

Dominicans. There were 19 churches in the Diocese, and he estimated the Catholics in the state of Kentucky at not fewer than
10,000. In the state of Tennessee he estimated that there were 25
Catholic families. He had found 50 Catholic families in Ohio on
his return to Baltimore in 1812. In Indiana he found 130 families
in Vincennes. There were Catholics at Cahokia, Kaskaskia, and
Prairie du Rocher in the Illinois country. He mentioned two missions in Detroit; St. Ann's with 1,500 souls and La Rivière aux
Raisins with 500 souls. He had heard of other French congregations in the Northwest Territory but he had no chance to visit them.

By the treaty of San Ildefonso of October 1, 1800, Louisiana
had been ceded to France, but France sold it to the United States
on April 30, 1803. Before his departure in 1801, Bishop Peñalver
had named Fathers Patrick Walsh and Thomas Hassett as Vicars
General. Hassett wrote to Carroll about the religious condition of
the newly acquired territory of the United States, and Carroll sent
this word to Rome. Father Walsh also wrote to Rome about the
insubordination of Father Anthony De Sedella, the Capuchin who
resisted his authority and who was assisted by the American Governor, Claiborne. Propaganda gave jurisdiction over the region to
Carroll but, before he could appoint an administrator, De Sedella
renewed his schism. To administer the territory, Propaganda asked
Archbishop Carroll to appoint Father Charles Nerinckx, but
Nerinckx, backed by the Kentucky clergy, begged to be excused.
Carroll finally persuaded Father Louis William DuBourg to accept
the appointment. DuBourg left Baltimore on October 18, 1812,
for Louisiana. After the victory of Andrew Jackson at New
Orleans in January 1815, Father DuBourg went to France and to
Rome where he was consecrated Bishop of Louisiana on Septem-
ber 24, 1815. Bishop DuBourg left France on his return journey
July 1, 1817, accompanied by twenty-nine recruits—five priests,
four subdeacons, nine clerics, three Christian Brothers, four ecclesiastical students, and four workmen. He arrived in Louisiana,
January 5, 1818.

Archbishop Carroll had retained jurisdiction over Maryland,
the District of Columbia, Virginia, North and South Carolina,
and Georgia. His cathedral, after some discussion and disagreements, was finally begun on July 7, 1806, on Charles Street. The
Archbishop appealed at home and abroad for the financial means
to complete it, but it was not completed until six years after his
death. He continued to live at St. Peter's rectory with Father
Beeston, the Pastor. When Father Beeston died in 1809, Father
Enoch Fenwick succeeded him.

Father Francis Nagot, the Sulpician, had acquired a farm at Pigeon Hills, Adams County, Pennsylvania, and gathered around him a few seminarians preparing for the collegiate seminary. Father John Dubois, the Pastor at Frederick, had also acquired some land in what was called Emmitsburg near a former chapel of the Elder family. He urged Nagot to bring there his seminarians from Pigeon Hills. Father DuBourg joined them, and they acquired five hundred acres near the church on which they erected two rows of long buildings in 1808. Mt. Saint Mary's College had forty pupils by 1810 and twice that number by 1813. Nearby, Mrs. Elizabeth Seton took over the log building formerly used by Father Dubois as the site of her own foundation, which in time became Saint Joseph's, the Motherhouse of the Sisters of Charity.

There were in the Diocese the same congregations begun by the Jesuits at Frederick, Emmitsburg, Hagerstown, Leonardtown, Bohemia, Washington, D. C., and Georgetown, D. C. In Virginia there was a church at Alexandria and one at Norfolk, but none in Richmond. The Catholics at Norfolk did not cooperate with the clergy sent them during the first decade of the century. In Charleston, South Carolina, a port town, there were several Irish and French families. When Archbishop Carroll replaced Father Felix Gallagher as Pastor there, Gallagher had appealed to Rome and Rome asked Archbishop Carroll to reconsider. When Father Gallagher, supported by the trustees, refused to accept Father LeMercier although sent by Bishop Carroll, Bishop Carroll suspended Father Gallagher. Father Gallagher set up a chapel in his home and, with the Trustees, went into schism. Gallagher was supported by Father Robert Browne, O.S.A., whom Father Carroll had appointed to Augusta, Georgia. In 1812 the Archbishop sent also Father Joseph Pierre Picot de Clorivière, a former French Army officer, to Charleston. He remained until 1815 and then went to France, but by November 28, that year, he was back in Charleston.

Archbishop Carroll received the pallium on August 18, 1811, from Bishop Neale. But the plans for a council in 1812 were upset by the troubles that eventually led to the War of 1812. Apparently Archbishop Carroll had little sympathy with those who wanted to go to war against England, whom he regarded "as the bulwark of the public welfare." When President Madison called for a day of prayer, Archbishop Carroll issued a pastoral calling Catholics to join in the supplications for peace and prosperity. He ordered a solemn *Te Deum* on July 10, 1814, on the liberation of Pope Pius VII. He remained in Baltimore during the attack on Fort

McHenry in August 1814, and he ordered a solemn *Te Deum* of thanksgiving on October 20 after the deliverance from the attack. With the return of peace, he was eighty years of age, and he began to show his years of service. Bishop Concanen's death had delayed the arrival of a bishop for New York. Bishop Egan had died on July 22, 1814. The holding of the Council, prevented by the War of 1812, was postponed indefinitely. The Archbishop was invited to give the discourse at the laying of the cornerstone of the Washington Monument of July 4, 1815, but declined. He went to Georgetown in July for his health, but his health did not improve. By November his decline was very evident and on November 22, Bishop Neale was summoned to give the Archbishop the last sacraments. He anointed the Archbishop the next day. The Archbishop died December 3, 1815.

In Archbishop Carroll's last years the wars and the imprisonment of the Holy Father interrupted his correspondence and reports to the Holy See. The death of two of the first appointees as Suffragan Bishops upset his plans for the organization of the Church in the United States. Declining health and advanced age rendered him incapable of travel and personal administration. Had there been a Provincial Council in 1812 with the Archbishop and his four Suffragans back from their Dioceses, and perhaps the Administrator, Father DuBourg from Louisiana, the problems that were to face the nascent Church between the death of the Archbishop and the First Provincial Council of 1829 might have been faced. At least the effects of some scandals might have been prevented.

When the Archbishop died, Roman Catholicism was rising rapidly in the United States, chiefly by immigration in most of the port towns. The heart of the Catholic organization was still in Maryland and Pennsylvania. There had been defections, particularly through mixed marriages in some of the planter families of Maryland, but the Archbishop and his relatives and some Catholic families of Maryland were respected citizens. This was evident in the invitation to him to give the discourse at the laying of the cornerstone of the Washington Monument in 1815. Philadelphia offered the first example of urban Catholicism and, while the Catholics were not the wealthiest of that city's citizens, there were professional men and literary men such as Matthew Carey and Robert Walsh in Philadelphia who could be depended upon to uphold the Catholic viewpoint. In New York where the increase in Catholics was largest, the social position of Catholics was helped at first by the participation of the Spanish and French ministers and consuls, but the majority of the immigrants were of the lower classes. In Boston the missionaries of the first decades of the nineteenth century, after the episodes involving La Poterie, Rousselet, and Thayer, were of high character. Father Matignon and Bishop Cheverus were respected by the Yankees, but the Irish citizens were not, and the Yankee prejudices against Roman Catholicism were very strong. The same contrast between Catholics of English descent and Irish immigrants was found in the port towns all along the coast. In the West, the French villages were not important, except as foundations for later Catholic communities, outside of, perhaps, Detroit and New Orleans, which had some urban culture. The Kentucky settlements, coming mostly from Maryland, shared the English-American character of the mother state, but few of the wealthy Maryland families went west. The Kentucky Catholics were children of yeomen and redemptioners, but they were at home in the frontier of American life. They did not become wealthy plantation owners, but their Catholicity was to be the cornerstone of Middle Western Catholicism. The conservative ideals of the disappearing English clergy were upheld by French and Irish clergymen. The French were mostly Sulpicians and other followers of the reform movement in France, trained in the tradition of the French seminary of the eighteenth century. Besides establishing the chief training school of American clergymen, they kept alive the missions of the distant towns during the period when native vocations were few. Of the Irish clergy there were many illustrious men but there were also almost as many, in these early years, who brought disgrace on the Church. Bishop Carroll and his Suffragans tried to turn away the unworthy ones and to encourage the zealous Irish priests.

The need for discipline in the young Church was evident in the display of nationalism. Besides the English, the Irish were the first, but because they spoke English the charge of nationalism is not so clearly evident. For them the mixture of trusteeism and rebellion seemed less nationalistic. But in the Germans, the first large group of priests and people who did not speak English, the difference of language brought out the same problems with the added factor of a foreign language.

Carroll had failed to solve the problems of either trusteeism or of nationalism, but he had neither the time nor the means to deal with them. He had yielded to lay trusteeism as a solution for the problem of the lack of an establishment, and perhaps his ideals could have been carried out. But Bishop Carroll had no precedents to show him how to guide a Catholic church in a free country without state aid. The Archbishop had established Georgetown and St. Mary's and had aided in the establishment of Mt. Saint Mary's and the convents of Sisters. There were not many parish schools in existence, but the organization of the Church could not really reach the parish level for many decades. All told, Archbishop John Carroll had created the Catholic Church in America and had set up a Christian pattern. But the growth of the Church was not to be something planned, nor a growth from within.

CHAPTER FIVE

The Trustee Controversy 1815-1828

WITH THE PASSING OF ARCHBISHOP JOHN
Carroll the newly organized American Church lost a certain dignity which his personal and social prestige shed upon it. Probably
Carroll's choice of Father Leonard Neale as his Coadjutor and
successor was determined by his hope that Neale, coming from a
distinguished Maryland family, could continue this social recognition of the office. The choice had been made approximately
twenty-two years before and, while Father Neale even then had
continued to suffer from diseases contracted in the tropical swamp-
lands of Guiana, Carroll certainly did not foresee the sad condition in which his successor would be at the age of seventy when he
was called to assume the actual direction of the Archdiocese.
Leonard Neale was mentally and spiritually well qualified for the
tasks assigned him by Carroll, although as President of struggling
Georgetown College he insisted on a too rigorous discipline. He
lived an austere life even as Bishop in a room at Georgetown that
served during the day as his living room and at night for a bed-
room when a folding bed was lowered for him by the caretaker.[1]

After being relieved of the presidency of Georgetown, he lived
until his death near the convent of Sisters whom he had brought
from Philadelphia. These Sisters, Teresa Lalor and her companions, lived for a while with the Poor Clares until that community returned to France after the death of Mother La Marche.
They continued, however, as a religious community with annual

[1] John M. Daley, S.J., *Georgetown University: Origin and Early Years*
(Washington, 1957) pp. 102–104.

vows, and Neale tried to have them formed into a convent of the Visitation order. The papal indult for this Neale obtained shortly after he became Archbishop in November 1816. Mother Teresa Lalor, Sister Frances McDermott, and Sister Agnes Brent took their solemn vows on December 28, and the rest of the community made their profession on January 23 and 28, 1817. This accomplishment was perhaps the most consoling event in Neale's career as Archbishop. The rest of his career, while spiritually meritorious, was filled with trials.

There are many reasons why lay trustees attempted to take over the government of the newly organized Catholicism in America.[2] The basic reason was that the rise of the Church in the United States, unlike the conversion of western Europe by some great apostle, began when lay Catholics came together and provided a center where a congregation could be assembled and a church built. Then they waited for a traveling missionary for Mass and other services. The chief exception to these developments were the missions attended by the Jesuits who supported themselves by their plantations and came at the same time that the laymen organized congregations, or even before. In several port communities the erection of churches was aided greatly by the French and Spanish consuls. Lacking a resident pastor, or a formally erected parish, the congregation in a community consisted of a group of lay people. The fact that the Church was not recognized in law meant that even when parishes were organized the church as a church could not incorporate the physical properties of the congregation. This did not create too much of a problem in congregational Protestantism, or even in other forms of American Protestantism, because the control of the church and its property was usually in the hands of lay trustees. How much this American Protestant situation inclined the Catholic lay trustee to seek similar control is not clear. There was the usual desire of the members of an organization to control the resources of the organization. The preservation of national traditions and foreign languages was an important factor where the members of a group were of the same national origin and language. However, practicing Catholics knew that Catholicism without the Mass and the Sacraments would not be Catholic, and therefore to succeed in their

[2] John Gilmary Shea, *History of the Catholic Church in the United States, 1808–1843*, Vol. III, 25–38. The best account of Neale is Sister M. Bernetta Brislen, O.S.F., "The Episcopacy of Leonard Neale," *Historical Records and Studies*, United States Catholic Historical Society (New York, 1945) XXXIV, 20–111.

plans they had to have the cooperation of a priest or bishop.

Archbishop Carroll, when faced with the first lay rebellions in New York, Baltimore, Philadelphia, and Charleston stressed the fact that these laymen could not have spiritual power over the Church. At least at the beginning he seemed to think that a suitable solution of the American problem lay in the use of lay trustees to secure incorporation and to handle the physical and financial problems of the congregations. As his health began to decline, the friction between some trustees and their pastors was becoming acute. His Coadjutor and successor, Archbishop Neale, was not physically capable of solving the problem. One of Neale's first acts as Archbishop had been the appointment of Father James Lucas, a Frenchman, to take the place of Father Lacy, who had died at Norfolk. Lucas arrived on December 18, 1815. The Trustees received him coldly and did not invite him to their next meeting. On December 30, hearing of a second meeting of the Trustees at the home of Doctor J. F. Oliveira Fernandez, he went uninvited. The Trustees offered Father Lucas the chairmanship of the meeting, but he refused, and Doctor Fernandez was elected chairman. The doctor intended to exclude the priest from the physical administration of the church and to leave him only the spiritual powers. He claimed that the Trustees had the right to reject a priest sent by the Bishop. The Trustees wrote the Archbishop claiming their right to reject Father Lucas. They also told Lucas that he could not celebrate Mass or preach in any other congregation, such as Richmond, without their consent. The Archbishop wrote to Lucas making light of the claims of the Trustees on the ground that they were not patrons of the Church as recognized by the Council of Trent and advising him to have patience in this trial. In the meantime the Archbishop wrote to Rome of his infirmities and begged for the immediate appointment of a Coadjutor. He asked first for Bishop Cheverus, but that Bishop objected.

In desperation Lucas wrote to the Archbishop, April 10, 1816, asking permission to abolish the Board of Trustees. Neale's answer pointed out that the Trustees had power only to act in the name of the Pastor and to turn over the funds to him. To this message, when communicated to them, the Trustees answered on May 6 that the Pastor was merely commissioned by them to provide such things as were necessary for the use of the altar. Lucas answered by declaring: "MM. J. Herron, Th. Moran, Eug. Higgins, B. M. Mulhollan and J. Donaghey that they are Trustees no more. . . ." He did not make the announcement publicly but did make his position clear to the Trustees after the next Sunday Mass.

On May 16, the Trustees again appealed to the Archbishop. Neale wrote to Lucas enclosing a letter to the Trustees. To Lucas he advised mildness without giving up the proper system of holding property. To the Trustees he expressed regret that his letter had disturbed them but rejected their contentions because for trustees to have full power to transact all temporal business by majority vote would be unjust and an inversion of the order of nature. He added that this kind of power was not granted by the Church to the laity. He denied that Father Lucas had written derogatory accounts of them or criticized anyone except those who were trying to excite schisms and disturbances. The Trustees in answer insisted that they had handled the business of the parish correctly and asked that Father Lucas call a meeting of the pew-holders to discuss their work.

The Trustees then prepared a longer appeal to the Archbishop, which was in the main the work of Dr. Fernandez, who manifested a knowledge of many books on Church law and history, especially Febronius, Gerson, Mosheim, and Paolo Sarpi. The letter represents the most theoretical assertion of the rights of laymen over the clergy that appeared during the trustee controversy. Most of the trustees who were insisting at that time on the right to appoint and remove pastors would have been incapable of such an intricately documented paper. The first part, based on Gerson, argued that the authority of the Holy See in temporal matters was based on ignorance and superstition and "above all, by an uninterrupted system of Machiavellic politics in the Roman Curia." The implication was that princes and people had a sovereign right over the affairs of the nation and the inherent right over ecclesiastical disposition. Besides, he argued, there was another right enjoyed by certain laymen called the right of patronage acquired by those who support and maintain benefices. He quoted decrees on these rights of patronage which he said included the right to remove unworthy pastors as well as to appoint worthy pastors. Then Fernandez added an attack on Fathers Lacy and Lucas to show that they were unworthy. He also argued that the power exercised by clergymen in this country was contrary to the national Constitution.

On December 18, 1816, Father Lucas wrote to Archbishop Neale that he had appointed a new set of Trustees. This had resulted in a disturbance in the church and the publication of a pamphlet against the action by the Trustees. When Lucas did not listen to the old Trustees, they demanded the keys of the church and, on being refused, barred the windows and doors and put a chain and lock on the churchyard gate. Father Lucas then changed a large room in his house into a chapel and had services there for the faithful who had not followed the schismatics.

Archbishop Neale, in the meantime, was distracted from writing to Norfolk by the schism of Fathers Gallagher and Browne in Charleston and by his efforts to obtain a coadjutor. A fact that must have disturbed him also was the letter from Cardinal Litta obtained by Browne from the Sacred Congregation of Propaganda during his visit to Rome ordering Neale to reinstate Gallagher and Browne with the proviso that if he did not they would *ipso facto* be reinstated. Neale wrote immediately to Pope Pius VII, outlining the real reasons for the suspension of Gallagher by Carroll and himself and the great scandal which had resulted from the letter of Cardinal Litta. The Cardinal in answer excused himself on the grounds that he could not judge the case properly because Neale had not sent documents about the case; but the Holy Father wrote an understanding answer which arrived, however, after Neale's death.[3]

Neale had appealed to the Sacred Congregation of Propaganda on February 4, 1816, stating that the unanimous opinion of the bishops and priests was that Cheverus should be appointed his Coadjutor. As an alternative Neale proposed Father Ambrose Maréchal, a professor of theology at St. Mary's Seminary. Maréchal had already been suggested for Coadjutor of New York by Bishop Concanen, but he avoided the appointment and, when appointed on January 16, 1816, to Philadelphia, he had declined on July 3 and sent back the bulls. Maréchal suggested Bishop Cheverus for the Coadjutorship, but again Cheverus declined. Rome then appointed Maréchal as Coadjutor on July 14, 1817. But, before the bulls reached the United States, Neale was dead.

In the intervening months, the Trustees had tried to bribe Father Lucas to join them, offering him $1,200 a year. Lucas told the Archbishop of this on December 30, 1816. Neale wrote him a letter of consolation on January 14, 1817, in which he urged him not to give the keys of the church to Fernandez, adding an interdict of the church until the church and the premises were restored to the administration of the Archbishop.

When the father-in-law of Eugene Higgins, one of the Trustees, died, one Jasper Moran tried to bribe Lucas to go to the home and conduct a funeral. Lucas refused and told about the attempt at Mass the next Sunday. Moran then printed a defense of his

[3] Brislen, note 2 above, Chapter V, "Schism in Charleston," pp. 76–93.

action and an attack on the priest. Higgins wrote on April 8, 1817, to Neale attacking the conduct of Lucas in the trouble with Jasper Moran. Neale in his letter to Lucas on March 26 admitted that Lucas had been imprudent in the manner in which he had treated Moran but advised Lucas that a new church should be conveyed to the Archbishop which was the new method used in the State of Maryland to avoid disturbances. On May 4 Lucas wrote to Neale that the Norfolk Trustees had written to the Charleston schismatics asking them to send a priest to Norfolk. That same day Bishop DuBourg from Paris had written to Cardinal Litta warning him that his actions were doing great harm in the United States. Neale performed his last episcopal act on May 31, 1817, in ordaining four priests. June 16 he fell into a coma and died June 18, 1817. Maréchal was consecrated Archbishop of Baltimore on December 14, 1817.

The Norfolk Trustees decided to carry their appeal to Rome in the way that Father Browne had appealed the Charleston case. Two remarkable documents were prepared by Fernandez and sent to the Congregation of the Propaganda. They are dated May 31 and June 1. The Trustees alleged that they had not been visited by any bishops during their twenty-two years as a congregation and that since the death of Fathers Lacy and O'Brien they had been subject to foreign priests who did not conform to the customs of the country. They said that they knew that the Pope would understand the evils of foreign domination, that as a result of it conversions were few and losses of faith frequent. The only answer was for the Pope to give them a bishop of their own for the States of Virginia and North Carolina, and they suggested for this see Father Thomas Carbry, a Dominican in New York. They promised to cooperate with Father Carbry for the Church and to establish a seminary and a school. They admitted that they had not consulted the Archbishop about this because he would not recognize their right of patronage; nor had they consulted the French who were taking all the episcopal sees because the people, being mostly Irish, were attached to Irish clergy. They referred to the letter of Cardinal Litta to Neale about Fathers Gallagher and Browne. Their own letter was signed by Thomas Reilly, John Donaghey, Eugene Higgins, Bernard Mulhollan, Jasper Moran, and John F. Oliveira Fernandez, M.D., Secretary to the Board of Trustees.

A second letter sent with the petition was addressed to Donaghey and Moran who had volunteered to go to Rome with the petition. It outlined the arguments they should offer in support of the petition and the system of election and education they intended to follow if they were supported by Rome. It even listed the courses to be taught in the seminary to be established at Norfolk, the salary rates to be established for all officials of the diocese, and prizes to be offered for the pupils after a public examination.

Father Thomas Carbry, O.P., had been a friend of Bishop John Connolly in Ireland and renewed that friendship when the Bishop came to New York. Connolly had achieved the election of a favorable group of Trustees for St. Patrick's Cathedral when he divided the two parishes into St. Peter's and St. Patrick's. The Trustees of St. Peter's remained opposed to him. In the beginning of the troubles with the Trustees, Father Carbry had been on the side of Bishop Connolly along with other Dominicans, and it is doubtful that Carbry went to Norfolk to join any rebellion against the Archbishop, although Maréchal placed that interpretation on his coming. In search of an Irish bishop for their proposed See in Virginia, the Trustees found Carbry suitable for their plans. Donaghey had also secured letters of recommendation of Carbry for the Bishopric from three other Dominicans, one in Ireland, his former Provincial, and two in Rome.

Father Ambrose Maréchal had no choice but to accept the office of Vicar General and Administrator of the Archdiocese, but he did hope to escape the Archbishopric because he felt that taking himself out of St. Mary's seminary would ruin the seminary. When Eugene Higgins wrote to him as Administrator asking for a solution of the Norfolk schism, he told Higgins that he was not the Archbishop but would do all in his power to restore peace. In the meantime Maréchal received the letter addressed to Neale by Pope Pius VII making amends for the letter by Cardinal Litta in which he had restored Gallagher and Browne. Also Cardinal Litta had written endeavoring to explain his mistake by the lack of documents from Neale to enable him to judge the situation properly. On July 21, 1817, the Sacred Congregation wrote to Maréchal that he had been appointed the Coadjutor to Neale. In the meantime, as Administrator, Maréchal had written to Cardinal Litta complaining of the encouragement given to all the discontented groups in the country by his letter on the Charleston Trustees, noting especially the encouragement derived by the Norfolk dissidents.

Donaghey apparently had received a welcome at the Sacred Congregation because on September 20, 1817, Cardinal Litta, the Prefect, wrote a letter to Fernandez thanking him for his letter and praising his good work for the Church in Virginia. Donaghey must have had Irish friends in Rome. However, the Cardinal noted that since Virginia was a part of the Archdiocese of Baltimore that prelate would have to be consulted. He seemed to say that the Archbishop would be pleased to give up a region so distant from his own see. While awaiting the opinion of the Archbishop, the Cardinal would consider the person suited for the new see, and, since the people were mostly Irish, the suggestion of Father Carbry was fitting. However, the Cardinal noted that, even if the Trustees were recognized as having a right of patronage in the canonical sense, this privilege would not extend to spiritual matters, but he was sure that such fervent men would not demand more. The Cardinal wrote two letters to Maréchal telling about the mission of Donaghey and indicating that, since Virginia was so far away, Maréchal would not object to the separation and would not object to the appointment of Carbry. Donaghey in the meantime was carrying as messenger a letter sent from Rome by Father John Grassi, S.J., as agent for Maréchal to the Archbishop in which Grassi spoke disrespectfully of the Sacred Congregation. Since the letter was unsealed he took the liberty of copying the critical passage and sending it to the Cardinal Prefect.

On July 14, 1817, the Sacred Congregation decided that Maréchal was Coadjutor Archbishop of Baltimore. Although the Sacred Congregation did not know it then, he became by that decision the Archbishop of Baltimore because Neale had died. On September 25, 1817, after he had been informed by Bishop DuBourg of his appointment Maréchal wrote a letter to Gallagher and Browne demanding their submissions. Browne gave his submission, but Gallagher remained contumacious. The bulls for Maréchal arrived on November 10, and on December 14 he was consecrated by Bishop Cheverus, with Bishop Connolly and Father de Barth as assistants, in St. Peter's Church in Baltimore. The sermon was preached by the Augustinian, Father Michael Hurley.

Maréchal has been described as a small energetic person with the mannerisms of a college teacher, and the printed portrait makes him a pleasant person with small face, deep-set eyes behind his spectacles, and large nose. He has been dealt with sharply by partisan historians because he fought Irish nationalism. The underlying factor in his troubles was the absence of capable administrators among the English and American clergy to assist him and the ambitions of the Irish who felt that he was unfair. Just as Germans were later to resent being Americanized by an Irish clergy, so the Irish then resented being Americanized by a French clergy. The French, by their associations with the English and Americans and by their labors in the seminaries and missions, had in this case inherited the mantle of the Anglo-American founders of American Catholicism.

In the manuscript[4] of the sermon given by the new Archbishop in St. Peter's Church, December 20, 1817, is a note that, because of the inclemency of the weather, he did not give the second part of the sermon in which he had prepared a statement of the evils that threatened the American Church, namely, the shortage of clergy, the evils of too great wealth, and the dissensions that were arising. The first part of the sermon dwelt chiefly on the magnificent progress of the Church during the preceding fifty years and on the progress since he first came to Baltimore in 1792.

Twenty-five years ago, when I first entered Baltimore, this temple of God, how small soever it may now appear to us, was much too large for the congregation. Yet this was the only Catholic church in the city. Three others have been since built, all of which are now too small and if any apprehensions are entertained respecting the magnificent metropolitan church, they are grounded upon the idea not of its being too extensive, but of its being laid out upon too small a scale to contain the Catholics of this city, who may crowd under its roof on great solemnities.

One of the first actions of the new Archbishop was to publish the acts of the Synod of 1791, with the regulations adopted by the Bishops in 1810, to which he added certain regulations of his own on the preparation for marriage, on erecting churches, on permitting strange priests to officiate, and on the proper memorials for Archbishop Neale.[5] He wrote to his friend Cardinal Dugnani, the former Nuncio, that he had accepted the Archbishopric to prevent the disorder that might follow his refusal.[6] He complained of the harm done to church discipline by Father Gallagher in Charleston and by the hearing obtained by Donaghey of Norfolk at the Sacred Congregation. He exposed his suspicion that some translators of documents were imposing on the Sacred Congregation. Maréchal probably understood that the Italian prelates did not understand English and were really at the mercy of the Irish translators as interpreters of the reports and letters in English.

[4] The manuscript is in the Baltimore Collection of the University of Notre Dame Archives.

[5] Copy in Propaganda Archives. Microfilm copy in the University of Notre Dame Archives.

[6] Since there is no biography of Maréchal, the best account of these troubles is in Guilday, The Church in Virginia (1815–1822) (New York, 1924) Chapters IV and V "Archbishop Maréchal and the Norfolk Schism," pp. 63–123.

Dr. Fernandez encouraged by the letter of Cardinal Litta wrote an insulting letter to Maréchal informing the Archbishop that he was demanding a separate bishopric and that in the meantime he demanded the removal of Father Lucas. Maréchal again exchanged letters with Cardinal Dugnani about the Archdiocese and detailed the causes for the Norfolk trouble. He complained again about the interpreters for the Sacred Congregation. Bishop Connolly of New York also had written to Rome on February 25, 1818, recommending a separate diocese in each of the seventeen States if the Irish there could support a church in the State as the Irish in Norfolk had done. Connolly claimed that Jasper Moran and his seven children had left the Church because of the events in Norfolk. He recommended Father Carbry for Bishop of the Diocese of Virginia. On February 26 he wrote again claiming that Archbishop Neale could have been condemned legally for his actions in Norfolk. Cardinal Litta, however, had received Maréchal's letter of October 21, 1817, and was more friendly in his answers. He admitted that he had received Donaghey but said that he had insisted on the consent of Maréchal before any change would be made. He asked Maréchal for advice on the proposals of the Trustees of Norfolk. On April 9, 1818, Bishop Connolly wrote a letter to Maréchal urging the appointment of Carbry as Bishop of Virginia.

In March Maréchal started on a visit to the Archdiocese. Accompanied by Father James Whitfield he visited besides Baltimore, Georgetown, Washington, Alexandria, Port Tobacco, St. Thomas' Manor, and Newport. On June 11 they left Baltimore for Norfolk. There on June 12 he confirmed eighty prepared by Father Lucas. He called also a meeting of the pewholders, but a fourth of them stayed away and some did not remain in the meeting. While Maréchal was at Norfolk, Fernandez published a broadside containing the previous resolutions of the former Trustees and their charges against the Archbishop and Father Lucas. In answer Maréchal wrote a letter to Father Lucas telling him that he could excommunicate the leaders of the rebellious group but would not do so. In reply Fernandez published a second broadside repeating the charges of the Trustees, insisting that they would continue their position until their appeal was answered by the Holy See.

In Charleston the Trustees under the leadership of Dr. Matthew O'Driscoll acted as if they did not believe that the Apostolic rescript allowing Maréchal to suspend Gallagher and Browne really existed; instead they insisted on the removal of Father Clorivière according to the previous document brought back by Donaghey. Their argument for their right of patronage was based on the history of the concordats between Rome and the French monarchs.

Your memorialists beg leave to suggest to your Reverence, that that part of the sovereign people of these United States, in communion with his Holiness the Pope, as their government interferes not in matters of religion, think, and hold themselves, *immediately* intitled, to the same benefits and immunities in their religious concerns, as are established between the court of Rome, and the Sovereigns of Europe, *intermediately* negotiating for the interests and religious liberties of their subjects.[7]

During the spring of 1818 Maréchal and the recalcitrant Gallagher and the Trustees of Charleston exchanged letters without effect. Then the Trustees appealed to Rome. Their long letter of May 13, 1818, really joined the two schisms of Norfolk and Charleston by asking for a new bishopric consisting of all the Archdiocese south of Maryland with Father Thomas Carbry, O.P., as Bishop. When Maréchal heard that Carbry had been invited by the refractory Trustees, he wrote to him on July 17, 1818, threatening him with excommunication if he ministered to the schismatic group. At the same time, the Archbishop had sent out a questionnaire to the clergy of the Archdiocese and from his answers he prepared a report for Propaganda on the condition of the Church in the Archdiocese, dated October 16, 1818. Meanwhile Carbry had acted as pastor for the schismatics in Norfolk, and he remained in the Diocese until the arrival later of the first Bishop of Richmond.

Maréchal began this report[8] with a brief statement of the relation of the Archdiocese to the other dioceses. Then he turned to his own diocese where, he said, there were 52 priests: 1 Italian, 3 Germans, 4 English, 7 Belgians, 12 Americans, 11 Irish, and 14 French. Each priest had a church but many attended also two or three other missions at least once a month. The foundations of the Cathedral had been laid but for lack of money the building had not been completed, although he hoped to dedicate it within eighteen months. He mentioned the two seminaries, St. Mary's and Mt. Saint Mary's at Emmitsburg. Georgetown College was established near Washington, and he did not understand why the Jesuits in Rome did not send six or eight additional teachers there.

[7] Peter Guilday, *The Life and Times of John England, First Bishop of Charleston (1786–1842)* 2 vol. (New York, 1927) I, 225. These volumes are the richest source for the period 1815–1842 and surpass Shea.

[8] This report is in *Catholic Historical Review* (1915–1916) I, 439–453. Microfilm of original in University of Notre Dame Archives.

He mentioned three convents of nuns, the Carmelites at Port Tobacco, the Visitandines at Georgetown, and the Daughters of St. Vincent de Paul near Emmitsburg.

Characterizing the non-Catholics in the Archdiocese he noted that there were representatives of nearly every kind of sect, but that they all tended toward Unitarianism. There was a deep prejudice among the people against Catholicism, which these Protestants had inherited from their cradles. Nevertheless there were converts—at Taneytown he found that a third of the Catholics were converts. There were many immigrants coming into the country, about 40 or 50 a day, and many of these were Catholics. He did not find any deep culture among the Americans but on the whole the Americans were above the Europeans in general culture. The Americans had too great a desire to acquire wealth, and this hindered their contributions to the building of churches. They lived chastely, but the women, he found, dressed richly and read love stories. Americans observed the Sundays strictly because they had formerly been required to do this by law. Books were numerous, including those published in England and France, and the liberty of printing was strongly defended. Maréchal observed that that there were as many daily newspapers as in Italy and France combined.

In another part of his report Maréchal stressed the need for native priests. Those that they had were not deeply versed in learning but, with their knowledge of moral and dogmatic theology and their piety, they rendered great service. After the Americans the most useful priests were the English, of whom he had only four, one of whom, Father James Whitfield, came to help him when he heard that he had been made a bishop. The Belgian, French, and German priests, while they did not speak English perfectly, were well received by the faithful, despite the charges of Fathers Gallagher and Browne. Of the pious Irish priests, there were several who rendered great service, but there were other Irish priests not so pious whom he could not entrust with the care of souls. Nevertheless, he marveled at the power these bad clergymen had among their own people, who regarded drunkenness as only a light fault. All the schisms of recent origin arose among these Irish. Lately the Irish priests had also accused the French Bishops of Boston, Bardstown, and himself of trying to set up a French hierarchy and to expel all Irishmen. Maréchal pointed out that he had given faculties to eleven Irish priests and most of the seminarians were Irish. Of the fourteen French priests, eight worked entirely in the two seminaries.

Maréchal said there was no country where Catholicism could be more easily spread than in the United States since there was no danger of persecution. Every religion was protected by law. The only threat to Catholicism was internal dissension. The schisms arose: (1) from the great liberty given to Americans, which Protestants exercised in choosing their ministers and which led Catholics to want the same freedom; (2) also because when a church was built the Catholics in the region collected the funds and chose some persons to put in charge of the property. These incorporated themselves and claimed for themselves rights over the congregation. When a bad pastor had been installed, the Bishop could not remove him without the consent of these Trustees. This had happened in Norfolk where an impious doctor, Fernandez, and two dissolute Irishmen opposed Father Lucas. Maréchal added that in some cases bad priests could persuade the Trustees to block their removal by the Bishop. There was nothing in American law to prevent this.

For the states of North and South Carolina, Georgia, and the territory of Mississippi, he suggested that these be erected into a Vicariate Apostolic and that a priest experienced in the American missions be made Vicar Apostolic, as was done in Louisiana with the appointing of Bishop DuBourg. The See for this Vicariate would be in Charleston. He did not know the proper person for the office but suggested that he be English and be able to speak French because there were French-speaking people in the area. He had recalled Father Clorivière because he had been so badly attacked and had sent in his place two Jesuits. He did not know whether the Jesuits would be able to restore peace. The Irish of Charleston were trying to deceive the Sacred Congregation as they did in the case of Norfolk and as Father Browne did on his visit, and they hoped to obtain the right to elect their pastors by getting their countrymen throughout the country to demand it. Maréchal closed his letter with a statement of the number of orders he had conferred, the faculties he needed, and a list of the priests of the Diocese. He noted also the vacancy in Philadelphia since the death of Bishop Egan.

Bishop Connolly had faith in his former classmate, Father Thomas Carbry, and recommended him to Maréchal on October 31, 1818, for the proposed See of Charleston. He sent a similar recommendation to the Cardinal Prefect. The two Jesuits sent by Maréchal to Charleston were Fathers Benedict Fenwick and James Wallace. They arrived November 10, 1818. Clorivière was still there, and so were Gallagher and Browne, although they were not active. The Trustees received them and asked for the removal of the interdict on the church, but the Jesuits refused until the Trustees signed an agreement that was proposed to them concerning their submission. Clorivière left Charleston in December and spent the rest of his life working in Georgetown. As soon as Father Benedict Fenwick raised the interdict, the Trustees packed the election of January 1819 and manifested their intention of demanding again the right of patronage. In May 1819, Father Browne left for Rome to further the establishment of the See of Charleston and the appointment of Father Carbry. On January 4, however, the schismatics of Norfolk had sent through Father Carbry in New York a letter to an Irish Franciscan, Father Richard Hayes, who was in trouble in Rome because of his action on the Veto Question in Ireland, asking him to go to the Jansenistic Bishop of Utrecht to receive consecration as Bishop of South Carolina in North America. He was to proceed after his consecration to Charleston and be ready to consecrate other bishops. Father Hayes immediately sent a copy of the letter to Archbishop Troy of Dublin, denouncing the invitation, and also a copy to the Holy Father. Carbry had gone from New York to Norfolk when he heard that Maréchal had appointed Father Nicholas Kerney to the church in Norfolk. On June 8 Maréchal wrote to Carbry challenging his right to come there. At Norfolk the Trustees had prepared in December 1818 their long letter to Thomas Jefferson, copies of which they sent to various governmental persons.

This letter to Jefferson[9] began with a statement about religion that could have been written by Deist Jefferson. By contrast to this notion of freedom, the letter spoke of the temporal dependence of the American Church on the Pope and his dependence on European monarchs. The letter then included a diatribe against the Jesuits, accusing them of covetousness, which had been imitated by the Sulpicians. The American way of electing ministers they praised, saying that this discipline was once part of the Catholic Church. The Irish suffered in America because of the lack of this manner of election since they were the most numerous but had only about one twentieth of the membership of the clergy appointed in the country. They listed the possibility of the Church's imposing royalist doctrines on this country through its subservience to the British government and insisted that such a foreign power must not be allowed to function in the United

[9] This letter is printed in Guilday, *Church in Virginia*, note 6 above, pp. 93–101.

States. Copies of this letter were sent to members of the Congress then in session.

With the arrival of Carbry, the Trustees prepared a letter to Maréchal dated June 14, 1819, in which they related the events since the coming of Father Lucas and quoted various authorities, civil and ecclesiastical, supporting their right of patronage and threatening legal action if the Archbishop tried to act against Carbry or their associates. Carbry appeared before the Norfolk magistrate and was recognized there as the Pastor of the church. He then said Mass in the interdicted church. To Maréchal he claimed he did not need authorization from him in the United States.

In June 1819, the Sacred Congregation of Propaganda held a meeting to discuss the condition of the Church in the United States. They accepted Maréchal's recommendation that there be a see in Charleston, but they accepted also another opinion that there should likewise be a new see in Virginia. Seven priests were mentioned as suitable for these sees, two for Virginia and five for Charleston. On August 2, 1819, they decreed the establishment of the See of Charleston, but they delayed the erection of the Virginia See. On September 11, Maréchal received news of this action with the added sentence that they were not certain whether to establish the see in Richmond, Norfolk, or Washington. On September 13, the Congregation asked the Provincial of the Dominicans to order Carbry out of America. Maréchal wrote to Cardinal Litta suggesting that the new Prefect of Propaganda, Cardinal Fontana, seek information before acting.

Meanwhile Maréchal published his *Pastoral Letter to the Roman Catholics of Norfolk* dated September 28, 1819, an answer to the *Letter to Thomas Jefferson*. The Archbishop summed up the argument against the Trustees from the institution of the priesthood, the practices of apostolic times, and the constitution of the Church as set forth by the Council of Trent. He claimed that the Trustees wanted the priest to be merely a hireling, with the obvious implication that they had such a hireling in Father Carbry. He further pointed out that there were no real parishes or benefices in this country and that nothing in the Constitution of the United States interfered in the proper administration of the Church's laws. Father Carbry, he said, had no jurisdiction and had not received any secret appointment from the Holy See. The solution of the problem, falsely represented by the Trustees who went to Rome, had been turned over to him by the Sacred Congregation.

In his letters to Rome, Archbishop Maréchal told how the French bishops had been accused of trying to set up a French hierarchy in the country and to throw out the Irish clergy. In his letter of September 18, 1819,[10] he expressed severe criticisms of the Irish clergy in the country. He admitted that he had some Irish clergy who were very good, but he added that, out of ten Irish priests who came, only one or two were successful while eight of them turned out badly. He hoped that soon the Americans would have a native clergy. He welcomed English and Scotch priests and would accept Irish clergy but only after careful scrutiny. He could say that practically all the scandals of the day were caused by Irish priests in Philadelphia, Norfolk, and Charleston and now by the attempted marriage of Father Egan in Richmond. He further pointed out that, although Bishop Egan had a majority of Irish clergy, he too had troubles and dissensions among them. And the same was true of Bishop Connolly in New York, where the Irish predominated. Maréchal wrote on April 28, 1820, recommending Father Fenwick, his Vicar General at Charleston, as the Bishop of the new see. Maréchal was unprepared for the appointment of a succession of Irishmen whom he did not know to the vacant and newly erected sees.

Pope Pius VII had already on November 26, 1819, appointed Father Henry Conwell, Vicar General of Armagh, to the See of Philadelphia. On July 1, 1820, the Holy Father at the suggestion of the Congregation of the Propaganda erected the two Sees of Richmond and Charleston. Father Patrick Kelly of the Diocese of Ossory, the appointee to Richmond, was a learned man who had taught for a time at the diocesan seminary. He was forty years of age and a good preacher. But he wrote to his friends that he did not have the money to pay even for his passage to his new See. He was consecrated on August 24, 1820, in St. James Chapel, Dublin, by Archbishop Troy. On September 21 he took part in the consecration of the Bishop-Elect of Charleston, John England, a brilliant Irish priest of Bannon. A writer and orator of ability, Father England had opposed the Veto and was recommended by the Bishops of Ireland for promotion to a foreign see. Ireland's loss in this case was a gain for the Church in the United States. On November 11, Propaganda sent Bishop Kelly a subsidy of one hundred Irish pounds to pay for his journey to Richmond. On the same day it sent letters to Charleston, to Norfolk, and to Maréchal.

On October 17, Archbishop Maréchal wrote a letter of protest

[10] Microfilm copy from Propaganda Archives, University of Notre Dame Archives.

against the erection of the Virginia See. On November 20, Father Malou, the Jesuit who was leading the anti-Irish faction in New York against Bishop Connolly, wrote to Maréchal that Father Browne had arrived there and had been reinstated in the Diocese of Charleston by Bishop England. On November 21, Bishop Conwell arrived in Baltimore to confer with the Archbishop. Their relations, however, seem to have been cordial. On December 29, Bishop Kelly also arrived in New York. Father Carbry was still in Norfolk defying the Archbishop. When Bishop Kelly arrived in Baltimore, Maréchal read to him a formal protest against his attempting to set up the See of Richmond, adding: ". . . But to assure the tranquility of our conscience we hereby distinctly declare to your Lordship, that we in no wise give or yield our assent positively to this most unfortunate action of the Sacred Congregation de Propaganda Fide. . . ."[11]

Father Louis de Barth had just been made Vicar General of the Philadelphia diocese before the death of Bishop Egan, and Archbishop Carroll naturally chose him as the Administrator of that vacant see. Father De Barth, however, was insistent that he would not accept the Bishopric for himself and actually asked to be released from the Administratorship. He and Father McGirr were the two clerical members of the Trustees of St. Mary's Church, and the lay Trustees, led by Augustine Fagan and John Doyle, strongly supported Father William Vincent Harold and proposed that the charter be amended so as to exclude the clergymen from the management of the temporal affairs of the church. Father Harold hoped to be named Bishop of Philadelphia. However, although the Trustees voted for the change, no action was taken then with the state legislature. During March 1820, Father William Hogan from Ireland came to Philadelphia, after failing to be accepted by Archbishop Maréchal in Baltimore where his cousin was accepted as a seminarian. He did not have credentials but, on the representation of the cousin, Father De Barth allowed him to preach in St. Mary's. He was so eloquent that the Trustees elected him Pastor instead of Father Felix Gallagher, who was to come from Charleston. Besides his oratorical ability, Father Hogan was a handsome man with a becoming head of brown hair, blue eyes, and fair skin. He paid careful attention to the members of the parish and was invited to their homes. While Father De Barth was absent from the city, unsavory rumors about Hogan's conduct began to spread and, although Fathers McGirr and Cummiskey

[11] Guilday, *Church in Virginia*, note 6 above, p. 134.

objected, he did not listen to them. He moved into a separate house which was redecorated and repaired by the congregation. On December 2, Bishop Conwell arrived in Philadelphia. He was described as tall, straight and muscular but was already seventy-five years of age. On December 3 he took possession of his See and at the High Mass Father Hogan preached. The sermon to the surprise of all was a bitter attack on Father De Barth. The Bishop, who had heard reports of Hogan before he left Ireland, advised Hogan to leave the separate house and live with the other clergymen and to change his ways. Hogan refused and the next Sunday, December 12, the Bishop called the priests together and suspended the faculties of Hogan. Hogan's friends, including Matthew Carey the publisher, held a meeting and protested his suspension, saying that the penalty was too severe for the offense given by the sermon. Bishop Conwell, however, had also in mind the immorality of the priest in his separate residence and would not reinstate him.

The Irish were having troubles in other dioceses also. In New York, Bishop Connolly had managed to separate the incorporation of the two churches. The Trustees of St. Patrick's cooperated with him, but the group opposed to the Bishop got control of St. Peter's Church. The supporters of the Bishop there were mostly Irish and included Father Michael O'Gorman, whom he had brought with him from Ireland, and the Dominicans Fathers Charles L. Ffrench and Thomas Carbry. The Trustees opposing the Bishop were supported by Fathers Peter Malou and William Taylor. The Trustees of St. Peter's brought charges against Father Ffrench of misconduct in Canada before he came to New York and asked the Bishop to remove him. The Bishop refused. The Trustees threatened to withold Ffrench's salary and even that of the Bishop. Father Taylor went to Rome on behalf of the Trustees, and, when he returned, the Bishop refused to allow him to remain in the Diocese. He withdrew also the faculties of Father Peter Malou. The Bishop, meanwhile, visited the Diocese as far west as Buffalo and founded churches in Utica and at Carthage and placed them under the care of Father John Farnan. Father Carbry meanwhile went to Norfolk, Father Ffrench was ordered by Rome to leave the Diocese, and Father Malou was recalled by his Jesuit superiors. Their departures brought peace to the Diocese. The depletion of the clergy was repaired chiefly by the arrival of the eloquent and learned Father John Power in 1819 and the ordinations of Fathers Richard Bulger and Patrick Kelly.

In Boston, Bishop Cheverus was watching with interest the

troubles of Archbishop Maréchal in Norfolk and Charleston and wrote with some amusement of the charge of the Irish Trustees that the French bishops were trying to set up a French hierarchy and to expel the Irish. On September 19, 1818, the Bishop lost his great friend, Father Francis Matignon, by death. The Diocese grew in population through immigration, chiefly from Ireland. Churches were established at South Boston, New Bedford, and Salem, Massachusetts; North Whitefield, Maine; and Claremont, New Hampshire; and other missions were begun. The number of Catholics in the diocese in 1820 was estimated at 3,850 plus about 750 Indians in Maine. There were a small number of adult converts from among the Yankees. The Bishop, however, had only five priests in all New England to help him. In June 1820, the Bishop went to Montreal to bring back two professed and two novice Ursulines to take over the house and school prepared by the inheritance of Father John Thayer who had died in Ireland.

In the vast territory under the administration of Bishop Flaget, pioneers were gradually making progress, especially after the Indian power had been broken during the War of 1812. In Bardstown the Bishop laid the cornerstone for St. Joseph's Cathedral on July 16, 1816. In 1818 Fathers Charles Nerinckx and Robert Abell visited the missions in western Kentucky. Flaget opened his house to Father Felix De Andreis, Father Joseph Rosati, and other members of the Congregation of the Missions on their way to Louisiana, who were desirous of learning English before entering their mission field. On Flaget's request, Rome made Father John David (the Coadjutor of Bardstown) Bishop of Mauricastro on July 4, 1817. Learning that Father Gabriel Richard was having difficulties with his trustees in Detroit, the Bishop wrote them a pastoral on February 24, 1817, and decided that he should visit them. He visited the missions of southern Michigan and returned by way of Pittsburgh and Cincinnati. On August 7, 1819, he moved his seminary from St. Thomas to the cathedral residence. On August 8 he dedicated St. Joseph's Cathedral in Bardstown, and Father Robert Abell, a noted orator, preached the sermon on the occasion. The next Sunday Bishop Flaget consecrated Bishop David. At Flaget's suggestion, Rome erected the See of Cincinnati to have jurisdiction over Ohio, Michigan, and the Northwest with the Dominican Father Edward Fenwick as Bishop.

In 1817 Bishop DuBourg made his way back to his strife-torn diocese of Louisiana, arriving in St. Louis on January 5, 1818, where he was welcomed by the people as well as the clergy.[12] He was accompanied by Bishop Flaget to officiate at his installation. For the time DuBourg ignored the southern part of his diocese where the rebellious Capuchin, Antonio de Sedella, was in charge of the Cathedral and made light of DuBourg's episcopal powers. DuBourg established his seminary among the Vincentians at the Barrens, near St. Louis, and also established the home of the newly founded Madames of the Sacred Heart at St. Charles. De Sedella, "Père Antoine," had drawn two unworthy priests to him as his assistants in the Cathedral. He received and gave generously but he was likewise careless about Church law. He let the Marguilliers or Trustees have their way, and as a result they supported him in his rebellion. Father Sibourd, whom DuBourg had named his Vicar General in New Orleans, lived in the city and merely tolerated the activities of De Sedella.

Father Bertrand Martial had come from Paris with the Religious of the Sacred Heart. He remained in New Orleans and undertook the education of young boys. He became popular, a real rival of Père Antoine. Père Antoine, when he saw his popularity vanishing, submitted and at the request of the Marguilliers, Bishop DuBourg sent three of his best priests to care for the Cathedral, Fathers Louis Moni, Bertrand Martial, and Angelo Ferrari, who had come with the Bishop from Italy. But reform in the city itself was badly needed. Finally, since the strife seemed subdued, the Bishop went to New Orleans just before Christmas in 1820. After Christmas he called a Diocesan Synod with twenty of his priests, although this was not accepted as a real synod by Rome. He returned to St. Louis in the summer but was back again in New Orleans in 1822.

In 1822, there appeared the first real directory of American Catholicism, *The Laity's Directory to the Church Service, for the Year of Our Lord MDCCCXXII*. There had been an earlier version of this published in 1817, but the information about the contemporary churches was very meager. There was to be a regular *Directory and Almanac* after 1833 but this one in 1822, revised from that of 1817, by Father John Power of New York gave one of the best summaries of the progress of Catholicism up to what was probably the peak year of the trustee controversy. Besides the

---

[12] The only history of the Church in Louisiana is Roger Baudier, *The Catholic Church in Louisiana* (New Orleans, 1939). For this period see pp. 260–295 and Shea, note 2 above, III, 356–394.

usual almanac materials, the booklet contained a brief account of the establishment of the episcopate of the United States and a copy of the *Brief* of that establishment, a statement of the present condition of the Church, an account of the reestablishment of the Jesuits, and the obituaries of the more important deceased American prelates. Under the account of the Archdiocese of Baltimore, which included Maryland and the District of Columbia, the book listed the two colleges, Georgetown and St. Mary's, Baltimore, two seminaries at the same places, the newly planned college at Mt. St. Mary's at Emmitsburg, the novitiate of the Jesuits at Whitemarsh, two religious female institutions, one at Georgetown under the Visitandines and the other at Emmitsburg under the Daughters of Charity, and a convent of Carmelites at Port Tobacco. There were four churches in Baltimore, including the new Cathedral. In Washington there were two; in Georgetown two; one each in Frederick, Emmitsburg, and Alexandria; with twenty-eight scattered throughout the rural parts of the Archdiocese. There were two charity schools in Baltimore and two in Georgetown.

In the account of the Diocese of Boston, which included all of New England, the book noted that, before the arrival of Matignon and Cheverus, Catholics in Boston were scarcely known but now they had two churches, Holy Cross and St. Augustine, besides one at Salem and one at New Bedford, and two in Maine at Damariscotta and Whitefield, besides the Indian Mission in Maine. There was also a new house of the Ursulines in Boston. The directory tells us nothing about the laity, who were mostly Irish.

The Diocese of New York comprehended the State of New York and the northern part of New Jersey. In New York City there were two churches, one the Cathedral of St. Patrick, the other St. Peter's, and two charity schools, both receiving funds from the state. There were also Albany, Utica, Auburn, and Carthage in the state with one church each, and there was one also in Paterson, New Jersey. It was worth noting that all the priests were Irish.

In describing the Diocese of Philadelphia, which included Pennsylvania, Delaware, and the southern part of New Jersey, the book noted four churches in Philadelphia and eleven other churches in Lancaster, Conewago (with five priests), Reading, Carlisle, Chambersburg, Loretto, Greenburgh, Pittsburgh, Cochinhopen [sic] in Pennsylvania; one in Wilmington, Delaware, and one in Trenton, New Jersey. The Sisters of Charity from Emmitsburg had an orphanage in Philadelphia, and there was a charity school at St. Joseph's in that city. The last sentence of the section on Philadelphia expressed the hope "that peace, good-will, and harmony, may once more prevail among them" who were then one fifth of the city of Philadelphia.

As the book says, the Diocese of Bardstown was "of prodigious extent," including Kentucky, Tennessee, Indiana, Ohio, Illinois, and the territories of Michigan and the Northwest. The Cathedral was in Bardstown, and the book says there were sixteen or eighteen churches in the Diocese. There were some Indians in the Diocese, some of whom had obtained the Faith from the Jesuit missionaries of the seventeenth century. There was a seminary at Bardstown. There were several large congregations in Ohio, Indiana, and Illinois, a college run by the Dominicans in Kentucky, and an academy at Frankfort. There were four houses of female religious according to the book: the Daughters of Charity, at that time a branch from Emmitsburg, *The little congregation of the Friends of Mary beneath the Cross of Jesus; . . .* Apostolines . . . and the Cloister of Loretto . . ." but the last two are not mentioned in any other account, although the first might refer to the Dominican Sisters founded at St. Catherine's in 1822. The second probably refers to the group who became the Lorettines, already mentioned.

The account of the "Bishopric of Louisiana" in the *Directory* stated that it included the territory bought from France as Louisiana and the Floridas, which had two sees in St. Louis and New Orleans but only one bishop. The book described the seminary of the Vincentians at the Barrens and a College of St. Louis under the Bishop. The upper part of the Diocese had churches at St. Genevieve, Kaskaskia, Prairie du Rocher, Cahokia, St. Ferdinand, and Portage des Sioux, besides the Cathedral at St. Louis, although the spelling of these names in the *Directory* had many imperfections. The Ladies of the Sacred Heart were in the village of St. Ferdinand. The State of Louisiana had eighteen ecclesiastical parishes, New Orleans, St. Bernard, St. Charles, St. John the Baptist, St. James, St. Michael, Ascension, Assumption, St. Joseph, St. Gabriel at Iberville, Baton Rouge, Point Coupée, St. Martin and St. Mary, St. Landry (Attacappas), St. Charles Borromeus (Opeloussas), Avoyelles, and Natchitoches, and Natchez in Mississippi. The Ursulines were in New Orleans with their seminary and a public church. There was also a college near New Orleans under the direction of Father Martial. The Ladies of the Sacred Heart had a school for young ladies at Opeloussas. A priest was to be sent to Florida, which had just been acquired by the United States.

There was one priest in Arkansas, and others were being sought for the Indians of the area.

The description of the Diocese of Richmond emphasized the bad situation of Bishop Patrick Kelly, since his See was Richmond and his residence was in Norfolk. There were six other churches in the new Diocese: in Portsmouth, Richmond, Martinsburg, Winchester, Bath and Shepherdstown, although the last four were to be attended by a priest from Winchester.

The Diocese of Bishop John England comprised the three states of North Carolina, South Carolina, and Georgia. A cathedral was being built in Charleston. There was no church in North Carolina, although there were Catholics at Newbern, Wilmington, and Washington. In South Carolina, churches were planned at Columbia and in Chester County. In Georgia there were three churches, in Savannah, Augusta, and Locust Grove. There were no Catholic schools in the Diocese. The account gave the Constitution of the organization in Charleston for the dissemination of good literature.

The Floridas were mentioned with some indication that they would become a separate diocese. There were two Catholic churches in Florida, at St. Augustine and at Pensacola. Most of the population in both places were Catholic. The *Directory* had its imperfections, but it gave a good outline both for the existing Church and the future development.

A document in the Propaganda Archives[13] in Rome drawn up at approximately the same time as the 1822 *Directory* estimated the total Catholic population of the country at 163,500 as compared to the 17,000 in 1783. These figures placed the population of the Archdiocese of Baltimore at 80,000; that of the Diocese of Boston at 3,500; of New York at 24,000; of Philadelphia at 30,000; in Virginia (Richmond) 2,400; in Kentucky, 20,000; and in Charleston 3,600. The Catholic population of Ohio (Cincinnati) was unknown. The report added a descriptive phrase on the condition of religion in these dioceses. Baltimore was noted as having peace and great prosperity, Boston as all prosperous, New York as having grave dissensions, Philadelphia as having the greatest confusion, Virginia as having confusion, Kentucky as enjoying peace, and so, also, Charleston. But even these witnesses of dissension and difference fail to show how these scattered groups of Catholics, constituting less than five percent of the people, did not have unity or a workable cohesion.

[13] Microfilm copy, *Congressi*, vol. VII, ff. 167–170, University of Notre Dame Archives.

The dissension and confusion in New York, Virginia, and Philadelphia had many causes. There were laymen who wanted to take charge of the temporal affairs of the churches. The most important disturbing factor, however, was the existence of several unruly Irish priests who were usually allied to these rebellious lay elements. Opposed to them, besides a few English and American priests, were the conservative French clergymen who had fled from the Revolution in France. The Irish priests, who felt at home in the English-speaking world, considered the French priests and bishops as foreigners and accused them of plotting to gain control of the American church and to exclude the Irish. The difference of language was merely a confusing issue. There were also two more serious issues. The first contest between the laymen and clerics was to determine who would control the spiritual life of the Church in the United States, the second was to determine who would control the material goods of the Church. The theoretical lay rebels, such as Fernandez of Norfolk and Augustine Fagan of Philadelphia, would have claimed for the laity at least some spiritual power but chiefly control of the material welfare. The more conservative bishops, such as Archbishops Neale and Maréchal, felt that the power to control the material welfare of the Church would lead to control of the spiritual life of the Church. The bishops were supported by Rome in the eventual solution of the trustee controversy.

Bishop Patrick Kelly arrived in Norfolk on January 19, 1821. Those who had supported Father Lucas resented the fact that the Bishop listened to Fernandez and reinstated Father Carbry. Next the Bishop ordered all to attend St. Mary's Church. Father Lucas stayed in Norfolk only to complete the year at the school he had begun. His followers, however, on May 25 sent a letter to Bishop Kelly demanding his reinstatement. This the Bishop answered with a refusal on June 7. The followers of Lucas wrote again and received a second refusal. There was a third plea that was apparently not answered. In the meantime Bishop Gradwell in England and Bishop Plessis in Quebec had taken the side of Archbishop Maréchal and written to Rome. Propaganda, however, on July 21, 1821, rejected Maréchal's complaint on the grounds that the Archbishop of Baltimore had no right to be consulted in the election of his suffragan bishops. Bishop Kelly had, in the meantime, written to Rome of the collapse of the Norfolk schism, although Father Carbry had withdrawn from the Diocese after a disagreement with the Bishop. Bishop Kelly began to look for a better See, but American bishops would not consider him for an American diocese because he had publicly opposed the incorporation of the trustees by the American state governments. On January 28, 1822, Propaganda transferred Bishop Kelly to the Diocese of Waterford-Lismore in Ireland, returning Virginia to the administration of Maréchal. Bishop Kelly left in June 1822, taking with him Father James Walsh and leaving Virginia without any priests.

Bishop John England arrived in Charleston Saturday, December 30, 1820, where he was welcomed by Father Benedict Fenwick and took possession of his cathedral the next day. Immediately on his arrival, he had made Father Denis Corkery, who came with him, his Vicar General, as well as Father Fenwick, and gave the faculties of the Diocese to Fathers Felix Gallagher and Robert Browne. With these he had six priests in his diocese. The other three were Father James Wallace in Columbia, Father Samuel Cooper in Augusta, and Father Denis Corkery. The Bishop issued a well-written pastoral to the Diocese and began his visitation on January 15, sailing for Savannah with Father Browne, whom he intended to assign there. After visiting Savannah, the Bishop with Father Browne went to Augusta, where Father Samuel Cooper and the Trustees received him, and on January 29 to Locust Grove, where lived some descendants of the first settlers of Maryland. The Bishop then went to Columbia, where he found that Father Wallace was also a member of the faculty of Columbia College and not active as a missionary, although he did say Mass for the Catholics of the area.

Bishop England seemed never to stand still. Besides his pastoral visitations, he prepared a small catechism and sent a report on the diocese to Rome. He then visited the northern part of the Diocese, where there were no priests. He was at Wilmington, South Washington, North Washington, and other towns looking for Catholics and preaching for all in the public halls. He visited Bishop Kelly at Norfolk. From Norfolk he went to Baltimore, New York, and Philadelphia. At the suggestions of friends, he tried to settle the Philadelphia schism but was less than successful. When he reached Baltimore on his return trip, Maréchal had gone to Rome. Bishop England soon proposed to publish a new edition of the Missal but was checked for a while by Roman authorities, who felt that he was moving too fast. On January 8 he opened a diocesan seminary and on June 5, 1822, he published the first number of *The United States Catholic Miscellany,* a weekly newspaper. This first American Catholic newspaper contained explanations of Catholic doctrine and practice and claimed the protection of the Constitution on its front page. Bishop England then tried to settle the trustee issue. The Trustees, protected in their office by law, held out against him, but he threatened to abandon St. Mary's and even took a separate house for his home. After much discussion the Trustees capitulated in 1824.

Bishop England, after his own experiences in Charleston and his visits to the troubled churches of Philadelphia and New York, felt that a solution to the problem of lay trustees was needed and prepared a solution for his own diocese. He drew up a "Constitution for the Roman Catholic Church for the States of North Carolina, South Carolina and Georgia."

The Constitution recognized two parts of the Church, that which was of divine institution and that which was of human regulation. The latter was divided into ecclesiastical discipline and the regulation of temporalities. The ecclesiastical discipline belonged exclusively to the Church. The Constitution consisted of seven titles: Doctrine; Government; Property; Membership; District Churches; the Convention; and Amendment of the Constitution. The title on property decreed how funds were to be raised and handled and called for the creation of a General Fund for the Church of Charleston to which all were obliged to contribute. The Convention was to meet once each year and consisted of the Bishop, the House of the Clergy, and the House of Lay Delegates. The Constitution was indeed a democratic organization although there were clauses safeguarding the rights and supremacy of the Bishop. The Constitution was published before the first Convention of the Catholics of South Carolina, which met on November 24, 1823. Eventually, there were Conventions in North Carolina and Georgia, and the final form of the Constitution was not settled until 1839.[14] The word that the Bishop had adopted a democratic constitution aroused the opposition of the conservative bishops to the north, and the constitution did not survive him even in Charleston.

There were many reasons for Archbishop Maréchal to go to Rome in 1821, especially since no American Archbishop had been to Rome since the establishment of the American hierarchy thirty years before. The Archbishop did not give his reason except to say that he felt someone in Rome was interfering in American affairs. He probably knew that the Vatican officials were generally ignorant of English and were dependent on Irish clerics for trans-

[14] Guilday, *England*, note 7 above, Chapter XII "The Constitution of the Diocese of Charleston (1823)," I, 342–379. Ignatius A. Reynolds, ed., *Works of Rt. Rev. John England*, 5 vol. (Baltimore, 1849) V, 91–108.

lations and for information about American affairs. The principal problem pressing the Archbishop had to do with the arrangements with the Jesuits about the property of the Archdiocese. A second problem was to arrange the elimination of the Diocese of Richmond. A third was to get a ruling from Rome on the trustee controversy. In the decision on the Jesuit estates, Maréchal told Propaganda that there were rumors that the Jesuits would no longer pay the $1,000 a year that they had been giving him and that such an action would leave him destitute. He argued that, after the suppression of the Society, the property of the clergy belonged to the Diocese. The Jesuits objected, and a compromise was effected whereby the property at Whitemarsh should go to the Archdiocese. Eventually this was accepted by the Jesuits. As a result of this controversy, the Jesuit novices were taken from Whitemarsh to the diocese of St. Louis. As to the Diocese of Richmond, Bishop Kelly was transferred to Ireland, and the Archbishop of Baltimore was made administrator of the vacant see.

On the third point, brought to a head when the Trustees of St. Mary's in Philadelphia tried to force the retention of Father William Hogan, the Bishop received from Pope Pius VII *Non Sine Magno,* an apostolic letter, on August 24, 1822, addressed to the Archbishop and to the American bishops.[15] The Papal Brief expressed the Pope's sorrow on hearing of the conduct of Father Hogan, especially since he had continued to act as a priest despite his excommunication. The Pope said that he had heard that the priest with his followers had gone so far as to deny the Bishop his support, which action was a grave injury to the Bishop and to the Holy See. These laymen had dared to take over matters that were reserved solely to the Bishop and to the Holy See. The Pope was further distressed to learn that these things had happened not only in Philadelphia but in other cities of the country. The Trustees must remember, he told them, that what is given for the Church passes over to the power of the Church and that the Trustees must accept the will of the Bishop in their administration. He added that it is unheard of in the history of the Church that the Trustees should have the power to install a priest who lacks the faculties of the Church, which was the case with Father Hogan. Such action constituted an attempt to usurp the power of the Bishop. The Pope advised the bishops to draw up rules on caring for material goods to avoid such happenings. To this

---

[15] Shea, note 2 above, III, 243–246. Reynolds, ed., *Works of John England,* V, 178–179.

Papal Brief the Sacred Congregation added a letter to the Archbishop setting forth four rules on trustees: (1) to choose only upright and honest men as trustees; (2) to limit the power of the trustees so that they could not refuse the rightly appointed pastor his church and sustenance; (3) to see that pastors were independent of the trustees in the administration of their ministry; and (4) that the trustees must be of the same mind as the Bishop in these matters. To give the trustees too great authority, he said, sows the seeds of future dissensions. Hereafter this determination of authority must be taken care of before the building of churches or purchasing of property. The property acquired was to be in the name of the Bishop, and to prevent other troubles the Bishop was to make his will with two copies, one for himself and the other for a proper witness. If the laity was unwilling to accept these rules, the Bishop was to get the agreement limited by a civil contract that would prevent the abuses mentioned above, and the church should not be blessed until such an arrangement had been made. Basically, when this rule was decreed by Rome, the trustee controversy was over so far as American Catholicism was concerned. But carrying out this decree was not easy in several instances, especially in Philadelphia.

Bishop England went to Philadelphia late in 1821 and proposed to settle the conflict by accepting Hogan into his own diocese. Hogan, on his knees before the Bishop and before witnesses, made his submission. The Trustees asked Bishop England to preach the next Sunday at St. Mary's. He could not accept the invitation, but he was amazed to learn that Father Hogan was going to preach. He forbade Hogan to do so, but Hogan resigned his membership in the Charleston Diocese and conducted the services on Sunday. The attempts of the Trustees of St. Mary's to eliminate the clergy from the board had come before the Pennsylvania Supreme Court, which had rejected their proposal on the grounds that the Trustees were not the corporation and therefore could not change the rules of the corporation. At this point Father William Harold returned to Philadelphia and, although unwelcome, joined forces with the Bishop. The Trustees in their pamphlets now attacked Harold as well as the Bishop and increased the number of electors to control the election of Trustees. Instead, there were two elections, and two sets of Trustees were elected. On Tuesday, April 9, 1822, riots broke out between the two groups. The courts upheld the Hoganite Trustees in the election of their supporters. Just then the Papal Brief on the scandal arrived. Hogan submitted to the Papal condemnation but then retracted his submission. The Trustees then got a bill passed by the State Legislature changing the charter, but the Governor vetoed the measure. By August 1823, the fervor of the rebellious Trustees was beginning to cool, especially as the debts were mounting. A Father Angelo Inglesi, an itinerant priest, tried to intervene and was accepted by the Trustees, but Father Harold, acting for the Bishop, rejected him. Then a Father Thaddeus O'Meally from Limerick came and replaced Hogan, who left the country. Bishop Conwell excommunicated O'Meally, who appealed to Rome. Bishop England came again but failed to solve the problem. Hogan too had gone for a while to England and then to Charleston. He returned to Philadelphia on June 25, 1824, and ejected O'Meally. The Trustees, however, upheld O'Meally and rejected Hogan, who preached in Protestant churches and married before leaving the city. The Trustees appealed unsuccessfully to Father Gabriel Richard, who passed through the city at that time, and to Bishop Edward Fenwick, another visitor, to help them. Both refused. O'Meally finally went to Rome to carry their appeal. When he arrived in Rome in July 1825, the Propaganda refused to see him. The Jesuits, in the meantime, had given to the Bishop their legal title to the property of St. Mary's. In the election of Trustees in 1826 the rebellious Trustees were again victorious and proposed a truce to Bishop Conwell, who accepted. The agreement between the Bishop and the Trustees gave the Trustees the right of recommending the pastor, although his appointment was to be made by the Bishop, and the Bishop's right to remove was subject to limitations. Another document drawn up by the Trustees restated their claim to the right of presentation and denied the right of the Bishop to appoint without them. According to this agreement Fathers Harold and Hayden were removed without the consent of the Trustees, and Father John Hughes, ordained on October 15, 1826, and Father O'Reilly were appointed by the Bishop. The agreement between the Trustees and Bishop Conwell had been reported to Rome. The Sacred Congregation sent for a copy. Pope Leo XII notified Bishop Conwell that, by the decision of the Sacred Congregation of April 30, 1827, the contract between the Bishop and the Trustees was null and void. The Bishop notified the Trustees and made his own submission to the decree in the pulpit on July 22, 1827. At the invitation of the Pope, Bishop Conwell went to Rome in August 1827, and Father William Matthews of Washington was named Administrator of the Diocese. Bishop Conwell sailed from New York, July 15, 1828. When he heard of the Provincial Council to be held in Baltimore the next year, he wanted to attend but his place was taken by Father Matthews.

Bishop England had been constantly urging a Provincial Council to meet and discuss the problem of trusteeism and to decide on common regulations for the growing Catholic Church body in the United States. There had been some suggestions of the need for the Council in the letter to Maréchal from the Propaganda in 1822. Bishop DuBourg also expressed the opinion that such a council would be proper.

Archbishop Maréchal, on the contrary, never granted the need for such a council. He had little in common personally with the other members of the hierarchy except the two former Sulpicians in Bardstown. He had lost a close friend and helper in any provincial council when Bishop Cheverus accepted the invitation to return to France in 1823. In the choice of Cheverus' successor, the Archbishop and the Bishops agreed on Father Benedict Fenwick for Boston and Father John Dubois of Mt. St. Mary's for New York. The choices were approved by Rome. The consecration of Fenwick in the Cathedral at Baltimore was the only time that the Archbishop and Bishops England and Conwell were together. At Maréchal's consecration of Bishop Dubois in the Baltimore Cathedral on October 29, 1826, Father John Power, the Administrator of the vacant New York Diocese assisted with Conwell, and Father William Taylor preached the sermon. But Bishop Dubois did not attend the Council in 1829 having made plans for more than a year to go to Rome.

Bishop Edward Dominic Fenwick of Cincinnati had been consecrated on January 13, 1822, at St. Rose's Church in Kentucky by Bishop Benedict Flaget of Bardstown with Fathers Wilson and Hill, Dominicans, as assistants. His installation took place in a little chapel of Northern Liberties, two miles outside of Cincinnati, with the aid of Bishop Flaget. The chapel was then moved into the city but collapsed and had to be rebuilt. In 1822, Bishop Fenwick made a visit of his Diocese around Ohio and to Detroit. He felt that he needed aid and sailed from New York early in July. The Pope, Pius VII, had died while Fenwick was on his way to Rome and was succeeded by Pope Leo XII on October 5, 1823. Fenwick returned from Europe later in 1824 but delayed his return from the East until March 1825. He proceeded to erect his Cathedral of Saint Peter in Cincinnati, which he dedicated in December 1826. Plans were made at that time for another bishop in Detroit, but the appointment was delayed.

Archbishop Maréchal was afflicted with asthma, and his general health showed a notable decline in 1826 and 1827. Although he continued to give Confirmation and Holy Orders during 1827 he did not pontificate in the Cathedral. On August 5 the Pope named him Administrator of strife-torn Philadelphia, but his health permitted him to escape the problems. He received Viaticum on December 12. In October he had asked for Father James Whitfield as his Coadjutor, and on January 8 Whitfield was elected in Rome. On January 29, 1828, however, before the bulls arrived for that consecration, Ambrose Maréchal died. He had met manfully the problems of organization, except for what could be accomplished by a provincial synod. The sealing of his victories would take place under his successor, Archbishop Whitfield, in the First Provincial Council.

CHAPTER SIX

The Formation of the Catholic Minority

JAMES WHITFIELD, MARÉCHAL'S SUCCESSOR, was a native of Liverpool, England, born November 3, 1770. His father, a prosperous merchant, had died when James was only seventeen years old. To assist his mother during her period of mourning, as well as for her health, he moved to Italy, settling with her at Leghorn until 1803. While returning to Liverpool, Whitfield was detained for some time in Lyons where he became acquainted with Father Ambrose Maréchal, then a professor at the Seminary of Lyons, where sometime later Whitfield returned to study for the priesthood. He was ordained in 1809 in Lyons, and, after his mother's death on July 4, 1810, he returned to England and engaged in pastoral work at Little Crosby near Liverpool. He was invited to the American missions by Father Maréchal, and before Father Maréchal was elevated to the Archiepiscopal See of Baltimore, was on his way to America, arriving September 8, 1817, where he was appointed an assistant at St. Peter's Cathedral in Baltimore. Archbishop Maréchal asked the Propaganda to grant Father Whitfield and three other Baltimore priests honorary doctorates in theology, and he conferred the degrees in the Cathedral on January 25, 1824.

When the Archbishop felt his health beginning to fail he also asked Propaganda to make Whitfield his Coadjutor Bishop with Fathers Samuel Eccleston and Michael Wheeler as other choices. Propaganda delayed, electing Whitfield as Bishop of Apollonia only on January 8, 1828, and Coadjutor on January 11. Pope Leo XII confirmed the election on January 19 but the news reached Baltimore after the death of Maréchal. In the meantime, Whitfield had been elected Administrator of the Archdiocese. On March 29, Propaganda wrote to him as the Archbishop of Baltimore, and he received consecration from Flaget on May 25. The coconsecrators were Bishops Conwell and Dubois, and the sermon was preached by Father Samuel Eccleston. Apparently Bishop England of Charleston was offended that he had not been notified of the approaching consecration in time to attend. He complained of this in a letter of June 2, 1828, to Whitfield and also of a similar neglect of Bishops Edward Fenwick of Cincinnati and Benedict Fenwick of Boston. Bishop England repeated also the request he had made to Archbishop Maréchal that there be a Provincial Council. He repeated his contention that such synods were the only cure for the troubles of the American Church and implied that he had written this opinion also to the veteran of the hierarchy, Bishop Flaget, to be passed on to Whitfield.

That Whitfield and Maréchal were of the same mind about the government of the Church in the United States was quite apparent, although, since they lived within the same community, there existed no need of letters between them to convey their agreement. However, they expressed approximately the same opinions in their letters to Rome. In his discussion of the clergy in his letter to Cardinal Capellari, Maréchal had insisted that English and American priests were the best pastors for the American scene.[1] He clearly indicated a feeling against the multiplication of Irish clergy, and, despite his own French nationality, he said that the successful priest should speak well the language of the country. Whitfield in one of his early letters to Propaganda and in another letter to Father Nicholas Wiseman, the Rector of the English College in Rome, made the same points.

There was a possibility that Archbishop Maréchal would have called a Provincial Synod had his health not failed so rapidly after 1826, but he was opposed to calling one. How soon Archbishop Whitfield agreed to the holding of the Synod is not evident. Bishop Benedict Fenwick of Boston also wrote to the new Archbishop on September 10, 1828, asking that he call a synod. He added:

The fact is, as we go on at present we shall never be able to effect other than partial good each one in his own Diocese: whereas were we

[1] Propaganda Archives, microfilm copy, University of Notre Dame Archives.

to unite in one settled plan of operations, assist one-another & pull together, what a happy difference would it not make in the general result. I am sure if y^r Grace will but weigh the matter for a moment in your mind, you will be convinced of it. If so; ought it not to be done?[2]

Fenwick listed four problems that were demanding solutions: (1) the preparation of Catholic school books; (2) the forming of a mode of proceedings that would modify the "abominable system of Lay Trustees introduced in some Dioceses (happily not in mine . . .)"; (3) the devising of some "cheap and efficient plan" for training up priests; and (4) the establishment of a Catholic press in a central situation.

How many other bishops wrote to Whitfield urging the calling of a council is not certain, but the Archbishop sent out to the bishops on December 18, 1828, an announcement that the Provincial Synod would be held the next year, opening October 1. He likewise asked of them suggestions on matters to be discussed in the Council. There seems to have been no one in the hierarchy who opposed the meeting. Bishop Conwell when he heard about the Council hurried back from Rome, contrary to his instructions, but, although he went to Baltimore, he was not permitted to act in the Council since Father William Matthews had been named by Propaganda as Administrator of the Diocese of Philadelphia. Bishop John Dubois of New York was called to Rome and did not return for the Council; nor did Bishop Portier who had been named in Rome the first Bishop of Mobile. Bishop John B. David, the auxiliary of Bardstown, did not attend because of ill health. The *Catholic Miscellany,* dated October 3, 1829, the day of the opening of the session, contained an editorial probably written by Bishop England expressing the high hopes for the success of the Council. The advance of the Church in the country signified by the Provincial Council, the first in the English-speaking world since the Reformation under conditions of freedom, was suggested in these words of the editorial:

. . . A few years ago, where our very name was used, but for ridicule and contempt, there are we now respected, and though, public profession is not immediately a religion which declares an eternal war on the passions, imposes a constant restraint on the senses, and what is most painful to human pride, requires the submission of the understanding to the belief of mysteries above man's comprehension, still conviction of the truth of our tenets and acknowledgements of our unanswerable

[2] Baltimore Cathedral Archives.

arguments are daily expressed. What cheers us most of all in our flattering anticipations of the future advances of the Catholic religion in this country, is the idea of the happy effects likely to result from the Synod of our Bishops, to be held this present month in Baltimore. The deliberation and mutual consultations of the truely pious and learned Hierarchy of the Catholic Church of these States, will be productive of much good and create a unity of action hitherto so desirable in matters of ecclesiastical discipline. . . .

The column noted also that Bishop Flaget of Bardstown and Bishop Rosati of St. Louis had arrived in the archiepiscopal city on September 24 and that Bishop England of Charleston had arrived even a week before that.

While awaiting the opening of the Council, the prelates held frequent informal meetings with the Archbishop to discuss the formalities to be observed and sources of information on topics to be discussed. The *Miscellany* reported on October 10: "The Archbishop has fully proved himself to be an excellent prelate of business, and is said to have developed information and talents which his great modesty had hitherto concealed." The Archbishop was probably the only member of the hierarchy who had a claim to some wealth and culture independently of his clerical position. The paper described Bishop Benedict Fenwick of Boston as not "fallen away either in his corpulency, his good humor, or his fine flow of spirits, and his zeal and piety are as conspicuous as his figure." Unfortunately the writer gave no pen pictures of the other bishops, except to refer to the venerable figure of Bishop Flaget.

The Archbishop, in the meantime, also held conferences with the theologians of St. Mary's Seminary on the organization of the Council. There were to be two kinds of meeting each day: one to be called a preparatory conference to be held in the Archbishop's house in the afternoon and the other a formal session to be held in the sanctuary of the Cathedral in the morning. The officers were to be a promoter and a secretary. Father Matthews as Administrator of Philadelphia was to have a decisive vote. The meeting of the Bishops before the Council was held on the afternoon of September 30 at the Archbishop's house to decide the final preliminaries. They elected Bishop Fenwick of Boston Promoter of the Council, Father Edward Damphoux, S.S., Secretary, and Father Francis P. Kenrick Assistant Secretary. Father John J. Chanche was elected Master of Ceremonies, and Fathers Francis Lhomme and John Radanne were appointed chanters. Especially invited to attend were Father Joseph Carrière, the Visitator of the

Sulpicians, and Father Dzierozynski, S.J., the Superior of the Jesuits in this country. The theologians of the Archdiocese were Fathers John Tessier, S.S.; Louis R. Deloul, S.S.; and Edward Damphoux, S.S.; and, for the other bishops Fathers Francis Patrick Kenrick for Bishop Flaget, Simon Gabriel Bruté for Bishop England, Louis de Barth for Bishop Edward Fenwick, August Jeanjean for Bishop Rosati, Anthony Blanc for Bishop Benedict Fenwick, and Michael Wheeler for Father Matthews. On October 5 Father John Power was admitted as the representative of Bishop John Dubois of New York.

Beginning with the first private conference of October 3, there were thirteen of these private conferences and thirteen public sessions. The Council enacted thirty-eight decrees besides asking the Holy Father for three special permissions: (1) to use the form for baptizing infants in the baptisms of adults; (2) to use the briefer form for blessing the baptismal water; and (3) that the time for making the Paschal Communion be extended to the period from the first Sunday of Lent to Trinity Sunday.

Had Maréchal lived to preside over this Council, its importance as the first step in Church organization might have been more explicit. The fact that the presiding officer was an English-born prelate who had been in the country for only about twelve years symbolizes the fact that the Catholic Church organization in the United States was destined to be adapted to the dominant Anglo-American culture and that both the Irish who spoke English and the French and others who did not would have to reform themselves according to the Anglo-American cultural tradition before they would be accepted socially in the country. Although Catholics were already estimated as numbering nearly 600,000, the Catholic Church was not regarded as an important force in American life. The significant Catholic fact in 1829 in the Catholic history of the English-speaking world seemed to be the Catholic Emancipation Act of the English Parliament and the important facts in the United States were the inauguration of Andrew Jackson as President and the political battles looming on the horizon over nullification and slavery. Few people paid any attention to this small group of twenty-two huddled in the sanctuary of the Baltimore Cathedral. Instead, this small group while representing the unchanging doctrines of Roman Catholicism was affected by the events of the country such as the westward movement down the Ohio, over the Appalachians, and across the Great Lakes; the modifications resulting from the influx of hundreds of thousands of immigrants; the divisions between North and South; the rise of manufacturing; and the revival of American Protestantism.

In a country of about thirteen millions, there were fewer than 600,000 Catholics and slightly fewer than 300 priests. The Catholics were mostly in Pennsylvania, in Maryland, and in port towns in other states. There were small groups of French around the Great Lakes and down the Mississippi Valley with a concentration of Catholic migrants from Maryland around Bardstown, Kentucky, and scattered groups of Catholic pioneers invading Ohio, Indiana, Illinois, and Missouri. There were seminaries of limited development established in Baltimore, Charleston, Philadelphia, Bardstown, Mt. St. Mary's in Maryland, and near St. Louis. There were nine collegiate institutions, three of which called themselves universities. Within the United States there were already thirty-three communities of religious women and four communities of religious priests. There were eleven dioceses, counting that of Bishop Leon De Neckere who had been appointed to New Orleans unbeknownst to the Councillors.

While Bishop Fenwick in his letters before the Council had pointed out the chief needs of the young Church, the basic problem was discipline. This problem arose from the diversity of national backgrounds of the bishops and priests as well as of the faithful, the influx of thousands of poor and ignorant peasants, and the movement of those who had the means to the new lands in the west. The bishops had first to seal the victory achieved by the intervention of Rome in Philadelphia over lay trusteeism, to establish their jurisdiction over their priests, and to regulate their relations with religious priests in their dioceses. They endeavored also to choose the manner in which they could assist in the election of bishops and to determine which national customs were to be followed in the administration of the Sacraments and in public worship. The decrees of the Council numbered thirty-eight. The first three decrees forbade the migration of priests from one parish to another and insisted on their incardination in a diocese. The fourth decree called for the appointment of one pastor in a parish. To strengthen the bishops on the question of trusteeism, the Council ruled that there was to be no right of patronage and that no churches were to be blessed unless the deeds to them were in the hands of the bishop. Further, faculties were not to be given to clergymen who supported lay trustees in their opposition to these decrees.

The ninth decree called for the use of the Douay version of the Sacred Scriptures, and the tenth for the use of the Roman Ritual. The next decrees called for care in the choice of sponsors and in the choice of names in Baptism, and for keeping registers for baptisms, confirmations, marriages, and burials. Other decrees called for the proper blessing of the baptismal font and keeping the baptismal water under lock and key and prescribed rules for baptisms. Further decrees prescribed the churching of women and gave permission to repeat in the vernacular the prayers at Baptism and burial. Other decrees said Confirmation should not be given before the age of seven, that the celebration of Mass should be in church, except on the missions. Care was demanded in providing cleanliness of the altar linens and in the proper setting up of confessionals. Some basic rules were made governing the clothing of priests, their public conduct, especially the avoidance of games, on their obligation to preach, and on their religious practices. The final group of decrees recognized the need for Catholic schools and Catholic books and for the preparation of a catechism modeled after that of Cardinal Bellarmine. Finally these decrees were not to be published until they were approved by the Holy See, and there was to be another Council in three years. At the conclusion of the Council, two pastorals were issued in the name of the hierarchy, one for the clergy and one for the laity.

The pastoral to the laity was quite important. It began with a survey of the growth of the Church in the country and of the problem of supplying priests. The pastoral warned that the failure of the parents to provide Christian education would lead to disaster in their children. The pastoral regretted the unfortunate increase in the number of attacks on the Church in the pulpit and press and the malicious misrepresentation of her true character. The faithful should read the Scriptures but only in authorized versions. In reference to the trustee schism, the laity should guard the unity of the Church and guard against those false reformers who try to set up independent churches through exaggerated claims over the material goods of the Church and claims to the right of patronage in the appointment of pastors. They should also be on their guard against that false liberalism that maintains that all religions are alike, no matter if their Protestant neighbors do hold that notion. The two pastorals were dated October 17. In relation to the pastoral to the laity it was significant that at the ninth public session on October 13 three prominent laymen were invited to join in the discussion of legal questions, especially concerning the incorporation of church property. They were the United States Attorney-General, soon to be Chief Justice, Roger B. Taney, and John Scott and William G. Read, prominent Baltimore attorneys.

In theory the Catholic minority in the United States had achieved in this Council a national unity and an organization; in fact the outlines of a national organization functioned for the first time. If we assume that the Roman decree and the Council had ended the threat of lay trusteeism, the main problems were the frictions of nationalisms, and the lack of means, primarily the lack of wealth, which made very difficult meeting the other needs of schools, teachers, and the products of those institutions, additional priests, religious teachers, and educated Catholic lay leaders. Not unrelated to the internal problems were the external problems which can be described as the care for Catholic immigrants, the friction within and outside the Church between natives and the new arrivals, and the westward movement of the population and its effect on the Catholics who joined it. Two other national developments affected Catholicism as they affected all social organizations of the day, the rise of manufacturing and the existence of Negro slavery, although the bishops proposed no solutions for these problems.

Of all these problems, the first that touched the Catholics of the country was the conflict between the Irish clergy and the Anglo-American and French who had occupied most of the higher offices of the Church until the Council of 1829. Archbishop Whitfield gave one of the best outlines of this problem in 1833 in his letter to Father Nicholas Wiseman, the Rector of the English College in Rome and his agent, on June 6, 1833.

It seems proper for me to make to you some remark concerning the views of Dr. England, Dr. Kenrick & c. These two Bishops are both warm headed Irishmen, & have it seems, strong Irish predilections in favor of Irish Bishops & Irish discipline for the U. States. They have both recommended for the vacant see of Cincinnati, Irishmen, & I believe that the three names on each list were all Irish Priests. They have united in using every effort, even by publications in their newspapers, to make me hold another Provincial Council; which notwithstanding all they have exposed before the public, I have not consented to convoke, because such is the agitating disposition of Dr. England, that he would be restless in proposing changes in our discipline until it were reduced to the standards of Ireland or reformed according to his republican notions. Before I knew that Dr. England was going to Rome, I wrote to the Cardinal Pref. Prop. some of my reasons for not complying with their wishes adding I would not, until commanded by the S. Cong. I am sorry that any more Irish Bishops are added to our Hierarchy, as I fear their increase in number will have power to have others of their countrymen nominated thereafter & bring over to this country a great number of Irish priests whilst I wish, with a few exceptions, they would all stay at home. . . .[3]

Bishops England and Kenrick had different notions. In 1834, after the Council had been brought about by Bishop England's intervention in Rome, Bishop Kenrick also complained to the Rector of the Irish College in Rome, Father Paul Cullen, against the stand of Archbishop Whitfield and the French Sulpicians:

The Bishop of Charleston's proposal to supply this Country with Missionaries from Ireland found no favor with the Council. *There was,* as a French Bishop writes me, an evident *disregard and defiance of the Irish interest in the Council.* God forbid that I should indulge any national resentment when our common Religion is at stake. . . .[4]

In 1835, discussing with Father Cullen the nomination of Father Anthony Blanc for the see of New Orleans, Bishop England, the other leader of the Irish clergy, gave vent to feelings that he had experienced for several years.

They go here upon the principle that no one but a Frenchman is fit to be a bishop of New Orleans, though at present one third of the Catholic population is Irish. And the majority of the inhabitants are Irish Americans & still they appoint French bishops in New York where almost all are Irish, in Bardstown where there are not ten French, in Mobile where the French are unintelligible and useless & this is a small specimen. I do not wish to point the waste of means & the want of exertion to which this system gives rise.[5]

Bishop England accused the Sulpicians particularly of trying to keep the Irish from controlling the American Church. He blamed the choice not only of Whitfield as Coadjutor but the later choice of Samuel Eccleston as Coadjutor to Whitfield on Archbishop Maréchal and the French Sulpicians. Eventually as these exiles from the French Revolution died out, the French dominance in the hierarchy died also, and, as there were too few native bishops to take over the hierarchy, the dominance became Irish. That there was any real difference in the religious character and the theological learning of any national group at this time is very doubtful. The cause of friction was simply nationalism, and it

[3] Letter in English College Archives in Rome, microfilm in University of Notre Dame Archives.

[4] Letter in Irish College Archives in Rome, Microfilm, University of Notre Dame Archives.

[5] Letter in Irish College Archives in Rome, Microfilm, University of Notre Dame Archives.

hampered the efforts of the bishops when they did assemble in the
Second Provincial Council of 1833. In that Council they agreed
only on noncontroversial items. They suppressed the See of Richmond, defined the geographical limits of the older dioceses, set up
the new See of Vincennes in Indiana, suggested a new plan for the
nomination of American bishops, placed the Indian and Negro
missions under the Jesuits, appointed a committee to edit an
American version of the Ritual, and urged the setting up of diocesan seminaries, the promotion of Catholic publications, and the
suppression of the exchange of faculties between dioceses that
had been set up in the decrees of 1810. They set 1837 for the next
Council. There were no decrees concerning the internal frictions
or against the attacks of bigots. There was little these men could
do to offset the anti-Catholic reaction to the manifest growth of
Roman Catholicism in what most Americans considered Protestant
United States. The pastoral letter of 1833, again composed by
Bishop England, was addressed to both clergy and laity and consisted mostly of exhortations to the higher ideals. It also recognized
anti-Catholic manifestations in American public life.

This anti-Catholicism had been growing steadily. In 1787, to
most of the natives of the thirteen original states of the United
States, Roman Catholicism was something medieval and foreign.
When Bishop Carroll returned from England in 1790 there were
some Catholics in most of the port towns, usually Irish immigrants. These Irish immigrants were most numerous in Boston,
New York, and Philadelphia. English and native Catholics were
centered in Maryland and southeastern Pennsylvania, where there
were also some German Catholics. Catholics of social prominence
such as Roger Taney, the Digges, and the Spaldings lived mostly
in Maryland, and there also were some yeomen Catholics living on
small farms or working as tenants. There had been Catholics in
both the Continental Congress and the Constitutional Convention, but when the references to religion were written into the
Constitution Catholics were not expected to be an important force
in the new country.

Religion in general had suffered in the laxity of war times,
especially since the struggle was revolutionary in character. But as
the nineteenth century opened there was a revival of interest in
religion that manifested itself in strong emotional movements
among the common people particularly in the new settlements
west of the Allegheny Mountains. The awakened religious feeling
had more intellectual manifestations in the older communities of
New England. The first manifestation was the movement for the

establishment of seminaries, or colleges devoted primarily to the training of clergymen, separated from the older colleges which had become quite secularized during the decline of religious expression during the Revolution and had changed their purpose to the training of civil leaders. Another manifestation of this religious sentiment was the publication of countless religious tracts intended to arouse the common people. Comparable to New England's interest in far eastern trade was the new interest aroused in foreign missions. One phase of this religious revival that directly affected the growing Catholic Church in the country was the fervent appeals of some pulpit orators to seaboard Protestants to check the growth of Roman Catholicism in the west. Some of the pamphlets and books printed at this time had a similar purpose.[6] These preachers and writers could appeal to the English Protestant tradition that Roman Catholicism was the enemy of their faith and culture, and some Catholic orators in their zeal and in their bursts of oratory occasionally answered these appeals in kind. Roman Catholicism which had been at best a tolerated small minority had grown in numbers from something less than 30,000 to an estimated 600,000 in 1830 with over 300 priests and with multiplying seminaries, colleges, and convents. Further, the agitators noted that this increase had not been simply by conversion or by the arrival of English Catholics but by the arrival of thousands of Irish, chiefly, who were hostile to English Protestantism and whose cultural and economic status was very low. Sometimes in New England these Irish immigrants competed with natives for jobs, and in some communities in their poverty they were filling the poorhouses. Even if they were living well, that fact did not decrease their threat to the security of the Protestant majority. Thus, the formation of the Home Missionary Society in 1826 with its appeals for missionaries for the western missions represented at the start a manifestation of the revived Protestantism; later this and similar societies appealed for means and missionaries to save the West from the invasion of foreign Catholics.

The growth in virulence of the attack on Catholicism at the end of the 1820s seems to have been nurtured by the bitter campaign literature against Catholicism in England in the fight over the Catholic Emancipation Act. The first Catholic newspapers, *The United States Catholic Miscellany* founded at Charleston in 1822, the *Truth Teller* in New York in 1825, and the *Jesuit* of Boston in

---

[6] The classic study of the anti-Catholicism is still Ray Allen Billington, *The Protestant Crusade* (New York, 1938).

1829, while they contained much news from Ireland, also devoted many columns to the defense of the Catholic Faith against the Protestant attacks. Against the Catholics there already existed the *Boston Recorder* founded by Presbyterians in 1816, *The Christian Watchman* edited by Baptists founded in 1819, and *The New York Observer* founded by the Morse brothers in 1823. But the formation of the Protestant Association in New York in 1830 and the beginning of the publication of *The Protestant* in January of the same year marked a new intensity in this reaction to the growth of Catholicism in the country. Significantly the *Miscellany* carried in large print on the top of its first page the first amendment of the Constitution forbidding any religious establishment. In a humble rebuttal of the attacks on the Irish immigrants the editors of the *Miscellany* pointed to the menial jobs immigrants had accepted.

Led by the *Miscellany,* Catholics at first tried to answer the published charges against them. In 1833 when Father John Hughes of Philadelphia was challenged by the Reverend John Breckinridge, a Presbyterian minister of Philadelphia, the *Catholic Herald* was founded to publish the Catholic account of the controversy. The Hughes-Breckinridge exchange and similar discussions in public halls continued for a few years until the Catholic bishops began to forbid priests to join in such discussions. The less respectable of these Protestant publications began to charge the Catholic Church with idolatry and immorality and to make crude charges of immorality against priests and nuns. In Boston there had been a series of incidents between Irish and native firemen, bitter exchanges between Catholic and Protestant publications, and misrepresentations of the running away of a deranged nun from the Ursuline Convent in Charlestown. Boston newspapers carried charges of mysterious events at the Ursuline Convent. On Sunday August 10, 1834, the Reverend Lyman Beecher had given three anti-Catholic sermons in Boston churches. A mob gathered before the Convent on the night of August 11 and eventually burned the Convent and another building on the Convent grounds. Prominent New England clergymen and the Boston press expressed shock at this violence, and there were promises of restitution that were not fulfilled. This incident marked the intensity of a movement that was partly anti-Catholic and partly nativistic that spread throughout the country and continued for twenty years until the public was distracted from the growth of Catholicism by the national crisis over slavery.

Within a week after the burning of the Charlestown convent there appeared two new anti-Catholic newspapers: *Downfall of*

Babylon edited in Philadelphia by Samuel B. Smith, an ex-priest who had worked in Michigan; and *The American Protestant Vindicator* edited by the Reverend W. C. Brownlee of New York City. Brownlee was one of the more effective of the Protestant agitators against Catholicism. An ex-nun, Rebecca Theresa Reed, whose stories had been told to excite mob violence such as the Charlestown incident, published her story under the title *Six Months in a Convent* early in 1835. The false charges in it unfortunately were answered by the Ursulines who thus gave occasion to additional anti-Catholic pamphlets. The next year appeared Maria Monk's infamous *Awful Disclosures of the Hotel Dieu Nunnery of Montreal.* Maria Monk had not been a nun but had been sent to a reformatory conducted by nuns. Her tale was sensationally obscene and was widely sold, proving a major factor in arousing the anti-Catholic feeling of the day, even though it was disproved by prominent non-Catholic writers. In *The New York Observer* Samuel F.B. Morse, a New England artist, had published twelve letters under the pen name of Brutus, based on the activities of the Leopoldine Foundation of Vienna which was sending money to the Catholic missions in the Middle West. These letters were published in 1834 in book form under the title *A Foreign Conspiracy against the Liberties of the United States.* They charged that there was a plot by imperial Austria to capture the West for Catholicism. The next year the Reverend Lyman Beecher, the President of Lane Theological Seminary in Cincinnati, who had helped cause the riots in Boston, published a similar plea but this time against the threat of losing the Middle West to Catholicism under the title, *A Plea for the West.*

The avalanche of anti-Catholic publications increased; the near acceptance of Roman Catholicism as a rightful religious society that may have seemed possible during the first two decades of the century faded away before such a violent reaction. Against this attack, the small Catholic minority could muster only a few weekly newspapers and a small number of pamphlets and books. In 1837 Bishop John B. Purcell of Cincinnati engaged in a public controversy with the Reverend Alexander Campbell, a Protestant leader, with doubtful results. In the next few years the image of the Catholic minority and its position before the American public was lowered by the increasing influx of poor and illiterate Irish immigrants most of whom were loyal Catholics whose leaders were the Irish priests and bishops in the cities where they tended to congregate.

The western bishoprics of American Catholicism seemed to go to foreign-born bishops at this time. Bishop Richard Miles, the

Dominican at Nashville and Bishop John J. Chanche at Natchez, both native Americans, seem to be exceptions. Flaget had outlived two French coadjutors. Portier remained in Mobile. Blanc despite England's criticism was named to New Orleans. Rosati, a Vincentian and an Italian, was in St. Louis. John Odin, also a French Vincentian, was made Vicar Apostolic in Texas. Mathias Loras was appointed in 1837 Bishop of Dubuque. Bruté, appointed to Vincennes in 1834, was succeeded by de la Hailandière in 1839. Résé, a German and leader in the formation of the Leopoldine Foundation of Vienna, became the first Bishop of Detroit and was succeeded by Bishop Lefevere, a Belgian, as Administrator in 1841. Of the origins of the Catholic clergy in 1835 Bishop Bruté wrote that the diocese of Bardstown had the most native clergy and Baltimore about the same. In St. Louis and New Orleans the priests were mostly Italians. The clergy of Philadelphia were almost all Irish and those of New York more so. Only in Vincennes and Mobile were the priests nearly all French.

Archbishop Whitfield died October 19, 1834, and was succeeded by his Coadjutor, Samuel Eccleston, a native American of English ancestry, who had studied after ordination at St. Sulpice in Paris. He had been President of St. Mary's Seminary when chosen by Archbishop Whitfield as his successor and was only thirty-three years old when he became Archbishop. He was described as a tall man with a large frame but not strong. His demeanor was pleasant, he had a large forehead and round chin with eyes and a small mouth inclined to smiles. He was the last of the Anglo-American-French line of Archbishops of Baltimore. In 1830 Father Francis Patrick Kenrick, the Irish theologian teaching in Bardstown, was made Coadjutor to Bishop Conwell of Philadelphia with full administrative powers, and in 1837 Father John Hughes, the Irish clerical leader in Philadelphia, was made Coadjutor of Bishop Dubois of New York, succeeding Dubois in 1842. Father Richard Vincent Whelan was made Bishop of Richmond in 1841, and Bishop Benedict Fenwick of Boston was succeeded by Bishop John Bernard Fitzpatrick. Both Whelan and Fitzpatrick were native Americans. William Tyler, also an American, was named Bishop of Hartford in 1843, and Irish-born Father William Quarter was named Bishop of Chicago. Of the influx of the Irish clergy into the country, there are no exact numbers, but the Irish names whether of immigrants or sons of immigrants soon filled the rosters of the clergy in New England, New York, Philadelphia, and Baltimore, as well as in the other towns along the coast and also followed the Irish who went inland. There was scarcely a diocese in the West that did not have some of these zealous Irish priests. There were also many German priests coming into the country, and their numbers increased with the coming of the Redemptorists and the Precious Blood Fathers and with the increase in German lay Catholic immigration. There was always a number of French priests, chiefly in the French-speaking regions of Louisiana. There were several Belgian priests and some missionaries from the lands of the old Austrian-Hungarian Empire in the missions of Michigan and the near Northwest. However, the most significant immigration of Catholics in these early decades of the century was that of the Irish.

One estimate of the Irish immigration into the United States during the decade after 1830 was 207,381. Most of these came directly to the port towns on the east coast. The number arriving in New York in 1826 was estimated as 4,255 and ten years later in the year 1836 at 15,135. There were many more during these years arriving in Canada, either at Quebec or Montreal, and many of these later crossed into the United States. The first immigrants were comparatively poor but not destitute. They found employment in building the new roads across the country and in digging the canals. It was said that there were 5,000 working on the Erie Canal alone, and Bishop Bruté found nearly 2,000 working along the Wabash-Erie Canal in Indiana in 1835. While many of the immigrants, lacking means to go West, remained in the city, others made their way into the interior of the country working at building canals and later railroads. Some, when they acquired a bit of wealth, bought lands along the roads and canals and turned to farming. A few opened stores. There is no record of the numbers of these immigrants who could read and write, but the percentage was very low. They had no technical skill, and even their notion of farming was quite primitive. Generally they had no money with which to buy farms or to join in the western movement into the fertile lands. They had to take the first job offered and live in the kind of shelter their limited means could afford. Irish shanty towns appeared along the railroads and canals and in the neighborhoods of mills where they were employed, and their homes in the larger cities were the worst of slums. But these earlier arrivals were generally better off than those who followed them after the great Irish famine of 1845 and 1846.[7]

The numbers of Irish who came during the decade from 1840

[7] Irish immigration into the United States still awaits a historian. George Potter, *To the Golden Door* (Boston, 1910) might have been one had the author lived to document his rich materials. On the famine, the best source is R. Dudley Edwards and T. Desmond Williams, *The Great Famine* (Dublin, 1956).

to 1850 jumped to 780,719 and in the decade before the Civil War (1851 to 1860) to 914,119. To understand the increase in the Irish population and in that sense in the Catholic population before the Civil War, these figures must be added together along with the increase by birth also. There had, in fact, been a higher immigration from the United Kingdom also during these decades but generally those other immigrants were possessed of some wealth and means of subsistence, had a higher percentage of literates, and were equipped with some skills. Furthermore, few of them were Catholics, and most of them were more readily absorbed by the nation. Of the Germans who came in increased numbers, most of them came in colonies and either went into the better farming lands or practiced their trades, especially milling and brewing, and small businesses in the cities of the interior. There is no sure way of determining the percentage of Catholics among the Germans. All told, the effect on the Catholic Church of this huge immigration was to change its complexion in the eyes of the native Americans. The smaller percentage of English and native Americans was swallowed up in this mass immigration which appeared to be not only Catholic, but illiterate and hostile to the English culture. Before long these new arrivals not only competed with the lower classes for jobs but the Irish, since they spoke English (with a brogue), began to participate in local politics. The Church was not concerned with the politics, but clergymen could not help admiring the civic progress of some members of their flock who managed to be elected to local positions of trust in the political organizations. The clergy were grateful also to those politicians, not necessarily Catholic, who helped the poorer immigrants in their flocks with food and shelter and warmth during the cold winter months and with picnics for the children in summer. When the clergy appealed to these politicians to help give these youngsters a Christian education they were not so successful. This was an open and public problem and there were unfriendly reactions to this desire for Catholic schools among the nativistic groups that at times deserved the name of persecution.

The problems of Irish immigration to the United States were manifold. Among the Catholic clergy the Anglo-American-French group dominated by Sulpician-trained clerics saw themselves soon outnumbered by the many Irish clergymen coming into the country. When Bishop England offered to hasten the immigration of the Irish priests, Archbishop Whitfield objected. Certainly there did not seem to be any tradition of strictness among the Irish immigrant clergy such as later Irish clergymen were said to have inherited from French-trained Jansenistic professors. There is no question that, while there were zealous and well-disciplined Irish priests, many of the clergy who were readily given permission by their bishops or superiors to come to America were not well disciplined or self-disciplined. The Irish clergy who came were not all John Englands or John Powers, and not all the William Hogans received public notice.

Of the Irish immigrants coming before the famine, some were able to pay their way over to Quebec or New York on the sailboat and perhaps have something with which to sustain themselves until they could obtain work. Some, however, were the victims of the Irish landlords who were clearing their land of tenants so that they could raise sheep or cattle. When the lease expired, these landlords simply refused to renew it. The victims of this eviction had no funds and lived in poverty along the roads of Ireland or huddled in the towns until they could get means to go to America. When they arrived in Quebec or Boston or New York, they had to take the first job offered them if they were not sent immediately to the poorhouse.

The Irish generally felt that they were suited for the United States because most of them spoke English. There are no statistics about the percentage of literacy among them, but the extreme poverty of these former tenants would scarcely allow for the maintenance of schools. Generally speaking the Irish immigrants were faithful to Catholicism, and this kept them from being absorbed socially into the poorer classes of the new country. The crux of the problem of Catholic immigration came in the field of education. The building of parochial schools to care for these immigrants was clearly impossible in the chief centers of immigration because there the poverty was greatest and the funds offered to the Church by the immigrants who obtained employment, added to the gifts of the Society of the Propagation of Lyons and Paris, scarcely enabled the clergy to erect churches and orphan asylums for the destitute. The public schools were still in the formative state in larger cities, but they were expected to teach the common morality as well as the beginnings of reading and writing and arithmetic. That morality was derived from reading the Bible. It was also contained in the moral teachings of readers and spellers, but the obvious cause of contention by the Catholics was the use of the King James version of the Bible in the schools.

The character of the conflict between the Irish and the Nativists differed according to the position of the immigrants. In general the Irish concentrated in the new cities or in milling towns where

unskilled labor was in demand. The New England states under-
went the second colonization when the Irish came sometimes
directly from Europe to Boston and sometimes in equal numbers
by boat or on foot from the first landing points in Halifax,
Quebec, or Montreal. Thomas Grattan has correctly said that the
hardest soil on which the Irish immigrant tried to take root was
that of Puritan New England, and yet it seemed that that was the
first center of Irish settlement. The Yankees did not help them,
but they did let them work. The impoverished immigrants could
not of themselves build up a Catholic school system, and they
eventually sent their children into the public schools as students
and later as teachers. The conflict of cultures broke out eventually
into violence that reached its peak in the burning of the Charlestown convent. When Bishop Fenwick helped his fellow Jesuits to
establish Holy Cross College, the State legislature refused it a
charter, and in its first years its influence was more as a beacon
than as a successful college in the land of the Anglo-American
Congregationalist. The Irish of Massachusetts, Connecticut, and
the neighboring states were the hewers of wood and the carriers
of water. Their chances of attaining the upper levels of society
were slight before the end of the nineteenth century. Their only
avenue of advance was in politics, where sheer numbers counted.
The Whig politician, Harrison Grey Otis, could speak contemptuously of the wild Irishman with scarcely a shirt on his back, but
he soon had to recognize the value of the Irishman's ballot, at
least in local politics. New England was an area of cultural hostility, of Yankee financial and cultural domination against which
Irish poverty and ignorance faced a long uphill struggle.

Writing in his *Review* in 1845 about the Native American Party,
Orestes A. Brownson spoke as a fellow nativist of the nativists'
attitude towards the Irish:

But the objection to foreigners is not exclusively political, nor chiefly
political. The Whig leaders are opposed on political grounds, because
a large portion of foreigners are supposed to vote for the Democratic
party. But below this is another objection, which operates chiefly
amongst the laboring classes. The mass of the people, especially of
those who live on from father to son in the same position and pursuit,
retain almost forever their primitive prejudices. The great mass of
what may be called the common people in this country are of English
descent—for we are all of foreign extraction; and they have inherited
from their ancestors, and still retain, two strong prejudices,—contempt
of the Irish and hatred of the French. There is no use in disguising the
fact. The assistance the French rendered us in the Revolution has molli-

fied our feelings somewhat towards them, but we still bear them no real good-will. But the national English contempt for the Irish has been reinforced in America. The Yankee hod-carrier, or Yankee wood-sawyer, looks down with ineffable contempt upon his brother Irish hod-carrier or Irish wood-sawyer. In his estimation, "Paddy" hardly belongs to the human family. Add to this that the influx of foreign laborers, chiefly Irish, increases the supply of labor, and therefore apparently lessens relatively the demand, and consequently the wages of labor, and you have the elements of a wide, deep, and inveterate hostility on the part of your Yankee laborer against your Irish laborer, which manifests itself naturally in your Native American party.

But the real objection lies deeper yet. The Native American party is not a party against admitting foreigners to the rights of citizenship, but simply against admitting a certain class of foreigners. It does not oppose Protestant Germans, Protestant Englishmen, Protestant Scotchmen, nor even Protestant Irishmen. It is really opposed only to *Catholic* foreigners. . . .

. . . The majority of the American people have descended from ancestors who were accustomed to pray to be delivered from the flesh, the world, the Devil, and the *Pope*; and though they have in a great degree rejected the remains of faith still cherished by their Protestant ancestors, they retain all their hatred of Catholicism. If they believe nothing else, they believe the Pope is Antichrist, and the Catholic Church the Scarlet Lady of Babylon. When the Catholic Church is in question, all the infidels and nothingarians, to use an expressive term, are sure to sympathize with their Protestant brethren. . . .[8]

In the Middle States the next concentration of Irish immigrants in time and number was chiefly in New York and Philadelphia. At the beginning of the century the prospects for Catholicism seemed better in Philadelphia than in New York, because there were more Catholics of some social and cultural standing in the area where Catholicism had existed for nearly a century. Philadelphia represented the first urban area of American Catholicism, although the more prominent Catholics were mostly Irish or Germans. Unfortunately Philadelphia Catholicism was disturbed by the bitterest quarrels over trusteeism and the scandal of the Hogan schism. Eastern Pennsylvania and Philadelphia were also dominated by a different form of opposition at first. The Quaker dominance was tolerant, but overwhelming. The other Protestant element in Pennsylvania was Congregational among the Yankees and Presbyterian among the Scotch-Irish, and these were militantly anti-Catholic. In New York there was less of this solidarity of Yankees. Further in New York, the Irish found a leader capable

[8] *Brownson's Quarterly Review*, "Native Americanism," II (1845), 76–98.

of directing them. Irish leadership was at first political and was accompanied by some financial improvement. The New York Irish also had capable clerical leaders first in Father John Power and later in the outstanding Catholic priest of the day, Bishop John Hughes. Bishop Dubois had refused to recommend Father John Power as his successor. He sought Bishop Francis Kenrick and then Father John Timon unsuccessfully. Then he accepted John Hughes, who became Bishop in 1838. Hughes had helped Bishop Kenrick in his defenses of the Church and by publicly debating the Reverend John Breckinridge. Bishop Dubois was not necessarily happy with his Irish Coadjutor but he became incapacitated in 1839, and Bishop Hughes took charge. Bishop Dubois died in 1842.

In Philadelphia, Bishop Kenrick, as titular Bishop of Arath and Administrator of Philadelphia, had begun his regime by forcing the submission of the Trustees of St. Mary's in Philadelphia. Also he erected the new church of St. John the Evangelist over which he appointed Father John Hughes. In 1832 he held a Diocesan Synod to enforce the regulations of the Provincial Council and began St. Charles Seminary. The Bishop also visited the regions under his jurisdiction around Pittsburgh and in Delaware. By 1838 the Bishop's brother, Father Peter Richard Kenrick, visiting in Rome reported that the vast Diocese, encompassing more than 50,000 square miles, had more than 120,000 Catholics. Despite this, Bishop Kenrick failed in his efforts to divide his task by the establishment of the Diocese of Pittsburgh in the West. In 1837 when Father Hughes was made Coadjutor of New York, Bishop Kenrick changed his Cathedral to St. John's. Finally in the Baltimore Council of 1843 the division of the diocese was accepted by the Bishops, who asked Rome to create the Diocese of Pittsburgh. The Bishop of the new See, elected that year, was Father Michael O'Connor, an Irish theologian who had been at one time the rector of the Philadelphia seminary. Bishop O'Connor felt the same nativistic attacks that rocked Philadelphia in 1844 but had a smaller and less qualified flock to endure them.

Philadelphia had had a series of riots during the first four decades of the century, chiefly because the outskirts of the city had separate and mismanaged local governments which did not function properly in times of crises. There had been labor riots, nationalistic riots, and race riots. In the later thirties the Nativists began to organize in the city against the Irish, who they knew were growing in number because of the number of their votes and because of the increase in the number of Catholic churches. Part of their religious feelings against the Irish could be attributed to a revival about this time in fervor among the Presbyterians. Pamphlets attacking Catholics were distributed in the city. Also in 1842, acting upon the plea of some Catholics who had children in public schools, Bishop Kenrick addressed a letter to the Board of Controllers of the Public schools against making Catholic children read the King James version of the Bible and against other practices likely to injure the faith of Catholic children.[9] He claimed correctly that such practices were contrary to the school law. The teachers in suburban Kensington disregarded the ruling of the Controllers. Kensington was settled mostly by immigrants from North Ireland. Protestant groups, informed of the Bishop's letter, held public meetings in which Catholics were accused of trying to take the Bible out of the public schools. Kenrick protested in the newspapers that Catholics were not opposed to the Bible but merely wanted Catholic children to read Catholic versions. Alderman Clark, also, called the attention of the teachers in the Kensington schools that they were not keeping the law. This brought about a protest meeting on May 3, 1844, in a lot near the public school. During the meeting an Irishman drove his horse and wagonload of sand through the crowd. Another meeting was held on May 6 which broke up with disorders. Some houses were burned, and a party of Catholics attacked the rioters with stones and guns, killing a youth holding an American flag.

The riots continued throughout the night. Bishop Kenrick posted placards the next morning asking the Catholics to avoid public meetings. The Native Americans met again that afternoon. The trouble continued through that day and the next and on May 8 St. Michael's Church was burned. Then a convent was burned. That evening the mob attacked St. Augustine's Church in Kensington and, despite the protection of the police, set fire to it. The riots were subdued the next day but guards were stationed about other Catholic churches and Bishop Kenrick was prevailed upon to take refuge with a Protestant clergyman. Property worth $250,-000 was destroyed, sixty persons were seriously injured and forty killed. Riots broke out again around St. Philip's Church after July 4 and only the intervention of the military and the Governor of the State prevented further burning of churches and ended the riots. The riots tended to disgrace the Nativists. In general Bishop Kenrick tried to calm his flock and keep them from par-

[9] A good account of the Philadelphia riots is in Joseph L. J. Kirlin, *Catholicity in Philadelphia* (Philadelphia, 1909) pp. 304–339.

ticipating in the riots. He was a scholar and not a militant leader like Bishop Hughes of New York around whom the Irish of that city more securely defended themselves.

In 1840 when Bishop John Hughes returned from a trip to Europe he found that the Catholics of New York under Father John Power had become embroiled in an unsuccessful attempt to get a share of the funds appropriated by the city for schools.[10] It was estimated that of about 12,000 Catholic children of school age in New York only about 4,000 were in Catholic schools—mostly schools for girls—and about 300 were in the public schools. The rest received no schooling. With government aid, some Catholics thought this condition could be remedied. Their efforts to get this aid became mixed with political agitation before the Bishop returned to take charge. In August and September the Bishop published his objections to sending Catholic children to the schools maintained by the Public School Society, which he said were not neutral on religion, and he asked for a share of the common school fund for Catholic schools. There was a public meeting attended by the Bishop, the school officials, the aldermen, and representatives of the chief Protestant churches. There were efforts to compromise the positions of the Bishop and the public school officials, but finally the Bishop's petition for a share of the funds was rejected on January 11, 1841. The Bishop then appealed to the State Legislature, which postponed discussion until after the coming election. When there seemed to be no one on either Democratic or Whig tickets who would support the reform that the Catholics wanted, the Bishop was urged to form an independent ticket composed of some independent candidates and some of the Democratic candidates. The ticket got only 2,200 votes in the election—not enough to win for its own candidates but enough to decide the election of some nominated on other tickets. The result was the enactment of a school bill by the legislature which provided a neutral public school. The Bishop had not won the battle but he had demonstrated his leadership of the Irish Catholics of the city. The Bishop held the first Diocesan Synod at the end of the annual retreat, August 29, 1842, in which, besides the

[10] Because a new biography is lacking, the best account of this controversy is in John R. Hassard, *Life of Most Reverend John Hughes, O.P.,* (New York, 1866). Supplementary is Henry J. Browne, "Public Support of Catholic Education in New York, 1825–1842: Some New Aspects," *Historical Records and Studies* (1953) XLI, 14–41. Vincent P. Lannie, *Public Money and Parochial Education: Bishop Hughes, Governor Seward and the New York Controversy* (Cleveland, 1968) is a fine account of the events in 1840–1842.

usual legislation, the power of lay trustees was limited, and they were threatened with loss of priestly services if they did not accept the decrees of the Synod. This led to a revolt by the Trustees of St. Louis Church in Buffalo, but the Bishop by building a new church and refusing to appoint a new pastor to replace the one they had—who had gone to Europe—forced them to submit.

The rise of the Native American Party which had brought about the riots in Philadelphia had begun to show itself in New York, instigated chiefly by the accusation in *The New York Herald* by James Gordon Bennett that the Bishop was trying to organize a Catholic political party. In April 1844, mobs of Nativists paraded through the Irish sections of the city trying to arouse the Irish, but, at the command of the Bishop, the Irish remained off the streets. The Bishop set armed men to guard the churches. When Nativists came from the Philadelphia riots in May to continue their work in New York, he warned the mayor to prevent any burning of churches by use of troops. The Bishop published several severe letters attacking the Nativists, and the editors, James G. Bennett and William K. Stone. In the face of Bishop Hughes' actions the threat to burn the Catholic churches in New York was dissipated.

The character of growing Catholicism in the eastern cities was shaped chiefly by immigrants and their efforts to rise to some economic and social position from the poverty and ignorance with which they arrived. The port towns farther south ceased to be important ports of entry, and the number of Catholics in them did not greatly increase. The exception was New Orleans, which became a regular port of entry through which Irish, German, and other immigrants made their way into the Mississippi Valley.

The Maryland Catholics of colonial days had been chiefly agrarian in character, and their chief colonies in Kentucky and Ohio were of the same character. From the region of Bardstown, the principal colony, they moved in many directions, especially when it was discovered that the soil there was not too fertile. Filial settlements were established in Union County, Kentucky; about Washington, Indiana; at Paris, Illinois; in Missouri; and in Tennessee. These Anglo-Americans prospered but seldom became an important influence in their new settlements because they were not numerous. They were usually joined by some immigrants, Irish and German, particularly, but not in great numbers. The number of converts to the faith from Protestantism made by these groups was proportionately rather large, but there are no accurate statistics for them. Bardstown continued to be the center of western

Catholicism only so long as western Catholicism was mostly English, and this explains the existence of the motherhouses of several religious communities and the establishment of Catholic colleges in early Kentucky.

The second great force affecting the character of the western settlement was the existence of the great natural resources, the most accessible of which were the fertile valleys of the Mississippi basin. Catholics who had the means joined in the westward movement, where they became the nucleus of the new Dioceses of Nashville, Natchez, and Little Rock. Later when Texas became part of the United States there was established the Vicariate of Texas and the See of Galveston. North of the Ohio the growth of Catholic settlements resulted first from some migrations from around Bardstown and its environs and from some direct settlements from Maryland. Usually, they sought Catholic mission centers which in later years became the parishes of the Diocese of Cincinnati. The Dioceses of Detroit and Vincennes established in 1833 and 1834 had as their nucleus the remnants of French settlers of colonial days to whom were added some American pioneers. Dubuque, made a Diocese in 1837, became the starting point for the missions of Iowa.

The route of the first Catholic pioneers to the West was over the mountains by the old trails. Very soon they went by boat down the Ohio, both priest and laity seeking homes in Kentucky, Indiana, and beyond. After the opening of the Erie Canal, the great flood of pioneers through the Great Lakes brought with it not only some Catholics from the old settlements but many of the new immigrants from the ports of entry. Some Irish came directly from Canada to the Middle West. The Irish came mostly to build the canals and later the railroads, down the Ohio, then from Canada directly across the Great Lakes and some up the Mississippi from New Orleans. Few of them had the funds to buy the fertile farmlands, although some saved enough from their pay to buy small farms. Many of them settled in the towns along the way. The Germans came better prepared both in financial resources and in skills in farming or trades. They brought with them also the tradition of a parish school and of parish activities. Nevertheless, the percentage of Catholic immigrants who settled in the Mississippi Valley and on the southern shores of the Great Lakes before 1860 was small. Even when the number of Catholics was multiplied by the immigrants, they did not have many compact settlements like the concentration of Irish immigrants in the cities of the eastern seaboard. As a result the Catholics in the new states of Ohio, Indiana, Illinois, and Michigan had to show more self-assertiveness and to compete with their farmer Yankee neighbors for their social and economic welfare without much political support. Their advancement in western society was possible because, despite the transplanted Yankee prejudices, there was in the newly settled areas a less compact social order, and there were better chances for the industrious worker to forge ahead.

In one sense the agitation of the eastern Protestants against the growth of Catholicism in those parts where missionaries went was justified because the progress of the Church on the frontier was rapid and if properly sustained might have made the Mississippi Valley a great Catholic country. The great western migrations were not Catholic, and, despite the aid from the Austrian, Bavarian, and French mission societies, the rural areas of the Middle West never became predominantly Catholic except in some small colonies. In the first place the Irish flood of the 1840s and 1850s did not come west because they had no savings with which to buy the rich lands; further, they were not experienced farmers as were so many of their non-Catholic neighbors who had previously farmed in the eastern regions of the country. The result was that even those Irish who went into farming regions seldom remained there and tended to go into the towns and later to the cities.[11] The Germans more commonly settled in comfortable rural communities but their retention of their German language and customs kept them from having great influence outside of their own groups. Despite their poverty, the Irish were generous toward the Church, but they did not advance socially. The German colonies in the Middle West were more successful in agriculture, but the Catholics who achieved social recognition in the western states before the Civil War were those of English ancestry and American birth. These did not have numbers and were widely scattered in the rural areas of the South and Middle West. Socially and culturally, these Anglo-Americans reinforced by some Irish and Germans who had become quite Americanized were the nucleus of future American Catholic cultural leadership. Their centers were Mt. Saint Mary's and Mt. Saint Joseph at Emmitsburg, Georgetown, and St. Joseph's College and St. Mary's in Bardstown. These centers were strengthened by well-trained clerics from Europe. St. Louis, Detroit, and Notre Dame as colleges of Catholic intent helped raise the cultural position of Catholics in the Middle West.

[11] Florence E. Gibson, *The Attitudes of the New York Irish Toward State and National Affairs, 1848–1892* (New York, 1951) does not say much about religious affairs.

The majority of American Catholics by 1850 were immigrants, and, while they commanded political recognition in the cities of the east, they lowered the cultural position of Catholics in the country. These immigrants were lacking in education and higher culture, but they were loyal to the religious faith which was their great consolation and their chief hope for a better life. Most of them had suffered in their persons or their ancestors for their faith and they were determined to drink to the full their draft of American religious freedom. From their poverty, they built churches and orphan asylums and hospitals. By their numbers, in compact areas, they began to demand political recognition. They gave to American Catholicism something that the Anglo-American Catholic minority did not have, a determination that they would not be second-class citizens. This had its effect also on the ecclesiastical organization of the Church in America, which was formed during these decades.

The story of that ecclesiastical organization is recorded chiefly in the action of the Provincial Councils. When John England died in 1842 Bishop Kenrick came to preach at his funeral and called him the "Father of the Provincial Councils." Kenrick knew how great a part this Irish Bishop England had played in forcing the Archbishops of Baltimore to hold the councils of 1829, 1833, and 1837. He knew also that the zealous and capable Bishop had dominated the hierarchy during that time. Unfortunately, England's "republicanism," and his democratic solution of the trustee problem as well as his undisguised favoritism for the Irish kept him from being moved to a more important see than Charleston. In the Council of 1833 the influence of England and Kenrick was just sufficient to prevent Whitfield from having his way. In the Council of 1837 most of the legislation was intended to shore up any defects in the legislation of the previous Councils by calling for greater uniformity in rule and in public liturgical services, asking for better church music and for the abrogation of certain feasts and fasts that were not suitable to the country. Bishop England in the pastoral wrote eloquently against the rising clouds of persecution. He regretted that the old tales against the Church had been revived. "The people of other nations," he wrote, "are astonished at beholding those charges renewed here, in language far more vulgar and obscene than ever disgraced their worst exhibition in Europe. . . ." He noted also the actual low state of the immigrants.

We are indeed comparatively few amongst the millions of our fellow-citizens; the greater portion of our flocks are in the humble, laborious, but useful occupations of life: we do not aspire to power, we do not calculate by what process we should be able, at some future day, to control the councils of the republic, neither do we combine to raise the members of our society to places of trust, of honor, or of profit: we seek not to make friends for our church by exhibiting the ability of our party to reward and to sustain its benefactors; but, relying upon the protection of our God, we endeavor to live in peace with our brethren whilst we are occupied in our several appropriate duties. . . .[12]

By the time of the Council of May 17, 1840, there were sixteen sees from which twelve bishops were in attendance. Bishop Hughes, who was to achieve his dominance among the Bishops in later meetings, was in Europe. The decrees outside of stringent rules about mixed marriages and legislation to promote temperance seemed to manifest an awareness of the anti-Catholic crusade that was being waged against the Church in the nation. The clergy were admonished to see that Catholic children were not forced to read non-Catholic versions of the Bible or books imbued with Protestant doctrines. The faithful were warned against secret societies, and the clergy were to see that the church properties were safeguarded in law, according to each state. The pastoral letter, the last one by Bishop England, spoke of the failure of Massachusetts to redeem its good name by making restitution for the Charlestown outrage, complained of the libels against the Church, especially against religious and clergy, urged the establishment of Catholic schools, the study of the Sacred Scripture as the best means of refuting the confusion existing in the minds of those opposing the Church, and touched on the topics treated in the Council, such as intemperance, secret societies, and the danger of the confusion in the rough presidential campaign of 1840. The letter of Pope Gregory XVI prohibiting the slave trade was read and discussed in the Council, but no decree about it was included in the results of the Council.

The Council of 1843 was the first without Bishop England and the first attended by Bishop John Hughes upon whose shoulders seemed to fall the mantle of episcopal leadership. Archbishop Eccleston was a capable prelate, but he did not have the qualities of leadership exhibited by these two natives of Ireland. That the judgment of England and Hughes was better than that of Eccleston can well be doubted. Both were undoubtedly influenced by their devotion to Ireland and to their fellow immigrants. But since the great mass of the Catholics were now immigrants, the

[12] Peter Guilday, ed., *The National Pastorals of the American Hierarchy, 1792–1919* (Washington, 1923) p. 83.

leadership of Bishop John Hughes was what enabled his fellow immigrants to enjoy the fruits of the rich country.

The decrees of the Council of 1843 were not significant. The earlier decrees about the holding of the Church properties had to be modified to fit the legal situation in the various states. In general the decrees of the Council of Trent, which had not been enforced in the nation, were not to be enforced—only in the city itself of the Detroit Diocese was the *Tametsi* decree on marriage to be allowed. As a sign of greater permanence in the diocesan organization, the Council required permanent residences for pastors and the erection of permanent confessionals in churches and forbade the holding of nonreligious meetings in the churches. This last rule arose apparently from a disturbance in a meeting in a New York church. The Council recognized the works of the Catholic publishers of Cincinnati and Baltimore. The Pastoral of the Council lacked the flowing sentences of Bishop England. It mentioned the need for Catholic education, the necessity for avoiding secret societies, and urged the practice of temperance and the avoidance of public scandals. The writer of the pastoral urged prayer for the Indian and Liberian missions and the support of Catholic institutions and praised the activities of the contemporary Oxford convert movement.

The Provincial Council of 1846 was rather a perfunctory meeting, since there were really no pressing problems to be solved. Present were the Archbishop, Samuel Eccleston, and twenty-three bishops. The records of the meeting are sparse, and there were only four decrees, the most important of which asked that the feast of the Immaculate Conception be made the patronal of the Church in the United States. The decrees were not approved immediately, but the reason for the delay was the death of Pope Gregory XVI and the election of Pius IX.

Actually the assembled bishops unofficially had much to discuss. The riots of Philadelphia were not forgotten nor the continued publication of bitter anti-Catholic books and pamphlets such as that of the ex-priest, Anthony Gavin, *A History of Popery* to which was appended *History of the Papacy in the United States*. But there were also consoling events to discuss such as the conversions from the Oxford Movement in the country, and the remarkable converts, Isaac Hecker and Orestes A. Brownson, whose influence on American Catholics would be very great. The number of secular clergy in 1846 in the country was estimated at 508 and of religious clergy as 193 with 36 religious brothers and 1140 women religious. The new Dioceses erected since the previous Council,

Pittsburgh, Little Rock, Chicago, Hartford, and Milwaukee, indicated only imperfectly the rapid growth of the Catholic organization, despite the nativistic and anti-Catholic opposition. There was nothing said publicly about the slavery question. The Pastoral to the faithful by the Council spoke of the converts, defended the dignity of the Holy Father which had been attacked in the anti-Catholic propaganda, and thanked the Society of the Propagation in France for its benefactions to the Church in the United States. Before the next Council, Pope Pius IX was driven from Rome.

The Seventh Provincial Council of Baltimore in 1849 was in a sense a National Council since there were two archbishops in attendance, and the third had been invited. Oregon City was made an archdiocese in 1846 under Archbishop Norbert Blanchet with seven proposed suffragan sees. The next year, to correct the fact that the new Archdiocese had belonged to the Diocese of St. Louis, that See was also made an Archdiocese with Peter Richard Kenrick as the first Archbishop. The chief work of the Council was to seek other hierarchical reorganizations with three other Archdioceses, New York, Cincinnati, and New Orleans, and to discuss the Dioceses suited to be suffragans to each Archdiocese. The assembly also called for a National Council for 1850. The pastoral, besides defending the rights of the Pope, solicited funds for his relief. As a kind of climax, the Council asked that the Archbishop of Baltimore be made the Primate of the country. These were hasty measures by which the bishops tried to catch up with a Church body that had grown too fast. The Roman authorities refused the establishment of a primacy, without giving a reason. The attempt to organize the national Church within itself was symptomatic of the formation of the Catholic minority in the United States.

In the Catholic organization in the country, the new Archdioceses of Oregon City and St. Louis represented the spread of the Church throughout the western frontier, including even the new territories of California, New Mexico, and Texas. The setting up of the new Archdioceses of New York and Cincinnati represented in their leaders, Archbishops Hughes and Purcell, the body of Irish immigrants that had overwhelmed the Catholic organization along the eastern seacoast and in the Ohio Valley. Cincinnati might well have had a German Archbishop, but the massive German immigration came after Archbishop Purcell had gone to Cincinnati and was perhaps symbolized by the See of Milwaukee, where German immigrants had gone in great numbers, and by its Bishop, John Martin Henni. Archbishop Anthony Blanc represented the territory of old Louisiana and the Floridas. The Archdiocese of Baltimore and the southern states remained mostly Anglo-American in character because the Irish immigrants remained mostly in the north. In 1851 Archbishop Samuel Eccleston died, and his replacement by an Irishman symbolized a change that had already taken place in the government and public character of the American Church. The Anglo-American clergy and laity did remain the social and cultural leaders of the Catholic faithful, but the main task facing the hierarchy in 1850 was the Americanization as well as the sacramental administration of the more numerous immigrants who lacked social and cultural prestige. The immigrants, especially the Irish, were to lead the reaction to the nativistic persecution that had arisen in the two preceding decades and give the American Catholicism a forwardness and aggression that it had lacked under the leadership of the Anglo-American-French hierarchy. The formation of the Catholic minority while fully outlined by 1850 would not be complete for more than another generation because of the continued influx of so many non-English Catholics.

The story of the Catholic Church in America during the Middle Period relates how the small Anglo-American group was gradually overwhelmed in numbers by the Irish and German immigrants, although the newcomers did not rise to the social importance achieved by the higher ranking families of the native group. But during this time there were movements into the Church from the Protestant majority that have never been fully told. Probably every Catholic pastor in the rural areas could speak of non-Catholics, one or more, who had come into the Church. Bishop Bruté in his report to Rome spoke of conversions.[13] His successor in Vincennes, Bishop Hailandière, made some effort to explain the causes. He gave marriage with non-Catholics as one of the chief factors, along with the care given by Catholic religious women in hospitals and schools. Some Protestants were led to the Church by the books and discussions of Catholic faith. There were two examples of conversions to Catholicism at this time that can be considered as distinct movements.[14] The first was the Oxford Movement, which although a movement in the Anglican Church in England, caused a parallel movement in this country. The second was the conversions of Orestes A. Brownson and Isaac

[13] Thomas T. McAvoy, ed., "Bishop Bruté's Report to Rome in 1836" in *Catholic Historical Review* (1943–1944) XXIX, 177–233, on conversions, pp. 229–232.

[14] Hailandière Papers, University of Notre Dame Archives.

Hecker, the most important converts of the day, and of those who followed them.

Among the parallels of the Oxford Movement in England and America perhaps the most important was the parallel between the lives of Hurrell Froude in England and Arthur Carey in America since neither lived to reach the fulfillment of the movement they hastened. There is hardly a parallel in America to John Henry Newman, because the man who has been called the American Newman, Orestes Brownson, reached the Church through other channels. There is no way of measuring the importance to the Church of this American Oxford Movement.[15] Among those who did not become priests were James A. McMaster, later the mighty editor of *The New York Freeman's Journal*, and William Richards, among whose sons was Father Haven Richards, S.J., the President of Georgetown. With McMaster came Clarence Walworth, later a Redemptorist and Paulist, and Edgar Wadhams, later the Catholic Bishop of Ogdensburg. Augustine L. Hewit, who became a Redemptorist and Paulist, entering the Catholic Church in 1846, was undoubtedly one of the leading minds of the group. A close friend who followed him in 1853 was Father Francis Baker. Father Dwight Lyman, also a close friend of Hewit, had come in shortly after Hewit. Other noted converts attributed to the movement were Thomas S. Preston, later to be one of the leading clergymen of the New York Archdiocese, William Everett, who served as a priest in New York City, and John Murray Forbes who later returned to Anglicanism. Another Anglican convert was Levi Silliman Ives, Bishop of the Episcopal Church in North Carolina, who had formed an Anglican religious community, the Order of the Holy Cross, and whose conversion to Catholicism, followed by the conversion of some of his friends, created a sensation among Anglicans. Among his fellow converts was Donald McLeod, who wrote much about the Blessed Virgin after becoming a priest. James Roosevelt Bayley, a relative of Mother Seton and a New York pastor, left the Anglican Church in 1842 and later was ordained a priest and bishop and eventually became Archbishop of Baltimore. Two who did not become priests after their conversion were William Henry Anderson, a professor at Columbia University, and Jedediah V. Huntington, a brilliant journalist and novelist who became editor of *The Metropolitan*. From West Point came General William Rosecrans and George

[15] Clarence E. Walworth, *The Oxford Movement in America* (New York, 1895).

Deshon, later a noted Paulist priest. These were leading converts of the time, but there were literally thousands of others,
who probably offset the thousands of Catholic immigrants who
wandered from the fold.

The conversions of Isaac Hecker (1819–1888)[16] and Orestes A.
Brownson[17] came from a group of people associated with the
Transcendental movement, a romantic episode of religiously
minded Congregationalists around Boston. Hecker had been born
in New York, December 18, 1819. Under the influence of his
mother, he was raised a Methodist. When the father of the family
died in 1832, the Hecker brothers went into the baking business.
Isaac was not successful as a worker in the bakery but spent much
of his time reading philosophical works. He was interested in the
workingman's movement. Although not old enough to vote, he
became interested in the antimonopoly factions and the Loco
Focos. He met Orestes A. Brownson at a lecture at the Mercantile
Library, and they exchanged ideas. At Brownson's suggestion
Hecker was for a while at Brook Farm and at Bronson Alcott's
Fruitlands. When Hecker talked of entering the Anglican Church,
Brownson told him that the Roman Catholic Church was the only
one that would satisfy his yearning for spiritual security. Hecker
then visited Bishop Fitzpatrick of Boston and was baptized con-
ditionally on August 2, 1844, by Bishop John McCloskey in St.
Patrick's, New York. In 1845 he entered the Redemptorist novitiate in Belgium and was ordained a priest by Bishop Wiseman on
October 23, 1849. After a brief period in England, he came back
to the United States. His work of giving missions to Americans, in
which he was joined by some of the converts of the Oxford
Movement, led to his leaving the Redemptorists and the founding
of the Paulists. Hecker was an idealist who seemed to have little
difficulty finding his way into Catholicism, but his one-time advisor, Orestes A. Brownson, had a harder way, the route of the
logical reasoner.

Orestes A. Brownson (1803–1876) was born in Stockbridge, Ver-
mont. When his family was broken up, he went to live with an
elderly couple at Royalton. He had little formal schooling but
developed a great interest in philosophical and theological study.
He became a Presybterian and began to teach school. In 1825 he

[16] Vincent F. Holden, *The Yankee Paul, Isaac Thomas Hecker* (Milwaukee,
1958) tells the story until 1858.

[17] There is not yet a satisfactory life of Orestes A. Brownson. The most
acceptable is Theodore Maynard, *Orestes Brownson, Yankee, Radical, Catholic* (New York, 1943).

became a Universalist and was ordained at Jaffrey, New Hampshire, in 1826. He married Sally Healy, a pupil, and became editor of the *Gospel Advocate*. For a brief time he was associated with Fanny Wright, and in 1829 he resigned from the paper and joined the Workingman's Party. He came under the influence of William E. Channing in 1829 but professed to be an agnostic for the next few years, although he was a preacher in Ithaca in 1834. In 1831–1832 he edited *The Philanthropist*. In 1832 he became a Unitarian and preached in Walpole, Massachusetts. He was later in Canton and Chelsea, Massachusetts, and then came into contact with the Transcendentalists. In 1838 he began to edit the *Boston Quarterly* and accepted some form of Cousin's Religion of Humanity. He participated in the presidential election of 1840, writing some radical essays on the Working Classes which some claimed lost New England for the Democrats. As a result of the fakery of that election, Brownson turned against democracy. He began to read Pierre Leroux. He ended the *Boston Quarterly* in 1842 and founded the *Brownson Quarterly* in 1844. He became a Catholic in 1844. His was one of the great original minds of the era, but his turning to Catholicism cut him off from the dominant cultural leaders. Even Emerson refused to deal with him after his conversion. Brownson was a severe critic of Catholic writings and of the low cultural status of the Catholic immigrants. Although he admired the Irish, he reproached them for their withdrawal into their isolated groups. His position in the Native American era lost him the friendship of both the Irish and the Nativists. He supported Fremont in 1864 and criticized the Jesuits and the Catholic press in their attitudes toward the Civil War. His *Review* lost most of its subscribers, and he ceased to publish it in 1864. He later wrote *The American Republic,* which was his chief interpretation of the theory of government. He revived his *Review* in 1873. When his orthodoxy in 1860 was questioned because he refused to consider the Papal States as essential to the Papacy, he insisted that he was and would remain a faithful son of the Church. His influence was strong over his faithful readers and he became an ideal Catholic lay leader, but he suffered from the opposition of the leaders of the Irish immigrants and the bishops who felt the sting of his stark criticisms.

A leaven in the mass of immigrant and native Catholic body which developed from the very blood and flesh of the poor Catholics of the era was the beginnings of Catholic education. Georgetown, St. Mary's, and Mt. St. Mary's dated from the first decades of American church organization. Even before Carroll had been consecrated, the Select Body of the Clergy had urged the necessity of a system of education at least to educate the priests of the nation. Several bishops tried to establish seminaries in their cathedral rectories. By 1840 there existed small colleges such as Mt. St. James, later Holy Cross College, in Worcester, Massachusetts; St. Phillip's University in Detroit; the College of Vincennes; St. Mary's College at the Barrens in Missouri; St. Louis University in Missouri; St. Charles College at Grand Coteau, Louisiana; the College of Spring Hill in Alabama; St. Joseph's College, Bardstown, and St. Mary's College, Kentucky. The Brothers of Holy Cross came in 1841 and the Brothers of the Christian Schools arrived in 1846. Academies for young ladies were more numerous and existed in New York, Boston, Philadelphia, Baltimore, Cincinnati, St. Louis, New Orleans, and in other concentrations of Catholics who could support a band of religious women. Communities of Sisters, which began with Visitandines and Carmelites, the Sisters of Charity of Emmitsburg and Bardstown, and the Lorettos, were joined by Charity Sisters, Dominicans, Visitation nuns, Ursulines, and St. Joseph Sisters. St. Mary's of the Woods in Indiana was founded by the Sisters of Providence in 1840 and Notre Dame by the Congregation of Holy Cross in 1842.

These institutions multiplied within the next decade, and, while some of these academies and colleges were much less than they were planned to be, the *Directory* of 1852 claimed the existence of 47 male literary institutions and 100 female academies. They lacked both the financial support and the trained personnel of the older American colleges and academies, but they did enable hundreds of the children of immigrants to prepare themselves not only for the priesthood and sisterhood but also for the professions and for positions requiring advanced education. *The United States Catholic Magazine,* the chief literary organ of Catholics, was published through most of the 1840s but was dependent upon translations from Europe. Even the essays by Americans in the magazine seemed to pay little attention to the American scene. The news items about foreign and American Catholic events were meager but do indicate an awareness of the problems of this minority group.

The Catholic minority in the United States had begun below the Mason-Dixon line, and, even when the Catholic population in the North had outgrown in numbers that in the South, before the Civil War in one sense the Catholic minority was socially a Southern group. In discussing the favoritism of so many Catholics for the South at the beginning of the Civil War, Orestes A. Brownson said in his July 1863 *Review:*

The public opinion of the Catholic body is formed mainly by the Catholics in the Border Slave States, and the Catholics in these states, including the District of Columbia, are intensely Southern in their character and sympathies, and bitterly hostile to New-England, or to the "Yankees." Their Southern sympathies, and hatred of Yankees or New Englanders are diffused through the entire Catholic body even in the New-England States themselves.

There were other reasons than the Southern outlook to explain why the Catholic minority did not take a clear stand against the retention of slavery in the country. In the first place the Catholic minority was not capable of changing the nation's opinions. Catholics of some social and political position were mostly in the Southern States where they were even more of a numerical minority. In the places where the Catholics lived in compact settlements sufficient to have political power, slavery was not a question, but the persecution by the nativistic and antislavery Yankee was. There was also a very important political factor; the Democratic Party, which had become the party of the South, had for more than a generation been also the party of the immigrant in the Northeast.

The Catholic theology on slavery did not consider slavery in itself as sinful; further, slavery itself had to be the result of sin because, by the scriptural story, in man's original innocence there was no subjection of one man to another.[18] Even though theologians regarded slavery as existing ultimately as the consequence of original sin, all Catholic theologians, following St. Thomas, insisted that human slavery had to be mitigated so that the slave could attain his eternal salvation. Thomistic thought recognized two sources of slavery: the enslavement of offenders in war and the traditional institution of slavery that had come to be by economic circumstance and was retained because of the fear of the evils that would follow liberation. Under this second category might be considered slavery as it existed in the Southern states in its better forms and perhaps the serfdom of the Middle Ages. Although early in the nineteenth century there had been movements even in the South to free the slaves, they had declined after the Nat Turner rebellion in 1831. The most forceful argument for the continuance of slavery was the social argument, the fear

[18] One of the best pre-Civil War discussions of the Catholic position is in *The Metropolitan* (Baltimore, 1858) III, 265–273.

of what would follow liberation unless the Negroes were removed from the country. The great fear of the hard-core slaveholders has been characterized as that of "the man holding the wolf by the ears: dangerous to hang on, but still more dangerous to let go."

There had been Catholic slaveholders throughout the South. The Jesuits in Maryland had been slaveholders since colonial days. Members of the hierarchy had owned slaves, and so had the Ursuline nuns of New Orleans. In the "black code" of Louisiana, slaves were to be allowed a certain mitigation of slavery so that they could preserve the bonds of marriage and observe the holy days of rest. The Provincial Councils had insisted that *servi* be allowed to fulfill their religious obligations and also be instructed in all that pertains to the Catholic Faith, but there is considerable evidence that these laws were not always observed. Some Catholics participated in slave trading and the secret importation of slaves. The complicating factor in American slavery was that the slaves had black skins and that, even in the North, the Negroes were not accepted fully as equals. In the period of early settlement both whites and blacks could come into the colonies as redemptioners and earn their freedom. But most of the black slaves were brought from Africa, bought from other black slaveowners and sold for profit. The justification for slavery was not a moral argument: that labor of slaves alone could do the mass manual labor required at the time to make the plantations profitable. As a matter of fact, at the same time there were Southern authors arguing before the Civil War that slavery was not profitable in the long run. The fact of the matter was that slavery as the great problem in American history was Negro slavery. The situation was not the creation of the Catholic minority.[19]

Before exonerating the Catholic minority for its failure to lead in freeing the slaves, one must remember that the dominant culture of the country, North and South, was a notion of Anglo-Saxon-white-Protestant supremacy. In modern times the Anglo-Saxon had never had to accept persons of color as equals. The lack of Negro slavery in the North by the time of the Civil War can be explained simply by the fact that it was not profitable there. The servants needed in the industrial world and mill regions of the North were a bit higher type than the manual slave. The same Puritan consciences who did not themselves own slaves were will-

[19] The most balanced discussion of the Catholic position is Madeleine Hooke Rice, *American Catholic Opinion in the Slavery Controversy* (New York, 1944) although she expected too much from a minority group.

ing to haul and sell slaves to the Southern planter or slave trader. In the South many of those who felt that liberation must eventually come were afraid of the black slave, especially in regions where the slaves were more numerous than whites. Whether this was a just argument or not, it did fit in with the Thomistic argument against abolition that the change might upset the social order. There were other specious arguments offered by religious people: that the slave was better off in his new state because he had been Christianized in his new surroundings and that he was better off in some respects than the mill worker of the New England slums who had to fend for himself in sickness and in childhood and old age.

The position of American Catholics on slavery was brought into the political arena by Secretary of State John Forsythe in the campaign of 1840 after the letter of Pope Gregory XVI in 1839 against the slave trade.[20] The Pope had been explicit:

We ... do vehemently admonish and adjure in the Lord all believers in Christ, of whatsoever condition, that no one hereafter may dare unjustly to molest Indians, negroes, or other men of this sort; or to spoil them of their goods; or to reduce them to slavery; or to extend help or favor to others who perpetrate such things against them; or to exercise that inhuman trade by which negroes, as if they were not men, but mere animals, however reduced into slavery, are, without any distinction, contrary to the laws of justice and humanity, bought, sold, and doomed sometimes to the most severe and exhausting labors; and, moreover, the hope of gain being by that trade proposed to the first captors of the negroes, dissensions, also, and as it were, perpetual wars are fomented in their countries. . . .

Bishop England maintained that the Pope had merely forbidden reducing free men to slavery or being cruel to those already in slavery and that the encyclical did not apply to "domestic slavery." He admitted that he himself was not friendly to its existence. But its abolition he regarded as a political question.

There was another angle about the question of abolitionism as it affected the Irish immigrant. Not only in the South was the slave a competitor for the immigrant's job but also in the North. The freed slave would have been a competitor for the lowest jobs, which were then the chief means of a livelihood for the unskilled and uneducated Irish peasant. This must be added to the fact that, in the eyes of the Irish immigrant, abolition was being advo-

[20] John England, *Letters to the Hon. John Forsythe on the Subject of Domestic Slavery* (Baltimore, 1844).

cated by their chief persecutor, the "Yankee." In some cases the agitator for abolition was also an agitator against the Catholic foreigner. When the Irish heroes, Daniel O'Connell, the Liberator, and Father Theobald Mathew, the great temperance worker, urged their Irish friends in the United States to join in the movement for abolition, the American Irish immigrant told O'Connell and Father Mathew to mind their own business. Some hinted that England was supporting abolition solely because slavery was no longer profitable in England. At least the Irish immigrant in the North did not feel that freeing the slave was his problem.

There were others who were pushed to this neutral position by the rise of Garrisonism and the publication of Garrison's *Liberator,* which demanded the abolition of slavery and the freeing of the slaves even contrary to the Constitution if necessary. The Irish poor in the United States were very grateful for the freedom guaranteed to them by the Constitution of the United States. They did show at times less than respect for some who administered the laws based on that Constitution, but they manifested a great respect for the guarantees of the Constitution. They may have manifested envy toward those who were in possession of the property of the country; but they realized that the law that protected their employers also protected them in what they had and in their religious and political freedom. They were not going to join any movement that had openly declared its intention of breaking the Constitution when it stood in the way of their plans. This legal argument seems to have been very important among the Catholics of the North who had no friendliness to slaveholding. Such an important Catholic voice as Orestes A. Brownson accepted this argument. As to the theological argument, Bishop England quoted the chief American Catholic theologian, Francis Patrick Kenrick, later Archbishop of Baltimore, who regretted the American laws restricting the liberty of slaves yet added:

. . . Nevertheless such is the state of things, nothing should be attempted against the laws, nor anything be done or said that would make them bear their yoke unwillingly. But the prudence and the charity of the sacred ministers should appear in their effecting that the slaves, imbued with Christian morals, render service to their masters, venerating God, the supreme Master of all; and that the masters be just and kind, and by their humanity and care for their salvation, endeavor to mitigate the condition of their slaves.

In an article in *The Metropolitan* of June 1855, an unsigned article on "The Catholic Church and the Question of Slavery" might be taken as expressing the opinions of the Archbishop in whose jurisdiction it was published. Archbishop Kenrick was quoted within the text. The conclusion of the article is rather typical of the opinions of Maryland-Kentucky Catholicism.

The present abolition movement began several years ago, and has produced only one result, the stability of slavery. Since the agitation began no state has enfranchised its slaves; on the contrary, Texas, Missouri, Kansas and Nebraska, which would naturally have been free territory, have all been added to the domain of slavery. And in these slave states the laws against the slaves are more severe than ever, and all attempts to ameliorate the condition of the negro have been neutralized. In one word, the emancipation of the slave has been retarded, perhaps for a century.

Convinced of this, that abolitionism is in itself wrong, that it is injurious instead of beneficial to the slave; that moderation and the exercise of Christian charity alone will effect the liberation and what is more, the elevation of the negro slave, Catholics must ever stand aloof from the abolition movement, and in their own way labor to effect the great end; and few we think who have followed us through this article, will entertain any other opinion than our own, that if slavery ever is abolished, it will be by the Catholic Church in her own calm, steady, lawful way.

But the Catholic way of these border-state bishops was not to be followed. Nor did the bishops state any positive Catholic way. Although the question was undoubtedly debated in the Provincial and the First Plenary Councils, no declaration on the subject was issued. That the other Churches of the country split over the question can be explained by the fact that under English Protestantism, especially in the United States, the state had become the chief moral authority, and the Protestant Churches followed the local civil power. So long as Catholics regarded the question of the liberation of slaves not as a moral question but as a political question under the guise of abolitionism, Catholics did not divide over it. Most Protestant Churches had no choice but to follow their accepted moral authority, the local government, into division and Civil War.

On the eve of the Civil War, Bishop Martin John Spalding of Louisville in his letters blamed the approach of war on the New England Protestant preachers, and in his efforts to prevent the war Archbishop Hughes came close to a defense of slavery, although he became a participant in the war effort for the North once the war had begun. Archbishop Purcell, who had also opposed abolitionism before the war, became definitely antislavery once the conflict had begun. In general the Catholics were not numerous or influential enough to support an independent opinion in the nation. Their participation in antidraft riots arose from other reasons. In the political argument they generally followed the opinions of their local community, especially since most of them felt that the question was being argued as a political and sectional issue and not as a moral problem.

In one sense, the older English and American nucleus of this Catholic minority was being buffeted by many forces. The Catholic minority had been increased in actual size by the influx of hundreds of thousands from Ireland, Germany, and other parts of Europe, with most of the new arrivals caught in the rise of manufacturing in the North or in the movement to the frontier in the West. The older Catholic families in the South were entangled in the problems of slavery. Catholics generally had been encouraged by the notable number of conversions from the Anglican Oxford Movement and from the American vagaries of Transcendental Protestantism because these converts gave a real spiritual and intellectual uplift to American Catholic life. The Catholic minority was being formed by this buffeting of external forces.

Fundamentally, there was a basic reason for the strong fidelity of American Catholicism to the papacy as a kind of guide amidst these stormy gusts. The dominant trends of spiritual life among Catholics seem to have been reformist, and perhaps a bit Jansenistic. The Sulpician piety that permeated the clergy had more than an accidental leaning toward the rigorism of Father Jean Joseph Surin, S.J. The fact of being a minority increased the external expressions of fidelity of the loyal Catholics and permitted those who wished to forget the Church to drop out. The exceptional care of the bishops to train up their own clergy prevented wide variations in services. The lack of freedom and security of the ordinary clergy, and the missionary canon law under which they lived, helped maintain an almost military subjection of priest to bishop. Happily, the bishops were for the most part themselves exemplary in priestly virtue. This Catholic organization had little time and few means to develop the higher spiritual and intellectual possibilities of traditional Catholicism.

CHAPTER SEVEN

The Immigrants Dominate
the American Church 1850-1866

AS IN THE CASE OF THE BURNING OF THE Charlestown convent, the violence of the Philadelphia riots embarrassed those who had been so strong in attacking the Catholic immigrants. In fact, Nativism was comparatively quiet between 1846 and 1852, when the Native Americans became a national party. The immigrants in New England had been securely put in their place from which they would rise only after another generation or two, when pure ballot strength enabled them to enter the city offices and eventually the state and national offices open to this kind of power. In New York the leadership of Archbishop John Hughes had given the Irish immigrants and other Catholics a chance to show resistance to persecution. In Philadelphia the reaction to the riots of 1844 was a kind of armed truce.[1]

It is true that there had been a sudden national friendliness toward Pope Pius IX for a short time after his election in 1846 because he seemed to be leading the Italian states who were fighting Austrian domination of the Italian peninsula, and this sudden admiration for the Pope did not sour until after the end of his exile to Gaeta and his return to Rome. Even the war with Mexico, a Catholic country, excited little anti-Catholic feeling compared to the antislavery opposition to the war. President Polk had asked

[1]Ray Allen Billington, *The Protestant Crusade* (New York, 1938) pp. 238–261.

163

Bishop Hughes to go to Mexico to avert any religious opposition and had two Jesuits sent as chaplains with the troops not only to care for the Catholics, who volunteered readily for the war, but also to give some religious assurance to the Mexican Catholics. There was also the fact that even in the colorless political campaign of 1848 the American voters tended to vote for either of two parties and to ignore any third party as a means of reform. The Whigs were then not much of a party, and the Republican Party had not yet become the chief opposition to the Democrats. It is true also that the peak Irish famine immigration in 1848 aroused sympathy as well as opposition.

Whatever the reason—perhaps ennui in the agitators—there were not many startling manifestations of anti-Catholicism for a few years. Yet it was estimated that in the one year 1849 of this comparative silence, 2,200,000 pages of pamphlets attacking the Church were published in the country. Nicholas Murray's first series of letters to Bishop John Hughes over the name "Kirwan," published first in the *New York Observer* and later in book form, had been published in 1847. Murray, a prominent Presbyterian clergyman who came to this country as an Irish Catholic boy wrote a rather intellectual attack on the Church with a kind of inside information based on the knowledge of a former Catholic. "Kirwan" was the name of a noted earlier convert from Catholicism to Presbyterianism. Bishop John Hughes tried to ignore the attack at first but finally answered some of the charges in letters in *The Freeman's Journal*. When Kirwan's identity became known, Hughes attacked him personally.

The off years between presidential elections have frequently witnessed the rise of third parties and political movements of protest which disappear in the presidential elections when the major parties take over the more important proposals for reform. In 1848–1852 underneath the surface in the country the major struggle was becoming the problem of slavery. Even the Catholic Church had seemed to be ensnared in the discussion when Pope Gregory XVI had condemned the slave trade in 1839. The Papal letter against the slave trade was read to the Bishops in the Council of 1840, and Bishop England had given some rather careful answers to Secretary of State John Forsythe in 1840–1841 which kept the Catholics in the South from being called abolitionists, but which some thought were a defense of the slave system to which the Bishop himself was opposed. That exposition of the problem and the theological opinion of Archbishop Francis P. Kenrick of Baltimore made slavery acceptable while condemning the excesses of slavery that did not treat slaves as human beings. Despite the Wilmot Proviso, the general attitude of the country at the time was one of not fighting even over the slavery issue, and this benevolence even seemed to touch the issue of Nativism.

There is no proof that the Know-Nothing party of the 1850s arose from the native American or American Republican Party of the 1840s. Both have their roots in the deeply imbedded feeling of English Protestantism that Roman Catholicism is not only against the Protestant churches, but full of corruption, priest-craft, and idolatry. A second feeling which supported attacks on the Church could be called a notion of Anglo-Saxon supremacy which regarded the non-English as inferior and was forcibly applied especially to Irishmen (the non-English closest at hand), the Germans, the French, and, in another setting, the Negro.

The factors of English-American prejudice and Anglo-Saxon-ism had varying effects on the new American Catholic Church. The unity of the Catholics was based on the essential doctrines contained in the Apostles' Creed, the Ten Commandments of God, the so-called six precepts of the Church, the Seven Sacraments, and a devotion to the Pope—possibly in reaction to the English attack on that personage. On practically all other questions—some of them very close to Catholic doctrine—the American Catholic minority in the United States had about as many opinions as there were groups of Catholics. It was rather significant that, just before the holding in 1852 of the first council of the Church that was really national, Archbishop Samuel Eccleston, in a sense the last direct heir of the Anglo-American-French directorate of the Church, should die on April 22, 1851. The official notice in the *Directory* described him as "tall and commanding, and remarkable for his graceful deportment and ease in conversation. . . ."[2] He was also described as corpulent but of delicate health.

Immediately after his death there arose a discussion about the choice of a successor. The American-born bishops in their correspondence insisted that the holder of the chief, if not primatial, see should be a native of the United States.[3] Even Bishop Kenrick, although sensitive to the opposition of Maréchal and Whitfield to the Irish, felt that Bishop John Timon, a native American then in the See of Buffalo, should be transferred to Baltimore; and Archbishop Eccleston had named three native Americans in

[2] *Metropolitan Catholic Almanac and Laity's Directory for 1852* (Baltimore, 1851) p. 61.

[3] Correspondence of Bishop John McGill, Richmond Diocesan Archives.

suggesting his successor. The other native-borns suggested included Bishop John Chanche of Natchez and Bishop Vincent Whelan of Richmond. But the two outstanding Bishops of the day were the daring John Hughes of New York and the scholarly Francis Patrick Kenrick of Philadelphia, both of Irish origin. Rome elected Francis Patrick Kenrick Archbishop of Baltimore on August 3, 1851. On July 19, 1850, Rome had also made New York, Cincinnati, and New Orleans Archdioceses. There were rumors in Europe and America that Rome had decided to recognize further the growth of the Church in the United States by raising one member of the American hierarchy to the rank of Cardinal. Both Kenrick and Hughes were mentioned, but Kenrick noted in reference to the suggestion that Hughes was about to be made a Cardinal that the raising of an Irish-born prelate to cardinalitial rank would not be the way to recognize the American Church. Later in 1854 when rumors arose of this Nativism among the Catholic hierarchy, Archbishop Hughes denied in *The New York Times* that it existed. The Council of 1849 had proposed a national council. On August 19, 1851, the Archbishop-Elect of Baltimore was also appointed by Rome Apostolic Delegate to preside over the first American National Council in 1852. Significantly in that Council there were to be six archbishops, and none of them was a native American.

The solemn procession of the First Plenary Council to the Cathedral on May 9, 1852, in full ecclesiastical splendor with six archbishops, twenty-six bishops, and more than fifty priests for the first public session of the Council was an impressive show of force. But such a show was not the purpose of the Council; the Archbishops and Bishops were striving for uniformity and unity. Of the hierarchy, only eight were American-born, eight were born in Ireland, and the rest were mostly of French or Belgian origin with but two Germans. According to this same source, *The Metropolitan Catholic Almanac* for 1852, there were 1,421 priests serving 1,411 churches. The Catholic population was estimated at 1,600,000. Of the 34 Dioceses and 2 Vicariates Apostolic, some were among the more populous regions of the East, others were on the frontier, which then included New Mexico, California, and Oregon; some were in the South where the Catholic percentage of the population was small. Others in the Northeast were filled with newly arrived and mostly poor and illiterate Catholic immigrants. The variety of Catholics almost defied any general characterization outside of their adherence to the rites and doctrines of Roman Catholicism. Probably the most numerous Catholics were the Irish, who were gathered chiefly in the cities and along the newly constructed roads, canals, and railroads. In the cities, the Irish were crowded into the poorest and least comfortable tenement areas. In the rural areas, the Catholic farmers were English or natives in the South and German in the Middle West and Northwest with a few Irish farmers who came before the famine. Of the nationality of the priests, there is no clear record. The majority were probably Irish by birth or descent whether trained in this country or in Ireland. The German Catholic colonies that were found occasionally in the Middle West usually brought their German priests with them or obtained them through the German mission societies of Munich or Vienna. There were many French and Belgian priests throughout the country, some of whom had followed the American bishops from their native regions, and others had come through missionary zeal. To form this assortment of nationalities, social variations, and economic differences into a Catholic unity was a baffling task for a group of bishops who were themselves united only by their appointments.

When the preliminary meeting of the Council was held in the Archbishop's house on May 8, it was the first meeting between many of the bishops because ten new dioceses had been erected since the last Provincial Council of 1849. The Council produced twenty-five decrees counting the last, which stated that the acts were not valid until approved by the Holy See. These decrees, besides professing the bishops' union with Rome, made the decrees of the previous Provincial Councils binding on the nation and prescribed the use of the common ritual and manual of ceremonies. Concerning the organization of the dioceses, the Council forbade absences of bishops from their dioceses for more than three months of the year, asked that the bishops choose a council of consultors from among their priests to be consulted once a month, set up a chancery office, and choose censors for publications, especially books of prayers. The bishops were urged to set up regular districts for priestly jurisdiction, to require the publication of banns of marriage, and to provide Christian instruction for all their young people. The Council urged the bishops to set up schools in connection with the churches, and to create a diocesan seminary or send their seminarians to a provincial seminary. It insisted on an annual account of all financial transactions. It requested the transfer of ownership of church goods to the bishop and care to prevent lay usurpation of the administration of church property. Among other acts of the Council there were decrees on uniformity in ceremonies and on societies. Later, in approving the decrees and arranging for the erection of new sees suggested by the Council, the Sacred Congregation warned the bishops against making too many exceptions to universal church customs that might lead to a "national church." This reference to a national church together with the Roman refusal to set up a primatial see witnessed the fear of the Roman authorities that a national church in the United States would be a dangerous thing. The Roman authorities did not explain their fears but evidently there was chiefly the fear of a national church such as had arisen in earlier centuries in Europe. An American national church would be "republican" and permeated with the spirit of the English-speaking world. Strangely also within the groups constituting Catholicism in the United States these issues of democracy and language became the chief points of division and argument.

The Pastoral of the Council, written by Archbishop Kenrick, while it urged the same points commanded by the decrees of the Council stressed also the need to show obedience to the State, that Catholics by their prompt compliance with civil requirements might "refute the idle babbling of foolish men."

Writing to the Society of the Propagation of the Faith in Paris in March 1852 Bishop Michael O'Connor related a story of harassment and persecution by non-Catholics in Pittsburgh which, while somewhat personal in that the Bishop himself was the victim, was representative of the basic hostility between the immigrant Catholic and the native Protestant in many parts of the country. In Pittsburgh there were few Catholics of any prominence; most of the Irish and Germans were ordinary workers, chiefly on the rivers and canals. The social leadership was Scotch-Irish Presbyterian or Methodist. The harassment of Catholics was public and continuous. Once the public abuse was so obscene that the leader of it, Joe Barker, was jailed, only to be nominated and elected Mayor of Pittsburgh while in jail. When freed he had Bishop O'Connor arrested for allowing sewage from the Sisters' hospital to empty into the public sewer. Acting also as judge, Barker fined the Bishop $20. There were many such incidents when the Irish canal or railway workers came to live in Protestant communities in the Middle West.

There were many reasons why the native Americans continued to oppose the growth of the immigrant population.[4] The cause for immediate reaction was the immigrant competition for the jobs of the unskilled. The Order of United Americans, founded

[4] The best treatment of the Know-Nothings is still Ray Allen Billington, The Protestant Crusade (New York, 1938) pp. 380–436.

in New York in 1844, had for its purpose the care of the poor, especially against immigrant competition, and its members professed to be organized to protect the welfare of the country against foreign influences. By 1855 chapters of the Order had been founded in sixteen states and its membership had grown to 50,000. Other organizations of a similar type were being formed, such as the United Daughters of America in 1845, the Order of United American Mechanics and the United Sons of America. They also had their publications: the *Order of the United Americans,* begun in 1848; *The Republic,* begun in January 1851; and *The American Mechanic,* begun in 1849. In 1849 also Charles B. Allen of New York formed a secret patriotic society, The Order of the Star Spangled Banner. Originally the Society was not to enter politics but to function outside other parties aiding those opposing the immigrants and especially Catholics. In April 1852, James W. Barker took over the Society, and the Society showed some influence in the elections that year. That year Franklin Pierce was elected President, notably with immigrant votes, and he appointed James Campbell, a Catholic, to be Postmaster General, the first Catholic to hold that office. By the close of 1853 branches of the Order of the Star Spangled Banner existed in New Jersey, Maryland, Connecticut, Massachusetts, and Ohio as well as in New York, where the party was temporarily divided. Their first call for a national convention of the American Party, as it was officially called, on May 14, 1854, did not attract many attendants but they called a second meeting in June, and delegates from thirteen states assembled in New York. They set up district or local councils who were to send delegates to the State Council, over which was a National Council. The society adopted an oath of secrecy and a ritual with two degrees of membership. The first degree of membership required, among other things, that the member be a native and not a Catholic. In the second degree the members were eligible for office in the society. While nativism was one of the principles of the society, the organization was basically a no-Popery party and was organized against Roman Catholics.

In 1854 the society made its first effort to influence the elections. Members voted for their own candidates, even writing in their candidates when not on the ballot, and in some localities they elected their whole program. Since they would admit nothing about this society they became known as the Know-Nothings. They prepared to act strongly in the fall election that year. Not everyone they supported was a Know-Nothing candidate, but they were quite successful in electing officials in Massachusetts and Delaware and, in conjunction with the Whigs, in Pennsylvania. In Massachusetts they claimed the governor, the whole Senate and all except one Whig and one Free Soiler in the House of Representatives. The next year the Know-Nothings claimed victories in Rhode Island, New Hampshire, and Connecticut. Maryland and Kentucky also elected Know-Nothing officials, and the party gained partial victories in Tennessee, New York, California, Georgia, Alabama, Mississippi, Louisiana, and Texas. With these victories the Know-Nothings were sure that they would put their candidate in the White House in 1856.

But the victories of the Know-Nothings in the years 1852–1855 were not based on nativism and bigotry alone. The whole nation was confused politically because of the Compromise of 1850, the Kansas-Nebraska Act, the decline of the Whig Party, and the reorganization of the Democratic Party going on throughout the country. There were really many other parties besides the Know-Nothings in various regions bidding for the votes of the confused electorate. It is true that in the confusion many voted for the American Party or the Know-Nothing party because they thought that the nation's ills came from the influx of foreigners and foreign ideas. Others who did not vote for the many other splinter parties voted for the Know-Nothings because they did not know where else to turn.

It was evident in the election of 1856 that the country had not fallen for the bigotry and attacks on Catholics. In 1856, the American Party captured the electoral vote of Maryland only. That was because the Maryland voters were searching for a compromise party. Willard Fillmore, the American Party candidate for President, did not stress nativism in his campaign, and while he received about 800,000 votes or about one-fourth of the votes cast, many of these votes were cast by persons who were trying to find a compromise on the main issue of slavery. In the National Congress the Know-Nothings had been more successful in 1855 when they had 43 Know-Nothings in the lower House. But their bills were not voted on even when they were approved by the committees. The peak year of the movement was probably 1855, which saw the passage of a convent inspection bill in Massachusetts that made the members of the Assembly look ridiculous. Riots over nativism took place in many cities in 1854, and on Bloody Monday, August 5, 1855, twenty were killed and many wounded in Louisville. The election of 1856 was marked by violence in many cities. In Baltimore where the name "plug uglies" came into use, eight were killed and fifty wounded on election day; in New Orleans four were killed.

There existed at this time a political relationship between the United States and the Papal States. This did not necessarily have any religious meaning, since the proposal of diplomatic relations with the Papacy arose chiefly from those Americans who, greatly interested in the liberation of the Italian peninsula from Austrian rule, saw in the reforms instituted by Pope Pius IX in 1847 in the Papal States a movement toward democracy in the papal dominions. There had been some form of American consulship in the Papal States since the 1790s but liberal groups began to agitate for regular diplomatic relations. A public demonstration was held in New York in the Broadway Tabernacle on November 29, 1847, and in Philadelphia on January 6, 1848, in favor of opening diplomatic relations. President Polk in his message to Congress asked, among other diplomatic appropriations, for an appropriation for the establishment of American diplomatic representation with the Papal States. Immediately some members of the American Party in the House of Representatives challenged the proposal, and it was defended by non-Catholics on business and political grounds, while the bill establishing the mission passed. On April 1, 1848, Jacob L. Martin, the Secretary of the American Legation in Paris and a convert to Catholicism, was named chargé d'affaires of the United States to the Papal States. Martin died and, when his successor, Lewis Cass, Jr., was appointed, the Pope had gone into exile at Gaeta during the regime of Mazzini. Cass protected from mob threat the College of the Propaganda at which Americans were studying. To offset any charge of favoring Catholicism, Cass obtained permission to establish a Protestant Chapel. When the Pope returned to Rome in April 1850, Cass presented his credentials. In 1853 the representative to the Papal States was raised to the rank of Minister, and Cass was raised to that rank in 1854. He was succeeded in 1858 by John P. Stockton, but the popularity of Pius IX among the liberals in the United States had declined shortly after his return to Rome.

In 1853 officials of the Roman Court decided to have Archbishop Cajetan Bedini, the newly appointed Nuncio to Brazil, pay a visit to the United States. The idea apparently had no origins among the American bishops, who learned of the plan only when the Sacred Congregation of Propaganda sent them a letter, dated April 5, 1853, about the visit.[5] The announced purpose of the visit was to settle some current Church difficulties in the United States and to sound out the possibilities for the establishment of a nunciature in the country. The Archbishop was to present a letter from the Pope to the President. In his instructions he was told to observe the conditions of religion and to refer back to Rome only outstanding problems. He was advised to reiterate the refusal of Rome to establish a primatial see, to examine into the care of the Indians, to work with Bishop Timon to settle the trustee controversy in Buffalo, and to study the conflict between the immigrants and natives among the clergy.

After Bedini arrived in New York June 30, 1853, he went first to Washington to present the papal letter to President Pierce. From Washington he went to Baltimore and Philadelphia, where he tried unsuccessfully to settle the difficulty between the Trustees of Holy Trinity Church and Bishop Neumann, and to Milwaukee where he consecrated the new Cathedral. After that he visited the Indians at Arbre Croche, Michigan, and went on to Detroit. From Detroit he went to New York and then to Montreal. In the meantime an ex-priest, Alessandro Gavazzi, a former Barnabite who had arrived in New York about that time, accused Bedini of being responsible for the execution of some rebels in Bologna, including an ex-priest Hugo Bassi. Bedini was threatened with assassination on his return to New York. From Montreal, Bedini went to Boston on September 24. In his subsequent report Bedini expressed anxiety at the poverty of the Cathedral and Rectory in Boston, the cultural center of America, and proposed the erection of a better one, but his plans were opposed by Bishop Fitzpatrick who felt that additional churches were more necessary. From Boston he went to Providence, New Haven, and New York. The Nuncio was obviously worried. Despite a visit to Buffalo, he failed to solve the trustee controversy there and returned to New York to preside at the consecration of Bishops De Goesbriand, Loughlin, and Bayley on October 30.

The agitation aroused by Gavazzi against him continued in the press, but the Nuncio decided to visit the West and South. He went to Pittsburgh, Louisville, and Cincinnati. In Cincinnati the press had renewed its attacks, backed by some German and Italian freethinkers. On Christmas night there was a demonstration

[5] The best account of Bedini is James F. Connelly, *The Visit of Archbishop Gaetano Bedini to the United States, June, 1853–February, 1854* (Rome, 1960).

against him in Cincinnati in which he was burned in effigy, and the police fired into the mob, injuring some.

Bedini changed his plan to make a trip to the South and returned east to Wheeling and Washington. In Washington the Senate debated whether the mission of Bedini was diplomatic or not, but the debate indicated only the goodwill character of the visit. Bedini returned to New York and was put aboard his steamer secretly for his return to Europe. It was a strange episode. The bishops did not speak out in defense of Bedini, and he criticized the position of Catholicism in the country. The visit probably increased the agitation of the Nativists in the contemporary Know-Nothing era. It certainly showed that there was no place for an apostolic nunciature in the United States.

The report of Bedini to the Sacred Congregation of Propaganda was based on a planned investigation despite the short time that he spent in the country. He admitted that, since he did not have any announced appointment to investigate the Church in the United States, the bishops had treated him cordially, regarding his visit as a sign of the benevolent interest that the Pope had in them. He felt that his silence in the face of the lies of his detractors also endeared him to the American Catholics. He estimated that of the 24,000,000 people in the country, 2,000,000 were Catholics and that of the 22,000,000 non-Catholics 17,000,000 really belonged to no church. The other 5,000,000 were divided into many sects. The 17,000,000 felt and showed less antagonism towards Catholics, but were really indifferent in religion. He felt that Protestantism in American was not fervent and that the American universities did not support it.

Catholicism he found respected by persons of the upper class, but, because they saw Catholicism only among the Irish, who were the lowest class and living in poor conditions, they considered Catholicism as the religion of the poor and something not for the better people. While there was little to fear that Protestant teaching could draw people away from Catholicism there was much to fear from Protestant fanaticism which was derived from old sectarian heretical, diabolical hatred. This had been fed by Catholic scandals. He found that the American bishops were respected. The higher classes had a good opinion of Catholics but seldom allowed Catholics into lucrative jobs or into higher government positions. There were no Catholic officers in the Army, but there were some Catholic officers in the Navy. There were few Catholic justices, but the chief exception to this was the Chief Justice of the Supreme Court, Roger Taney. Bedini mentioned the failure of Catholics to eliminate the state schools and the great sacrifices Catholics had to make to have their own schools without state aid. He mentioned the growth of the Church by Irish and German immigration, but added a note about the free-thinking German immigrants, some of whom had tormented him in Cincinnati. Archbishop Bedini said that many immigrants had lost the Faith. He admitted that he did not know how many but thought that those who lost the Faith were more numerous than those who had joined other churches.

Speaking of the bishops, he criticized Bishop James Vandevelde of Chicago as wanting in prudence, but was strong in praise of Archbishop Hughes. Next he praised Bishop Michael O'Connor of Pittsburgh and Bishop John B. Fitzpatrick of Boston. He praised also the scholarliness of Archbishop Francis P. Kenrick of Baltimore. He lauded the charitable institutions and seminaries which had been erected, but he thought the churches were too sparsely decorated and that the practice of collecting pew rent was abominable. He recognized the insecurity of the priests since in a mission country they did not have the rights of parish priests. He discussed three possible faults in priests: selfishness, immorality, and a spirit of independence. On the first fault he thought the Irish priests were too greedy. On the second he said the charges of immorality among the clergy were very few, and on the third he thought the spirit of independence was innate in every American but excused it because the American priest had to make greater sacrifices in this new country in becoming a priest. Referring to the arbitrary rule of bishops he regretted the lack of cathedral chapters to check the bishops. He mentioned the strong rule of Archbishop Hughes and the friction between him and the Jesuits. When he was in Vienna, he had formed a bad opinion of the American priests who came there to get money to pay their debts, but now he understood how necessary those debts were if the priests were to have churches. He praised Bishop Martin Henni of Milwaukee for building a good church and felt that the Bishop of Boston was too timid in building his Cathedral. He further noticed the difference between native and foreign-born bishops and suggested that the bishops should be natives. He said that the bishops were friendly until the riots of Cincinnati and that they then advised him to return to Europe. He complained that they did not defend him because of the trouble in Cincinnati but admitted that it was not wise for bishops to take sides in the slavery controversy.

In discussing the priests, he admitted that the Irish priests had the veneration of their people and that they in turn loved their people but he said they did not seem well educated. The German priests did not suffer by comparison with the Irish priests, but the Germans were too nationalistic. Bedini rejected the prediction that the Church in the United States would be divided into two parts, one English and one German, because eventually all would be speaking English. The French priests were associated with seminary work, which they had carried out well. There were few Italian priests. In general the priests were too few and each did the work of three or four. As a solution to this shortage of priests, he urged the establishment of an American college in Rome, maintaining that those trained at Propaganda were the best among the American clergy. Propaganda, however, could not handle enough Americans to meet the problem. The Archbishop argued at great length the need for this American college in Rome and the usefulness that it would have. He talked about American nationalism, which he said was growing prematurely and had shown itself by a lack of appreciation of the Irish clergy. In general he found the American clergy good and loyal to the Holy See.

On the subject of the religious, the Archbishop wrote at length about the Jesuits who had more Americans in their order than did the other communities, and he praised their work at Georgetown, St. Louis, and Fordham. He praised the work of the Redemptorists for the Germans and also that of the Benedictines of Latrobe, Pennsylvania. He mentioned other communities of men, including the Christian Brothers. He spoke of the Sisters of the Visitation, the Madames of the Sacred Heart, and the Sisters of Charity. He did not approve of the separation of the New York Sisters of Charity from the mother community, without blaming Archbishop Hughes explicitly. In an additional report he weighed the question of establishing a nunciature in the United States. He dismissed the arguments against the establishment, such as the predominance of Protestants in the population, and he insisted that the hostility of Protestants had weakened, and he claimed that, because of the American democratic system, Catholics could defend themselves against discrimination. He suggested a temporary nunciature, preferably in Washington. He insisted on the great future of the United States and indicated that a nuncio would play an important part in the growth of the American nation. He felt that the nuncio would be able to counteract the renegades and apostates from Europe who were spreading lies against the Pope and the Church. He rejected the arguments of some American bishops against the nunciature, that there would be interference by the Government in ecclesiastical affairs. On the contrary he thought that the nuncio would prevent interference by government officials in such matters. The Archbishop thought that the low social status of Catholics would be raised by having a representative of the Pope, a temporal ruler, present. He finally argued that the protection given him amidst the riots came because of his diplomatic status, and the nuncio would also be protected. The Archbishop again recognized the low social status of the Catholic minority and repeated the suggestion that the establishment of the nunciature would change this.

The bishops of the country did not know the real purpose of the Archbishop's visit. Rome could hardly have picked a more inopportune time for him to visit the country because the Know-Nothing Movement against the Church was then reaching its peak. Further the friendly attitude of non-Catholic Americans toward the Pope had already changed, and the Pope was no longer considered a friend of democracy. What troubled the bishops most was the fact that they could not clear him from the charges that he had some part in the political persecutions of the papal legations in Bologna. They were used to enduring persecution and public attacks, and they felt that he did not stand up well in the face of the attacks aimed at him. Archbishop Purcell, who had been his friend before the visit, spoke rather contemptuously of the fears of the Archbishop. It is quite probable that the Irish and German bishops had no idea of his criticism of their nationalism that he sent to Rome. All told, it was to them a quixotic adventure.

Outside of their theological doctrines at the time of the visit of Bedini, the unity of the Catholic hierarchy was built on many accidental relationships. The basic unity arose from the practice of allowing the bishops to nominate the candidates from which the Sacred Congregation elected the new bishops. Aside from this, the metropolitans were for the most part leaders among the bishops in their provinces. In the Province of New York, John Hughes undoubtedly was also the outstanding prelate, and, while a majority of his suffragan bishops were of American birth, they were of Irish descent, and their priests and the majority of their faithful were either of Irish birth or descent. Archbishop Hughes was regarded as the chief spokesman for American Catholicism. When suggestions were made that he and Archbishop Kenrick did not agree, he published a denial of the charge as he also denied that there was any real friction between the native and Irish-born bishops. In the Province of Baltimore, although there were some native bishops, the two outstanding bishops were the Irish-born

Archbishop Kenrick and his close friend, Bishop Michael O'Connor of Pittsburgh. Kenrick and O'Connor were the most erudite of the American bishops, but neither seemed to be able to reach the American non-Catholic public. In the Province of Cincinnati, Purcell was the guiding pastor at this time, and Bishop Martin John Spalding, in the center of the transplanted Marylanders at Bardstown and Louisville, was the only native bishop. Spalding was erudite but he lived in a poor and rural diocese. In the Province of St. Louis, except for Bishop Miles of Nashville, the prelates were all of foreign birth. Their task was that of frontier missionaries. The distant provinces of Oregon and San Francisco were also led by foreign-born, but the vast majority of the bishops of the sees of those provinces had served some time on the missions in the American dioceses before being presented by their fellow American clergymen for bishoprics. Across the country between the bishops were bonds of friendship based upon seminary associations, common problems, and personal affection. Archbishop Purcell, for instance, was revered as a kind of fatherly guide by many of the younger bishops.

Irish nationalism in American Catholicism was very noticeable among the Catholics of the New England port towns and their neighboring mill regions and in New York and Philadelphia. In New England, especially, the Irish faced a closely aligned and bitterly hostile Yankee social order which kept them down for several decades. Only in New York did there seem to be any leadership around Archbishop Hughes or among the Irish politicians who served themselves as they organized their fellow immigrants. German leadership was mostly in the Middle West, where the peaceful farmer of the Rhineland had gone to get away from the marching armies of central Europe. Also the Germans were found in noticeable numbers in certain cities such as Cincinnati, St. Louis, Milwaukee, and Buffalo. Of the two German Bishops, John Neumann, the Redemptorist in Philadelphia, and Martin John Henni of Milwaukee, Henni was the more active in public affairs; in the eastern cities and many midwestern communities, the Redemptorists and Precious Blood Fathers were the most attentive to the needs of the German-speaking people. Some of the German colonies were accompanied by their own priests. The German traditions were supported by four weekly journals, *Der Warheits Freund* of Cincinnati, *Der Religions Freund* of Baltimore, *Katholische Kirchen Zeitung* of New York, and *Der Herold des Glaubens* of Saint Louis. The only French newspaper was *Le Propagateur Catholique* of New Orleans, edited by Father Napoleon Perché.

Some of the English publications were accused of being more Irish than Catholic. Such indeed were the *Pilot* of Boston and *The American Celt* published in Buffalo by Thomas McGee. More definitely Catholic with a broader base nationally were *The United States Catholic Miscellany* of Charleston, which had survived Bishop England, *The Catholic Telegraph and Advocate* edited by the brother of the Archbishop, Father Edward Purcell, *The Catholic Herald* edited by the convert Henry Major in Philadelphia, *The Freeman's Journal and Catholic Register* published by the convert James A. McMaster, *The Pittsburgh Catholic*, *The Catholic Mirror* of Baltimore, *The Western Tablet* of Chicago, *The Catholic Instructor* of Philadelphia, *The Catholic Vindicator* in Detroit, and *The Shepherd of the Valley* of Saint Louis. Some of these lasted only a few years during the 1850s but they served several purposes. They answered the Protestant attacks on the Catholic faith, they supplied instruction to Catholics who lacked the means of formal Catholic instruction, they kept Catholics aware of what other Catholics were doing, and they provided for the bishops a means to reach the scattered faithful. They were an important network in uniting the Catholic minority especially in their mutual exchanges of local information. They supplemented in a very important way the provincial councils and the diocesan synods which directed the patterns of public service among the clergy under the local bishops. The chief Provincial Councils at the time were those in Baltimore in 1855 and 1858, in New York in 1854 and 1861, in St. Louis in 1855 and 1858, and in Cincinnati in 1855, 1858, and 1861.

The external forces which hammered unity into the Catholic minority were the nativistic and no-Popery reactions which rose and fell throughout the period. Even in the bishops there was some division between the native and Irish prelates. This division had manifested itself in the time of the election of Bishop Kenrick to the Archdiocese of Baltimore. The feeling arose chiefly from a desire to give a more native appearance to those outside the Church. The friendships of Archbishop Purcell with Archbishop Blanc, Bishop Henni, and Bishop Martin Spalding show that nationalisms were not taken too seriously by them in the period of nativistic persecution. Bishop Kenrick presented native-born Bishop Timon for Baltimore in 1851. A more definite manifestation of nativism came from the great publicist, Orestes A. Brownson. In his *Review* he began to lecture the Irish for not being more American, while condemning at the same time the excesses of the nativists. Brownson tried to make a clear distinction between nativism and religion. He felt as an American that the national traditions, especially in politics, were English modified by the American experience. He foresaw that if the Catholic Church was to prosper in the country it had to accept the political milieu in which it was to live. He was a fierce antagonist against no-Popery and wanted to take away its nativistic disguise. He went even farther in expressing his belief that only when the United States became Catholic would it reach the perfection of the American political and social life. His distinctions were not acceptable to some of the Irish-born clerics, especially to Archbishop Hughes, the articulate Bishop Michael O'Connor of Pittsburgh, and the long-time American but still Irish John Baptist Purcell of Cincinnati. They and some other Bishops began to exert pressure on Archbishop Francis Patrick Kenrick, also Irish but no longer Irish minded, to take away from Brownson the written approval given him in the Council of 1849. It was true that in this as on another occasion Brownson had been offering his own ideas about the temporal power of the Pope, but it is hard to believe that the other essays on nativism published at the same time were not the more important cause for such episcopal disapproval.

Brownson had, indeed, insisted on the indirect papal power in temporal matters in his *Review* in 1853, at the very time that the Know-Nothing movement was very strong and growing stronger. The bishops felt that this was the wrong time to propose such an opinion—just when the apologists for Catholics were trying to repel any charge of papal aggression in the United States. Brownson, like many a convert, did not fear any reprisal for the doctrines he really held and felt that the doctrine of the indirect power was the only sensible one if one really held the absolute spiritual power of the Pope. The bishops accused him of failing to distinguish between the spiritual and the temporal.

Brownson's views on the indirect power of the Pope in temporal matters were attacked by an article in *The Metropolitan*,[6] the monthly Catholic magazine published during the fifties in Baltimore. The editor then was Jedediah V. Huntington, but it was generally understood that the article attacking Brownson was written not by Huntington but by Bishop O'Connor of Pittsburgh. Archbishop Hughes refused to intervene in the dispute and conceded Brownson's freedom to write what he thought. Archbishop Kenrick was sympathetic to Brownson but did suggest that the formal approval of the bishops be dropped from the back cover of

[6] II (1854) 351–362.

the magazine. In 1854 Brownson removed his editorial offices from Boston to New York and then to New Jersey, but, in the change, there does not seem to be any objection by Brownson to Bishop John Fitzpatrick of Boston. Brownson and Hughes did not always agree, but Hughes never threatened Brownson with suppression.

Brownson was the intellectual giant of American Catholicism in the 1850s. He towered over the other converts, James A. Mc-Master of *The Freeman's Journal,* Henry Major of *The Catholic Herald,* and Jedediah V. Huntington of *The Metropolitan.* These three men had one talent in common, they had studied theology before they entered the Catholic church and did not become priests afterward. Instead they devoted themselves to literary works. Their theological studies made them the ideal Catholic newspaper editors because, besides having literary zeal, they could enter the field of theological controversy with some confidence. All had close clerical friends to whom they could turn in case of doubt, but they were willing to enter controversy not only with other lay-men but, if the occasion offered, also with bishops. Brownson's chief episcopal opponent at this time was Bishop O'Connor of Pittsburgh, a brilliant man whose talents seemed wasted in tasks for which he had no attraction. Brownson's chief advisor at this time was the first American graduate of the Propaganda College, Father Jeremiah W. Cummings of New York, likewise a brilliant fellow, whose life ended prematurely at forty-six.

Cummings joined with Brownson in criticizing the first efforts at Catholic higher education. Brownson had been deprived of higher education. He was really a self-made man, with all the crudities that implied, but he had learned his lessons well. Proba-bly he had also learned something from the attendance of his sons at Catholic colleges. He understood the financial handicaps of the Catholic college and did not approve of the use of reli-gious fervor as a substitute for scholarship. Brownson's terminol-ogy was not technical, but he objected to the many tasks that the religious teacher tried to perform, both within the college and in the neighboring missions. He was skeptical of the courses that were supposedly taught by men who were not fully prepared. Although not expressing his criticism in these words, he did object to the use of theology students to teach the college students while they were studying their theology and the mixture of religious direction with matters of secular information. He felt that the mere impowerment by a legislature to give degrees was not suffi-cient justification for founding a college and that the means at hand were not sufficient for the number of students then in these Catholic colleges.

On the major problem of the day, slavery, Brownson and the Catholic press generally agreed to reject abolitionism but not necessarily for the same reason. Brownson did not support the abolitionist movement because he considered it contrary to constitutional government. Later, when the Civil War began, he changed his position in favor of using abolition as a threat to force the rebelling States back into the Union. On the topic "The Catholic Church and the Question of Slavery," *The Metropolitan* of June 1855, which was *the* Catholic monthly journal of the time, as has been noted, praised the failure of the Catholic Church to become embroiled in the controversy over slavery. In this *The Metropolitan,* published as it was in a border state, seemed to hold the common opinion of Catholics of the time. When Daniel O'Connell urged his exiled countrymen in America to join the abolition movement, the American Irish would not listen to him.

In *The Metropolitan* of August 1857, another writer began a bitter criticism of the recently published *The Roman Catholic Element in American History* of Justin D. Fulton. The writer admitted that most of the book was taken from the writings of Bancroft and Prescott to which had been added writings of Brooks, Kirwan, Gavazzi, and other Know-Nothings. The reviewer first summed up the true history of Catholicism in the United States. In the second part of the review, in the October issue, he discussed the "present position of Catholics":

. . . Catholics are a minority totally disregarded by all political parties who legislate about the administration of Catholic churches, the education of Catholic children, the worship of Catholic paupers, as though they, as Protestants, had a right to settle all these matters. A Catholic remonstrance is hailed with contempt in legislative halls. We are *helots*. Once only have we stood aloof. This was in the great controversy as to the public schools in New York. . . . We have several wrongs to be redressed, and if neither party will give redress, we should stand aloof.

And what are these wrongs? 1st. The State interference with our church discipline as to church property. 2nd. The exclusion of Catholic priests and teachers from the eleemosynary institutions. 3rd. The force resorted to to compel Catholic children in such institutions to attend Protestant worship and to receive Protestant instruction, and the preventing of such children attending Catholic worship. 4th The hardship of compelling Catholics to contribute to the support of free schools which they conscientiously believe bad in system and which are Protestant in their textbooks. 5th. Compelling Catholics to contribute, by tax, to school libraries filled with books representing the Catholic religion as false. 6th. The exclusion of Catholics from being actually represented *pro rata* in legislative bodies.

The writer was not too clear but he did mirror the hurt feelings of the Catholics in the country.

Yet Catholicism continued to grow and to develop into a force within the nation. *The Catholic Almanac and Directory* at the end of the decade, 1859, gave some statistics which are clues to the growth of the Church in the United States. Including San Francisco, there were seven Provinces, although the *Almanac* does not mention that none of the presiding Archbishops were natives of the United States and that the most vocal—Archbishops Hughes and Purcell—were Irish, even though they had spent most of their lives in this country. There were a total of 43 dioceses with two vicariates apostolic with a total of 45 holding episcopal rank. There were 2,334 churches attended by 2,108 priests. There was no estimate of the number of Catholics in the country, since the figures for many of the important dioceses, such as New York and New Orleans, had not been supplied. Statistics on the number of schools and colleges that might here give a cross section of the internal progress of Catholicism in the country were likewise lacking. In the Middle West there were already serious efforts to build parish schools for each parish, but this was not true in either New England or the far West.

In comparing the Catholic minority to the non-Catholic majority in the United States in the decade before the Civil War, the chief point of contrast was the lack of independent moral authority in the churches of American Protestantism. Throughout American Protestantism, North and South, there was, indeed, a note of Puritan morality, a certain strictness in public conduct, which was to be taught by the kind of minister or church to which the individual chose to give his adherence, but decisions in matters of public morality were left to the State. This was not new and could be traced without much effort to the kind of church-state relations that were worked out with some slight modifications both north and south of the Mason-Dixon line in the colonial period. After the enactment of the Constitution and the first Ten Amendments, the separation of the churches and ministers from the State became more and more a fact, yet the kind of morality that was to be demanded by the laws of the country was expected to be Protestant. Opposed to this notion was the general Catholic doctrine that, while the State had its own sphere in which it was supreme, only the Church could decide the morality of an institution or a practice. This difference between Protestants and Catholics on the role of Church and State in morals, especially the Catholic submission to the Pope, was at the heart of the anti-Catholic or no-Popery agitation following the sudden growth of Catholicism in the United States by immigration in the 1840s and 1850s. The earnest Protestant regarded the Catholic immigrants as a threat to his way of life by threatening to take over the State. There were also differences in the kinds of Sunday service and in the use of vestments and ceremonies, but the major difference was in practice, centered on this criterion by which a custom or institution was considered good or bad. When the slavery issue was discussed as a moral problem, the attitude of Catholics and Protestants necessarily differed on what should determine its goodness or badness but, as *The Metropolitan* of June 1855[7] proudly boasted, Catholics were not divided on the political question of abolitionism.

The beginning of the opposition to slavery in the country could be attributed to the Quakers, and there had been a general feeling in the country during the first decades of the nation that slavery would eventually be abandoned. The invention of the cotton gin gave a new value to slavery on the southern plantation, and the whole character of the discussion of slavery changed about 1830 with the founding of *The Liberator* and the agitation of William Lloyd Garrison and other abolitionists, who claimed that slavery was an intolerable moral evil and demanded its abolition. Most Catholics did not regard slavery as evil in itself and in general opposed abolitionism because Garrison and his followers not only held slavery as in itself sinful but also demanded that the State abolish it. In the reform movements of the 1820s and 1830s northern Protestants turned against slavery. Abolition societies spread throughout the North and West, but, after the Nat Turner Rebellion in Virginia in 1839, the movement for abolishing slavery lost supporters in the South. The abolitionist agitation continued to gain momentum, and, while efforts were made to avoid the issue in most of the elections of the 1840s and early 1850s, by 1856 the existence and the extension of slavery was the chief question before the nation. Interest in Know-Nothingism declined, and the new Republican Party adopted most of the doctrines of the Free Soil and Liberty parties. Then came the Dred Scott Decision of Chief Justice Roger B. Taney in 1857, the Lincoln-Douglas debates of 1858, and the publication in 1860 of Hinton Helper's

[7] *The Metropolitan*, III (June, 1855) 265–273.

The Impending Crisis of the South: How to Meet It. In the background was the tremendous effect of Harriet Beecher Stowe's *Uncle Tom's Cabin,* published in 1850, and of the radical editorials of editors like Horace Greeley. When the election of 1860 brought about the split of the Democratic party and the election of Abraham Lincoln, the South seceded rather than permit the Federal Government to solve this problem by law even though the newly elected President promised not to take such steps.

Bishop Martin John Spalding of Louisville in his letters to Archbishop Purcell repeatedly blamed the approaching war on the New England Protestant ministers.[8] In a sense he was right because it was the agitation chiefly from New England that called for the governmental abolition of this moral evil that produced the crisis of 1860–1861. In the South the answer had to be an appeal to the same kind of moral authority, that is, to the local governments in the South, later aligned in the Confederate States of America. Almost before the American public could understand, the argument became a war.

There were many Catholics both in the clergy and in the laity who disapproved of human slavery. Pope Gregory XVI in 1839 had condemned the slave trade and even Bishop England, explaining this to Secretary of State Forsythe, in denying that the Pope had opposed the slavery in the United States admitted that his own personal feeling was against the existence of slavery. Many Catholics in the South merely accepted the common practice. Theoretically Catholics were commanded to be mindful at all times that the slaves were human beings and to make sure that the slaves in their service had the freedom necessary to save their souls with particular emphasis on the protection of the marriages of slaves. Some Catholics were very faithful in the observance of these rules, but not all. Some Catholics accepted the argument that the slaves in a Catholic household were better off than they had been in their pagan jungles. There were no Catholics taking the lead in the South in the efforts to abolish slavery. This fact was important because the intellectual and social leadership of the Catholics in America, except for Orestes A. Brownson and his friends, was mostly in the Southern States, particularly in the border states of Maryland and Kentucky. For them the agitation over slavery was a political question, an interference of the Yankees in a Southern problem. In the heat of the final arguments some clerics, includ-

[8] Cincinnati Papers, University of Notre Dame Archives. Cf. also, David Spalding, C.F.X., "Martin John Spalding's 'Dissertation on the American Civil War,' " *Catholic Historical Review,* LII, 66–86.

ing Bishops Augustin Verot[9] and Augustus Martin, even defended slavery.

In the North the leadership of the abolitionists was coupled very often with the leadership of the nativist and no-Popery agitation. The Irish immigrants in New England had no real affection for the Protestant clergymen who treated them as if they were the scum of the earth, and yet the leaders of the abolition movement were often the same clergymen.[10] When Daniel O'Connell urged the American Irish to join with the abolitionists in their fight against slavery, American Irish rejected the suggestion. The leading Catholic newspaper was probably *The Freeman's Journal and Catholic Register* of New York, edited by the convert James A. McMaster. McMaster spoke the minds of the vocal Irish just beginning to emerge from their ghetto. They were mostly members of the Democratic Party who did not want to go against their political allies in the South and above all did not want to align themselves with their persecutors in the North. McMaster found it easy to reject abolitionism as immoral because it called for forceful deliverance of the slaves without recompense to the slave owner. The Abolition Movement had become openly against the Constitution since the Constitution was used by the courts to defend slavery. McMaster pinned his hopes on Stephen Douglas as the candidate for the Presidency in 1860 as did many Catholics in the North. McMaster's *Freeman's Journal* and the *Catholic Mirror* of Baltimore were openly and strongly against the effort to abolish slavery by force. But Douglas split the Democratic ticket and Lincoln won. The few words of McMaster about the new Republican President were not complimentary. He quickly attacked the war measures of Lincoln as unconstitutional. The result was that the Postmaster General gave orders that *The Freeman's Journal* was not to be accepted for mailing, and, when *The Freeman's Appeal* was published instead, McMaster was arrested and imprisoned in Fort Lafayette. In the meantime, the Archbishop of New York, John Hughes, had made *The Metropolitan Record* his official journal and was not involved in the McMaster episode.

In the period of decision, the Catholic hierarchy restrained itself from all pleadings except for peace and for prayers for peace and for the observance of law and order. Since the chief

[9] Michael V. Gannon, *Rebel Bishop, The Life and Era of Augustin Verot* (Milwaukee, 1964) pp. 31–56. Verot wanted reforms in slavery.

[10] Madeleine Hooke Rice, *American Catholic Opinion in the Slavery Controversy* (New York, 1944) pp. 102–103.

prelate, Archbishop Francis Patrick Kenrick, had said in his manual on moral theology that Catholics were not permitted to break the law to end slavery, the general Catholic attitude toward slavery was that, while its excesses were condemned, the institution itself was permissible. The Catholic bishops generally supported the State or government to which each gave his allegiance. Most of the Northern bishops immediately stood by the Federal Government, and those of the South defended the Southern governments. Of the two pivotal sees, held by the two Kenricks, Archbishop Francis Patrick Kenrick of Baltimore remained silent in the crisis, as one would expect in a scholar, and so did Archbishop Peter Richard Kenrick in St. Louis, although some thought him to be privately sympathetic to the Southern side. Bishop Martin John Spalding of Louisville, while blaming the war on the agitation of preachers in New England, was slightly partisan for the South. Bishop Whelan of Wheeling followed his State into secession. So also did Bishop John McGill of Richmond followed by Bishop Patrick N. Lynch of Charleston, Bishop Augustin Verot—with some strong sermons—of Savannah, Bishop John Quinlan of Mobile, Bishop William H. Elder of Natchez, Bishop Augustus Martin of Natchitoches—also strongly—and Archbishop John M. Odin of New Orleans. Archbishop Blanc of New Orleans died before the election was held. Whelan, Quinlan, and Elder were to have some troubles with the Union troops later in the war, and Archbishop Peter Richard Kenrick was to carry his quarrel over the Blair oath of loyalty to the Supreme Court at the end of the war.

In the episcopate of New England, Bishop John Fitzpatrick was definitely pro-Union and gave useful support to the Union cause in Belgium while on a trip to Europe during the war, but the remainder of the bishops, while loyal and anxious about the Catholics in the war, did not give notable leadership during the conflict. Archbishop John Hughes tried at first to prevent the conflict, so much so that he was even accused of defending slavery, but, once the war had begun, even though he was already in declining health, he supported the Union side, making a journey to Europe where he defended the Northern side of the fight in Ireland, at the Imperial Court in France, and in Rome. In Rome, where there was a belief during the first years of the war that the Union had been irrevocably split, some fear was expressed that Hughes' activity would hurt the Church in the new Confederate States. Other Northern bishops who showed partisan feelings during the war were Bishop John Timon of Buffalo, Bishop Michael O'Connor of Pittsburgh, and his successor, Bishop Michael Domenec (who went to Spain in support of the North), and Archbishop John B. Purcell of Cincinnati. The Cincinnati *Catholic Telegraph* seemed to approve of almost every Northern decision.

Just how many Catholics served in the armies of the Civil War cannot be told. The frequency of Irish regiments and Irish Brigades are measures of efforts to enlist volunteers rather than a measure of the Irish participation in the war. Colonel Corrigan of the New York Sixty-Ninth, the most famous of the Irish regiments, was captured in the first battle of Bull Run, and there are many tales of Irish volunteers on both sides, the most sad being that of the Irish who fell uselessly in the battle of Fredericksburg on December 13, 1862. Because of the presence of Catholics in the armies, chaplains were necessary to attend to them. The laws about chaplains were rather vague at the start of the war. Some commissions were given to priests by the State governments, and some who served were never really commissioned by the armies to which they gave service. Governor Oliver P. Morton of Indiana asked Lincoln to appoint Father Edmund Kilroy a chaplain in the Navy, but Kilroy changed his mind, and did not accept the appointment. Thus there was no Catholic Navy chaplain in the war. In the northern armies there were over fifty priests who served in the field or in hospitals, the most famous of these was probably Father William Corby, C.S.C., of Notre Dame who gave the dramatic general absolution on the battlefield of Gettysburg. His fellow religious, Father Peter Paul Cooney, C.S.C., gave a similar but less renowned general absolution at the battle of Stone River, Tennessee, and was cited for bravery in the battles in the West in the *Official Records*. Other Northern chaplains who were recognized for the devotion to their men were Father Jeremiah Trecy, who served at different times both Northern and Southern troops,[11] Father Joseph Carrier, C.S.C., who served with Missouri troops under General Hugh Ewing, Father Thomas Scully who attended the Irish from Massachusetts, Father Thomas Willet, S.J., Father Costney Egan, O.P., and Father Richard Christ of Pennsylvania. In the Southern armies Father James Sheeran, C.Ss.R., rendered heroic services in the bloody battles in Virginia and later in Tennessee and other parts of the South. Father Egidius Smulders, C.Ss.R., served in many places. Others whose work has not been properly recorded were Father Hippolite Gache, S.J., who served Louisiana troops, Father Charles P. Heuzé and Father Ghislain Bohème, an elderly missionary, who died in the service.

Of the work of the Sisters in the hospitals there are only dis-

---

[11] Unpublished manuscript by David Powers Conyingham, "The Soldiers of the Cross," University of Notre Dame Archives.

connected accounts, but their good and constant service earned them the title of "The Angels of the Battlefield."[12] In the North, the Sisters of Charity from Mt. St. Joseph in Cincinnati served especially with the armies in the West. Of the Sisters of Mercy, members came from houses in St. Louis and New York. The Sisters of Holy Cross from St. Mary's, Notre Dame, led by Sister M. Angela, C.S.C., began their work in the hospitals of Mound City but extended these services to many other hospitals. Also the Sisters of Charity of Nazareth, Kentucky, and the Sisters of St. Joseph of Wheeling, the Dominican Sisters of Kentucky, and the Sisters of St. Francis of Cincinnati worked long hours in the hospitals. The Daughters of Charity of St. Vincent de Paul alone furnished 231 nurses. In the South, besides some of the communities already mentioned, the work of the Sisters of Mercy of Charleston was very important. Aside from the great charitable work accomplished by these volunteer nurses, the Sisters in the war were credited also with a great work of practical apologetics for the Catholic Faith.

The leaders in the Civil War were mostly from the ranks of those trained in the military academies or leaders in prewar civil societies. There were some prominent Catholics, such as General William D. Rosecrans who had been converted while a student at West Point, General Philip Sheridan, and Generals Hugh and Charles Ewing, about twenty other major generals, and at least eleven brigadier generals. In the South the most noted Catholic generals were Pierre Beauregard and William J. Hardee. The full list of Catholic officers in the Confederate armies has not been compiled.

The Civil War was not a religious war, and the moral problem of slavery was submerged in the great sectional dispute. The causes of the war had not been clearly stated before the fighting began, and when the fighting ended there was to be a long dispute on how the conflict should be settled. Slavery did end, but the social problem of the people of color was not solved. Much of the wealth that had been concentrated in the plantations was destroyed. The North—except for its losses in manhood and the costs of war—emerged almost untouched from the war. The expansion into the West and the beginnings of industrial America received a great help from the wartime legislation. In the sense that the Catholic Church was mostly a Southern institution in its social and cultural leaders before the war, the Church suffered

---

[12] *Ibid*. has a treatment of the services of the Sisters in the war.

from the war. In the industrial and commercial North, which won the war, there were not many Catholics in positions of leadership or wealth, and the same was true of those who were forming the mind of the victorious North in the influential secular press. Among the masses of the Northern workers there were many Catholics, and they would be reinforced by more Catholic peasant immigrants in later decades. The heroic services of masses of Irish immigrants in the war were not long remembered. The revival of anti-Catholicism after the war grievously disappointed the Irish who had served in the war.

Within the Catholic body itself there were more important events that changed the Catholic group. In one sense the years of war marked the passing of some of the greatest leaders of American Catholicism. Archbishop Anthony Blanc, the leader of Southern Catholicism for twenty-five years, died on June 1, 1860. His successor, Archbishop John M. Odin, a great missionary, did not have the influence of his predecessor. On July 6, 1863, died Archbishop Francis Patrick Kenrick, who occupied the chief see of the American Church. His leadership was intellectual rather than political. He had become the spokesman for the Catholics in the border states, but his neutrality was distressing to those who wanted active leadership. In New York Archbishop John Hughes died on January 3, 1864. Some did not approve of his active leadership in all matters. His action in the Carroll Hall slate in the 1841 election will be debated indefinitely in its effects on Church and State, but his leadership in the riots of 1844 was unquestioned. He may have given Orestes A. Brownson some of that critic's saddest hours, but he never suppressed him. Archbishop Hughes was proud of the political advancement of the Irish Catholics in his archdiocese and hoped for social and economic advancements as well. He was the leading Catholic prelate while he lived.

There was one incident in which Archbishop Hughes figured that did not reflect glory on the Irish Catholics during the war. When the draft laws were enacted, they were not equitably enforced. The Irish workers in New York resented them not only because of the unequal way in which they were enforced but also because they were added in their minds to other injustices which they thought they saw in the war. The Civil War was for them fought to free the slave in whom they had no great interest. Further, after the Negro slaves had been freed, they would probably come North to compete with the poor Irish immigrants for their jobs. Actually Archbishop John Hughes of New York had advocated conscription as a just way of getting troops. But the

Irish of New York followed their own opinion of the law that had been enacted. On July 13, 1863, they carried on riots in the streets of New York in which property was destroyed and Negroes killed. Horace Greeley, pointing out that the Archbishop had approved conscription, challenged the Archbishop to quell the riots. The Archbishop called a meeting of the Irish at his home and made a dramatic appeal to them from the balcony of his home on Friday, July 17, 1863. That was his last public appearance, but it was successful.

The contrast between Archbishops John Hughes and Francis Kenrick was clear. Kenrick, a scholar, was not permitted to pursue his studies in this missionary country. Further, his attitude on the slavery question, while theologically correct, did not allow Catholics to claim leadership in the elimination of this great evil of American life. Archbishop Hughes was not so careful or scholarly at all, but he was forceful in whatever he did or said. He was the hero of the Irish Catholic immigrant.

In the war, Brownson's *Review* was one of the casualties. Brownson seemed to be scolding everyone. He persisted in telling the Irish to become Americans, he criticized Catholic education, he accused the Jesuits of trying to play both sides in the war. He blamed his troubles on his supporting Fremont in the election of 1864, but actually he had criticized most of those who were trying to help him. Having alienated his subscribers, he had to end his *Review*, at least temporarily, because he had no other financial support. Of all his troubles, his attack on the Irish and his criticism of schools were his most improvident actions. He was reported to Rome for his writings about the temporal power of the Popes in which he did not share the opinion that the temporal power was necessary, but the reporting seems to have been done by Irish critics of his *Review*. When he explained his real views to Cardinal Alexander Barnabo, the Prefect of the Congregation of Propaganda, the Cardinal expressed regret that he had listened to the criticism. *Le Propagateur Catholique* of New Orleans in which Father Napoleon Perché had defended the Southern point of view, was also a victim of the war. But in 1865 two new publications began in the North. In New York in April the *Catholic World*, a monthly magazine of culture and religion, was begun by the Paulists, and in May of the same year the *Ave Maria*, the first periodical in the country devoted to the Blessed Virgin, began its career as a weekly family magazine at Notre Dame, Indiana.

In the hierarchy Martin John Spalding of Louisville was chosen to replace Archbishop Francis Patrick Kenrick, and this marked the return of that primacy of honor to native Archbishops. Spalding had been critical of Kenrick during the war because of Kenrick's failure to lead. But Spalding himself found no great opportunity to direct the Catholics of the country until the war ended and he could summon a new plenary council. Bishop John McCloskey became the new Archbishop of New York. He was likewise a native, although of Irish ancestry. He was a gentle person, who obtained the respect and affection of his flock, but was not a great leader. The saintly Bishop, John N. Neumann of Philadelphia, had died suddenly on January 5, 1860, and his successor was Bishop Frederick Wood, likewise a native and a convert. The Church in the country was facing a reconstruction, not much like that of the country, but one derived from the first Americanization of the first great flood of immigrants who had come before the Civil War.

CHAPTER EIGHT

Martin John Spalding in
Baltimore 1864-1872

ARCHBISHOP MARTIN JOHN SPALDING HAS been compared to Archbishop Kenrick by his nephew, later Bishop John Lancaster Spalding.

Both, [he said,] were gentle and simple, innocent and good in themselves, and unsuspicious of evil in others. Archbishop Kenrick was reserved. He gave expression to his sentiments in a quiet, subdued way, as though the outer world were not his home; and he seemed at once, without effort, to sink back into the sanctuary of his inner life. Archbishop Spalding, on the contrary, was demonstrative. There was a merry ring in his laugh, suggestive of the undeceived heart of childhood. He had not the art of concealing anything—he thought aloud. . . . Archbishop Spalding probably knew more of men, and understood better how to develop and put to proper use the energies of those whom he governed, whilst Archbishop Kenrick was the profounder scholar. . . ."[1]

Both men were writers and both good theologians. One represented the best of Irish ecclesiastical scholarship, the other was the preeminent clergyman of the Anglo-American group. Kenrick was Archbishop when the attack on the Church in America was violent, and he was aware that he was not a native. Spalding was a native and was desirous of making Catholicism understood by his fellow Americans.

[1] J.L. Spalding, *The Life of Most Rev. M.J. Spalding, D.D., Archbishop of Baltimore* (New York, 1873) pp. 261–262.

On July 13, 1864, with the cooperation of Archbishop Purcell, Spalding met with the bishops of the Cincinnati Province in Detroit to discuss various problems including the choice of his successor in Louisville. The Civil War was entering its final phase when he took over his Baltimore See on July 31, 1864. He came from one border state to another and was very alert to the problems of the Catholics in the war, but there was little he could do about them, since he knew that this was not a religious war. In his diary, however, he did record his objections to the partisanship of Archbishop Purcell and Bishop Rosecrans for the North. He publicly deplored the assassination of Lincoln the next spring, and he was also well aware of the lawlessness that was abroad in the country in the wake of the war. Outside of the completion of the Cathedral his chief pastoral work in the first years consisted mainly in assisting Catholic efforts to meet the moral and physical disturbances resulting from the war, which were far more important in the urban concentration of Catholics in the East than in the rural areas of the West.

Archbishop Spalding faced several major problems, some of which defied solution during the eight years of his regime in Baltimore. Some of these difficulties had international complications. The American bishops, for instance, had been very active in the first years of the 1860s defending the Pope and his temporal power, at one time proposing to raise a battalion of troops to go to his aid, but more wisely changing their interests to financial aid and papal loans. In their defense of the Papal States, they were caught unprepared for the Encyclical *Quanta Cura* and the *Syllabus of Errors,* which was interpreted by some writers as a condemnation of democracy. The criticism of this famous document was very sharp in England, and American periodicals active in cultural affairs soon joined in the attack. In announcing the jubilee of 1865, most of the bishops issued letters supporting the papal decrees, but most of them did not publish the encyclical and *Syllabus* with their letter. Archbishop Spalding did. He rejected directly the general charge that the Pope had even implicitly condemned American democracy, American religious freedom, or even modern living. Most American defenders of the papal pronouncement were at a disadvantage because few of them had close acquaintance with the previous documents from which the statements of the *Syllabus* were culled or with the attacks on the Church by the extreme socialists of Europe. Spalding spoke of the "howl of indignation with which the world has received the document"[2] and "the pains taken by the English press—from which a great portion of the American press has copied—to mutilate and disfigure its meaning through a faulty translation." The Archbishop was careful to point out that the men who were being attacked in the *Syllabus* were holders of "Naturalism," who required "human society to be constituted and governed without any regard whatever to Religion, as if this did not even exist, or at least without making any distinction between true and false religions." He said that it was in this sense that the Pope condemned the proposition that claims " 'that the liberty of conscience and of worship is the peculiar (inalienable) right of every man, which should be proclaimed by law, and asserted in every well constituted society, and that citizens have the right *to all kinds of liberty (omnimodam libertatem), to be restrained by no law, whether ecclesiastical or civil. . . .'* " This the Archbishop said amounts to "anarchy and Jacobinism in politics, and to radicalism, rationalism, and infidelity in religion." Further he said that to apply the papal condemnation to "our Noble Constitution" was "manifestly unfair and unjust."

In the first Amendment to the Constitution, Spalding said the fathers of the Constitution did not intend "to pronounce all religions, whether true or false, equal before God, but only to declare them equal before the law. . . ." He further noted that the condemned propositions must be understood in the context from which they had been chosen and also that they bore different degrees of censure "according to their intrinsic nature and their extrinsic bearings: some are censured much more mildly than others," and some were condemned not so much for their intrinsic reasons but because of the dangerous interpretations to which they were susceptible.

Whether the *Syllabus* had any influence on the Archbishop's desire to have the approaching Council set forth a statement of Catholic doctrine for the United States or not is not clear. Since he had come to Baltimore with the desire to make this statement, the suggestion for holding the council probably arose more from his own Americanism and his desire for a restatement of the doctrines of the Church in the American environment.

In the reconstruction of the Southern States most of the Catholic press remained, as it had been before the war, sympathetic to the South. Certainly there was no real participation by Catholics

---

[2] *Pastoral Letter of the Most Rev. Martin John Spalding, D.D.* Second edition revised, with a supplement (Baltimore, 1865) p. 6.

in the radical movement. The Catholic press generally supported those moves of President Johnson to restore the governments of the Southern States. In its greeting to the New Year of 1866, the *Catholic Tablet* of New York said:

. . . It is not enough that they are with us again beneath the folds of the old Flag. They must not be meanly taunted with their error, not wantonly reminded of their vain resistance to a Power of which they had not calculated the extent. . . .

Another subject of congratulation in the past and of supplication for the years to come, is to be found in the generous policy of the honored Head of the Republic. . . . He has steadily refused to play the miserable part of an organ of that turbulent minority which absurdly claims to speak in the name of the people of the United States. . . .

Later on January 6, reviewing Brownson's *American Republic* with apparent agreement the *Catholic Tablet* noted:

. . . Dr. Brownson holds that all the laws in force at the time of secession remain in force till suspended or abrogated by competent authority, and that there is no authority competent to the abrogation but the United States acting in all the plenitude of their powers. In this respect he is far more liberal than Mr. Senator Sumner, whom we think the learned Doctor, in his generous frankness, has honored with unnecessary praise. . . .

Among the first problems faced by Archbishop Spalding in Baltimore was one pressing for solution in most of the urban centers where the Irish immigration was producing in its second generation countless youths with little or no education, many of whom had also lost their parents. Orphan asylums had been founded in many dioceses in which small boys and girls could find a home for a while. In the cities, for those a bit older something more, a protectory, was required. Father John L. Spalding described the situation as faced by his uncle, the Archbishop:

. . . He frankly admitted the melancholy fact that a large proportion of the idle and vicious youth of our principal cities are the children of the Catholics.

Day by day these unhappy children are caught in the commission of petty crimes, which render them amenable to the authorities, by whom they are placed in sectarian or public reformatories, to be thence transferred by hundreds to distant localities, where they are brought up in complete ignorance of the religion in which they have been baptized. Numerous and active societies also exist, whose sole aim is to snatch from the church these helpless and unfortunate little ones.

. . . and he had also learned that the chief source of the evil is in the large cities of the East, where the church finds it impossible to provide for the great number of orphans and indigent children who are each year thrown upon her.[3]

When the Archbishop proposed that the Archdiocese erect and support a protectory, he met opposition from the conservative wealthy Catholics of his see city. Undaunted he made his plans, obtained a grant of land from the McTavish family, and invited the Xaverian Brothers to take charge of the protectory. In Boston Father George Haskins had begun a similar work. In New York the convert, Dr. Silliman Ives, with the assistance of the clergy and under lay direction, founded what in time became the New York Protectory. Father John Spalding was mistaken when he said this problem existed only in the East. Father John McMullen of Chicago carefully pointed out that the Irish were entering into all phases of American life.

. . . They are found in every grade, in every station putting forth an energy, and manifesting a spirit of enterprise, not easily rivaled and certainly not surpassed. . . . They are, in a word, numerous amongst those who deserve to be called the pride and hope of our country, numerous among her best citizens and bravest defenders. We should not be astonished, when we consider that most Catholic parents are emigrants, and contemplate the restless, progressive spirit of their children, that not a few irregularities should necessarily result. The parent will sometimes depart from the virtuous habits in which he grew up in his fatherland, and the active, enterprising youth will seek to free himself from parental control, and long to try his strength and wits amidst the struggles for wealth and fame. Many children are left orphans at an early age; and before the parents had acquired a sufficiency to support them in such an emergency. Some parents are incapable of holding the reins of domestic government with a steady hand; some children by evil associations, will not brook control.

Neither are such cases few, nor confined to certain localities. It is a common fallacy to judge that they are found only in large cities. They are met with in the village and rural district; and if not observed in these places to any great extent, we should call to mind, that our country friends are ever willing to provide a facility of transport to all such unfortunates, to the larger cities, when [sic] it is believed that there are, or should be, institutions to provide for them.[4]

Father McMullen was disturbed because these youngsters were exposed to capture by what he called "philanthropists" of two kinds, those who were without any religious faith, and religious

[3] J. L. Spalding, note 1 above, p. 288.
[4] James J. McGovern, *The Life and Writings of the Right Reverend John McMullen, D.D.* (Chicago, 1888) pp. 135–136.

people who made their livelihood by creating benevolent institutions. He added: "View them as we will, they are enemies to the welfare of your boys, who need the protection of the Asylum or the Reform School. They would prefer that the little unfortunates were anything but Catholics."

These protectories of Baltimore, Boston, New York, and the work of Father McMullen in Chicago were the headliners in the efforts by the Church in the United States to take care not only of the indigent immigrants but more especially of their children. This attendance on the homeless and orphaned children as well as the care of the adult sick and indigent was a tremendous burden, to which the immigrants themselves were seldom able to contribute support and which made almost impossible the erection in the first three quarters of the century of those advanced educational institutions for which the provincial and plenary councils were pleading.

Another activity among the Irish immigrants received a forthright condemnation from the American hierarchy. The Fenian Brotherhood had been founded in Paris in 1848, organized in Ireland in 1853, and in the United States in 1857.[5] Many Irish enlisted in the Union and Confederate armies in the hopes of receiving training and even arms by their service. The Fenian leaders were quite sure that the United States would go to war with the English over their interference in the Civil War and hoped to take advantage of the conflict to help Ireland. When no war developed with England, they undertook ineffectual raids against Canada. The American hierarchy, following in the wake of the Irish hierarchy, condemned the Brotherhood because it maintained a secret oath which it regarded as above the religious obligations of its members. Despite public denials, the existence of the oath was certain. Then in 1865 an Irish newspaper carried a story that a decree from the Holy See had ruled that the Fenians were not to be disturbed by the bishops.

Archbishops Purcell and Spalding were immediately concerned and asked for a clarification from Rome. Rome immediately denied that such a decree had been issued and eventually condemned the Brotherhood formally on January 12, 1870. These and other activities of violence, particularly in the mining regions of Pennsylvania, were ample justifications for those Nativists who

---

[5] Fergus Macdonald, C.P., *The Catholic Church and Secret Societies in the United States* (New York, 1946) pp. 33–34. Cf. William D'Arcy, O.F.M., *The Fenian Movement in the United States 1858–1886* (Washington, 1947).

regarded the Irish as opposed to law and order. *The Atlantic Monthly* in May 1866 in an article on "The Fenian 'Idea' " observed: "Devotion to an idea, to a constitution, to a flag; respect for law *as* law; sturdy independence and self-reliance; regard for others' rights and jealousy of a man's own,—all these true republican characteristics are most rarely to be found in Irishmen." These events and ideas soon led to a renewal of social persecution of the Irish immigrant that had been held in abeyance by the patriotism and generosity of the Irish volunteer in the Civil War.

After the death of President Lincoln the administrative conflict between the moderates and the radicals for the control of Congress and the plans for reconstruction were mentioned frequently in the Catholic press and in the correspondence of the bishops. The bishops were outspoken in their regrets over the assassination of Lincoln, but Lincoln had hardly been an object of affection during the war. There was no Catholic idea on reconstruction any more than there had been a Catholic opinion on the war itself. Just as there had been no real Catholic position on slavery and abolition, there was no Catholic program to care for the "freed blacks," as they were referred to in the Catholic papers. Some letters of priests working in the South at the end of the war expressed fear of what might happen when the Northern armies were withdrawn, although the same letters spoke of friendly relations with Negroes whom the priests themselves had hired. The Catholic Church, which was the religion of only a small minority of the South, did not have a workable solution for the problems of Southern reconstruction. The Catholic press generally opposed the radicals. Archbishop Purcell felt that the country, despite Congress, would sustain President Andrew Johnson in his opposition to them. Orestes A. Brownson had published his *American Republic,* but there was no general agreement among Catholics on reconstruction. *The New York Tablet,* published by Sadlier, supported President Johnson's veto of the Freedmen's Bill.

Archbishop John McCloskey, the successor to Hughes in New York, condemned a meeting of Fenians held March 4, 1866. Bishop Patrick Lynch, for whom Archbishop Spalding had obtained a presidential pardon, was invited by McCloskey to give the St. Patrick's Day sermon in New York. When he was challenged by the *New York Tribune* on his loyalty to the Union during the war, he published an answer defending his actions as taken for the public welfare of his flock. He denied that he was responsible for any papal intervention in favor of the South. The *Tribune* merely answered that this was not for want of trying on the Bishop's part. On January 8 the death of Father Jeremiah Cummings, the close advisor of Orestes A. Brownson, ended a long illness. Bishop John Fitzpatrick of Boston died on February 13, 1866. On May 26 Father Constantine Pise died. These incidents and deaths were not related, yet together with the changing conditions in the country they witnessed an unsettled feeling among the leaders of the Catholic minority and a change in leadership for a while. This probably explains why so many bishops were anxious to hold a national council to consider these developments, but just why Archbishop Purcell should suggest that the council be held in Rome is not clear. Archbishop Spalding had given several reasons in his letter to Rome on June 14, 1865, why there should be such a council. He wanted a national Catholic university; he wanted a meeting on the problems resulting from the war; he thought there should be a new effort to achieve uniform discipline in the country; and he wanted to work out some solution for the handling of the "Freedmen." "We have a golden opportunity to reap a harvest of souls, which, neglected, may not return."

Pope Pius IX, in a letter of February 16, 1866, approved the holding of the council and appointed Archbishop Spalding as Apostolic Delegate to preside over it. On March 19, 1866, Spalding sent out to the hierarchy an announcement that the Second Plenary Council would open in Baltimore on the first Sunday of October and that he had been appointed Apostolic Delegate to preside over it. In assigning certain topics to be prepared by each Metropolitan and his suffragans, he took the first two for himself and his suffragans. He called to Baltimore also a group of theologians to prepare the matter to be discussed in the Council after the various topics had been prepared by the other bishops. The hierarchy assembled in Baltimore on October 7, the feast of Our Lady of the Rosary—seven archbishops, thirty-eight bishops, three mitered abbots, and over one hundred and twenty theologians.

Archbishop Martin John Spalding wanted to hold the Second Plenary Council to write a statement of Catholic teachings and to put into a definite body of legislation the experiences of Roman Catholicism in the United States. The decrees of the previous Councils of Baltimore he called "rudimentary" and proposed that all the previous Conciliar decrees be embodied in a kind of American *corpus juris*. After his consultation with the theologians, all proposals were really in almost definite form when the hierarchy opened the Council with a formal procession to the Cathedral on that first Sunday in October.

Probably the tone and emphasis of the Council and its decrees came from the Archbishop himself. This very intelligent and articulate priest had proved himself a capable theologian as a student in Rome and a capable writer in his histories of Kentucky and in his apologetical writings. He represented in a special way the rural, native Anglo-American group within the Catholic minority. Thus, while the acts of the Council were in full harmony with the universal Church, there are in the decrees definite points of awareness of special American conditions. The same is true of the pastoral letter issued after the Council, which was written by young Father James Gibbons with the advice and direction of the Archbishop. Of the group, two archbishops and twelve bishops were American, and three were converts, Wood, Bayley, and Rosecrans. Two archbishops and nine bishops were Irish, but Patrick Lynch and Bishop John Loughlin had come to this country as boys, and Archbishop Purcell, also, had been so long in this country that some of his confreres had forgotten his Irish origins. Three, the two Blanchets and Demers, were of Canadian origin, nine were French, two were Flemish, one Swiss, one Austrian, and two were Germans.

The Archbishop in his schema chose those points that were important for the American scene. When the schema was presented to the council, Archbishop Peter Richard Kenrick tried to have the schema thrown out as an imposition by Spalding on the bishops, but only a small minority of the bishops supported his suggestion. The decrees restated the existence of the divine revelation, the role of the Church as the one infallible agency, and the nature of Faith.[6] Other basic doctrines of the Catholic Faith were succinctly stated, including the formal acceptance of the decree about the Immaculate Conception of the Blessed Virgin, which had been issued in 1854. The special errors of the day that were appearing in the country were briefly discussed and condemned. The first error consisted in the rejection of the authoritative guidance of the Church, which had resulted in the confusion of the sects. The proximate error arising from the confusion of sects was indifferentism, which taught that it made no difference what a man believes so long as he is honest and upright. The next errors were Unitarianism and Universalism, American names for old heresies that denied the fundamentals of the Christian religion. Derived from them with scarcely any trace of Christianity were

---

[6] *Councilii Plenarii Baltimorensis II . . . Acta et Decreta.* Editio Altera (Baltimore, 1877).

the errors of Transcendentalism and pantheism, to which the Council noted very learned people had given their adherence. The Fathers of the Council condemned also the false science of those days called "magnetism," which they said consisted of tricks and sleight of hand by which persons tried to know secret things through dreams and superstitious practices. Also the bishops condemned spiritism, to which nervous persons and especially women had attached themselves recently.

The Council professed faith in the Supreme Pontiff and expressed the need of the present pontiff for his patrimony, although the patrimony was not of the essence of the primacy. Further, the bishops condemned those who had sacrilegiously taken away from this patrimony. For the Pope's aid, they decreed an annual collection. The rules for provincial councils and diocesan synods were outlined. In the dioceses themselves, there was to be a group of consultors chosen from the priests of the diocese who were to meet at stated times with the bishop, a vicar general, a chancellor, a secretary, a notary, and rural deans. There were to be six diocesan examiners to examine candidates for pastorates and judges of the diocesan courts. The Council then spoke of archbishops, bishops, the election of bishops, and the duties of pastors. While asking that parish lines be drawn, the pastors of the church would be permanent but not irremovable.

The obligation for preaching was treated at length, with insistence on proper preparation for the task. In treating of the lives and conduct of the clerics, note was made that they were not to attend shows or dances or bear arms. The acceptance of deposits of money by them was forbidden without special permission.

In the decrees on the Sacraments, pastors and superiors were not to interfere with frequent and even daily Communion if the confessor of the penitent approved. First Communion was to be made not before ten nor after the twelfth year. The decrees on the Sacrament of Penance contained rules for the guidance of the confessor. There were also decrees about Mass, forty hours' devotion, and the Sunday vespers. Under the title of "Regulars and Nuns," the relations between bishops and exempt orders were briefly discussed, and special problems concerning communities of religious women were treated. One title was devoted to the instruction of youth, and the Council urged the erection of a parish school for each church. Where these schools could not be built, there should be special care for those who attend other schools. Parents of children who have attained the use of reason were to see that the children attended the Sacraments of the Eucharist and Confession. Since some children will always get into trouble, industrial schools and protectories were to be erected as soon as possible for delinquent and needy children. The Council went on record also as urging the founding of a Catholic university for the nation. This university would not interfere with the support also of the American colleges in Rome, Louvain, and Dublin.

In another title they spoke of zeal for souls, especially among priests. The priest was to be impervious to rank, color, condition, and without earthly ambition or avarice. The decrees then discussed the new and pressing problems of the freed Negro slaves. Catholics were bound to do all they could to save these souls, who are redeemed by the blood of Christ. The condition of the freed men was different in different communities. Where the pastors judged best, separate churches were to be constructed for them, but, where the bishop thought best for white and Negro to worship together, no separate churches were to be built. If no new churches were erected for the Negroes, the bishop was to make sure that the Negroes were really invited to come so that no blame for their not coming would be on the conscience of the Church. The Council urged that special mission centers be erected for the Negroes, and, since there might be a shortage of priests for this work, priests were asked to volunteer for this work, and their bishops were urged to permit them to go. Schools for the Negro children were especially important, and religious communities were urged to found such schools and especially to gather Negro orphans into charitable institutions.

The decrees spoke of books and periodicals. The decrees praised the Catholic Publication Society which had been founded in New York. The Council recognized the need for a Catholic press and lauded those dioceses that had official organs, while admitting that not everything published in such a paper should be attributed to the bishop. The Council stated that it would like to see one national publication published each week and also a suitable quarterly review.

The decrees spoke of condemned secret societies. The Masonic sect had been condemned by the popes with the gravest censures, and this had been reinforced by the Baltimore Councils. The Odd Fellows at the request of Archbishop Francis Patrick Kenrick had been included by Rome among the condemned Masonic societies. Other societies which were condemned by the general decrees against societies for having secret oaths, or whose pledge was against Church or State, were to be considered as condemned. The condemnation was not to be extended to societies of workers so long as they did not use forbidden oaths.

Title Thirteen discussed the new sees that the bishops wanted erected, asked for a coadjutor for Bishop Baraga, and asked that the sees of Philadelphia and Milwaukee be raised to archiepiscopates.

The Pastoral Letter of the Council was representative of the newly acquired status of a national church, just beginning to think in terms of the new world and its problems. The Pastoral speaking for the assembled bishops spoke first of the authority of the plenary councils and of the character of the authority of the Church and the obligation of the faithful to listen to her. On the relation between that Church authority and the civil power, the Pastoral denied that there was any conflict between the power of the Church in church matters and the State in civil matters.

. . . The Church, indeed, does not proclaim the absolute and entire independence of the Civil Power, because it teaches with the Apostle, that "All power is of God"; that the temporal magistrate is His minister, and that the power of the sword he wields is a delegated exercise of authority committed to him on high. For the children of the Church obedience to the Civil Power is not a submission to force which may not be resisted, nor merely the compliance with a condition for place and security; but a religious duty founded on obedience to God, by whose authority the Civil Magistrate exercises his power. This power, however, as subordinate and delegated, must always be exercised agreeably to God's law. . . . The Catholic has a guide in the Church, as a divine Institution, which enables him to discriminate between what the Law of God forbids or allows; and this authority the State is bound to recognize as supreme in its sphere—of moral, no less than dogmatic teaching. . . .[7]

The Pastoral went on to regret that in some states the Church was not permitted to protect its property according to the laws of the Church and also mentioned particularly the Blair oath prescribed in Missouri as a condition for the exercise of ecclesiastical ministry.

The Pastoral then praised the faithful for their generosity toward the Pope and suggested that there be a special collection for the Pope annually. The Pastoral praised the dignity and sacredness of Christian marriage that had led to the Pope's defying the King of England and in more recent times Emperor Napoleon. As to the Catholic press, the Pastoral repeated the urging of the earlier conciliar decrees about the need of the Catholic press, and asked for support for the Catholic Publication Society. The Pastoral continued its parallel with the decrees by insisting on Catholic schools and Catholic protectories and industrial schools.

[7] Peter Guilday, ed., *The National Pastorals of the American Hierarchy, 1792–1919* (Washington, 1923) p. 205.

It urged the fostering of vocations to the priesthood but at the same time urged the laity to greater attendance at the Sacraments. The clergy were urged to be an example of devotedness.

The passages about the emancipated slaves expressed regret that the emancipation had not been more gradual, such as when the serfs of medieval Europe only gradually obtained freedom. But the Pastoral recognized that the evils of the existing situation must be met and urged clergy and people alike to give the most generous cooperation to the plans the bishops had drawn up for the welfare of these newly freed slaves. The final passage was a tribute to the zeal and sacrifices of the religious communities of women.

The Pastoral was published widely, but the decrees, even when finally approved by Rome after some delay, were not translated from the Latin. The whole council remained a kind of wasted effort by Archbishop Spalding and his co-workers to set before the Catholic faithful the eternal doctrines of the Church which they must accept and carry out in this new world in which they were a small minority without having the corresponding wealth or social dignity that a minority should have if it were to survive. The period immediately after the Civil War was more or less just a breathing space in which the old Catholic families and those who had been in the country for a generation tried to adjust themselves and the recent Catholic immigrant to the American scene. But the flood of immigrants had not stopped. The later flood of Catholic immigrants, while it continued to have a certain number of Irish and English who spoke the English language, was to have a further handicap, for the most part, of foreign languages and sometimes of aroused national loyalties to their fatherlands.

Even most of the older Catholics were not so well settled and comfortable that they could think primarily of religious ideas. The dominant quality of the Catholic group during the succeeding decades had to be the effort to take advantage of the expanding opportunities that followed the Civil War to gain economic and social welfare and position for themselves and their children. The cultural leaders of these millions of Catholics remained the Anglo-American group, increased within by thousands of converts and by those earlier immigrants who had been economically successful and were able to attend to the problems of cultural and social advancement. This cultural nucleus was larger than it had been fifty years before but proportionately was overwhelmed by the large mass of Catholics of 1870.

The Catholic population was not evenly distributed. Even at

this early period, Catholicism was predominantly urban in its concentrations, and the establishment of new sees was not the cure for that problem. Elsewhere, when the growth of Catholic population justified hope for episcopal support, the faithful could be better served by the establishment of new sees. In the New York Province, the See of Rochester was set up and assigned to the zealous and outspoken Bernard McQuaid of Seton Hall College. In the proposed Province of Philadelphia, two new sees were set up in the mining regions at Scranton and at Harrisburg with Bishops William O'Hara and J. Shanahan. Both Bishops were to witness trouble between the Irish miners and their employers. Philadelphia, however, did not become an Archdiocese until 1875. Also in the Province of Baltimore the See of Wilmington was erected in the area about the Delaware and upper Chesapeake Bays and assigned to the convert Thomas Becker. The State of North Carolina was made a Vicariate Apostolic and assigned to the young and capable James Gibbons, who had assisted the Archbishop so much in the Council. In the Province of Cincinnati, Columbus was made a see and assigned to the Auxiliary Bishop of Cincinnati, Sylvester Rosecrans. In the Province of St. Louis, the new Diocese of St. Joseph was assigned to John J. Hogan. The Council requested that Omaha be made an episcopal see under Bishop James O'Gorman, the Vicar Apostolic, and that Vicariates Apostolic be set up for the Territory of Montana, comprising that part of the Montana Territory east of the Rocky Mountains, for the Territory of Colorado and Utah, for the Territory of Arizona, and for the country around El Paso in Texas. Rome decided in 1868 to erect only the Vicariate of Idaho and Western Montana in 1868 under Louis Lootens and the Vicariate of Colorado and Utah under Joseph Macheboeuf. Milwaukee was to be raised to an Archdiocese with two new Sees, Green Bay and La Crosse, as part of its province. The new province was not established then, but Joseph Melcher was appointed to Green Bay and Michael Heiss to LaCrosse. The Vicariate of Grass Valley in California was raised to the rank of Diocese under Bishop Eugene O'Connell. In some of the new sees there was only a handful of priests, but the bishops assigned soon gathered from Europe new helpers and in time established regular missions and eventually resident pastors.

The growth of Catholicism in the United States attracted the attention of James Parton writing in 1868 in *The Atlantic Monthly,* that paragon of American culture, on "Our Roman Catholic Brothers." The center of Parton's story was a visit to St.

Stephen's parish in New York during a mission. While he marveled at the crowds of faithful who attended successive Masses in the early morning and returned for sermons in the evening, he was more impressed by the evidence that the Catholic Church was gaining control of considerable property, not only in this sample parish but by the multiplication of parishes and by the ease with which the pastors raised the money to pay for building the churches and parish buildings. He was also greatly impressed with the work of Father Isaac Hecker, tracing his career from the New York bakery through Transcendentalism to the Redemptorists and the founding of the Paulist community. He was deeply impressed with the confidence of the parish priests in the ultimate conversion of the country to Catholicism. He found the Catholic Sunday school at St. Stephen's remarkably like those Sunday schools he had witnessed in Protestant churches, but he described the attendance at the Mass as something entirely different from Protestant worship. He noted the absolute power of the Archbishop:

The Archbishop, be it observed, is the almost absolute ruler of the priests of his province. He places them, removes them, suspends them, according to his own good will and pleasure, subject to the laws and usages of the Church. There is no appeal against his decisions, except to Rome; and this resource is seldom within the compass of a priest. Rome is far away, and a priest appealing against the judgment of his superior must have a very good case or a very good friend, in order to obtain a favorable judgment. . . .[8]

Parton insisted, however, that the Bishop was really elected by the men whom he was to govern in the existing manner of nomination, since he had been told that the appointment almost invariably followed the nomination sent to Rome. He was disturbed that Catholics still believed in miracles. He was impressed by the converts made in the private schools and the convent schools conducted by religious. Parton raised the possibility that in 1945 Protestants and Catholics would be united by laying aside their separate claims to orthodoxy and by becoming "Americanized."

Parton's smiling tolerance of Catholicism as seen in this prosperous parish in New York or in the enlightened missions of the Paulists hardly represented the general attitude of American Protestants toward Roman Catholics after the Civil War. The Protestant attitude toward Catholicism drew its source chiefly from the Protestants' own ideas of Christianity. The literary group

[8] James Parton, "Our Roman Catholic Brothers," *The Atlantic Monthly*, XXI, 432–451 and 556–574.

for whom Parton spoke were tolerant for the most part toward Catholics, a group they did not regard as their equals in either learning or culture. Living in New England's literary "Indian Summer" they maintained the "genteel tradition." They were Brahmins, with their household gods, Emerson and the Transcendentalists. They wrote very chaste prose and very formal verse, and, while they had little to talk about, they went on chattering about the external virtues of manhood and courage, falling into plain naturalism with only a faint trace of Christianity. They captured the universities and the public forums and regarded the more theological Protestants as merely the more fervent of their group. A second classification of important Protestants included the faculties of the theological seminaries, the pastors of prominent churches, and theological scholars who were the remnants of the Protestant counterreformation of pre-Civil War times. They had no counterpart in Catholicism because the Catholic missionary bishops and the overtasked teachers in Catholic academies had no time for scriptural or theological study. Archbishop Spalding, an exception to this generalization, wanted a Catholic university to provide a Catholic counterpart.

The third and most numerous group of Protestants was nontheological and generally less literate than the two preceding groups. They were numerous in the lower classes of the East and in the Middle West and South. They were evangelicals who received their inspiration from reading their Bibles and listening to sermons from their slightly better informed clergymen. They had baptisms, and usually adult prayer meetings, sermons, and singing services. They recognized no infallible authority in religion outside the democratic leadership found in their synods and conferences, which usually drew up rules of conduct and appointed ministers. Their denominations multiplied in the land, and it was regarded as the badge of superior citizenship in the lower classes of society to belong to one of these churches. If the evangelical Protestant could not find a church of the denomination to which he originally belonged he often joined the one most akin. Outside of these formal Protestants, perhaps as many as one third of the non-Catholics of the country, especially those who had moved from their original American locality, had failed to revive the denominational adherence of their parents or ancestors but if questioned would say that they were Protestants and would, perhaps, even claim their ancestral denomination.

There was one common belief in these Protestant groups: that the Catholic authority exercised by the hierarchy and from the

Pope had no jurisdiction over them and was never to have any power over them. Many of them did not have any obligatory service on Sunday except such as was demanded by the Ten Commandments and the Bible but they were inclined to make the Sunday a real biblical Sabbath. Their attitude toward Catholicism was that it was a secret movement contrary to the national culture, a foreign and idolatrous invasion. The Catholic organization to them was predominantly foreign. To them the Irish were not accepted as English because of their strong Catholic traditions and because so many of the Irish were of low cultural attainment. Even the Germans and other later immigrant Catholic groups from eastern and southern Europe were definitely considered inferior to the Anglo-Saxon leaders of the Americans. All Catholics were definitely superstitious to the Protestant, who did not believe Catholics understood the Latin services at which they attended. As Parton had observed, the Catholic still believed in miracles.

There were many ways in which the Catholics, especially the Irish in the cities, felt this rejection by the majority of their fellow citizens. In the business world, where they were fewer, they got fewer chances for promotion, and the same handicaps were even more noticeable in the field of finance. In employment the signs "No Irish need apply" were perhaps more numerous in New England, but the prejudice existed also where the Yankee or Southern Protestant, white, Anglo-Saxon majority ruled. There was one notable exception to this handicap. Once the Irish became citizens, they could vote. The political machines first used these immigrants, then the immigrants began to gain control of the machine locally and then higher. Eventually Irish Catholics became mayors of the larger cities, but the charges of graft and bribery made against these machines were often quite exact. Thomas Nast in his bitter cartoons in *Harper's Weekly* pretended he saw a papal plot in the rise of Tammany.

Writing to his agent in Rome, shortly after his return from Europe in 1862, Archbishop Hughes noted that New York hardly seemed to know that a war was going on, in the burst of prosperity and expansion that followed the change in government during the war. The National Bank Act, the Morrill Tariff Act, the Homestead Act, and the issuance of greenbacks, followed by the change in the iron and steel industries and the rapid expansion of the railroads immediately after the war, plunged the North into a period of grand expansion. In this expansion of finance and business, Catholics took a minor role. There were two special reasons why Catholics could not participate. Aside from the fact that the Catholics were not numerous in what might be called the upper middle class, under the existing system of "rugged individualism and exploitation" in the country only those who had wealth could participate in this expansion. The same Yankee families that had control of the wealth east of the Mississippi controlled the railroads and businesses west of the river. A second reason, of some validity, for Catholic absence from the "great barbeque" of the public resources was that Catholics did not believe in the wild and cruel exploitation that took place during this era. Some Catholics with wealth acquired in mining used their family fortunes to advantage, but the spirit of the financial adventurer was certainly not typical of the Catholic morality of either the Irish worker or the German farmer.

The Catholics who had wealth before the Civil War were for the most part in the South, and their region suffered during and after the war. The Catholics in the North were generally of two types. The first type was chiefly the impoverished Irish in the cities or working on the railroads, who earned little more than weekly wages which afforded them very little for saving or investment. The second was the farmers, especially the Germans, who settled in the more fertile regions of the Middle West and sought the peaceful prosperity of the farming communities. Neither group was inclined to corporative exploitation which became all conquering in the United States at that time. Catholics who left the cities and did not go into farming usually followed the railroads, still using the pick and shovel but occasionally rising in the organizations, and sometimes saving enough money to buy a farm along the railroad. In the new cities of the Middle West the Irish continued to work for the railroads or to do similar labor, and the Germans in these towns engaged in small businesses or built themselves breweries or meat-packing businesses.

The Catholic Church in the United States had obligations of charity toward two other groups—the Indians and the Negroes. The Catholic mission to the American Indians had suffered from a lack of priests until the Jesuits assumed the task. Led by such men as Fathers Pierre De Smet and John B. Miège, French, Belgian, and Italian Jesuits traveled over vast regions of the upper Missouri and Mississippi valleys and into the mountain areas. They were assisted by Benedictines and Franciscans and Sisters of Mercy, Charity Sisters, Sisters of Loretto, and Ursulines but none of these had great wealth, despite the donations to them by the French Society of the Propagation. The ratio of Indians who were

Catholic in the decades after the Civil War was scarcely one in eight.

The effort of American Catholics to care for the Catholic Negroes is not a success story. The numbers of Catholics among the Negroes has been estimated at four percent, and this has not changed even in the twentieth century. In this effort, as in that for the Indians, there was simply no financial aid proportionate to the task. Besides, the continued flood of immigrants swamped the limited means of the older Catholic agencies and left little for expansion into the apostolate opened by the freeing of the slaves. The plea of the Second Council for zeal for the freedmen did not fall only on unheeding ears. Archbishop Martin John Spalding before his death did secure the Josephite Fathers from England, who have devoted their services chiefly to the colored. Father John Lancaster Spalding volunteered to establish a Negro parish in Louisville. There were other efforts to retain the Catholic Negroes in the Faith, but the vast majority of Southern Negroes, like their former white masters had little if any experience with Catholicism. The fear on the part of the Irish immigrants about competition for their jobs from the freed Negroes was not ended by the war. The pleas for the Negroes of such bishops as William H. Elder of Natchez and Augustin Verot of Savannah were not heeded, and the limited means of the northern immigrant in the cities went mostly into building churches in the North.

Aside from the consecration of the new bishops chosen as a result of the 1866 Plenary Council, the most important ecclesiastical functions in the years following the Council had their center in Rome. On the feast of the Immaculate Conception, December 8, 1866, the Pope issued an invitation to the bishops of the world to assemble in Rome for the celebration of the eighteenth centenary of the martyrdom of Saints Peter and Paul, June 29, 1867. Many other ceremonies, including the canonization of Japanese martyrs, were planned for the occasion. The appeal seemed to be of great interest to most of the American hierarchy and as many as could arranged their work to go to Rome, some taking trips to other parts of Europe or to the Holy Land at the same time in the interest of health or piety. Archbishop Spalding, despite a recent recovery from a serious illness in which his death had been announced in parts of the United States and in Europe, set out in May for Rome. In one of the assemblies Pope Pius IX announced that he would convene an ecumenical council in Rome in the near future. Several of the American hierarchy who had heard of the proposed council had already expressed their approval of the project and before their departure from Rome five American Archbishops, Alemany, Odin, Kenrick, Purcell, and Spalding, and eighteen Bishops, Amat, Bayley, Conroy, Domenec, Elder, De Goesbriand, Grace, Juncker, Loughlin, Lynch, McGill, Quinlan, Rappe, Williams, Wood, Lefevere, and Rosecrans signed the letter from the five hundred bishops present for the many ceremonies approving of the Pope's suggestion that a General Council be called. The large number of American bishops in attendance probably was meant as a manifestation of the loyalty of the Catholics in America to the Holy Father who was being slowly hemmed in by the approaching armies driving for Italian unification. There were few indications that the American prelates were much concerned at the time with what was to be the main subject of discussion in this first council since the Council of Trent (1545–1563). When the Pope asked the bishops to send to Rome expert theologians to help in preparing the schema for the Council, the American bishops were generally agreed in sending Dr. James A. Corcoran of the Diocese of Charleston, who had been one of the chief consultants of the hierarchy in the Second Plenary Council. The convocation of the Council to open on December 8, 1869, was made on June 29, 1868, to the Churches in union with Rome (*Aeterni Patris*), to the nonuniate Orientals on September 8 (*Arcano Divinae Providentiae*), and to Protestants on September 14, (*Iam inter nos*). Of the 1,002 persons eligible to attend, there were 689 present, counting cardinals, patriarchs, primates, archbishops, bishops, abbots, and superiors general. From the United States there were six archbishops, forty bishops, and one mitered abbot, Wimmer of St. Vincent's of Latrobe, Pennsylvania.[9]

The American hierarchy had not been particularly helped by the encyclical *Quanta Cura* and the *Syllabus of Errors* of 1864. The attacks on the *Syllabus* in England had been repeated in American periodicals. Although most of the attacks on the Church in the United States were on a lower level than that of the doctrines expressed in the *Syllabus,* the prospect of further declarations of dogma—especially of a dogma of papal infallibility—aroused some fear among the American prelates. Few American bishops had any doubts about the infallibility of the Pope, but many did not wish to have the doctrine proclaimed as a matter of Faith amidst the unsettled world of 1869. In this matter the posi-

[9] The best account of American participation in Vatican I is James Hennessey, S.J., *The First Council of the Vatican: The American Experience* (New York, 1963).

tion of Archbishop Martin John Spalding, the leading prelate of the American hierarchy, was of special interest. He was popularly supposed to be among the bishops opposing the proclamation of the dogma of infallibility and to be at least among the Americans holding the inopportuneness of the declaration of the dogma. Actually, he accepted infallibility but did not want to use the word "infallibility" which he felt would provoke Protestants and others outside the Church unnecessarily. He wanted the dogma defined negatively without the use of the positive formula.

There was a first informal assembly of the prelates on December 2. When the Council opened, there were two types of assemblies, common general congregations and solemn public sessions. The first schema considered in the Council was on *De Fide*, consisting of eighteen propositions. In general these were definitions about the doctrines which the Pope had discussed in the encyclical *Quanta Cura* and the *Syllabus*. On the committee of thirty-five preparing this schema were two American prelates, Peter R. Kenrick of St. Louis and Augustin Verot of Savannah. Verot had been trained in the Sulpician Seminary at Issy near Paris and had taught the natural sciences in St. Mary's in Baltimore.[10] His statements and questions seemed to have the quality of scientific love of accuracy. He wanted clearer statements about the nature of the human species against slave owners, and of the doctrines summed up from the decrees of the Council of Trent. He entered also into the discussion of the schema in the sixth General Congregation. Bishop Thaddeus Amat also criticized the text parts of the schema. When the discussion was finished, the schema was adopted by a vote of 515 *Placet,* and 80 *Placet juxta modum.* Among the objections were some offered by seventeen Americans, mostly to the phrase "Roman Church" which was then modified to read "Holy Catholic Roman Church" and to the use of the word "Anathema" which they thought too hostile. In the public session, the constitution, *De Fide Catholica,* was adopted unanimously. There were thirty-eight American bishops present and Abbot Wimmer. The next schema discussed was that on discipline and canon law in which Bishop Verot took a very active part, expressing his desire to prohibit clerics from hunting, attending theatres, and other pastimes which he considered as unbecoming to the clerical state. He wanted also stricter requirements about clerical retreats. In the discussions about missions, Bishop Elder raised the question of the

[10] Michael V. Gannon, *Rebel Bishop, The Life and Era of Augustin Verot* (Milwaukee, 1964) pp. 192–227.

unequal distribution of the aid from the mission societies and proposed that better methods of distribution be adopted. But the main subject of the Council was not what was being discussed in these general sessions, but the doctrine of papal infallibility, which was being discussed avidly in private groups.

Papal infallibility had been implicitly stated in the decrees of the Second Plenary Council of Baltimore and in the letter of that Council to the Supreme Pontiff, and American bishops generally had been very loyal to the Supreme Pontiff. Likewise, the statement of the 500 bishops, including several Americans, presented to the Pope at the celebration of the centenary of the martyrdom of Saints Peter and Paul in 1867 had implicitly professed faith in papal infallibility. The first formal *Postulatum* for the definition was drawn up on January 1, 1870. It was signed by 389 Fathers, including from the United States two archbishops (Blanchet and Odin), seven bishops (Dubuis, De Goesbriand, Heiss, Lootens, Martin, Miège, and O'Connell), and Abbot Wimmer. Archbishop Spalding was in a peculiar position.[11] In a document prepared before he started for the Council, he had suggested an implicit definition without formally stating infallibility. But at the Council he was on the committee *De Postulatis* and felt that he could not continue if he presented such a document. Bishop Wood, his senior suffragan, presented the document, and it was signed by Bishops Conroy, Elder, Quinlan, and Williams. Five separate petitions were sent to the Committee *De Postulatis* against the definition. Bishop Mrak signed one of these. Another petition stressing the inopportuneness of the definition received the signature of Archbishops Kenrick, McCloskey, and Purcell and of Bishops Amat, Bacon, Bayley, Domenec, Feehan, Fitzgerald, Hennessey, Henni, Hogan, Lynch, McFarland, McQuaid, Melcher, Mullen, O'Gorman, Verot, and Whelan. This petition gave three reasons for their stand: that the discussion would show a lack of union; that in the regions where they lived, with heresies dominant, the definition would alienate non-Catholics rather than draw them to the Church; and because they feared that the strife within the Church resulting from the definition would hurt the Church.

When the news of the opposition of the American prelates to the definition was rumored in the United States, James McMaster in the *Freeman's Journal*, following the lead of Louis Veuillot of the *Univers* in Paris, began to berate the bishops who opposed the definition. On January 21, the schema *De Ecclesia Christi* was

[11] J. L. Spalding, note 1 above, pp. 379–429.

presented. It consisted of twenty-one canons and fifteen chapters on the nature of the Church, her power, the primacy of the Roman Pontiff, and the Temporal Dominion of the Church. Among those who presented written criticisms of parts of this schema were Archbishop Alemany, and Bishops Elder, Domenec, Lynch, Mullen, Verot, and Whelan. On March 7 a formula for the definition of papal infallibility was distributed to the Fathers as an additional chapter of the schema. Since word had gone out that the question of infallibility would be treated immediately, other matters were set aside. On March 10 a letter asking for immediate study of the proposal was presented. Among the signers of this petition were Bishops Miége and Dubuis. On March 15 Archbishops Kenrick and Purcell and Bishop Fitzgerald signed a petition against such action, asking that the topic be treated in its proper place. In the meantime Bishops Amat and Whelan had submitted criticisms of the earlier chapters of the schema *De Ecclesia*. The documents of March 7 had asked for observations on the added chapter. Archbishops Alemany and Spalding and Bishops Conroy, Elder, Quinlan, De St. Palais, and Williams asked that a special paragraph be inserted in which the assent to papal definitions was required to be internal as well as external. Other American prelates offered their separate observations and suggestions for changes.

Chief among those American bishops who opposed the definition of infallibility was Archbishop Peter Richard Kenrick of St. Louis, whose conduct was not always admired by the other Americans. He insisted that the opinion that the Roman Pontiff and he alone without the consent of the other Bishops is infallible was not so certain that it could be defined as a dogma of the faith and that it was inexpedient to define it even if it were true. He attacked the arguments in support of the dogma drawn from the Scriptures, found incompatibility between the dogma and the writings of the Fathers and other Councils, and questioned some of the theological opinions offered in support of the dogma. He warned about schisms that would result from the definition.

The opinions of the other American bishops who opposed the definition varied. Amat held only to the inopportuneness, Bishops Domenec, McQuaid, and Verot also felt that the doctrine was not certainly evident in Scripture and Tradition. Bishops Mullen and Whelan tried to propose a milder definition. In the discussion of other parts of the schema the dogma was kept in mind, especially when some Bishops, including Archbishop Purcell, and Bishops Fitzgerald, Verot, and Whelan endeavored to say that unanimity was necessary for definition. Archbishops Purcell and Kenrick tried to delay the discussion of the topic. On April 22 Bishops Dubuis, De Goesbriand, Miége and Rappe signed a petition to hasten the definition, but the presidents of the Council at that time would not change the order of discussion. A later petition to hasten the discussion was more successful, and on April 29 the debate on the Catechism was interrupted to discuss the dogma of infallibility. The first report was made on May 13, and the discussion began the next day. The second speaker on the schema was Archbishop Alemany, who wished to limit the extent of the papal power but rejected the fears expressed that the doctrine was not really revealed. Verot opposed the definition but drew laughter rather than support. Archbishop Spalding, besides maintaining that his predecessor (Archbishop Francis Patrick Kenrick) had supported infallibility, insisted that refusal to vote the acceptance of the dogma would be equivalent to accepting the declaration of the Gallican clergy condemned by the Holy See. Archbishop Purcell first criticized some statement of the Patriarch of Jerusalem, who seemed to brand the opponents of the definition as heretics, and then asked for a more limited definition of the dogma. Bishop Domenec opposed the definition on the grounds of inopportuneness and made some comparisons between Catholicism in America and Italy that brought an admonition from the presiding officer. On June 3 a petition that the discussion be closed was accepted by a majority of the Council, although a petition of protest against this, signed by several American bishops, was presented the next day. When Archbishop Kenrick realized that he would not be allowed to speak again he published on June 8 his *Concio*[12] or speech against the definition in Naples.

Several American bishops took part in the remaining discussion. On the preamble, Bishop Amat made several suggestions, some of which were ultimately accepted. Bishop Verot made such strong remarks against the dogma that audible murmurs against him were heard. Bishop Whelan also made some criticisms of the preamble. The discussion continued on the first three chapters of the schema. On July 13 votes were taken on Chapters Three and Four of the schema. The votes were 451 *placet,* 63 *placet juxta modum,* and 88 *non placet.* Four American prelates, Archbishops Blanchet and McCloskey and Bishops Amat and Demers, voted *placet juxta modum* and suggested minor modifications. On Sun-

[12] Raymond Clancy, "American Prelates in the Vatican Council," *Historical Records and Studies,* XXVIII, 7 to 135, gives the "Concio," pp. 93–131.

day, July 17, a letter was sent to the Holy Father which pointed out the 88 who voted against the definition, the 62 who had reservations, and the 76 who were absent and asked that the fourth public assembly be canceled. Among the signers of this were Archbishop Kenrick and Bishops Domenec and Verot. They announced that they would not attend the session if it were held. The final public session was held July 18. Of the American prelates who had voted *placet juxta modum*, all voted *placet* in this public session. Bishops Conroy and O'Connell, who had been absent at the general congregation, voted *placet* in the public session. Of those who had voted *non placet*, McCloskey changed to *placet* in the public session, and Fitzgerald voted *non placet* but immediately submitted. Of the others who voted *non placet*, Archbishop Kenrick, Bishops Domenec, McQuaid, Mrak, and Verot absented themselves. Archbishop Purcell had gone home June 30, but would probably have voted *non placet*. When Purcell announced that he would speak publicly in Mozart Hall in Cincinnati on his return, Bishop Lynch wrote him pleading that he, the Dean of the hierarchy, not publicly oppose the definition. Apparently Purcell had no intention of opposing the definition. He supported the definition in his speech and sent in his submission to Cardinal Barnabo. The Cardinal suggested that the submission be sent also to the Holy Father. The other bishops sent in their submissions individually later. War then broke out between France and Prussia, and Victor Emmanuel took over Rome. The formal suspension of the Council was declared in a letter dated October 20, 1870. Archbishop Kenrick sent in his adherence to the definition on January 13, 1871. There is some doubt that he ever accepted the reasons advanced for the definition, but he did accept the definition as decreed by the supreme magisterium of the Church. The charge that some of the American bishops were Gallican could be explained in his case, as he himself pointed out in his *Concio,* because he had been trained by Irish theologians of an earlier age who had been formed by French theologians.

There was general agreement that the Council was rudely interrupted by the invasion of Rome. Later, in Vatican Council II, it was maintained that the interruption prevented the Council from balancing the doctrine of papal infallibility with a statement of the collegiality of the bishops, but the times of the two councils were different. In 1870 the Pope was attacked, and there was a desire on the part of many bishops to show that they stood with the Pope against those who were invading his dominions and questioning his power. But there was a paradox in the fact that the

American episcopate, which had always been so loyal to the person of the Pope, was mostly opposed to the declaration of the doctrine of papal infallibility at least at the time.

Before some of the hierarchy, including Archbishop Spalding, had left Europe the Italian troops had entered Rome, and the Holy Father had become the "Prisoner of the Vatican." Spalding was still in Switzerland when the Holy City was taken on September 20. Any hopes that the Council would resume was then ended, and he left for Liverpool and New York. The greeting for Archbishop Spalding in Baltimore and later in Washington, while at the time a welcome for the returned Council leader, was turned also into a protest meeting against the seizure of the Papal States. The resolution of the large assembly that greeted him in Baltimore said that they wished "to avail themselves of this impressive occasion to give expression, in the face of all Christendom, to our earnest, solemn, and unanimous protest against the late invasion of the Roman States by the Florentine Government." A few weeks later in a public meeting in Philadelphia the Archbishop himself made a forceful protest against the seizure of the Papal States, arguing that this was not the wish of the people of Rome but a conquest by arms. In 1871 on the occasion of the silver jubilee of the pontificate of Pope Pius IX, the Archbishop arranged a general Communion for the Pope on Sunday, June 17, after which a letter of congratulation was sent to the Pontiff. The Pope responded with a special letter of gratitude to Spalding and his flock.

Spalding had suffered from recurring illness frequently in his later life. He was so ill in the spring of 1867 that rumors arose that he was dead, just before he went to Rome. In October 1871, he had another relapse but again recovered after hope of recovery had been given up. He himself described his sickness as "a kind of gastric affection." Recovered, he began to plan a new church in Baltimore and to revise his books on Kentucky. Just before Christmas he went to New York to attend a meeting of some bishops and caught a cold. He said Mass for the last time on Christmas morning, at a side altar, and his life gradually ebbed away until his death on February 7, 1872. There seemed to be a kind of consensus that his successor was to be Bishop James Roosevelt Bayley, the successful Bishop of Newark. There were other rumors that Archbishop McCloskey of New York would be transferred to Baltimore. Baltimore was really a primatial see, but New York was actually a more important city, and such a change does not seem to have been seriously considered. What does seem to have weighed importantly in the decision was that, as an American and a relative of Mother Seton of Maryland, Bayley was peculiarly fitted to become the next Archbishop of the Maryland See. In later appointments to Baltimore, this factor was not important, but in 1872 with friction against immigrants still very much in the air, there is definite evidence that nativism was an important factor in the choice. When Bayley heard of the possibility of his promotion he made some efforts to avoid it. He received letters from friends in Rome on August 10 that he had been elected Archbishop of Baltimore on July 21, at the same time that Bishop Gibbons had been named to the See of Richmond. The official documents arrived on September 2, and after some delay he accepted the appointment. He publicly took over his archiepiscopal cathedral on October 13.

While the hierarchy was in Rome for the Council, there was no great change in the internal operations of the Catholic Church in the United States. Many of the bishops were back in nearly six months; and only in those missionary dioceses where the bishop performed part of the local pastoral duties was their absence of great importance. There were actually no decrees enacted in the Council that affected the internal life of the Church in the United States, even though the much discussed doctrine of infallibility may have induced controversy on some higher levels in this country. It was certainly less troublesome than the criticisms that had arisen over the *Syllabus of Errors*. The all absorbing problem of American Catholicism was how to furnish the Sacraments and Christian education for the mass of continually arriving Catholic immigrants. The multiplication of dioceses that had followed the second Plenary Council was part of the answer; the increase in seminaries and of seminarians to fill them was another.

The seminary program of study was nearly always the same, including a foundation of classical education—normally consisting of six years, two years of philosophy and four of theology. In some seminaries where priests were gravely needed, the classical program was shortened by two years. Where the bishop had the means or could get the prospective priests, he sent the more promising youngsters to Montreal, to Louvain, or to Rome to study. Within the country, the general traditions of the Sulpician seminary were imitated. In the farming regions of the Middle West, compact German settlements were able to secure German-trained seminarians or young German priests and set up Catholic communities, occasionally totally Catholic. Even when the neighborhood was only partially Catholic, the German priest tried to imitate within his parish all that he could of the Catholic parish he had known in the German Catholic Rhineland. Usually, the German language and local customs became strong bonds of religious fidelity as well.

The story of the Irish, especially the recently arrived, was a bit different. There were a few attempts to establish Irish communities, particularly after the famines of the 1870s, but most of the Irish immigrants lived in the poorer slum sections of the large cities, in shanties along the railroad tracks, or worked as laborers in the coal mines. Probably the most beneficial of these outlets for Irish labor was that offered first by the canals and then by the railroads. Through employment on the railroads and also on boats, some of the Irish made their way into the interior of the country. If the Irish women came with them, the couples soon acquired some kind of farm and began to achieve respectability in their communities. Some Irish, of course, continued to work on the railroads and eventually their sons and grandsons rose to positions of some honor and earned higher pay. If they remained as workers on the railroad, they had regular employment in a work that was a bit romantic at that stage of rising industrialism, but they continued to live in the poorer sections of the railroad towns. Later they joined railway unions, but they ceased to manifest any tendency to violence.

In politics the leadership in a precinct or a ward in the over-populated slums was not an introduction to higher society, but it did bring the Irish immigrant into some political power of a kind of brutal form, a form associated with big city politics for several generations. Although most of the Irish were Catholics, and their Catholicism was as much a badge of loyalty as any political arrangement, in the beginning the chief bond of loyalty among them was their common Irish backgrounds. Later alignments were made frankly for the reward the winning politician could hand out. As the political leader needed votes, he had to recognize the groups of voters by giving them the lower offices. Eventually the lower officers demanded a share of the higher offices, and soon there were Irish Catholic politicians in the aldermanic councils and later in the mayoral seats. There is no question that the Irish pastor was pleased to see his parishioners advance in political power. No harm was done, apparently, when the politician or his "boss" helped the pastor care for the poorest families in the parish. Gratitude from those befriended called for votes for the benefactor at the next election. Some have maintained that the "boss" system was evil in itself, but no one seemed able to invent a better system that would win. In some cases the poorer persons did advance and the invasion of poorer and less sure people into political offices did promote a rough kind of real democracy in the larger cities. Later when these machines became all powerful and were openly involved in graft, the position of the churchmen who had influence in politics was called in question. The American Puritan tradition did not accept any right of the politician to get rich on his political service. Some Catholic politicians felt that their circumstances justified their deeds.

The third focus of Irish immigrant activity was not one learned in Ireland. The Irish, having no skill except with the pick-axe and shovel, were among the first recruits in the development of the Pennsylvania coal mines that accompanied the expansion of the iron and steel industries. The working conditions of the miners were bad throughout the world; even a century later, despite all the improvements in techniques, an explosion may happen far below the earth, and the maimed bodies that are brought to the surface cause some rethinking about the necessity for men to undergo these dangerous conditions. In the 1860s, after the railroads began to make the large deposits of coal movable and the new uses of coal in the production of iron and steel created a new market, larger numbers of workers were recruited for the anthracite coal mines of northeastern Pennsylvania. Some Europeans came to America with a family tradition of working in the mines of Great Britain, and some Irish had gone to work in the English mines. But the Irish brought with them something different, a tradition of physical violence against cruel oppressors. To protect themselves against their employers and spies, the members of these groups formed secret alliances and took a pledge of secrecy.

In the case of the Fenian Brotherhood, the attitude of the Church against these secret Irish societies was made plain. It is a paradox of Irish Catholicism that, while it resents the cruelty and oppression imposed on them by economic or political force, the Catholic doctrine forbids retaliation in kind. The Fenian movement, by its violence and its secret oath fell afoul of the traditional Church laws against Masonic societies. When Archbishops Purcell and Spalding finally obtained a Roman ruling on the Fenians, the Brotherhood did not survive as a real force in American Irish life. The ban against secret societies was a major problem in Catholic life during the second half of the nineteenth century. Secret societies, with their rituals, have had their appeal to non-Catholics, as a kind of replacement for the liturgical splendor taken away from English Protestantism by the Puritans. The opposition of the Catholic Church to secret societies was manifold. Not only did these societies make their secret oath superior to religious obligations, the societies themselves were frequently founded on principles contrary to civil as well as religious authority. Finally some, such as the Freemasons, tended to set up a rival religious faith.

The Freemasons had their origin in a guild of masons of medieval times; but by the nineteenth century they accepted members other than mason workers and began to hold services which had nothing to do with the mason trade and which included a kind of natural and deistic religion. They adopted secret oaths and a ritualism similar to the religions of the Far East. On April 29, 1738, Pope Clement XII in the Bull *Eminenti* had condemned the Masons for their tendency to undermine Christianity and because of their oath of secrecy. Although there are Masonic emblems in many old Catholic cemeteries in the United States, before the Civil War, the attitude of the Church toward even the American kind of Masonry was clear. For most Catholics there did remain those societies on the verge of Masonry. First the Odd Fellows were condemned, and then the Sons of Temperance, a society which, from being a reform movement, had become a society with other religious implications.

Among the immigrants who professed to be Catholics, there were some who had inclinations toward these Masonic groups, chiefly those societies which were opposed to both Church and State in south Europe. There were some Italian Carbonari who were active in the regions about New Orleans. In the Bedini incident in Cincinnati, there was a show of German freethinkers, but whether any of these were Catholics is not evident. The problem of secret societies immediately following the Civil War was raised again among the Irish immigrants, although Catholic migrants to the West tended to join for social reasons whatever social lodges they found. The chief reason for organizing societies in the industrial and mineral regions was the need among the workers of mutual aid and protection.

Not all associations of this kind were necessarily bad. The political organizations in the large cities could be classified also as social organization against oppression, although they did not attract the condemnation that labor organizations had because they were presented more in the aspect of political clubs, even when their practices were illegal and perhaps violent. The Irish organizations which attracted the ire of the bishops were the Fenians, the Molly Maguires, the A.O.H. (Ancient Order of

Hibernians—some forms), and later the Irish Land League. The hierarchy in Ireland and America condemned the secret oaths of these societies and their resort to violence.

The Molly Maguires were a vaguely defined group of Irish Catholic miners in the anthracite coal mines of Luzerne and Schuylkill counties, Pennsylvania. They were apparently members of the Ancient Order of Hibernians, although probably a group within the local chapters of the order. After some members of the group were betrayed, a common defensive silence among the families of those involved has made further research among the character of the group almost futile. Members of the A.O.H. in other parts of the country were quick to disown any relationship to the violent group. There had been organizations for violence in Ireland, but these had been condemned by the Irish hierarchy. In the late sixties and early seventies violence and murders were being committed in the coal mining regions of Schuylkill and Luzerne Counties, and seven Catholic priests of the region published in *The Freeman's Journal* on October 10, 1874, a statement accusing the A.O.H. of being responsible for the violence, noting that their practices had been condemned in Ireland, and demanding the elimination of the condemned practices. The seven priests served in the neighborhood. They were: Fathers Michael Sheridan of Ashland, Joseph Bridgman of Girardville, Edward Field of Centralia, Joseph Koch of Shamokin, D. O'Connor of Mahanoy Plane, Henry O'Reilly of Shenandoah, and D. McDermott of New Philadelphia. Father McDermott gave an interview to the press in which he claimed that the members of the secret organization had joined the A.O.H. The actual existence of a separate society remained unproved.[13]

Eventually Frank G.B. Gowan, the President of the Philadelphia and Reading Railroad decided to break the power of the Molly Maguires with the aid of detectives, some of whom infiltrated the Molly Maguires. Twenty of the Irish workers were convicted and hanged. The role of the Church in this was clear insofar as the seven priests had condemned the group, and Bishop Frederick Wood of Philadelphia had issued a pastoral condemning both the violence and secret oaths. These actions, in turn, caused some to claim that the Church was unsympathetic to labor and to the sad conditions of laborers in the mines. Others hinted that only among Irish Catholics who could easily obtain forgive-

[13] The latest and probably the best account of the Molly Maguires is Wayne G. Broehl, Jr., *The Molly Maguires* (Cambridge, 1964).

ness and absolution in the confessional was such violence possible. In fact the priests were bound by the secrecy of the confessional. Nor could they at the time do anything about working conditions in the mines. The story of the Molly Maguires hurt the reputation of the Irish Catholic worker in the press and convinced the more conservative members of the hierarchy that secret labor organizations were necessarily evil. In the rise of the Knights of Labor the bad recollections of the Mollies and the fear of Masonic secrecy had much to do with the opposition of many American bishops to the Knights.

There were always some Catholic farming communities in the Middle West; most of them were formed by successful farmers from the Rhineland.[14] The Catholic immigrant who had the means to buy a farm in the new country sought first to find a suitable location in the vicinity of a Catholic mission or endeavored to get enough Catholics to go with him into a neighborhood so that they could secure the promise of a visiting missionary. No one can tell how many Catholics lost the Faith because they could not obtain this assurance. Father Andrew A. Lambing, the Pittsburgh pastor and chronicler, wrote several articles in the *Ave Maria* in 1872 on "The Grievances of the Church" in which he gave a contemporary evaluation of the chief obstacles to the growth of the Church in the United States. Besides treating of public opposition to the Church, the problem of mixed marriages, and other "grievances," he wrote on March 2 on "The Defection of Immigrants."

There are in nearly if not every State of the Union persons who never saw a Church nor heard Mass on Sunday. How, it may be asked could they have the practical knowledge of religion to bear them safely through the stormy sea of life in America? No: it is a tear and a prayer that I have for the poor immigrants, rather than a word of censure or blame. Their great numbers, the unexampled growth and spread of Catholicity in this country, and the inability of the Church to furnish a sufficient body of laborers for the "Fields already white for the harvest," precluded the possibility of meeting the wants of the numerous and widespread flock. . . .

Persons may differ widely in their estimate of the numbers lost to the

[14] For a good account of Catholics on the farming frontier in Nebraska, one may consult Henry W. Casper, S.J., *History of the Catholic Church in Nebraska,* 3 vol. (Milwaukee, 1960–1966), especially volumes II and III. James P. Shannon, *Catholic Colonization on the Western Frontier* (New Haven, 1957) treats of the colonies in Minnesota. For earlier colonies, there is Sister Mary Gilbert Kelly, O.P., *Catholic Immigrant Colonization Projects in the United States 1815–1860* (New York, 1939).

Church in this manner, but all must admit them to have been considerable. The one least competent to decide may safely set them down at many thousands, basing his conclusions on the well-known nature of the causes at work. The late Archbishop Hughes—certainly no mean authority—declares that we have lost hundreds of thousands by defection, and though he undoubtedly made the most of it, I am inclined to think, from the opportunities I have had of judging, that he is not so wide of the mark as some persons imagine.[15]

But the great body of Catholic immigrants did not go into the countryside, except those who followed the railroad builders into the interior. Most of the Catholic immigrants went into the cities and later into the mill towns of the East and the Great Lakes region. There they finally achieved some political power by sheer numbers, achieving the mayor's desk in Boston and New York in the 1880s and many other local positions. In the revival of bigotry after the Civil War, the essential point of conflict between Catholic and Protestant was not in employment or in politics, although religious prejudice was often bitterly manifest in those spheres. The essential conflict outside of religion itself was in the matter of education. The failure of the mass of Irish immigrants in New England to achieve social heights earlier could be attributed to the lack of educational achievements among the Catholic workers whether Irish or of other nationalities. Perhaps the bitterest writings against Catholicism centered about the Catholic efforts to get public support for their parochial schools. In 1872 the editor of *Harper's Weekly* defended the magazine's opposition to Francis Kernan, the Democratic candidate for Governor of New York in 1872, on the grounds that he was a Catholic, adding: "Now the Roman Catholic Church in this state is a political party. . . ." Quoting Father Thomas Preston's charge that the common schools were in fact sectarian, *Harper's* added:

Thus the object is plainly avowed. It is not the Bible in the schools, it is the very secular intention of the schools, which is the real argument in favor of the exclusion of the Bible, which is the object of the hostility of the Roman Church. Its real argument is that the common public schools must be sectarian, and therefore that they are inconsistent with the constitutional guarantee of religious liberty and equality. It is the schools, not the Bible in the schools, to which the Roman Church is opposed. To destroy the system is its political object. . . .[16]

Earlier in discussing the quarrel between Father Michael P.

---

[15] *Ave Maria*, VIII, 137–139.
[16] *Harper's Weekly*, November 16, 1872, p. 890.

Stack of Williamsport, Pennsylvania, and his Bishop, William O'Hara of Scranton, the editors of *Harper's Weekly* went out of their way on February 3, 1872, to distort the absolutism of the Catholic Church. Using the current quarrel as an occasion, they attacked the laws that had been passed shortly before in the state of New York for the incorporation of Catholic property.

The danger of this unprecedented law, this gross departure from the principles of equality and freedom, is increased by the fact that the Romish priesthood have formed themselves into a distinct political party. Not content with humane toleration accorded them among us, they labor to control the elections, and rule by the disunion of their opponents. Of all the religious sects they alone enter into the strife of parties as a united and well-organized body. They make no secret of their purpose. They propose to destroy the common schools, and to gain such an influence in the State as shall best serve to advance the interests of their Church. If they obey the papal syllabus they must labor to make their religion the religion of the State, to the exclusion of all others.

The editors of *Harper's Weekly* pretended that they were defending American institutions against a degrading influence. They were at the same time defending the Republican opponents of the Irish Catholic candidates. Many other attacks against Catholicism were less careful in framing their charges against the Church. Scurrilous books and pamphlets were very much available. In the rural areas where the Catholics had not gone, the absent Catholics were sometimes made into ogres. In the cities, the evils of ignorance and poverty were mixed in with the corruptions of city political machines and attributed to Catholicism. The Church leaders, now that they had returned from Rome, were heavily burdened with the task of supplying churches, orphanages, hospitals, and perhaps schools for the hundreds of thousands who had come before the war but had not yet achieved economic or social security and who were now being followed by other hundreds of thousands who had sometimes even less. Soon the immigrants would have to assume the leadership in these tasks.

CHAPTER NINE

The Rise of the American
Irish 1872-1884

BISHOP BAYLEY PROTESTED HIS NOMINA-
tion to the See of Baltimore. At that time his health did not
bother him, but apparently he honestly felt that he was not the
man for the office, perhaps because he was a convert. He was a
member of a prominent American family, and while he had given
up his inheritance in becoming a Catholic he was regarded as of
aristocratic rank. The Healy portrait shows him to have been a
well built individual, a bit inclined to flesh with a full face, high
forehead, and medium nose and mouth. In his installation sermon
he spoke of his ancestry:

. . . We—and I use the word we, because though not born among you,
I stand here today on account of my position as good a Marylander as
if my ancestors came over in the Ark and the Dove—We Catholics of
Maryland, have a glorious record; of suffering for conscience sake, en-
dured patiently and courageously; of great principles asserted, vindi-
cated, and lived up to. There are bright and glorious names among the
clergy and laity, who are venerated all over the land.[1]

On October 20 the new Archbishop went to Richmond to install
his friend, James Gibbons, as Bishop of Richmond, and on No-

[1] Sister M. Hildegarde Yeager, *The Life of James Roosevelt Bayley, First
Bishop of Newark and Eighth Archbishop of Baltimore 1814–1877* (Washington, 1947) p. 345.

vember 2 he made his first official visit to Washington. He began to assay the prospects of the Archdiocese. Baltimore itself had eighteen Catholic churches and there were prominent Catholic families there, more probably than in any other American city. Besides the Carrolls and Jenkinses the families of the O'Donnells, the Harpers, the McSherrys, the Spaldings and the Foleys were also important. Washington had also some prominent Catholics, but the other portions of the Archdiocese were not prosperous. Agricultural Maryland was a former slave state which had suffered during and after the war; its chief port, Baltimore, was no longer a notable port of entry for immigrants. In its tradition as the first see of the Church in America, Baltimore had in its Archdiocese the two chief Catholic cultural institutions of the country, Georgetown College and St. Mary's Seminary. Close to these in rank were Mt. St. Mary's at Emmitsburg, which had declined because so many of its staff had been recruited for the hierarchy, and Mt. St. Joseph, the mother house of the Daughters of Charity of Mother Seton. Calvert Hall was conducted by the Christian Brothers in Baltimore and in the Diocese were houses of the Redemptorists, Jesuits, and Passionists and female academies conducted by the Visitandines, the Daughters of Charity of Mother Seton, the Sisters of Mercy, the Sisters of Notre Dame, and the Sisters of Holy Cross. Baltimore's influence in the Church, however, did not correspond to the shift in leadership in the United States generally. The economic and political forces determining the future of America after the Civil War were centered in the northern and eastern states. In the northern states must be included the old West better known as the Middle West, which began to play an important part in national politics and in the welfare of the nation. It was also an important part of American Catholicism.

On November 21 the Archbishop went to St. Mary's Seminary to conduct ordinations. He already had a slight cold when he arrived, and he spent a busy day. There was no fire in the chapel, and the next day the Archbishop developed a more serious cold throughout his body. He did not leave his room for several weeks. As his recovery was delayed, his physician advised him to go to Florida during the cold season. The Archbishop went to Washington and then visited Richmond, Wilmington, Charleston, and Savannah on his way to St. Augustine, where he stayed until March 26. At the beginning of April 1873, feeling sufficiently recovered, he returned to Maryland and began his tasks as Archbishop. Also on April 27 in Baltimore he consecrated Bishop

William H. Gross the new Bishop of Savannah and went on to Newark to attend the consecration of his successor, Michael A. Corrigan. But he did not return to good health.

The failure of the Roman authorities to erect Baltimore into a primatial see did not make much difference as long as they acted as if the Archbishop were the primate in most national problems and the hierarchy was closely united. Bayley was not the oldest member of the hierarchy and did not try to assume any national authority, and his bad health kept him from much active leadership. He did consult the other archbishops about certain problems that remained from the Second Plenary Council, particularly the erection of Milwaukee and Philadelphia as archdiocesan sees. A second problem faced by the Archbishop as quasi-primate was the support of the North American College in Rome. Here again Bayley acted as if he were a primate in a meeting called in Washington.

Another problem calling for a supradiocesan decision was the relations between the Catholic bishops and the Federal Government on Indian affairs. In 1870 President Grant had announced a policy of leaving the supervision of the Indians to the religious denominations. This so-called "Peace Policy" seemed a proper solution of the complicated problem by which religious groups would care for the education and direction of the Indians, until the question arose as to which denomination would have charge of certain Indian nations. There was no Catholic member of the Indian Commissioners working under the direction of the Department of the Interior and no Catholic authorized to act for the bishops. President Grant had not carried out some promises made to Catholics who had spoken to him. Although all the Catholic bishops having Indians under their care were interested, Archbishop Norbert Blanchet of Oregon City was the one most concerned; however, the Washington phases of the dealings were within the archdiocese of Archbishop Bayley. Archbishop Bayley opposed setting up a Catholic lobby to intercede for the Catholic interests. General Charles Ewing had been voluntarily interceding for the Catholic interests and finally, with the consent of the other bishops, Archbishop Bayley appointed him on January 2, 1874, as Catholic Commissioner of Indian Affairs, a title he held until his death on June 23, 1883.[2] In the meantime Father George Deshon, a Paulist who had been a West Point classmate of Presi-

---

[2] This matter is the subject of Peter J. Rahill, *The Catholic Indian Missions and Grant's Peace Policy 1870–1884* (Washington, 1953).

dent Grant, was asked to talk to him about the Catholic problem, and Father J. A. Brouillet was assigned to work with General Ewing. In 1879 the office of Catholic Indian Commissioner was changed to Bureau of Catholic Indian Missions.

When Cardinal Barnabo of the Congregation of the Propaganda asked Bayley to call a meeting of the bishops of the country to discuss the new episcopal and archiepiscopal sees, Bayley thought such a meeting unnecessary and proposed instead that a meeting be held of the holders of the proposed new archiepiscopal sees and the bishops and archbishops whose status would be changed. The meeting was to be held in Cincinnati early in May 1874. Archbishop Kenrick of St. Louis quickly agreed to the proposal because he had already approved the erection of Boston and Philadelphia to archdiocesan rank, and he added now that he thought Milwaukee and Santa Fé should also be advanced to that rank. Archbishops Kenrick and McCloskey and Bishop Wood joined Bayley and Purcell and several other bishops at Cincinnati on May 4. They agreed on the four new archiepiscopal sees and the division of the suffragan dioceses. With him, Archbishop Bayley had brought a questionnaire that he had received from the Sacred Congregation of the Propaganda on the question of the attendance of Catholic children at public schools. Archbishop Bayley was plainly irritated by the questionnaire and by the writings of James McMaster that had occasioned it.[3] There was never any doubt in the minds of the American bishops that a full Catholic system of education was desirable, but generally where the Catholic people were most numerous, as in the cities along the eastern coast, they were also the poorest and unable to erect and maintain a functioning Catholic school system. The Catholic schools that did exist in the East depended to a great extent on the zeal of the individual pastors and bishops and the financial advancement of the parishioners. Among the Germans in the farming communities of the Middle West, these two factors of zeal and support were backed by immigrant nationalism and farmland prosperity, and there the Catholic parochial schools began to multiply.

James McMaster, the editor of *The Freeman's Journal*, had always advocated the establishment of Catholic parochial schools but seemed to have been inspired anew by the irreligious events of the Paris Commune of 1871. He declared war formally on the

[3] Thomas T. McAvoy, C.S.C., "Public Schools vs Catholic Schools and James McMaster,"*Review of Politics* (1966) XXVIII, 19–46.

godless public schools and against those priests and bishops who allowed Catholic children to attend them. Quoting from articles forty-seven and forty-eight of the *Syllabus of Errors* and the papal letter to the Archbishop of Freiburg from which they were taken, he maintained that the Pope had decided the question and that bishops and priests had no choice but to remove the Catholic children from the public schools. Further through his Roman agent, Miss Ella B. Edes, and Father Edmund DePauw of Chateaugay, New York who visited Rome in February 1874, McMaster had presented a petition to the Sacred Congregation of the Propaganda and its Prefect, Cardinal Franchi, for a clarification of the law. McMaster, in his presentation of the problem, made the public schools proximate occasions of sin because of the qualities of the teachers and the circumstances of the schools. As a result of this petition, apparently, the Sacred Congregation sent on April 10 a letter to the Archbishops of the United States asking five questions.

1. Precisely for what reasons do the faithful permit their children to attend non-Catholic schools?
2. What sort of means are there whereby young people can more easily be kept from schools of this sort?
3. What are the reasons why some up to now hold that sacramental absolution must be denied to Catholic parents who send their children to non-Catholic schools whereas others think that absolution should be granted?
4. Whether by the denial of the sacraments it can be easily brought about that parents will not allow their children to attend such schools?
5. Finally, whether, and with what difficulties, could a remedy of this sort be harmful, with due regard to the circumstances of places and persons?[4]

The archbishops meeting in Cincinnati decided to answer this questionnaire by a common basic agreement and to allow their suffragans, who might disagree, to send in their own answer to Rome. The "Minutes" of the opinions of the Archbishop and Bishops said that the public schools were not of their very nature opposed to the Catholic religion but that they were, instead, secular; that the bishops were really desirous of erecting Catholic schools and of sending all their children to them but that was impossible in some areas and that the bishops were opposed to denying absolution to parents who sent their children to the public schools because there were many circumstances which excused

[4] *Ibid.,* 30–31.

such actions. In the specific answers to the five questions, the bishops noted the fact that sometimes the teachers in the Catholic schools were inferior to those in the public schools, simply because the Catholic schools could not afford to hire better ones. Further they thought that denying absolution generally would be unfair in some cases and would merely stir up feelings against the Church.

The questionnaire and its answers seemed to have had no immediate effect, although the answers of the Bishops were turned over by Propaganda to the Sacred Congregation of the Inquisition. That Congregation gave a ruling on November 24, 1875, which disagreed with the "Minutes" of the bishops and seemed to hold the public schools as proximate occasions of sin. The Inquisition ruled that, unless the proximate occasions could be made remote, Catholic children should not be sent to them. However, the Sacred Congregation insisted that Catholic schools must be the equal of the public schools and that religious communities must be encouraged to provide the necessary teachers. Admitting that all Catholic children could not be sent to Catholic schools, they insisted that there be a just reason for sending children to the public schools instead. This decree was not sent to the United States until one year later, November 24, 1876. It caused no great change in the Catholic practice but was the basis for the later legislation on parochial schools in the Third Plenary Council of Baltimore.

Archbishop Bayley was not a fluent orator, but he was a well educated man who had sound opinions and could express them. Undoubtedly he was conservative in his political opinions. In a notable speech to the Irish Catholic Benevolent Union of Baltimore on October 21, 1874, he praised the Union for its offering of opportunities for culture and for community charity.[5] He advised its members to be very careful about the opportunities for culture that they provided for their children and to promote worthwhile associations. Specifically he urged them to avoid the associations of mechanics which had a "communist or international character." In saying this the Archbishop was within the recommendations of the Second Plenary Council against secret associations except that the Council had urged that no prohibitions should be placed in the way of workingmen forming associations for bettering their working conditions. The Archbishop certainly was aware of the evil doings of the Molly Maguires and the Fenians and may have found in them evils of secret organization. Archbishops and bishops, like other clergymen of the day, gave encour-

[5] Yeager, note 1 above, pp. 386–388.

agement to those good social organizations springing up like mushrooms over the country which furnished entertainment for the workers when not at work and added opportunities of cultural advancement. In fact the formation of Catholic Unions was attempted in many dioceses in answer to the plea of the Holy Father himself for the formation of Catholic unions in defense of the Holy See and the rights of the Church which the Pope had made to the Belgian Union after the seizure of the Papal states. However, since these were lay organizations, some bishops did not encourage their formation.

When the English controversy over Papal infallibility attracted attention in the American press, Archbishop Bayley was asked to give his opinion on the question. In answer to an article on November 17, 1874, in *The New York Herald* on the Manning-Gladstone controversy, Bayley refused to enter into the controversy itself, but he called Gladstone's argument a form of the old charge that Manning was not "a friend of Caesar." He added: "It is indeed sad to see a distinguished statesman like Mr. Gladstone, who has always enjoyed the reputation of being a high-toned and honorable man, putting on 'the cap and bells' and attempting to play the part of Lord George Gordon."

In writing in this fashion, Bayley was following the path of his predecessors, Archbishops Francis Kenrick and Martin J. Spalding. But he would not carry on long in this vein, as he was already suffering from recurring sicknesses. He wrote on July 22 to Bishop Gibbons—when because of illness he missed the funeral of Bishop Whelan at Wheeling—that his health kept him from fulfilling his duties and that he wanted Gibbons to be appointed his Coadjutor. While he continued to be very active, ill health—a combination of nephritis and rheumatism—began to dog his steps. There was, however, no obvious connection between his ill health and the Roman decision to make Archbishop McCloskey, instead of Bayley, the first American Cardinal. Archbishop McCloskey presided over a more important see and one that was growing even more prosperous.

Perhaps in choosing the New York prelate Rome was emphasizing her refusal to make Baltimore a primatial see. In fact a kind of titular leadership of American Catholicism at this time was given to the well-liked Archbishop of New York, John McCloskey, when he was named Cardinal by Pope Pius IX. Rumors of McCloskey's nomination had come from Rome constantly since the first of the year, 1875, and the editor of *The Freeman's Journal* professed to have word of the impending election from his Roman agent on March 9 and gave the news out as authentic. The naming took place at the Consistory on March 15, 1875, which made the word official that McCloskey was the first Roman Cardinal in the New World. The biretta brought from Rome by Monsignor Caesar Roncetti was imposed on the new Cardinal by Archbishop Bayley in St. Patrick's Cathedral, New York, on April 27, and the new cardinal visited Rome to complete the ceremonies in September. McCloskey did not have the strong personality of his predecessor John Hughes, about whom predictions of a similar promotion had not proved true, but he was older and more experienced than the holder of the first see, Archbishop Bayley. American-born and not a convert, he represented better than Bayley the flourishing Catholicism of the United States, and the fact that he was of Irish parentage, although a native, made him a kind of type of the new rulers and guides of the American Church. A small man with a thin face, G.P. Healy's portrait makes him a sweet tempered, but reserved and thoughtful prelate. His archiepiscopate was justly peaceful and happy at a time when hard decisions were not taken. Somehow the Church in America seemed to share in the expansion and prosperity of the nation.

Any attempt, however, to picture the Catholic Church in America as a strong unity would not correspond to the facts. Archbishop Bayley, the holder of the titular primacy, was an American and in his cultured, even aristocratic, way represented the basic English and American cornerstone of the Church edifice, but that cornerstone was being lost to view most of the time in the unplanned growth of American Catholicism. The public was mostly aware of the Irish Catholics who had come in such great numbers in the 1840s and 1850s and who, while legally equal to the native Americans, had not really ceased to be poor, peasant minded, and unskilled for the most part. The desire for a national organization to work for the betterment of Irish immigrants led to the formation of the Irish Catholic Benevolent Union in 1869, an attempt to unite the many parish and district societies into a national union. Its peak membership of 30,000 was reached in 1876 with 304 member societies. In its *Journal* and annual meetings, the Union fostered Catholic schools and Catholic colonization projects and helped many Catholics achieve local, political, and social distinctions, but internal dissensions and political factions kept its attainments meager. Some of its members became congressmen, local judges, and mayors of cities.[6] The Irish immigrants seemed very eager for public offices and for free public

[6] The history of this effort is told in Sister Joan Marie Donohoe, S.N.D., *The Irish Catholic Benevolent Union* (Washington, 1953).

education. Wealth and education they did not have, but numbers they could marshal. They did not represent any notable moral betterment although they were faithful and generous to their priests.

The German Catholics among the immigrants kept more to themselves. The hundreds of thousands of Germans who had begun to come before the Civil War and continued to come through the war and after did not usually go to the cities, but to the small towns or to the rural areas, sometimes in compact communities. Thus they did not disturb the politics of the native population nor did they want the natives to bother them. But they were too prone to maintain a foreign language and to remain in isolated communities. In some rural communities both Irish and German Catholics could be found, and frequently in cities and even small towns each group had its own church, with the English-speaking congregation called the "Irish" church.

The Catholics in the United States in the 1870s were a greater force numerically than they had been before the immigration of midcentury, but they did not wield a cultural influence proportionate to their numbers. Where the Catholic immigrants were the most numerous, along the eastern shores of New England, in the mill regions of New York and Philadelphia, in the mining regions, and even in the second so-called "mill zone" stretching around the Great Lakes, they were expected to be workers, mill hands, and farmers of small farms with little education and practically no wealth. The compact German settlements were exceptions to this, but, because of their sticking to the German language and customs, the German Catholics were not influential outside the local community. As the railroads spread across the plains, the Irish went with them, building and maintaining the railroads and their services.

The pleas of the Baltimore Councils for a Catholic press and for Catholic education represent in a forceful way the bishops' sense of the need for cultural elevation for the immigrants. The older Catholic families, especially the Maryland and Kentucky families and their relatives in neighboring states, were almost lost to sight in the millions of non-English immigrants who had come to represent American Catholicism in the press and in the public opinion. There were, indeed, some evidences of Catholic culture. *The Catholic World,* the *Ave Maria,* after 1876 the *Catholic Quarterly Review,* and for a few years in 1870–1873 the revived Brownson's *Review* were the chief literary efforts of Catholics. The Catholic weekly press was well edited but poorly supported. *The New York Tablet, The Freeman's Journal, The Catholic*

Telegraph, the *Western Watchman, The Western Catholic, The Catholic Vindicator,* and others like them were sprightly and interesting but had to be edited by clergymen who had other work to do or by laymen without special literary talents. *The Atlantic Monthly, The North American Review, Harper's, The Living Age,* the official organs of American culture, occasionally mentioned the Church, chiefly in stories about Rome or southern Europe, but not with notable respect. If the Catholics were to rise from their lowly status, Catholic schools had to be created and eventually Catholic colleges and universities.

The center of the Catholic school system before the 1880s was the seminary and the "college" which led to the seminary. Catholic education was expressed chiefly in terms of "classical" education, and there is no reliable standard by which we can measure the success of the existing colleges in teaching that classical course. The Jesuits led the way at Georgetown and Holy Cross in the East, at St. Louis, and Detroit in the Middle West. There were a few other small colleges directed by seculars, the chief of which was Mt. St. Mary's at Emmitsburg, and the painful efforts at Vincennes, Bardstown, and St. John's, Fordham. Notre Dame, chartered as a University in 1844, was a boarding college of limited means. Most successful in operation in the Catholic system were the private academies which, with the convent schools for girls, were dependent on the support of a religious community. The convent schools were aided by the attendance of daughters of wealthy non-Catholics. Parish schools existed where the pastor was zealous and managed to get the means. In the farming communities of the Middle West a parish school was the common achievement of a resident pastor. Sometimes these parish schools were held in the basement of the church, but, as the Sisters' communities began to come from Europe, separate buildings, often part of the convents of the Sisters, were set aside for classrooms. Catholic readers, spellers, and catechisms began to be printed. But the supposition that there could be a Catholic school for each parish seemed realistic only in the small Catholic communities of the Middle West, especially those having a German pastor and a community of German Sisters at hand. Actually there were few generalizations about the Catholic parish schools that were valid. Where the schools were most needed in the crowded slums of eastern cities, there were fewer financial means with which to build and maintain them. Also, most of the clergy of eastern dioceses felt that the preparation of orphanages and protectories for the orphans and the handicapped was more important, given the limited means

at hand. Bishop Bernard McQuaid of Rochester, himself an educator before his promotion, was rather an exception in his devotion to the building and staffing of Catholic parish schools.

The statistics on Catholic schools were not carefully gathered
in the 1870s. A sampling in the *Catholic Directory* for 1875 gives
some indication of the trends. In the Diocese of Boston only 14
parochial schools were listed. In the Archdiocese of New York
there were 93 parish schools and several private academies. In the
Diocese of Cleveland the *Directory* says that there was a parish
school in almost every parish in which there was a resident pastor.
In the Diocese of Alton among the Germans of southern Illinois
there were 83 parish schools, in the Diocese of Milwaukee the
parish schools are grouped according to the community of Sisters
conducting them, but they were apparently very numerous. To find
out where there were no parish schools, the reader would have to
subtract the schools listed from the number of parish centers. The
number of children in these parish schools ran from fewer than
thirty in some of the small parishes in the countryside to two
thousand or more in some of the cathedral parishes in the larger
cities. There are some indications that where there were no Catholic parish schools but Catholic churches there were often some
Catholic teachers in the public schools. Where there was a strong
system of parish schools, especially where the Catholic community
was made up of German immigrants, the public schools were not
attended by Catholic students nor did they have Catholic teachers,
and this situation gave some basis for the charge that Catholics
were opposed to the public schools—a charge that was very common as Catholic schools increased in the last decades of the
nineteenth century. One of the most important elements in
the creation of Catholic schools was the arrival from Europe of
communities of Sisters and, in lesser number, religious Brothers.
In the ranks of these communities there frequently were superior
teachers, some of whom were American converts from socially
superior families. Others were members of communities that were
engaged in teaching in Europe.

During the last years of Archbishop Bayley's life the feeling
against Catholics received special prominence in the renewed agitation over the schools and public institutions. There was the
usual accompaniment of dullness in political discussion during
the Grant administration and a general prosperity of the country
despite the setback from the panic of 1873. In this new attack on
Catholics there was none of the violence like the burning of the
Charlestown Convent in 1834 or the destruction of the churches

in Philadelphia in 1844, or the Black Monday riots of Louisville in 1854. By the 1870s there were some Catholics with political power in some localities having a large concentration of Catholics, but the reputation of Tammany Hall in New York and of other political machines in which Irish Catholics were prominent did not lessen the expression of bigotry against Catholics. The attacks in *Harper's Weekly* which connected Catholicism with the corruption of New York politics, echoes of the controversy between Gladstone and Manning over the dogma of papal infallibility, the excitement over the elevation of Archbishop McCloskey to the rank of a Roman Cardinal, conflict between Church and State in Italy resulting in the seizure of the Papal States and the conflict between the Church and the German government in the *Kulturkampf* were recorded in the American press. In the revival of bigotry after the Civil War, public controversy over the religious instruction of the Indians, revival of anti-Catholic writing about monasteries and convents, some new charges that Catholics were opposed to the reading of the Bible, assertions in the press that Catholics held all Protestant marriages invalid, and repeated charges that the Catholics were producing the majority of public criminals, marked a new intensity of anti-Catholic feeling. Bigotry was manifested notably in efforts to enact laws against allowing religious institutions to share in public funds. In New York and Michigan proposed amendments against aid to sectarian institutions were defeated, but a discriminating amendment was enacted in the Illinois Constitution of 1870. The Pennsylvania Constitution of 1873 forbade the appropriation of money to any institution not entirely under state control and added, "No money raised for the support of the public schools of the Commonwealth, shall be appropriated to or used for, the support of any sectarian school." Colorado adopted a similar amendment to its Constitution in 1875. In Ohio an attempt to include an amendment to tax religious institutions in the Constitution of 1874 was defeated, and in New Jersey such an amendment was defeated only when submitted to the people in 1875. The Republican Party platform of 1876 forbade the application of public funds or property for the benefit of any school or institution under sectarian control.

The name of President Grant was attached to the opposition to Catholic schools because of his several careless utterances against the appropriation of public money for religious institutions, particularly in a statement before Army veterans in Des Moines, Iowa, on September 27, 1875. Grant in his message to Congress in

1876 also gave support to the proposed sixteenth Amendment to the Constitution introduced by James G. Blaine which passed the House and nearly passed the Senate that year:

No state shall make any law respecting the establishment of religion, or prohibiting the free exercise thereof; and no religious test shall ever be required as a qualification to any office or public trust under any state. No public property and no public revenue of nor loan of credit by or under the authority of the United States, or any State, Territory, or municipal corporation, shall be appropriated to or made or used for the support of any school, educational, or other institution under the control of any religious, or anti-religious sect, organization, or denomination, or wherein the particular creed or tenets of any religious or anti-religious sect, organization or denomination shall be taught. And no such particular creed or tenets shall be read or taught in any school or institution supported in whole or in part by such revenue or loan of credit; and no such appropriation or loan of credit shall be made to any religious or anti-religious sect, organization, or denomination to promote its interests or tenets. This article shall not be construed to prohibit the reading of the Bible in any school or institution; and it shall not have the effect of impairing rights properly invested.

Section 2. Congress shall have power, by appropriate legislation to provide for the prevention and punishment of violations of this article.[7]

But after the election of 1876 the anti-Catholic agitation subsided, although it did not disappear.

In the controversy over government aid to religious institutions the Archbishop of Baltimore does not seem to have taken a very important part. Typical in this attitude of the Anglo-American members of the Catholic minority, Archbishop Bayley was not aggressive and showed no desire to force recognition of Catholic rights. Although his ill health has been given as the reason for this quiet acquiescence before the dominant Protestantism of the day, he seemed to have been active enough in other matters. He did see to the formation of the Bureau of Catholic Indian Missions, giving it his own character; although he admitted that he was not well informed in Indian matters he would not permit the formation of a formal lobby to deal with the government because of the criticism he thought such action would cause. In the meeting about the financial problems of the North American College in Rome, in answering the Roman questionnaire on public schools, and in setting up new ecclesiastical provinces, which were strictly ecclesiastical matters, he acted as the leader of the Church in America.

[7] *Congressional Record*, August 11, 1876, p. 5453.

Despite his ill health he made the journey to the West to visit the troubled See of Louisville and to confer there with Bishop George McCloskey, went on to St. Louis after conferring with the other archbishops in Cincinnati, and visited his brother in Illinois before returning to Baltimore. Neither did he neglect the regular visitation of the parishes of the Archdiocese, despite the protests of the neighboring bishops who were aware of his physical discomfort. Nevertheless it was quite apparent that his health was seriously damaged and that he seemed unable to avoid catching colds. The symptoms were those of acute nephritis with other complications which he described as "rheumatism." He admitted to other bishops that he needed aid in the administration of the Archdiocese and told Bishop Gibbons that he would ask for him as coadjutor. However, when he wrote to Cardinal Franchi, the Prefect of Propaganda, the Cardinal saw no reason for haste and asked the Archbishop to follow the regular procedure and send in a terna and get the recommendations of other Archbishops. This merely delayed the appointment of Bishop Gibbons. In the meantime the Archbishop's health began to fail very fast, and he decided to go to Vichy in the spring of 1877 on the advice of friends to try the baths. This trip was an error and seemed to hasten his decline. Late in August he returned to America and went into seclusion in Newark where he died on October 3, 1877.

Bishop Gibbons had been named Coadjutor Archbishop with the right of succession before the death and presided at the funeral of Archbishop Bayley. He returned to Richmond to close his episcopate there and left for Baltimore finally on October 19. Because of the illness of Pope Pius IX, the pallium was not actually conferred until February 10, 1878, a few days after the death of the Pope. Archbishop Gibbons, then in his forty-third year, was a native of Baltimore who had been taken to Ireland three years after his birth but had returned with his family to New Orleans in 1853.[8] After deciding to study for the priesthood, he made his studies in the Sulpician seminaries and was ordained by Archbishop Francis P. Kenrick on June 30, 1861, in the Baltimore cathedral. His first assignment was to care for St. Bridget's parish in Baltimore; then the new Archbishop of Baltimore, Martin John Spalding, had made him assistant secretary and attached him to the Cathedral staff. Active as Secretary in the Second Plenary

[8] John Tracy Ellis, *The Life of James Cardinal Gibbons Archbishop of Baltimore, 1834–1921*, 2 vol. (Milwaukee, 1952) is the latest and most complete biography of Cardinal Gibbons and covers much of the history of Catholicism in the nation also.

Council of 1866, Father Gibbons was credited with writing the pastoral for the hierarchy under the direction of the Archbishop. He was made a Bishop and appointed Vicar Apostolic of North Carolina in 1868 and was the youngest Bishop at the Vatican Council in 1869–1870. He was promoted to the See of Richmond in 1872. While he had many interesting and varied experiences both in the missions of North Carolina and in Virginia, he had also developed an interesting manner of preaching and writing. Just before his appointment to Baltimore he completed *The Faith of Our Fathers,* a simple exposition of the Catholic beliefs which became the chief tool of Catholic apologetics in the country for more than a generation.

Archbishop Gibbons was a slender man of moderate height with a small head whose long thin lips and smiling eyes gave him a look of gentleness and understanding. His slimness fulfilled the American notion of a spiritual man, and his gentleness was becoming in a chief pastor. Although the Roman officials persisted in their refusal to make Baltimore a primatial see, so long as Archbishop Gibbons lived the See was primatial in fact if not in name. But, beyond the common essential doctrines, the unity of the American Church, numbering as it did persons of widely differing national origins and traditions, consisted of little more than fidelity to the Holy See and the use of the same Latin rites.

Any effort to gather all the activities of the burgeoning nation into a unified picture at this time was very difficult, and the delineation of the Catholic minority presented even greater difficulties because the Catholics were distributed unevenly about the country, already tending to form an urban Church. The United States in 1877 could be regarded as yet a Protestant country in cultural tradition, even though the nation had just celebrated the centenary of political independence in which religious liberty was an essential glory. There were some sections of the country in which the Catholic American was unknown or if he existed was regarded with patent suspicion. The most important cause of this feeling against Catholics must be described in negative terms, especially in the lack of Catholic lay leadership in civic affairs. Where the Catholic population was found in large numbers in the cities of the eastern seaboard, their prominence was chiefly in politics. Moreover they did not manifest in this rise in political power any dedication to literature or to art, but chiefly a subservience to the Roman Catholic religious organization which to the ordinary American was the enemy of Anglo-American cultural tradition. In Boston, where the Irish had begun to achieve power, there were soon such outstanding Catholic laymen as Patrick Donohoe, John Boyle O'Reilly, Thomas R. Looby, Patrick Collins, Hugh O'Brien, Charles Francis Donnelly, Theodore Metcalf, but these few, respectable though they were, were scarcely noticeable in a community that had its cultural center in Harvard and Yale and among so many families of wealth and tradition that had produced the literature of America for more than two centuries. These leading Catholics had, indeed, been joined by several converts from older American families such as Henry L. Richards, Dr. Horatio Robinson Storer, Dr. Hasket Derby, General Charles P. Stone, Emma Forbes Cary, and others, but the total of Catholic lay leadership failed to change the estimate of Catholicism as the religion of the lower classes and, in one sense, of the uncultured. Another important absence of Catholics in New England was in the financial and industrial world which was rising to dominance over the manufacturing areas of the East, for there were few Catholics with the capital either to join in the expansion after the Civil War or to aid their fellow Catholics in business.

So also in New York, the unsuccessful efforts of Francis Kernan to win the governorship were balanced against John Kelly's rise to the leadership of Tammany and the election of William R. Grace as Mayor in 1880.[9] In business there were such Catholics as the Develin family, Henry Hoguet, Felix Ingoldsby, and Alexander Patton. Among the publishers of Catholic materials there were the Sadliers, the Benzigers, and Lawrence Kehoe. There were other Catholics who achieved minor recognition in the New York society of the time, but, while New York did not present the solid phalanx that Yankee society achieved in New England, the leaders of New York society were of old Protestant families for the most part.

While it was true that the more successful families of the eastern states did not find it convenient to go into the newer states of the West, the lesser families and the younger generations of those older families did take over the leadership of the cities and manufacturing areas of the Middle West. There were some rural colonies in the Middle West possessing a common Catholic settlement, but generally physicians, lawyers, schoolteachers, and the more successful merchants of the Middle West in the first decades after the Civil War were uniformly born in the East or were the first Yankee generation in the Middle West. Because of the less com-

[9] Reverend John Talbot Smith, *The Catholic Church in New York*, 2 vol. (New York, 1905) Chapter XIX, "The People and their Parishes."

pact Yankee society in which they lived, the Catholic farmer and small businessman, and the ambitious children of the Irish immigrants, did have a higher hope of attaining wealth and social position in the Middle West than their contemporaries in the older communities of the East. The fact that the dioceses of the Middle West could build and maintain so many parish schools along with their churches and orphanages indicated a general higher level of accomplishment for the Catholics of the region. There were a few organized Catholic rural colonies in Illinois, Minnesota, Kansas, and Nebraska, but they were always outnumbered by their Protestant neighbors in state politics, even though these Protestant neighbors were divided into a wide variety of religious denominations.

Some of the Catholics, Irish, German, or of other national origins, lost the Faith, partly because of the economic handicap of maintaining the Faith amidst an overwhelming majority that seemed not only of higher culture but also more successful. Sometimes also the fewness of Catholic neighbors led to a gradual drifting away over a generation. There were, indeed, converts in the communities where Catholic social life existed, especially where that life was sustained by a parish school or where in a community, such as Baltimore, conversion was no social handicap.

The Catholic home of the era after the Civil War in the United States was the basic unit of Catholicism. This Catholic home had a remarkable similarity whether the members spoke English with or without a brogue, German, Polish or other Slavic tongue, French, Spanish, or Italian. There were family prayers at meals, frequently a common recitation of the Rosary, and evening prayers. Where a parish school existed, instruction in the principles of the Faith and the preparation for Confession and Communion were not difficult. In families in parishes without schools the instruction came from the remembrances of the parents, with occasional sermons and instructions by visiting or resident missionaries. Catholic books were few. Prayer, especially in time of trouble, was the chief bond of unity. Much of the loyalty to Catholicism was a combination of social and religious loyalty. The Catholic immigrants had come into a country where there was religious liberty, where for the first time citizenship was not attached to external religious observance; this liberty, by eliminating European bonds of unity, served in many instances to heighten the loyalty to the religious as well as the social practices brought from Europe.

Many Irish immigrants who could scarcely be said to practice the principles of their Catholic faith were intensely loyal to the Irish and Catholic group. The same could be said of the members of many other non-English Catholic settlements throughout the country. The problem of the Catholic hierarchy insofar as it was a directorate endeavoring to guide the five or six millions of the Catholics into respectable American life was essentially to keep these people faithful to their religious practices while they acquired the economic means to live comfortably. A second problem of the hierarchy was to provide the social means for their immigrants to elevate themselves into the better society possible in the freedom of the New World. The prime work of the bishops and their clergy was to provide sacramental services for the Catholic multitude. Never oversupplied with priests, the Catholic clergy of the United States, trained mostly in the reformed discipline of St. Sulpice, worked hard and ceaselessly to build churches and orphanages and to give instructions in the Faith.

Some of the new American cathedrals and churches were expensive imitations of European churches, justified in part by the clergymen's desire to emphasize the higher ideals of Roman Catholicism. Other churches were just barnlike structures, used only during the early hours on Sunday. Some were of ugly red brick with senseless towers, and some were decorated with statues that were utterly lacking in artistic value. But the universality of the Sacraments, and the insistence on strict conformity in essential ceremonies, in all sections of the country allowed for little differences in the Catholic services whether the Cathedral was on Fifth Avenue in New York, in the German countryside in Indiana, or in an Irish settlement in Iowa. But to erect a Catholic school alongside the church was costly to the former peasants, who could build churches only by sacrificing a part of their meager earnings.

The conflict in state legislatures and in the national party conventions and the Congress in the 1870s over constitutional amendments against aid to sectarian schools was argued chiefly by politicians, and the chief restraint on such legislation was the threat of a loss of Catholic votes. The more important arguments on Catholic education, however, were carried on in a few Catholic publications and in the public forum by such forceful speakers as Bishops McQuaid and Ireland. The arguments of Catholics on the public school question were not always the same. The basic contention of the theologians was that the state did not have the right to educate the child except when the parent failed to do his duty. This argument had a basic defect in that the argument denied the state the right to educate while trying to impose at the same time an obligation of the state to pay for the education.

This may have been perfectly logical for those trained to believe that the first duty of parents was to provide religious education for their children, but it sounded strange to the ordinary Yankee who had acquired the American Puritan notion of the duty of the state to educate. These American Puritans interpreted the Catholic argument as an attack on the public schools and a desire to force the state to support the Catholic schools. In vain did a few Catholic speakers argue that under existing laws Catholics were forced to pay for two schools in order to have the kind of education they felt was their right. For the Puritan majority, public support of any Catholic institution was wrong. Perhaps this support of a separate system of schools would not have been so unacceptable to Catholics if they had been the more prosperous citizens of the country. Private schools among the wealthier people had always found support. Nevertheless the fact was that the Catholic minority for the most part belonged to the underprivileged of the country. Even in those communities where Catholic parish schools had been erected, this additional expense was a notable handicap, and in many areas of the country the maintenance of separate Catholic academies and colleges had been considered impossible. Many Catholic academies and colleges had been founded throughout the country chiefly by religious communities or by bishops who sought to establish a source of diocesan clergy, but very few of these academies or colleges could sustain themselves from the tuition, even with the contributed services of a religious society. None of these colleges had any endowment, and in some instances the training of the teachers in these colleges amounted to no more than the priestly studies that they had obtained in the seminaries where they had received their only collegiate education. The ambitions of Catholics to improve their situation caused the economics of the Catholic school system to become an increasing problem as did the demands from Rome for more Catholic parish schools. Thus the strain of maintaining Catholic schools and Catholic opposition to the public schools continued to be sources of friction between Catholics and Protestants.

The reaction of the Protestant majority to the growing Catholic minority was again one of deepening alarm. There were two qualities in the Catholic minority that stood out: subservience to the priesthood, and the overwhelming predominance of Irishmen and their descendants in the Catholic hierarchy. A fear of this subservience of Catholics to their clergy had been ingrained in the English Protestant by two centuries of constant repetition of charges of evil priests and descriptions of the foreign idolatrous faith, with its Latin prayers, and its multicolored vestments. The word "transubstantiation" of the old Puritan oaths had probably ceased to have much meaning to most American Protestants, and the word "Mass" was used to describe the Latin rite to which Catholics came every Sunday. The fact that the clergy held the title to all the church property of the Catholics and wielded all official power was also a sign of "priestcraft" to the ordinary American Protestants whose notions of religion, besides the Bible, the hymn, and the sermon, were not very extensive. The feeling of Anglo-American Protestantism about the growing menace of Roman Catholicism was well stated by James Anthony Froude in *The North American Review* in December 1879 under the title "Romanism and the Irish Race in the United States." He said:

The Catholic revival is a fact, and it will serve, among other purposes, to clear our minds on the real meaning of modern self-government. . . . The Catholic Church stands ready with its code of duties and its formulas of faith—formulas which were once co-extensive with Christendom. . . . That the Church has refused to fraternize with the modern spirit is no longer its crime but its credential; and it can be encountered only by spiritual convictions of the same nature as itself which face it on its own ground. . . .[10]

The other quality of American Catholicism—its dominance by the Irish—was not exactly new because, wherever Roman Catholicism had flourished in the English-speaking world since the Reformation, the most faithful group had been the Irish. Most of the clergy had been Irish, and the most aggressive Catholicism had been led by Irish leaders. Not every improvement in American Catholicism in the nineteenth century can be credited to the Irish. The cultural nucleus of American Catholicism had remained the Maryland-Kentucky Anglo-American group, plus other successful Catholics, usually of English background, who had prospered in small groups or individually, notably in some parts of the South and occasionally in the Midwest. Also the Germans in the colonies and settlements in the farming regions of Ohio, Indiana, Illinois, Missouri, and especially Wisconsin regarded themselves as superior to the Irish worker on the canal or the railroad who did not bring with him any of the more artistic traditions which the Germans had known in the Rhineland or along the Danube. Again Froude may be accepted as a hostile but creditable witness to the role of the Irish in American Catholicism:

[10] *North American Review,* CXXIX, 519–536 and CXXX, 31–50. These quotations are from CXXIX, 533–535.

. . . Roman Catholicism, which grew sick and stagnant in power and prosperity, has in Ireland been braced into vigor by calamity. Like the mythological monster, it has been in contact with the hard soil of fact, and has gathered fresh life from it. With an energy infinitely creditable to them, when they reached the New World, the Irish clergy and people set themselves to meet their new circumstances. There was money in plenty. The old six-pence-a-day wages of Ireland was turned into as many shillings, and out of the shillings the Irish boys and girls parted cheerfully with as many as were needed for a faith which was second nature to them. Thousands, perhaps tens of thousands, were lost at first into the huge cities of the enormous continent, but the Church soon overtook its straying sheep. It watched over their marriages: the Irish in America marry wholly among themselves and within their creed. It kept its hold on the children, and furnished them with antidotes to correct the poison of the secular schools. The lapses from the faith, once relatively large, have now wholly ceased, and after thirty years the Roman Catholic body is the largest, strongest, and wealthiest in the Union. Its members are the most perfectly organized, and the most completely obedient to their spiritual chiefs. . . .[11]

Froude was witness to the facts as they appeared to many of English Protestant background. In his assessment of the Irish-American he implicitly brought into the picture the old English prejudice against Roman Catholicism, which prejudice had become a positive faith among the English common people. For the Protestant of English descent in the United States, the notion that England had once been really Roman Catholic was unbelievable, and the essential contradiction between English democracy and Roman Catholicism was unquestionable. As a matter of fact the unfriendly attitude of many Roman and south European Catholics of that day toward English democratic traditions served to confirm this prejudice. The mystery of American Catholicism, however, was the fidelity of the Irish to Catholicism when a lapse from the Faith could have been not only easy but generally profitable.

By 1879 there were hundreds of thousands of Irish in the country, many of whom had long since become Americanized politically. There was also at that time at least one generation of Irish descendants native to the country. The most honored of the American Catholic clergymen bearing Irish names, Cardinal John McCloskey, Archbishop Williams, Archbishop Corrigan, Bishop McQuaid, Archbishop Gibbons, Bishop McNeirny, and many others had been born in the United States. Somehow, because of the close associations of their nationality and their religion, the

[11] *Ibid.*, CXXIX, 522.

American public made little distinction between the Irish by descent and the Irish born. The prejudice against the Irish was generally not shown against the Germans, partially because so many of the German immigrants, especially the most vocal ones, the "Forty-Eighters," were not Catholic. Yet there were also hundreds of thousands of non-Irish Catholic immigrants, particularly in the Middle West. The Catholic of English descent objected to them, too, but the opposition to the German Catholics seems to have been local. The Germans did not usually go into politics and seemed content, most of the time, to have their own parish schools, nor did they try to change the character of the state schools. Later the German parish schools were attacked because of their dedication to a foreign ideology.

Just how this mass of Catholic people, most of whom came from a variety of lands and many of whom were not literate in English, could be formed into a working unity as one Church was a marvel that was not always correctly understood by non-Catholics. Some Catholics also misinterpreted their growth in number. In the first place the growth in number was not actually an increase in the Catholic Church. How many of the immigrants, Irish and non-Irish, left the Church after they reached the American ports cannot be estimated with any accuracy. In nearly every generation there were observers who lamented the losses to the Church of hundreds of thousands and even millions. But while the numbers of those who lapsed may have been greater than in Europe, there was an astonishing practical virility in the faith of those Catholics who remained faithful. Despite their poverty and their lack of education, the Irish and Germans and other groups from Catholic European regions became active members of the Church and gave from their scarcity to building churches, orphanages, hospitals, and schools. In their fidelity a definite factor was their being Catholic because they belonged to a Catholic neighborhood, but very often social advancement could have been a reward for their leaving the Church, so that this fidelity was not merely perfunctory.

Catholicism in nineteenth century America was not the result of the conversion of a people by missionaries as in the conversion of western Europe in the dark ages but of the hurried efforts of the Church organization in the nineteenth century to get priests into the new settlements where the Catholic laity had gone. As a result of this situation, there developed certain characteristics of American Catholicism, not all of them good, which distinguished American Catholicism from that of Europe.

The chief characteristic of American Catholicism was a kind

of unquestioning faith. The ordinary Catholic immigrant and his children were too busy acquiring the essentials of a good living to think much about or to study his faith. He depended upon the priest for his instruction, and later upon the parish schools to take over the task of teaching his children and inculcating the principles of Catholicism. It seldom occurred to him to question the faith which had given him so much consolation in trial. Quite important in his reliance on the priest was the rule of the Church established in the trustee controversy that the church and the school and other church property were to be administered entirely by the clergy, presumably for the preservation and spread of Catholicism. Despite the differences in language there was little difference in the Catholicism that was preached in the churches or taught in the elementary parish schools across the country, it was the elementary doctrines of the penny catechism for the most part. The manner in which the congregations expanded in the cities differed only slightly from the more direct missionary growth on the frontier. In the city when the number of Catholics in a congregation became unwieldy and the funds could be had for construction, the parish was subdivided. In the less populous places, as soon as the number of Catholics in the community could support a priest, the bishop endeavored to send out a missionary who might have to care for more than one congregation at first. The farther west the Church moved, the scarcer normally would be the Catholic population and the more widely scattered would be the mission centers of the Church, except along the far western coast where the prosperity of California after the gold rush, which had its Irish clergy, had begun as it were a countermovement toward the east. There were of course local variations to all these patterns, but a Catholic could hear Mass and receive the Sacraments according to the Roman rite in any Catholic church or chapel.

Sometimes in these pioneer decades the personality of the ruling prelate of a diocese gave the tone to the Catholicism of the area. Archbishop John Williams, much like his predecessor Bishop John Fitzpatrick, was a moderating influence on the Irish Catholics of Boston. He spoke publicly on very few occasions, but was always with his people. He did not insist on building parish schools, and seemed to take for granted that the Irish were to continue in the humbler roles in the community. Archbishop Bedini had complained of this timidity of the Boston Catholics in 1853, and there was little done to change the situation in the subsequent decades. Holy Cross College in Worcester was the exception rather than the rule in this cultural submission. Williams' suffragans, the Bishops in Hartford, Providence, Burlington, and Springfield, were uniformly good priestly men who lived close to their flocks, but none of them gave strong leadership in cultural or social affairs. Undoubtedly the task of elevating the immigrant Catholics of New England amidst one of the most closely knit American societies was very difficult, yet when the Irish of New England began to acquire some property and to advance in education they tended to imitate the society in which they lived. Only in politics did they seem able to gain power, but there, the confusion of nationality, religion, and politics did not always advance Catholicism. In Boston more than almost anywhere else Catholicism in politics meant sheer voting power. In the second half of the nineteenth century New England society manifested toward Irish Catholics probably the most devastating kind of bigotry, which they supported by economic and social discrimination. The political victory of the immigrant in this milieu was shallow because it was bereft of most social gains.

Cardinal McCloskey in the neighboring Province of New York and New Jersey was of the same kind of serene, quiet, spiritual type as Archbishop Williams. There seemed to be no real connection between the victorious Irish politicians of his day and this clerical leader, but there was no notable effort by the Cardinal to disown the Catholic politicians. There were more successful Catholic businessmen in New York than in New England, there was a more outspoken Catholic press, and a more active group of clergymen. Some of these priests who felt free to speak out under the Cardinal were checked by his successor, Archbishop Corrigan. Among the active clergymen in New York there was the first American group of religious priests, the Paulists, among them Fathers Isaac Hecker, Augustine Hewit, and George Deshon, and such noted secular priests as Fathers Edward McGlynn, Richard Burtsell, Thomas J. Ducey, Thomas Preston, and Henry A. Brann. Of McCloskey's suffragans, two were very active. Bishop Michael Corrigan of Newark and Seton Hall, later Archbishop of New York, had been a successful student in Rome whose notions of orthodoxy went more in line with the traditional Catholicism of southern Europe. The other notable suffragan was also a product of Seton Hall. Bishop Bernard McQuaid, an orphan who rose by his talent, was like Corrigan in many of his ideas, but was a more active pastor. Bishop McQuaid lost no opportunity to preach or teach his notions of Catholic life, supported strenuously the building of Catholic schools, and was a forthright administrator of his diocese. His seminary, St. Bernard's in Rochester, became under his planning the outstanding seminary of the country. Defenders of orthodox Catholic principles found in him a militant ally. Bishop Stephen Ryan of Buffalo and Bishop Conroy of Albany were good pastors but not remarkable leaders.

In the Province of Philadelphia, a tradition of Catholicism dating back to the early eighteenth century did not seem to become strong or forceful. The trusteeism and Hogan schisms had been, indeed, blights on the Philadelphia Church for many years. Despite the lack of a strong Catholic educational institution as well as the lack of forceful clerical leadership, Catholicism in the Province of Philadelphia displayed a quality of sturdiness and deep spirituality but also mildness and conservatism. In the western regions of Pennsylvania, the Catholicism of Pittsburgh was that of hard working and fervent faithful, and the Catholics there faced a permeating anti-Catholicism based on active Presbyterianism and later of Methodism. The activity of St. Vincent's Abbey and Seminary in Latrobe supported this work-a-day Catholicism but neither was renowned for the traditional Benedictine liturgical splendor or traditions of study.

In the Ohio Valley the outstanding prelate was the aging Archbishop John Baptist Purcell, whose thirty years of residence in the Middle West had caused his friends occasionally to forget his Irish birth. The story of his long and fruitful episcopate was soon to be tarnished by a tremendous financial failure. The Archbishop and his brother, Father Edward Purcell, had zealously but inexpertly tried to be bankers for many of the faithful and had been ruined in the panic of 1873 and its aftermath. Nearly all the suffragans in the Province were priests of Purcell's choice. The most zealous of them, Bishop Amadeus Rappe in Cleveland, had resigned under a cloud, and his successor Bishop Richard Gilmour, a convert of Scottish background, was a stern ruler. Bishop Sylvester Rosecrans was nearing the end of an undistinguished career. In Detroit, in the absence of Bishop Frederick Résé in Germany, Bishop Caspar Borgess, an active missionary who had succeeded Bishop Peter Paul Lefevere as administrator, worked hard with uneven success to govern a group of priests and laymen of various national origins. In Marquette, Bishop Frederic Baraga, the saintly missionary, was succeeded by zealous Bishop Ignatius Mrak and later by Bishop John Vertin. In Indiana Bishop Joseph Dwenger, C.Pp.S., of Fort Wayne sought priests from Europe to attend the German farmers and Irish railroad workers who had come into his diocese, and Bishop Francis Chatard had moved his see from Vincennes to Indianapolis in an effort to raise the social position of his flock. George William McCloskey of Louisville had difficulty handling the administrative problems of this oldest center of frontier Catholicism. Farther west, as Coadjutor of Bishop Grace in St. Paul, John Ireland was already recognized as an outstanding speaker and leader, and in Wisconsin the aging Archbishop Martin Henni was being replaced by the younger German Bishops Michael Heiss and F. X. Krautbauer. The Benedictine Bishops Rupert Seidenbush and Martin Marty, combined work with the Indians with attendance on the German immigrants. In the Province of St. Louis, Peter Richard Kenrick continued as the chief prelate. His suffragans in Alton, Chicago, Dubuque, Nashville, Leavenworth, St. Joseph, Missouri, and the Vicariate of Nebraska were missionary bishops with zeal, but they were not forceful leaders with the exception of Bishop James O'Connor in Nebraska. In the Province of Santa Fé was the good missionary Archbishop John Lamy, and Bishops John Salpointe in Arizona and Joseph P. Machebeuf in Colorado. On the west coast Archbishop Joseph Alemany of San Francisco, Bishop Eugene O'Connell of Grass Valley, and Bishop Francis Mora of Monterey were poorly prepared for the vast changes brought about by the discovery of gold and the influx of so many strangers.

In setting up so many dioceses and vicariates apostolic and forming them into provinces, the archbishops under their Roman supervisors had given to the Catholic Church in the United States a semblance of the organization of their European contemporaries, but most of the European supervisors and some of the European-born bishops of the United States did not really understand what had taken place in the Catholic Church in the United States. This had been quite clear in the brief archiepiscopate of Archbishop James Bayley. At the meeting of the Archbishops and Bishops in Cincinnati in April and May 1874, the prelates had discussed several problems and proposed some solutions. However, the chief prelate, Archbishop Bayley, was not a forceful leader, and his subsequent ill health prevented his solving the major problems. While Rome did agree to the new provinces and set up the requested archiepiscopal sees, this concession was rather the acceptance of the fact, after some obvious failures, that the Americans knew more about the geography of the country than did the Roman prelates who had scarcely been out of Italy. On the school question, the rejection of the milder opinions of the archbishops and bishops about the nature of the public schools manifested in the Instruction of 1875 merely added new and severe handicaps to the solution of a peculiarly American problem and sowed the seeds of many bitter controversies in the subsequent decades. But the prelates discussed another question that appears regularly in the extant correspondence of the bishops of the day and of decades before and after the 1874 meeting. The fact that the Church in the United States was considered a missionary organization meant that permanent relations between the priests and the bishops had not been established and gave the bishops arbitrary powers in the assignment and the removal of their priests.

The problem had been brought forward in the first decades of the century by Archbishops Leonard Neale and Ambrose Maréchal in their rejection of the right of patronage claimed by the trustees of Norfolk and Philadelphia. Both prelates pointed out that there could not be any right of patronage because the conditions for a true parish or benefice were not established in these congregations. To have a real parish or benefice, there must be definite limits, a sure income, and permanence of title. Basically according to Church law, since the United States was considered a missionary country and the priests were ordained under the title of the mission, they, therefore, were removable at the will of the Bishop. While some of the Councils of Baltimore had suggested that definite limits be established for parish responsibility, that one priest be named pastor, and that there be a definite income attached to the rectorship of the parishes in the more populous centers, these circumstances did not change the fact that the clergy were ordained under the missionary title and could be moved at the will of the Bishop. This was a necessary condition in the early decades of the Church in this country as in all missionary countries. Nevertheless, as the Catholic population increased, some priests achieved recognition among the people to whom they were assigned, and the older priests naturally resented their own complete dependence on the will of the Bishop.

Most of the bishops knew that something was needed to give greater security to the more important priests in a diocese, but most of them were unwilling to give up their right to move the priest when they so desired. With the opening of the North American College in Rome and the return of American priests after study in Roman colleges, appeals began to go more frequently to Rome against the arbitrary power of the American bishops. The American civil courts had in general recognized the rights of bishops to rule their property and their clergy according to the laws of the Church. Further, there was no provision in

Canon Law whereby a priest could appeal to another bishop against his own superior, although under various excuses such appeals were being made. Shortly after the Second Plenary Council a movement was begun among some American priests to secure some redress from this situation. The priests found a voice, for a while, in the columns of *The Freeman's Journal* before the Vatican Council. One of the agitators was a priest of the diocese of Cleveland, Father Eugene O'Callaghan, who wrote under the name of "Jus." The major handicap of such agitators was that they had no protection from arbitrary punishment by their bishop. Finally in an Instruction[12] of 1878 the Sacred Congregation of the Propaganda ordered the American bishops to set up a commission of priests of the diocese who were to hear the cases of priests who, for a cause, had been removed by the bishop from their churches when the priest objected to the removal. Since the results of such a hearing were to be committed to written record, there was some semblance of a regular trial. However, the commissioners were to be chosen in a diocesan synod or temporarily by the Bishop, and, in the opinion of some, the Instruction was not a real solution to the problem. The Instruction caused considerable talk among American clergymen, and was criticized by some of the bishops, especially Bishop McQuaid in letters to Rome.

The two Instructions on the schools and on clerical rights were the most important actions taken by Rome toward the American Church since the condemnation of trusteeism in 1822. They were the preliminaries to a continued interest of Rome in the Church in the United States that would lead eventually to the Third Plenary Council.

There is also in this picture something that caused confusion to the casual observer, and that was the general subservience of the Catholic laymen to the priest and the priest to the bishop. Some hostile critics thought this subservience to the clergy was a manifestation of peasant mentality which would disappear when the immigrant really enjoyed American freedom, and the persistence of the loyalty even generations after the immigrant had arrived aroused further charges of superstition and ignorance, which were not allayed in any way by the failure of the peasants to produce civic and cultural leaders in proportion to their numbers.

The fact that the public schools of the country were forced by law to exclude the teaching of religion had brought about attempts in many parts of the country to have Catholic parish

[12] This Instruction was published in *The Pastor* (April 1883) I, 170–178.

schools. The Catholic parish school was an added financial burden that called for the aid of religious teachers and for ability to pay the additional funds, but those helps did not exist everywhere. Beyond the elementary school, many communities of religious women had established academies for girls, and priests, secular and religious, had established colleges for young men. Far too many of these colleges, already numbering seventy-five by 1875, did not have the means or the teachers to survive but their efforts were an indication of the desire of the Catholic immigrant to rise socially and culturally.

There were some Catholic writers, such as Mary Sadlier, Anna Hanson Dorsey, J. Vincent Huntington, but they did not belong to the mainstream of American literature.[13] The best of Catholic writing was to be found in *Brownson's Review, The American Catholic Quarterly Review, The Catholic World,* and the *Ave Maria.* There were many Catholic weekly newspapers, the most noted of which were *The Pilot* of Boston, *The Freeman's Journal* of New York and *The Catholic Telegraph* of Cincinnati. In the Catholic press there was much discussion of the need for a Catholic university to direct these efforts to create an American Catholic culture.

In the longer-settled dioceses of the eastern part of the country the bishops were not inclined to ask any Roman interference to solve their problems. When Archbishop Gibbons visited in Rome and on the occasion of visits of other prelates to Rome after that, the Roman authorities had suggested that there should be a new Plenary Council in which the current problems might be solved. Archbishop Gibbons consulted with Cardinal McCloskey, Archbishop Williams, and Archbishop Corrigan, and they agreed with him that such a Council should not be held for some years. In Rome, itself, there is available very little documentary material to explain why Rome urged the Council. When Bishop McQuaid returned from Rome in 1879 he was quoted as saying, "There in Rome are high ecclesiastics not of our nationality, who are anxious to know about America, its churches, schools and institutions. They want to know of our young, growing, and already grand Church of America."[14] Since the unpleasant experiences of Archbishop Bedini in 1853, the Roman authorities had not pushed

[13] John O'Kane Murray, *A Popular History of the Church in the United States* (first published in New York, 1876) contains a contemporary evaluation of the Catholic literary effort.

[14] *Freeman's Journal and Catholic Register,* May 10, 1879.

any plans to establish an apostolic delegate or nuncio in the United States, although Archbishop Gibbons thought it necessary to tell the Roman authorities during his European trip in 1880 that there was still no need for such a delegate. Nevertheless some prelates had suggested that the American bishops should have some representative in Rome who could be a spokesman for the Church in the United States. As matters stood, the only American of even the rank of Monsignor in Rome was Monsignor Louis Hostelot, the rector of the North American College. One American correspondent complained because there was no American prelate there to whom appeals could be made for special favors for pilgrims. Nevertheless it is quite clear that some American bishops were writing complaints to Rome.[15] The German bishops of the Milwaukee Province had expressed their opinion to Archbishop Gibbons that they were in favor of a new Council, and some other western bishops had sent to Rome their approval of the venture.

Judging from the manner in which the Roman officials acted, however, it is quite apparent that the chief movement for holding the Third Plenary Council originated in Rome. Stated briefly the Roman officials had been troubled by the frequent appeals of American clergy to Rome against their bishops, and by other reports from the country, and felt that the time had come for the enforcement of full Roman discipline on the American Church. It was significant that this was similar to the reason advanced by Archbishop Martin J. Spalding for holding the Second Plenary Council, although Spalding's interest seemed to have been more American, as he wanted to draw up not only a brief statement of Catholic doctrine for America but also a set of rules suitable to the American scene. On May 22, 1883, Cardinal Simeoni sent a letter to Gibbons and to most of the other archbishops and to some bishops of those provinces of the United States inviting them to Rome in November 1883 for a series of conferences to prepare the agenda for a new Plenary Council of the Church in the United States. The archbishops and bishops invited to Rome met first in September at the residence of Archbishop Gibbons to discuss their plans. They took as their canonical advisor, Doctor James Corcoran of St. Charles Seminary, Philadelphia.[16] When the prelates arrived in Rome they found prepared for them a series of thirteen proposals which the Roman authorities sug-

[15] Ellis, *Gibbons,* note 8 above, I, 204–208.
[16] *Ibid.,* 203–257 is the best account of the Third Plenary Council.

gested be made into the decrees of the Council. The meetings were held under the supervision of the Sacred Congregation of Propaganda and were presided over by Cardinal Simeoni, the Prefect, with Cardinal Franzelin, Cardinal Ludovico Jacobini, Archbishop Domenico Jacobini, the secretary of the Congregation, and Bishop Luigi Sepiacci, O.S.A., a consultor, in attendance. It was rumored that Bishop Sepiacci would be sent as Apostolic Delegate to preside over the Council, but when the American prelates objected Archbishop Gibbons was named Delegate to preside. Cardinal McCloskey was not appointed because of his health.

At the first session on November 13, the Cardinal Prefect said that Pope Leo was pleased with the decrees of the Second Plenary Council but thought the decrees were not sufficient and for that reason he desired the new Council. In the discussion that followed, probably with the consent of the other prelates, Archbishop Gibbons took the lead in expressing American objections to certain proposed decrees, although Archbishops Seghers and Corrigan and Bishop O'Hara also asked frequent questions. The matters prepared for the consideration of the prelates covered chiefly the education of the clergy, especially the erection of seminaries and vacation villas for seminaries, the establishment of cathedral chapters and irremovable rectorships, the regulation of episcopal visitations, the organization of chanceries and ecclesiastical courts for the clergy, the regulation of clerical garb, the setting up of rules on Catholic participation in non-Catholic organizations, the provision of Catholic education according to the Instruction of 1875, the care of Italian immigrants, and the provision for Indian and Negro missions. The American prelates were most vocal against the establishment of cathedral chapters and the establishment of irremovable rectorships. The singling out of Italian immigration for special mention was a rather bleak admission of the lack of balanced information by the members of the curia who had prepared the topics. Italian immigrants may have been neglected, but their number was as yet a small item in the problems compared to the Irish and the Germans in the Church in the United States. Not all the suggestions were acceptable to the American prelates. They succeeded in limiting the proposals about seminaries, particularly about the provision of villas for seminarians in the summer. They also prevented the requirement of cathedral chapters and preserved the growing American custom of having episcopal consultors. Nevertheless the program for the Council was imposed from Rome. With Archbishop Gibbons as the presiding bishop instead of an Italian prelate or the ailing Cardinal McCloskey, the guidelines were set for the Third Plenary Council to be called for the next year.

Archbishop Gibbons had played a very important part in the meetings in Rome, speaking frequently in the name of the other American prelates. In the closing conference on December 10 he thanked the Roman prelates in the name of his confreres. Since he did not return immediately, he was appointed by Pope Leo to officiate at the St. Mary Major Basilica on Christmas. Undoubtedly he conferred during his stay in Rome with the Roman officials about matters proposed for the Council. On January 4, 1884, the Pope addressed a letter to him summoning the American hierarchy to a plenary council to be held in November of that year and naming him as the Apostolic Delegate to preside because Cardinal McCloskey's health would prevent him from performing that function. The Archbishop wandered leisurely through Europe and reached Baltimore on March 13, and on March 19 he sent out the summons for the Council to meet in Baltimore beginning November 9.

While the revised proposals drawn up after the Roman conferences were made available to the hierarchy, there was further work required to get these matters into schematic form for the Council. Archbishop Gibbons invited a theologian from each province to meet with him in Baltimore on August 16. He further began to draw up the assignments of preachers for the public sessions of the Council and to invite those others who had a reason for attending. To allow for new ideas on the problems prepared for the Council, the Archbishop assigned a chapter to each province for study before the meeting of the theologians and also invited suggestions for new matters. He appointed also the Committee on New Matters consisting of the Archbishops Williams of Boston, Heiss of Milwaukee, and Feehan of Chicago. A committee on the preparation of a catechism was also appointed. It was headed by the Archbishop of San Francisco and included Bishops Stephen Ryan, Dwenger, Spalding, Kain, and Janssen. Also appointed to compose the letter to the Holy Father was the Delegate himself. Archbishop Corrigan headed the committee to prepare the pastoral for the clergy and people. The Archbishop was aided by Bishops O'Farrell and Keane. The committee to prepare the letter to the Society of the Propagation of the Faith consisted of Archbishop Seghers and Bishop Moore. The examination of the other topics for the Council was assigned to committees consisting of an archbishop as chairman with assisting bishops, a notary, and a group of theologians. There were twelve of these committees. In their reports on the topics assigned to them, some of the archbishops suggested minor changes, but for the most part the change did not modify extensively the proposals agreed upon in the Roman sessions, and the schemata for the Council were in readiness before the prelates came to Baltimore. The first private meeting was held on November 6 in the Archbishop's residence and consisted of the archbishops. The second, held in St. Mary's Seminary on November 7, consisted of the archbishops and bishops, and in it all the preliminary steps and the rules for the assembly were announced and approved. Among these decisions were the approval of the right of coadjutors to vote and the right of bishops-elect to full power in the council. The committees previously appointed were also listed and approved, the manner in which the sessions would be conducted, the assignment of the public sermons, and certain special tasks were also approved. On Saturday, November 8, there was a preliminary meeting in the Cathedral of all members of the Council in which the matters approved by the bishops the previous day were announced and the pledge of silence was imposed. Then the Archbishop announced formally that the first session would take place the next day.

The newspapers estimated that when the procession to the Cathedral began at nine-thirty the next morning there were approximately 30,000 people crowding the streets around the Cathedral. The members of the procession sang the *Veni Creator,* the *Ave Maris Stella,* and Psalms 80, 83, and 86. The celebrant of the Mass was the venerable Archbishop Peter Richard Kenrick with Archbishop Gibbons presiding on the throne. The sermon on "The Councils of the Church" was preached by Archbishop Patrick Ryan. The decree opening the Council was then read, followed by the roll of members of the Council. There were fourteen archbishops, fifty-eight bishops and one abbot, Isidore Robot as Prefect Apostolic, one administrator, and three procurators of dioceses, one archabbot, and six abbots, seven domestic prelates, and three very reverend monsignors, thirty-one superiors of religious communities, eleven superiors of major seminaries, and eighty-eight theologians. Also mentioned were the seven prelates who were absent and seven who were invited but could not come, and Bishop Peter Maria Osouf of Japan who was present. The officials of the Council were announced: Bishops Kain and Janssen as Promotors; Loughlin, De Goesbriand, McCloskey, and Fink were made judges of excuses and complaints. The other minor officers of the Council were also announced. The Secretary then read the profession of faith and the members made their profession of faith with the Delegate. There were thirty-one private and five public sessions—the last on December 7.

The discussions in the Council were apparently quite frank and, while all the bishops were not fully satisfied, there was general agreement on the matters contained in the published decrees. There were some decrees that were formulated because they were in the matter submitted by the Roman prelates to the Council, although they had no special urgency. Of all the matters presented to the Council the most important were education, both of the clergy and of the faithful, methods of nominating candidates for bishoprics, and the establishment in the dioceses of a certain number of irremovable rectors. Since the general purpose of the Council was to bring the American Church under standard canon law practices, special American problems were not brought up. The question of secret societies was left to a committee of archbishops. The decrees in final form were divided into eleven titles preceded by one confirming the decrees of the Second Plenary Council. In all there were 310 paragraphs in the decrees. There were some minor modifications of the decrees made in Rome before they were finally approved.

The first title affirmed that the decrees of the Second Plenary Council remained in force except where modified by the Third. The first regular title was an acceptance of the decrees of the Councils of the Vatican and Trent. The second title on ecclesiastical persons, set up rules on *ad limina* visits to Rome, the frequency of the episcopal visitations of dioceses, the choice of consultors, and the manner of nominating bishops.

Title three treated of public worship including bination on Sunday, the feasts and fasts, and the music in the church and the observance of Sundays. Title four dealt with the Sacraments, with special rules about the baptism of converts and about mixed marriages. Title five concerned the education of the clergy, opening with a passage from a letter of Pope Pius IX comparing the clergy to leaders of an army. The decrees called for training of seminarians from the early years and suggested that there be a minor seminary in every diocese, while insisting that the teachers be of the highest quality. There was to be set up in the country a central seminary which would become the center of a Catholic university. Nevertheless the bishops were to continue to send qualified students to the American Colleges in Rome, Louvain, and Innsbruck.

In title six, on the education of Catholic youth, the chief provision required that there be attached to all existing churches a parochial school within two years after the promulgation of these decrees. The pastor who failed to build this school would merit removal, and parishes which failed to supply the means for erecting such a school were to be reprimanded by the Bishop and induced to comply. All Catholic parents were required to send their children to these schools unless they could take care of this duty of Catholic education in their homes or in other schools. The decree, while quoting the Instruction of 1875 and a letter of Pope Leo to the French Bishops of February 8, 1884, noted that, while the need of Catholic education was clear, some Catholic parents would have to send their children to public schools. Such parents were to see that the proximate danger of perversion be made remote. But the decree warned bishops and pastors against being too severe with the parents when the children attended public schools and especially against being too severe with these children.

Title seven on Christian doctrine stressed the need for preaching, the provision and the study of the catechism, and the preparation of books of prayers especially those prayers from the missal and breviary. The books of prayers were to be carefully examined by the proper authority. The title included a plea for Catholic books and for a Catholic press, urging that there be at least one newspaper for each province. The best solution would be a newspaper under Catholic auspices which would be a regular newspaper but which could on occasion defend the Catholic viewpoint.

Title eight on immigrants departed from the proposal of the Roman suggestion about Italians to speak particularly about the Irish and Germans and suggested that societies, such as the St. Raphael Society, be established to care for immigrants at the ports of entry. The education of Negroes was especially urged, and, where necessary, separate schools and churches were to be erected for them. The decrees urged the bishops to allow zealous priests to devote themselves to the Negroes, who were for the most part not members of the Church. The care of the Indians was also specially recommended. A collection was decreed to be taken up for the Indians and Negroes in all dioceses on the first Sunday of Lent. In this title the Council discussed societies also, repeating the condemnation of secret societies, but asked that no prohibition against doubtful societies be made without consulting the committee to be appointed among the archbishops for that purpose.

Title nine discussed the administration of the temporal goods of the Church, distinguishing the rules of bishops, priests, and laymen. In the regulations about collecting funds, the collection of money at the doors of the church was forbidden. Sunday picnics and excursions to raise money were forbidden, and, where circumstances allowed exceptions, wines and liquors were not to be permitted at picnics and excursions.

Title ten set up the rules for ecclesiastical trials, called for the erection of curias, and set up rules in line with recent Roman decrees for trying delinquent clergy and for judging efforts to obtain release from the marriage bond. Title eleven treated of Christian burial, the care of Catholic cemeteries, and of the arrangements to be made in the burial of Catholics in non-Catholic cemeteries. Title twelve insisted that these decrees were in force once they were promulgated by the Apostolic Delegate but that the provinces and dioceses also should promulgate them in their own territory. Because of some departures in the decrees from what had been prepared in Rome, the final decrees were not approved until 1885.[17]

The decrees, which were never published in translation, were directed to the clergy of the country. The decrees that had most direct effect on the Church in the United States were those on parochial schools, the decision to establish a Catholic university, and the provisions for curial offices and ecclesiastical trials. The Pastoral was written for the American public and was probably read by many people. The chairman of the committee that composed it was Archbishop Corrigan.

The Pastoral opened with a statement on the reasons that the decrees of the Second Plenary Council should be revised, not the least being that the Pope had ordered the hierarchy to revise them. Since that Council there had been an Ecumenical Council in which papal infallibility had been proclaimed. While giving their adherence to the decisions of that Council, the Bishops of the Council thought it proper to repeat their own rejection of the two great heresies of the day: rationalism, which had crept into American non-Catholic institutions of learning, and materialism, arising from the comfort and luxury of modern progress. Further, while giving their adherence to the Vatican Council, the Bishops rejected any charge that there was any conflict between the doctrine of infallibility and the power of the civil state. "We repudiate with equal earnestness the assertion that we need to lay aside any of our devotedness to Our Church to be true Americans, and the insinuation that we need to abate any of our love for our country's principles and institutions, to be faithful

---

[17] *Acta et Decreta Concilii Baltimorensis Tertii* (Baltimore, 1886).

Catholics. . . . No less illogical would be the notion, that there is aught in the free spirit of our American institutions, incompatible with perfect docility to the Church of Christ."[18]

The Pastoral then turned to the subject matters of the conciliar decrees such as those on clerical education and the rights of the clergy, discussing these matters insofar as they affected the laity. The Pastoral insisted on the need for Christian education. "No parish," it said, "is complete till it has schools adequate to the needs of its children, and the pastor and people of such a parish should feel that they have not accomplished their entire duty until the want is supplied."[19] Much space in the Pastoral was given to the Christian home, the sacredness of marriage, the need for good reading, especially of the Sacred Scriptures and of Catholic publications. The Pastoral gave special attention to the proper observance of the Sunday and warned against profanations by too great indulgence in amusements and in the selling and drinking of liquors. There was a special passage urging the workers to take home their wages on Saturday night for the benefit of their families. The faithful were urged to avoid forbidden societies and to give their attention to Catholic societies, especially the "Catholic Young Men's National Union" and associations of Catholic workingmen. Finally the Pastoral urged support of the home and foreign missions.

The Pastoral was dated December 7, 1884, and signed by the Archbishop as Apostolic Delegate in the name of all the Fathers of the Council. It was a document for the occasion, and spoke of those things on which the hierarchy were particularly united. But, while the decrees and the Pastoral were what the Roman authorities desired, for the most part there were many problems very close to the assembled bishops that were not really touched which would become the basis of sharp controversy within a few years after the Council.

[18] *Ibid.*, LXXV.
[19] *Ibid.*, LXXXVI.

CHAPTER TEN

An Era of Catholic
Growth 1884-1895

THERE OCCURRED, JUST WHEN THE THIRD
Plenary Council was about to open, an incident that was given far
greater importance than it deserved. In the presidential campaign
between James G. Blaine and Grover Cleveland, Cleveland had
been regarded as less than friendly to Catholics. James G. Blaine,
who, although born of a Catholic mother, was not a Catholic, had
introduced the proposed Constitutional Amendment against aid
to denominational institutions in 1876. The campaign of 1884
had been conducted on a low plane and Catholics had not gained
friends in either party. Just a few days before the election Blaine
permitted in a public meeting the Reverend Dr. Samuel Burchard
to call unchallenged the Democratic Party the party of "Rum,
Romanism, and Rebellion." Since the Democrats carried the State
of New York by scarcely 2,000 votes, those who wished credited
the decision to the resentment of the Irish Catholics to this charge.
The cause of the defeat remains uncertain but these events portray
the political atmosphere surrounding the Church in this country when the bishops assembled for the Third Plenary Council.[1]
But the bishops did not gather to consider problems in American
politics, and the election campaign had no effect on their delib-

---

[1] Florence E. Gibson, *The Attitude of the New York Irish Toward State
and National Affairs 1848–1892* (New York, 1951) pp. 390–391.

erations. There were other problems facing the growing Catholic minority.

Somehow, although the Third Plenary Council was in itself a period of intense activity for the Catholic hierarchy in America, the work of the Council seems to have had very little direct effect on American Catholicism. It is true that the decrees of the Council became law once they were approved by Rome, and anything contrary to them no longer had the force of tradition. Also because the decrees were in essence dictated from Rome without a deep consideration of American conditions, they did not create any startling changes in the Church in America. Nevertheless the period of the Council can be considered a kind of watershed or dividing line in the history of the Church in the United States.

The most important fact of the Council was the formal unity of the hierarchy into a working body for a few weeks. Of the seventy-two prelates in the Council only about two dozen were American born, although some others had lived in the country from childhood. The largest group of the foreign-born were from Ireland, some of whom had become militantly American. But there were also nine Germans, four Belgians, seven Frenchmen, two Spaniards, and one each from Scotland, Holland, Switzerland, and Slavonia. Their education had been obtained in many countries and circumstances. They had unity in the essential matters of the Faith, but wide divergencies in matters of custom and culture. Since no one knew outside what was said in the Council the chief effects of the Council came from the externals of the Council.

In connection with the Council there was a series of public sermons by the prelates. Under these circumstances this was one of the finest series of sermons ever offered to an American Catholic audience.[2] Some titles such as those on the Councils and the Mass did not allow for much personal opinion. Three of these sermons had special meaning in any effort to measure the position of the Catholic minority at this critical era, and they were given by persons who were very active in the formation of the growing Church in the United States.

Bishop McQuaid[3] of Rochester spoke on "The Catholic Church

[2] The sermons were published in *The Memorial Volume, A History of the Third Plenary Council of Baltimore* (Baltimore, 1885).

[3] Frederick J. Zwierlein, *The Life and Letters of Bishop McQuaid*, 3 vol. (Rochester, 1925–1927) is the best life of McQuaid and is good for the conservative side of most of the controversies. Zwierlein, *Letters of Archbishop Corrigan to Bishop McQuaid and Allied Documents* (Rochester, 1946) is supplemental.

in the United States." He quoted the statistics from the *Catholic Directory,* including the estimate of a Catholic population of 6,623,176, which he said was inadequate since he felt that there were at least eight millions. But even the correct figures, he maintained, did not give credit to the amount of work performed and the "sacrifices of the poor people who furnished the money, often drawing out of purses all but empty." He continued:

. . . If non-Catholic America can with just pride call attention to its colleges and universities, the noblest of modern times in wealth of endowments, the gifts to learning of its millionaire friends and patrons, so can Catholic America bespeak consideration for what zeal, devotion and the generosity of the poor have brought into existence. . . .

But he admitted losses:

. . . We frankly admit that we have not always held our own. But we in America do not take reproof from our brethren in Europe with amiability and good grace. Many of the Christians they have turned out on our shores have not been models of piety and holiness; nor does the light of faith burn brightly in their souls. . . . We cannot just ask: Are there no losses to the Church on the other side of the ocean? Corrupted in faith and morals before they leave home they bring corruption with them.

Finally McQuaid found the chief glory of American Catholicism in the Catholic school raised up amidst hardship.

. . . Without further argument or dispute, but, nevertheless, grieving and groaning under the wrong put upon us by process of law and the vote of the majority, Catholics gathered their children into their own schools, that therein they might breathe a Catholic atmosphere while acquiring secular knowledge. Without these schools, in a few generations our magnificent cathedrals and churches would remain as samples of monumental folly—of the unwisdom of a capitalist who consumes his fortune year by year without putting it out at interest or allowing it to increase. The Church has lost more in the past from the want of Catholic schools than from any other cause named by me this evening. The 2,500 schools, with a half million of scholars, which now bless our country, tell Catholics and non-Catholics that the question of religious education is settled, so far as we are concerned. The good work so well advanced will not halt until all over the land the children of the Church are sheltered under her protecting care. . . .

The short stocky Irish-American Bishop with the strong chin and strong voice represented the true conservative clergy in the country. He expressed not a timid fear of the majority; he was a leader who insisted on aggressive Catholicism that was at the same time uncompromising.

There was another speaker whose life at this time seemed to be deeply involved in one important national undertaking—the establishment of a Catholic university. Bishop John Lancaster Spalding,[4] a rather tall slender bishop of English ancestry, with his erect carriage, high forehead, and thoughtful mien, wrote and thought far ahead of most of his episcopal confreres on the need of intellectual leadership among the hundreds of thousands whom Bishop McQuaid was shepherding into the parochial schools. His topic was "University Education." He said he had been asked to speak of priestly higher education. But, since the higher education of a priest meant to him higher education itself, he devoted his sermon to an appeal for a Catholic university, which was his special interest. He seemed at first impelled to prove the need for higher culture. He admitted that intellectual culture could not replace religion, but he added: "No excellence, as I conceive, of whatever kind, is rejected by Catholic teaching, and the perfection of the mind is not less divine than the perfection of the heart." He continued that Catholicism must either hold that learning is a hindrance to teaching religious truths or insist that mental culture is most helpful. Spalding's long sentences with their ponderous arguments were not easy to grasp but as they rolled along they built up a strong argument for the intellectual formation of Catholic priests.

In whatsoever direction we turn our thoughts, arguments rush in to show the pressing need for us of a centre of life and light such as a Catholic university would be. Without this we can have no hope of entering as a determining force into the living controversies of the age; without this it must be an accident if we are represented at all in the literature of our country; without this we shall lack a point of union to gather up, harmonize and intensify our scattered forces; without this our bishops must remain separated and continue to work in random ways; without this the noblest souls look in vain for something larger and broader than a local charity to make appeal to their generous hearts; without this we shall be able to offer but feeble resistance to the false theories and systems of education which deny to the Church a place in the school; without this the sons of wealthy Catholics will, in increasing numbers, be sent to institutions where their faith is undermined; without this we shall vainly hope for such treatment of religious questions and their relations to the issues and needs of the day, as shall arrest public attention and induce Catholics themselves to

[4] The most recent biography of Bishop Spalding is David Francis Sweeney, O.F.M., *The Life of John Lancaster Spalding, First Bishop of Peoria, 1840–1916* (New York, 1965).

take at least some little public notice of the writings of Catholics; without this in struggles for reform and contests for rights we shall lack the wisdom of best counsel and the courage which skillful leaders inspire. . . .

Ah! surely as to whether an American Catholic university is desirable there cannot be two opinions among enlightened men. . . .

These speeches of McQuaid and of Spalding outlined the chief positive work of Catholicism in the United States during the next two generations. But these proposals were to be handicapped, as they were already being hindered, by the new influx of peasant Catholic workers from Europe who would not only increase the burden to the breaking point but would create a more dangerous problem by resisting the education proper to the new country into which they had come.

Already countermovements defending foreign nationalities were in evidence, and it was in the face of such problems that the presiding Archbishop had chosen one of his favorite speakers, Bishop John Ireland,[5] to speak on "The Church—The Support of Just Government." Bishop Ireland's first words indicated his task. "I do not, I think, mistake the feelings of many of my fellow-countrymen in presence of the Plenary Council now holding its sessions in Baltimore, when I ascribe to them the desire that a statement be made as to the bearings of the Catholic Church in her teachings and her practical acting towards civil society, and notably, perhaps, towards the form of government for society which obtains in the United States of America. . . ." Bishop Ireland was a naturalized citizen who had become deeply enamored of his new fatherland. He continued:

. . . I speak beneath this cathedral dome not less as an American citizen than as a Catholic bishop. The Church is the mother of my faith, the guardian of my hopes for eternity: America is my country, the protectress of my liberty and of my fortunes on earth. I could not utter one syllable that would belie, however remotely, either Church or republic, and when I assert, as I now solemnly do, that the principles of the former are in thorough harmony with the interest of the latter, I feel in the depths of my heart that I speak the truth.

Bishop Ireland called anarchy and despotism the Scylla and Charybdis of the civil community—communism or Caesarism. Against the teachings of Hobbes and Rousseau, he pointed to doctrines printed in the encyclicals of Pope Leo XIII of 1879

---

[5] The only biography at present of Ireland is James H. Moynihan, *The Life of Archbishop John Ireland* (New York, 1953).

against socialism and of 1884 against naturalism. He called on Catholic doctrine to bring about a true union between liberty and authority. Above all he rejected the charge that the Catholic Church was the enemy of liberty. Pope Leo had said in his encyclical of 1881 that nations can choose for themselves the "sort of government which befits their temper or accords with the traditions and customs of their race." But Bishop Ireland added, "The choice once made, the conditions of government once traced, the people cannot at will, through mere whim or fancy, dethrone their rulers or revoke their constitutions. . . ." The bishop then turned to Saint Thomas Aquinas and defined the nature of law and the relation of human law to the divine law. He added: "Liberty we take to be the alliance of special protection and individual rights with as little curtailment of the latter as the case may permit. The Catholic definition of law is the consecration of this alliance."

Ireland continued to point out the meaning of true liberty and to indicate the kinds of tyranny that can be imposed in the name of liberty. He further indicated that some have claimed that the Catholic Church interferes with the duty of citizenship. In answer he said: "The Church simply proclaims the principles of justice and of morality which are binding upon men, whether as individuals or as communities." He reviewed the Church in its passage through the centuries and as it existed at the time in other parts of the world. He admitted that Catholics at all times and everywhere had not his love and admiration for the republican form of government. But he left no doubt concerning his own feelings about the relations between Catholicism and the government of the United States:

. . . To Americans, then, who love the republic, I fearlessly say, your hope is in the Catholic Church, because she is the mighty power today to resist unbelief and vice. Do you not see that outside of the Catholic Church the most important doctrines of Christianity are melting away, and that a moral chaos is threatening, most of vital virtues said to be no longer of significance, and the fount of all social life, the family, breaking up under the pressure of violent passion? The most valued aids to the republic from the Church are not her direct enunciations of liberty, but her powerful labors in the cause of religion, of purity, of honesty, of all the heavenly virtues that build up the Christian man and the Christian family.

Republic of America, receive from me the tribute of my love and of my loyalty. I am proud to do thee homage, and I pray from my heart that thy glory may never be dimmed—*Esto Perpetua!* . . .

These three sermons of McQuaid, Spalding, and Ireland were the ones most alive on the underlying problems facing Catholicism in America. The sermon of Bishop Becker on "The Church and Science" was out of touch with the rising controversy over evolution and some other sermons arranged by the Delegate were at best abstract and routine. Even the sermon of Bishop John J. Keane on "Catholic Societies" avoided the disturbing question of labor unions and the subject of the non-Catholic secret societies, which was not brought to the floor of the Council.

There was, indeed, a strange contrast between the strong unity and peaceful tone of the Council and the rising national and social dissensions that were to break out immediately after the Council. There was a fitting contrast in this of the strong bond of Roman discipline written into the decrees of the Council at the request of Rome and the unruly and disquieting social and national practices which these laws would try with only limited success to reduce to order. Already some German priests of St. Louis and Milwaukee were beginning to protest against the domination of non-German prelates, the prelates opposed to Catholic membership in certain secret societies were demanding prohibitions, and the signs of labor unrest were disturbing those prelates who feared an introduction into the United States of European socialism.

The first problem of the Apostolic Delegate after the Council was to get the Roman approbation. The two bishops chosen to take the decisions to Rome were Bishops Moore of St. Augustine and Dwenger of Fort Wayne. The choice of these two did not meet universal approval because there was some worry about the departures from the original proposals from Rome introduced in the decrees. There was, also, some worry on the part of the bishops that Bishop Dwenger as a member of a religious community would not support the interests of the bishops who were having difficulties with the religious priests in their dioceses. Rome did, indeed, insist on the "consent"—rather than the "counsel"—of the consultors for episcopal action in financial matters of some moment, although even this difference was compromised by an agreement permitting such action for ten years with counsel. Further, Bishop Chatard of Vincennes complained by letter to Rome against the failure of the Council to make a decree against certain secret societies.

When approval was delayed there was a suggestion that Bishop Gilmour should go to Rome to hasten the consent of the Sacred Congregation. After some hesitation Archbishop Gibbons asked

Bishop Gilmour to go to Rome on his *ad limina* and hasten the consent of the Sacred Congregation. Eventually the decrees were approved and presented to the Pope for final approbation on September 10, 1885. Also at that time, when Monsignor Hostelot, the Rector of the North American College, died, Father Denis O'Connell was named Rector at the nomination of Archbishop Gibbons.

The quiet that followed the first months after the Council was rippled by a few minor problems such as the crisis over the diocesan debt in New Orleans and the new arrangements at the Bureau of Catholic Indian Missions. But the calm was only temporary. Within a few years the deeper problems facing the American hierarchy had begun to come to the surface. Probably the first was that of foreign nationalism.

Most of the earlier nationalistic problems that had troubled the American Church had not involved the question of language because most of the incoming foreigners in the early decades of the nineteenth century spoke English, albeit with a slightly different order and usually with a brogue. But because the Irish had generally lived among English-speaking people and since there was religious freedom in the new country, the Irish coming into the United States before the famine and after, as late as the Civil War, seemed to be aware of no cultural barrier besides their religion. The opposition of the French Sulpicians and the English prelates of Baltimore to the appointment of Irish bishops and to the influx of large numbers of Irish clergy was resented by the Irish Bishops England, Kenrick, and O'Connor, because to them the French who were being made bishops did not speak English well and were not so adaptable to the English-speaking world. The first crisis was solved easily; the French clergy were not replaced after the French Revolution, and the Anglo-American priests whether of English birth or American born were not numerous enough to care for the quickly expanding American congregations. Outside of Louisiana and, for a time, Kentucky, the Irish or sons of Irish began to be appointed to the American sees. That the chief spokesmen for American Catholicism at the outbreak of the Civil War were Archbishops John Hughes, the two Kenricks, John Purcell, and Bishop O'Connor seemed quite natural to the Irish majority of American Catholics and the usual thing for the non-Catholic Americans, who judged American Catholics in a numerical or political way as primarily an Irish church. There were, of course, French prelates in Louisiana, a German bishop in Milwaukee, and occasionally elsewhere a Belgian or French or

Spanish bishop who had been promoted because of his zeal in the missions, but the rank and file of the hierarchy were either Irish or American-Irish.

By the beginning of the Civil War, however, the number of German people coming into the country outnumbered even the Irish. Truly, they were not all Roman Catholics, but great numbers of them were. Some of them did go into the small towns and into the larger cities of the interior, such as Cincinnati, St. Louis, Milwaukee, Buffalo, and Cleveland, but the chief colonies were rural, and most of the Germans came with enough wealth to buy a farm and usually in such numbers as to to be able to set up their own German Catholic community. Some secular German clergy came with these communities, and in other cases there were available German religious such as the Redemptorists, the Jesuits, and the Precious Blood Fathers.

As Archbishop Bedini had noted in his visit in 1853, the German clergy on the whole gave an impression of having had better training. Their knowledge of German gave them a sense of superiority, which in their minds made up for a deficiency in English. Most of the Germans who settled in communities brought with them not only a language but songs, prayers, and social and religious customs from their native lands. The fact that they could live among themselves in their communities prevented them from having many of the social and cultural conflicts with the American and English natives that the Irish, whose poverty and ignorance forced them to work for and in a sense against the natives, had experienced. But within the Church a conflict soon arose between the German invaders, no matter how successful and self-complete they were, and the Irish, who had taken to themselves the dominance of the American Church. The American Catholics of English and Anglo-American backgrounds, while they had become accustomed to sharing their churches with the Irish and especially the children of Irish immigrants, were less inclined to demand that the Germans give up their native language. These Anglo-Americans, indeed, were the cultural nucleus of growing American Catholicism because to them the English language and the traditions of English literature and politics were native. In the American clergy they were represented by archbishops, bishops, and priests, such as the Spaldings, the Elders, the Mattinglys, the Jenkinses, and, among the converts, Bishops Josue Young of Erie, Alfred Curtis of Wilmington, and Thomas Becker of Wilmington, and Archbishop Frederick Wood. Their contribution to the trickle of American Catholic literature was far beyond their number, yet they did not seem to take part in the conflict between the Irish and the Germans. This conflict was in fact a difference between two groups, neither of which was native in culture, although the Irish felt native because of their English speech. For the remainder of the century the protests of the Germans against being American-ized by the Irish were growing in volume, while in the same era the Irish, mostly by descent, were insisting that they were in fact the American Church.

The chief historian[6] of these German immigrants speaks of the German triangle, roughly from Cincinnati to St. Louis to Milwau-kee. But in fact the Germans were also in considerable number outside this triangle in Buffalo, in western Pennsylvania, in Cleve-land, and along the upper Mississippi. Even before the Civil War there had been some complaints sent to the Austrian and German mission societies that the money sent by them to America for the German missions was being spent for others, but the com-plaints were scarcely justified. When the aging Archbishop Henni named three German bishops for Rome to choose one of them as his coadjutor, Rome, as in the case of Bayley, insisted that the regular procedures be followed. Bishop Heiss, his first choice, was actually named to succeed him.

Then in St. Louis, just before the Third Plenary Council, the existing rule was imposed, that national parishes did not have regular parish status but were only succursal. The rule had not been harshly imposed by Archbishop Kenrick, but the German priests regarded such a rule as unfair and they appealed directly to Rome for redress. The Cardinal Prefect of the Propaganda referred the complaint back to Archbishop Gibbons, the Apostolic Delegate of the Council, who did not think the complaint was justified. He referred the complaint to the committee of bishops on new matters, presided over by Archbishop Heiss, but nothing was done about it in the Council.

When Bishops Moore and Dwenger arrived in Rome to present the decrees of the Council they discovered that there were many complaints of German priests about the neglect and oppression of Germans by the English-speaking bishops and priests. Bishops Moore and Gilmour, when Cardinal Franzelin insisted on the validity of the German charges, wrote a plain answer to him in which they said, "The Germans demand absolutely that the priest and the school should be German. To keep peace with the Ger-

[6] Colman J. Barry, O.S.B., *The Catholic Church and the Germans* (Milwau-kee, 1953) Chapter II, "The German Triangle of the West," pp. 44–85.

mans, injustice is often done to other nationalities. In such circumstances the Irish usually submit, while the French generally cease going to church. The number of German priests is far greater than the number of German Catholics requires."[7] They went on to say that a spirit of nationalism was being introduced into the American Church which would eventually lead to a conflict that would cause loss to religion and piety.

The bishops thought they had satisfied the Cardinal, but the Cardinal wrote to Archbishops Williams and Gibbons asking them to answer two problems presented by another American prelate, who was, it seems, Archbishop Kenrick: whether several independent parishes of different nationality could be erected in the same vicinity and whether the children of a parish must remain members of that parish until they attained their majority or contracted marriage. Archbishop Williams thought there could be several independent national parishes in the same area and was inclined to make the children stay in the national parish until majority or marriage. Gibbons agreed on the first point but did not see how the second could be enforced.

Father Peter M. Abbelen of Milwaukee had been Archbishop Heiss's theologian in the Plenary Council. In October 1886 he wrote to Gibbons asking for a letter of recommendation to the Roman authorities, since he was going to Rome to discuss some of the problems of the German pastors. Receiving the letter of recommendation, Abbelen sailed on October 12 for Rome. With him he carried a petition from prominent German priests of Milwaukee, Cincinnati, and St. Louis demanding equal rights for German parishes and the German people in the Church in the United States.

Father Denis O'Connell, the close friend of Gibbons and now the Rector of the North American College in Rome where Abbelen was staying, learned from Abbelen the reason for his visit and sent word to Bishops Ireland and Keane who were in London on their way to Rome. Ireland hurried to Rome and obtained a copy of the Abbelen petition. He had it printed and sent copies to all the archbishops and those bishops whom he felt would want to know about it. Abbelen's letter, added to the other petitions in Rome, aroused Ireland and Keane. They prepared their own answer to the German priests and handed it to the Propaganda on December 6. Bishop Keane wrote of it to Gibbons himself because the petition had cited the Baltimore synod ruling

[7] *Ibid.*, pp. 60–61.

of 1876 refusing to accord to German pastors exclusive rights over German children, which had been corrected by the Baltimore Council of 1886. Bishops Ireland and Keane also sent cablegrams to all the archbishops and several bishops asking that they answer the Abbelen petition immediately.

Father O'Connell, Gibbons' representative, had sent word to him to get some response from the archbishops to Rome before the meeting of the Propaganda on January 3. Cardinal Gibbons sent word to Archbishops Elder, Williams, Ryan, and Corrigan to meet in Philadelphia on Thursday, December 16. Elder could not attend, but the others came. They drew up a message to Propaganda in which they denied any unfair treatment of the Germans and said that, in the Council, the German prelates had not used the ample opportunity that had existed to discuss this matter. Gibbons followed this document with a personal letter supporting Bishops Keane and Ireland. He was to be in Rome himself before the Sacred Congregation met on the question on April 11. After hearing Cardinal Gibbons, the Sacred Congregation on June 7 answered three of the nine questions raised by Abbelen. They allowed the erection of independent national parishes, permitted bishops and priests to require children to attend the services of the parents' church except where the parents decided otherwise, and asserted that national parishes could be declared irremovable. The other six questions were not considered, and these three did not change any of the previous practices.

In the meantime Cardinal McCloskey had died on October 10, 1885. A premature cablegram to Archbishop Corrigan from Europe in January 1886 said that Archbishop Gibbons had been named a Cardinal. Archbishop Gibbons received many congratulations to his embarrassment, but his embarrassment was changed when he received official word of his nomination as Cardinal on May 4, 1886.

There seemed to be no doubt that Archbishop Gibbons was destined to be made a Cardinal, and the embarrassments of the premature announcement produced only premature congratulations for the most part. When the actual announcement was made, the Pope chose Monsignor Germano Straniero to bring to Gibbons the formal notification of his appointment and the biretta. Gibbons chose June 30, the silver anniversary of his ordination, for the formal ceremony. An informal ceremony took place on June 29, and the formal reception of the red biretta from the hands of Archbishop Kenrick took place the next day in the Cathedral before ten archbishops and twenty-four bishops. Gibbons then awaited word as to the time of the consistory in which he would receive the red hat and fulfill the other ceremonies. On January 17, 1887, he received a cablegram from Cardinal Jacobini that the consistory would be held late in February or early in March and that the Pope wanted him to come to Rome. The new Cardinal started for Rome later in January, but before going he arranged for a conference in New York at the residence of Archbishop Corrigan with some archbishops and bishops to consider problems that might be raised on the occasion of his visit to Rome. There were several such problems facing the Church in the United States since the close of the Council.

One of the first of these problems to arise after the Council was the setting up of a Catholic university. The Cardinal-Elect was not one of the early enthusiasts for the project. The sermon of Bishop Spalding on university education had been followed by an offer of Miss Mary Gwendoline Caldwell of $300,000 as the initial donation for the university. In the Council, Archbishop Gibbons, as the Apostolic Delegate, had appointed a committee to study the problem, and they had recommended the founding of the university and the acceptance of the gift. The committee consisted of Archbishops Corrigan, Kenrick, Alemany, and Ryan and Bishop Spalding. When Archbishop Gibbons suggested that Miss ·Caldwell turn over the funds to him, she refused and insisted on further decisions. The first decision was on the site of the university. Previously Bishop Spalding had suggested that the Cincinnati Provincial Seminary be purchased to relieve that archdiocese of part of the great debt incurred in the financial collapse of 1879. This had been rejected by the hierarchy. Miss Caldwell, backed by Bishop Spalding and Bishop John Ireland, suggested Washington. Archbishop Elder objected to Washington. At that time Seton Hall College in Jersey City was in deep financial trouble, and a proposal was made that the committee purchase that college as the site of the university. Miss Caldwell objected, and so did some of the bishops. In a meeting of the committee in Baltimore on May 7, 1885, with Archbishop Gibbons as chairman, Washington was chosen as the site of the university. On May 12, 1886, the committee met to choose a rector. A subcommittee to choose the rector first asked Bishop Spalding to accept, but he refused. They then chose Bishop John Keane, and he accepted. Keane was asked, then, to go to Rome to present to the Roman officials the problems of the proposed university, and, since Bishop Ireland was to make his *ad limina* visit that year, he was suggested as a collaborator with Keane. In Rome, Keane found some opposition to the founding of the university aroused by the Archbishop of New York, who had consulted with the Provincial of the Jesuits on a proposal to establish a university in New York.

Arising from the growing concern in the country about economic and social reform, two other problems had appeared on the ecclesiastical horizon: the question of secret societies and the single tax movement. The committee of archbishops was scheduled to meet with Cardinal-Elect Gibbons on October 28 to discuss the proper measures to take on the condemnation of secret societies. This problem had been complicated by the decision of Archbishop Taschereau, Cardinal-Elect of Quebec, to ask Rome for a decree of condemnation against the Knights of Labor. The Knights of Labor, who had been in existence since 1869, had grown in numbers very rapidly during the 1880s. At their head was Terence V. Powderly, a machinist and one-time mayor of Scranton, Pennsylvania. The Knights had endeavored to shed any connection with the Molly Maguires and other violence-using labor organizations. But they did have a secret oath and a secret ceremony modeled after the masonic societies.

In the 1880s the Knights had begun to spread into French Canada, and the French Canadian bishops had ruled that the Knights fell under the condemnation of all secret societies. Taschereau had been named Cardinal and was going to Rome, actually on the same boat with Gibbons, to get the red hat. He proposed to obtain a formal condemnation of the Knights at the time. Cardinal Gibbons and several of the American hierarchy were endeavoring to prevent any condemnation of the Knights because there were so many Catholic members, and Gibbons and his close friends felt that condemnation would cause only harm. The Knights held their convention of 1886, October 4–20, in Richmond. In Richmond, Powderly, a Catholic, attended Mass at the Cathedral and called on Bishop Keane. Keane conferred with the officers of the Knights and eventually arranged a meeting of Powderly with the committee of the archbishops[8] in Baltimore on October 28. The events of the meeting and the contents of the exchange between the labor leaders and the prelates were not recorded, but the archbishops decided against condemnation, only two archbishops, Kenrick and Salpointe, being in favor of condemnation.

The other problem involving economic and social conditions

[8] Henry J. Browne, *The Catholic Church and the Knights of Labor* (Washington, 1949). On the meeting between Powderly and the Archbishops, pp. 208–227.

was really a local issue but had national repercussions. Father Edward McGlynn,[9] a graduate of Propaganda, was a successful pulpit orator and a leader in popular causes in New York. He did not believe in a separate Catholic school system but desired rather to support programs of social reform. He was reported to his alma mater, Propaganda College, several times, notably for supporting the Irish Land League in 1882, and, after a silence, again in 1884. His chief critic was the coadjutor Archbishop, Corrigan. In 1886 Henry George ran for Mayor of New York against Abram S. Hewit. George had elaborated in his books and speeches his theory of a single tax which, according to some, denied the right of private property. Catholic followers of George insisted that he did not deny the right of private property. When Father McGlynn publicly supported George, Corrigan suspended him for two weeks and reinstated the suspension when Father McGlynn resumed his political speaking during the very heated campaign. George lost the election to Hewit. Archbishop Corrigan's pastoral on religious matters shortly after contained an implied condemnation of Henry George's proposals. McGlynn publicly criticised the pastoral, and his suspension was continued. In the meantime the Sacred Congregation of Propaganda summoned "alumnus McGlynn" to Rome. He refused to go and, when he continued in his refusal, was excommunicated on July 3, 1887. He remained out of the Church until 1892, a cause of much scandal and dissension among the Catholics of New York. Meanwhile Archbishop Corrigan tried to have the teachings of Henry George condemned in Rome. Cardinal Gibbons, who feared the popular effect of such action, opposed the condemnation. Rome eventually compromised, condemning the doctrines of George but leaving the condemnation a secret of the Holy Office. The Cardinal never publicly took the side of McGlynn but Archbishop Corrigan accused him of supporting the suspended priest.

The meeting of the archbishops on October 28 had been called primarily to discuss the question of secret societies—a topic which had been deferred to the committee by the Council. There was disagreement among the archbishops on the condemnation of secret societies. On the Knights of Labor, the archbishops disagreed seven to two, Kenrick and Salpointe favoring condemna-

---

[9] John Tracy Ellis, *The Life of James Cardinal Gibbons, Archbishop of Baltimore, 1834–1921*, 2 vol. (Milwaukee, 1952) I, 546–594, treats the McGlynn episode as it affected Gibbons. Cf. Zwierlein, *McQuaid*, note 3 above, III, 1–83, for the Corrigan side of the story.

tion; on the Grand Army of the Republic, which some prelates had desired to have condemned, no action was taken because an agreement eliminating compromising ceremonies seemed probable; and on the Ancient Order of Hibernians, whom some associated with the Molly Maguires, the archbishops disagreed and did nothing. The question of condemning the Odd Fellows and Knights of Pythias was postponed through the efforts of Gibbons, who did not want to alienate common people by being too prescriptive. But these gentle actions of the archbishops were not approved by some other prelates. Archbishop Heiss of Milwaukee, who could not attend the meeting, and Bishop McQuaid were incensed by this lack of action.

Cardinal Gibbons left Baltimore on January 26 for New York, sailing from there on January 29 and arriving in Rome on February 12, 1887. Awaiting him were his faithful friend, Monsignor Denis O'Connell and Bishops John Ireland and John Keane. Bishop John Ireland had emerged in the Council as the most promising of the western bishops of the United States, a gifted orator and a magnetic leader. His eloquent speech in praise of the American form of government and his espousal of the cause of the Catholic university were milestones in a career that had been remarkable already in civic and religious undertakings in Saint Paul, and he was beginning to attract attention nationally. There were two differences between him and most of the other bishops. He was a Republican in politics, and not exactly a silent one, and a westerner in mannerism and forcefulness. His companion, in Rome, the Rector-Elect Bishop Keane of the Catholic University of America, was a kindred spirit in many ways. He made friends readily, was zealous, and self-sacrificing. While he was not the philosopher of education that Bishop John Lancaster Spalding was, he had elaborate ideas of how the University should function if it was to succeed. Of Monsignor Denis O'Connell, it can be said that besides being a devoted assistant to Cardinal Gibbons he was thoroughly acquainted with the way of Roman ecclesiastics. He had large plans for the Church in America and for his friends, and he had hopes that he himself would play a large part in them. Like the other two prelates, although born in Ireland, he was deeply in love with his adopted country and gloried in American freedom and prosperity.

The secret consistory in which the new Cardinals would be received had been set for March 17, and on that day seven new Cardinals went through the ceremony of sealing and opening of the lips, the reception of the large red hat, and the assignments to

their titular churches. Cardinal Gibbons was assigned the Basilica
of Santa Maria in Trastevere and also given a place on the Congregations of the Propaganda, of Religious, of Indulgences, and
of Studies. The Cardinal took over his titular church on March
25. On the suggestion of Monsignor O'Connell, he made a formal
speech on the occasion in which he praised the cordial relations
that existed in the United States between the Church and the Government. He noted that he belonged "to a country where the civil
government holds over us the aegis of its protection without interfering in the legitimate exercise of our sublime mission as ministers of the Gospel of Jesus Christ." He also thanked Pope Leo
for his recognition of American Catholicism in his appointment,
indicating that non-Catholics in the United States also shared in
his pleasure at the recognition. The speech was reprinted widely
in the United States and received laudatory comments in the secular press. Gibbons left Rome on April 18 and on June 7 arrived
in Baltimore, where a grand civic and religious welcome awaited
him.

Shortly after the Cardinal had arrived in Rome in February
1887, he had been confronted by Roman action on at least two
American problems. On the question of national parishes, no
decision was announced until after the Cardinal had returned
home, although he had an opportunity to present his side of the
question at the meeting of the Congregation of Propaganda on
April 11. Also, the question of the Knights of Labor was brought
to the fore by the fact that his companion on the way to Rome,
Cardinal Taschereau, was bent on securing a papal condemnation
of the Knights during his visit. Bishops John Ireland and John
Keane, who were in Rome on business about the new Catholic
University, together with Monsignor O'Connell, were very active
in preparing Cardinal Gibbons's side of the American problems
that had been appealed to Rome.[10] They had already prepared
a memorial for the Sacred Congregation on the Knights and to
this the Cardinal gave his signature, although he had some fear,
according to Keane, that he might be endangering his Cardinal's
hat. The Memorial, dated February 20, 1887, reviewed the actions
of the archbishops in Baltimore on the previous October 28 and
then outlined the case against condemnation. The document said
that the Knights were not a secret society since their pledge of
silence was not absolute, and the General Master Workman, Powderly, had given his pledge of devotion to the Church. Neither

[10] Browne, note 8 above, pp. 228–274.

did the Knights of Labor plot against the Government, as President Cleveland had assured Cardinal Gibbons. Catholic members had joined the Knights to protect their interests. The Memorial made light of the danger resulting from Catholics' associating with Protestants in the society, or with radicals. On the contrary, the Memorial appealed to the example of Cardinal Manning, pointed to the beginning of a new age in which it was necessary that the Church manifest its affection for the people in helping them attain their reasonable demands. Any condemnation of the Knights would appear to be unjust and would cause a loss of the faithful to the Church, as well as a loss of the contributions of the workers to the Church, which were so important for building churches and even for the support of the Pope from America. Finally, the Memorial pointed out that the Knights would soon pass away and any action taken against them would do only harm to the Church after they had gone.

Some correspondent of *The New York Herald* obtained possession of the Memorial and on March 3 printed an abbreviated version of it, including the arguments against condemnation. It was claimed that the correspondent of the *Herald* had obtained a copy of the Memorial by bribing a secretary, and such occurrences were relatively common in Rome. The result was twofold. As Bishop Ireland observed to Bishop Gilmour, any condemnation was averted for the time, and Cardinal Gibbons and the American bishops generally were recognized by the American public as friends of organized labor. Only the conservative members of the Catholic press seemed unenthusiastic about the Memorial. When Cardinal Manning read the newspaper accounts, he wrote a letter in support of the Cardinal's action. The most important impact of the publication of the Memorial was undoubtedly in the United States, because up to that time the public statements of the hierarchy had not given the American prelates any reputation for friendliness to labor. The general attitude expressed in the Catholic statements on labor organizations had been in the spirit of the conservative attitude typical of south Europe. The answer given to Taschereau by the Congregation on March 10 was not clear but was clarified by further statement after a March 30 meeting of the Sacred Congregation which allowed the Knights in Canada to receive the Sacraments if they expressed a willingness to accept the decisions of the Holy See. Gibbons did hand in another document against the condemnation of the Knights in April. One passage of Gibbons' Memorial had not been included in the translation reported in *The New York Herald:* that which referred to the bad public effects of the condemnation of Father Edward McGlynn by Archbishop Corrigan. This passage about McGlynn was sent to Archbishop Corrigan, who pretended to ignore it when he greeted the Cardinal on his return from Rome.

The official decision of the Congregation of the Propaganda in answer to the petition of Father Abbelen and the other German priests was dated June 8. There were some minor errors in the answer, and the petitioners were not certain who had won, except that any further division of the American Church by nationalities was rejected. But in the meantime the petition itself and the strong answers of Bishops Ireland and Keane had been printed and distributed. The latter brought out stronger protests in the German Catholic press. Some German priests, however, took the side of Gibbons and Ireland against the appeal of Abbelen. Most prominent among them was Father John Gmeiner of Milwaukee, the editor of *Der Seebote*, who argued that it was impossible to perpetuate the German language in this country and that the Germans should thankfully accept their conditions in the New World. But most of the German writers turned against Gmeiner, who moved to Saint Paul. Especially bitter were the pamphlets of Nicholas Gonner, the editor of *Katholischer Western* of Dubuque and Father Anton H. Walburg of St. Augustine's Church in Cincinnati. Walburg's pamphlet in English attacked the new nativism in the Church in the United States. He considered the Germans the best Catholics in the world and said that knowing two languages would help the American people. He praised the German nationality and the Irish nationality, but had little to say in praise of American nationality. Admitting that eventually all the immigrants would become American, he gave a general defense of foreign nationalism in the Church in the United States:

However, the transition from one nationality to another, is always a dangerous process, and it will not do to hasten it, and to force foreigners to Americanize. For the present we should remember that the American nationality counts for little or nothing in the American Church, and if it is ever converted, it must be done by the clergy and population already Catholics. The most efficient portion of our Catholic body are of foreign birth and training, and will be for some time to come.[11]

Walburg was stating in reverse the fact that the Catholics in the United States would achieve importance culturally only insofar as they accepted the American or, as he called them, "the Anglo-

[11] A. H. Walburg, *The Question of Nationality* (Cincinnati, 1889) p. 61.

Saxon" traditions. But at the time Walburg and the other German leaders did not intend to hasten the change.

As early as 1883 a zealous German Catholic merchant of Limburg an der Lahn, Peter Paul Cahensly,[12] had interested himself in improving the reception of German immigrants, especially in the port of New York. He was a member of the St. Raphaelsverein, an organization devoted to the emigrants from Germany to the New World. The next year, as a result of his interest, the layman who had been in charge of the New York office was replaced by a priest, Father John Reuland. There was some dissension over the move but Father Reuland took over. Cahensly continued his interest in the German-American Catholic immigration, especially through the periodical, the *St. Raphaels Blatt*. Also, on February 16, 1887, there was formed in Chicago the first conference of the Deutsch-Amerikaner Priester-Verein, which decided to meet with the Central Verein, a union of German Catholic societies in the country, in Chicago on September 6. An interview with Archbishop Heiss on the proposed meeting on August 18, 1887, appeared in the *Milwaukee Sentinel* in which he remarked about the fewness of the German bishops in the United States and indicated that the coming meeting would discuss the perpetuation of the German language in the schools and whatever else the people desired. Some bishops were alarmed by the interview and protested to Cardinal Gibbons, but the *Katholikentag* or German Catholic General Assembly was held beginning September 9 in Chicago. There were some indiscreet things said in the meetings, but the group did vote to support the St. Raphael's center in New York. A second assembly was arranged to be held in Cincinnati on September 3, 4, 1888. Archbishop Ireland sent a protest through Monsignor O'Connell against granting a papal blessing to the Cincinnati meeting, but the blessing had already been sent. A proposal was made in the meeting that there be a general Catholic assembly, modeled after the German *Katholikentag,* in which all languages would be represented, but such a meeting was never held. That fall the German Catholics of Minnesota asked permission of Archbishop Ireland to have such a Catholic day in Chaska, Minnesota. In answer, Ireland praised the zeal of the German Catholics and gave permission but attacked the leaders of the movement. He attended the meeting on October 18 and in his speech attacked the purposes of the assemblies of Chicago and Cincinnati. The 1889 meeting of these German societies was held

[12] Barry, *German Americans*, note 6 above, p. 20 ff.

in Cleveland, and that of 1890 in Pittsburgh. In the Pittsburgh meeting, there appeared on the stage Monsignor Joseph Schroeder, a newly arrived professor of the Catholic University in Washington who was soon to become the intellectual leader of the German Catholic societies in the United States.

When Bishops Ireland and Keane had arrived in Rome to discuss with the Roman officials the problems of the Catholic University, they found much opposition and little encouragement. They counted on support from Cardinal Gibbons when he arrived, but he had not been too favorable to the project even though he was chairman of the Episcopal Committee on the University. Archbishop Heiss of Milwaukee had withdrawn from the Committee with some hint of a lack of German support. Then it was discovered that Archbishop Corrigan had written a letter to Rome opposing the foundation of the University.[13] When Bishop Ireland learned of this, he merely reinforced his intention to establish the University, and he demanded that Cardinal Gibbons and Bishop Keane join with him in a fight to the finish. Gibbons then wrote a letter to Pope Leo XIII outlining the proposal and urging the necessity of founding the University. Within a short time the Pope issued a formal letter dated April 10, 1887, heartily approving the foundation. Gibbons then became a strong supporter of the University and told the other archbishops that the Pope was set on its establishment and that they must not disappoint him.

The opposition came not only from Archbishop Corrigan but especially from Bishop McQuaid, who regarded the University as a rival for his own newly established seminary. The University Committee met on September 7, 1887, and the Cardinal announced that the bishops had voted for Washington as the site of the University. He also announced publicly the choice of Keane as the first rector. Then Archbishop Corrigan, with the backing of McQuaid, resigned from the University Committee.

The laying of the cornerstone of the first building of the University was set for May 1, 1888. Actually the ceremony, attended by the President of the United States and several cabinet members besides many bishops and distinguished visitors, took place on May 24. In July 1888, Archbishop Corrigan returned to the University Committee. McQuaid, however, published a letter against the project. Bishop Keane, besides speaking in the Middle West on the University, spent some time on the campus of the Univer-

---

[13] John T. Ellis, *The Formative Years of the Catholic University of America* (Washington, 1946) pp. 217 ff.

sity of Notre Dame composing a first draft of the statutes of the University. He asked Gibbons to ask the Sulpicians to take over the administration of the discipline of the University. In a meeting of the Committee on November 13 the proposed statutes were approved and on November 17 Keane sailed for Europe. On March 7, 1889, Pope Leo issued an apostolic letter *Magni nobis gaudii* giving his final approval to the University. The formal opening was set for November 1889 to coincide with the celebration in Baltimore of the centennial of the establishment of the hierarchy.

When Henry F. Brownson, the son of the renowned editor, heard of the celebration planned for the centennial to be held in Baltimore, he suggested that there be a lay congress in connection with the celebration. He found a sympathetic friend in Archbishop Ireland, and a co-worker in William J. Onahan of Chicago. Cardinal Gibbons was at first hesitant to approve but was won over by Ireland, and a committee of bishops was appointed to oversee the papers to be presented. Onahan and Brownson were joined by many other prominent laymen from various parts of the country representing many groups and classes of persons.

The solemn celebration of the centennial of the foundation of the American hierarchy was held in the Cathedral of the Assumption in Baltimore on November 10, 1889. The Pope sent Archbishop Francesco Satolli, the Archbishop of Lepanto, as his delegate to the ceremonies. Archbishop Williams sang the Mass, and Archbishop Ryan preached. In the evening at solemn vespers, Gibbons again presided and Archbishop Heiss was celebrant. Archbishop Ireland gave one of his startling sermons.

Commenting on the accomplishments of the past century, Archbishop Ireland turned more to the future and gave to Catholics in the United States a new work. "It is two-fold: to make America Catholic, and to solve for the Church universal the all-absorbing problems with which religion is confronted in the present age."[14] He proceeded to show that it was God's will that America become Catholic and that America was destined to be important for the Church. He further insisted that American Catholics were called to reconcile the Church and the Age. He listed the watchwords of the age as "reason, education, liberty, the amelioration of the masses," and proceeded to show that the Church had the true answers to these demands. He went on to show that American people were not hostile to the Church and that the Church was

[14] John Ireland, *The Church and Modern Society*, 2d ed. (Chicago, 1897) p. 55.

free to enjoy the liberty of the country. As assurance of the Catholic victory, he demanded earnestness and aggressiveness. He said that the age was one of intellect and for that reason the Catholic University was destined to be of great service. It was also an age of democracy, and Catholicism in the United States would show the countries of Europe that Catholics had the answer to this demand for democracy and for social improvements. Finally, recognizing the laymen who were there for the Congress that would open the next day, he made to them a special appeal.

... Priests are officers, laymen are soldiers. The hardest fighting is often done by the soldier; in the warfare against sin and error, the soldier is not always near the officer, and he must be ready to act without waiting for the word of command. Laymen are not anointed in confirmation to the end that they may merely save their own souls, and pay their pew rent. They must think, work, organize, read, speak, act, as circumstances demand, ever anxious to do good to their fellowmen....[15]

He concluded with an apostrophe that the Church in America would be "first in civil liberty and social happiness, first in Christian loyalty among the nations of the earth."

On the next morning there was a Mass in the Cathedral to open the Lay Congress, after which 1,500 delegates assembled in Concordia Opera House for the opening session. John Lee Carroll, the former Governor of Maryland, presided, and Cardinal Gibbons welcomed the assembly. The opening speech was a review of the history of Catholics in the United States by Daniel Daugherty. Among other speakers at the Congress were Henry F. Brownson, Charles J. Bonaparte, Honoré Mercier, Peter Foy, and Edward F. Dunne. The topics discussed included "Lay Action in the Church," "The Independence of the Holy See," "The New Social Order," and "Education." At the close of the second day of the Congress, the resolutions of the Congress were presented by Daniel A. Rudd, the Negro editor of the *Cincinnati Catholic Tribune*. Archbishop Ireland in closing the Congress expressed the feeling of many clergymen when he said:

... As one of your bishops I am ashamed of myself that I was not conscious before of the power existing in the midst of the laity and that I have not done anything to bring it about.... Say to your fellow Catholics that there is a new departure among Catholics of the United States. Tell them hence-forth you are going to do great things.[16]

[15] *Ibid.*, p. 81.
[16] *Souvenir Volume—Three Great Events in the History of the Catholic Church in the United States*, 2d ed. (Detroit, 1890) p. 82.

On Wednesday the assembled clergymen and laymen were in Washington to dedicate the new Catholic University of America. The ceremonies were held in the newly completed Caldwell Hall. The Mass in the hall chapel was celebrated by Archbishop Satolli, the Papal Delegate, and the sermon was preached by Bishop Gilmour. Bishop Gilmour said that "the science of sciences," theology, was above the arts and the sciences, indicating perhaps the immediate aim of the new university. This supremacy of theology did not exist in university learning in the United States, for few American universities had theological schools in their faculties. At the dinner after the Mass, President Benjamin Harrison and several members of his cabinet were present. All went well except for a bit of unprepared humor at the dinner by Archbishop Patrick Ryan of Philadelphia in which he made among other remarks a reference to someone's meeting his Waterloo. Waterloo, in the Rochester Diocese, was the city in which Father Louis Lambert, a priest who had appealed to Rome against McQuaid, resided.[17] McQuaid was not present nor was Archbishop Corrigan, his ally in his opposition to the University. The University began to function on the following Monday, November 18, with forty-six students in theology.

The staff of the University did not include many of the European scholars that Bishop Keane had sought. Father Philip G. Garrigan, Irish-born pastor of St. Bernard's Church, Fitchburg, Massachusetts and former Director of the seminary at Troy, was Vice-Rector. Monsignor Joseph Schroeder from Cologne was Professor of Dogmatic Theology; Dr. Henri Hyvernat was Professor of Biblical Archeology; Dr. Thomas Bouquillon from the University of Lille was Professor of Moral Theology; Dr. Joseph Poehle of Fulda was Professor of Philosophical Apologetics; Dr. John Hogan, S.S., the Irish-born former Rector of the Boston Seminary was made President of Divinity College; Father Alexis Orban, S.S., was made temporary librarian; Father George M. Searle, C.S.P., was Professor of Astronomy and Physics; Charles Warren Stoddard was Professor of English Literature. At a later date Dr. Sebastian Messmer of Switzerland and of Seton Hall College was Professor of Canon Law; Dr. Thomas O'Gorman of St. Paul was Professor of Recent Ecclesiastical History; Dr. Thomas J. Shahan of Hartford was Professor of Early Ecclesiastical History; and Dr. Charles P. Grannan was Professor of Old Testament Exegesis.

In the generally laudatory descriptions of the opening of the

---

[17] Ellis, *Formative Years*, note 13 above, p. 387.

University, there were also references to Archbishop Ryan's un-
guarded reference to Bishop McQuaid and some hints of criticism
that so many of the professors had come from Europe. Cardinal
Gibbons wrote a glowing account of the series of events to the
Holy Father, but he could hardly have been ignorant of the disagreements that were soon to be manifested within the University,
as if it were a microcosm of the problems of the Catholic minority in the United States. In his zeal to get outstanding men to teach
in his University, Bishop Keane had had to sacrifice the unity that
might have been formed had the faculty all been of American
origin. The necessity for going to Europe for so many of the
faculty can be understood as an indication that American Catholics were not ready for a university.

The opening of the University, the holding of a national Congress, and the recognition of Archbishop Gibbons as a kind of
national leader by his election to cardinalitial rank gave the
Church in the United States an appearance of unity that was
deceptive. Nevertheless, for the next thirty years Cardinal Gibbons would be looked upon by Americans outside the Church and
unofficially by Rome as a kind of central authority in the Church
in the country. The Cardinal seemed to enjoy the role. His slight,
ascetical figure which seemed majestic in his cardinalitial robes,
his realization that he was the only Cardinal in the country for
many years, and, particularly, the fact that the Roman documents
addressed to the whole Catholic Church of the country were
usually addressed to him made the Cardinal act at times as if he
were a real primate. Certainly being Archbishop of the rather poor
See of Baltimore, even if it did contain the national capital, did not
add much to the Cardinal's stature, and he did not spend as much
time attending to his Archdiocese as some other prelates did to
theirs. Bishop Bernard McQuaid, who was restive under these
tendencies toward a primacy manifested by the Cardinal, raised
his own diocese to a high level of accomplishment by sheer personal power and active pastoral labors, pushing aside or out priests
who opposed him, building up an excellent seminary, setting up a
first-rate system of schools with teaching Sisters, erecting good
parochial buildings, and inspiring a very active clergy. He was
probably the most successful American bishop and wanted no
outside interference in his diocese. There were other bishops just
as jealous of their episcopal prerogatives and autonomy who made
the appearance of national unity deceptive.

For the most part the bishops of New England usually followed
the lead of the Archbishop of Boston. In this case it was John

Williams, a fine pastor but not a strong leader. In general meetings he opposed attacks on the public schools and pleaded for a closer understanding with the non-Catholic majority. He did not have the means to build parochial schools for all his Catholic children and did not want to attack the public schools which he had to use. There were some critics who thought he yielded too quickly to the dominating "Yankees," but he thought and acted in terms of what he considered best for his own people. Harvard and Yale and lesser colleges had Catholics in their student bodies, but very few of these students expected to mount the social ladder of New England.

Archbishop Corrigan, according to his friends, should have been made a Cardinal as soon as, if not before, Cardinal Gibbons, because New York was certainly a much more important see, and the city had much more influence on the nation. He always had the backing of Bishop McQuaid and usually of his other suffragan bishops, and there was a feeling among them that New York should lead in public matters. Only in New York were there Catholic clergymen and laymen who had more influence in local and even national matters than did the ordinary layman. Sometimes they asserted this notion of superiority in the press, as in the case of Dr. Edward McGlynn and his formal resistance to the Archbishop. For the rest of the Middle Atlantic States Province, the hierarchy had the canonical superiority of bishops over the priest, and archbishop over bishop, but most of the activities of the clergy in these Middle States and even in dioceses of the Middle West at this time were devoted to sacramental ministrations, the building of churches and schools, and the supervision of the religious who were themselves mostly engaged in conducting Catholic institutions.

Further west, Cincinnati was suffering from the financial disaster which darkened the last years of the Purcell regime.[18] Archbishop Elder, Purcell's successor, was a capable administrator and a man of ideas, but both in Natchez and in Cincinnati he was handicapped by administrational problems. The See of Chicago was also handicapped by the mental illness of its Bishop who lived on for twenty-five years in an asylum. St. Louis had prospered under the overaged Archbishop Peter Richard Kenrick, who had become a difficult person in his advanced years. The Archdiocese of New Orleans, likewise, was laboring under heavy indebtedness.

[18] A brief account of the disaster is told in John H. Lamott, *History of the Archdiocese of Cincinnati 1821–1921* (New York, 1921) pp. 189–207.

Of the other western bishops, the new Archbishop Patrick Riordan of San Francisco gave great promise, but, despite the transcontinental railroad, San Francisco was almost outside the country.

There remained then in the northwestern part of the Middle West the center of the German clergy with a German archbishop in Milwaukee, other German bishops and many restive German priests and several lay leaders of some literary ability in German. There were many non-Germans in the area, but the chief diocesan seminary was in Milwaukee, and the members of most of the religious communities and of the clergy of several dioceses were predominantly German. The "German triangle" between 'St. Louis, Milwaukee, and Cincinnati was real at this time. Archbishop John Ireland in St. Paul had some Irish clergymen with him, but he was literally surrounded by German prelates, and those who might have helped him in his attempt to hold the German clergy in check, the prelates in Chicago and Detroit, were not noted for forceful activity. The timidity of his confreres did not check Ireland when he soon found himself involved in further controversies.

The friction between Catholic and non-Catholic over the American schools had been of varying intensity ever since the Catholic attempts in the 1840s, in New York and Philadelphia, to get state aid for Catholic schools and to eliminate the reading of the Protestant Bible by Catholics in the public schools. In many communities of the Middle West where parochial schools had become a regular part of the parish life, especially when the community was German, the public schools were loudly condemned by the Catholic pastor as "godless." The Roman Instruction on the public schools of 1875 and the decrees of the Third Plenary Council had strengthened the position of those who wanted a complete and separate Catholic school system. But the financial means to erect such as independent system did not exist, especially among the Irish immigrants who thronged the Catholic churches of the eastern states.

In New England, particularly, the Catholic youngsters who went to school had usually to go to the public school. There were lacking the financial resources to build a school for each parish in New England and to a certain extent in the Middle Atlantic States. There had been a few efforts to obtain limited state help, such as that at Poughkeepsie, New York, in which the religious exercises and teaching were done outside of regular school hours to obtain public financial assistance. Usually, however, Catholic prelates when they were asked to comment on public school education insisted that education without religion was in their minds defective. This insistence on the "godlessness" of the public school by those clergy who had built parish schools served merely to antagonize further those who were opposed to state aid for religious schools because the public school had become a permanent institution in the United States. The chief organization on the other hand formed by the teachers and administrators of the public schools was the National Education Association. Under these circumstances the fact that Cardinal Gibbons and Bishop Keane were invited to discuss the position of denominational schools at the annual meeting of the National Education Association in Nashville on July 16, 1889, was a milestone in the tolerance of Catholicism in the country despite the hearty rebuttal offered to the Catholic speakers by the two opposing speakers, on this occasion.[19]

Cardinal Gibbons did not attend in person but had Bishop Keane read first his brief paper in which he said, ". . . But it is not enough for children to have a secular education; they must have religious training . . ." and concluded:

The combination of religious and secular education is easily accomplished in denominational schools. To what extent religion may be taught in the public schools without infringing the rights and wounding the conscience of some of the pupils is a grave problem beset with difficulties, and very hard to be solved, inasmuch as those schools are usually attended by children belonging to the various demonimations, by Jews also, and even by those who profess no religion whatever.[20]

Bishop Keane when he read his own paper limited the term "denominational schools," which was the topic assigned for discussion, to "Christian schools" and to Christian parents. He developed his argument on the obligation of Christian parents to secure a Christian education for their children. He further noted that being an American did not change this obligation. Nor, he argued, can that Christian education be completed in the home. He denied that denominational schools encouraged sectarianism because all must seek truth as they see it. On the failure of the public schools to teach Christian morality, he referred to criticisms of the public school that had been heard during the previous twenty years. Finally he concluded with a statement that "in all our land there is no element more identified with America, more devoted to our country and her institutions, than the clergy and the people of the Catholic Church; . . ."[21]

[19] National Education Association, *Journal of Proceedings and Addresses . . . at Nashville, Tennessee* (Topeka, 1889) pp. 111–179.

[20] *Ibid.*, p. 43.

[21] *Ibid.*, p. 121.

The answer to the prelate's paper by Edwin D. Mead of Boston began with quotations from *A Catholic Dictionary* edited by William E. Addis and Thomas Arnold which stated the Catholic doctrine of exclusive possession of divine truth. Mead said he liked that statement, which had the imprimatur of Cardinal Manning. He gave as his own purpose to show ". . . that this interference with liberty of conscience and family choice, with which Cardinal Manning charges the state, but of which the state is not in the least guilty, is in truth the capital sin of the Roman Church, pervading its whole policy in the establishment of parochial schools in this country, from New England to New Mexico."[22] He quoted in support of his thesis, Father Thomas Conaty of Worcester, Massachusetts, Bishop Baltes of Alton, the Catechism of the Council of Baltimore, Bishop Gilmour, and the pastorals of several bishops commanding attendance at Catholic schools under threat of various penalties. He particularly stressed statements of *The Catholic Educator's Manual* of Thomas J. Jenkins. Mead maintained that the coercion existing in the Catholic school could not be carried out in a state school. He then turned against the charge that the public schools were not equal in every moral quality to the Catholic school or that they were "godless." He maintained that "a parochial school can never give anything else than a parochial education." His final objection was, "I find in most of the Catholic utterances on education no sense of obligation to the whole, no civic breadth, no thought of any children but their own."[23]

Bishop Keane gave a brief rebuttal in which he defended the honesty and logic of Cardinal Manning. He made fun of Mead's attempt to interpret the meaning of Pope Leo XIII. He affirmed that the Catholic insistence on Catholic education was not different from the policies of other Christian churches who insisted on Christian education. To prove the evil possibilities of state control of education he quoted Massachusetts laws in which that state had lately attempted to legislate against parochial schools. He interpreted the philosophy of Mead's speech as agnosticism.

Another paper presented in this meeting was "Public and Parochial Schools" by John Jay of New York City, who tried to destroy the arguments for Catholic schools by statements of Catholics. He entered into his argument with great gusto within the second paragraph of his speech, crediting Roman Catholics who accepted the public school as having common sense and inveighing against

[22] *Ibid.*, p. 129.
[23] *Ibid.*, p. 146.

"Jesuitical methods resorted to in the corruption of our legislatures" for concessions and the attempts to denounce the public schools as godless. He accused Catholics of attempting to exclude the Bible from public schools. He spoke of the need of the common school to Americanize the tidal wave of immigrants. He then proceeded to quote various Catholic writers to prove that Roman authorities intended to destroy the public schools and to enforce censures on Catholics who did not join in the effort. He gave a long historical defense of the American public school and then pictured the parochial school as aimed to destroy that school, quoting criticisms of Catholic schools from Brownson, Father McGlynn, and Father Hecker. He concluded that it was the obligation of public authorities to protect naturalized Roman Catholic children from every foreign prince and potentate.

The controversy on the relative value of Catholic and public schools was argued with more heat than understanding, but the problem did not apply equally in all parts of the country. In those dioceses where there existed the means to set up a system of Catholic parochial schools, pressure was used by the bishop and the priests to make the parents send their children to the parish school. This expense of a separate school was a handicap to the poorer Catholics in the Middle West, especially where Catholics were in a minority. But in other sections, especially in the eastern states, the erection of a system of parochial schools without state aid was practically impossible. Thus there were many kinds of writings on the question of Catholic education. Those who had parochial schools tended to call the public schools "godless" and to demand that Catholics avoid them. Others who did not have parochial schools used similar arguments against the public schools in the hope of getting state aid to build denominational schools. There were others who sought some middle ground, in which state aid could be had for the teaching of secular subjects and for physical maintenance of the Catholic schools, with the right to teach religion secured. There were actually more bishops who believed in this solution than dared to say so publicly because of the Instruction of 1875 and the decrees of the Third Plenary Council.

In Wisconsin the question of public and private schools was argued from a different angle. In a few German communities English was taught only as a secondary language in some elementary grades, and in others German was considered at least an equal medium of speech. The Wisconsin state legislature passed, on

April 18, 1889, the so-called Bennett Law,[24] which required the attendance for part of the year of the youngsters of the state at a "school" and defined that such a "school" according to that law must include "as part of the elementary education of children, reading, writing, arithmetic and United States history, in the English language." There were other rather arbitrary provisions in the law among which one prohibited educating a child outside its district, and another gave the public school officials certain rights to interfere, to investigate, and even to determine textbooks in any school in these districts. In reaction Archbishop Heiss and Bishops Katzer and Flasch published a joint letter of protest in which the law was declared (1) an unnecessary law, (2) an offensive law, and (3) an unjust law. In the bitter controversy that followed, the charge was made by the German bishops against Archbishop Ireland that he supported the Bennett law, if not publicly at least in private, and there were some hints that Archbishop Ireland was not in favor of the parochial schools. The next year, in 1890, the Republicans, who were in the majority in the state when the law was passed, lost the election, apparently because the German Catholics shifted their votes to the Democratic candidate for governor. The Bennett law was repealed in 1891. In the meantime in July 1890, the National Education Association held its annual meeting in St. Paul on July 8, 9, 10, and Archbishop Ireland was invited to give one of the major addresses of the convention on July 10.[25]

Archbishop Ireland took as his topic the question "Is Union Possible Between the State School and the Parish School?" The companion paper discussed laws on compulsory education. Archbishop Ireland began his speech with an affirmation of his support of the Constitution and with an assertion that he was "a friend and advocate of the state school." As to the parish school, he wished that it did not have to exist. The archbishop went on to explain why he supported the state enforcement of education, despite the fact that the primary right belonged to the parent of the child. Without the state law, he said, thousands of children would not receive education. Then he returned to the parish

[24] A good account of the Bennett Law as it affected Catholics is in [Henry H. Henning] *The Catholic Church in Wisconsin* (Milwaukee, 1895–1898) pp. 286–287.

[25] Cf. National Education Association, *Journal of Proceedings and addresses . . . at Saint Paul* (Topeka, 1890) pp. 179–199 for Ireland's speech and the discussion.

school. The Catholic schools taught an estimated 750,000 children. Lutherans, Episcopalians, and other Protestant denominations also had some parish schools. His grievance against the state school was: "The state school tends to eliminate religion from the minds and hearts of the youth of the country." In rolling sentences the Archbishop indicated how this situation was giving indifference as a creed to the youngster who in manhood would be estranged from "God and the positive influences of religion." Further, he said, it is not enough that the state schools teach morals. "Christians demand religion." He admitted the rights of secularists and unbelievers, but neither would he let them impose their secularism on him. He appealed to the fair play of Americans to be just. He insisted that there be some compromise. He suggested, first, that the state pay for the secular instruction in the private school; or, secondly, that some such program as that adopted in Poughkeepsie be adopted in which the parish schools were public schools between 9:00 A.M. and 3:00 P.M. to get the necessary aid for buildings and faculty; or some other such compromise. Above all, he insisted, it was unfair to say that Catholics were opposed to the American school system. They merely wanted to add to that system the "splendor and majesty" of religious instruction. In the discussion that followed, the discussants were very respectful of Archbishop Ireland, but indicated that they did not know how to achieve the compromise. One speaker made doleful references to the Bennett law and the strict enforcement of the requirement for parochial schools in La Crosse.

When Archbishop Ireland's speech was reported in the Catholic press, he was accused of regretting the existence of the parochial school and of giving the state the supreme right to educate the child. Some prelates lost no time in reporting the speech to Rome with accompanying accusations that Ireland was opposed to the parochial school.[26] Cardinal Gibbons read the speech carefully and wrote to Rome in defense of the Archbishop. Writing to Cardinal Gibbons in his own defense, the Archbishop pointed to the 63 Catholic schools in his archdiocese with over 12,000 children in them. Despite rumors in the Catholic press that Archbishop Ireland would be called to Rome to explain his position on the schools, no such summons came. As the accepted leader of the Americanizing members of the hierarchy he became aware of another action of German Catholics affecting the country.

[26] Daniel F. Reilly, O.P., *The School Controversy 1891–1893*, p. 49. This study usually takes the side of Archbishop Ireland.

On December 8 and 9, 1890, the representatives of the branches of the St. Raphael Societies of Europe, interested in German migrants to the United States, held a convention in Lucerne, Switzerland. The leader in this meeting was Peter Paul Cahensly, who had visited the United States on this matter as early as 1883. On the second day the assembly adopted a resolution presented by Marchese Volpe-Landi, a delegate from Italy. This resolution was a Memorial to the Pope and was signed by all delegates.[27] It was presented to the Pope actually by Cahensly on April 16. The preamble of the resolution stated that the losses to the Church among the immigrants exceeded ten millions. Among the recommendations of the Memorial was the setting up of separate national churches in the United States and, where the immigrants were not numerous enough for a separate parish, the appointment of an additional priest in the parish of that nationality, and that in the episcopate there be several bishops of the countries from which the immigrants had come.

Word of the Memorial reached America first on May 4 and other dispatches elaborated on the purpose of the Memorial and aroused serious reactions among the Catholics of the country. When Archbishop Ireland was interviewed by the press on the Memorial he denounced Cahensly as a meddler who was mistaken. The non-Catholic press applauded the Archbishop's Americanism and praised his denouncement of Cahensly. In the meantime, when Cardinal Rampolla asked Cahensly to give more of the information on which the Memorial was based, Cahensly presented a second Memorial in which he listed six reasons for the losses to the Church among the immigrants, increasing the number of immigrant losses to the Church to twenty-six millions. The chief reason, he alleged, was the lack of protection for the immigrants, the lack of priests and parishes for the different nationalities, the financial sacrifices demanded of them, the public schools, the lack of societies and unions for them, and the lack of representatives of the various nationalities in the hierarchy. When Archbishop Ireland obtained a copy of the Memorial he released it to the press with denunciations. Many American bishops were thoroughly aroused, and Pope Leo sent assurance through Cardinal Rampolla on June 28, 1891, that the Holy Father had received the proposals of the immigration societies but had found them "neither opportune nor necessary."

A few days later Cardinal Gibbons was vacationing at Cape

[27] Cf. Barry, note 6 above, pp. 313–316 for these Memorials.

May, New Jersey, and happened to meet the President of the United States, Benjamin Harrison. In the conversation Harrison expressed some concern that foreign countries should treat the United States as a mission country, and the cardinal told him of the reassuring message he had recently received from Cardinal Rampolla. With the President's cooperation, the statements of the interview were released to the newspapers.[28] In reply the German language newspapers defended Cahensly, and the newly appointed Archbishop Katzer of Milwaukee issued a pastoral before leaving his former see stating that he was the spiritual father of all without regard to nationality or birth. Katzer then invited Cardinal Gibbons to preside at his reception of the pallium in Milwaukee on August 20. Gibbons accepted and in his sermon attacked anyone who would try to sow dissension in the American Church, adding: "Let us glory in the title of American citizen. We owe our allegiance to one country, and that country is America." The sermon was directly opposed to what was called Cahenslyism. Peter Paul Cahensly, the German merchant, had intended no evil, but his name had become attached to divisive German nationalism in the Catholic Church in the United States. This divisive force was destroyed by the Pope's decision, but the animosity aroused by the discussion manifested itself on a new occasion in Archbishop Ireland's diocese.

On August 22, 1891, Father James J. Conry, the pastor of Immaculate Conception Church at Faribault, Minnesota, in Archbishop Ireland's diocese, with the Archbishop's consent, approached the public school board of Faribault with a proposal that the public school system take over Immaculate Conception parochial school.[29] The proposal as formulated in writing agreed that for a nominal fee the public school would furnish the equipment and pay the salaries of the teachers and the religious exercises and teaching would be done before or after the regular school hours. On October 14, Father Charles Corcoran of St. Michael's Parish in Stillwater made a like proposal to the school Board there. The two agreements became known throughout the state and through much of the nation. Catholics attacked them as granting too much to public school education, and non-Catholics attacked the proposals as contrary to the traditional separation of Church and State. The State Superintendent of Instruction of Minnesota laid down a rule that there could not be any implied

---

[28] Ellis, *Gibbons*, note 9 above, 1, 373–374.
[29] Reilly, note 25 above, p. 78 ff. treats of the proposals.

agreements on religious matters in such a contract. The contract in Stillwater lasted one year, that in Faribault for two years, when disagreements between the contracting parties brought about cancellation of the contracts. Similar agreements between public and private Catholic schools had been made in other parts of the country but the importance of these contracts arose from the personality of Archbishop Ireland, who had authorized the priests to make the contracts and who was accused of being opposed to parochial schools.

Two other events that year added to the importance of the discussion of the Faribault-Stillwater agreements. In August Doctor Thomas Bouquillon, the moral theologian of the Catholic University wrote an article, "Education, To Whom does It Belong?" for the *Catholic Quarterly Review*. When the *Review* refused to accept it, he published it as a pamphlet. In it Bouquillon argued that the State as well as the parents and the Church had a right to insist on the education of the child, although he denied the right of the State to insist on a certain determined school if the parent chose some other school. Bouquillon had no intention of entering into the Faribault-Stillwater controversy, but the opponents of Archbishop Ireland hurriedly printed a reply under the signature of Father René Holaind, S.J., *The Parent First,* which insisted on the prior right of the parents. The Holaind pamphlet was intended for the archbishops, who held their annual meeting on November 29, 1891, at St. Louis, so as to join the meeting with the celebration of the golden jubilee of Archbishop Kenrick as Bishop on November 30.

The Archbishops discussed the Cahensly Memorials and objected to the high estimate made in them of losses among the immigrants and the threat of foreign governmental interference in ecclesiastical matters. In the meeting also Archbishop Ireland explained his experiments at Faribault and Stillwater apparently to the satisfaction of the Archbishops present. In answer to a request by Monsignor O'Connell and later at the request of Roman authorities, Cardinal Gibbons sent a report to Monsignor O'Connell on the meeting and on Archbishop Ireland's experiments. But Monsignor O'Connell warned Archbishop Ireland that he should come to Rome to defend his position. *The New York Herald* of December 12, 1891, had published a report of the archbishops' meeting with great emphasis on Father Holaind's pamphlet. Archbishop Ireland was in New York and gave an interview to the *Herald* the next day in which he denied the part of the article of the previous day that said the archbishops had spent their time discussing who should educate the child and had deferred the question to Rome. He also defended his agreements in Faribault and Stillwater, praised the pamphlet of Bouquillon, and belittled that of Holaind. Then, on January 16, he did sail from New York for Rome.

On the way Ireland attended a social Congress in Liège. At this time, also, his friends in Europe had arranged to have sent from Berlin a press statement attributed to a Catholic prelate, which was carried widely in the American press, that in Europe the Church did not contest the right of the State over primary schools and that this was especially notable in German-speaking countries, that the Church always tried to have religious instruction in public schools, and that State schools in which religious instruction was given was the practical ideal of the Catholic parties on the continent. The other side of the argument, however, was being developed under Father Salvatore Brandi, S.J., the editor of the *Civiltà Cattolica,* who had taught for some time in the United States. In the *Civiltà* there appeared a criticism of Bouquillon's pamphlet and a news commentary criticizing Archbishop Ireland. In the United States, a whole series of criticisms and rejoinders on the question appeared in various publications, which served chiefly to sharpen the feelings on the issue. The pamphlet of Bouquillon had an importance not immediately grasped in the United States because the canonist was a personal friend of Cardinal Rampolla, the Papal Secretary of State, who at that time was trying also to offset the influence of the Triple Alliance of Germany, Austria, and Italy against the Papacy. Thus, aside from the school question itself, Archbishop Ireland's opposition to any influence, real or imagined, that the German imperial government was exerting in the United States certainly did him no harm with the Cardinal. Nevertheless, the charges against him on the parochial schools had reached Rome, and the Pope appointed a special commission to consider them. In his own defense Archbishop Ireland prepared a long Memorial in which he reviewed the story of the Faribault and Stillwater agreements, the Bennett Law affair, and his speech to the National Education Association. He concluded with a statement that he was regarded by non-Catholics as the leader of those who were supporting the United States Government, rather than being one of those who might combine foreigners into a threat to the republic.

The decision of the Propaganda was made on April 21, 1892, and announced on April 30, to the effect that the plan of the Faribault-Stillwater agreements could be permitted (*tolerari*

potest). The first reports from Rome on May 4, including an un-
clear telegram to Archbishop Corrigan, claimed that the Faribault-
Stillwater plan had been condemned, but on May 11 *The New
York World* announced the actual decision, which was interpreted
by the friends of Archbishop Ireland as a victory. Critics of the
Archbishop tried to interpret the decision otherwise, but the public generally accepted the opinion of the Ireland followers. Archbishop Ireland demanded that the *Civiltà Cattolica* publish Cardinal Gibbons's letter to Monsignor O'Connell of the previous
year in which the Cardinal had explained the actual opinion of
the archbishops in the St. Louis meeting. When the *Civiltà* gave an
unfriendly interpretation of the decree, Cardinal Rampolla published a letter to Ireland that the *Civiltà* was not an official paper
of the Vatican, and, when the Bishops of New York under Archbishop Corrigan sent a letter implying that Archbishop Ireland
had obtained the decision by threatening an American *Kulturkampf,* the Pope sent them a letter denying that Ireland had made
any such threat. Archbishop Ireland left Rome in triumph. On
his way home he accepted an invitation to visit France.

Besides supporting the policy of the Pope in seeking to hold in
check the Triple Alliance, Archbishop Ireland had other special
instances of agreement with the Holy Father. He could refer to
a series of lectures he had given on labor relations the year before
the Pope's *Rerum Novarum* which were much along the line of
the Pope's encyclical, and his support of the American republic
was much in line with the policy advocated for France in the
papal letter of the previous February 10 to the French bishops, *Au
Milieu des Sollicitudes,* which advocated reconciliation between
the bishops and the Republic in France. Archbishop Ireland
seemed to go to France with the special blessing of the Pope. To
the Frenchmen who welcomed the Pope's invitation for French
Catholicism to be reconciled with the French Republic, Ireland
was the chief Catholic from the prosperous and growing Catholicism of the United States. Archbishop Ireland acted the part,[30]
appearing in a simple cassock in the hall of the Société de Géog-
raphie on the evening of June 18 and praising the progress of
the Church in the United States, especially the advantages that
had accrued to the Church from its democratic surroundings. The
French press carried long excerpts of his speech and reported
another talk given to the young university students a week later.
Other reports were published of a talk to the young clergy of

[30] Moynihan, note 5 above, pp. 136–145.

Paris, given subsequently, in which he urged the French priests to get out of their sacristies and to work with the people. Ireland immediately became a symbol of American democracy in the field of religion to both friend and foe in Europe. Some of the French already knew of his speeches in Baltimore and of his association with Cardinal Gibbons in preventing the condemnation of the Knights of Labor. His opposition to the Germans did him no harm in France.

When Archbishop Ireland arrived in New York on July 8, he learned that someone had obtained a copy of his Memorial to the Pope in his defense and had published parts of it in *The New York World* on June 26. Archbishop Corrigan was using the published portions to support his claim that the *tolerari potest* had been obtained by the threat of a *Kulturkampf*. Archbishop Ireland rejected a proposed conciliation meeting between the two archbishops and instead allowed Father McGlynn, the excommunicated opponent of Archbishop Corrigan, to visit him in his hotel room. He went on to Baltimore to see Cardinal Gibbons and then returned to St. Paul in triumph. In the meantime the new Prefect of Propaganda sent a letter on July 1 to Cardinal Gibbons asking that the archbishops discuss the school question with their suffragan bishops before the annual meeting of the archbishops in November.

Archbishop Ireland had discussed with authorities in Rome the proposal of Pope Leo XIII to establish an Apostolic Delegate in the United States. There was no clear indication that one would be sent immediately, but Archbishop Ireland had left suggestions with friends that a likely person for such an appointment would be Archbishop Francesco Satolli, who had been the papal legate to the centennial celebration of the American hierarchy and who had written in the German press in defense of Archbishop Ireland. The Pope suddenly found an occasion to send a special representative to the American Church through whom he hoped to reconcile the two opposing groups of the hierarchy. A world's fair was being planned for Chicago to commemorate the 400th anniversary of the landing of Columbus in the New World. The formal opening of the fair was to be on May 1, 1893, but the main fair building was to be dedicated on October 21, 1892. The managers of the fair sought certain maps and charts from the Vatican Library for exhibition at the fair. After certain preliminary discussions, Secretary of State John W. Foster wrote on September 15, 1892 to Cardinal Rampolla, the Papal Secretary of State, asking for the loan of the maps and charts. The Cardinal answered promptly on September 28 that the Pope would not only make the loan but would send his personal representative to accompany them. That Ablegate was Archbishop Satolli. Accompanying the Papal Ablegate was Monsignor Denis O'Connell, who was assisted by Archbishop Ireland in planning the itinerary of the Ablegate. The Archbishop with the cooperation of Cardinal Gibbons had a revenue cutter meet the Ablegate's ship and bring him to port. After a cursory visit to Archbishop Corrigan, Archbishop Satolli was taken by train to Baltimore and then to Chicago to assist at the dedication of the main fair building on October 21. On that occasion Cardinal Gibbons gave the closing prayer. After that the Ablegate went to St. Paul for a visit with Archbishop Ireland while awaiting the annual meeting of the archbishops in New York.

The annual meeting of the archbishops opened on November 16. Archbishop Satolli not only went to the meeting but on November 17 presented to the American archbishops two proposals. The first was a fourteen point solution of the parochial school question which seemed to be approximately what Archbishop Ireland had advocated.[31] Catholic schools, he said, must be as good as public schools in subject matter, Catholic children were to be permitted to attend public schools when other plans could not be carried out, pastors were to be forbidden to refuse the Sacraments to parents who did not send their children to Catholic schools, and under certain circumstances compromises such as those used by Archbishop Ireland in Faribault and Stillwater were to be permitted. While the Ablegate insisted that the Baltimore decrees remained in effect, he elaborated ways in which exceptions would be allowed. In the second proposal, the Ablegate suggested that there be established a permanent Apostolic Delegation in the United States. On the first proposal the archbishops were all but unanimous in rejecting it and in agreeing on a reassertion and slight implementation of the Baltimore decrees. On the second, they voted that Cardinal Gibbons should send a letter to the Pope thanking him for his kindness in sending the Ablegate but suggesting that the proposal of a resident delegate was inopportune. Apparently the Ablegate was not present when these actions were taken, as he went on to Washington, D.C., where he took up residence at the Catholic University.

On December 3, the Ablegate announced that he had received some extraordinary powers to handle certain American problems.

[31] Zwierlein, *McQuaid*, note 3 above, III, 181–186.

Under these powers he arranged a hearing for Father Edward McGlynn, the excommunicated New York priest. When McGlynn subscribed to the Leonine doctrines about private property and promised to make the journey to Rome to submit to the Propaganda as he had been commanded before his excommunication, the Ablegate released him on December 23 from his censures. Archbishop Corrigan had to receive him back into the Archdiocese but did not give him the same parish. Then on January 14, Archbishop Satolli announced that by a letter from the Pope he had been named permanent Apostolic Delegate to the United States with his office in Washington.

The appointment of the Apostolic Delegate did not stop the protests of the bishops to Rome against the fourteen points of the Delegate's proposal in the November Council of Archbishops. The Pope then asked each bishop to write to him on the subject. There is no record of the number of protests that were sent to Rome, but they were sufficient in number and fervor to have Pope Leo send on May 31, through Cardinal Rampolla, a long letter to Cardinal Gibbons and the other American bishops in which he reviewed the purpose of Archbishop Satolli's appointment: not only to prove his affection for American bishops but also to work for the elimination of the dissensions among them. He said that the propositions on the school controversy of the Delegate given in the November New York meeting had been published inopportunely and subjected to malign interpretations. The Pope wished to acknowledge the letters which he had received in answer to his request for them and said that from them he had learned that they thought the Delegate had abrogated the rules promulgated in the Third Plenary Council on Catholic schools. Such an interpretation he said was alien to the meaning of the Delegate. To make this matter clear, the Pope then affirmed that the decrees of the Baltimore Council were still in force. He hoped that this letter would put away any error that had risen on the subject and that the hierarchy would strive to eliminate dissension. The Pope repeated the same ideas in a letter to the bishops of the Province of Cincinnati on August 28. The school controversy was closed, and the situation before the Faribault-Stillwater agreements was restored.

CHAPTER ELEVEN

A Period of Conflict 1895-1907

THE ROLE OF THE APOSTOLIC DELEGATE in the United States was not clear by any means when Archbishop Satolli made the announcement of his appointment. To the anti-Catholic organization called the American Protective (or Protestant) Association, he had come as the Pope's agent to take over the American government, and on April 8, 1893, the *Patriotic American* of Detroit published an alleged papal encyclical calling for the massacring of all American Protestants on the feast of St. Ignatius the following summer. To some of the American Bishops the appointment was annoying because they felt that the Delegate would take over jurisdiction within their dioceses and interfere in their disciplinary problems to the loss of prestige and perhaps power of the Bishops. To Archbishop Ireland and Bishop Keane, the appointment could mean only that the wishes of the Pope would be carried out, that the Catholic University would be supported, that foreign nationalisms, especially the German, would be checked, and that there would be an increase in Americanism with greater Catholic participation in movements for social reform. To Archbishop Corrigan, and Bishop McQuaid also, the fact that the Delegate arrived and traveled under the guidance of Archbishop Ireland meant that support would be given to those forms of American nationalism that Archbishop Corrigan and Bishop McQuaid opposed: centralization under the Cardinal Archbishop of Baltimore, the strengthening of the Catholic University, and the liberal tendencies of the Americanizing prelates.

The object of all this thought was a short, stocky Italian clergyman of decidedly south-Italian characteristics and mannerisms, scarcely literate in the English language and therefore much dependent on his English-speaking advisers. He was undoubtedly a capable theologian and had been in the country before as a legate to the celebration of the centenary of the hierarchy and the opening of the Catholic University in 1889. Probably he was the only Roman prelate with experience in the United States that the Pope could send to calm down the multiplying dissensions within the American Church. The ideological distance between Rome and the United States had decreased greatly since the mistakes of the Sacred Congregation of Propaganda in 1820 in dealing with the United States but there were lacking in Rome men experienced with the way of life in the New World. The Pope's commending the Delegate to Monsignor O'Connell's care seemed a good move, because the Monsignor was at that time the chief representative of the United States in Rome. It is doubtful that the Roman officials understood that while Monsignor O'Connell was a personal friend of Cardinal Gibbons he had become also a strong partisan of Archbishop Ireland and Bishop Keane ever since they had worked together in 1886. Once the Delegate set up permanent headquarters in the country it was quite natural for him to ask for one of his former students who had been working in America for several years to come and be his secretary. The former student was Father A. H. Minckenberg, then working in the Archdiocese of St. Paul. For the first year the Delegate was so generally accepted as a partisan of Archbishop Ireland that those who disagreed with Archbishop Ireland did not conceal their hostility to him. Soon the Pope had to ask Cardinal Gibbons to arrange friendly exchanges between the Delegate and Archbishop Corrigan.

Despite the disagreements among themselves, which seemed natural enough among persons of so many different origins and traditions, the Catholics in the United States were also a cause of concern to non-Catholic Americans who thought of them as foreign, superstitious, and members of a secret organization, opposed in its very essence to the American Protestant Anglo-Saxon cultural tradition. There were no reliable statistics on the number of Catholics, but it was said that Catholics were about one sixth of the population, numbering between eight and ten millions. There were in the country fourteen archbishops and seventy-three bishops and over nine thousand priests. Although there were Catholics in nearly every section of the country, the concentrations of Catholics were in the large cities and in factory towns, leaving some rural areas where Catholics were mostly unknown except through their damaged reputation among Anglo-Saxons. Americans of the rural areas were not the only ones who feared Catholicism. The "No-Irish need Apply" signs had not disappeared from the Boston area, where Catholics were numerous, and there were few Catholic names on the social registers of the eastern communities. The creation of the Catholic University was a real *tour de force* which promised to give to American Catholicism an intellectual quality that the mass of its peasant immigrants had failed to create. Although a survey taken in the 1890s by Professor Austin O'Malley, M.D., found more than a thousand Catholics in attendance at the existing non-Catholic colleges and universities of the country, the sprinkling of these better educated Catholics seemed to have had little effect in raising the cultural standards of Catholic society.[1] There were many Catholic academies and colleges but, lacking endowment and filled with students without intellectual background, they were gravely in need of the leadership that the Catholic University proposed to give. Some of these institutions were obviously intended to be feeders to the seminaries and offered mostly the traditional renaissance course of the humanities, with a pretence of mastering Latin and Greek, history, and English composition but with little attention to physical science or the newly formed social sciences. The University of Notre Dame with its science program since 1865 was an exception, as was its chief product, Father John A. Zahm, C.S.C., who was writing and lecturing strenuously to prove that there was no real conflict between science and religion. His efforts were not praised by most of the American clergy, although he found support and friendship in Archbishop John Ireland and Bishops John Keane and John Lancaster Spalding.

Of the Catholic lay leaders of the period, we have knowledge mostly by their participation in the two lay Congresses in 1889 and 1893, and while these events were remarkable demonstrations they seem to have had little permanent effect. In estimating Catholic influence on the intellectual leadership of the United States, we are led to the conclusion that the clergy, the chief Catholic intellectuals, had little influence in public affairs for the most part. Archbishop Ireland, Cardinal Gibbons, Bishops Keane and Spalding almost completed the list of those who could expect invitations to the public forums. Thomas Dwight, Professor of Anatomy at Harvard; Professor Charles G. Herbermann of City Col-

---

[1] Austin O'Malley, "Catholic Collegiate Education in the United States," *Catholic World* (June, 1898) LXVII, 289–304.

lege, New York; Professor Martin J. Wade of the Law School of the University of Iowa; and Professor Thomas J. Semmes of the Law School of the University of Louisiana were exceptions to the lack of Catholic professors in the chief educational institutions of the country. Most of the Catholic students attending non-Catholic colleges went into the professions but even they were seldom leaders in Catholic activity among their professions. There were some Catholic writers of literature, but the majority were women or clergymen. John Gilmary Shea, the chief Catholic historian, was by profession a journalist. Richard Clarke, a lawyer in New York, was also an exception in his work in Catholic history and in his efforts to create a Catholic Union in the 1870s and 1880s. Since the Catholic colleges had no endowment, the faculties in them tended to be clergymen or religious, with an exceptional layman, usually unmarried, who received his salary from the earnings of the religious. The majority of the Catholics were working people, very few of whom had received more than elementary education, but who were regular in attendance at the local parish church which had been erected chiefly from their hard-earned contributions.

Because this mass of Catholic laymen had no higher education, they took very little part in the theological controversies that were creating dissensions within the ranks of the clergy except insofar as foreign nationalisms were involved. Because the clergy were the protagonists in several controversies, they quickly drew into the discussion the faculty of the institution founded to give intellectual leadership, the Catholic University. Not all took sides. Of the eighty-seven archbishops and bishops of the country, probably sixty of them were not much excited by problems of nationalism and liberalism. They had plenty to do begging for their poor parishes and supervising the building of churches, schools, hospitals, and orphanages. They were moderately interested in speculative matters and watched with care the local politics insofar as it affected the welfare of their flock and their church property but they had little interest in international affairs or even ordinary American national politics. Some bishops, of course, seemed quite aware of the problems of national and international interest but had no desire to argue publicly about them. This left but a handful of Catholic prelates, mostly bishops, to furnish the active leadership in one of the most exciting periods of American Catholic history.

Gradually these episcopal leaders tended to be divided into two groups, although the groupings were not the same on all questions. The first problem, the perpetuation of foreign nationalisms, left the German clergy almost alone, since there were few representatives of other nationalisms in the hierarchy, and even the other conservative bishops opposed the trend called Cahenslyism after the well intentioned and maligned German businessman, Peter Paul Cahensly. The Germans may have lost the war in the 1880s but they did win some battles when their opponents failed to make Bishop John Lancaster Spalding Archbishop of Milwaukee, when German Bishops were named to the other Wisconsin sees, and when Bishop Ignatius Horstmann was named to Cleveland. The sharp antagonisms aroused in this nationalistic controversy made certain also that the German bishops would be opposed to Archbishop Ireland on most of his other proposals. There were German professors on the faculty of the Catholic University, but it was regarded primarily as an institution of Archbishop Ireland and his friend Bishop Keane and therefore received only grudging support from the German bishops and Ireland's opponents, Archbishops Corrigan and Ryan and Bishop McQuaid. The conservative bishops led by Archbishop Corrigan were suspicious of all secret societies and wanted them condemned; and here they received constant support from the German bishops who regarded these societies as inimical to religion. Although Archbishop Ireland denied that he was opposed to the parochial schools, his opponents in their defense of parochial schools seemed to feel that they were scoring against him. On the vaguely defined question of cooperation with non-Catholics in civic and social progress, the conservatives, especially the German bishops, professed to see in this cooperation with non-Catholics the forbidden liberalism of the *Syllabus of Errors,* while Archbishop Ireland and his friends insisted that in such cooperation they were just following the encyclicals of Pope Leo XIII. They called their opponents *réfractaires* like the French Catholics who would not cooperate with the papal *ralliement* program in France.

Undoubtedly the most interesting manifestation of the progressive spirit of American Catholicism at this time was the Catholic Columbian Congress in Chicago in 1893. During the Baltimore Congress of 1889, resolutions were taken to hold another Congress in connection with the proposed World's Fair to celebrate the fourth centenary of the discovery of America. Eventually the site for the Fair was set at Chicago, in 1893, and William Onahan, the chief manager of the Baltimore Congress, became not only the chief planner for the Chicago Catholic Congress but also a member of the World's Fair Auxiliary.[2] A committee of Catholic laymen headed by Onahan was present at the archbishops' annual meeting in Boston in 1890 to discuss the Chicago Congress, and an episcopal committee headed by Archbishop Ireland was appointed to work with the laymen led by Onahan. But the arrangements for planning were not satisfactory.[3] Other meetings of the committee were held occasionally in 1891 and failed to attract proper cooperation. At one time Onahan was deserted by all his friends and at another Archbishop Ireland seemed about to disapprove of the project. The dioceses were asked to hold congresses from which delegates would be sent to the national congress. Some bishops refused to cooperate, and others could not get lay cooperation, but when the Congress opened on September 4, 1893, there was present a representative group of Catholic laymen.

In general, good papers on many topics were presented. The first day was devoted to the commemoration of Christopher Columbus. On the second day the topics took up social reform under the headings of pauperism, charities, men's societies, pensions, insurance, trade, strikes, immigration, colonization, drunkenness, Indians, Negroes, the independence of the Holy See, and capital and labor. Also, as promised, the Apostolic Delegate appeared with Archbishop Ireland on the stage of the main hall and gave a speech in which he was quoted as telling the members of the Congress to go forward "in one hand bearing the Book of Christian Truth and in the other the Constitution of the United States."

In their speeches on capital and labor, O.E. Browne and John Gibbon of Chicago stressed the rights of the laboring man while Colonel Robert M. Douglas, the son of Stephen A. Douglas, presented a reasonable case for the business corporation. Father James M. Cleary of St. Paul gave a strong case for Catholic temperance. Eleanor C. Donnelly and Rose Hawthorne spoke for the role of women in Catholic public life; Maurice Francis Egan, Bishop Keane, Brother Ambrose of LaSalle College, and others gave speeches on the problems of Catholic higher education. Mary Elder of New Orleans shocked the audience by estimating Catholic losses in the United States as twenty millions and blaming them

[2] Sister M. Sevina Pahorezki, O.F.M., *The Social and Political Activities of William James Onahan* (Washington, 1942) treats of Onahan and the Congress, pp. 131–168.

[3] The story of the Congress is told in *Progress of the Catholic Church in America* and *The Great Columbian Catholic Congress in 1893*, 2 vol. in 1, 4th ed. (Chicago, 1897).

on the concentration of Catholics in the cities. Charles H. Butler of Washington spoke on "The Future of the Negro Race." Of the general addresses, besides that of Archbishop Satolli, the most important were given by Archbishops Ireland and Corrigan. In the resolutions adopted on the last day, September 9, a general progressive program was adopted along with resolutions of loyalty to the Holy See and of adherence to the teachings of the Pope's encyclicals. There seems to be a bit of disorderliness in the published proceedings, which gives the impression of many fine things well said but not coordinated. For some reason the end of the Congress was the end of the American lay congress movement. The victory for the progressive Catholics in this assembly was really quite hollow.

In connection with the World's Fair, a National Catholic Educational Exhibit was planned under the supervision of Bishop John Lancaster Spalding and Brother Maurelian of the Christian Brothers' College of Memphis, Tennessee. While all types of Catholic educational projects were represented, the chief exhibits endeavored to show the accomplishments of the parochial schools. Also from Notre Dame, Professor James F. Edwards furnished many examples of books, manuscripts, and other relics of American Catholic history. September 2 was a day of special celebration at the Exhibit with speeches by Archbishops Feehan, Hennessy, and Ryan and by Judge Morgan O'Brien and the Honorable Thomas Gargan of Boston, but the effort had little real impact on American Catholicism.

Before his appearance at the Catholic Columbian Congress, the Apostolic Delegate had made some progress in the assignments given him by the Pope. On June 16 he began a tour of the West, visiting Chicago, St. Paul, and certain other places west of the Mississippi where difficulties had risen between the bishops and the clergy, especially between the Diocese of Lincoln and Bishop Bonacum. In St. Paul he repeated in public his praise of Archbishop Ireland. Meanwhile, the unfriendliness between the Delegate and Archbishop Corrigan became public knowledge, and Cardinal Gibbons was asked by the Pope to heal the breach between the two prelates. Cardinal Gibbons arranged that Archbishop Corrigan give a public reception for the Delegate in St. Patrick's Cathedral in New York on August 15. On his way back to Washington, the Delegate also visited Archbishop Ryan in Philadelphia, by these two visits balancing his friendship toward Archbishop Ireland.

Although the Delegate went to Chicago under the guidance of

Archbishop Ireland, he did not make any other manifestations of attachment to the St. Paul prelate besides his speech at the Columbian Congress. He made no new proposals at the annual meeting of the archbishops which was held in Chicago before the Congress. The archbishops, however, took the occasion to protest the bitterness appearing in the Catholic press and the criticism by Catholic editors of members of the hierarchy and invoked the decrees of the Third Plenary Council against the wayward editors. The Delegate also refused to participate in the other main event of the Fair, the Parliament of Religions, held from September 11 to 18 as the culmination of all the other religious congresses.

In planning the World's Fair, the managers felt that there should be a proper representation of religion. They encouraged all religions to have their congress at the Fair, and at the end they planned a Parliament of Religions in which all forms of religion might stand together against all forms of irreligion. The general promoter of the Parliament of Religions was Charles C. Bonney, the President of the World's Congress Auxiliary, and the chief organizer was the Reverend John Henry Barrows, a Chicago Presbyterian minister. Archbishop Feehan was named a vice-chairman of the Advisory Committee on the Parliament of which Cardinal Gibbons was a member. The request that Catholics cooperate was presented to the archbishops in their 1892 meeting in New York and the archbishops appointed Bishop Keane to organize the Catholic representation. The archbishops at their Boston meeting in 1893 had asked Bishop Keane to see to the Catholic participation in the Congress. The proposal of Catholic participation, however, was handicapped because of the simultaneous participation of Buddhists, Shintoists, Parsees, and other Asiatic sects as well as Protestant and schismatic churches. Bishop Keane did what he could to keep Catholicism from being put on the same level as these other religious organizations.

The Parliament was planned to last seventeen days.[4] On September 11, after the singing of an English version of the one hundredth psalm, Cardinal Gibbons opened the Parliament with the Lord's Prayer. In the ceremonies of the opening day Archbishop Feehan, Cardinal Gibbons, and Archbishop Redwood gave brief addresses along with representatives of many other religions. Each day there was a general theme. On the second day the theme was the existence of God. The Catholic paper was given by Father

[4] The best account of the Parliament is *The World's Parliament of Religions*, edited by John Henry Barrows, 2 vol. (Chicago, 1893).

Augustine Hewit, C.S.P. On the third day the Catholic paper was given by Father Thomas Byrne. Other papers were given by Father Walter Elliott, C.S.P., Monsignor d'Harlez of Louvain, Monsignor Robert Seton, Professor Martin J. Wade, Professor Thomas Dwight, Father D. J. Kennedy, O.P., the Honorable Charles J. Donnelly of Boston, Father J.R. Slattery, the Honorable Thomas Semmes, Father Thomas O'Gorman, Father John Gmeiner, Father Thomas E. Sherman, S.J., Bishop Keane, Bishop John A. Watterson of Columbus, Archbishop Ireland, and Archbishop Chapelle. During the meeting Bishop Keane spoke three times, on "Truth, Grace and Holiness through Jesus Christ," "The Incarnation Idea in All History and in Jesus Christ," and, on the last day, on "The Ultimate Religion." In addition to these Catholic papers a special hall was set aside where Catholics could answer queries about their religion. The numbers that came to this hall were quite large, and a special lecture was given every afternoon at four o'clock for those in attendance.

As if he knew that he and the others who participated in the Congress were to be criticized, Bishop Keane wrote a summary of the Parliament in the *Catholic Family Annual* of 1894 in which he concluded:

. . . They will consider the Church degraded, because she stood there in the midst not only of her own truant children but even of heathens. But the dear Lord, who has said that his Church must bring forth from her treasure "*new* things and old," and who has made her, as St. Paul says, "a debtor" to all outside wanderers and gropers, will be sure to view the matter differently. For him alone was the work undertaken and carried on; to His honor and glory may all its results redound.[5]

The Chicago Congresses were not the only manifestation of Catholic progress during this financially bad season of 1893. The Catholic Summer School had been organized during the spring of 1892 as a kind of expansion of the Catholic Reading Circle Movement. It was directed by Warren E. Mosher but chiefly was under the leadership of priests and laymen of New York. Its first session was held at New London, Connecticut,[6] from July 30 to August 30, 1892. Although the planning time was short, the combination of recreation and instruction was successful. Among the lecturers were Father H.A. Halpin of Fordham on ethics, Maurice Francis Egan, Malcolm Johnson, and Ernest Lagarde on Shakespeare, and

[5] *The Illustrated Catholic Family Annual for 1894* (New York, 1893) p. 140.
[6] *Ibid.*, pp. 68–75.

Richard Clarke on historical subjects, particularly on Columbus. There were six hundred present on the opening day.

In 1893, despite the Panic, the second session was held at Plattsburg, New York, beginning July 16. The sponsoring organization, which had by that time been formally chartered, was headed by Father Thomas Conaty of Worcester, Massachusetts, as President, Father Joseph McMahon of New York, as Vice President, and Warren E. Mosher, the editor of *The Catholic Reading Circle Review,* as secretary. There was ample episcopal support and attention. In the 1893 meeting there were forty-two lectures, eight sermons, five conferences, and a reception. Highlighting the lectures were four on "Science and Revealed Religion" by Father John A. Zahm, C.S.C., one on the authenticity of the Gospels by Father Augustine F. Hewit, C.S.P., and others on a variety of topics given by other specialists.

The Summer School set up a permanent home near Plattsburg and subsequently held other sessions in Madison, Wisconsin, and in New Orleans. The movement was another manifestation of the premature golden age of American Catholic activity that glowed at the turn of the century.

On October 18, 1893, Cardinal Gibbons celebrated in the Baltimore Cathedral the silver jubilee of his episcopal consecration. In the morning, before thirteen archbishops and fifty bishops, the Cardinal celebrated the Mass, and Archbishop Corrigan gave the sermon on the dignity of the office of bishop. Later that day at a vesper service celebrated by Archbishop Redwood of Wellington, the preacher was Archbishop Ireland on the theme, "The Church and the Age."[7] In his opening paragraph the Archbishop said that he was surfeited with common men and wanted a man among men and such a man was Cardinal Gibbons. He then turned to the spirit of the times and the great discoveries and inventions that were taking place. ". . . Let all things be new, is the watchword of humanity today, and to make all things new is humanity's strong resolve. . . ." To this he added: "To conquer the new world to Christ, the Church must herself be new, adapting herself in manner of life and in method of action to the conditions of the new order, thus proving herself, while ever ancient, to be ever new, as truth from heaven is and ever must be." Yet he said that the age and the Church were at war because the age is proud and exaggerates its intellectual successes, and the leaders of the Church

[7] The sermon is printed in John Ireland, *The Church and Modern Society,* 2 vol. (New York, 1903) I, 105–131.

have been too slow to extend to the age "the conciliatory hand of friendship." He regretted the fact that "The age, abandoned to itself and to false and mischievous guides, irritated by the isolation and unfriendliness of the Church, became hardened in its secularism, and taught itself to despise and hate religion. . . ." This, he said, was a mistake and a misfortune. He distinguished what was good and what was bad in the age, what was permanent and what was transient. He went on, "I preach the new, the most glorious crusade. Church and age. Unite them in the name of humanity, in the name of God." He enumerated the characteristics of the age: ambition for knowledge, an age of democracy, an age of social justice, and an age of material progress. He urged Churchmen to have zeal with human prudence, seeking the things that the age sought. He praised the Catholic leaders of the age: Von Ketteler, Lavigerie, Manning, Gibbons, and Pope Leo XIII. He praised the work that the Pope was doing for France and urged Americans to be loyal to him. Cardinal Gibbons he called the providential leader of America and praised his work. The phrases that echoed from this speech were his pleas that Catholics be patrons of knowledge, models of patriotism, and active in social justice. His friends in France read his speech joyfully and had it translated for wider reading.

During the winter months of 1893–1894 the excitement that had moved the Church in the United States seemed to die down. The Apostolic Delegate bought property in Washington and moved from the Catholic University. In some respects the Apostolic Delegate seemed to have attained his purpose and that of the Pope. There was much discussion and considerable criticism of the Catholic participation in the Parliament of Religions, but Cardinal Gibbons sent to Cardinal Rampolla a favorable account. There were no open hostilities between the followers of Archbishop Ireland and those of Archbishop Corrigan. The Catholic press continued to carry articles critical of members of the hierarchy, and the *Ecclesiastical Review* published articles on the relations between science and the scriptures. The articles in the *Catholic Quarterly Review*, prepared by the most learned clerical and lay Catholics, maintained an open approach to the chief scholarly questions of the day, publishing chronicles of the latest scientific discoveries, articles on the latest scriptural advances, on themes of evolution, and historical studies that were scholarly but not technical. The Church in America seemed to be following the advice of Archbishop Ireland.

It is an interesting fact that this period of progress of Catholicism in the United States was also the period of the final rise of the American Protective Association.[8] The A.P.A.'s successes were national only in the sense that they were widespread. Actually they were mostly local and partially confused with other contemporary issues and movements. The success of this anti-Catholic movement could hardly be described as a reaction to Catholic successes. The arrival of the Apostolic Delegate, and some stories of his interference in local Catholic squabbles in his trips around the country did have some influence in the general excitement, but there is no indication that the leaders of the A.P.A. had any real knowledge of what was going on within American Catholicism.

It is quite clear also that the rank and file of American Catholics were not much aware of these dissensions between the bishops. The Catholic University, for instance, had not yet weathered the trials surrounding its foundation, but the ordinary American Catholic was not interested in university affairs. Bishop Keane continued to have a difficult time getting funds to pay the current expenses of the University. The nationalistic discussions on the faculty began to be noticeable when Dr. Poehle decided to return to Europe and accepted a position in the University of Münster. His German associate, Monsignor Joseph Schroeder, while unhappy, refused to resign despite some provocation. For some reason the new Catholic University *Bulletin* carried no article by Schroeder, or Abbé Georges Périès, his friend. There were no other real Catholic universities in the country in the American acceptation of the title. The Catholic colleges of high caliber were few because these colleges did not have any real endowment, and there was no other graduate school in the country where a faculty could be trained under Catholic auspices. Most faculties of Catholic colleges were made up of clergy and religious, with a few dedicated laymen who could manage to live on meager salaries.

In the spring of 1894, charges were made by Bishop McQuaid in New York that Archbishop Ireland had interfered by correspondence with Republican leaders to have Father Sylvester Malone chosen a member of the Board of Regents of the University of New York to replace the deceased Bishop McNeirny instead of Bishop McQuaid, who was the choice of Archbishop Corrigan. Then in the summer Catholic efforts to get the Repub-

---

[8] Humphrey J. Desmond, *The A.P.A Movement* (Washington, 1912) has been superseded by Donald L. Kinzer, *Episode in Anti-Catholicism, The American Protective Association* (Seattle, 1964), which has some minor errors.

lican Party to condemn the A.P.A. organization were unsuccessful, although the Democratic Party did. Later Archbishop Ireland appeared in New York during the latter part of the campaign and supported the Republican program. Deeply offended by this, Bishop McQuaid on November 25 denounced from the pulpit of his own cathedral the interference of Archbishop Ireland in matters of another diocese. In his conclusion he said:

I also wish it to be understood that this meddling in the political affairs of another state by Archbishop Ireland is altogether exceptional,—as he is the only Bishop who interfered with others, that this scandal deserved rebuke as public as the offense committed. I sincerely hope that the Church will be spared its repetition.[9]

When the Apostolic Delegate heard of the McQuaid speech he sent for a copy of it and reported the matter to Rome. Rome asked Archbishop Corrigan to reprove Bishop McQuaid, and in so doing gave Bishop McQuaid an opportunity he desired to present his full complaint against Archbishop Ireland to Rome a few months later.

During the summer of 1894 Bishop Keane and Father Thomas O'Gorman, one of the professors of the Catholic University, went to Rome to report on the progress of the University and to counteract complaints against the University that had been sent to Rome by some prelates who were not satisfied with its progress. Bishop Keane had two interviews with the Pope. The Pope promised him that in an encyclical soon to be issued he would urge full support for the University. The Pope had shown himself quite disturbed also about the growth of secret societies in the United States which were attracting Catholic memberships. Bishop Keane tried to reassure the Pope on this matter but knew that he had not succeeded. On August 20, the Congregation of the Holy Office sent a decree to Archbishop Satolli, condemning the Knights of Pythias, the Odd Fellows, and the Sons of Temperance.[10] However, the decrees were to be referred to the meeting of the archbishops to be held in Philadelphia beginning October 10. In that meeting, under the leadership of Archbishop Ireland, the majority of the archbishops voted against the immediate promulgation of the condemnation but that, instead, the faithful were to be

[9] Frederick J. Zwierlein, *The Life and Letters of Bishop McQuaid*, 3 vol. (Rochester, 1925–1927) III, 210.

[10] *Ibid.*, II, 471–474. These and other matters involved in the Americanist controversy are treated in T.T. McAvoy's *The Great Crisis in American Catholic History* (Chicago, 1957).

warned against joining such societies. Some bishops, however, had already issued the condemnation, and in December the Delegate wrote to the archbishops that he had been told by Rome to proclaim the condemnation publicly. Archbishops Ireland and Reardon and the Cardinal, who were very conscious of the violent campaigns of the A.P.A. at that time, thought that the decree would do no good but would probably incite further action against the Church. But their protests to Rome accomplished nothing. Even when Cardinal Gibbons endeavored to have the decree softened during his visit to Rome during the summer of 1895, he knew he could not change the Pope's alarm.

While Bishop Keane was in Europe during the summer of 1894, the Catholic participation in the Parliament of Religions in Chicago, 1893, was widely discussed. In the Cologne *Katholikentag*, Father William H. Tappert of Covington, Kentucky, attacked the Catholic participation, accusing the Catholics who took the part of condemned Liberalism and of Americanism. But at the Third Scientific Congress of Catholics held in Brussels, September 3 to 8, Bishop Keane boasted of the good accomplished by Catholic participation in the Parliament of Religions.[11] Not only did he say that Catholicism was presented to people who would otherwise never know of it, but that this was possible only in the United States where the old national and racial lines of Europe were disappearing. Keane's words on the Chicago Congress were printed in the *Bulletin* of the Institut Catholique in Paris by Abbé Felix Klein. Other accounts of the Parliament were published in France and a movement was begun to have a similar Congress of Religions in Paris at the World's Fair in 1900.

On January 6, 1895, the long awaited Encyclical to the Catholics in the United States appeared under the title *Longinqua Oceani*.[12] The Pope opened with his first separate salutation to the Catholics in America, although he noted that he had recognized them already on the occasion of the Columbian celebration in sending a special legate to that celebration. He praised the liberty and independence of the country and recalled the friendship between George Washington and Archbishop John Carroll. He praised the progress not only of the country but of Catholics in the country

[11] *Compte Rendu du Troisième Congrès Scientifique Internationale des Catholiques tenu à Bruxelles du 3 au 8 Septembre, 1894,* 9 vol. (Brussels, 1895) I, 67–74.

[12] Published with a translation in the *American Catholic Quarterly Review,* XX, 346–368.

amidst its freedom of religion but added a note of warning: ". . . It would be very erroneous to draw the conclusion that in America is to be sought the type of the most desirable status of the Church or that it would be universally lawful or expedient for State and Church to be, as in America, dissevered and divorced."

On his own part the Pope claimed that he had sought two things for the Church in America: the advancement of learning and the perfection of Church management. The first he had sought in the establishment of the Catholic University, which he admitted was slowly growing but which he hoped the American people would support. He added to this a plea for the support of the North American College in Rome, which he had canonically recognized in 1884. The second contribution he had made was the establishment of the Apostolic Delegation in which he had recognized that the United States was the equal of any other nation or empire. He denied that the Delegate's power lessened that of the bishops and urged that the faithful show their appreciation of this by their proper submission to the representative of the Holy See. In civic affairs the Pope warned against joining societies that were opposed to the government or which were condemned by the Church. He suggested that Catholics form their own societies and that in their societies they must not violate the rights of others. He urged also that Catholic journalists labor zealously for the Church and that they observe the moderation suggested by the Baltimore councils in the treatment of bishops and of each other, as this was suggested by the archbishops in their meeting of September 1893. He further advised charity toward those outside the Church but suggested that the leadership in this be taken by the bishops and the clergy. Finally he suggested zeal for the welfare of the Indians and Negroes.

The encyclical was welcomed in itself as high praise for the American Catholics and as a plea for support for the Catholic University. Archbishop Ireland and some others, however, did not like the passage in which the Pope made reservations about the American relations between Church and State. In the *Catholic Quarterly Review* for April, Monsignor Joseph Schroeder wrote a commentary on the encyclical in which he saw warnings by the Pope against what he called minimism and liberalism. Schroeder noted that the Pope urged support of the Catholic University as an answer to rationalism and that he warned against attributing the growth of the Church in America to the regime under which it lived; that he urged social justice as opposed to socialism; and finally that the Pope told the journalists that they belong to the hearing not to the teaching part of the Church.[13]

New information, however, was being sent to Rome to Cardinal Ledochowski at Propaganda. In February 1895, Bishop McQuaid sent a long and detailed defense of his attack on Archbishop Ireland. Besides giving details of the interference of the Archbishop in the politics of New York, he accused Ireland also of a constant harassment of Corrigan, so much so that Corrigan's health had suffered. Apparently Archbishop Ireland was unaware of this document.[14]

Also on April 21, 1895, the Apostolic Delegate had gone to Pottsville, Pennsylvania, a German community, to attend the laying of the cornerstone for the parochial school of St. John the Baptist. The Delegate had come in the company of Monsignor Schroeder. The Monsignor gave the sermon in the morning Mass in the presence of the Delegate and said that the Delegate had come to this German community to show that the evils of so-called Cahenslyism were not real and to testify to the devotion of the Germans to the parochial schools. That afternoon at the actual cornerstone laying the Delegate also gave a speech in Latin—later translated into German and English—in which he upheld the right of the Germans to retain their language and customs and praised their loyalty to the Holy See and to the parochial schools. The news of the Delegate's speech was widely noticed in the press, and in some cases heralded as a change in papal policy on liberalism and on the Triple Alliance, since Archbishop Satolli represented the Holy Father.

The Pope had told Bishop Keane in 1894 that he wanted to see Cardinal Gibbons and suggested that he come to Rome that fall. Because of the difficulties of winter travel, Cardinal Gibbons delayed his visit to Rome until the following spring, sailing from New York on May 18.

On June 7 Monsignor Denis O'Connell wrote to Cardinal Gibbons that he was resigning as superior of the North American College, on the plea of ill health. It was generally accepted that he had been forced to resign, some said because of too many absences from Rome but more claimed because some of the bishops charged that he was too much a partisan of Archbishop Ireland and Bishop Keane. The news reached Gibbons on his

[13] Ibid., pp. 369–388.
[14] Zwierlein, note 9 above, III, 216–225 gives the whole letter.

return from Rome and he immediately made Monsignor O'Connel the rector of his titular church, Santa Maria in Trastevere, so he could stay in Rome. The removal of O'Connell was a hard blow to the Cardinal. On top of that, he had to proclaim the Roman decree against secret societies. A third blow to the partisans of Archbishop Ireland came on September 15 when a letter from Pope Leo to the Delegate, Archbishop Satolli, forbade Catholics to participate in international congresses of religions such as the Parliament of Religions, and suggested that they hold their own congresses separately with the exception of the conferences for non-Catholics held by the Paulist Fathers. The Apostolic Delegate had requested this letter, but the occasion was the growing movement in France for a Congress of Religions at the 1900 Paris World's Fair led by Abbé Victor Charbonnel. In Charbonnel's program, all religions were to be considered equal. Archbishop Ireland at first tried to deny the obvious purpose of the papal letter, but the impact of the papal message on the liberal group was undeniable.

In November word came from Rome that Satolli had been named a Cardinal, and the biretta was conferred on him by Cardinal Gibbons in Baltimore on January 6, 1896. The *Civiltà Cattolica* of January 4 announced that the tide had changed and that the conservatives who had been overshadowed during the first year of the Delegate's life in Washington were now regaining lost ground by the actions of the Delegate. The article stressed the evils of the Parliament of Religions which it called a manifestation of neo-Pelagianism. The writer also accused the Americanists of a kind of separatism, which the article tried to connect up with the nativism of the A.P.A.

On April 19, 1896 in St. Patrick's Church in Washington, D.C., Father Thomas O'Gorman, the professor of History at the Catholic University, was consecrated Bishop of Sioux Falls by Cardinal Satolli. The preacher on the occasion was Archbishop Ireland. He began with a statement of the dignity of the episcopate and the need for it and noted that the lack of an active episcopate had caused great losses to the Church in the critical ages in Japan and in England. This seemed to many a criticism of the Jesuits, and he followed this praise of the episcopate with praise for the diocesan clergy, saying that the bishop could not depend on the religious clergy because he did not form them and because they had their own work to do. He praised the Apostolic Delegate saying that the Delegate had been successful in his mission and asked him to tell the Pope of the progress of the Church in the United States. He then went into a long description of the harmonious relations between Church and State in the United States.

> . . . The Church recognizes as her own sphere faith and morals. She possesses and claims no mission in civil and political matters. The State appropriates to itself civil and political matters and assumes no authority in the domain of faith and morals. There is no room for conflict between Church and State; both move in separate and distinct spheres.

Expanding this idea he repeated several times the phrase "Separation of Church and State! Most assuredly. . . ." He concluded with a word of praise for the Catholic University and for the new Bishop. In view of later charges against the Americanists, it is notable that in this daring speech he did insist on the need for the supernatural and on the insufficiency of the natural before entering on his apostrophe on the separation of Church and State.

The speech produced many reactions. Father Havens Richard, S.J., of Georgetown, felt called to answer the attack on religious orders the next week in a reception for Cardinal Satolli at Georgetown. Other religious communities expressed their resentment. But the more important charge that the speech aroused was that the Archbishop was guilty of the false liberalism condemned in the *Syllabus of Errors*. His friend, Father John A. Zahm, C.S.C., of the University of Notre Dame, was also under attack for his advanced scientific opinions.

In the early months of 1896, Father Zahm's *Evolution and Dogma* was published in Chicago. Zahm had played a prominent part, while Vice President and Professor at the University of Notre Dame, in the Plattsburg Summer Schools and had given speeches before learned bodies in Europe as well as in the United States in his efforts to prove that there was no real conflict between science and religion. In his new volume he did not intend to defend Darwinism, but merely to show that there was no real essential conflict between the revealed truth and the concept of evolution. He did not believe in the evolution of the whole man. Even some of his friends, while admitting his orthodoxy, did not accept his arguments, and many conservatives, who had no attraction at all toward modern science, regarded him as plainly heretical. The bitterest opposition was aroused by his efforts to prove from Catholic authorities, such as St. Thomas and St. Augustine, that the possibility of limited evolution was always part of the Christian faith. The Catholic press openly debated the book, and some secular periodicals did not help him when they ascribed to him a defense of the whole theory of evolution, even of Darwinism. In May 1896, Father Zahm went to Rome as the Procurator General of the Congregation of Holy Cross at the Holy See. This appointment had nothing to do with his teachings on evolution, but in the excitement of the controversy was interpreted by some as a recognition and by others as a summons to judgment. *Evolution and Dogma* was being translated into French and Italian, and the Italians were not prepared for his advanced opinions.

In the Catholic press, and to some extent in the secular press, there was speculation as to when the first Apostolic Delegate would go back to Rome and even more speculation about his successor. *The New York Sun* through its Roman correspondent "Innominato" insisted that the new legate would not be a monk, despite rumors that the delegate would be Archbishop Diomede Falconio, a Franciscan. But the new Apostolic Delegate was a monk, the Augustinian, Sebastian Martinelli, who was not yet a bishop. He was consecrated in Rome and came to the United States in September as Cardinal Satolli prepared to leave.

In a sense the new Cardinal, by his speech praising the Germans in Pottsville and some subsequent praise of the Germans in St. Louis, had balanced the effect of his earlier friendliness toward Archbishop Ireland. Archbishop Ireland still considered him a friend, but was not certain. The religious controversy was ignored for the summer and fall because the country, and Catholics as well, was very much excited about the 1896 presidential election and the political issue of free coinage of silver. The traditional party of the Catholics of the country was the Democratic, but Archbishop Ireland was notably a Republican. Usually, the Archbishop, when he gave a political opinion, warned his hearers that he spoke as a citizen and not as an archbishop, but the feelings of those who heard were not so quickly quieted by his disclaimer.

Suddenly Cardinal Gibbons received from Rome a letter to Bishop Keane dated September 15, 1896, saying that it was not the custom to let rectors of papal universities continue in office without limit and that Bishop Keane would be removed to make way for his successor. There was no disguising the fact that Bishop Keane's removal was an act of discipline. His friends were stunned. For once Archbishop Ireland had nothing to say. Whether Cardinal Satolli really admitted that he was responsible for the change is not clear, but the public accepted the opinion that he had been the cause of the removal. The papal letter had suggested that the American hierarchy could nominate Bishop

Keane for an archiepiscopal see in America or he could go to Rome where he would receive a titular see and be appointed to the Congregations of Universities and of Propaganda. Keane, in the first feelings of shock, decided rather that he would retire. He immediately notified the student body which had assembled for the new scholastic year and turned over the administration of the University to the Vice-Rector, Philip Garrigan. Even Cardinal Gibbons, who was present when the Bishop told the students on October 4 of his removal, could not refrain from tears. When the Washington people learned of the papal action, there was a public reception on October 8 honoring him and expressing regret at his removal. The *Baltimore Sun* correctly described the situation when it said: "The removal of Bishop Keane is regarded here as the most serious and far-reaching change which has taken place in many years. . . . The blow is a terrible one to the Catholic University, and to the progressive party in the Church. . . ."

The *Sun*, perhaps unwittingly, had predicted the real result of the change. The University was not yet financially viable, did not have a strong staff or proper support from the hierarchy, and had a divided faculty. The change was intended to cure the last problem but actually made the condition worse. The friends of Bishop Keane on the University faculty and in the hierarchy determined that Monsignor Joseph Schroeder must leave the University. They accused him unofficially of having made in Rome, during the preceding summer, the charges against Keane that led to the removal. The other charges against Schroeder were meagre, and the Roman Cardinals objected to his removal from the University.

As the new Apostolic Delegate was crossing the sea from Rome, Cardinal Satolli began his departure. The Trustees of the University met to nominate a successor to Bishop Keane. They chose Father Thomas Conaty as the most worthy, and their choice was confirmed in Rome. Archbishop Martinelli was installed as Apostolic Delegate in Washington on October 4, and Cardinal Satolli departed, visiting on the way the Archdiocese of New York where he was cordially received by Archbishop Corrigan. Archbishop Ireland also spoke to him a few moments before he sailed from New York. Archbishop Ireland admitted that he was mystified by the recent turn of events. He was not certain that Cardinal Satolli had been responsible for the removal of Bishop Keane, nor whether the former Delegate had really turned against him.

Since the new Apostolic Delegate had left Rome before the removal had been announced, he could talk openly with reporters and express complete ignorance of the meaning of the change.

He did say that there would be no change in policy in the Apostolic Delegation. Archbishop Martinelli had lived earlier for a short time in the United States. He was a quiet person, and his role in the Delegation was not to be the public one of Cardinal Satolli. The argument on the school question had quieted down, the opposition to the University was muted, and the liberal tendencies implied by the participation in the Parliament of Religions and in the toleration of certain secret societies had been removed. Satolli had achieved not peace as he thought but an armed truce. His success was limited probably because he never really understood the United States.

Whether Cardinal Satolli said all that was credited to him or not, he was reported to have taken credit for the removal of Bishop Keane from the rectorship of the Catholic University, and when he arrived in Rome there was a rumor published in *The New York Journal* of November 12 and 13 that he had also recommended censoring Archbishop Ireland and the removal of three other progressive professors at the Catholic University, Fathers Bouquillon, Thomas Shahan, and Edward Pace. In *La Vérité,* the conservative Catholic journal of Paris, the disasters that had happened to the progressives were outlined with glee by "St. Clement," later identified as Abbé Georges Périès, the dismissed canon law professor from the Catholic University. Archbishop Ireland in Saint Paul and Cardinal Gibbons in Baltimore denied the charges, especially those concerning the Archbishop. The rumors continued, and the *Western Watchman* of Father David Phelan quipped on November 26: "Not a cardinal nor an archbishop nor a university professor has been deposed in this country for a week. Even a sense of relief can become monotonous." Finally Archbishop Ireland sent a protest to Cardinal Rampolla, who sent a cablegram to Archbishop Martinelli denying the rumors. In the meantime Bishop Keane had thought more about his letter of removal and, on the advice of friends, decided to accept the invitation of the Pope and go to Rome. Some of his friends even implied that he had misread the papal letter and that it was simply a letter of promotion, but most observers continued to regard the letter as a kind of reprimand.

Abbé Georges Périès in *La Vérité* hastened to enlarge on the significance of the removal of Keane, because at that time in France there was a strong contest in the press between the progressives, who advocated the *ralliement,* and the conservatives, who rejected the Republic. In this controversy, the progressives were using the progress of the Church in the United States as an argument for democracy in France. Périès in his articles described the removal as a disgrace because he claimed the two archbishoprics proposed for Keane did not exist. Also he said that Keane was known in France for his participation in the Parliament of Religions which had been advocated for the World's Fair in 1900 by Abbé Victor Charbonnel and Abbé Felix Klein but was now condemned by the Pope. On October 24 writing as "St. Clement," he quoted an interview with himself in which he made Satolli responsible for the deposition of Keane and praised the constancy of Archbishop Corrigan. Abbé Klein immediately published a letter denying his connection with the proposed Congress of Religions in Paris in 1900. "St. Clement" renewed the charge against Klein noting also that Klein had said that he agreed with Archbishop Ireland in his introduction to the collection of Ireland's speeches. In subsequent issues of La Vérité, Périès gleefully gathered all the rumors in American papers against Archbishop Ireland adding that, since Cardinal Gibbons had been implicated, he, too, would receive a Coadjutor Archbishop of Baltimore. The cablegram of Rampolla to Martinelli denying the rumors kept Périès quiet for a short time, but on December 28 he began the attack on Ireland and Keane again accusing them of favoring secret societies, Protestant ideas of religious congresses, and the public schools; further he insisted that Ireland and Keane were opposed by the Germans and the French and the majority of the American episcopate. He quoted selected American journals to show the split in the American hierarchy and insisted that the conservative majority would prevail in the end. L'Univers-Monde, the paper of the ralliement, denied his charges, but Périès replied with quotations from the Washington Herald affirming the split.

The attack of the conservatives on Archbishop Ireland and his friends in the United States had continued. In the American Ecclesiastical Review of February 1897, "Tharseus," probably Périès, wrote on "Elements of American Liberalism" characterizing this liberalism by (1) its efforts to nationalize the Church, (2) its impatience with tried ways of acquiring knowledge, (3) its disrespect for authority, (4) its willingness to identify Protestantism with the true religion.[15] Monsignor Schroeder had also published without his name in the Katholisches Familienblatt of Pittsburgh, a series of articles containing similar charges against Ireland and the progressives. These articles were republished in English under Schroeder's name by Arthur Preuss in his Review.

[15] American Ecclesiastical Review, XVI, 147–154.

On January 9, 1897, Bishop Keane received from Pope Leo a promotion to the titular Archbishopric of Damascus and was made an assistant to the pontifical throne and a canon of St. John Lateran. Eventually after he protested he was also made a consultor of the Sacred Congregations of Studies and of Propaganda. In Washington on January 19, 1897, Thomas Conaty was installed as the second Rector of the Catholic University.

Archbishop Ireland decided to answer his critics. On March 28, 1897, he gave a sermon in St. Patrick's Church, Washington, under the title "The New Age," in which he called his opponents *réfractaires*, the name given to the opponents of Pope Leo in France. He added:

"Réfractaires," rebels against Leo, are found outside France. They are found where we should least expect to find them—in America. There are, unfortunately, divisions among Catholics in America; not, indeed, in strict matters of faith and morals, but in tendencies and movements, and in adaptations of actions to modern circumstances and surroundings. . . . It is thought sometimes that Catholics in America are divided sometimes on lines of race and language. It is not so. So far as they may be divided, the line of division is that the great majority follow Leo's direction and some hold themselves aloof from him. The loyal Catholics and the réfractaires are confined to no one language. I speak now for myself, but in what I say, I know I speak for all the loyal Catholics in America. There is for me no race, no language, no color. I rise above all such accidentals. In seeking out my brethren, I wish to find those who work for God and for truth, those who work with Leo. . . .

This was a daring speech which aroused his opponents and cheered his followers. The Germans denied that they were attacking Archbishop Ireland because he was opposed to Germans, but because of his liberalism. In France the publication that spring of the French translation of Father Walter Elliott's biography of Father Hecker and the reaction to it made the similarity of the *réfractaires* and their opponents in France into a closer resemblance to the opposing forces in the United States.

After the death of Father Isaac Hecker (1819–1888), the founder of the Paulist Fathers, Father Walter Elliott of the Paulists prepared a biography of Hecker which ran in consecutive issues of the *Catholic World* beginning in April 1890. Archbishop Ireland was invited to write an introduction for the biography, but since his manuscript arrived late it did not appear until the June issue. The next year the biography with the Introduction was published in book form in New York with the approbation of

Archbishop Corrigan and attracted only minor attention. The biography was filled with quotations from the diary of Hecker and from his letters, but Elliott had put them together in such a way as to show that Father Hecker was a very spiritual person with a special mission in the modern world. Hecker, besides being a convert, with experiences among the Transcendentalists in New England, had been for a time a Redemptorist until his efforts to have the Redemptorists establish a special kind of mission work among Americans had led to his expulsion from their ranks. With the approval of the Roman authorities, Father Hecker and the group of the Redemptorists who had been associated in the project were released from their vows as Redemptorists and founded the Congregation of St. Paul, the Paulists, a community without vows, dedicated especially to the conversion of America. Hecker had written and preached on the special compatibility of Roman Catholicism with American political institutions and had published an essay which was critical of the condition of the Church in western Europe. Elliott had indicated that the Paulist community had been raised up by God to meet modern problems and situations and that the absence of the usual religious vows was suitable to the greater independence of the individual in modern times. Besides stressing Hecker's insistence on devotion to the Holy Spirit and his new techniques in making converts, Elliott devoted a whole chapter to the essay composed by Hecker in his last illness in which Hecker had blamed the defeats of the Church in modern times on the defensive actions of the Church and called for more active virtues suitable for the modern age.

When Father Elliott asked his friend, Vicomte de Meaux of Ecotay, to have the book translated into French, de Meaux and his friend, Count Guillaume de Chabrol, asked a cousin of the latter to prepare the translation. The translation was too long for the kind of public to whom these Frenchmen wanted to appeal, and they asked Abbé Klein, the translator of the speeches of Archbishop Ireland, to cut and improve the text. Klein shortened the volume and improved the style and then added a short preface of his own. Ireland had indicated in his Introduction that Hecker was an example of the reconciliation of the Church and the age of which he had spoken in his own sermons. Klein compared Hecker to such American heroes as Franklin and Lincoln and to St. Augustine and St. Theresa and said he was in a sense a doctor of the Church in exposing his mystical experiences. He quoted from one of Hecker's friends, Abbé Dufresne, that Hecker was the ideal type of the modern priest. Klein emphasized Hecker's insistence on a more direct relation between God and the soul, his greater insistence on internal direction and personal freedom. In this Hecker manifested the superiority of the Anglo-Saxons, with their insistence on internal guidance, to the Latins, who relied more on external manifestations.

On the publication of the book, Chabrol and Klein and their friends arranged a campaign of publicity in the French press, which included two articles by Chabrol in *Le Correspondent,* Klein's preface in *La Revue du Clergé Français* and Ireland's Introduction in *La Quinzaine.* Briefer notices appeared also in many other papers, and there were only a few critical reviews. The Fourth International Scientific Congress was being held that year in Fribourg in Switzerland, and Father Zahm and Monsignor O'Connell were scheduled for papers. For his paper, O'Connell, who had not really studied the Elliott biography but who recognized the value of the great publicity given the book in France, prepared a paper entitled "A New Idea in the Life of Father Isaac Hecker." O'Connell boasted to his friends that the Hecker biography would accomplish what they had failed to do themselves so far, that it would sell the way of American Catholicism to France as well as to America. His paper was really a postscript to Archbishop Ireland's sermon against the *réfractaires.* In it he distinguished between political and ecclesiastical Americanism. The political Americanism was found chiefly in the Declaration of Independence and the Constitution, and these he found superior to ancient Roman law because they recognized the dignity of man and guaranteed his liberty and dignity. In discussing ecclesiastical Americanism he admitted that the ideal state, the "thesis," was for the state to accept the Church as the religion of the nation or in a special relationship to the state, but since this was not possible in practice in the United States because of the First Amendment the actual freedom enjoyed by the Church in the United States, the "hypothesis," was the best practical solution. He pointed out that the Pope himself had praised the American Constitution. O'Connell insisted that Hecker had accepted both Americanisms and that these were free of the condemned liberalism and constituted a loyal devotion to the Constitution under which the Church had prospered. Bishop Charles Turinaz of Nancy, a conservative, gave a refutation to the Congress in answer to O'Connell, but his remarks were erased from the proceedings.

In the meantime in Rome on May 15, 1897, the *Civiltà Cattolica* had published a couple of paragraphs in its chronicle in which the question was asked whether the United States was a Christian nation. *The Freeman's Journal* in New York, on June 19, attacked the article and called it an attack on Ireland, Keane, and Gibbons. Other American papers continued to carry attacks or answers on the question of the progressives' liberalism. Ireland and his friends endeavored to confine the discussions to political Americanism or to cooperation between republican government and the Church, rather than making the discussion a religious question. But the conservative American press continued to charge him with the condemned liberalism. In Washington, after the University began its fall sessions in October, the University trustees met and, by a vote of ten to four, voted Monsignor Schroeder's dismissal, to be effective in the spring of 1898. Monsignor Conaty accepted the decision of the trustees, thereby incurring the displeasure of the Germans, who no longer supported the University. Schroeder accepted a position at the University of Münster for the next year.

In Europe the opponents of the *ralliement* and some who disagreed with Klein's appraisal of Hecker were beginning to react to the publicity campaign about the biography. The most notable of the first critical reviews was one by Father A. de La Barre, S.J., in *Etudes* on September 20, 1897. Klein, however, published an even more laudatory account of Hecker in the *Revue Française d'Edimbourg*. On November 10 in the Church of Saint Sulpice in Paris, Père Coube, S.J., in a sermon celebrating the feast of St. Charles Borromeo, opened an attack on four evils that he said threatened the Church. These four most dangerous evils were the Parliament of Religions, an article by Brunetière on the Bankruptcy of Science, Maurice Blondel's philosophy, and Father Hecker's Americanism. A summary of the sermon with the names of the persons attacked was printed in *Le Peuple Français*. On the following Sunday a similar attack was made in St. Clotilde's Church by Père Gaudeau, S.J., at vespers. A third sermon was given later at Sacré Coeur by another Jesuit, and there was a rumor that only the intervention of Archbishop Richard stopped the series. There was another criticism of Abbé Klein published by Père Delattre, S.J. The movement headed by Ireland, Keane, and in France by Klein had acquired the name *"Américanisme"* in Europe.[16]

The newspaper discussion of the French translation of the biography of Father Hecker continued, and the pamphlet publication of Monsignor O'Connell's paper also attracted attention. On

---

[16] The most complete account of the Americanist controversy is T. T. McAvoy, *The Great Crisis in American Catholic History, 1895–1900* (Chicago, 1957).

March 3, 1898, there appeared in *La Vérité* the first of a series of articles signed "Martel," entitled "L'Américanisme Mystique." "Martel" was Abbé Charles Maignen, a priest of the Society of the Brothers of Saint Vincent De Paul, who had acquired some notice by attacking previously Albert de Munn, a leader of the *ralliement*. Maignen had consulted Abbé Périès about the biography of Father Hecker. The first article indicated the importance of the book from the praise of Hecker by Klein and Ireland but asked if relations between God and man had really changed in recent times. The next article criticized the early life of Hecker. Other articles emphasized the limited education of Hecker and gave an adverse interpretation of his departure from the Redemptorists. "Martel" then began to attack the spiritual character of the Paulist founder, called his apologetics an attempt to make the approach of the rationalists to the Church easier, derided Hecker's sanctity, said that the call for abolishing the custom houses for converts was an attack on the defenders of the Church, and said that Hecker's teaching about the Holy Ghost was contrary to the encyclical on that subject by Pope Leo XIII. He then turned on Hecker's praise of the Anglo-Saxons over the Latins and his praise of democracy and American civilization. In later articles "Martel" attacked O'Connell's paper at Fribourg and Keane's speech at Malines on the Congress of Religions. He accused Keane of holding certain propositions condemned in the *Syllabus of Errors*. Finally, "Martel" on April 2 claimed that the biography was just the Trojan horse of *Américanisme*. On April 4 "Martel" began to describe the plot of the Americanists against the Church, of which the first campaign was the Chicago Parliament of Religions which they hoped to repeat in Paris in 1900. The third campaign described on April 9 was the proposal of Father Hecker as a saint. In an article on the Spanish-American war which began at the time, *La Vérité* pleaded for a defense of European civilization against the Americans.

News of these "Martel" articles had reached the United States, and Cardinal Gibbons prepared a preface to the sixth edition of the French biography in defense of Hecker. Klein wrote a defense of himself for *L'Univers* and the editors of that paper exposed "St. Clement," the author of the attack on the Catholic University, as Abbé Périès, the ousted professor. Maignen, however, sent an answer to *L'Univers* in which he supported his charges against the biography and its defenders. On May 28, *La Vérité* announced the publication of the articles of "Martel" in book form. In the book *Le Père Hecker est-il un saint?* Maignen admitted his authorship and added essays defending his actions. Maignen's book had been refused an imprimatur by the Cardinal of Paris, but with the permission of his superior Maignen took the book to Rome and, adding the name of a Roman publisher, obtained the imprimatur from Père Lepidi, the Master of the Sacred Palace. This action gave some grounds for the presumption of a papal approval of the book.

In the United States the American press had been advocating for months American intervention in Cuba where the natives had mounted an insurrection against the Spanish Governor. The Spanish Governor had tried to suppress the revolt by cruel methods. In the midst of this agitation the American battleship *Maine,* which had been sent to the harbor of Havana to protect American interests, was blown up. The cause of the explosion was not actually determined, but the press implied that the Spanish were responsible. As war between Spain and the United States threatened, European powers intervened, and President McKinley seemed desirous of avoiding conflict. On March 27 Cardinal Rampolla wrote to Archbishop Keane in Rome asking him to get Archbishop Ireland to use his influence in Washington to bring about a pacific solution of the problem.[17] Ireland went immediately to Washington but the President had already demanded that the Spanish government declare an armistice until October 1. The Spanish government had declared the conditions attached to the proposal inadmissible.

On April 1 Archbishop Ireland conferred with the President and cabled the Pope that action by Spain would have to be taken immediately. Ireland had favorable conferences with the Ambassadors of Spain and France and Senator Cushman K. Davis, the Chairman of the Senate Foreign Relations Committee, and so notified Cardinal Rampolla. Unfortunately the Spanish acted on this message and claimed that, because of the intervention of the Holy Father at the request of the United States, an armistice would be granted. This announcement was not true and merely worsened conditions. Spain laid down conditions for the armistice that the United States could not accept. Then the American Ambassador, Woodward, in Madrid made a demand that had to be withdrawn. The negotiations and the promise of an armistice were delayed until finally President McKinley felt that he had to give his report to Congress on April 11. Congress began the debate,

[17] Humphrey Moynihan, "Archbishop Ireland and the Spanish-American War—Some Original Data," *Ireland America Review* (1942–1943) V, 98–118.

but Spain, despite promises of an armistice, delayed the actual announcement from day to day. The House of Representatives on April 17 passed a resolution demanding the independence of Cuba, an act amounting to a declaration of war. The Senate concurred on April 19, and Archbishop Ireland's intervention was wasted by the Spanish delay. On April 21 Archbishop Ireland wired to Cardinal Rampolla that he had failed but had been honored to be of service to the Holy Father. He could justly say that Spain had acted too late in announcing the armistice, but he had to admit that he had failed, and his critics were not slow to charge that against him. Other events worked against the Americanists.

Father John A. Zahm, C.S.C., who had been the Procurator of the Congregation of Holy Cross in Rome since 1896, was named Provincial of the American Province to succeed the deceased Father William Corby, C.S.C., on January 22, 1898, and was elected to the position by the General Chapter in August. Monsignor O'Connell wrote to Zahm that the controversy over Americanism was becoming intense, that the Holy Father had reserved examination of the question to himself, but that an imprimatur was to be given to the second edition of Maignen's book. Then on September 10, 1898, the Sacred Congregation of the Index issued a prohibition against Zahm's *Evolution and Dogma*.[18] The decree, however, was not to be published until the Superior General of the Congregation of Holy Cross had been consulted and had answered a request for the correction of the book. The decree was sent through Father Gilbert Français, C.S.C., the Holy Cross Superior General. Zahm prepared to submit to the decree, claiming that his only purpose in writing the book was "the good of Souls & the glory of the Church." Actually Zahm felt that his involvement in the Americanist movement was the immediate cause of the condemnation and that others in Europe had written just as frankly on the subject. He urged his friends in Rome to prevent the decree from being published or that he be permitted to revise the book to meet the criticisms of the Sacred Congregation. Cardinal Serafino Vannutelli intervened with the Pope to prevent the publication of the decree. In the December 29, 1898, issue of *Civiltà Cattolica*, Father Salvatore Brandi, S.J., who had taught for some time in the United States, wrote a very critical review of the book, and privately to Archbishop Corrigan predicted its condemnation. Archbishop Ireland wrote a letter to

---

[18] Ralph E. Weber, *Notre Dame's John Zahm, American Catholic Apologist and Educator* (Notre Dame, 1961) pp. 99–128.

Cardinal Rampolla against the condemnation, and this with the intervention of Cardinal Serafino Vannutelli prevented the condemnation but did not prevent the secretary of the Sacred Congregation of the Index from demanding the withdrawal of the book in all languages. A letter of Zahm to his Italian publisher asking the withdrawal of the book at the request of the Holy See became public and gave pleasure to his opponents, but the actual decree was never published.

Meanwhile the publication of the Maignen book was announced on May 24. To the essays published in *La Vérité*, Maignen added some discussions of the more recent events in the controversy and gave a biased interpretation of Ireland's unsuccessful intervention to prevent the Spanish-American war. He noted also a newspaper story that Cardinal Gibbons might be made Pope and criticized certain other essays in French and English periodicals published under pen names of persons whom Maignen insisted were Americanists, using them to give a liberalistic interpretation of the speeches given by Keane at the Chicago Parliament of Religions. Archbishop Keane protested the granting of the imprimatur by Father Lepidi but Lepidi pleaded the right of writers to publish opinions. The letters published about the granting of the imprimatur left the knowledge of the Pope and Cardinal Rampolla about it uncertain. From St. Paul, Archbishop Ireland wrote a letter of protest to Cardinal Rampolla against the book and the granting of the imprimatur. He maintained that he was the chief culprit in the book and denied that Americanism had the bad meaning attributed to it by Maignen. Americans, he said, would be indignant at the charges, and this reaction would do harm to the Church in the United States. In June another book attacking Americanism appeared from the pen of A.J. Delattre, S.J., of Namur. Klein again defended his position in *Le Correspondent*. More articles appeared in the French press on both sides of the argument, and they began to appear also in the Italian press.

One of the more important articles was that by Père Hippolite Martin, S.J., in *Etudes*, which was frankly anti-Americanist and accused the Americanists of the condemned liberalism and attacked the character of Father Hecker as portrayed by the Americanists. During the summer months there was a lessening of activities in Rome but Cardinal Gibbons wrote a letter of protest to Cardinal Rampolla on August 27. But the Maignen book had been read widely in Rome and had considerable influence. Further the Spanish-American War did not help the Americanists in Rome nor did the movement later called "Modernism" which was already being attacked in Rome. The Pope appointed a committee of Cardinals to examine into the Americanist dispute.

In the United States the English translation of Maignen's book was rejected by the Benziger publishing house, and the name of an English publisher was pasted into the book. Father Walter Elliott, writing on October 20, 1898, could say that the European attack on the Americanists and Father Hecker had no echo in America except in *The Review* of St. Louis. Archbishop Ireland had received a letter from Cardinal Rampolla dated August 6 assuring him that he did not need to worry. Ireland was detained in Chicago and did not attend the meeting of the Council of Archbishops in Washington on October 12. A letter of protest and explanation from the Paulists to the Archbishops, entrusted by the Paulists to Archbishop Corrigan, was presented by him, but he did not support any protest. The Americanists in Rome had begun to think that they were to get a favorable decision from the Pope, but Archbishop Ireland decided to go to Rome as soon as he could arrange the trip. He arrived in Rome on January 27. Cardinal Gibbons also sent a cablegram on February 7 asking for a delay in any decision. The copy of the Apostolic letter to Gibbons on Americanism was sent from Rome on January 31, that to Archbishop Martinelli on February 1. The papal letter, *Testem Benevolentiae*,[19] was dated January 22. Both Ireland and Gibbons were told that their protests came too late, and Gibbons was told by Cardinal Rampolla in his cablegram that Gibbons would find the letter acceptable.

The letter began with a statement that this letter was a witness of affection but that the Pope wanted to list some matters to be reproved and corrected and that he wrote to end certain contentions. Gibbons, he said, was aware that certain doctrines had been introduced concerning the Christian life in connection with the publication of the biography of Father Hecker, especially in the translation. These doctrines advocated changes not only in methods of teaching the doctrines of the Church but even in the "Deposit of Faith" as an indulgence to modern life and discoveries. Such changes in doctrine were contrary to the decrees of the Council of the Vatican. Further the Pope added that changes in discipline must be made by the Church, not by individuals. The Pope specified certain special doctrines to which the name "Americanism" had been attached: (1) the rejection of external guid-

---

[19] The letter was printed in many journals and as a separate pamphlet. Cf. McAvoy, *Great Crisis*, note 16 above, pp. 379-391.

ance and dependence instead on the internal guidance of the Holy Spirit; (2) the extolling of natural virtues above supernatural virtues; (3) a distinction between active and passive virtues and the preference of active virtues where the Pope said all virtues were active; (4) the rejection of the evangelical virtues and the vows of the religious life as passive virtues; and (5) the adoption of new ways to bring converts into the Church. New changes, the Pope said, must be made under the direction of the local bishop and be accompanied by the wise observance of the sacred ceremonies and by good lives. The Pope added that by this condemned "Americanism" he did not mean the characteristics of the American people. He said also that, if the reproved doctrines were taught in America, he was sure that American bishops would reject them. While the doctrines called Americanism were reproved, the Pope did not condemn the biography of Hecker or say that anyone held the condemned doctrines.

Archbishop Ireland immediately published his acceptance of the letter but denied that he had ever held the doctrines condemned. Archbishop Keane made a similar statement. Later on March 17, 1899, Gibbons wrote to the Pope that no educated Catholic in the United States held the condemned doctrines. Abbé Klein sent in his submission to the pope and withdrew the French biography from sale, contrary to the wishes of Archbishop Ireland.

The anti-Americanists boasted of their victory, and the controversy was dead. Ireland, before he left Europe, allowed himself to be interviewed by the press and claimed that the whole heresy was a creation of Abbé Georges Périès and his co-worker, Abbé Maignen. The reaction of the American bishops was interesting. Of the fourteen archbishops, three, Feehan of Chicago, Hennessy of Dubuque, and Bourgade of Santa Fé made no public statement. Four, Elder of Cincinnati, Chapelle of New Orleans, Christie of Portland, and Ryan of Philadelphia, simply thanked the Pope for his letter but did not admit the existence of the heresy. Riordan of San Francisco, Kain of St. Louis, Williams of Boston, and Gibbons of Baltimore denied that the heresy existed in the country. Two, Corrigan of New York and Katzer of Milwaukee, thanked the Holy Father for checking the growth of the heresy. In Rome, the *Civiltà Cattolica* accused the Americanists of a Jansenistic mental reservation in their denial that they held the reproved doctrines. This charge was repeated in the letter of the archbishop and bishops of the Milwaukee Province to the Holy Father.

Since the Americanists did not admit the existence of the condemned heresy and their opponents insisted that it did exist, the subsequent discussion which was maintained by a few Catholic papers on both sides of the Atlantic was about the existence of the heresy. No one defended the doctrines reprobated by the Pope.

In France the controversy over the *ralliement* was continued, but *l'Américanisme* as a factor was dead. In the United States defenders of Archbishop Ireland even insisted that the Apostolic letter was a blessing since it freed the Americanists from the heresies which they did not hold. After he returned to St. Paul, Archbishop Ireland answered the Wisconsin bishops in an article in the *Northwestern Chronicle* under the initials "H.M.," pointing out particularly that the Pope in his letter did not say that anyone held the heresy, and that the denial that they held the heresy was not like the Jansenistic denial, which was a denial of established facts. Later, when Ireland attended the meeting of the archbishops at the Catholic University on October 12, he tried to get a resolution adopted challenging the statement of the Milwaukee bishops about the existence of the heresy but his resolution was lost by the intervention of Cardinal Gibbons after a tie vote. An article on "The End of 'Americanism' in France," published in 1900 in the March *North American Review* by Monsignor Péchenard, was answered by J. St. Clair Etheridge, in "The Genesis of 'Americanism' " in the May issue. Apparently the author of the latter was Archbishop Ireland, and it contained a forceful defense of his position in the controversy.

Archbishop Keane was asked to return to the United States in the fall of 1899 to beg for the Catholic University. He opened his campaign in Washington at St. Patrick's on Sunday, October 22, and after another sermon in that city went on to Philadelphia, Boston, Providence, Springfield (Massachusetts), and New York. On March 4, 1900, Archbishop John Hennessy of Dubuque died. The terna proposed by the Archdiocese listed Keane in the second place. In the bishops' terna he was first. Cardinal Gibbons wrote a letter to Cardinal Rampolla asking for Keane's appointment, and he was named Archbishop of Dubuque on July 24, 1900. To his dismay a personal letter from Pope Leo accompanying the bull urged him to preserve his flock from the dangers of Americanism mentioned in the Apostolic letter.[20] The formal notification came to Keane on September 12, while he was resting at Bad Nauheim in Germany. Whether the appointment was a full restoration of the

---

[20] The letter as well as the rest of Keane's correspondence has not been preserved.

Archbishop or not was not clear because of the papal personal letter. But his close friend, Archbishop Ireland, claimed that Americanism was triumphant in the appointment. Archbishop Ireland was even more emphatic when Monsignor Denis O'Connell was made the Rector of the Catholic University in January, 1903.

As in all periods of crisis, events affecting the Catholic Church in the United States had happened with lightning rapidity during the last five years of the century. The papal letter written to end the controversy in Europe had the intended effect also of stopping the public controversy in the United States. But while the question of Americanization and its correlative cooperation in social reform were just accidental problems in the European controversy between two parties of the *ralliement* in France, they were at the heart of the dissensions in the United States. In the so-called Cahensly controversy, the non-English Catholic groups had been defeated in their efforts to achieve an independent government but, at least, the Germans had succeeded in calling attention to their second-class status in the hierarchy and obtained more German bishops. The friction between the Irish and the Germans and French Canadians, however, was not ended by the papal letter. The embers of old fires were not out. There were even new developments of the same discussion when the flood of Polish, Hungarian, and Italian immigrants of the last decades of the nineteenth and the first decades of the twentieth centuries brought new nationalistic and linguistic problems. The Americanist crisis in the United States involved these linguistic and nationalistic problems and in its positive side concerned the participation of Catholics in the public life of the new American nation, particularly in the social and economic movements at the turn of the century. The divisions on these problems continued on even after World War I but were not discussed as religious Americanism.

Archbishop Ireland may have been too enthusiastic about the future of the United States, but he was certainly in tune with the mood of the Progressive Era in American politics and social and economic reform. Archbishop Keane and he thought very much alike on these matters, although Keane had a more gentle personality. Both associated freely with non-Catholic religious and social leaders. Bishop John Lancaster Spalding was classified generally with them but had arrived at his position independently of the political leadership of Ireland and Keane. He was recognized generally as the best thinker among the hierarchy of that day and as one who cooperated with public authorities in the social and economic reforms advocated in the Progressive Era. The most important Catholic prelate politically was Cardinal Gibbons, whose reputation as a diplomat rested upon his ability to deal intimately and cordially with the political chiefs of the nation. Although Roman authorities would not give him the title of primate, he functioned in public as the head of the Church in America. His graciousness and his stately appearance were of great service in promoting better public relations between Catholics and non-Catholics in the country. Archbishop Michael Corrigan represented the conservative mind which hesitated to cooperate with non-Catholics even in matters of public need. His career was suddenly interrupted by a fall followed later by complications that resulted in death in 1902. His successor, Archbishop John Farley, had neither the zeal nor the qualities of leadership of Corrigan. There were a few promising younger men in the hierarchy, such as Bishops John J. Glennon of Kansas City, Sebastian Messmer of Green Bay, and James McFaul of Trenton, but for the most part the leadership remained for another decade with older prelates who had carried on the controversy over cooperation with non-Catholics during the five years from 1895 to 1900. The papal letter, by dragging in the French controversy, prevented the American controversy from reaching a clear decision in the United States, where it was important. Pope Leo's assertion that he was not writing about the real Americanism was forgotten in the denials and counterassertions over the mythical Americanism. Archbishop Ireland never admitted defeat, and the conservatives and many Germans kept insisting that the American way of life was not Catholic. The Catholic University, whose staff divided in the controversy, was perhaps the chief loser of the controversy by the departure of the German theologians and the withdrawal of support by the German-Americans. Yet the University did struggle on. The generally bad effects of this crisis without a decision were not immediately noticeable. The noticeable booming of interest in Catholic things that had brought on the controversies continued for a decade although new leaders in public life did not arise. The discussions of Catholicism in the secular press and in the Catholic papers during the 1900s were not really different from what had appeared in the 1890s except that there was a noticeable silence about "Americanism."

In *The Atlantic Monthly* of October, 1899, Henry D. Sedgwick, Jr., discussed the future of Roman Catholicism under the title, "The United States and Rome." He reviewed the startling growth of Roman Catholicism in the United States since the colonial period, looked abroad at the ability of the Church to survive the various crises of western European history, and spoke briefly of the Americanist movement in this country and the Anglo-Catholic movement in the Anglican Church in England. He judged that the conservatives had won the Americanism controversy. He noted also the care with which Cardinal Gibbons in the case of the Knights of Labor and Cardinal Manning in the great dock strike had taken in laboring classes. There had been no reversal in this field. He concluded:

. . . Who is so bold as to predict the future of the Catholic Church in America? At present she is the church of the ignorant, but her ambition seeks to extend her influence over the whole nation. There are but three classes of citizens, which, as classes, we are sure will not come under her sway. Men of scientific knowledge; men of independent character who are resolute to manage their own affairs, a class which is on the wane; and third, the negroes, with whom the Catholic Church has not been successful, but who, as a class, will never have a share in guiding our national life. Set these classes aside, and divide the remainder into thirds. One third, composed of the educated, will be divided among the disagreeing Protestant sects; but the remaining two thirds will be a great flock, now scattered and wandering, ready for a wise church to guide. The danger to the world from priestly intolerance and greed is practically past; the danger to the world from oligarchs, free from religious influences, is far greater. The church may well have this sympathy of the unbiased.[21]

Sedgwick saw another source of Catholic growth in the "tide of reaction against the materialistic beliefs of the passing generation" calling themselves, "Healers, Faith Curers, Christian Scientists." Sedgwick's assumption that outward opposition to the Church had disappeared was premature, as were his hints that Rome would accept the way of America because the Americans were so successful. The Americanists had had a vision of quickly converting the United States, but they had been rebuffed by Rome. The story of the Catholic Church in the United States during the next two decades is the story of the rejected Americanists hoping for changes that did not come and their opponents trying to solve the problem of getting Catholicism accepted in American circumstances without adopting the policies they had condemned in their opponents.

The geographical distribution of American Catholics in 1900 had very little in common with the political divisions of the country. The greatest concentration was around New York with about 825,000 in the Archdiocese of New York, 500,000 in the Diocese

[21] *The Atlantic Monthly*, LXXXIV, 458.

of Brooklyn, and another 272,000 across the river in the Diocese of Newark. In this group were represented all nationalities of Western Europe, often with national churches, but there was a predominance of Irish. Some were very poor, living in tenements. These had few chances of rising from their misery except through political deals. There were others who had worked up to better jobs and positions by which they could own or rent a suitable living place. Although there were several Catholic journalists of reputation, Catholics were fewer on the faculties of cultural institutions and on the boards of education than their numbers could justify. Even fewer had acquired real wealth and position.[22] Among these were the families of John McKay and his son, Clarence; the Iselin family; James McDonald, the builder of the subway; the Coleman brothers; William R. Grace; Joseph J. Donohue; Lawrence Callanan; Peter F. Collier, the publisher; John A. McCall, the dealer in insurance; John McAnerny; John B. Manning; John D. Crimmins; John Flanigan; Samuel Adams; Hugh King; George Hecker; Peter Doelger; George Ehret; the Travers brothers; Daniel O'Day; and Patrick and Stephen Farrelly. These men and others had made their way to the top of some of the many businesses in New York. Others who deserve notice in their fidelity and generosity to the Church include the orator, Bourke Cockran; Augustine Daly, the theatre manager; Thomas Fortune Ryan; Mrs. Kate Ashman; and Miss Annie Leary. The pastors of some of the larger parishes in New York were by that fact alone persons of importance in city life. Among these were, besides Father Edward McGlynn and Father Sylvester Malone, who died in 1900, Dr. Richard Lalor Burtsell, Father Joseph Mooney, Father James Flood, Father John Edwards, Father James McGean, Dr. Patrick McSweeney, and Father James Nilan. Fathers Frederick Wayrick, Anthony Kessler, and Anthony Lammel were leaders of their German-American flocks. Most of the larger Catholic societies of the country were represented in the New York area. The more important of them were the Catholic Foresters, The Ancient Order of Hibernians, The Irish Catholic Benevolent Union, The Catholic Mutual Benevolent Association, The Catholic Knights of America, and the flourishing Knights of Columbus. These societies, besides providing insurance benefits for their members, were service organizations within the Catholic community and agencies for defense in times of attack.

Boston, with an estimated Catholic population of 610,000, did

[22] John Talbot Smith, *The Catholic Church in New York,* 2 vol. (New York, 1905) II, 449–459.

not have as many Catholics successful in business as New York and, except for several converts, had few acceptable in Boston society. As in New York, the Irish began to make progress in political careers in Boston and its environs. In lieu of colleges, the Catholic weekly, *The Pilot,* seems to have been the center of Catholic cultural activities, having such staff writers as Patrick Donahoe, John Boyle O'Reilly, Katherine Conway, and James Jeffrey Roche. To these must be added Louise Imogen Guiney, the poetess whose origin was Boston. In professional life the name of the most noted lawyer was probably Patrick Andrew Collins, who served in the state legislature and as Mayor of Boston. Other Catholic lawyers of prominence were Charles Francis Donnelly, who also gave legal guidance to the Catholic clergy, Thomas J. Gargan, and John Francis McEvoy of Lowell. Catholic physicians of note were Dr. John G. Blake and Dr. Michael Gavin and Dr. Thomas Dwight, the Professor of Anatomy at Harvard. Among the few Catholics to rise in business were Thomas R. Looby and Thomas B. Fitzpatrick.[23]

Other large cities serving as centers of Catholic population were Chicago with 700,000 Catholics in the Chicago Archdiocese, Philadelphia with 460,000 in the area about Philadelphia, and Pittsburgh with 280,000 in its Diocese. In each of these communities there were a few Catholics who had attained prominence in the professions, usually a few journalists of ability, and a few businessmen of some success. By reason of the fewness and widely scattered locations, the Catholic laymen were unable to unite. The leaders of the Catholic minority were the clergy, who were classified as well educated by reason of the long period of formation and who had position and organization by reason of their office. Although many of these clergymen had special capabilities in the pulpit, they had little time for writing. Outside of a few journalists, there were very few laymen with the leisure or the financial means required for the pursuit of literature and the arts. The *Catholic Directory* of 1900 listed 178 colleges for boys and 662 academies for girls, but there were no definite meanings to the terms "college" or "academy." The first Catholic colleges for women were just beginning to take form, at Notre Dame in Baltimore, Trinity in Washington, and St. Mary's of Notre Dame, Indiana. The boys' colleges usually followed in theory the old classical college pro-

[23] The best account of Boston lay Catholicism at this time is Robert H. Lord, John E. Sexton, and Edward T. Harrington, *History of the Archdiocese of Boston, 1604–1943,* III, 382–415.

gram but neither the faculties nor the students were properly qualified for the program, although there were occasional exceptions. Most American Catholics belonged to the working class, and Henry Sedgwick could be excused for believing that the appeal of Catholicism was only to that class and that the intellectual and independent thinker would not enter the Church. At this time there was a flowering of Catholic culture—premature perhaps—but one that could have given the optimistic leaders of American Catholicism, Archbishop Ireland, Cardinal Gibbons, Archbishop Keane, and their friends, some real encouragement.

Of the eight or nine millions of Catholics, a very large percentage were in their first generation in the United States. There are no accurate statistics on Catholic immigrants, but in the previous decades 651,893 immigrants had come from Italy, 388,416 from Ireland, and 592,707 from Austria-Hungary. Poland was not an independent nation at the time and hundreds of thousands of the immigrants from Germany, Austria-Hungary, and Russia were Polish Catholics. There were also considerable numbers of Catholics from Bohemia-Slovakia, Lithuania, and other regions who had lost their national status in the formation of modern Europe. The population of the nation was already forty percent urban, but the Catholic urban percentage was much higher if the mill towns were included as urban. There were some Catholic farming communities in the Middle West and some other Catholics in rural communities, but most Catholic immigrants had neither the funds to buy lands nor skill in farming.

The common elements of this large Catholic minority, except for a few congregations of Eastern Rite Catholics, was the Latin Mass and the Sacraments, usually also conferred in Latin, and catechetical knowledge of the teachings of the Apostles' Creed. Their family prayers were often said in a foreign tongue. Parish grade schools and also a parish social hall were common in the parishes of the Middle West and in some regions of the eastern dioceses. Among the clergy there were religious communities of priests, chiefly of the old orders, Jesuits, Franciscans, Dominicans, Augustinians, Vincentians, and a few congregations founded in the eighteenth or nineteenth century, such as Holy Cross, the Marists, the Precious Blood Fathers, and the American-founded Paulists. Most of the collegiate institutions were maintained by the Jesuits or by diocesan clergy, with the exception of Notre Dame, St. Bonaventure, Villanova, and a few seminaries. Insofar as these religious communities were irregular in their location and worked mostly independently of the diocesan organizations, they were not a unifying factor in American Catholicism. There were about 200 Catholic newspapers, some in foreign languages and mostly weekly diocesan papers, but very few of them had more than a local circulation. The few Catholic magazines had a wider distribution but no definable clientele.

The fact of the matter was that, despite the supposed close organization of the hierarchy and the presence of a resident Apostolic Delegate, American Catholicism was not a real unity even with the Instructions of 1875 and 1878 and the decrees of the Third Plenary Council. The Catholic schools differed in quality and quantity from diocese to diocese and generally had no direct relationship to the Catholic University. The national societies included the growing Knights of Columbus and many national societies for the Irish, Germans, or Polish, which were usually regional in importance, if not very local. With this background and the division of the hierarchy during and after the Americanist controversy and related conflicts, united efforts in the face of opposition were rendered practically impossible.

After the Spanish-American War this divisiveness became very apparent. In the settlement of the Friars' Lands case in the Philippines, the Catholic editors were agreed that Catholics were not properly represented in the settlement and unpublished documents discovered later have confirmed their suspicions.[24] But neither the Apostolic Delegate nor the leading American prelate, Cardinal Gibbons, could speak for the Catholics of the country. There were two bishops, Sebastian Messmer of Green Bay in the German West and James McFaul of Trenton in the more Irish East, who felt that the needed unity could be found in the existing Catholic societies. There was scarcely a prosperous Catholic parish which did not have two or three of these societies, and usually they were associated with a diocesan or national organization of such local groups. Two societies with national functions were the Irish Benevolent Union and the Knights of Saint John. Superficially the federation of all these local groups into a unity seemed quite easy and would present a Catholic force of millions of Americans. But the planners of this federation could not forget that nationally the Catholics of the country had been divided on this very question of a forced unity and Americanization. Strangely the new effort at unity came from the very groups which had opposed centralizing ten-

<hr />

[24] Cf. John T. Farrell, "An Abandoned Approach to Philippine History: John R.M. Taylor and the Philippine Insurrection Records," *Catholic Historical Review*, XXXIX (January, 1954) 385–407.

dencies. The argument in favor of the federation of Catholic societies, however, was that each society by retaining its separate identity would avoid both the association with non-Catholics and the liberalism and centralization that had been charged against the Americanizers.

As a result of the Spanish-American War, the Catholic Church in the United States acquired some new members outside the continental United States. In the peace treaty, the American Government had accepted the Philippines and Puerto Rico and certain supervision over Cuba. One of the major problems involved in the Philippines was the transfer of ownership of great areas of lands that had become attached to monastic institutions in the Philippines, generally designated as the Friars' Lands, the replacement of Spanish bishops by Americans, and the separation of Church and State, especially in the provision for educational institutions. Some members of the American Catholic press and some of the hierarchy felt that Catholics in the Philippines were being unjustly treated by the American officials, despite the fact that some of the officials were Catholic.[25] On September 16, 1899, the Holy See appointed Archbishop Placide Chapelle as Apostolic Delegate to Cuba and Puerto Rico with instructions to care also for the Church in the Philippines. The Philippines presented a difficult religious problem, complicated by a schism led by Father Gregorio Aglipay of the Diocese of Nueva Segovia. Aglipay established the Filipino Independent Church, with members numbering somewhere between one and two millions, which was very much anti-friar. A new Apostolic Delegate to the Philippines, Archbishop Giovanni Guido, arrived in 1902 and began to work on the internal dissensions.

When the schismatic church lost in the courts their claim to the ownership of the Church properties, the schism received a mortal blow. The Spanish friars had, indeed, sacrificed much of their popularity in the War by supporting the old government, but many of the charges against them were not true. Nevertheless the American government decided they should not return to the Islands. Since they were not to be restored to their properties, the Commission appointed by the President of the United States to set up a Philippine government was faced with the problem of arranging a fair reparation to the friars for their lost properties. At this time President McKinley was shot on September 6, 1901, in

---

[25] The best account of these affairs is Frank T. Reuter, *Catholic Influence on American Colonial Policies 1898–1904* (Austin, 1967).

Buffalo and died on September 19. Theodore Roosevelt became President. The friendly exchanges between Cardinal Gibbons and the new President helped to erase the friction aroused between the hierarchy and the government about the Philippine question. Roosevelt sent a commission headed by Judge William H. Taft to Rome, and an agreement was made by which the government paid the Spanish friars $7,239,000 for a total of 410,000 acres of land. The question of the removal of the friars solved itself in time. Also at this time American bishops were appointed to important Philippine dioceses: Archbishop Jeremiah J. Harty of Omaha to Manila; Thomas A. Hendrick to Cebu; Monsignor Frederick Rooker to Jaro; and Dennis J. Dougherty to Nueva Segovia. There still remained to be settled the payment for the damage to church properties during the invasion of the islands. Through the new Apostolic Delegate, Archbishop Ambrose Agius, O.S.B., a payment of $363,030.19 was awarded, a very inadequate sum. This was later increased to $403,030.19, but was still inadequate. In Puerto Rico a proposal by Archbishop Chapelle to divide the Island into three dioceses was resisted by Bishop James Blenk, then Bishop, and the division was not made until after Blenk had been made Archbishop of New Orleans. The rights of the Church to certain acquired properties in the Island was upheld by the courts after considerable litigation.

The need for Catholic leadership in public affairs led to attempts to organize Catholic laymen. The Knights of Saint John in their general meeting at Cleveland in June 1899 had taken the initiative in seeking a federation of Catholic societies, and Bishop McFaul gave them the necessary episcopal sponsorship. Archbishop Ireland and his *Northwestern Chronicle* quickly opposed the movement because the federation as advocated by Arthur Preuss and *The Review* was becoming a kind of protest against the McKinley administration and tending toward the formation of a Catholic political party like the German Center Party. When the Knights of Saint John met in Philadelphia for their annual convention in June 1900, they had already drawn up a proposal for the federation and invited various societies to join with them. Nine societies sent delegates to discuss the plan with the Knights, and thirteen other organizations manifested an interest in the proposal. Also Bishop McFaul spoke to the Knights of Columbus at their annual meeting in Atlantic City in August 1900 about the injustice done the friars in the Philippines. The Irish Catholic Benevolent League in their summer meeting appointed a delegate to meet with the representative of the Knights of Saint John. The first formal meeting of delegates to the proposed federation was arranged for Philadelphia on September 16, 1900. This group proposed a larger committee meeting for Thanksgiving Day in New York. Cardinal Gibbons tried to discourage the movement, but fifty delegates from nineteen societies met in New York on Thanksgiving Day. ¯ .e next committee meeting was set for May 7, 1901, in Cincinnati, and a plan for federation by Bishop Messmer was suggested. On March 26, 1901, Bishop McFaul wrote to the hierarchy backing the plan for federation, but when Archbishop Ireland opposed the movement the meeting was postponed until the fall. Specially chosen committees worked at the difficulties in the way of the federation and prepared a tentative constitution. The date was finally fixed as December 19, the meeting to be held in Cincinnati.

The Convention of December 19, 1901, adopted the name "The American Federation of Catholic Societies" and stated its purpose as:

the cementing of the bonds of fraternal union among the Catholic laity and Catholic Societies of the United States; the fostering of Catholic interests and works of religion, piety, education and charity; the study of conditions in our social life; the dissemination of the truth, the encouragement and spread of Catholic literature, and the circulation of the Catholic press.[26]

Membership was open to all societies of Catholics whose constitutions were approved by the Executive Board but each society would retain its autonomy. It was a grand plan but lacked any disciplinary power. The Federation incorporated into its constitution decentralization and local autonomy which the conservatives and Germans thought were wanting in the plans of the Americanists. Since the national officers lacked power, the annual meeting became just a sounding board for grandiose plans in which the originators of the Federation spoke eloquently of the needs of the Catholic minority in the country and passed resolutions of protest against discrimination against Catholics in government and society and of praise for Catholic accomplishments. There were to be continued disagreements in the Federation about the power of the Federation over individual members and about the relation between various types of member societies. The omission of the clergy from the statement of organization indicated another very serious defect in the organization. It seemed to be a lay organization, but the clergy

[26] Sister M. Adele Francis Gorman, O.S.F., "Federation of Catholic Societies in the United States 1870–1920" (Unpublished Ph.D. thesis, Notre Dame, 1962) p. 113. Sister Adele's thesis is the best account of the Federation.

were always there because without them there would be nothing official in the Federation. Yet the Federation never had the backing of the entire hierarchy. At the third annual meeting the only bishops in attendance were Bishops McFaul, Messmer, Benjamin Keiley of Savannah, and Archbishop Ryan of Philadelphia. The Federation struggled on, never strong but offering a limited basis for action for those lay people with the necessary means and zeal to foster the advance of Catholicism in the United States.

There was another national Catholic organization formed at this time which was to play a more permanent part in American Catholic life but which also suffered from the decentralizing forces at work among the Catholic leaders of the country. Monsignor Thomas Conaty, the Rector of the Catholic University, had written to the Presidents of Catholic colleges suggesting that they meet with him to discuss cooperation among Catholic colleges. The meeting was arranged to be in a central place and was held at St. James Church and hall in Chicago[27] on April 12 and 13, 1899. Fifty-one delegates represented fifty-three colleges. The resulting organization was called the Association of Catholic Colleges, which adopted a constitution at its second meeting. The first four annual meetings of the Association were held in Chicago with the fifth at Philadelphia and the sixth in St. Louis. Among the topics discussed at these meetings was the failure of the Catholic colleges to draw Catholic students. Several thousand Catholic youths were attending non-Catholic colleges for various reasons, but many more Catholics were not going beyond high school. The most important result of these five meetings was the advocacy by Father James A. Burns, C.S.C., of the establishment of central Catholic high schools of size and quality. The Conference joined the Parish School Conference in the St. Louis meeting to form the Catholic Educational Association in 1904. The Constitution of the new association was adopted at the St. Louis meeting of July 14, 1904. The association under its early leaders was a strong force for higher educational standards, although like the Federation of Catholic Societies it lacked real disciplinary power over recalcitrant members.

In 1901 the annual meeting of the archbishops had authorized Cardinal Gibbons to salute the aged Pope Leo XIII on the silver

---

[27] Catholic Educational Association, *Report of the First Annual Meeting, 1904* (Columbus, 1904), "History of the Association of Catholic Colleges," I, 12–17. The story of the Association is told in the unpublished dissertation of James H. Plough, "Catholic Colleges and the Catholic Educational Association, the Foundation and Early Years of the C.E.A., 1899–1919" (Notre Dame, 1967).

jubilee of his pontificate in 1902. Gibbons wrote a letter in which he enumerated the accomplishments of the Church in the United States under the benign rule of Pope Leo. In return, the Pope wrote a letter in which he gave great praise for this same progress, adding, ". . . the state of your churches, in this flourishing youthfulness, cheers Our heart and fills it with delight."[28] Pope Leo died July 20, 1903. Notified of the approaching death of the Pope, Cardinal Gibbons was already on his way to Rome for the conclave which opened on July 31 and in which he was the first American to take part in the election of a Pope. In the conclave Cardinal Rampolla, the most likely successor and the friend of the Americanists, suffered from the veto of the Austrian Emperor. Cardinal Joseph Sarto of Venice was elected as Pius X. The change in pontiffs was to make great changes in the life of American Catholicism.

In the meantime the optimistic progress that had manifested itself during the last decade of the nineteenth century continued in American Catholicism. The Catholic University under Monsignor Denis O'Connell was handicapped by financial difficulties, but the opening of his rectorship took place while everything seemed prosperous for university activities.[29]

The Catholic University Bulletin, which had suffered in the Americanist controversy, received new life, primarily by the advent to the faculty of a group of exiles from France, such as the Marists, Dubray and Butin, and Georges Sauvage, C.S.C. *The American Ecclesiastical Review*, owned and edited by Father Herman J. Heuser at St. Charles Seminary in Philadelphia, was filled with interesting theological discussions, unsigned commentaries on recent scriptural studies and the higher criticism, and articles on the new apologetics by Father Francis P. Siegfried. The *American Catholic Quarterly Review*, established in 1876, was publishing articles by James A. Burns, C.S.C., Thomas Shahan, Walter Elliott, Richard Elliott, William Kerby, Charles P. Neill, and many others on science, history, and literature, which, while not technically perfect, showed some depth and critical ability. *The New York Review*, a theological quarterly expressing advanced Catholic opinions, was begun in 1905 at St. Joseph's Seminary in New York and obtained contributions from some of the better American, English, and French writers in apologetics and scriptural studies.

---

[28] John Tracy Ellis, *The Life of James Cardinal Gibbons, Archbishop of Baltimore, 1834–1921*, 2 vol. (Milwaukee, 1952) II, 80.
[29] Cf. T.T. McAvoy, "The Catholic Minority after the Americanist Controversy, 1899–1917, a Survey," *Review of Politics* (January 1959) XXI, 53–82.

Among them were Vincent McNabb, Pierre Battifol, Henri Bremond, and Wilfrid Ward, from Europe and Francis E. Gigot, William L. Sullivan, John A. Ryan, and Francis P. Duffy from the United States. At this time, also, because of a difference between superiors, the Sulpicians in charge of the New York Seminary withdrew from the Sulpician community and the diocesan priests conducted the Seminary under the direction of Archbishop Farley. In Philadelphia, there was a sign of progress; the editor of the *Ecclesiastical Review* began to publish the *Dolphin,* a layman's version of the clerical magazine with contributions from such writers as Agnes Repplier, Joseph McSorley, Vincent McNabb, and W.H. Kent. The *Sacred Heart Messenger,* the chief outlet for Jesuit writings in this country, was edited on a high plane for a few years and in its editorial columns participated in the current theological discussions. At this time also a most important contribution of American Catholics to scholarship, the *Catholic Encyclopedia,* was begun under the editorship of Charles G. Hebermann, Edward A. Pace, Condé B. Pallen, Thomas J. Shahan, and John J. Wynne, S.J. The formal work began at a meeting on January 11, 1905. The first volume appeared in March 1907. The final volume was completed in April 1914.

During the first years of the century, besides the Catholic Summer School at Plattsburg, additional summer schools were held at Madison, Wisconsin, and New Orleans. The Catholic Reading Circle under Warren Mosher continued until his death in 1906. The *Catholic World,* besides encouraging budding Catholic writers, in its editorial columns participated in the current apologetical and scriptural discussions. Among the Catholic writers of significance at the time were such novelists as Henry Harland, Anna Sadlier, and Christian Reid; such capable journalists as T.A. Hart, Katherine Conway, and Arthur Preuss. This intellectual flowering among Catholics at the turn of the century was probably a result of the sharp intellectual discussions and activities of the last decade of the nineteenth century when the American hierarchy exhibited front-page personalities who took a prominent part in public affairs and when the Catholic press was noted for its frankness and open discussion. It was probably a belated result, also, of the Baltimore Third Plenary Council, the founding of the Catholic University, the Lay Congresses of 1889 and 1892, and the Americanist movement. But it did not last beyond the first decade of the new century.

One of the limitations of this cultural flowering of the first decade of the century was that it lacked depth. Fathers Zahm,

C.S.C., in science; Charles P. Grannan and Francis E. Gigot in Scripture; John Hogan and Francis Siegfried in theology were scholarly men who understood and discussed the best thought of the day, but they really did not create anything. Zahm, who was probably the most original of the group, turned to travel writings after the rejection of his writings on evolution by Rome and his rejection as Provincial Superior by his own community. The Catholic lay writers, Charles Warren Stoddard, Maurice Francis Egan, and Henry Harland were not top literary figures of the day, although Stoddard's writings about the South Seas were first class.

A more fatal defect of this period of cultural growth of American Catholicism was that it had no basis in Catholic higher education. The Catholic University was handicapped by division in its faculty and financial disaster. Other Catholic universities had mediocre liberal arts colleges and a few second-rate professional schools. The actual financial burden of maintaining the parochial schools that were multiplying during the preceding and the current decades was heavy. Further, there was little cultural difference among Catholics in those areas where these Catholic schools did not exist. There were no Catholic high schools outside of a few private academies. Father James A. Burns began his arguments in the newly formed Catholic Educational Association for the erection of central Catholic high schools. He maintained that only about one third as many Catholic youths attended high school as should have according to the general trends of the country.[30] Another writer explained that the Catholics of prominence had not been trained in Catholic colleges. Actually in the Catholic colleges two thirds of the students were really following high school programs maintained by the same faculty, and the one third who followed the collegiate program were scarcely one third of the Catholic youth attending college. Another revealing figure indicated that most of the Catholics in these secular colleges were in technical schools and, therefore, would not become teachers or creative writers or wield intellectual influence in the country after they attained maturity.

Outside of the Catholic University, which was handicapped most of its first years by nationalistic disputes and then almost destroyed by the earlier faulty investment of its funds, the chief centers of Catholic intellectual endeavor were three seminaries, St. Charles Seminary in Philadelphia, St. Bernard's Seminary in

---

[30] James A. Burns, C.S.C., "Catholic Secondary Schools," in *American Catholic Quarterly Review* (1901) XXVI, 485 ff.

Rochester, New York, and St. Joseph's Seminary in New York. Father John Hogan of St. John's Seminary, Boston, and Fathers Thomas Shields and John A. Ryan of St. Paul's Seminary in Minnesota were really a part of this seminary effort. These seminaries were by their nature not universities, but professional schools. Even in their own fields of theology, scripture, and philosophy, however, this seminary effort received a crushing blow by the condemnation of Modernism and the rigorism that followed. The other Catholic universities and colleges were not endowed for graduate study. Their staffs were overworked, and most of their student bodies came from homes that had no intellectual traditions. Most of the clerical faculties of these colleges were also engaged in priestly work in the neighboring parishes, and the laymen received such meager salaries and had so much teaching to do that creative research was very difficult. Altogether, these handicaps meant that the forward movement in American Catholic cultural affairs was dying of internal difficulties at the time that the decrees against Modernism stopped the most promising clerical developments.

There is some doubt that what was condemned as Modernism by Pope Pius X actually had any followers in the United States. Some essays in the *Ecclesiastical Review,* in the *Catholic University Bulletin* at this time, and in the *New York Review* during the three years of its existence, some essays in the *Catholic World* and the scriptural textbooks of Father Francis E. Gigot were about the only manifestations of the "new theology." There was a real interest in the faculties of the seminaries in Philadelphia, New York, and Boston and at the Catholic University in the new apologetics that had manifested itself chiefly in France and in its chief exponents, Abbé Alfred Loisy, George Tyrrell, and Maurice Blondel. In the *London Tablet* of March 23, 1907, the basic ideas of this new theology were described briefly:

In altering the concept of Revelation, the New Theology has naturally made a corresponding alteration in the concept of Faith.

We have seen that by Revelation it does not mean any external communication of a message of truth from God to mankind, but merely an internal and personal experience, by which God or the divine which is immanent in man acts upon the individual soul, awakening it to a sense of a new life, giving to it a consciousness of right and wrong, and leading it upward and onward towards righteousness. If this be its notion of Revelation, or God's part, what does it mean by faith?

Faith is man's part. It is the response of his conscience or religious sense by which he acts in accordance with this manifestation of the divine will. It will be remembered that what is revealed to man is not any body of doctrinal truth which he has to believe, but simply a mode of life, action or conduct which he has to follow. It is not dogmatic but ethical. It is addressed directly not to the intelligence but to the will.

So far, we have two ideas which, divested of all word-dreaming and subtlety, are perfectly clear. First, God immanent in man makes Himself felt in the soul in the consciousness of right and wrong. That stands for Revelation. And man's religious sense responds to God's action by moving towards Him. That is Faith.

To these two ideas must be added a third, namely, the origin of Dogma.

When God has thus manifested His will, and man made his response, man using his intelligence begins to reflect upon the process. He "tries to explain it to himself by various religious conceptions and beliefs." He "tries to picture it and understand it, to invent a history or a philosophy to explain it." The strong emotion would produce conform imaginings much as it does in the poet, the dreamer or the delirious. Herein we have the origin of dogmatic beliefs and creeds. Dogmas are simply transformed religious sensations or emotions, and it is man himself who effects the transformation. . . .

There was no American Catholic historian of the depth of Louis Duchesne or scriptural scholar like Loisy or Père Lagrange, O.P. But European scholars were beginning to write in the American Catholic journals. The most sensitive field was that of the higher criticism of the Scriptures. Rome soon reserved to herself the giving of advanced degrees in scriptural study. The Archbishop of Paris had condemned Loisy and on December 17, 1903, Pius X signed the decree of the Sacred Congregation of the Index condemning five of Loisy's books. On July 3, 1907, the Sacred Congregation of the Holy Office issued the *Lamentabili,* a syllabus of sixty-five errors, taken mostly from the writings of Loisy. On September 8 Pope Pius issued his encyclical, *Pascendi Dominici Gregis,* which not only condemned the body of the doctrines of Modernism but recommended remedies against the spread of the heresy. These remedies included the revival of Thomistic studies, the study of positive theology, the introduction of scientific studies, a more careful choice of seminary faculty, greater vigilance by bishops and the setting up of committees of vigilance to detect the spread of the heresy, and more careful censorship of clerical publications. The Pope followed this encyclical on November 18, 1907, with a *motu proprio* in which he gave the Biblical Commission the same authority as any Roman Congregation and threatened with excommunication *latae sententiae* anyone who dared defend the propositions and opinions condemned in the two previous documents. The *New York Review* ceased publication, the other American Catholic clerical reviews abandoned the fields of scriptural and apologetical discussion. The first golden era of American Catholicism—perhaps prematurely formed—was over.

CHAPTER TWELVE

The Conservative Reaction
and World War I

THERE HAVE BEEN TIMES WHEN THE ACTIV-
ities of the Catholic Church in the United States seemed to parallel
the developments of the social and political life of the country.
In this sense the development of the progressive efforts of the
Americanists can be said to parallel the beginning of the Progressive Movement in American political life. But the parallel
stops rather quickly because the Americanist movement received
a severe check in the papal letter *Testem Benevolentiae* of January 22, 1899, while the Progressive Movement in American politics scarcely reached its peak before the election of Woodrow
Wilson in 1912. In a sense the flowering of Catholic cultural
efforts in the decade after the condemnation of Americanism can
be attributed in some part to the progressive reform movement
abroad in the country.

The strictly theological movements of Catholicism have not had
any close parallel to American political history. In the first place
the center of Catholicism has been outside the country in Rome
and secondly, in a country dominated by English Protestants, the
Catholic minority, in itself predominantly immigrants, especially
non-English immigrants, has consisted of a social and cultural
complex different from that of the country as a whole. Early historians of American Catholicism have sometimes been criticized
for writing their history in a vacuum, but they have had to be
excused for so writing because there seemed to be very little con-

nection between the general American cultural history and that of American Catholicism. The hope of Archbishop Ireland and his friends was to eliminate much of this lack of conformity between the Catholic people and the American way of life, and in so doing they hoped also that the Church universal would recognize the newer and better things in American civilization and accept and imitate them in matters that were not strictly theological.

The American public was aware only in part of the internal developments of American Catholicism. Few American newspapers could report properly the news about the administration of the Catholic Church organization. The condemnation of Modernism was reported in most of the more scholarly theological and philosophical journals as a return of Catholicism to the world of the *Syllabus of Errors* and a retreat from modern civilization. They could not find out much more about Modernism from the Catholic magazines. The *Lamentabili* was translated in a few Catholic magazines, and the encyclical *Pascendi Gregis* was circulated in a separate brochure. The subsequent condemnations of books and men and the decrees providing means for ensuring the orthodoxy of seminary professors, the exclusion of priests from editorial positions, and other measures drawn up to secure the complete eradication of all tendencies toward Modernism were known to only a few who could have access to official Roman periodicals or to one or two Catholic clerical magazines.

The most informative article on Modernism published in the country was probably one in the *Ecclesiastical Review* by Father Anthony Vieban, S.S.,[1] but he seemed to find few Modernists in the United States. Father Charles W. Currier in the *Catholic Quarterly Review* noted the critical comments in American Protestant journals and the resistance of Loisy and of the Italian Modernists, but gave no indication that any Americans held the condemned doctrines. A few other essays appeared in the *Ecclesiastical Review* and the *Catholic Quarterly* showing the contrasts between orthodox Catholic doctrines on faith and revelation and the teachings of the Modernists. Gradually critical essays on Scripture ceased to appear and were replaced with archeological essays, historical studies, and discussions of moral problems. The editors of the *New York Review* insisted that they had not been censured and that they were ceasing to publish because they had too few subscribers. The new Constitution of the Church reor-

---

[1] A. Vieban, "Who are the Modernists of the Encyclicals?" *American Ecclesiastical Review* (1908) XXXVIII, 489–507.

ganizing the Roman Curia published by Pope Pius X was discussed at considerable length although there was not much said about the statement in it by which the United States, with other countries of the western hemisphere, was removed from the list of mission countries under the direction of the Sacred Congregation of the Propaganda. The *Catholic Encyclopedia* continued to appear though there were rumors that the editors had made trips to Rome for consultation about some of the articles. The negative aspects of the condemnation of Modernism have been the most notable because the positive remedies were not carried out. How the councils of vigilance functioned is not recorded. Some seminary professors were retired to parish work and others had to prove their orthodoxy. Thomistic philosophy and theology were made mandatory in all seminaries and colleges, but the manuals were so rigid and the teachers so dogmatic that no living Catholic philosophy resulted.

In the field of positive theology, the decrees of the Biblical Commission and the restriction of scriptural degree-giving to the Biblical Commission in Rome left little for the American scriptural scholar to do. The history teachers at the Catholic University were mediocre and in most seminaries even worse. History in the English-speaking world had become something for which the Catholic teacher had to apologize since the good non-Catholic texts were not friendly to the Church, and the Catholic texts were miserable, usually translations from the German. Canon Law, which was to come alive after the promulgation of the new code of Canon Law, was still in 1908 more or less a jungle in which few knew the way. The training of the priest became a short trip through the old Latin and Greek classics, two years of Thomistic theses and syllogisms in philosophy, and four years of dogmatic and moral theology. The most exciting discussion in liturgy was on the use of the gothic vestments for Mass.

Although the *Catholic World* and the *Ave Maria* with a few other religious periodicals of literary ambition continued to be published, there was no great Catholic literature. Francis Marion Crawford wrote popular novels but not as a Catholic writer. In the sciences, the Catholic University struggled along with a few teachers such as Daniel W. Shea, John J. Griffin, and Albert Zahm but with little financial help. Notre Dame had an acceptable engineering school and a good undergraduate school in the physical and biological sciences. Georgetown, Creighton, St. Louis, and, for a while, Fordham, had successful medical schools. But the contribution to science from these Catholic universities was meager and had little influence on seminary training. There were two developments in Catholic life that were to have great importance during the later decades of the century; the first was the decrees of Pope Pius X on early first Communion and on frequent and daily Communion, which changed the character of Catholic living, and the second was the application, chiefly from the Catholic University, of the papal teachings on social justice.

The effect of the decrees on frequent and daily Communion had impact only where the local clergy explained them to the people and offered opportunity for frequent Confession. The Jansenistic notion that only the near-perfect should approach the Sacraments frequently was deeply imbedded in the traditions of American Catholicism. One of the first persons to break away from this tradition was Father Joseph Chartrand, first as pastor of the Cathedral in Indianapolis and then as Coadjutor Bishop. But eventually the practice became so common throughout the country that the test of a good Catholic became the attendance at the Sacraments instead of attendance at the Sunday Mass or the protestation of adherence. In some sections of the country where there were large parishes of urban people, the churches were unable to hold those who attended the Sunday services and had to be multiplied. Attendance at daily Mass and Communion multiplied generally.

An important extension of activity of Catholic churchmen in the domestic missions found expression in the formation of the Extension Society on October 18, 1905, under the protection of Archbishop James E. Quigley of Chicago and the presidency of Father Francis C. Kelley of Lapeer, Michigan. In 1907 the central office of the Society was moved to Chicago, but the mission activity of the Society was chiefly in the South and West where Catholics were few.

The friendship of the Catholic hierarchy to labor had its foundations in the defense in 1887 of the Knights of Labor by Cardinal Gibbons.[2] But there were some members of the hierarchy who were not reconciled to this friendly attitude toward labor unions and accused the unions of socialistic and anarchistic tendencies. Further, communistic and Marxist literature in the country had been propagated among some immigrant Germans, leading many of the German clergy and the Central Verein to be very much

[2] Aaron I. Abell, *American Catholicism and Social Action, A Search for Social Justice, 1865–1950* (New York, 1960) Chapter V, "Not Socialism—but Social Reform 1900–1917," pp. 137–188.

alert to the danger that German workers could be indoctrinated with socialism. The Catholic interest in social justice really stemmed from the study of the encyclical *Rerum Novarum* of Pope Leo XIII, although the American Catholics who took an active interest in the application of the encyclical to the American scene were quite few. As Cardinal Gibbons had predicted in his letter to the Propaganda against the condemnation of the Knights of Labor, the Knights soon began to decline in importance. In their place the trade unions were formed led by Samuel Gompers of the cigarmakers' union. Catholic membership in these labor unions of various kinds was quite high. Nevertheless the American Catholic interest in the problems of social justice in the twentieth century did not arise from any special effort by the hierarchy to influence the labor movement. Several members of the hierarchy had a real interest in social questions, but the most important efforts by Catholics were the products of the personal interest of priests and laymen.

Father John A. Ryan of the Archdiocese of St. Paul did have a personal interest in the rights of the laboring man which he had acquired in his youth on the farm in Minnesota and in the Seminary at St. Paul.[3] He had been influenced by the oratory of the Populist, Ignatius Donnelly, and by the speeches and activities of Cardinal Gibbons in the defense of the Knights of Labor. After Father Ryan's ordination in 1898 Archbishop Ireland sent him to the Catholic University to prepare for a professorship in the archdiocesan seminary. At the University he combined the special direction in moral theology of Doctor Thomas Bouquillon, his major professor, the teaching of Doctor Charles P. Neill, his professor in economics, and that of Father William F. Kerby, his professor in sociology. Already in Minnesota Father Ryan had read widely and followed closely the political battles of the Populist period. He took as the subject of his doctoral thesis an examination of the ethical and economic basis of the right to a living wage, the basic idea for which he took from the encyclical *Rerum Novarum*. The thesis was not finished until 1905. He defended it in May 1906 and the book, *A Living Wage*, was published in April 1906. Recalled to St. Paul to teach in the seminary by Archbishop Ireland, he took an active interest in the social and economic problems of Minnesota while teaching moral theology and later eco-

[3] John A. Ryan, *Social Doctrine in Action* (New York, 1941) is the best exposition of his ideals. Francis L. Broderick, *The Right Reverend New Dealer, John A. Ryan* (New York, 1963) is not so good on Ryan's formative years.

nomics in the St. Paul Seminary. His book, *A Living Wage,* had a wide and deep influence in the discussions of labor problems in the second and third decades of the century.

Another Catholic priest who became prominent in the problems of social justice was Peter E. Dietz[4] of the Diocese of Cleveland who was ordained December 17, 1904, by Cardinal Gibbons at the conclusion of studies at St. Mary's Seminary in Baltimore. A native of New York, he had acquired his education in many communities and countries before returning to the United States after his adoption into the Diocese of Cleveland. He suffered from nervous disorders which made the strict rules of seminaries and novitiates of religious communities quite unbearable and made him difficult and at times quick tempered but he had also acquired in his study and travel a desire to devote himself to carrying out the ideals of Pope Leo's *Rerum Novarum.* By reason of his German parentage he had a command of the German language without losing his ability to write English well. His first priestly assignment was a bit unusual. He was made an assistant at Elyria, Ohio, with a kind of chaplaincy at Oberlin College. Shortly after coming to Elyria he talked the priests of Lorain County into helping the Catholic laymen of the county form a Catholic organization which he proposed to affiliate with the National Federation of Catholic Societies. He joined that Federation himself in 1908, but, when it seemed unable to do anything, he later joined the Central Verein, which was at that time carrying on an active campaign against the inroads of socialism among the German-American Catholics. He became an active member of the Ohio Staatsverband, the Ohio branch of the Verein, and by lobbying in Columbus influenced state labor legislation. He became active also in the national Verein, and in 1908 he was appointed to a committee of the Verein headed by Nicholas Gonner of Dubuque which took over a magazine called *Central Blatt* and published it, beginning in 1909, as *Central Blatt and Social Justice.* Father Dietz wanted it to be entirely English, but it remained bilingual with Dietz editing the English half of the journal.

The Central Verein, which followed closely the activities of Bishop William E. von Ketteler and Father Adolph Kolping in Germany and the German Center Party, had for its special purpose to aid in the rejection of socialism by the German Catholic immigrants. Socialism did not make much progress among the other Catholic immigrants in the United States despite some

[4] Mary Harrita Fox, *Peter E. Dietz Labor Priest* (Notre Dame, 1953).

efforts in the first decade of the century to form a Catholic Socialist group. Two priests, Father Thomas McGrady of Kentucky and Father Thomas Hagerty of Chicago did leave the Church to follow the socialist leadership but they took with them few Catholic laymen. Father Dietz, as the editor of the English portion of the *Central Blatt and Social Justice,* had constant disagreements with Frederick P. Kenkel, the Central Verein Chairman of the Committee for Social Propaganda. In September 1909, Father Dietz organized a Social Institute at Oberlin and planned many other activities, but Kenkel as the head of the Central Bureau of the Verein continued to oppose his reformist position. Father Dietz then turned to the Federation of Catholic Societies and in their 1911 convention in Columbus suggested the formation of a Committee on Social Reform. In answer to his appeal a Social Service Commission was established under the chairmanship of Bishop Peter J. Muldoon of Rockford with Father John W. Cavanaugh of Notre Dame, Professor James E. Hagerty of Ohio State, Charles J. Denechaud of New Orleans, and Father Dietz who became secretary of the Commission. The editor of the *Bulletin* of the Federation allotted a portion of the periodical to Father Dietz and Dietz became the force behind the activities of the Social Service Commission.

In 1910 Father Dietz had taken another step toward fulfilling his ambitions to improve Catholic influence in the labor movement. At the annual meeting of the American Federation of Labor, with the approval of Archbishop John Glennon of St. Louis, he had organized the Catholic delegates into a society which he called the Militia of Christ for Social Service. The formal Constitution of the Militia was not adopted until 1912. It provided for a director as well as national officers with a central national organization rising from delegates of local chapters. The Militia met at the same place and time as the annual meeting of the Federation of Labor, and its members were practicing Catholics who accepted the principle of unionism. Its magazine, *Social Service,* began to appear in 1911.

At that time Bishop Farrelly thought Father Dietz should devote his full time to parish work, but Father Dietz felt that he should continue his special work. After he failed to get accepted on the staff at the Catholic University, Dietz was adopted by Archbishop Messmer into the Archdiocese of Milwaukee, where the Archbishop allowed him freedom to continue his program. But Father Dietz, as usual, soon developed friction with Anthony Matre, the secretary of the Federation of Catholic Societies, who felt that the Social Service Commission was only a part of the organization he was directing. Dietz, however, who had been the secretary and editor of *Social Service* of the Militia now combined it with his section of the *Bulletin* of the Federation. Thus there were really two editors of the *Bulletin*, Matre in St. Louis and Dietz in Milwaukee.

In the election of 1912 the Socialist Party attained its greatest voter influence, polling 897,011 votes for its candidate, Eugene V. Debs. But the Democratic Party won the election and inaugurated Woodrow Wilson as President the following March. Nevertheless, the threat of socialism and a papal letter to the German laboring people added interest to the work of the Social Service Commission at the Federation meeting in Louisville that year. The next year on January 18, the Social Service Commission issued its first *Newsletter* to the Catholic press. The Commission also published several pamphlets on social problems.

The twelfth annual convention of the Federation of Catholic Societies was one of the most impressive of its history. Meeting in Milwaukee on August 9, 1913, besides the host, Archbishop Messmer, there were present Cardinal Gibbons, Archbishops Glennon, Ireland, Quigley, Moeller, and Keane, and seventeen bishops. While the speeches were fine, the meeting harbored in its ranks much dissension and disagreements about the work of the Federation. The chief cause of friction was the parallel work of the Federation, the Social Service Commission, and the special service activities of the Central Verein under Kenkel. For the next year Father Dietz was editor of both the *Bulletin* and the *Newsletter*. The *Bulletin* showed the results of his superior editorship with articles by Father Edwin V. O'Hara of Oregon, Louis Budenz, Bishop John Carroll of Helena, Father John A. Ryan, and Louis Collins. Father Dietz was also active in the Wisconsin Federation of Catholic Societies and in the Militia of Christ.

Father Dietz had felt the need to establish a social service school in which Catholic leaders could be trained for participation and in a sense for leadership in social service. He had been offered property in Tennessee but had found it unsuitable for a school. In 1914 Mrs. Katherine Safford of Hot Springs, North Carolina, offered him property in that city, where he felt he could establish his school. The offer, later modified, was in fact so indefinite that Father Dietz could not get the Federation to support him in accepting it. Nevertheless he moved his offices to Hot Springs in April 1915 and eventually, on other property in Hot Springs, opened a school for training young ladies for social service. He called it the American Academy of Christian Democracy for Women. The school existed there for five sessions of varying length and varying content. He had difficulty securing a staff of teachers although the graduates gave a good account of their training later in the several cities in which they continued their work. The alumnae of the school he organized into an Association of White Cross Nurses. When he realized that he could not continue the school in North Carolina, he sought a new site for the school and eventually in 1917 Archbishop Moeller granted him the use of an abandoned hospital building in Cincinnati.

In September 1914, meanwhile, the Federation of Catholic Societies and the Social Commission and other associate Catholic societies met in Baltimore for the annual convention. Two important resolutions adopted at the meeting did not meet with approval by their host, Cardinal Gibbons. One Federation resolution asked President Wilson to end the persecution of the Church in Mexico and another asked that the Government forbid the use of the mails to the anti-Catholic paper, *The Menace*. Gibbons felt that the first resolution merely handicapped whatever good the United States government could do in Mexico and that the action sought against *The Menace* could be used later against the Church and that meanwhile other unfriendly publications would remain untouched.

With the outbreak of war in Europe in 1914, Dietz saw the necessity for the Central Verein to soften its German character and suggested closer affiliation of the Verein with the Federation of Catholic Societies, but his suggestion was rejected by Kenkel for the Central Verein and opposed by Matre in the Federation. At the 1915 Federation Convention in Toledo, the Social Service Commission devoted much of its time to the problems of the immigrant. At the general meeting of the Federation, speakers reported a decline in bigotry and praised the report of the Knights of Columbus of their investigation into the causes of religious bigotry, which was published in 1914. The action of the Federation in support of the proposed immigration restriction was a bit confused because the "literacy" clause in the immigration law could be used to keep out various groups for other reasons.

The 1916 meeting of the Federation was held in New York City during "Catholic Week," beginning August 20. Cardinal John Farley wanted a demonstration of Catholic unity and got it under the leadership of three cardinals and the Apostolic Delegate and with the cooperation of the many Catholic societies represented within the State. In the convention many resolutions were adopted on various matters, but underneath the oratory the old internal dissensions and jealousies had full sway. The Federation did propose censorship of movies, protested the persecution of the Church in Mexico, and passed other similar resolutions, but it did not have internal unity. Outside of the personal work of Father Dietz, his Social Service Commission, and his other operations which it would not sponsor, the Federation accomplished practically nothing between meetings. During the winter of 1916–1917, various plans for a reorganization of the Federation were discussed in committee meetings, in the pages of the *Ecclesiastical Review,* and in the meeting of the archbishops in April 1917 in which the archbishops promised their support to the President in the newly declared war. The annual meeting of the Federation was held on August 26–28 in Kansas City and was well attended, but while there were the usual solemn services presided over by the Apostolic Delegate and the usual well attended assemblies, nothing was really accomplished. Actually the Federation faced serious competition from the gathering of the National Catholic War Council that was taking place that summer in Washington. Monsignor Splaine of Boston announced to the Federation that John Whalen of Brooklyn, the President of the Federation, had attended the Washington meeting as their representative. To the convention came a message from Father John J. Burke, C.S.P., the secretary of the new War Council, thanking the Federation for its cooperation and for the aid rendered by President Whalen. The Federation after discussing the various plans for reorganization adopted a diocesan plan of organization as opposed to a federation of societies or the proposal of dissolving entirely. This meeting was really the end of the Federation of Catholic Societies and with it the work of the Social Service Commission under Father Dietz. The Federation had failed, and the War offered an opportunity for American Catholics to try some other agency to unite the forces of American Catholicism.

The confusion within the Federation of Catholic Societies was indicative of the lack of actual unity among American Catholics at the beginning of the twentieth century. The threat of socialism was being discussed in some of the Catholic press and there were some local victories won by the Socialist Party. The more important problem facing Catholicism in the United States was the absorption of the final wave of immigrants from eastern and southern Europe. The theological silence that had settled over the Catholic University and the seminaries of the country after the condemnation of Modernism was broken chiefly by those who were concerned with social reform, under the leadership of Fathers William Kerby and John A. Ryan at the Catholic University.

Father John Ryan had been repeatedly invited by interested persons, including Cardinal Gibbons, during the decade after the publication of his book on the *Living Wage,* to return to the Catholic University as a professor. Archbishop Ireland would not consent to this, because he did not have a replacement handy and because he had already given Father Thomas Shields and Father William Turner to the University. He did not want to establish a precedent in the Archdiocese of having the better men going away from the diocese. Finally, however, he gave Father Ryan permission in 1915, and Father Ryan went to Washington in September of that year. Also, Ryan published that year another notable book entitled *Distributive Justice* on the proper distribution of wealth. Not only was it well received by Catholics but it was recognized by social scientists outside the Church. With the outbreak of war, Father Ryan's interest was attracted by the activities of wartime and the efforts to restore the peace. He upheld, particularly, the conditions for a just peace as proposed by Pope Benedict XV on August 1, 1917.

The events of the summer of 1917 mark a change in the history of the Catholic Church in the United States. The involvement of the country in a war with Germany was not in itself an ecclesiastical matter, although it coincided more or less with the death of Pope Pius X and the election of Pope Benedict XV. But just at this time the Federation of Catholic Societies, the chief effort at unity during the previous sixteen years, was falling apart from internal and external difficulties. The Central Verein, the unifying organization next in importance, suffered vitally because the war was against Germany, and like most German organizations, it was forced to prove that it was American and patriotic. The war itself proved to be the occasion for the first really unified action that the Catholic Church in the United States had achieved since the Third Plenary Council of 1884. That unity in 1884 was superficial and was dissipated soon after by the quarrels over foreign nationalism and Americanization. The difficulties in the way of unity manifested in the attempt to support the war effort emphasized in some ways the division and dissensions which were hindering Catholic unity.

Although Cardinal Gibbons often acted in the name of Catholicism in the United States, when war was declared against Germany on April 6 there was no national organization in the country that could speak for Catholics. On April 14 the Knights of Columbus, the largest organization of Catholic laymen, through their Supreme Board of Directors meeting in Washington, promised to President Wilson "the patriotic devotion of the four hundred thousand members" of the order. Their message was sent to the President, April 17. The next day, April 18, the Council of Archbishops meeting in the annual session, as the nearest to an official group, pledged the loyalty of American Catholics:

. . . Our people as ever, will rise as one man to serve the nation. Our priests and consecrated women will once again, as in every former trial of our country, win by their bravery, their heroism and their service new admiration and approval.

They added:

We are all true Americans, ready as our age, our ability and our condition permit, to do whatsoever is in us to do, for the preservation, the progress and the triumph of our beloved country. . . .

The statement was more laudatory than helpful, because American Catholicism, despite its record of loyalty, was not united outside of the official doctrines of the Church.

Prior to the actual declaration of war, there had been a large portion of American Catholics who opposed going to war. There were large numbers of Germans who felt strong ties to their mother country or the country of their ancestors and were sympathetic to the German war effort. Also the Irish and those of Irish descent in this country were a bit reluctant, for the most part, to have the United States enter the war as an ally of England. When after Germany invaded France the President of the Federation of Catholic Societies, John Whalen, sent a message of sympathy to the lay Catholics of France, some members of the Federation openly criticized him, although he was promptly praised by Bishop McFaul, the sponsor of the Federation.

Already there were two Paulist Fathers directly concerned with the ecclesiastical phase of the military preparations. Father Lewis J. O'Hern, C.S.P., of St. Paul's College, Washington, served as a clearinghouse for applications and appointments of chaplains in the Army and Navy, and Father John J. Burke, C.S.P., the editor of the *Catholic World,* had established the Chaplains' Aid Association to supply vestments and other needs of the Catholic chaplains in the service. It was significant that the one functioning national Catholic fraternal organization, the Knights of Columbus, took the lead in looking after the Catholic men who would be called into the service. It had rendered a similar service to the Army in the punitive expedition into Mexico in 1916.

Father Burke was joined by Father O'Hern, C.S.P., the representative of the hierarchy in dealing with chaplains in the services, Father William Kerby of the Catholic University, and Charles P. Neill, a member of the Government Commission on Training Camps, in an effort to form a Catholic agency to represent the Church in the many problems arising as a result of the War. Father Burke with this backing sought the aid of Cardinal Gibbons. The Cardinal approved of his calling, in the name of the three American Cardinals, Gibbons, Farley and O'Connell, a general convention of Catholic representatives at the Catholic University on August 11 and 12. Father Burke wrote first to all the archbishops and bishops asking each one to send to the meeting one cleric and one layman. He sent a second letter to each of twenty-seven Catholic national societies asking them to send two representatives to the meeting. In his invitation to the delegates Father Burke, with a remarkable appreciation of the situation, stated:

. . . Our resources are great, our societies many, capable and zealous. We must not work at cross purposes, nor overlap one another's work. Through ignorance of what other individuals or societies among ourselves are doing we will forfeit just so much of the salutary work we would otherwise do.

It is time when we should "get together" as speedily as possible; learn, if we do not know already, the problems and the needs we must meet, the common policy we ought to pursue, and how, working with one another, we can best meet them. Generous cooperation is the only road to the right solution. . . .

The spiritual and moral welfare of the Catholic soldiers is in our hands. In every camp established or to be established by the government we must build a recreation hall that will give to the soldiers the opportunity of fulfilling their religious obligations and of enjoying such healthy recreation as will help them to forego evil company and sinful occasions. These halls must be well built, so that they may be used in winter as in summer. In many camps more than one will be required. These all must be well furnished and equipped. Priests—outside of the regular army chaplains—will have to be provided and supported that they may minister to the soldiers.

Some of the new camps will number 40,000 men; of these 15,000 will be Catholics. How are all of them to have the opportunity of assisting at Mass on Sundays?

The salaries of those assisting priests must be furnished for the dioceses are as a rule too poor to provide it.

The spiritual work of the priests must receive the assistance of the laity—local committees will assist in providing suitable recreation, bringing something of the home life into the lives of those who have been for the time deprived of it.

The halls must be furnished with suitable means of recreation.

The Chapels should be furnished with all the necessities for divine service. Literature—prayer books, catechisms, devotional articles—must also be provided.

Post libraries of good books should be furnished.

All this must be done to anticipate, to provide for the moral and spiritual care of 1,000,000 men in which there will be at least 300,000 Catholics. . . .[5]

In these lines Father Burke placed the problem before the Catholic authorities.

The response was limited. At the meeting there were representatives of sixty-eight dioceses and twenty-seven societies, a total of one hundred and fifteen delegates. But all the dissensions that had been hampering the progress of Catholicism during the previous two decades permeated the convention. Against these disconcerting forces, Father John J. Burke took the floor and propounded the needs of the crisis. He called the war a test of American democracy. "The entry of our country into the war has presented a challenge to the Catholic Church of America more serious than she has ever known in her history. If we fail to meet it, the progress of the Church will be fatally affected for the next quarter of a century. . . ." He then appealed to the delegates to forget their individual parish, social, and diocesan differences and to create a larger Catholic unity. He outlined the results to be expected from the drafting of men into the services and the needs of the servicemen that he had listed in his letters.

Father Burke, with the cooperation of such men as Monsignor Splaine of Boston, Monsignor Michael Lavelle of New York, Father Kerby, and others, then appointed a committee to present a plan of action. On this committee were Father P. P. Crane of St. Louis, John Whalen of New York, Patrick H. Callahan of Louisville, Jack Spalding of Atlanta, J. H. Lyons of Seattle, Robert Biggs of Baltimore, Michael J. Slattery of Philadelphia. That committee in turn produced three resolutions by which they announced the need for a national Catholic organization and suggested that this organization should be called The National Catholic War Council and that it should be composed of delegates from the diocesan councils appointed by the bishops and be led by an executive committee consisting of one delegate from each arch-

[5] Michael Williams, *American Catholics in the War, National Catholic War Council, 1917–1921* (New York, 1921) pp. 110–113.

diocese. Further, under the direction of Father Burke and his collaborators, the convention recognized the Knights of Columbus as the representative Catholic body for the special work they had undertaken in meeting the moral problems arising out of the war. The President of the War Council chosen in the convention was Father Burke; the secretary, Robert Biggs of Baltimore; and the treasurer John G. Agar of New York. Six committees were established and a chairman was appointed for each. Father Burke then sought the cooperation of similar non-Catholic religious organizations to meet the problem of safeguarding the moral welfare of the American troops. The General Wartime Commission of the Federal Council of Churches of Christ and the Jewish Welfare Board of the Army and Navy cooperated quickly at his suggestion and a "Committee of Six" was formed which represented the chief Catholic, Protestant, and Jewish religious organizations throughout the war. The Government at that time had not yet formed a certain policy regarding chaplains, their number, or their training, although by the end of the war a settled policy based upon wartime experiences was in operation.

Actually this National Catholic War Council had no real authorization because neither Father John J. Burke nor Cardinal Gibbons had any real authority to call the convention that created it. It represented more or less the feelings of the patriotic mass of Catholics led by the Knights of Columbus in their desire to fulfill their duties in the war effort. This was an awkward situation and when the trustees of the Catholic University met in mid-November Cardinal Gibbons, the unofficial primate, discussed with the other bishops a solution of the problem. They agreed that the only official organ of the Church in the country was the Board of Archbishops. Acting on the advice of the assembled episcopal trustees of the Catholic University, the Cardinal sent a letter to the archbishops on November 21 stating that they should constitute themselves the Catholic War Council and assume the direction of the National Catholic War Council which the priests and laymen had organized as their representatives. He also listed two problems that this Council would have to face, the first, the organization of the Council and, the other, to decide the status and sphere of activity of the Knights of Columbus. When the archbishops sent their agreement to Cardinal Gibbons, he sent another letter to the bishops of the country announcing that, with the consent of the archbishops, he had appointed an episcopal committee consisting of Bishops Patrick Hayes of New York, Joseph Schrembs of Toledo, William T. Russell of Charleston, and Peter

J. Muldoon of Rockford to act in the name of the hierarchy. Bishop Muldoon was appointed Chairman. The Committee was requested to meet with the Cardinal at the Catholic University on January 9, 1918. Because of the death of Bishop Foley of Detroit, the actual meeting was delayed until January 16. In a letter of January 12 to the Committee, the Cardinal announced that the archbishops assumed responsibility for the earlier War Council and wanted it to continue in existence. The Knights of Columbus were also to be brought into the conference because their work was greatly needed. Finally all other Catholic societies were to be asked to cooperate in the war effort.

This action ratified the first steps of the Knights of Columbus and Father John J. Burke and his collaborators and set up an official national Catholic organization. The organization consisted first of the National Catholic War Council composed of the four-teen archbishops and, secondly, of the Administrative Committee composed of the four bishops who derived their authority from the Board of Archbishops. Thirdly, there was set up the Executive Committee composed of the four bishops, six members of the Committee on Knights of Columbus War Activities, and six mem-bers of the Committee on Special War Activities which had been set up in the August convention. The Executive Committee was an Advisory Board and met regularly for the general discussion of all national Catholic war activities. Two principal committees were appointed through the National Catholic War Council. The first was the Knights of Columbus Committee on War Activities, which had complete authority assigned to it by the Administra-tive Committee of the National War Council over the operation of the special work that the Knights had undertaken and for which they had been given official sanction by the government, namely, the great task of providing recreation centers for the en-listed men in the camps at home and abroad. The other commit-tee appointed through the National Catholic War Council was the Committee on Special War Activities, which had charge of all other matters, especially of the appointment and provision of chaplains. Father John J. Burke became the chairman of the Com-mittee on Special War Activities and William J. Mulligan in New York acted as Chairman of the War Activities Committee of the Knights of Columbus. The most critical problems of the War Activities Committee were those which came under the direction of Charles P. Neill: the supervision of entertainment and amuse-ment and, specifically, the work of the Commission on Hygiene and Sanitation. The government's Committee on Training Camp

Activities asked and obtained the cooperation of the National Catholic War Council in meeting the moral problems traditionally associated with army camp life. There were incidental problems of cooperation by the Catholic committees with other religious organizations in raising funds and in camp activities. Generally among Catholics, acting as Catholics outside of the national committees and their associates, the unit of activity was the parish. On November 24, 1917, Bishop Patrick Hayes, the Auxiliary of New York, was made the Chaplain Bishop of the United States. He took over the direction of the chaplains in January and appointed five vicars general with authority over five district areas of Army centers. In April Bishop Hayes sent a letter of instruction on the conduct of the chaplains in the service. At the beginning of the war, there were about twenty-five chaplains in the service, and at the time of the Armistice on November 11, 1918, there were one thousand and twenty-six chaplains in active service and four hundred and ninety-nine whose application had been approved. Bishop Hayes retained his jurisdiction over the chaplains after he became Archbishop of New York on March 10, 1919.

The eight archbishops whose signatures were attached to the letter of loyalty sent to President Wilson on April 18, 1917, represented in many ways the divisions of the Church which only wartime enthusiasm could mould into a practical unity outside of essential religious matters. Some archbishops, of course, were absent from the meeting because they were too far away or were constrained by other business. The old divisions of the American controversy were represented by Archbishop Ireland and Archbishop Messmer. Archbishop John J. Keane was living in retirement and his namesake, James John Keane, was in the See of Dubuque. The second Keane, Cardinal Farley, and Cardinal O'Connell represented a later type of American-Irish prelate who had a sense of loyalty to Irish traditions but who regarded himself as fully American. The same could be said of Archbishops Moeller and Mundelein who had definite sympathy with the Germans but who were fully American in patriotism and in their hopes.

About the ninety-six bishops ruling eighty-six dioceses or serving as auxiliaries, few generalizations could be made outside of their official work. The new rule about the choice of bishops in the United States, enacted in Rome on July 25, 1916, did not really become effective until after the War.[6] Consequently most

[6] Cf. Francis J. Weber, "Episcopal Appointments in the U.S.A.," *American Ecclesiastical Review* (1966) CLV, 178–191.

of them had been nominated locally by their own clergy and fellow bishops. They represented many types of American Catholics. The most common source of their seminary training was Rome, but there was not the predominance of Roman-trained men that one might have expected after the condemnation of Modernism and the care in choosing candidates demanded by Pope Pius X in his Modernism message. There were many Bishops who had received their training in seminaries in the United States and several who had studied in the Sulpician Seminary at Montreal. The predominant characteristic of the group was a strong fidelity to the care of the flock entrusted to them, a zeal of the missionary rather than that of the bishop of a long established see. Their chief duty was still the building of churches and the provision of priests to attend them. Except for Cardinal Gibbons, the growing importance of the diocesan rule gave them less and less opportunity to extend their influence outside of their diocese or province.

The annual meetings of the archbishops were rather perfunctory, as can be seen in the 1917 resolution on the war which did nothing to face the real problem of Catholic participation. The Catholic press of that day consisted for the most part of diocesan weekly newspapers. They lacked a common news agency and seemed too careful to reject criticisms and discriminations against the Church and were filled with excessive praise for all Catholic accomplishments. The Federation of Catholic Societies which met in Kansas City in August 1917 was sadly characteristic of the lack of forceful leadership. There were archbishops, bishops, priests and laymen there, but all they accomplished besides oratory were a few resolutions of loyalty to the Pope, to the government, and a criticism of the questionable movies that had begun to appear. The Code of Canon Law which was being printed and would be put into effect after the war was a needed stimulus to functioning ecclesiastical organization and the creation of diocesan chancery offices. The Code of Canon Law with the new decree removing the appointment of bishops from local influence, and the clarification of jurisdiction were to create a more efficient ecclesiastical organization, but reduce the local incentives to Catholic effort. However, in 1917 the hierarchy was held down by local prejudices and foreign nationalisms which tended to perpetuate extremely patriotic foreign nationalisms as well as local prejudices. There were a few of the younger prelates who would leave their names on the Church history of the next decade, among them Archbishop Mundelein, Bishop Peter J. Muldoon, Bishop Michael Curley, and Bishop Joseph Schrembs, but the already distinguished prelates were few. That the efforts toward Catholic wartime cooperation should arise rather from the laymen and priests than from the bishops was an indication of the conservatism of the hierarchy of the period.

Of the lay organizations, the Knights of Columbus were undoubtedly the most successful, and their membership and physically active trends were admirably suited for war work. The next largest organization was probably the Central Verein, but their dedication to German ideas resulted in a sort of semiparalysis in a war against Germany. The Federation of Catholic Societies, and the societies that joined it were in the process of losing what little force they had attained.

Outside of the diocesan organization, the chief nondiocesan clerical society was undoubtedly the Society of Jesus which supported most of the colleges of the country and several private classical academies. Their organ after 1909 was *America,* which tried to speak for American Catholicism in words of a certain conservatism. The Dominicans, likewise numerous throughout the country, devoted themselves to parish and missionary work mostly. The Franciscans had some colleges but had as their best reputation a great devotion to the poor and to the missions. The Vincentians and Sulpicians were devoting their efforts chiefly to seminaries. There were several other smaller communities, the most notable of which was probably Holy Cross because of the University of Notre Dame. But Catholic colleges, with a few exceptions, such as Holy Cross, Georgetown, and Notre Dame, had scarcely attained full college viability, having no endowment worth mentioning and lacking highly trained specialists in most college subjects or the financial means to produce them. The Catholic University, because of the Americanist controversy and subsequent dissensions, had never attained the promise of its founders, but was becoming notable for its moral theologians, Fathers William Kerby and John A. Ryan. Permeating the whole problem of Catholicism in the United States was the internal difficulty of the Americanization of the millions of immigrants who constituted so much of the body of American Catholicism in 1917. The census of 1920, while taken three years later, is quite useful in weighing this problem since the war interrupted immigration during those three years. That census listed 1,139,979 Americans as born in Poland—a Catholic country. It listed 575,627 as natives of Austria and 397,283 as natives of Hungary—a large percentage of which were probably Catholic—1,037,234 as natives of Ireland, and 1,610,113 as natives of Italy. There were hundreds of thousands from other Catholic regions of Europe even though the number of practicing Catholics from Catholic countries may have been much smaller than the total immigration from these areas. In a nation which was just reaching national maturity, this large foreign-born mass meant that the Catholic body as a whole was not yet ready for those positive advances in culture and education that might have been expected from a minority of 17,000,000 or more inhabitants in a nation of 105,000,000. There was a heavy concentration of these immigrants in the cities and in industrial centers. Attending the Catholic population, the *Catholic Directory* of 1917 listed 19,983 priests. There were 10,190 parishes with resident priests of whom 5,687 had parish schools caring for 1,537,655 children. The *Directory* did not distinguish the foreign language schools from the others or the schools in slum areas from those among middle-class Catholics. The *Directory* for 1917 also listed the diocese of the Ruthenian Greek rite, which had been established in 1913, with a membership of 500,000. The first priest of this rite came in 1884. The first bishop was Soter Ortynsky, O.S.B.M., who was consecrated in 1907 and given a regular see in Philadelphia in 1913. He died on March 24, 1916, and was succeeded by Constantine Bohachevsky.

The story of Roman Catholicism in the United States during the war, besides the increased attendance at Holy Communion resulting from the decrees of the previous decade, was a litany of drives for funds for the service organizations, for the Red Cross, and for the sale of Liberty Bonds. While there were efforts for provincial and diocesan drives, many of which were hampered by the influenza epidemic of 1918, the chief unit for Catholic effort was the parish, although the actual measurement of sums was by civic unit. There were no quotas for soldiers or sailors based upon religion, but each parish soon had its service flag with gold stars for the dead. There was a higher percentage of Catholics in the service than the accepted Catholic percentage of population. Some of this difference probably arose from the definite identification or religious affiliation in the service by those who did not admit religious affiliation in civilian life, but the higher percentage was accepted as manifesting the loyalty of the Catholics in the nation. To the Knights of Columbus went the chief burden and the chief honor for service to the Army and Navy during the war.[7] The huts

---

[7] Maurice Francis Egan and John B. Kennedy, *The Knights of Columbus in Peace and War,* 2 vol. (New Haven, 1920) gives much information but is not a good history.

erected in camps and posts by the Knights of Columbus, in which the motto was "Everybody Welcome Everything Free," consisted of a long wooden building containing recreational facilities, offices for the Knights' secretaries and workers, and a chapel. Huts were also erected in larger cities and in transportation centers where servicemen would be expected to gather. More important later were the huts built in Paris and in the camps overseas. The huts provided the scene, the Chaplains' Aid Association furnished the sacerdotal equipment, and the Military Ordinariate furnished the priests for attendance at Mass. What was needed beyond that for relief and recreation was supplied also by the Knights. One feature that was peculiar to this war was the presence of the Knights of Columbus chaplain-priests, who were supported and transported by the Knights in addition to those who were inducted into the regular military services. The work of the Knights of Columbus priest and worker did not end with the armistice but continued until the servicemen had returned to their homes. The Knights of Columbus then assisted in the demobilization and in the plans for reconstruction. When the war ended, the Knights had 250 points of operation overseas with a thousand secretaries and in this country they maintained over 360 buildings with 750 secretaries. To help the discharged servicemen get jobs, the Knights employed 27,250 volunteer workers on this very important work.

One of the most important wartime developments under Catholic auspices was the National Service School for Women established under the National Catholic War Council at Clifton, a forty-acre tract on the outskirts of Washington, D.C. Raymond B. Fosdick, the Chairman of the Committee on Training Camp Activities and the leader of the Big Six in charge of the war workers, asked in a letter of March 31, 1918, that Father Burke secure some women to join in the service overseas in the K. of C. centers. By the end of June 1918, three overseas units had been sent in addition to those who were assigned to work in this country. The training course varied with the individual and with the needs of the government, but in general the course lasted seven weeks and included classes and lectures proper to the special kind of social work they planned to do. Besides the resident faculty, lecturers were supplied from the Catholic University and Georgetown faculties and from suitable government offices. There were in all twelve units of these women service workers trained in the Clifton school. The small number of Catholic women already trained in this kind of work before the war pointed up the need of a permanent school of social work and the founders of Clifton had this in mind in establishing the wartime institution.

There were other wartime innovations that were to affect Catholicism after the war, as well as some temporary measures like the Student Army Training Corps, established ineffectively in about 55 Catholic colleges. The Student Army Training Corps ended almost as soon as the war. The ratification of the prohibition amendment to the Constitution, which was generally not well received by Catholics, might not have taken place in peacetime with the soldiers at home. The women's suffrage amendment proposed and enacted shortly after the war was something that was not dependent on the war and was rather an expression of the advance of American women in freedom and in active participation in public life. It cannot be said that Catholics were in the van in the movement for women's suffrage and in the so-called emancipation of women. But when women were needed in the war service the Catholic War Council cooperated. The communities of Sisters who had done war work in the Civil War were not in a position to render similar service in the modern way, except in their own hospitals. The graduate of the Catholic Service School was one answer to this need. The problem that Catholic moralists faced as a result of the war was the invasion of public offices and factories by women during war times. Conservative Catholic moralists wanted to stem the tide and return the women to the home, but the invasion by women into business was permanent and was to grow.

Accidental to the change in the spirit and action of the public leaders of the Church was the passing of many old leaders. The chief losses were Archbishop John Ireland, who died September 25, 1918, and Cardinal John Farley, who died September 17, 1918. Archbishop John J. Keane died June 23, 1918, Bishop Francis S. Chatard of Indianapolis died September 7, 1918, Archbishop Edmond Prendergast died February 26, 1918, and Bishop Cusack, July 12, 1918. New Ordinaries of importance who arrived on the scene included Archbishop Dennis J. Dougherty, transferred from Buffalo to Philadelphia; Archbishop John W. Shaw, transferred from San Antonio to New Orleans; Archbishop Austin Dowling, transferred from Des Moines to St. Paul; Archbishop Patrick J. Hayes, the Military Ordinary made Archbishop of New York; and Albert T. Daeger, O.F.M., Archbishop of Santa Fé. New bishops included Bishop Edward Kelly of Grand Rapids, Bishop Michael J. Gallagher of Detroit, Bishop Joseph Chartrand of Indianapolis, Bishop William Turner of Buffalo, Bishop John

T. McNicholas, O.P., of Duluth, later of Cincinnati, and Bishop Thomas J. Walsh of Trenton. The national unity of the country that had been created by wartime propaganda had begun to have adverse effects on the position of Catholicism despite the acknowledged patriotism during the war. The passage of the prohibition amendment was one symptom, the attempt to nationalize the school system with a cabinet minister at the head—called by the editors of *America* a "Prussian system"—was another. There had been some interference with civil liberties during the war, as there seems to be in every war, but the combination of a revival of the Anglo-Saxon-Protestant-white cultural myth with the strengthening of the police arm of the government gave rise to a nativistic movement whose crudest manifestations were the new Ku Klux Klan and the police crusade against political radicals.

In the National Catholic War Council under the Committee on Special War Activities there had been a Subcommittee on Reconstruction which was intended to plan for postwar problems. The chairman of this subcommittee was Dr. John O'Grady. Dr. O'Grady turned to his fellow faculty member at the Catholic University, Dr. John A. Ryan, who had been working out a program for social reconstruction.[8] Father Ryan polished up his notes before turning them over to Father O'Grady. Father O'Grady in turn submitted the program to the four episcopal members of the Administrative Committee of the War Council, under Bishop Muldoon as Chairman. After a few verbal changes, the Committee of Bishops issued the program on February 12, 1919, under the title, "Social Reconstruction: A General Review of the Problems and Survey of the Remedies." Father Ryan had drawn his program from a study of various proposals for reconstruction, especially those of the British Labor Party and of Cardinal Bourne as well as of the American Federation of Labor, the British Quakers, and the United States Chamber of Commerce. The program was, as Ryan claimed afterwards, the best program offered at the time. The document first examined and criticized the chief proposals for reconstruction which Father Ryan had been studying and then outlined an American Catholic program of social reconstruction. The chief positive statements were:[9]

It is not to be expected that as many or as great a social change will take place in the United States as in Europe. Neither our habits of

[8] John A. Ryan, note 3 above, pp. 144–148.
[9] The statement is printed in *Our Bishops Speak,* edited by Raphael Huber, O.F.M., Conv. (Milwaukee, 1952) pp. 243–260.

thinking nor our ordinary ways of life have undergone a profound disturbance. . . . The first problem in the process of reconstruction is the industrial replacement of the discharged soldiers and sailors. The majority of them will undoubtedly return to their previous occupations. However, a very large number of them will either find their previous places closed to them, or will be eager to consider the possibility of more attractive employments. . . .

One of the most important problems of readjustment is that created by the presence in industry of immense numbers of women who have taken the places of men during the war. One principle is clear: no female worker should remain in any occupation that is harmful to health or morals. . . . Another general principle is that the proportion of women in industry ought to be kept within the smallest practical limits. . . . Those women who are engaged at the same tasks as men should receive equal pay for equal amounts and qualities of work.

. . . The War Labor Board ought to be continued in existence by Congress, and endowed with all the power for effective action that it can possess under the Federal Constitution. . . .

The general level of wages attained during the war should not be lowered. . . .

Even if the great majority of workers were now in receipt of more than living wages, there is no good reason why rates of pay should be lowered. After all, a living wage is not necessarily the full measure of justice. . . .

Housing projects for war workers which have been completed or almost completed by the government of the United States, have cost some forty million dollars, and are found in eleven cities. . . . The great cities in which congestion and other forms of bad housing are disgracefully apparent ought to take up and continue the work, at least to such an extent as will remove the worst features of a social condition that is a menace at once to industrial efficiency, civic health, good morals, and religion. . . .

During the war the cost of living has risen at least 75 per cent above the level of 1913. Some check has been placed upon the upward trend by government fixing of prices in the case of bread and coal and a few other commodities. . . . If the extortionate practices of monopoly were prevented by adequate laws and adequate law enforcement, prices would automatically be kept at as low a level as that to which they might be brought by direct government determination. . . .

More important and effective than any government regulation of prices would be the establishment of cooperative stores. The enormous toll taken from industry by the various classes of middlemen is now fully realized. . . .

. . . The several states should enact laws providing for the establishment of wage rates that will be at least sufficient for the decent maintenance of a family, in the case of all male adults, and adequate to decent individual support of female workers. . . .

. . . The State should make comprehensive provision for insurance against illness, invalidity, unemployment, and old age. So far as possible the insurance fund should be raised by a levy on industry, as is now done in the case of accident compensation. . . .

. . . Municipal clinics where the poorer class could obtain the advantage of medical treatment by specialists at a reasonable cost would likewise seem to have become a necessity. . . . Free medical care should be given to those who cannot afford to pay.

The right of labor to organize and to deal with employers through representations has been asserted above in connection with the discussion of the War Labor Board. It is to be hoped that this right will never again be called in question by any considerable number of employers. . . . The establishment of shop committees, working wherever possible with the trade union, is the method suggested by this group of employers [English Quakers] for giving the employees the proper share of industrial management. . . .

The need of industrial, or as it has come to be more generally called, vocational training, is now universally acknowledged. In the interest of the nation, as well as in that of the workers themselves, this training should be made substantially universal. . . .

The question of education naturally suggests the subject of child labor. Public opinion in the majority of the states of our country has set its face inflexibly against the continuous employment of children in industry before the age of sixteen years. . . .

Nevertheless, the present system stands in grievous need of considerable modifications and improvement. Its main defects are three: Enormous inefficiency and waste in the production and distribution of commodities; insufficient incomes for the great majority of wage earners, and unnecessarily large income for a small minority of privileged capitalists. . . .

. . . The majority must somehow become owners, or at least in part, of the instruments of production. . . .

The second great evil, that of insufficient income for the majority, can be removed only by providing the workers with more income. . . .

For the third evil mentioned above, excessive gains by a small minority of privileged capitalists, the main remedies are prevention of monopolistic control of commodities, adequate government regulation of such service monopolies as will remain under private operation, and heavy taxation of income, excess profits, and inheritances. . . .

In the conservative reaction that seized the country during the reconstruction period, at least some termed "socialistic" this progressive proposal of the Executive Committee of the National Catholic War Council. Actually it wrote into more concrete form the reputation the hierarchy had won through Cardinal Gibbons' intercession in the 1880s for the Knights of Labor as a friend of the working people. The reasons for the statement were about the same: most Catholics were in the wage-earning classes, but this time there was additional support for the proposals in the *Rerum Novarum* of Pope Leo XIII.

While this statement on social reconstruction was being prepared and issued, the efforts at national unity in the Catholic Church in the United States were undergoing a severe crisis. There was something sad in the failure of the Federation of Catholic Societies to unite American Catholics. The idea of federation did not work because the societies in it were not able to bring united societies to the Federation, with the exception of a few nationalistic groups such as the Central Verein, which was so strongly united that some members resented any direct control from the Federation. The other weakness was the lack of real episcopal support. The fact that the German-Americans, including many members of the Central Verein, had opposed the Americanists in the previous decade invited coolness toward the Federation on the part of the espiscopal leaders of the Americanists, such as Archbishop Ireland. The strong support of Bishops Messmer and McFaul did not attract other bishops except the few who appeared at the National conventions.

The two best qualities of the Federation were its fostering of social reform under Father Dietz and its encouragement to leadership by laymen. To the personal disappointment of Father Dietz the Catholic social reform program was taken over by the new National Welfare Council under the leadership of Bishop Muldoon and Father John A. Ryan. The lay leadership of the Federation had been handicapped by the failure of the most active lay group of national importance, the Knights of Columbus, to really enter into the Federation. As a matter of fact the Knights of Columbus by their success during the war had made the efforts of the Federation look almost useless. The leaders of the Federation in their final meetings after the American entrance into the war had manifested a consciousness that the Federation would have to be reformed essentially to survive the war. The Federation did receive an invitation to join the new National Welfare Council but as a member of a subcommittee. The *Bulletin* of the Federation gave the program of the new Council in the final issues in 1919. There was nothing left for the Federation to do.

On August 16, 1918, Cardinal Gibbons, a beloved leader of American Catholicism, highly respected by Catholic and non-Catholic alike and respected abroad for his leadership in peace and war, reached the golden anniversary of his priesthood.[10] A celebration of the event planned for October had to be cancelled because of the influenza epidemic, although at St. Mary's Seminary in Baltimore there was a private celebration on October 20 attended by the seminarians, the Seminary faculty, and some friends including representatives of the American, French, and English hierarchies. Messages of congratulation were sent from the President of the United States and from Cardinal Mercier. On November 16 Ambassador Jules Jusserand of France conferred on the Cardinal the decoration of Commander of the Legion of Honor. Other hierarchies and governors sent felicitations. On February 20, 1919, at the Franciscan Shrine Church in Washington the Cardinal sang a Mass as the public celebration of his golden jubilee in the presence of Cardinals O'Connell and Begin, of twelve archbishops and of fifty-eight bishops, as well as of a large gathering of other clergy and laymen. Archbishop Mundelein gave the sermon for the occasion. This Washington celebration was the occasion of a very important change in the Catholic organization in the United States.

The representative of Pope Benedict XV at the jubilee celebration was Archbishop Bonaventura Cerretti, Secretary of the Congregation for Extraordinary Affairs. On the occasion of the celebration, February 20, Archbishop Cerretti addressed the American hierarchy in the chapel of Caldwell Hall of the University. While praising the hierarchy and telling also of the work of the Pope in the recent war, he suggested that the Pope wished the American bishops to form some kind of organization which would help the Pope in his efforts to secure a lasting peace and which would at the same time participate in the application of Christian ethics in the fields of education and labor. This new organization would have to be a replacement for the annual meeting of the archbishops and the National War Council.[11] Cardinal Gibbons immediately appointed a committee to act on the Archbishop's suggestions and to report to the annual meeting of the archbishops the next day. At that annual meeting of the archbishops, the committee suggested that there should be an annual meeting of the whole hierarchy each year and that a standing committee of five bishops be appointed to act in the name of the hierarchy

[10] John Tracy Ellis, *The Life of James Cardinal Gibbons, Archbishop of Baltimore, 1834–1921*, 2 vol. (Milwaukee, 1952) II, 433–437.
[11] "The September Meeting of the American Hierarchy," *American Ecclesiastical Review* (July 1919) LXI, 1–19 and Ellis, *Gibbons*, note 10 above, II, 298–302.

between the annual meetings. Undoubtedly the suggestion came from Pope Benedict. The Archbishops accepted the suggestion and asked the secretary of the meeting to write to the bishops not present at the meeting asking them to join in the proposal. Cardinal Gibbons then appointed the four members of the Executive Committee of the National War Council and himself to be the provisional committee to plan the annual meeting and the program for the hierarchy. Later, because Bishop Hayes, one of the four members of the Council, was appointed Archbishop of New York on March 10, the Cardinal replaced him with Bishop Joseph C. Glass, C.M., of Salt Lake City at the suggestion of Archbishop Hanna so that there would be a representation from the West on the committee.

After Archbishop Cerretti had returned to Rome, Pope Benedict XV sent a letter dated April 10 to Cardinal Gibbons, Cardinal O'Connell, and the other archbishops and bishops of the country in which he told of his pleasure in the report of Archbishop Cerretti about the celebration and particularly their decision on that occasion to have an annual meeting of the American archbishops and bishops. He expressed agreement also with their decision to appoint two committees, one on educational problems and the other on promoting the interests and welfare of the Church. The Pope praised the good that could come from such an annual meeting of the hierarchy, especially in fulfilling the principles of the *Rerum Novarum* of Pope Leo XIII. He urged the bishops to take a special interest in Catholic education and in the Catholic University and commended their plans to erect at the University a shrine to Our Lady of the Immaculate Conception. In answering the Pope's letter, Cardinal Gibbons spoke of only one committee, "The Committee on General Catholic Interests and Affairs," and said that three resolutions had been taken: to help the Pope who had been impoverished by the war, to have an annual meeting of the hierarchy, and to appoint the committee of five prelates.

In his letter on May 5 to the members of this Committee, the Cardinal called for the setting up of a central bureau and listed eleven topics to be examined by the Committee when they should meet and appointed Bishop Muldoon to be the chairman of the Committee in his absence. The topics were: "1. The Holy See, 2. Home Missions, 3. Foreign Missions, 4. Social and Charitable Work, 5. Catholic University, 6. Catholic Education in General, 7. Catholic Literature, 8. Catholic press, 9. Legislation, 10. A Catholic Bureau, 11. Finances." The last two items offered the hardest problems because already the National Catholic War

Council was being criticized by some bishops for interference in diocesan matters and for their efforts to centralize authority. The finances were important also because without financial aid from the dioceses the central bureau would die because of lack of means to operate. On the question of social and charitable work, the Cardinal praised the Social Reconstruction Program published by the Committee and the work done by the Knights of Columbus in the war. On May 17 the Cardinal sent out another letter to the hierarchy announcing that the Committee of Bishops under Bishop Muldoon had met in New York on the occasion of the conferring of the pallium on Archbishop Hayes. At this first meeting the Committee had taken notice of the proposed laws, of laws proposed about federal aid to education, of problems that had arisen in connection with the new Code of Canon Law, and of the need for finances for the Committee. On May 24 the Cardinal sent a further letter to the hierarchy announcing that the first annual meeting of the hierarchy would be held beginning on September 24 in Divinity Hall at the Catholic University. He then sent to the bishops the program he had earlier sent to the Committee with its eleven topics.

In preparation for the September meeting the Committee of four bishops held a meeting on July 22, 23, and 24 at the University of Notre Dame attended by prominent specialists in the topics listed in the Cardinal's original letter to the Committee. No list of those in attendance at the meeting was published but Father Dietz was among those consulted on the question of social reform. He was encouraged by Bishop Muldoon to continue his work in social reform but his special activities were not accepted as part of the new program. Some representatives of the Federation of Catholic Societies who attended were encouraged to report to the Committee on Catholic Lay Activities, an invitation that actually ended the Federation even though some of the officers were elected to offices on the new National Council of Catholic Men. The meeting decided that there were three fields of concentration for Catholic activity: the mission field (both domestic and foreign), the Catholic press, and Catholic social work. The results of these three days of consultation were drawn up in schematic form for presentation to the first annual meeting on September 24. Another meeting of the officials of the new organization was held in New York on August 28. The transition from the Catholic War Council to the National Catholic Welfare Council, except for the activities of the Knights of Columbus, was declared immediately, but the definite lines of the new organization were not clear for some months.

When the bishops assembled in Washington on September 24, there were ninety-three members of the hierarchy present.[12] By secret ballot they elected the officers of the Council. Archbishop Edward J. Hanna was elected chairman of the Administrative Committee and Bishop J. F. Regis Canevin of Pittsburgh was named a member of the Committee. The chairmen of the five Committees of the Council elected were Archbishop Dennis Dougherty of the Department of Laws and Legislation, Archbishop Austin J. Dowling of the Department of Education, Bishop P.J. Muldoon of the Department of Social Action and Vice-Chairman of the Administrative Committee, Bishop Joseph Schrembs of the Department of Lay Organizations, and Bishop William T. Russell of the Department of Publicity, Press, and Literature. Father John J. Burke, C.S.P., was elected General Secretary and the personal representative of the Chairman of the Administrative Committee. These committees began to organize their forces. One of the first to begin operations in the national headquarters at 1312 Massachusetts Avenue, Washington, was the Social Action Department with its director Father John A. Ryan assisted by John A. Lapp of Chicago. Their appointments unfortunately marked the further eclipse of Father Peter Dietz and the Social Service Commission of the Federation. Father Edward A. Pace of the Catholic University was named the Director of the Education Department, and Justin McGrath and Michael Williams began the direction of the Press and Publicity Department. In the Department of Lay Organizations, Michael Slattery was named Executive Secretary of the Laymen, and Agnes Regan of San Francisco was named Executive Secretary for Laywomen.

The lay organizations were expected to support themselves from contributions from the societies associated with them. The funds for the operation of the Administrative office and for the headquarters of the other committees were to be drawn from voluntary contributions from the dioceses. The Administrative Committee and the other four committees were to operate on a budget approved by the annual meeting of the Bishops. The Council itself was to be a voluntary organization and had no legislative or mandatory power. The Council did not have universal support in the hierarchy even during these first years, but chiefly because of the remarkable men who headed the Council during its first years, plus the support of the aging Cardinal Gibbons, the Coun-

[12] N.C.W.C. Bulletin, "The National Catholic Welfare Council" (October, 1919) I, 10–13. The story of the formation of the Council has not been written yet.

cil was in many ways effective at the start. The first important achievement was the issuance of the Pastoral Letter of 1919, the first pastoral since the Third Plenary Council of Baltimore. Composed apparently by Father Edward Pace, it was signed by Cardinal Gibbons in the name of the whole hierarchy, and, while not as startling as the Bishops' Program for Social Reconstruction, it contained many of the same proposals.[13]

The Pastoral began with a brief survey of the thirty-five years since the Baltimore Council of 1884 noting an increase from seventy-five to one hundred bishops. The Pastoral then renewed the exhortations of other pastorals to the practice of faith, the reading of the Sacred Scriptures, the development of a Catholic spirit, the practice of prayer, the use of the Mass and the Sacraments, devotion to Our Blessed Mother, support for Catholic education, especially the Catholic University as the home of all the sciences and the center of all Catholic education, the support of Catholic societies, the support of home and foreign missions (particularly the Indian and Negro missions), the encouragement of priestly and religious vocations, and the support of the Catholic press. Then the Pastoral turned to changes in world conditions since the Baltimore Council, especially to the advance in technical means and the wider diffusion of knowledge. The Pastoral praised the work of Catholics during the war and the formation of the new Catholic Welfare Council. The lessons of the war, the Pastoral pointed out, should incline American Catholics to remember that the war was a punishment for human failures and that Catholics should be thankful for the country's deliverance from many other evils and for the fine spirit manifested by the faithful during the war.

The rest of the Pastoral took up the problems of reconstruction from the evils resulting from the war and from certain evil factors that even preceded the war. The Pastoral acknowledged also that "intelligence, initiative, and energy have been exerted to accomplish higher and worthier aims" but that these efforts could not obscure the fact that they were "facing grave peril." The country must face the need for reforms. These reforms must be based on the recognition of the position of Christ and His Church but include a realization that the sources of evil listed by Pope Benedict XV as " 'Lack of mutual good will, contempt for authority, conflict of class with class, and absorption in the pursuit of the per-

[13] There are many printings of this Pastoral. Cf. *Our Bishops Speak*, note 9 above, pp. 3–65.

ishable goods of this world, with utter disregard of things that are nobler and worthier of human endeavor.' " The fundamental error, said the Pastoral, was to become "absorbed in worldly pursuits and to neglect those which belong to our eternal welfare." Fundamental in reform must be the recognition of God as the Supreme Ruler.

The Pastoral then took up the obligations of justice in the contemporary world and insisted that the same spirit of justice that condemned dishonesty in private dealings must also condemn "more emphatically any and every attempt on the part of individuals to further their interests at the expense of the public welfare." Thus God must be recognized as the origin of all authority. The State has a sacred claim on respect and authority but "it is the means to an end, not an end in itself; . . . Where the State protects all in the reasonable exercise of their rights, there liberty exists." The State must also be the first to appreciate the importance of religion for the preservation of the commonwealth.

The Pastoral then turned to the obligation to exercise charity. "As commonly understood charity is manifested in deeds that tend to the relief of suffering in any of its various forms, or that provide opportunities of advancement for those who have none, or that add somewhat to the scant pleasures of many laborious lives. . . . By its very nature, charity is also social virtue." Charity is the law of the Gospel and will become less apparent as the world moves away from the Gospel. Discussing social relations, the Pastoral stated:

The security of the nation and the efficiency of government for the general weal depend largely upon the standards which are adopted and the practices which are admitted, in social relations. . . .

The esteem in which marriage is held furnishes an index of people's morality. . . .

It is essential, in the first place, that clean living before marriage be equally obligatory on men and women. . . .

On the other hand, it is idealism of the truest and most practical sort that sees in marriage the divinely appointed plan for cooperating with the Creator in perpetuating the race, and that accepts the responsibility of bringing children into the world, who may prove either a blessing or a curse to society at large. . . .

There is need of greater vigilance in protecting the home at this time, owing to conditions which tend to weaken its influence. The demands of industry, of business, and of social intercourse subject the family tie to a strain that becomes more severe as civilization advances. . . .

Concerning divorce the Pastoral said that no sane man or woman regards divorce as a good thing and the Church, under certain circumstances, permits only separation to meet extreme difficulties. The Pastoral regarded the growth of the divorce evil as evidence of moral decay.

The Pastoral recognized the need for social intercourse and called attention to the good contributed during the war by those who furnished entertainment for war workers and for the armed services. It urged that the same spirit prevail in the peace but that the prescriptions of plain decency should not be set aside in these matters. The Pastoral also recognized that in all civilized countries the tendency had been to give women a larger share in pursuits and occupations that were formerly reserved to men, such as the learned professions, the field of industry, and the forum of political life. It suggested that women's influence in public affairs would purify and elevate public and political life.

The Pastoral gave great importance to the problems of industrial relations, quoting from the encyclicals of Pope Leo XIII, emphasizing that the events of recent months (apparently the bitter strikes of 1919) proved that something was needed besides material factors. The Pastoral insisted with Pope Leo that the social question is more than a question of economics, that it is a moral and religious matter. The Pastoral insisted also that the people as a whole had a prior claim in these disputes which unnecessary strikes abuse. The trouble in these disputes, the pastoral said, is "that men fail to see their obligations to one another and to the public, or seeing them, refuse to fulfill them except under threat and compulsion." Mutual obligations must be recognized. Pope Leo had already pointed out the right of labor to organize, but, while labor has the right to organize, the employer has the right to the faithful observance by labor unions of all contracts and agreements.

Continuing to quote from the *Rerum Novarum* of Pope Leo XIII, the Pastoral urged the benefits of mutual understandings and associations between worker and employer by associations, conferences, and sharing of management. Above all, under the American form of government, the people must not resort to revolution to solve their economic problems.

The Pastoral then turned to the general condition of the country and the obligation of loyalty and the avoidance of sectional divisions, racial hatred, strife among classes, and purely partisan conflict. Americans should avoid proposals of reform that invade the rights of conscience. They should also help the immigrants to prepare themselves for the duties of citizenship. These new citizens, and old citizens, must adopt right principles in politics, in the choice of candidates for office, and in serving the true welfare of the country. This effort in turn calls for an enlightened public opinion, and, because of that, the publicist has both influence and responsibility. The press which does not safeguard the home is guilty of pollution, as bad as that of one who scatters germs in the water supply of a city. The Pastoral quoted the Popes on the need for international peace, especially in modern times. While protesting the elimination of the Pope from recent peace efforts, the Pastoral did note that "The success of these organized efforts [in former times] was due, in large measure, to the influence of the Church." The Pastoral noted that the Pope in 1918 had urged reduction of armaments and the establishment of international tribunals.

For the attainment of these ideals there must be education. "Democracy, understood as self-government, implies that the people as a whole shall rule themselves. But if they are to rule wisely, each must begin by governing himself, by performing his duty no less than by maintaining his right." For that purpose there must be sound education for all people. This duty is serious because of the complexity of modern civilization. Noting that the Catholic Church had maintained a separate system of education, the Pastoral stated the principles of true education.

First: The right of the child to receive education and the correlative duty of providing it are established on the fact that man has a soul created by God and endowed with capacities which need to be developed for the good of the individual and the good of society. . . .

Second: Since the child is endowed with physical, intellectual, and moral capacities, all these must be developed harmoniously. . . .

Third: Since the duties we owe our Creator take precedence of all other duties, moral training must accord the first place to religion, that is to the knowledge of God and His law, and must cultivate a spirit of obedience to His commands. . . .

Fourth: Moral and religious training is most efficacious when it is joined with instructions in other kinds of knowledge. . . .

Fifth: An education that unites intellectual, moral and religious elements is the best training for citizenship. . . .[14]

The Pastoral added that these convictions were shared by many not of the Catholic faith.

On the right to educate, the Pastoral said that Christ gave the Church the duty of teaching all nations. In the home, the parents

[14] *Our Bishops Speak*, note 9 above, pp. 59–61.

have both the right and the duty to educate. The school supplements the home but cannot deprive the parents of their prior right. Since the child is a member of the social group, his education must prepare him for his obligations to society and therefore the school bears a responsibility to the whole civic body. But "social righteousness depends on individual morality." As to the State, "the State has a right to insist that its citizens shall be educated." When the people failed in their duty, the State had the right to establish schools and to take legitimate "means to safeguard its vital interests against the dangers that result from ignorance." The Pastoral insisted that the State had the right and duty to exclude the teaching of doctrines "which aim at the subversion of law and order and therefore at the destruction of the State itself." But the State could not rightfully or consistently make education a pretext for interfering with rights and liberties which the Creator, not the State, has conferred. The spirit of the American people is adverse to State monopoly, and the "American Constitution provides that every citizen shall be free to follow the dictates of his conscience in the matters of religious belief and observance."

The conclusion of the long Pastoral restated the higher destiny of man and the oneness of Truth. It was dated September 26, 1919. While some of the passages were a bit high-flown, this document stated the platform for Catholic activity during the next generation. Neither all Catholics nor all prelates kept to its teachings at all times, but the higher attainments of Catholics between the two wars were possible chiefly because, for the most part, the leading Catholics followed this pastoral even when they may have forgotten its contents. In the direct application to current problems the most important part of the pastoral was that which dealt with citizenship and the relations between the government and its citizens, and many of the efforts of the agencies of the N.C.W.C. were directed in the next few years towards making good American citizens of Catholics who had been born abroad. Probably the next most important part of the program was that carried out by the Social Action Department under Father John A. Ryan in promoting the welfare of the laboring man and fostering industrial peace. At all times the problem of Catholic education in all phases including the promotion of higher studies was a major concern of the hierarchy both generally and locally. But the good feeling toward the Church which had been a natural reaction toward the generous and patriotic efforts of wartime was to fade in the reactionary and conservative mood that arose within the third decade of the century.

The death of Cardinal Gibbons on March 24, 1921, marked the passing of one of the most dramatic personalities in American Catholic history. Generalizations about his position and influence in the Church in the United States are not very valid because of the lack of any strong unity in the Church organization in the country, although he more than anyone else, after Archbishop John Carroll, could be said to have represented Catholic opinion in public affairs. It is not clear how many of the important documents on the war and the reconstruction were of his inspiration or composition, but, so long as he occupied the Baltimore See, documents issued with his signature were accepted as representing a united Catholicism in the country. Of the leaders of the previous generation, Ireland, Spalding, and Corrigan had gone, and the new leadership in the Church in the country was local if not parochial.

In New England, Cardinal William O'Connell,[15] while not a great personality, governed his archdiocese with power. He was a cultured gentleman and was unequaled among the Catholic clergy in expressing the Catholic opinions of New England. In New York Archbishop Patrick Hayes was an imposing pastor whose dignity and gentleness made his support for charity and goodwill very important, but he had neither the experience nor the executive ability to meet the problem of the shifting population to and within the metropolis. There was no new Bishop McQuaid among his suffragans. Cardinal Dennis Dougherty governed his Archdiocese and influenced his neighboring bishops for soundness and in doctrine and practice became with his clergy a stronghold of practical Catholicism without the intellectual spark of an earlier generation. The new Archbishop of Baltimore had been like his predecessor chosen for the episcopate while very young, but the similarities almost ended there. Where Cardinal Gibbons had been a gentle peacemaker and very considerate of others, Archbishop Curley seemed impulsive, daring, and fiercely competitive. Where the Cardinal in his activity in promoting national and international peace was inclined to pay less attention to his own archdiocese, Archbishop Curley was an excellent pastor, deeply interested in the spiritual welfare of all his flock, building schools, and insisting on full orthodoxy in all details.

In the Middle West, Archbishop Henry Moeller of Cincinnati headed the huge Province of Ohio, Indiana, Kentucky, Tennessee,

[15] Robert H. Lord, John E. Sexton, and Edward T. Harrington, *History of the Archdiocese of Boston, 1604–1943*, II, 487–773 is really a contemporaneous account.

and Michigan. Archbishop Moeller was a stolid churchman as were most of his numerous suffragans. Only two of his suffragans were better known for personal accomplishments; Bishop Joseph Chartrand of Indianapolis even before his consecration was an untiring promoter of frequent Communion, especially among young men. He encouraged his priests to carry on his crusade. As Bishop, however, he showed no business ability. Bishop Joseph Schrembs of Toledo and later Cleveland was a man of endless zeal and of superior intelligence, whose talents were probably greater than his opportunities to use them. He was active in the National Catholic War Council and its successor, the National Catholic Welfare Council.

In Chicago Archbishop George Mundelein, named a Cardinal on March 24, 1924, soon gave peaceful prosperity to a turbulent archdiocese. The Church in Chicago and its suburbs multiplied the number of its churches and schools, but the quality was not always maintained in the rapidly built schools, and there was little real intellectual leadership manifested by Catholics in the region despite the usual Catholic successes in big city politics. His suffragans, Bishops Peter J. Muldoon and Edmund Dunne, were strong personalities but did not create institutions of more than local influence. In Milwaukee the aging Sebastian Messmer was brilliant but seemingly disillusioned, like other prelates of German origin, by the war and the failure of the earlier promise of German Catholics in America. In Saint Louis handsome and capable Archbishop John J. Glennon had created a small Rome with his splendid Cathedral rising at its center, but the St. Louis leadership was confused over national and racial problems in this veritable crossroads of America. The South in 1920 was still a mission country for Catholics, and Archbishop John J. Shaw of New Orleans was the leader among several missionary bishops whose people were usually a minority and seldom capable of regional leadership. They relied much on the Society of the Propagation and the Church Extension Society. The Archdiocese of Dubuque under the second Archbishop Keane and his successors held the position of leadership of a Catholic minority in the rural north in which there persisted most of the old Anglo-Saxon farmers' fear of Rome but in which occasional hardworking Catholics could become prosperous if they imitated the Yankee thrift of their Protestant neighbors. The successful Catholic farmer, however, was usually German, except for a few communities of Irish colonization projects, and the bishops who directed them were worthy representatives of a beleagured minority. Most of these bishops were of Irish descent. In Santa Fé Archbishop Daeger, O.F.M., had an even poorer group of Catholics, in what was once Mexican country, whose Spanish traditions were not respected by the invading Yankees.

The Catholics of Colorado and other mining areas included some successful miners and farmers, but the railroad workers and farmers were seldom wealthy. In Oregon and the neighboring areas there was the dominance of the transplanted Yankees from the previous hundred years that the Irish in the mines and mills could outnumber but not offset. San Francisco and its Irish Catholicism was a kind of superior accomplishment, in which Archbishop Hanna had the support of some Irish Catholics who had made good in the mines. In much of Southern California the retired farmers were not very Catholic and certainly not respectful of either the Spanish or Irish Catholicism that they encountered there.

That all these archbishops of the country and their suffragans together with their flocks could form a single Catholic unity was a devout hope when one thought in terms of the essential doctrines of the Church but almost an impossibility when one considered how varied were their political and social backgrounds. There were, however, certain important changes taking place throughout American Catholicism that produced a definite uniformity beyond essential doctrines and the rules of the new Code of Canon Law that was baffling to those outside the Church. As was the case in early Catholic movements, some of the new manifestations came from the laity and lower clergy, although with support from the local bishop.

While the decrees of the Third Plenary Council had been in force since 1885 and while the general canon law of the Church had not changed much over the centuries, very few clergymen in America were familiar with canon law as such. In the seminaries and in common pastoral writings there was a general insistence on the study and practice of moral theology especially as it affected the confessional. For the rest, the limits of jurisdiction and matters of law were determined by the provincial and local synods. In this country there was a great need for the codification of church law that emerged from Rome in 1917 and became effective in 1918. But substitution of the new canon law for the old opinions took time. The priest or bishop who could quote the new canon law in a doubtful case had the final word.

The Ecclesiastical Review for the years following the promulgation of the code was filled with discussions of the applications of certain canons on marriage, on religious, on jurisdiction, and the like. Each Bishop made sure that one or more of his more suitable young priests went to Rome or to the Catholic University to study canon law to take over the offices in his chancery. The canon law faculty at the Catholic University quickly became one of the most important in the University. The chancery offices in even the smallest diocese became the center for the application of the code and in some of the larger dioceses each office of the chancery grew in importance in carrying out its proper function. Generally in the United States the chancellor rather than the vicar general became the chief agency of the bishop although the vicar general, usually one of the older priests of the diocese, could exercise the bishop's powers. Within a decade the new formulation of church law was being carried out in great detail. Sometimes the purpose of legislation seemed to be forgotten in the fulfillment of the law, and the distinction between the regulation and the moral law was sometimes obscured in the enforcement, but for the first time most of the clergy of the country knew clearly the legal aspect of their functions. Perhaps the excesses of legalism that sometimes developed could be blamed for some of the more unfortunate effects of the conservative wave that swept through the Church against the threat of Modernism. The decrees against Modernism were severe when enforced with strict canonical power. The rigidity of seminary training, the previous censorship of books and magazines, and the restrictions on permissions for clergy to write or to speak in public backed by the new canon law went far to explain the lack of much intellectual growth in American Catholicism between the two wars.

There were two positive developments of American Catholicism which, while not limited to these years, did have an important influence on the lives of American Catholics. The first was the growth of frequent and daily Communion especially among urban workers. Although the decrees on early first Communion and on daily and frequent Communion had been issued earlier, the general significance and usefulness seemed to wait until the boys of the first generation who had the advantage of early first Communion became priests. The renewed Eucharistic devotions carried with them an expansion of such devotions as that to the Sacred Heart and to the Blessed Virgin and in some localities to Saint Joseph, to St. Thérèse of Lisieux, and to St. Jude. Communion breakfasts, the devotions of the nine First Fridays, and other novenas and series of public prayers which had existed before became an important part in the lives of Catholics of the working class. There were two side effects of these personal devotions that were noticeable. The practicing Catholic was no longer the one who talked about the Church or went to the High Mass on Sunday, but the man or woman who was regular in the reception of the Sacraments. Churches were planned with these devotional services of the faithful more in mind and in some cases new churches had to be built when the entire Catholic population began to accept the new way of Catholic living.

Liturgical worship was not always a part of this strong Catholicism: the Mass was not neglected but the new opportunity for receiving Communion did increase attendance at Communion at times that Mass could not be attended. The Mass for most Catholics remained a brief Sunday interlude in Latin scheduled usually on the hour which included a brief instruction. The most important factor in this increased reception of Holy Communion was the greater opportunity provided for the people to go to Confession. The advocates of frequent and daily Communion defended themselves against any charges of creating too great a familiarity with the Sacrament of the Eucharist with the claims that so long as the recipients were in the state of grace no evil was being done. Further they claimed that devotion to the Mass followed devotion to Communion, an argument not accepted by the liturgists.

Undoubtedly the greatest manifestation of this new Eucharistic character of twentieth-century Catholicism in the United States was the Twenty-eighth International Congress held in Chicago, June 20—24, 1926. These International Eucharistic Congresses had been held since 1881 but none had been held in the United States, although there had been less significant national and local Eucharistic Congresses. The sublime element in the Eucharistic Congress was that it was a manifestation of faith in which the chief purpose was adoration and participation in the Eucharist. Plans for the Congress in Chicago, at which attendants were expected to number a million, were begun fully a year before. The Papal Delegate *a latere* from Pope Pius XI was Cardinal John Bonzano, the former Apostolic Delegate. Including the host, Cardinal Mundelein, there were twelve cardinals, hundreds of bishops, thousands of priests, and hundreds of thousands of laymen in attendance.

The formal ceremonies of the celebration began with a reception for Cardinal Bonzano in New York on June 6 at which city and state officials of New York joined Cardinal Hayes in doing honor to the Papal Legate. From New York there was a special "Red Train" across the country prepared by the railroad officials for the occasion. On that train were nine cardinals, five archbishops, six bishops, fourteen monsignors, and fourteen distinguished laymen. Besides Cardinal Bonzano, the Cardinals were Czernoch of Hungary, Piffl of Austria, Dubois of Paris, Von Faulhaber of Germany, Charost of Rennes, France, Casanova of Spain, Hayes of New York, and O'Donnell of Ireland.

There was a similar welcome in Chicago where the Mayor, as in New York, was a Catholic. The Congress opened in Holy Name Cathedral in Chicago and, after several meetings in mammoth Soldiers' Field in Chicago, ended with a public procession with the Blessed Sacrament in the Mundelein Seminary grounds outside the city. Merchandising and secular discussions were forbidden 'by Cardinal Mundelein. At the children's Mass on Monday, June 21, the attendance was estimated above 400,000. For the women's Mass, Tuesday, June 22, the estimated attendance ranged upward from 300,000, and for the men's assembly on Tuesday night, the number was estimated at about 275,000.

The Congress was something new to the United States. In the main, the country for the first time saw the massiveness of American Catholicism. The country was generally edified by the character of the ceremonies, the consecration of the services to the Eucharist, and the elimination of merchandising. There were plenty of sermons about the Eucharist, but the celebration grew out of the general religious atmosphere of American Catholicism of the day, and the characteristic note was one of personal and silent prayer, even in the public ceremonies. There was an unpleasant reaction that first manifested itself in some shock expressed in learned periodicals as if the majority of the country, especially those of long Protestant ancestry, could not believe that this had happened in Protestant America. The manifestation of Catholic numbers, if not of other kinds of Catholic power, helped to arouse the slumbering antagonism against Roman Catholicism that was to reach a new peak two years later, when a Catholic layman was nominated for the Presidency of the United States.

The other great manifestation of Catholic life after World War I was the growth of the Catholic school system. There had been a steady increase in Catholic parochial schools throughout the nineteenth century. The First and Second Plenary Councils had urged them, but the Roman Instruction of 1875, with its characterization of public schools as direct occasions of sin and its corollary that Catholic schools must be built to replace them, had been repeated in the decrees of the Third Plenary Council with a mandatory period of two years after the promulgation of the decree for the erection of the parochial schools. Yet ten years later the increase in schools was only about what might have been expected without the decrees of the Council. The major factor in this delay in building parochial schools was that where Catholics were most numerous they were also earning low incomes and had the least money for building parish schools, especially if the Catholic schools were to be as good in secular subjects as the public schools. This quality had been commanded in the Instruction of 1875 as well as in the Third Plenary Council decrees. The large number of parochial schools in the Middle West in the late nineteenth century was possible because there the rural Catholics generally were better able to support such a school and because in the centers of Germans, Poles, and other national groups there was a tradition of having a church school. Often these parish schools were as good as the public schools, if not better, during the first decades of the twentieth century because at that time in some communities the public schools were not well organized and had few devoted teachers, while the Catholic religious teachers were not only more inspired but had often superior background for elementary education. As civic consciousness began to insist on the improvement of the public schools and pedagogy became more technical, the religious zeal of the Catholic teachers could not make up for technical training or be multiplied to handle increased enrollments.

In 1918 the new Code of Canon Law with its unequivocal demand that Catholic children attend Catholic schools took away any excuse for sending Catholic children to a non-Catholic school where a Catholic school was available. Usually if Catholic schools were available the bishops were severe in punishing those who did not send their children to the parish schools. But in many parts of the country Catholic schools for all Catholic children could not be built with the available Catholic income. In theory canon law was observed, and the number of Catholic children in parish schools increased. The close observer knew, however, that there were many parishes without schools, particularly in the Northeast and in many manufacturing areas where there were thousands of Catholic children in public schools.

Under the direction of the newly formed Education Department of the National Catholic Welfare Council in 1921, the first definite attempt to estimate the size of the Catholic school system was made. The rules for defining elementary schools from high schools and academies were not always followed, but the published figures afford some basis for estimating the growth of the system before the depression of 1929. The *Directory* for 1921 estimated that there were in the system 16 universities, 51 seminaries, 62 colleges for men, and 52 colleges for women. The number of high schools was set at 1,552 with an enrollment of 129,838. The elementary schools were estimated at 6,551 with an enrollment of 1,795,673. Some of these high schools were two or three year extensions of elementary schools, and many of them had fewer than fifty pupils. Some parish schools offered practical courses, and some private academies prepared their students for college.

There were many developments in this vast system during the next seven years. State laws on teachers' qualifications, the erection of State superintendencies of education, and the establishment of accrediting agencies and educational associations with their requirements for teachers and pupils had a direct effect on the Catholic school system even when the Catholic teachers and schools were not subject to them. Despite the resistance to these agencies by some of the clergy, the need for accreditation for the schools if their students were to be accepted for higher studies gradually forced the accreditation of most Catholic schools. Accreditation, in turn, required normal training and higher degrees for the teachers and the improvement of school libraries and technical equipment. While this movement had considerable effect on the Catholic colleges and caused the opening of Catholic summer schools for the training of teachers who were employed in teaching during the year, the direct effect of this movement was felt chiefly in improving the teaching in elementary schools, the better planning of Catholic high schools, and the elimination of many high schools which had been lacking in equipment and teachers. The growth of the Catholic school system in the span from 1920 to 1928 involved an increase of 1,530 or 18% in the number of institutions; 28,561 or 53.5% in the number of teachers; and 557,521 or 28% in the number of students. By 1928 there were 10,236 institutions, 82,826 teachers and 2,538,572 students. Probably the most significant change was in institutions of secondary education. Under the urging of the Catholic Educational Association and its leaders, especially of the Educational Department of the N.C.W.C., Catholic youths were being urged to continue their education to fit themselves for better jobs if not for intellectual reasons. By 1928 the number of Catholic high schools and academies had increased from 1,552 in 1920 to 2,129 in 1928, the number of teachers in them had increased from 7,915 in 1920 to 13,489 in 1928, and the number of students had increased from 129,848 to 225,845. In this there was an increase also in the number of central Catholic high schools which allowed greater efficiency in teaching and also economies in construction and in the use of teachers. An important change took place in the provision of teachers. In 1928, of the 13,489 teachers in Catholic high schools, 11,543 were religious, whose salary problems were important but not as great probably as the salary problem for the 1,943 lay teachers, despite the fact that the salaries even for these were not high.

In the 1920s occurred the great test of the right of Catholics to maintain their system of parochial schools. In the state of Oregon, where Catholics were a small minority of the population, the Scottish-rite Masons placed on the ballot an initiative measure to compel children between the ages of eight and sixteen to attend the public schools of Oregon. In the November 1922 vote the measure won by a plurality of 15,000. It was to become operative in 1926. The newly formed National Catholic Welfare Conference immediately took an interest in the case at its meeting in Chicago on January 1923. In a suit brought by the Sisters of the Holy Names of Jesus and Mary the Federal District Court declared the Oregon law unconstitutional. The State of Oregon under Governor Pierce appealed to the United States Supreme Court, which also declared the law unconstitutional on June 1, 1925. The decision remained a landmark in the continuing discussion of the relations between the Catholic schools and the public schools.

The financial problems of collegiate and university education were already difficult to solve before the depression because of the rush of Catholic students into the colleges after World War I. By 1928 there were 163 of such Catholic institutions with a student body of 87,031 taught by 3,108 religious teachers and 3,337 lay teachers (with 384 additional teachers listed as unclassified). During this period the standards of teaching and equipment of these institutions were being raised, and there were increased expenses for training the religious faculty and for the higher salaries of the lay faculty. New buildings were needed for the increased enrollments in most institutions. The 1930 *Directory of Catholic Colleges and Schools* made no effort to give estimates on these financial matters, but the endowments of Catholic colleges were small when they existed at all. At the same time the accrediting agencies of schools and colleges began to enforce penalties against schools and colleges which did not adhere to the standards of the agency. The necessity for Catholic colleges and schools to meet those standards increased the financial problems. The depression, beginning in 1929, closed some of these institutions, not necessarily just those that were improperly financed. The grand dream of a self-supporting Catholic educational system was deflated by the depression but not destroyed, and as soon as financial conditions improved new institutions were created and old ones expanded. The Catholic educational system of the United States, as it existed, was the marvel not only of the country but of the Catholic world. Its internal problems, however, were not well understood even by some of those who sought to maintain it.

In the 1920s and 1930s some bishops tried to do without accreditation for their schools, but the schools and their students, when they sought entrance into higher institutions, were the ones who suffered from such efforts. At the same time the legislatures and city councils began to pour funds into the public schools. Older private schools increased their endowments. Catholic schools, existing chiefly by the sacrifices of religious persons who taught in them, had no reserve funds on which to draw to meet such competition. Where the religiously supervised schools were most needed, especially in the poorer sections of cities or mill towns, the funds were least abundant. In general Catholic parents and religious communities alike made great sacrifices, but the problem was beginning to be unsolvable especially when the new Code of Canon Law decrees began to be enforced.

The greater crisis of the American Catholic system of education came first to Catholic higher education. The chief institution, the Catholic University in Washington, had received a hard blow in the loss of some of its faculty in the struggles over nationalities in the 1890s. A second blow had been a financial debacle in the early 1900s plus the refusal of the German-American clergy to support the University and the condemnation of Modernism that stifled the growth of a strong theological center in Washington. Under the direction of Dr. William Kerby and Dr. John A. Ryan, the survival and growth of the moral theological faculty in the application of the Church's teachings to the economic problems and social welfare, especially as outlined in the *Rerum Novarum* of Pope Leo XIII, had given some recognition to the University beyond the mediocrity of many other departments. Then with the sudden demand for teachers with degrees and degrees for teachers, the Education Department and other departments with faculties for training teachers gained a new life and the Sisters' College was established. The University still lacked endowment comparable to its hopes, but in some fields, such as philosophy and the expanding school of canon law, good teachers and a good library were almost the only endowments necessary.

The hundreds of Catholic colleges that had been founded

throughout the country without a dollar of endowment were simply unprepared to meet the expanded enrollments and the new curricula after World War I or to face the competition of public institutions with public funds and public regulations on teaching certificates. Only a few private universities could meet the test in the 1920s. Notre Dame in 1922–1925 set up a board of lay trustees and, with the aid of the Rockefeller and Carnegie Foundations, raised an endowment of one million dollars and another million for new buildings, but most Catholic colleges tried to meet the new demands with the old resources.

The growing pains of Catholic institutions of higher learning during the prosperous days of the 1920s were much more in evidence than the growth itself. The increased enrollments were aids to prosperity so long as new faculty or new buildings were not needed, but once expansion was necessary the efforts to create an increased and properly trained faculty overnight and to acquire new facilities induced some neglect of standards in many schools and colleges. Catholic colleges were better known for their football teams than for scholars and there were debts on new buildings still unpaid even when the depression arrived in the winter of 1929–1930.

There were other manifestations of American Catholicism during the time of prosperity after World War I that deserve recognition. Father Edwin V. O'Hara of the Diocese of Oregon had begun to promote a Catholic study of the problem of rural life in 1919. To carry out his theories, he took a rural parish in Eugene, Oregon. He proposed the establishment of a Rural Life Bureau in connection with the N.C.W.C. and eventually became its first Chairman. He published *A Program of Rural Catholic Action* and in 1923 led in the holding of the first National Catholic Rural Life Conference. Later he taught classes in rural sociology at the Catholic University and at the University of Notre Dame until his election to the See of Great Falls in 1930.

Also Catholic interest in urban life was apparent in Catholic support of labor organization. Under the Department of Social Action of the N.C.W.C., a Conference on Industrial Problems was formed at a meeting of businessmen, labor leaders, and students of social affairs in Chicago on December 29, 1922. Professor David A. McCabe of Princeton was chosen president, and Father Raymond A. McGowan of the Social Action Department became secretary-treasurer. The Conference held its first public conference in Milwaukee under the sponsorship of Archbishop Messmer, June 27–28, 1923. Topics discussed at the meetings included

"Wages," "Collective Bargaining," "The Worker and Ownership," and "Women in Industry." Others who helped promote these meetings included Frederick P. Kenkel of the Central Verein, Patrick Callahan, a manufacturer of Louisville, and Father Joseph Husslein, S.J. There were many such conferences on industrial problems under the auspices of this group both before and during the depression. They did much to promote peaceful solutions of the conflicts between capital and labor.

At no time in the history of Catholicism in America have laymen failed to manifest some leadership, but, outside of the English and Anglo-American Catholics, the leadership of the laymen had been mostly in politics. At the turn of the century and during the next two decades, the chief manifestation of Catholic lay religious leadership was the ineffective Federation of Catholic Societies. Some of the federated societies were successful among their own members. Chief of these was the Central Verein, the editor of whose *Central Blatt and Social Justice*, Frederick P. Kenkel, was an ideal Catholic lay leader, exemplary in personal life, able to express his thoughts clearly in good English, and learned in the social problems of the day. But his was a kind of lonely life, and his associates seemed to blame him for the failures of the Verein, instead of helping him to overcome the obvious difficulties of a German language and cultural group in the English-speaking American world. His efforts to fight socialism and his embracing of Papal "Solidarism" were not understood by his American friends or his German associates.

The American Irish lay Catholicism never had quite the same kind of leader as Kenkel. Delightful John Boyle O'Reilly was a poet without a deep understanding of theological or economic problems. Peter Finley Dunne was a witty critic, but not a good writer. Of the Catholic political front men of the 1920s, James Curley of Boston and James Walker of New York were not exemplary Catholics. Edward Cermak and Edward Kelly of Chicago were a bit more of a credit to Catholics but were involved in machine politics. The exemplar of Catholic politicians was Alfred Emmanuel Smith, who rose without the benefit of higher education from the Fulton Street Fish Market to the governorship of New York. No one questioned his knowledge of the practical problems of American politics, but there were some questions raised about his associations with Tammany Hall, and his background of urban politics in general. Further he represented those who had no use for the Prohibition Amendment and the laws passed to enforce it. In 1924 an effort to nominate him as the

Democratic candidate for President was lost in a titanic struggle in the Democratic National Convention in Madison Square Garden. In Houston in 1928 Smith won the nomination easily and departed from the platform of the party in announcing his disapproval of the prohibition laws. Historians disagree as to exactly what factor was the chief cause of his defeat. He represented urban, machine politics, and opposition to the prohibition experiment, and he was also a Catholic. The rise of anti-Catholic bigotry after the war, the isolationism of the early 1920s, the revival of nativism had already made the name of Catholic feared in many sections of the country. The revived Ku Klux Klan united all these nativistic, anti-Semitic, and anti-Catholic feelings to claim a membership in the millions. The nomination of Smith gave these bigots the threat that they wanted to scare the ignorant masses of rural America. Smith did not carry even his own state, New York, and he lost in most rural sections of the country. He carried only eight states, including Rhode Island and Massachusetts which were dominantly Catholic and urban. They were also among the first states hit by the approaching depression in the movement of the cloth mills to the South. Many Catholics tried to be impartial in the campaign but found it very difficult not to defend Smith from the false charges that were distributed in many printed materials. Republican Catholics campaigned for Hoover but earned only the ill will of Catholics. As one good side issue of the anti-Catholic bigotry, many doubtful Catholics tended to return to the Faith in the face of such attacks, and there were many persons who entered Catholicism as a reaction to the bigoted propaganda. The Catholic bishops generally kept very still during the bitter campaign, and the depression that followed in 1929 not only seemed to still the bigotry but also made many Catholics grateful that the depression had not happened under a Catholic president.

Besides Catholics in politics, there were laymen who were achieving some position of prominence in Catholic higher education and a fewer number in secular and non-Catholic colleges and universities. The establishment of the weekly *Commonweal* in 1924 by the Calvert Associates, some of whom were not Catholics, as a Catholic lay magazine was a welcomed accomplishment but not a financially profitable adventure. The chief periodical for Catholics remained *America,* the Jesuit weekly, which was generally quite conservative at that time. During the decade the Catholic philosophers began *The New Scholasticism,* and the Jesuits at Fordham began *Thought* which was intended to be a national Catholic quarterly. However, American Catholicism was spread too far for one voice either by the week or by the quarter. Knute Rockne, the coach of the Notre Dame football team, and the Catholic actors in Hollywood were much better known than any Catholic professor, and many Catholic writers who achieved fame were defectors such as James Farrell, Eugene O'Neill, F. Scott Fitzgerald, Theodore Dreiser, and others.[16] The predepression era was a period of change.

The depression that began with the decline of the stock market in the fall of 1929 had religious repercussions. Financial losses, losses of employment, and accompanying hardships gave the faithful many additional reasons for prayer and the frequentation of the Sacraments. Financial difficulties necessarily checked the building of churches and schools and made difficult the payment of debts on them incurred in prosperity. College enrollments shrank. In general the bigotry and unfriendliness toward Catholics seemed to disappear in times of suffering. The work of the Social Action Department of the N.C.W.C. was increased by its efforts to foster solutions of the economic and social problems of the depression. The spiritual program of the Church did not change much in the depression, but the spiritual leadership that was required in order to rise from the depression was something different from that which had been expected in times of prosperity. Catholics suffered from the depression according to their location and circumstances. As a predominantly urban group, they felt a very severe jolt from the loss of employment and income. Even farm groups had to reconsider their programs. The active members of the clergy achieved distinction by working directly with their flocks for a solution of the economic and social problems of the 1930s.

[16] William V. Shannon, *The American Irish* (New York, 1963) makes a special plea to consider these wandering Catholic Irish as Catholic and Irish.

CHAPTER THIRTEEN

Hot and Cold War

TO SAY HOW MUCH THE INFLATED PROS-
perity of the late 1920s or the depression affected the Church in
the United States would require an excessive weighing of statistics,
many of which would probably not be available. The Catholic
publications of the prosperity era show evidence on the part of
the clergy, who wrote that the gaiety of the times and the spend-
thrift ways of the midtwenties were considered excessive. Even
before the crash there was general dismay about the effect of the
unenforceable prohibition laws on the younger generation, particularly because the so-called "smart set" carried hip flasks of
liquor and persons who would not have used hard liquors felt that
such drinking was the fashionable conduct. There were opinions
among Catholics that since the prohibition laws were penal laws
they did not have to be observed, and writers such as Father John
A. Ryan, who wrote to the contrary, accomplished little to make
Catholics keepers of the law. A greater scandal was the number
of persons of Italian and therefore Catholic names who were
engaged in the illegal production and sale of liquor and the gang
wars in New York and Chicago that accompanied the illegal businesses. It was said that only the Catholic Church prevented a complete moral collapse in the areas dominated by gangsters in Chicago, but that was not any great solace for those interested in
spiritual life.

There were many people with extra money for the first time
who had invested their savings in stocks and bonds because the
returns seemed good, and in their innocence they did not know

how easily all their earnings could be destroyed. There were some injudicious clergymen who had also been taken in by brokers and bankers who were occasionally as innocent as those they sought to guide. School buildings, hospitals, and churches had been built with the expanded money to be paid for by expanded salaries and from expanded employment. There were no notable Catholic clergymen among those persons who committed suicide but there were stories of Catholic executives, including clergy, who seemed to die prematurely under the weight of their unpayable debts. The interest owed on some diocesan and parish debts was tremendous. Teaching communities of religious generally did not have any great reserve fund before the depression and could scarcely survive when some pastors could not raise the money for meager salaries for their teachers. That the sufferings of the depression increased church attendance is doubtful, except where workers had more free time for church going or, in some cases, instituted novenas or other emergency prayer measures to obtain employment. There was undoubtedly a breaking off of entertainments and vacation travels for which there were no funds. But in general there were no changes in fundamental Catholic practice as a result of the depression. The breakoff was only in the means of support.

Despite the objections of some bishops to the centralizing effect of the National Catholic Welfare Council, there was no other organ capable of national Catholic action on problems that concerned the entire Catholic body. Fortunately the members of the executive committee during this first decade of its existence were men of vision who could see beyond their own local interests. Besides the bishops who had served on the Executive Committee of the National Catholic War Council with Cardinal Gibbons and formed the new organization, prominent members of the organization included Archbishop Hanna of San Francisco, who was for many years the Chairman of the Administrative Committee and Bishop Philip R. McDevitt, who devoted great efforts to improve the parochialism of the diocesan press. Nevertheless the Council was suddenly suppressed by Rome in the spring of 1922 after the death of Benedict XV. Quick action by several bishops, especially Bishop Schrembs, saved the organization. It was restored under the title of National Catholic Welfare Conference with strict limitations on its powers.

The Administrative Committee of the N.C.W.C. never had the backing of the whole American episcopate during these early years, but the efforts of the Committee to bring about better conditions for the persecuted Church in Mexico were the occasion of special recognition in the form of a letter of praise from Pope Pius XI in August 1927 addressed to the cardinals, archbishops, and bishops united in the National Catholic Welfare Conference. And to show that the praise was not just for that one instance of united service the Pope added:

Hence appears with abundant evidence how timely and useful was the organization of the National Catholic Welfare Conference which you so lately established, with its departments, the News Service, and the Bureau of Immigration. This organization is not only useful, but also necessary for you. Since you reside in cities far apart and there are matters of higher import demanding your joint deliberation—as, for example, those relating to the Christian family, the education of youth, public aid to private morality, care of numerous immigrants, and other problems of this kind—it is imperative that by taking counsel together you all agree on one common aim and with one united will strive for its attainment, by employing as you now do, the means which are adequate and adapted to present day conditions.

Cease not, therefore, to labor in this spirit of unity for the welfare of our holy religion, in that great Republic where the Church, under God's Providence, enjoys such wide freedom and such a degree of prosperity. . . .[1]

This letter effectively checked open episcopal opposition to the organization and made some reparation for the repression of 1922.

When the annual meeting of the hierarchy was held in Washington on November 12 and 13, 1930, the prosperity of the country had vanished, and a full year of the depression had begun to manifest itself in the work of the Conference.[2] Archbishop Hanna's report of the work of the Executive Department mentioned the dealings of the Committee with the American government on Catholic interests in China and Haiti, its continued cooperation with the hierarchy of the persecuted Mexican Church, the supervision of the speakers on the Catholic Radio Hour, which had been instituted by the National Council of Catholic Men, and the efforts to secure the war records of Catholic men.

The Legal Department, according to its report, had manifested Catholic interest in international affairs in Haiti and in the Institute of Politics at Williamstown, Massachusetts. The Education Department, besides its continued program for the improvement

---

[1] *American Ecclesiastical Review*, LXXVII (1927) 511.

[2] *N.C.W.C. Review* (December, 1920) II, 2–3. This publication, which later became *Catholic Action*, is a quasi-official source for the activities of the hierarchy.

of teacher training, reported its activity in opposing the proposed Federal Department of Education and Cabinet Secretary for Education. The Press Department reported on its efforts to improve the Catholic press despite the cost of its furnishing news reports, cables, and pictures. Of the Lay Organizations Department, the accomplishments of the National Council of Catholic Women was particularly noteworthy in furnishing Catholic representation alongside other women's groups in public discussion, although only forty-two diocesan councils of the N.C.W.C. had been organized. Bishop Schrembs, the Episcopal Chairman of the Department, noted the continued growth of the National Catholic School of Social Service which had forty-five students in 1930–1931.

The National Council of Catholic Men had begun with considerable success, probably as a result of an inheritance from the old Federation of Catholic Societies, and received the cooperation of many Catholic societies. The chief accomplishment of the Council of Men was the institution of the Catholic Hour on the radio on Sunday, which became a very important item in Catholic life in subsequent years. The program began on the National Broadcasting Company network on March 2, 1930, and was soon carried by forty-seven stations in twenty-eight states. The service was furnished by the radio network without cost, although the programs were under the supervision of a committee headed by Father Karl Alter. The outstanding personage during the first years was Father Fulton J. Sheen of the Catholic University. His Advent and Lent series attracted listeners not only among Catholics but also among non-Catholics.

Undoubtedly the most active Department in these depression years was the Social Action Department under the direction of Fathers John A. Ryan and Raymond A. McGowan. Bishop Thomas F. Lillis of Kansas City, the Episcopal Chairman, reported on the distribution of thousands of pamphlets, mostly containing the social programs based on the papal encyclicals and the reports of the five Conferences on Industrial Problems. Two other important activities of the Department were the promotion of civil education for the immigrants and the establishment of the Catholic Association for International Peace, which had to counterbalance the isolationist tendencies of many Catholic Americans of Irish and German descent who were opposed to the League of Nations as being English dominated. Under the Social Action Department was also the Bureau of Immigration. With the restrictive immigration laws passed in 1924 and 1928, this bureau did not have the volume of immigrants to deal with but was better able to handle the cases that were brought to its attention and to follow up cases of immigrants who were in difficulties. The report did not say what those dealing with immigrants' problems knew: that the restrictive immigration laws, while not intended to aid the Church agencies, did render a service by allowing the agencies to catch up with the heavy immigration of previous years.

In their meeting of November 1930, the bishops authorized Archbishop Hanna to issue in the name of the hierarchy a statement on the problems of unemployment. There were no figures available on the percentage of Catholics who were employed, but, since so many of the Catholic minority were engaged in the industries that were shut down by the depression and lived on wages that had ceased to be earned, the bishops could have written their own version of the general plea. The statement opened with the words "Again the United States is suffering the tragedy of millions of men and women who need work, who want work and who can find no work to do." The letter first praised those who had volunteered food to the hungry and clothes to the naked but added that more than charity was necessary, because the unemployment was a moral tragedy. "The failure is not due to lack of intelligence nor any more to ignorance. It is due to lack of good will. It is due to neglect of Christ." The bishops called upon Catholics to do more than give alms and more than to try to overcome the present difficulty. They added: "We are even under the call to do more and more, as one tries the best he can to live his Catholic morals, to try also to remold the institutions that surround work, ownership and trade to the image of the Saviour of the world." The bishops asked the faithful to study the *Rerum Novarum* of Pope Leo, the Bishops' Reconstruction Program, and the Pastoral Letter of 1919. In conclusion the letter quoted a passage from the bishops' program of 1919 about the necessity for more than the minimum wages to fulfill not only the principles of morality but also to preserve economic security. They added that following the principles in these documents would have saved the nation from many of the present troubles. " 'The human and Christian, in contrast to the purely commercial and pagan, ethics of industry,' to quote again, will both cure our country of our present malady and prevent its cruel recurrence."[3]

Probably for the first time in its existence in the United States, the Church was in a position to speak to the nation and to point

---

[3] *Our Bishops Speak*, edited by Raphael Huber, O.F.M. Conv. (Milwaukee, 1952) p. 193.

to a doctrine that was not formed just for the occasion but one that was already declared in the encyclicals and in the pastoral letters. And for the first time the people of the United States were really willing to listen to the voice of Catholicism. Perhaps the silence that had fallen over theological discussions after the condemnation of Modernism had providentially given American Catholic theologians a fruitful field for their efforts by causing them to concentrate on economic and social reform. The doctrines of Father John A. Ryan, Father William Kerby, Father Francis A. Haas, Father Raymond A. McGowan, and Father Joseph Husslein, S.J., were primarily theological and therefore sound principles, but, when they applied those principles to the question of the living wage, the organization of labor, and the distribution of wealth, they gave Catholicism a new meaning to the masses of the American people. There were others who called for social justice, but some unfortunately used the appeal for personal glory.

In the midst of the depression the leaders of Catholicism who had been urging the doctrines of the *Rerum Novarum* of Leo XIII as the solution for the depression and for their economic problems of the day were heartened when Pope Pius XI commemorated the fortieth anniversary of that encyclical on May 15, 1891, by one of his own, *Quadragesimo Anno*. The Pope first praised the timeliness of Pope Leo's action and the internal value of that encyclical. Then he examined the principles and applied them to the current crisis. The Pope reiterated the Church's position on the right to property but said that the obligation of ownership was both individual and social. He upheld the right of the Government to interfere for the common good. While rejecting socialism, the Pope suggested that the time had come for labor to share in ownership through participation in ownership, management, and profits. He insisted on living family wages, but not to the ruin of the employers. Above all he called for a renewal of the Christian spirit. Father John A. Ryan, Father Raymond McGowan, and their followers were happy to receive this papal support in their efforts to introduce the principles of the *Rerum Novarum* into the American depression. The N.C.W.C. republished the encyclical in pamphlet form with study guides for group study.

This work of the Catholic teachers stood out in what might be called applied theology of social and economic reform. This outstanding work of the Catholic teachers must be weighed against improvements, but at the same time against deficiencies in Catholic leadership during the decade before the depression. The

Catholic University did not have much money for research, but there were accomplishments worth noting. One notable effort came from Father Peter Guilday, who began his plans for a center of American Catholic history at the University in 1918. To widen his efforts, he changed in 1924 the *American Catholic Historical Review* from an American Catholic history journal to a journal of American Catholic historians. There was also formed in 1926 an American Catholic Philosophical Society with its journal, *The New Scholasticism*. Again this setting up of a separate organization was of doubtful wisdom, despite the need for self-examination of Catholic philosophers, which was not always present in their meetings. The presence of Catholic philosophers in the general philosophical society of the country would have eliminated much of the lifeless drill among Catholic philosophers and taught them how to bring their philosophy to the modern American scene. The same could be said of the Catholic Library Association which gave encouragement to struggling Catholic librarians, but did not make the Catholic libraries compete properly with other libraries. The Catholic Sociological Society which was begun in 1938 was preceded by the National Catholic Charities Conference where annual meetings were justified because they were meetings of Catholic institutions. But the Catholic Sociological Society and the later Catholic Economic Society were actually admissions that the social science departments of the Catholic colleges were not full competitors of their fellow workers in other colleges. It was unfortunately true that Catholic social scientists worked most of this time under the criticism of scholastic philosophers who tried to maintain that there were no real social sciences but simply applications of ethics or moral theology.

A very interesting phenomenon was that there was no isolating Catholic scientific society. One factor here was the lack in most colleges of financial means to compete with the large scientific laboratories of the great American universities, but there was also the wisdom of men like Father Julius Nieuwland of Notre Dame who knew that Catholics could achieve in science only by full participation in scientific activity. There was a good scientific tradition of many decades at Notre Dame, but Father Nieuwland, the inventor of the basic process for synthetic rubber, had to scrape and save as well as work long hours to achieve his successes. Such a harsh judgment of the zealous teachers who formed most of the Catholic scholarly associations should not overlook the fact that the founders of these associations were often doing all that they could to raise up scholarly traditions among good people who had no scholarly background. In most cases, the founders of these societies had no intention of isolating themselves from the general societies of scholars, but wanted chiefly to help each other attain the proper level of technical knowledge in their fields. That many of them failed to overcome their isolation is a fact that is part of the picture of Catholicism in the United States in the first half of the twentieth century.

In 1925 Professor George N. Shuster, after leaving his teaching position at the University of Notre Dame, wrote a sharp criticism of this Catholic failure in *America* of August 15, 1925, under the title, "Have We Any Scholars?" The criticism was resented. There were to be recurrences of this discussion at least once in each decade. Those who felt the sting of the critic's remarks sometimes gave sharp retorts, and usually relied on the excuses of the handicaps of immigrant and peasant backgrounds and the lack of finances. One such discussion that was sharp but failed to get down to statistics was contained in two articles in the *American Ecclesiastical Review*. In the first, Father John N. Cooper, the anthropologist of the Catholic University, wrote under the title "Christ and the Other Sheep" in May 1933. Starting with the innocent question, "In how far have we Christians done our part . . . to raise the position of women?" his implication was negative. Then he raised the question whether the public processions proved that Catholics were any better than non-Catholics, whether Catholic college students were any purer in language and conduct than other college students, whether Catholics really practiced the social justice they preached, whether Catholics had been friends of the poor, and whether the Church had retained the Catholic masses. Noting the few Catholic Negroes in the United States he asked whether the excuses for this were valid. He asked whether the Catholics did not practice birth control as much as non-Catholics; finally he raised the problem of the lack of Catholic scientists and Catholic scholars in other branches of learning. He admitted that he had been negative in his approach.

In reply to Doctor Cooper the scholarly Bishop McDevitt of Harrisburg in the July issue under the heading, "Aspects of Catholic Life in America" quoted printed accounts of Catholic respect for women, statements on the purity of Catholic college students, and defended the virtues of Catholics in political affairs. The Bishop was a bit sharp in his rejection of the charge that Catholics lacked honesty and other natural virtues or that they were indifferent in public affairs. He cited the evidences of anti-Catholic bigotry in such sources as *The Atlantic Monthly, The*

Harvard Journal, and *The Menace* as an excuse for Catholic tendencies to stay apart from general associations. He explained the lack of Catholic Negroes by the fact that before the Civil War most Negroes in America were in Protestant areas and explained Catholic failure to join in the abolition movement because of its policy of violence. The Bishop gracefully said he was not agreeing or disagreeing with the implications of Dr. Cooper's questions, but he felt that Dr. Cooper had implied an entirely negative answer to his questions about whether the Catholics were doing their share in these fields where they were associated with non-Catholics.

There were no statistics from which the questions of Dr. Cooper could be answered. *The Directory of Catholic Colleges and Schools* for 1930 published by the N.C.W.C. was tantalizing in its lack of definitions. There was practically no information about the curriculum of the 187 seminaries, although basically all followed the program outlined in the Code of Canon Law. Since most of them did not confer degrees and many of them were staffed by priests lacking degrees in the subjects in which they taught, they hardly deserved the first place which they received in the listing of Catholic educational institutions. Yet their being listed first indicates the basic orientation of Catholic higher education. So also many of the colleges were not accredited by proper educational associations, and perhaps only the Catholic University should have been designated properly as a university. Generally, no one questioned the religious atmosphere of the Catholic colleges and high schools, but there was an unwillingness to list the library holdings and the degrees held by staff members. A more serious defect in the colleges that was just beginning to manifest itself was a lack of financial endowment. The Catholic University had the highest endowment and the promise of an annual collection from the bishops, but, because it was primarily a graduate institution, did not have a large undergraduate enrollment, and lacked the contributed services available in educational institutions conducted by a single religious community, the endowment was more inadequate than was generally understood. Few other Catholic colleges had any notable endowment on which they could rely for hiring lay teachers or to repay the community for services so that the community faculty could obtain needed graduate study. Pressed by state requirements in 1920, the University of Notre Dame found that its total endowment acceptable by the State was $71,000, where the state required a productive endowment of $500,000 for an institution giving higher degrees. To meet this requirement Father James A. Burns, C.S.C., the President, appealed to a ruling of the North Central Association of Colleges which recognized the services of religious as "living endowment."[4] Father Burns evaluated the services of forty-seven religious at $93,800 and capitalized this at 5% to reach a sum of $1,876,000. The State allowed the statement of living endowment but suggested that the University try to get some financial endowment. Notre Dame, aided by the Rockefeller General Education Board and the Carnegie Foundation, raised one million dollars for an endowment in 1922 and another million for needed buildings. The modern Notre Dame began with that endowment, although even these sums did not place Notre Dame among the better American universities and colleges, which as early as World War I had been relying on endowment for over 50% of their annual funds.[5]

The fallacy hidden under the term "living endowment" was that there was no real provision in it for the higher training and eventual replacement of the religious teachers who were consumed in the process. The result was that the Catholic institutions of higher education were eating up the potential and at times the actual substance of the faculty. There were far more Catholic colleges than the financial means available could sustain, but there was no Catholic educational organization which had the power to say which institution should close or limit its efforts. In some instances the combining of high school and college in one unit disguised the fact that only the high school was properly sustained. The Department of Education in the N.C.W.C. had no authority in the matter at all, and the Catholic Educational Association dared take no punitive measures. At one time when the North Central Association placed four Catholic colleges on probation, a proposal was made that all Catholic colleges withdraw from the North Central, but wiser heads objected to the suggestion.

There were probably as many Catholics attending non-Catholic colleges as those attending Catholic colleges at this time, if not more, although exact statistics are not available. The depression increased the financial necessity for Catholics desiring higher education to take advantage of the lower tuition costs in state-supported institutions. Many bishops, recognizing their obligation to these Catholic youths, set up Newman centers at these non-

[4] T.T. McAvoy, C.S.C., "Notre Dame 1919–1922: The Burns Revolution," *Review of Politics* (October 1963) XXV, 444–446.

[5] Charles F. Thwing, *The American Colleges in the Great War, 1916–1919* (New York, 1920).

Catholic colleges which made some efforts to provide guidance and sacramental administrations to Catholic students. *The Directory of Catholic Colleges and Schools* for 1930 listed 168 of these Newman Clubs of varying completeness on the campuses of non-Catholic universities, colleges, and normal schools. The information about the training and progress of Catholics in these non-Catholic institutions is even less definite than that about those in Catholic institutions. Very few of the Catholic students of non-Catholic institutions were considered in the constantly recurring complaints about low attainments of Catholics in cultural life and in public affairs. One explanation claimed a great loss of faith among these students in non-Catholic colleges, but there was really no proof of such a contention. The better explanation maintained that the Catholic students at most non-Catholic institutions were technical or professional students who never became professionally known as Catholics. In addition it has been said that most Catholic graduates of both Catholic and non-Catholic institutions had no background of higher education or the leisure for cultural achievement. They were children or grandchildren of peasants who had to scrape hard to get the funds for higher education and intended that education to prepare them for better jobs. Both types left the profession of religious faith and teachings to the religious and clergy. Some of both groups went into the professions as lawyers, physicians, and technicians, but very few of them went into the teaching profession because it was not a way to wealth. The leaders in the professions, in government, and in education generally were still in great measure from the traditional Yankee families in the first decades of the twentieth century.

In politics the story of Catholic achievement was different, yet the greatest handicap of Alfred E. Smith in his campaign for the Presidency, besides his religion, was his lack of higher formal education. It was true that Catholic leaders were beginning to emerge in all lines of endeavor, but they were not in numbers proportional to the Catholic population. Some Catholic writers who seemed not to know that the Church had lost the leadership in the European universities and in the existing governments of Europe of the nineteenth and twentieth centuries, insisted that American Catholics were betraying the cultural tradition of Catholic medieval Europe. These critical remarks caused bruised feelings and savage retorts toward anyone who criticized the deficiencies of Catholic education. No one seemed willing to recognize the peasant backgrounds of these children of immigrants and to measure the gains and failures by objective standards.

The dropping of the religious issue from politics after the defeat of Governor Smith in the presidential election of 1928 was welcomed by Catholics. The Ku Klux Klan disbanded in many localities, and many who had joined it were ashamed of their former membership. The common problem of overcoming the depression left few occasions for such bigotry. The failure of the Hoover administration to overcome successfully the depression gave an occasion for Catholic writers to bring forward the Catholic teachings on social and economic problems. The Democratic party as the party of the immigrant had always had many members in the Catholic urban groups. The writings of Father John A. Ryan and his students at the Catholic University in demanding industrial reform, living wages, and improved living conditions were known to many labor leaders. Then in 1930 Father Charles Coughlin of Royal Oak, Michigan, who had been acquiring a reputation as a radio orator since 1926, began to offer the social teachings of the Popes as the real cure for the depression. At that time Father Coughlin preached in popular form chiefly the doctrines of the encyclical *Rerum Novarum* of Pope Leo XIII but he attacked also international bankers as the cause of the depression. Refused broadcast time by the Columbia Broadcasting Company and the National Broadcasting Company, he organized his own network of independent stations. Judging by the letters that were mailed at his urging on some occasions, his audience was numbered in the millions.

Father Coughlin was not accepted by many of his fellow priests, nor by many Catholics in the banking profession. But he had a popular subject, and his attacks on the international bankers and then the Hoover administration were very well received by his Sunday afternoon listeners. Father Coughlin appeared to be a friend of the new Democratic candidate for the presidency, Franklin Delano Roosevelt. In the Democratic National Convention he appeared on the platform while the Convention was waiting for the candidate to come and accept the nomination. How much influence Father Coughlin had in electing Roosevelt is uncertain. Roosevelt would undoubtedly have won anyway. Roosevelt did not discourage the aid of Father Coughlin at this time, although he never quite entered into any alliance with the priest. Father Coughlin had wandered, perhaps unconsciously, from the field of the social encyclicals into American politics and accepted a questionable theory of money and eventually fell into anti-Semitism, although he at first denied that he was anti-Jewish. He had the backing of his Ordinary, Bishop Michael Gallagher of

Detroit, and no other bishops could touch him although many undoubtedly reported his activities to Rome with some vehemence. And there were rumors of sharp words about him at the annual meeting of the hierarchy. When Roosevelt gradually refused to listen to him, he broke with the President and, with Reverend Gerald L.K. Smith, helped form a third party in 1936 headed by Representative William Lemke. Their party failed miserably in the election, and Father Coughlin temporarily ceased his broadcasts. The successor of Bishop Gallagher, Archbishop Edward Mooney, did not attack Father Coughlin but eventually forced him off the air for technical reasons. Whatever good Father Coughlin accomplished in his earlier talks on the social encyclicals was clouded by his mistaken notions of finance, some uncouth attacks on his opponents, and his stooping to anti-Semitism. However, he remained faithful to the Church and obeyed his superiors when they insisted that he sever his connections with *Social Justice* and the League for Social Justice. That publication, *Social Justice,* rose and fell with his national career. Some who lauded him when he began, regretted his later career.

There were many other Catholics who came into national prominence with the election of Franklin D. Roosevelt and the development of what was called the "New Deal." James Farley as Chairman of the National Committee of the Democratic Party became Postmaster-General. Senator Thomas Walsh was named Attorney-General but died before the inauguration. Frank C. Walker was the National Treasurer of the Party and a close associate of Roosevelt. So also was Thomas Corcoran an intimate of the Administration, but he and Walker were on opposite wings of the Democratic Party with Walker the more conservative.

Throughout the twentieth-century Mexican Revolutionary Movement, the Catholics in the United States had been interested watchers of events below the border. The interested Catholics in the United States, however, were not always well informed. There was no question that the regime of President Calles and his immediate successors was anticlerical and that it persecuted the Church. American Catholics paid little attention to the economic and social issues of the Revolution and insisted that if the American Government made the proper move the religious persecution would cease. Persons better informed on Mexican affairs knew that if the American Government interfered in Mexico in the interest of Catholicism, the Church would inherit the Mexican opposition to the "Gringos" as well as the anticlericalism of the revolutionary government. Through the ambassadorship of

Dwight W. Morrow the political and economic relations between the two countries had been bettered, but no real change had been made in the religious situation. When Josephus Daniels, the newspaper editor from North Carolina, was made Ambassador to Mexico by Franklin D. Roosevelt to carry out there his "Good Neighbor" policy, Daniels in his attempt to keep the goodwill of the Mexican government was accused by American Catholics of furthering the persecution of the Church by his efforts. In one speech he had innocently expressed with approval a quotation from Calles in favor of democracy in education in which Calles really was advocating the policy of the Revolution in education. Daniels was a Methodist but had many Catholic friends and was taken by surprise by the reaction to his speech.[6]

There seems to be no doubt that Daniels was interested in checking the persecution of the Church in Mexico, but he and other members of the Roosevelt administration felt that the American Government should make no open formal intervention. Daniels warned the Mexican government that, if the persecution of the Church continued, Catholic pressure on the American government would cause trouble. The Knights of Columbus in their meeting in Montreal in August 1935, formally demanded an investigation of the persecution and its Supreme Knight, Martin H. Carmody, sent a message on October 25 to the President asking that the religious rights of American citizens in Mexico be investigated. The effect of this public demand was to nullify the efforts that Daniels was making quietly to have the Mexican government check the persecution. Roosevelt on November 18 answered Carmody negatively. The lack of influence of American Catholics in the matter was written large in the inept protest of the Knights of Columbus. Democratic leaders were worried, however, about any general reaction of the Catholics against Roosevelt in the election of 1936. An unusual occasion to destroy this threat was offered to the Democrats by the University of Notre Dame.

On November 15, 1935, the Commonwealth of the Philippines was to go into existence. A suggestion had been offered to Notre Dame by Father James Drought of Maryknoll that Notre Dame hold a convocation in which the independence of the Philippines should be recognized and an honorary degree be given to the Honorable Carlos Romulo, a prominent Filipino Catholic, whom Drought wanted to see made President of the University of the

[6] E. David Cronon, *Josephus Daniels in Mexico* (Madison, 1960) pp. 92–111.

Philippines.[7] Father John F. O'Hara, C.S.C., the President of Notre Dame, accepted the idea at least insofar as recognizing the independence of the Philippines was involved. He sought to have Theodore Roosevelt, Jr., join with Notre Dame in the convocation of November 15. Roosevelt had already accepted an invitation to a Columbia University celebration that day. Through a Notre Dame alumnus, Frank C. Walker, President Franklin D. Roosevelt was asked to come to Notre Dame for the convocation. President Roosevelt accepted but asked that the date be changed because he would have to speak to a convention in Chicago in December. This was agreed and the date set for December 9. Plans were made to have Cardinal Mundelein of Chicago preside at the convocation at which Romulo and Roosevelt would receive honorary degrees and give speeches honoring the new Philippine Commonwealth.

Led by *America,* the *Brooklyn Tablet,* and the *Baltimore Catholic Review,* the Catholic press generally accused Notre Dame of having played into the hands of the President and given the President an easy out for not doing anything for the Catholics in Mexico. Father O'Hara refused to budge, since he personally was well informed in Latin American affairs and had insisted for some years that the worst thing that could happen to Catholicism in Mexico was to have an American formal intervention in the religious controversy. The convocation was carried by radio from coast to coast. What nettled the opponents of Roosevelt most was the laudatory speech about Roosevelt given by Cardinal Mundelein in his introduction of the President. If there was a threat of Catholic reaction to Roosevelt over his Mexican policies, it was killed by the Cardinal's words in which he denied the right of any group of Catholics to speak for the Church. Roosevelt's speech in general was a plea for religious freedom throughout the world.

According to the *Official Catholic Directory* of 1936, the total Catholic population of the United States, including Alaska and Hawaii, was 20,735,189. No one was really satisfied with this figure because it was not gathered with care or by an independent agency. Some Catholics claimed a Catholic population of nearly thirty millions or more, and some thought the *Directory* figures were too high. There were four cardinals, O'Connell of Boston, Hayes of New York, Dougherty of Philadelphia, and Mundelein of Chicago. Including these four, there were fifteen resident arch-

[7] T.T. McAvoy, *Father O'Hara of Notre Dame, the Cardinal Archbishop of Philadelphia* (Notre Dame, 1967) 161 ff.

bishops and two titular archbishops and 108 bishops including fifteen titular bishops. There were 31,108 priests of whom 21,378 were secular and 9,370 were religious. On the unity among this huge force there were divergent opinions.

To those outside the Church the common faith and practice of this huge throng of Catholic people was something mysterious and the bond of unity something to be feared. Even learned professors insisted that each priest was so close to the organization that any opinion he expressed was that of the whole body of the clergy. The Catholic "vote" was entered on many political charts, especially when a Catholic was a candidate for office. In some areas this Catholic vote was really a nationality vote by which an Irishman, a Polish immigrant, or a German or the like won a local election with the backing of his fellow Irish, Poles, Germans, or the like. But for the most part the non-Catholic majority did not know very much about the common faith or even the practices of American Catholics, except that Catholics generally went to Mass on Sunday and that they were subservient to their priests, who in turn were subservient to their bishops, archbishops, or cardinals and they to the Pope. The reaction of many to the liturgical splendor of the Chicago Eucharistic Congress in 1926 was that these golden vessels and silken garments were un-American. For Catholics, themselves, even when educated in Catholic schools, their Faith was little more than the contents of the catechism of the Council of Baltimore, although there was no universal understanding of its contents. As the century progressed, the spread of the practice of frequent and daily Communion added a new quality to the practicing Catholic. This Catholic minority continued to grow despite the restriction on immigrants from Catholic countries by the laws of 1924 and 1928. According to the Catholic estimate, the number of the faithful had increased more than two millions between 1915 and 1930.

The self-criticism of the Catholic masses that arose from time to time seemed of small moment because there was no way in which such criticisms would be conveyed to the more numerous lower class Catholic. Few Catholic newspapers had more than a local coverage, and the more national magazines had no subscription list comparable to the twenty millions of Catholics. While the myth of a Catholic vote had a warning power in politics, Catholic political power was usually local and backed by a local national group. Occasionally European Catholic visitors made fun of the subservience of American Catholics, their lack of universities of renown and writers and artists of national importance.

About the only retort of the American Catholic was to point to the known fidelity of the American Catholics to the Sunday Mass, and to the everyday virtues of life. Soon the flow of refugees from the persecution of Mussolini and Hitler, most of them university people, was to heighten the contrast between the Catholic intellectual of Europe and the common types of Catholic in the United States. Despite the often expressed desire by American Catholic intellectual or cultural leaders to direct the Catholic minority out of this mediocrity, no leadership arose. The drive for Catholic leaders had many handicaps. In the first place the Róman curia had never advocated any real national unity among American Catholics because of its fear of the evils of modern nationalism in a country predominantly non-Catholic. Archbishop Michael J. Curley, the holder of the titular primacy, was not made a Cardinal like his predecessor, and in most meetings the Cardinal took precedence over him. He was a zealous pastor but lacked the gentleness and the sereneness of Cardinal Gibbons. His blunt demands in letters published in the Baltimore *Catholic Review* for intervention by the United States into Mexican Church affairs and his hasty attacks on certain persons were not admired by those Catholics who were eager to promote the public welfare of the Catholic minority.

Of the cardinals, William O'Connell of Boston was regarded as formidable, a man of personal learning and culture, whose life had been crossed with personal tragedy, but not a person to give leadership or to encourage it in others. His flock were mostly the working people of eastern Massachusetts, almost in the position of the Irish workers in England. There were a few families both in and out of politics who were forging ahead, but their cultural traditions were "Yankee" if not "Puritan." His suffragan bishops, Rice of Burlington, Cassidy of Fall River, McAuliffe of Hartford, Peterson of Manchester, McCarthy of Portland, Keough of Providence, and O'Leary of Springfield, had few Catholics of wealth or high family tradition in their flocks. Actually by 1930 many of their people had suffered in the shift of the cloth mills to the southern states. They could be expected to exert power in local politics but not in Harvard, Yale, or Brown or on Federal Street, the banking center in Boston.

There was one new bishop on the Boston scene, Francis J. Spellman, auxiliary of Boston since 1932, who was considered a person of importance with a future because of his years in the Secretariat of State office in Rome. In August 1936 an announcement was made without much fanfare that the Papal Secretary of

State, Cardinal Eugenio Pacelli, was coming for a visit to his friend, Mrs. Nicholas Brady on Long Island, New York. His counsellor and guide in this visit, which included a transcontinental air trip to Cleveland, Notre Dame, Chicago, California, St. Louis, Cincinnati, and Washington was Bishop Spellman. Not only did the Cardinal visit cardinals, archbishops, and bishops and universities, but he made one notable visit to President Franklin D. Roosevelt at the home of Mrs. James Roosevelt, the mother of the President, at Hyde Park, New York. There were rumors that the purpose of the Hyde Park visit was to discuss Father Coughlin's opposition to Communism and the establishment of an American ambassador to the Vatican. So far as could be learned, this visit to America was a social trip in which the Cardinal Secretary of State got acquainted with the United States first hand, but the visit also marked the beginning of the influence of Bishop Spellman in American affairs.

The most beloved of the cardinals at this time was undoubtedly Patrick J. Hayes of New York, called also the Cardinal of Charity because of his interest in charitable works. He had a handsome face with soft lines and white hair befitting a kind father and spoke with a soft voice that was proper to his reputation of benevolence. Not an active man and without any real parochial experience, he was not too successful in leading his large flock through the trials of the depression. Of his suffragans, one did stand out by reason of his experience abroad. Archbishop Edward Mooney had served as Apostolic Delegate to India and Japan before being assigned to the See of Rochester to settle some financial problems. He had a grand manner of acting that was at the same time very democratic in the American sense. He was soon to be sent to the troubled See of Detroit where he eventually silenced Father Coughlin.

Cardinal Dougherty of Philadelphia was a worthy clerical representative of the common, workaday Catholicity of the Catholic people of eastern Pennsylvania. He had served for twelve years as missionary bishop in the Philippines and, after a brief term in Buffalo, had been made Archbishop of Philadelphia in 1919 and Cardinal in 1921. Philadelphia had splendid seminary buildings which symbolized the strong staff of teachers who formed the clergy according to the new canon law. But the intellectual and cultural life of the city and the community of Philadelphia was dominated by Quakers and by the chief educational institution of the area, the University of Pennsylvania. Under Father Philip McDevitt, later Bishop of Harrisburg, as Superintendent of

Catholic schools, the Philadelphia system had been one of the best in the country in the lower levels of education, but the Catholic colleges of the city had never gone beyond mediocrity. Of his suffragan bishops in Pennsylvania, Bishop Mark Gannon was an episcopal leader, and Bishop Hugh C. Boyle was a good pastor with a flock which included a variety of national origins and traditions.

The fourth cardinal, the first in the Middle West, Cardinal Mundelein, in his grand manner had something about him of the renaissance cardinals with his love of the arts. Under his benign influence the archdiocese prospered, and its school system grew. Here again outside of the seminary for which he obtained from Rome the power to given theological degrees, there was little intellectual leadership. Nor were any of his auxiliaries or suffragans noted for their scholarship or cultural leadership. Auxiliary Bishop Sheil was noted for his efforts to help the poor, for his Catholic Youth Organization, and his interest in social reform. As in many areas of the country, the intellectual leadership was held by the University of Chicago, by Northwestern University, and the University of Illinois, and a few old colleges such as Knox.

Of the archbishops of the country in 1930, John T. McNicholas, O.P., was a good pastor who achieved the improvement of his diocese and an advancement of his flock that was solid but not meteoric. Archbishop John Glennon of St. Louis was also a very successful pastor and under him the leaders of his flock were socially and intellectually acceptable. Archbishop Hanna of San Francisco had become a person of wide influence on the West Coast and in manners a worthy representative of the oldest western Catholic see. Bishop Cantwell of Los Angeles, Irish born like so many of his clergy, was the outstanding suffragan facing the sudden expansion of lower California.

To single out these men because of their prominence in leadership did not mean that the other bishops were mediocre. Some of them had not yet reached the opportunity in which they could show unusual ability or leadership. The bishops had to face two great problems. One was financial, the administration of the goods of the Church because the growth of the Church in the United States had been predicated on the right of property by which churches, schools, and other institutions could be built and operated without the danger of confiscation; but the actual administration of these institutions could and occasionally did limit the good accomplished. The debts encumbering some of these church properties in the depression and the extreme watchfulness necessary to prevent further indebtedness made the successful bishop too much of a real estate agent. The bishop's other problem was to see that the canon law of the Church was carried out in the diocese committed to his care. "Canon Law" was the majestic phrase by which the organization functioned so smoothly as to mystify the outside observer. Nearly every bishop had sent to Rome or to the Catholic University school of canon law in the 1920s certain promising priests to study the new legislation. These later took charge of the chancery office, handled marriage problems and pleas for dispensations, and solved most problems before the bishops had to intervene. The chancery office in the new code was something like a presidential cabinet of the diocese with each kind of spiritual work assigned to a secretary. Unfortunately some bishops never seemed to rise above the legalism of canon law and exerted no personal influence over their flock.

The sum total of this organized activity under the local bishop was the practical quality of American Catholicism, very strong on Sunday morning Mass attendance and quick to rally in case of outside attack, but neither very artistic nor intellectual. The effect of this efficient canonical administration on the lower class members had been remarkably successful in maintaining a practical but uninspired Catholicism—if one overlooks those impractical Catholics better known as Italian gangsters—but it was less successful with the growing number of Catholics who made their way through high school and perhaps college and sought to combine a higher cultural status with their Catholicism.

Running across diocesan lines, and in many cases holding certain exemptions from diocesan control were the religious communities of men and women. The societies of religious women had taken over almost completely the supervision of the parochial schools, but already they felt the need to supplement their services by lay teachers in the larger cities. The Sisterhoods also taught in many high schools and private academies throughout the country, and there were several Catholic women's colleges whose graduates were highly respected for their convent education. Not very many of their graduates, however, were interested in graduate education.

Of the male lay religious organizations the Christian Brothers, Marianist Brothers, Franciscans, Holy Cross Brothers, and Xaverian Brothers conducted a few parochial schools and conducted several private academies in the East, but they were engaged mostly in teaching in newly established centralized high schools. As the depression receded, new schools were being planned by bishops, particularly in the Midwest, to care for the multiplying products of the Catholic parochial schools.

The *Catholic Directory* for 1936 listed 9,730 religious priests, and these were for the most part in institutions operated by the religious communities to which they belonged. They represented a kind of mobile clerical force directed toward higher education and missions. The chief organization was that of the Jesuits, numbering approximately some 1,500 in the United States, conducting many colleges and universities in all parts of the country, and publishing *The Sacred Heart Messenger, America,* and *Thought.* The Benedictines maintained their tradition of monastic education in 21 abbeys but had also entered into much parochial work in the regions near these abbeys. The Dominicans, numbering over 700, likewise had departed from their traditional role as wandering scholars and preachers to take over the administration of Providence College. There were many monasteries of Franciscans, Capuchins, and Augustinians and centers of education and missionary activity under such congregations as the Vincentians, Holy Cross, Marists, and the like. The smaller communities usually operated one college or more and served a few parishes.

There had been no important dissensions between secular and regular clergy in the United States in the general expansion of the Catholic population from immigration and in the fewness of vocations in comparison with the needs. Here again nearly all contacts between the bishops and the secular clergy and the religious superiors and their subjects were governed by the precepts of canon law. Unfortunately the necessity for providing pastoral care for twenty millions of Catholics with all that was expected in the modern American parish or diocese did not allow much time or financial support for higher education or the means to recreate in the United States the old world Catholic traditions of art and culture. The bishops had other obligations, and the religious communities lacked the financial means. As a result, when the world entered the critical era that prefaced World War II, American Catholic leadership in matters of culture and education was mediocre and absent in most fields of modern science. The great step forward in American Catholicism of the vast multitude of former peasants in one generation did not conceal the fact that modern America had also gone farther ahead. There were a few Catholic voices of criticism but they spoke mostly in terms of the medieval philosophical ideals and of the glories of old cathedrals. Catholic writers neglected not only physical and biological sciences but also the social sciences which were becoming important factors in the workaday American way of living. The Rural Life Organization for Catholics produced a fairly well developed program but few American Catholics cared for farm life. For them as for most Americans the future lay in the cities. The major problem of American Catholicism was the impatience of the rising lower class to get the material means for modern living. Without any real family tradition of culture, most Catholic youths in the high schools sought mostly cash-paying jobs, and even those who went to college were still thinking only of an improved job. There was reason in these decisions because their parents, recently risen from poverty, had no family fortune to sustain them while they studied for the professions or for cultural positions. Recently arrived families worried about the news from Europe.

The peace of 1918–1919 that many hoped would be permanent was already overshadowed in 1936, and, as Europe prepared for war, the United States became an interested party. At least since 1917 the United States had become part of international affairs even though the American Congress had refused to join the League of Nations and had pretended that the country had gone back to the old isolationism. Some Catholics were probably among the most willing to stay out of European affairs, because they had no pleasant recollections of previous wars. For them the future of America at peace was the best future they could imagine. Only a small minority of American Catholics had any interest in the organizations for peace. Those of Irish and German descent were cold to the League of Nations or any plans in which England might profit. Yet no other organization in the country was in its essential policies as international or at least as supranational as Roman Catholicism.

In the period following World War I the opposition of Roman Catholicism to Russian communism had been very clear. The Soviet government had proclaimed its atheistic character and left no room for compromise. American Catholics held strongly that there could be no friendly dealings with communists. A harder line for Catholics to draw was that which would define the position of the Church on those political organizations which professed to be anticommunist. In the beginning many of these anticommunistic organizations sought the aid of the Church and, when in political power, passed laws giving support in some cases to Church activity. In the European political division between left and right, American Catholics were for the most part neither well informed nor deeply interested. They did accept the Church's opposition to communism as a matter of principle, and, when the Roosevelt administration established diplomatic relations with the Soviet Union, they expressed a general disapproval of the action, even though the action was recommended by such Catholics as Alfred E. Smith. On the other hand, American Catholics read with pleasure of the settlement of the conflict between the Vatican and the Italian Government by the Lateran Treaty because of their traditional devotion to the Pope, but they soon learned that all was not well in the relations between the Vatican and Mussolini's government. Nevertheless for most American Catholics there was this difference between the communist government of Russia and the fascist government of Italy, that the Church did exist in the fascist state. But there were two other fascist governments soon on the horizon.

Hitler had seized power in Germany and had begun to harass the Church. German Catholic refugees of Semitic ancestry, former members of the Catholic Centrist parties, and other political opponents of Nazism began to arrive in such numbers that the American bishops appointed a committee to give them aid. Then in the confusion surrounding the Spanish Civil War, the Republican Government of Spain began to impose harsh laws against the Church and was accused of planning to establish a communist state. The Spanish army revolted and, under the leadership of Francisco Franco, carried on an anticommunist crusade. The Civil War was carried on in brutal fashion with communists and liberals of western Europe supporting the Republican government and Hitler and Mussolini aiding Franco. Efforts were made to get American aid for each side.

This controversy over Spain in the United States was superficially Catholic versus Protestant, derived more from the old Anglo-Saxon legend than from contemporary conviction. Although the Basques, who supported the Republican government, were nearly all Catholics, American Catholics who supported Franco constantly described the Republican government as communist. Some Catholics, especially writers in *Commonweal*, opposed support for Franco. The official attitude of the American government was one of neutrality according to previously passed neutrality laws. The American hierarchy accepted the opinion of the Spanish hierarchy, who supported Franco. In the comparable Mexican persecution the hierarchy had protested the persecution of the Church by the Mexican government and had written a letter of sympathy to the Mexican hierarchy. Then in 1934 the American hierarchy opened a seminary for training Mexican seminarians in Montezuma, New Mexico. As the turmoil in Europe increased, the American press began to be filled with stories of the European political battles. Leaders in arousing Catholic interest in the European ideological struggle were the exiles from Germany and Italy, who were generally of high intellectual ability and quite vocal. They created a more active participation in world affairs among educated Catholics in the United States.

On July 1, 1937, the bishops of Spain published an address to the Catholic bishops throughout the world in which they surveyed the rise of the Spanish conflict, compared the military uprising and the communist revolution in their country, and stated their position in support of the Franco forces. The letter was printed in pamphlet form and sold by the N.C.W.C. On October 4 in *The New York Times* there was a letter of 150 Protestants attacking the position of Franco and specifically the letter of the Spanish hierarchy saying that they were "disturbed by the fact that no leaders of the Catholic Church in America have raised their voices in repudiation of the position of the Spanish Hierarchy." Monsignor Michael Ready, who had succeeded the deceased Father John J. Burke, C.S.P., as General Secretary of the N.C.W.C., published an answer to them in which he denied the charges made in the letter of the 150 that the Spanish bishops approved violence as a means of settling political disputes or that they rejected the Republic of Spain or that they condemned democratic institutions. Also, on October 14 a letter signed by 175 members of the Catholic clergy and laity was published in *The Times* in answer to the letter of the 150.

On November 17, 18, and 19, 1937, the American bishops held their annual meeting at the Catholic University. Besides the usual reports of the committees of the organization, the bishops issued two lengthy letters to the hierarchies respectively of Germany and Spain expressing their horror at the current persecutions. Of the Nazis, the bishops wrote:

. . . Today the sense of all religious-minded men and women throughout the world is outraged by the satanic resourcefulness of these leaders of modern paganism and by the incredible excesses committed by them in their attempt to exterminate religion and to blot out from the minds of the German people all true knowledge and love of God. . . .[8]

In their letter to the Spanish bishops the American bishops reviewed the contents of the Spanish bishops' letter and expressed their dismay at the murders of clergy and religious, concluding:

. . . God grant that once again you may be a powerful force to stem the tide of atheism, translated into social language and disguised with a

[8] *Our Bishops Speak*, note 3, above, p. 223.

diabolical ingenuity! In your sorrows and tribulations you may be comforted to know that we understand and sympathize with you. . . .[9]

In another document the bishops expressed their concern over the damage to American morality brought about by the "all-too-prevalent promiscuous and unwise use of intoxicant liquors . . . ," "unclean and immoral movies," and "suggestive, sensuous and unclean floor shows connected with many drinking places. . . ."[10]

On November 28, the Administrative Board of the N.C.W.C. issued a statement entitled "Christian Attitude on Social Problems." Addressed chiefly to the labor organizations, this document called attention to the two forms of the absolute state that threatened the world under the pretense of promoting the common welfare which they warned the workers to avoid. The bishops emphasized first the threat of communism:

In our country communist leaders see three things in their favor: first a sizable army of propagandists among left wing professors, teachers and intellectuals; second, the very real dangers to our financial and economic structure; third, the growing articulate discontent among the masses of the people. . . . [11]

The statement continued with an exposition of the dangers of the organizations called "peace and youth movements," sponsors of stage and screen entertainment, and so called crusaders for "democracy." Later the statement noted that "another method of destroying the liberty of the people, although it begins by lauding democracy and proclaiming freedom, is to establish the dictatorship of the absolutist State." The bishops added: "This kind of State is contrary to the letter and spirit of the American Constitution." Somehow in these and other condemnations of totalitarian regimes, the communists seemed to be the more strongly condemned.

In May 1937, Archbishop Edward Mooney was elected to the newly erected archdiocesan see of Detroit to succeed the late Bishop Gallagher. Already since 1935, Archbishop Mooney had been the Chairman of the Administrative Committee of the N.C.W.C., succeeding Archbishop Hanna. Under his influence the published statements of the hierarchy gave continued support to programs of social reform and for the healing of the suffering

[9] *Ibid.*, p. 221.

[10] *Ibid.*, p. 218.

[11] *Ibid.*, p. 315. The activity of Catholics in the New Deal years has been treated by George Q. Flynn, *American Catholics and the Roosevelt Presidency 1932–1936* (Lexington, 1968) and David J. O'Brien, *American Catholics and Social Reform; The New Deal Years* (New York, 1968).

and dislocations resulting from the depression. Archbishop Mooney did not write much, and his sermons and public speeches while clear were not forceful, but his influence was very great in private discussion and in the meetings of the hierarchy during the critical years that followed his appointment to Detroit. Closely associated with him in this progressive leadership of the Church in the Middle West was Archbishop Samuel Stritch, transferred from Toledo to the Archdiocese of Milwaukee in 1930. A quiet personality with a soft voice, Archbishop Stritch was a man of superior intellectual powers. He promoted in the N.C.W.C. and in the hierarchy the improvement of Catholic educational institutions. He was also a supporter with Archbishop Mooney of sound Catholic programs of social reform. The rise of these two newer leaders of American Catholicism came with the retirement of Archbishop Hanna to Rome, the death of Cardinal Hayes of New York on September 4, 1938, and the death of Cardinal Mundelein on October 2, 1939. Archbishop Stritch was transferred to Chicago on December 27, 1939, where he began to have a wider and stronger influence in Catholic affairs of the Middle West. Bishop Schrembs, the veteran of many campaigns, was named a titular archbishop and remained remarkably active. To New York the new Pope, Pius XII, brought his friend Bishop Francis P. Spellman from Newton Center, Massachusetts.

Bishop Spellman,[12] a graduate of Fordham University and the North American College, had served for a while in the office of the Papal Secretariat of State in the Vatican, notably in releasing outside Italy Pope Pius XI's encyclical against Italian Fascism, *Non Abbiamo Bisogno*. On July 30, 1932, the Pope named Monsignor Spellman auxiliary bishop to Cardinal O'Connell in Boston. It was in that capacity that he acted as guide to his friend, Cardinal Pacelli, on the Secretary of State's visit to the United States in the summer of 1936. With the death of Cardinal Hayes and Pius XI and the election of Cardinal Pacelli as Pope Pius XII, there was no great surprise when the new Pope made his friend Archbishop of New York on April 24, 1939. After the death of Cardinal Mundelein on October 2, 1939, because of his friendships at the Vatican throne, Archbishop Spellman became the chief channel for exchanges between official Washington and the Vatican. On December 11, 1939, the Apostolic Delegate in Washington announced that Archbishop Spellman had been appointed Bishop of the Armed Forces of the country and Father

[12] Cf. Robert I. Gannon, *The Cardinal Spellman Story* (New York, 1962).

John F. O'Hara, C.S.C., the President of Notre Dame, had been made his Auxiliary. He consecrated Bishop O'Hara at Notre Dame on January 15. In the meantime Archbishop Spellman had helped President Roosevelt arrange for a personal representative in the person of Myron Taylor at the Vatican court.

The three archbishops, Spellman, Stritch, and Mooney, were to be the recognized leaders of American Catholicism during the ensuing decade. Cardinal Dougherty in Philadelphia, Cardinal O'Connell in Boston, Archbishop John J. Glennon in St. Louis, Archbishop Cantwell in Los Angeles, Archbishop Mitty in San Francisco were important persons and successful administrators in their own areas, as were most of the archbishops and bishops of the day, but they did not command the national attention as often as did the Archdioceses of Chicago, Detroit, and New York. Archbishop Mooney and Archbishop Stritch were considered liberal in their approach to the social and economic problems of the day. Archbishop Spellman, because of his close friendship with the Pope and because of his very efficient administration of the difficult problems of the Archdiocese of New York, grew steadily in influence. He was considered less liberal than the other two.

When Pope Pius XII chose to honor the 150th anniversary of the foundation of the American hierarchy, he issued an encyclical on November 1, 1939, *Sertum Laetitiae,* in which he spoke of the progress of the country and of the Church's contribution to that progress. While honoring the good work of the Bishops, the N.C.W.C., the religious orders, the Catholic University, the Pope took occasion to regret the existence in the country of schools without religion and to warn the rich nation against sloth arising from pride in past accomplishments. At the celebration of the sesquicentennial in the Shrine of the Immaculate Conception at the Catholic University, Monsignor Edward P. McAdams outlined the growth of the Church in the country. At the end of 1939 there were 20 archdioceses, 91 dioceses, an Army and Navy Diocese, a Greek Rite, and a Ukrainian Greek Catholic diocese; 2 cardinals, 18 archbishops, 113 bishops, an abbott nullius, 22,569 diocesan priests and 10,971 religious priests, making a total of 33,540; a total of 13,114 churches with resident priests, 5,643 missions; 209 seminaries, 16,746 seminarians; 181 colleges for women; 1,362 high schools, 441,273 high school students; 7,561 parochial schools, 2,106,970 pupils attending parochial schools; 311 orphan asylums, 32,206 orphans; 167 homes for the aged; 679 hospitals; and a Catholic population of 21,406,507. While these figures were not necessarily accurate in every detail, they were close enough in all categories to give a fairly clear picture of the growth of the Church in the preceding 150 years. This was American Catholicism on the eve of World War II.

American Catholics who had little understanding of the internal politics of Europe were astounded when Hitler, after taking over Austria, forced the surrender of the Sudeten lands of Czechoslovakia. They were unprepared when he broke his promise not to seek other territory and took over the rest of Czechoslovakia March 1939. The Administrative Board of the N.C.W.C. did express its condemnation of anti-Semitism[13] on April 29, 1939. Before the bishops met in November, the troops of Hitler had conquered Poland. Writing to the suffering Polish bishops, the American bishops said mournfully: "Only yesterday, amidst the changes of the times, the Cross of Poland seemed the bulwark of Western Christian traditions against upsurging hordes. Like darkness came to Calvary, sorrow and suffering have come on the Church of Poland." The war had already included England and France, but there were many American Catholics who hoped that the United States would remain neutral. This was expressed in the Bishops' words:

. . . In the present crisis it is necessary for all men to devote their mightiest efforts to the reconstruction of a just order in society whose disruption has brought the world to its present pass.

Accordingly, we plead for a spirit of calm deliberation in our own nation. We beg our people neither to be carried away by intemperate emotion, nor to become victims of hate mongers who set loose the evils of cupidity, anger, envy and revenge. The first line of defense against the involvement of our own nation in the misery of war is aloofness from emotional entanglements. Our primary duty is that of preserving the strength, stability, and security of our own nation, not, indeed, in a spirit of selfish isolation, but rather in a spirit of justice and charity to those people whose welfare is our first and chief responsibility.[14]

On April 9 Nazi troops entered Denmark and later Norway. On May 10 the German troops struck through the Low Countries at France and on June 22, 1940, France capitulated. Italy struck at France from the South. The United States began hastily to arm, but England needed destroyers badly to fight the German submarines. Roosevelt made the deal of some "over-age" destroyers for certain outlying military bases from which the Western Hemisphere could be defended. Those who did not want the country

[13] *Our Bishops Speak*, note 3, above, p. 323.
[14] *Ibid.*, p. 226.

to go into war knew that we were drifting into the conflict. The Burke-Wadsworth Bill for the Selective Service passed in September and on October 16 all young men between twenty-one and thirty-five were registered for military service. In the election of 1940 many Catholics of German and Irish ancestry expressed their opposition to Roosevelt, who they felt was heading toward war on the Allied side, but the country overwhelmingly reelected Roosevelt.

The Administrative Committee of the N.C.W.C. under the chairmanship of Archbishop Stritch prepared a statement of the needs of the social order in a world that was still recovering from the depression. The statement, called "Church and Social Order"[15] and dated February 7, 1940, was prepared with the writings of the late Pope Pius XI before the committee that wrote it. It is essentially an American application of his theories, especially as stated in the *Quadragesimo Anno*. The document says that inasmuch as it is the right and duty of the Church to teach the moral law and in particular to deal authoritatively with social and economic problems, "we judge it wise and opportune to reaffirm the jurisdiction of the Church as the teacher of the entire moral law. . . ." The statement insisted that the bishops dealt only with the moral aspects of the problem and not with the matters proper to economic science and business administration. Following Pius XI the bishops discussed first the right to own private property and the two dangers affecting that ownership: the concentration of ownership and control and its anonymous character resulting from some existing business and corporation laws. The second part of the statement dealt with property and labor and called for the adoption of right principles for the distribution of the income of industry. The third part dealt with security and insisted that existing insecurity resulted from the inequal distribution of property. The proper distribution was to be obtained not only through mutual counsel and honest agreement between the employers and the employees but also by the regulation of government. This last clause was one that was not readily accepted by all American Catholic employers who thought such government interference was socialistic. The fourth part discussed wages and said that the first claim of labor, which takes priority over other claims, "respects the right to a living wage." That living wage is not only for the worker but also for his family and to meet future problems such as unemployment, sickness, old age, and death. The

[15] *Ibid.*, pp. 324–343.

fifth part dealt with the establishment of social order. The solution of that problem is not simple. In the establishment of this social order two extremes must be avoided: that which avoids all collective bargaining and government action and that which rejects all individual rights and rushes to the opposite extreme. The remedies were first the establishment of some kind of guild system and secondly a reform in morals and a renewal of the Christian spirit. This Statement of 1940 was one of the finest statements on social reconstruction published by the hierarchy of the United States but, coming as it did when the country was tending to be engrossed in the growing war, its fulfillment was delayed. The economic recovery which occurred at this time also took away the urgency of its program. In the meantime, the influence of the Church in America was enhanced by the decision of President Roosevelt to send Myron Taylor as his "Personal Representative" to the Holy See. After the preliminaries had been arranged through Bishop Spellman, the letter announcing his intention was issued on December 23, 1939, and was acknowledged in a letter by Pope Pius XII on January 7, 1940.

Cardinal Patrick Hayes had been the only Ordinary of the American Armed Forces. In December 1939, the Roman authorities decided to keep the office in New York and appointed Archbishop Spellman the Ordinary of the Military Diocese. He chose as his auxiliary Father John F. O'Hara, C.S.C., the President of Notre Dame. After Archbishop Spellman had consecrated his *Delegatus Castrensis* on January 15, 1940, he gave him a desk in the chancery office in New York and a chancellor, Father Robert McCormick. The *Catholic Directory* for 1940 listed the members of the Military Ordinariate as 34 commissioned chaplains in the Army, 19 in the Navy, 66 chaplains in veterans' hospitals, 21 auxiliary chaplains, 164 Military Reserve Chaplains, and 63 chaplains in the National Guard, a total of 367. The number of Catholics in the armed services was estimated at 50,000 but, in deciding the number of chaplaincies allowed, Catholics were estimated as one third of the services. The Military Ordinariate was still a peacetime force lacking applicants and not too well supported by the hierarchy. Bishop O'Hara, the famed former Prefect of Religion of Notre Dame, envisioned his task as being a prefect of religion to all the Catholics in the armed services. Whereas at Notre Dame his flock was well concentrated, his new flock was scattered through the world. Nevertheless, the new Bishop Delegate began traveling from one camp to another in an effort to become personally acquainted with the chaplains. On January 26, he wrote the first of many letters to bishops and religious superiors begging for additional chaplains and on January 30 he wrote the first of his noted Circular Letters to the chaplains themselves. These circulars were comparable to the *Religious Bulletins* he had used to direct the spiritual life of students at Notre Dame, only in these he tried to reach men whom he could not visit, occasionally pointing out mistakes, but usually encouraging men in trials. After the war had begun, he spoke of the deaths and injuries to chaplains and the need for greater efforts. The Bishop himself managed to visit most of the camps in the country, pleased occasionally to be able to perform some of the chaplain's tasks himself, while he begged the bishops and religious superiors for more help. After Pearl Harbor, Circular Letter No. 19, January 19, began:

A feeling of spiritual exaltation comes from observing your magnificent response to the intensified obligations that have been yours since the morning of December 7th. There is nothing new in the obligations: you are still priests, with the yoke of servants of God, ordained to save souls; you are still chaplains, charged by your government with the duty of maintaining a right spirit in the men you serve. But there is a new spirit in those men, and you are directing it to the glory of God, the good of your neighbor, and the salvation of your own soul.

Bishop O'Hara never went to the battlefield but carried on an endless task with the aid of his chancery office of interviews in his office or of trips, letters, admonitions, directions, and visits to camps on the mainland. He was later joined by Bishop William McCarty, C.Ss.R., who took over his office with Bishop William Arnold after Bishop O'Hara became Bishop of Buffalo in May 1945. On November 2, 1945, when Bishop McCarty drew up his summary of the service of the Military Ordinariate during the War, he listed 70 commissioned and 15 auxiliary chaplains who died in the service. The total number of chaplains in the service was 5,370 of whom 2,477 were Army commissioned, 824 Navy commissioned, 15 Merchant Marine commissioned and one in the Coast Guard. There were 2,018 civilian auxiliary chaplains, 12 in the chancery staff, and 23 vicars delegate. There was no way to estimate the actual services given by these men to their flocks. Only a few of their actions were recognized by Distinguished Service Crosses or medals or Silver Stars, and only a few stories have been written. Judging from the number of men who returned to the Sacraments there was a general spiritual revival during the war, giving rise to estimates of active Catholics in the country of over forty millions. Despite occasional mishaps and failures, the Church during the war functioned well but most of the events and services were unnumbered and only occasionally recorded in letters or stories.

During 1940 the work of the Church outside the armed services continued in much the same pattern that had developed since the depression. Most of the nonreligious activity of Catholic organization was shown in participation in movements for social reform and in the propagation of the notion of Christian social justice. One new manifestation was the first Liturgical Week in America, held in Chicago under the patronage of Archbishop Stritch, October 21–25, 1940. These "weeks" had been held in Europe for some years, and the Chicago meeting was modeled after the liturgical week that had been held each year at Louvain, centering chiefly in the liturgical parish worship.

On September 8, 1940, the President called for a day of prayer for peace, as the western world watched with worry the German victories. The Holy Father also asked for a day of prayer on November 24 for all those who had died as a result of the war. When the Annual Bishops' Meeting was held in Washington, the Administrative Board of the N.C.W.C., to cooperate with the United Service Organization in charge of relief services for the Armed forces, set up the National Catholic Community Service composed of the Administrative Board of the N.C.W.C. and the Military Vicar of the Army and Navy Ordinariate. The bishops announced also that $200,000 had been raised for the relief of suffering peoples abroad and that the Bishops' Committee on Polish Relief had raised $347,332.60 for their work. In the elections to the Administrative Board, Archbishop Mooney again became Chairman with Archbishop Spellman as Secretary.

In his Christmas message of 1939 Pope Pius XII had laid down five conditions for a just peace, and these were repeated in simple form by the Administrative Board of the N.C.W.C. headed by Archbishop Mooney in April, 1940:

First—The assurance of all nations of their right to life and independence—the will of one nation to live never justifying the death sentence of another.

Second—Progressive disarmament, spiritual as well as material, and security for the effective implementing of agreements to this end.

Third—Juridical institutions guaranteeing loyal fulfillment of peace terms and providing for revisions called for by changing conditions.

Fourth—Satisfaction of the fair demands of national and racial minorities.

Fifth—A deep sense of responsibility for the observance of the precepts of justice and charity among men and nations.[16]

In their pastoral letter of November 1941, the bishops issued a statement on "The Crisis of Christianity" in which they said that their "concern is the supreme interest of religion." Quoting the encyclicals of Pope Pius XI against Nazism and against communism, the bishops said that "neither system understands nor permits freedom in the Christian sense. Both systems usurp arbitrary power over the lives and destinies of men; their dictators assume a power which belongs to God alone." They showed that in these encyclicals the Pope had condemned Nazism while showing love for the German people; and, while expressing the most explicit condemnation of atheistic communism, he had expressed his "paternalistic and compassionate benevolence for the people of Russia." The bishops joined also in the Pope's commemoration of the golden jubilee of the *Rerum Novarum.* They repeated the three values the Pope insisted must be part of a sound world order: material goods must flow equitably to all; the duty and the corresponding right to work; and the possession of private property by the family. To this the bishops added: "An adequate solution of the problems of emigration is of major importance in bringing tranquility to a confused world." They added in reference to the sufferings of the war:

Our sympathy goes out again to the people of those countries who have been crushed under the heel of the invader, and, indeed, to all upon whom war has imposed so heavy a burden of suffering and sacrifice. We cannot too strongly condemn the inhuman treatment to which the Jewish people have been subjected in many countries.[17]

In the remainder of the Pastoral the bishops urged Catholics to support wholeheartedly the adequate defense of the country but felt it necessary to insist on the preservation of the authority of the Church in its own sphere. Nevertheless they urged the faithful to show proper respect for the civil authority and to be willing to bear the sacrifices that the crisis of the time required. Finally they urged peace among the American people. They repeated the Papal approval of the formation of labor unions but also expressed the hope that the unions would restrain them-

[16] The original is in *Catholic Action* (January, 1940) XXII, No. 1, 4. There are other adaptations of the five points.
[17] *Our Bishops Speak,* note 3, above, p. 106.

selves from anything contrary to the general welfare. Within a few days the Chairman, Archbishop Mooney, of the Administrative Board wrote another message of cooperation in the war effort to President Roosevelt after the attack on Pearl Harbor.

Not all that the bishops did for the welfare of their flocks during the war was recorded in the press. Through the Administrative Board of the N.C.W.C., the recognition of religious services by the Government as a part of the necessary war effort had to be demanded. Later, when those in charge of the physical welfare of the armed services tried to insist that the purposes of war took precedence over moral matters, the bishops forced those in charge of the military to admit that such an attitude was destructive of the purpose as well as the proper methods of war. But Bishop John F. O'Hara and Archbishop Spellman had to be constantly on the alert to keep the observance of these principles clear during the war itself.

In their Pastoral of November 1942, when the American troops had already entered Africa, the bishops insisted on the high purposes of the American entry into the war as stated by the President and warned that "secularism cannot write a real and lasting peace." They warned also about the effect of the war measures that had taken so many women out of the homes and expressed their concern about the youngsters in their teens who had been called into the service. They repeated their sympathy for the invaded countries, especially Poland, and for the persecuted Jews. They recalled also that Pope Pius XI had warned American Catholics to take a special interest in the welfare of the Negroes.

In October 1943, Archbishops Mooney and Stritch and Bishop Karl Alter as representatives of the hierarchy joined representatives of the Protestant and Jewish faiths in "An Introduction and a Statement of a Just Peace," consisting of seven principles for permanent organization. The statement called for the rule of moral law, the protection of the rights of the individual, including the rights of the weak and the oppressed and the erection of international institutions to promote international peace. Again in November 1943, the bishops issued a statement of the conditions which they as religious leaders felt they had a right to say must be included in a lasting peace. They insisted first on the recognition of the sovereignty of God and of the moral law. They insisted also on the recognition of the unity of the human race with the proper recognition of national rights and national sovereignties, properly interpreted. The nations must unite in setting up international institutions for the preservation of world peace.

Referring to domestic problems, the bishops expressed worry over the increase in crime that had appeared during the war and demanded that there be a greater recognition of the family and a rejection of planned parentage and other notions of marriage that they considered pagan. They called for the recognition of the rights of the Negro and the elimination of racial tensions; and they added a plea for the welfare of the Spanish-speaking members of the country's peoples.

Again in November 1944, as the European struggle was turning into Allied victory, the bishops issued a "Statement on International Order." In it the bishops claimed that the war had been the result of bad education. In the peace they wanted the Atlantic Charter to be carried out without equivocations, that might should yield to law, and that strong nations should help the weaker ones. They suggested that the international court have judicial power and that the sovereignty of nations should be recognized. But the bishops insisted on the innate rights of man on the grounds that free men mean free nations.

There were occasional problems of the war in which the question of Catholicism was accidentally involved. In the discussion of the Spanish Civil War, American Catholics generally seemed to show greater faith in Francisco Franco than his record deserved, and this support of Franco in turn caused some unpleasant exchanges between some Catholic writers supporting him and others. The uncertain situation in Yugoslavia also created misunderstandings that were increased when the Allied governments later recognized Tito. The bombing of Rome by the American forces brought out a protest from Archbishop Mooney in the name of the American hierarchy. To their credit Catholics helped promote goodwill with Latin America, particularly by an Inter-American Seminar on Social Studies in 1942, but the cooperation was not too well supported by the United States Government. In the American invasion of the Southwest Pacific, the American troops came in contact with many Catholic missions and with whole nations which had accepted Catholicism. American Catholic soldiers were surprised to find these brown and black people fervent Catholics and often contributed much to restoring churches and missions ruined by the war.

There were many accounts of the heroic service of Catholic chaplains on the sea and in battle. Bishop John F. O'Hara, the recipient of most of these reports from the front, was sure that the Church would receive a renewal of spirit from these years of trial. One of his circulars dated June 10, 1943, hints at this side of the picture.

. . . The Holy hour at jungle positions, the field Mass in magnificent parade grounds, Easter morning in an old Arab stable, Easter in the Coconut Bowl of Guadalcanal, shepherds and their flocks drifting by during Holy Week services in the fields of North Africa—a thousand letters from near and far tell the stories of the return of sinners to the life of grace, and of strengthening of grace in the hearts of the just.

Another interesting development of wartime that was especially dear to Bishop O'Hara was the granting in June 1942 of the privilege of the afternoon Mass. The Bishop's statistics on the increase in the reception of Holy Communion after the granting of the privilege showed that for the first five months of 1943 the increase had been 300% with an increase on weekday receptions of 360%. In Circular No. 41, February 10, 1945, the Bishop wrote sympathetically to his chaplains:

Sackcloth and ashes have been upon us for a long time now, and the forty days of Lent for most of you and your charges will mean no deepening of penance. It will take more than a lifetime to forget the horrors through which so many of you have lived since our last letter. Even those overseas who have escaped the ravages of a terrible winter have had their own problems; the tropics have seen much military action as well.

After the signing of the surrender of Japan on the battleship *Missouri* on September 2, 1945, American Catholics, like their fellow citizens, began the recoil from a tremendous war. The immediate problem for the superiors of the Church, episcopal and religious, was the transfer back to civilian work of the chaplains who had followed their young men into the Army, the Navy, and the Marines. Of the total of 5,370 persons associated with the chaplaincy in the services, many would remain in them because there would be no returning of the armed forces to the status before the war. As matters stood the services of the civilian congregations had been skimped a bit to meet the final efforts. Some ordinations by bishops and religious superiors had been advanced to fill the depleted ranks of the priests in civilian work. Some chaplains, who had died or been permanently disabled, would not return. Some clergymen who had become accustomed to the relatively freer status of the chaplain's life were not anxious to return; others were happy to get back to the old parish or community surroundings.

The colleges, perhaps, were the first civilian institutions to feel the effect of the changeover from war to peace with the rush of the discharged soldiers under the G.I. Bill to go to college. Catholic men's colleges, which had served for the training of Army and

Navy officers, disbanded their military officers and students and prepared for the returned veterans. Thousands of these young men, many of whom had not hoped to go to college before the war because they could not afford the expenses, decided to take advantage of the governmental assistance to get higher education. There were also the multitudes who had been able to get only one or two years of college work before going into the service or had gone into the service immediately after high school. To handle the rush, most colleges retained the speeded-up programs of wartime. Some smaller Catholic colleges, which had scarcely stayed open during the war, were suddenly bulging with young men, many of whom did not have the prerequisite training or perhaps even the mental ability to match their ambitions. There was some talk about the superior zeal for study among the returned veterans, but, while some were a bit more mature in their judgments, the five years without intellectual stimulus proper to college had really lowered the standards of intellectual achievement.

The older colleges of the country quickly reduced their enrollments to prewar numbers and were enabled to secure the cream of the returned veterans. Some of the other colleges obtained unforeseen geniuses, but most had simply older men who wanted to better their earning power. Colleges without endowment frequently made the mistake of trying to operate on the stipends of the students. Catholic colleges could supplement these fees with the unpaid services of religious so long as new faculty did not have to be hired or new buildings erected, but the actual figures showed that these colleges were giving away their futures to those young men because the fees of these students did not cover the advanced training of the religious faculty or the costs of replacing the equipment or buildings for future years. The returned veterans refused to accept the traditional Catholic college discipline, and infected the younger nonveterans with their complaints, so that the traditional discipline of Catholic colleges was permanently relaxed. After the first rush of veterans, the enrollments did decrease after the first years, but the numbers attending college were permanently increased. Catholic institutions were forced finally to seek permanent endowments as well as government loans to stay in business. Some members of the hierarchy and some religious superiors held out stubbornly against the obvious fact that higher education could not support itself.

The high attendance at the Sacraments among the troops reported to the Military Ordinariate had made Bishop O'Hara predict a great burst of Catholic fervor after the war. Many veterans did retain the fervor acquired during the threat of battle. The young couples in the new suburbia were a source of hope. But the home life of the ordinary Catholic young man had been changed by conditions of wartime. Wartime industry had given prosperity to millions of workers, and the return of industry to peaceful business brought millions of jobs with good pay.

The workers in these industries soon found the means to buy the new automobiles, new clothes, and the myriad new gadgets for the home which the factories began to turn out after the war. Many of the young men and women who had entered into war-time marriages and those who had delayed marriage until the end of the war brought an unpredicted increase in the number of marriages and a predictable increase in the number of children. Housing in every part of the country lagged far behind. People who had moved to the centers of war manufacture did not return to the countryside but added to the already complex housing problems of urban centers. The interest of the press and the advertisers, which had been concentrated on the teenagers because of the want of other public during the war, had found the younger market bigger and more profitable, so that they continued to cater to the young. The clergy, especially those chaplains who had similar experiences in the services, followed suit in their promotions of religious interests among young people.

For a short time the American people forgot about the war and began to revive the domestic prosperity. No one likes to blame the Government for yielding to this popular feeling and returning the soldiers from the fronts and for demobilizing the great army. Yet at least one of the war allies did not demobilize, and, before the people could be aroused, the Soviets had taken over much of Eastern Europe and under a new Marxist regime in China had seized the Chinese mainland. The postwar reconstruction at home continued, but the demobilization of the armed services had to be checked and finally reversed when war broke out anew in Korea in 1950.

In comparing American Catholicism of 1945 to that of 1919, certain differences are very clear between the two reconstruction periods. After World War II, the National Catholic Welfare Conference already existed, and the program of reconstruction announced in 1919 had already been clarified in the bishops' program of 1940. Where Catholics took the lead in economic and social reforms in the 1920s the threat of armed communistic nations, especially Soviet Russia in 1945, placed the Church in the less popular position of opposing all extreme socialistic reforms.

The bishops' program of 1940 was liberal in the good sense, but Roman Catholics were distinguished in the late 1940s as the group chiefly opposing the infiltration of communism. In education, instead of pleading with the Catholic youth to go on to college as in 1919, the bishops and their priests after 1945 were trying to maintain leadership among the mass movement to the colleges. The major problems of the Catholic position evolved in the home, promoting new housing and better housing, helping the returned veteran to remain religious in the ways of peace, and providing guidance against the two most dangerous threats to young Catholics: communism and secularism.

There was a brief flare-up after the war of the old anti-Catholicism of earlier eras, but it was short lived because, as Bishop O'Hara had said in his circulars, young men from the grassroots regions of the country had come in contact with Catholics and Catholic chaplains during the war and did not fall for the old propaganda. But there was a less definite and real difference arising between Catholics and their neighbors. The loyalty of the Catholic millions to the essential doctrines of the Church and their general fidelity to the practice of attending Sunday Mass, receiving the Sacraments, and accepting the authority of the hierarchy marked them off from the ordinary non-Catholic American who might or might not belong to a church organization, felt no strict obligation to go to church on Sunday, and did not admit that any religious organization could tell him what he had to believe or do. Probably the basis of the Catholic adherence to his formal religious practice was the enforcement of the canon law of 1918, by which bishops chosen for their orthodoxy had absolute control over their priests, and the priests held sway over the faithful by insisting on the conditions for admission to the Sacraments. The religious clergy more or less fitted into the same pattern: their superiors were not as absolute in power as bishops, and they were subject in many things to the bishops themselves. Catholic education was education colored with the purpose of teaching this discipline and the doctrines on which it was based.

Protestant observers frankly admitted that they could not understand this Catholic organism which seemed to function right down to the latest person receiving the Sacraments, going to Mass on Sunday, and not eating meat on Friday. Trouble began to brew when members of the Catholic organization began to object to any kind of Marxist or communist influence in public, that is, in politics or education, and when the Catholic organization decided to cleanse public entertainments, especially the moving picture industry, according to Catholic ideals. This Catholic submission to canonical order had its limitations. When the Pope proclaimed the dogma of the Assumption of the Blessed Virgin Mary, all Catholics accepted it without a murmur, and, when the rules for the Eucharistic fast were changed in 1955, that decree was something for Catholics alone and as such readily accepted. But when the Catholic practice or opinion affected their relations with non-Catholics or on matters which non-Catholics did not consider religious, there were differences of opinion and opposition. Catholics definitely refused to take their politics from their clergy and began more and more to demand freedom in social matters. Non-Catholics were still a majority and were not ready to accept Catholic dictation in public matters of morality and entertainment.

The bishops' Pastorals of 1919 and 1940 had given to these statements of the bishops a national significance that continued for the first years after the war. The statement of the Administrative Committee of the N.C.W.C. on November 18, 1945, was farseeing in its wisdom but went mostly unheeded. The bishops called attention to the unilateral actions of the Soviets and their setting up of puppet states in Eastern Europe. Some of the sentences were important:

. . . There are profound differences of thought and policy between Russia and the Western democracies. Russia has acted unilaterally on many important settlements.

* * *

There is a clash of ideologies. The frank recognition of these differences is preliminary to any sincere effort in realistic world co-operation for peace. The basis of this co-operation must be mutual adherence to justice. It would be unjust for us to be an accomplice in violating the rights of nations, groups and individuals anywhere in the world. . . . The charter which emerged from the San Francisco Conference, while undoubtedly an improvement of the Dumbarton Oaks proposals, does not provide for a sound, institutional organization of the international society. The Security Council provisions make it no more than a virtual alliance of the great powers for the maintenance of peace. These nations are given a status above the law. . . .

The bishops spoke of the broken pledge to the Polish people at Yalta and of the betrayal of the other Baltic countries. They spoke of the problems of Italy, Germany, Austria, and Hungary.

In November 1946, the Statement of the Bishops called upon the principles of the American Declaration of Independence and spoke of the conflict between Russia and the West. The bishops pleaded for the prisoners of war and for humane treatment of displaced persons. They called heartless the ruthless herding of uprooted people. The bishops, without naming the Germans, condemned the heartless brutalities committed by the Nazis during the war, which they said were contrary to human dignity. The Pastoral of 1947 on secularism was a more important statement that drew attention from other religious leaders outside the Church. Some of its sentences were very forceful in delineating the problems of the postwar world.

. . . Secularism, or the practical exclusion of God from human thinking and living, is at the root of the world's travail today. It was the fertile soil in which such social monstrosities as Fascism, Nazism, and Communism could germinate and grow. . . . Secularism, in its impact on the individual, blinds him to his responsibility to God. All the rights, all the freedoms of man derive originally from the fact that he is a human person, created by God after his own image and likeness. . . . The greatest moral catastrophe of our age is the growing number of Christians who lack a sense of sin because a personal responsibility to God is not a moving force in their lives. . . . Secularism has wrought havoc in the family. Even the pagans saw something sacred in marriage and the family. . . . In no field of social activity has secularism done more harm than in education. In our own country secularists have been quick to exploit for their own purposes the public policy adopted a century ago of banning formal teaching of religion from the curriculum of our common schools. . . . A philosophy of education which omits God, necessarily draws a plan of life in which God either has no place or is a strictly private concern of men. . . .

The bishops applied their criticism to the social and economic unrest of the day and to the troubles in international affairs and urged Catholics to be true to "our historic Christian culture" to offset this spread of secularism.

The first postwar decade saw the passing from the scene of several Catholic leaders of earlier decades and the rise of new personalities. After the death of Cardinal O'Connell on April 22, 1944, Cardinal Dougherty was the only American Cardinal until February 18, 1946, when Pope Pius XII raised Archbishop Mooney of Detroit, Spellman of New York, Stritch of Chicago, and Glennon of St. Louis to cardinalitial rank. The aged Glennon did not survive the return trip and died in Ireland on the way back. Two other archbishops of more than ordinary influence in the postwar world were Archbishop Richard Cushing, who succeeded Cardinal O'Connell in Boston, and Archbishop Francis McIntyre, who succeeded Archbishop Cantwell in Los Angeles.

When Cardinal Dougherty died in 1951, he was succeeded in Philadelphia by Bishop John F. O'Hara, C.S.C., of Buffalo, formerly of the Military Ordinariate. Archbishop Robert E. Lucey of San Antonio, while outside the center of American activities, was recognized for his care in handling his racial minorities in the South and his general interest in social reform. Bishop John Wright, Auxiliary of Boston and Ordinary of Worcester and later Pittsburgh, was recognized as a forceful speaker of progressive ideas who encouraged the rise of the Catholic laity. Archbishop Francis Keough of Baltimore suffered a heart attack shortly after his installation in Baltimore, which handicapped his public activities. Archbishop Patrick O'Boyle, who was elected to the new Archdiocese of Washington after the death of Archbishop Curley, had been active in social work in New York and found frequent need for social work in the troubled community of the nation's capital.

The senior Cardinal, Archbishop Mooney, also suffered a heart attack that limited his public activity, but he managed well his large archdiocese, the center of the automobile industry and of the complications of labor and capital involved in that industry. His written and spoken statements were forthright, although not numerous. In the postwar years undoubtedly the most outspoken member of the hierarchy was Cardinal Spellman. He was the head of the important Archdiocese of New York, the Bishop of the Military Ordinariate, and a close personal friend of Pope Pius XII; consequently his opinions were closely studied by both religious and civic leaders. When the Federal Congress began to prepare a national education program after the war, some congressmen tried to ignore the rights of the children in the parochial and private schools. Cardinal Spellman did not hesitate to speak out publicly on many occasions against these injustices, especially as contained in the bill proposed by Representative Graham Barden of North Carolina. This led to a public exchange between Cardinal Spellman and Mrs. Eleanor Roosevelt, who supported the legislation in her daily newspaper column and mentioned the Cardinal by name. In the exchange the Cardinal, irritated by her continued statements on the subject, denied that he asked the Government to erect buildings or pay salaries for religious purposes. He did insist that in other matters Catholic children should not be discriminated against. The Cardinal went to call on Mrs. Roosevelt to remove the bad feelings aroused but did not remove the public opposition to his action. Later the Education Department of the N.C.W.C. changed its position from opposition to all federal aid to education to a demand that Catholic schools participate in federal aid to education, which had become inevitable.

Cardinal Spellman was also outspoken in defense of the Catholic prelates who were suffering persecution in communist-dominated Europe, especially Archbishop Stepinac of Yugoslavia and Cardinal Mindszenty of Hungary. The Cardinal also led in the attack on the presentation of certain movies such as "The Miracle," "The Moon is Blue," and "Baby Doll" as offensive to public morals. His attempts to ban the showing of the play "The Miracle," which many considered blasphemous, failed when the exhibitors won in the courts in 1950–1951. In this as in his efforts for Catholic education, the common Catholic faithful were generally pleased by his leadership and comforted by his efforts, even when they were not entirely successful. While not defending Senator Joseph McCarthy in his charge of communist infiltration against the members of the Government, the Cardinal did give a tacit approval by his attendance at a Communion breakfast at which the Senator spoke. That action and his sending in seminarians to work during a strike of cemetery workers in a Catholic cemetery were opposed by those Catholics who considered themselves political and social liberals.

Cardinal Stritch of Chicago was accepted as a friend of Catholic higher education and a sympathetic worker in efforts to improve cultural positions of the Catholic minority. In educational matters his was the chief voice in the hierarchy. With Cardinal Mooney he was also the friend of those working for social and economic reform under the protection and guidance of the papal encyclicals. In a division of the hierarchy over the establishment of industrial councils, Cardinals Mooney and Stritch and Archbishop O'Boyle maintained that these councils were accepted by the papal encyclicals. Archbishop Cushing, already known as a generous friend of the Catholic missionary, was a sympathetic leader in many efforts to encourage the Catholic youth to be active in his religious faith. Likewise he was recognized by American labor leaders as a sincere friend. Archbishop Joseph E. Ritter in Saint Louis, Archbishop Rummel in New Orleans, and Bishop Vincent Waters of Raleigh attained prominence by their efforts to give Catholic leadership to the slowly moving campaign to obtain civil rights for Negroes.

The one notable Catholic heresy in the United States in the postwar decade was that of Father Leonard Feeney, S.J., who had previously been recognized as a leader of young people, a writer of ability, and, chiefly, the counselor at St. Benedict's Center near

Harvard. His actions apparently stemmed from his resentment of the student status and defensive position of Catholic clergymen and laymen in attendance at Harvard. From this resentment arose a conviction that the Church was giving in to the nonbeliever and violating the principle *extra ecclesiam nulla salus,* which Feeney interpreted rigorously. He began to attack Jews, Protestants, and even Catholics who did not accept his extreme views. Expulsion from the Jesuits and condemnation from Rome in 1949 and 1952 did not change his conviction. His group survives in Massachusetts, but after a few forays into other parts of the country the group settled outside Boston and has not had a very wide influence.

The life of American Catholicism in the years after the war was that of a loosely formed giant awakening from a sleep, each part of which had grown to tremendous size and was beginning to move one member at a time to see if they were really viable. Local censuses indicated that there were more Catholics in the country than anyone realized but that not all of them were at Mass every Sunday. The estimates of attendance at Sunday Mass ranged as high as sixty-five percent on the average in some tabulations, much less in others. New churches and schools were being built, but not enough schools to take care of the increased Catholic population and of those children whose parents had returned to the Church during the war. One important development in the movement to suburbia was the interest in the liturgy manifested by these families, particularly by younger families. The first great victory of the liturgical movement in the era was the restoration of the old Holy Week rites, but there was also a growing use of translated missals by the people attending Mass. There was an increasing number of Catholic books published and a few Catholic books reached the best-seller market, such as Thomas Merton's *Seven Story Mountain* and some books by Bishop Fulton J. Sheen and Fulton Oursler. While Catholic publications did not reach a wide public, there was a noticeable catering to Catholics by such widely circulated periodicals as *Life* and *Time,* although such magazines never accepted any Catholic authority even in religious matters. Catholic publications, books, or periodicals were read by a minority of a minority. The Catholic weekly newspapers, subsidized by the local Ordinary, had wide circulation when all the subscribers were added together, but they had little influence on the general public.

Whether Catholics numbered thirty millions or forty millions, they were the largest numerical minority in the country and naturally were watched carefully by those dependent on popular support. Any move by which Catholics could receive governmental support was attacked immediately by those who considered themselves watchdogs for religious liberty. When President Roosevelt appointed Myron Taylor as his personal representative to the Vatican, he did not name him ambassador and also notified the leading Protestant and Jewish authorities in the country that this was done for reasons of state. After Roosevelt's death, Truman continued the appointment and, when Taylor asked to be relieved, Truman asked Congress to approve the appointment of General Mark Clark as a regular ambassador to the Vatican. Most Protestant organizations, from Bishop W.B. Donegan of New York to the heads of various Methodist and Baptist organizations, protested. Congress did not act. Catholics had not sought the appointment and contented themselves with expressing resentment over the protests against what they considered a political and not a religious appointment.

On the question of federal aid to schools, the Catholic position seemed to change shortly after Monsignor Frederick Hochwalt succeeded Monsignor George Johnson as head of the Education Department of the N.C.W.C. from opposition to all federal aid to education to a position of asking that, since federal aid was to be, Catholic children be granted their share of the aid. Archbishop O'Hara of Philadelphia and some of his friends continued the old opposition to federal aid, and the old opponents of any aid to Catholics renewed their protests whenever the proposal of federal aid to schools was raised.

The principal political problem of most American Catholics after the war was the threat of communism. Atheistic communism had been condemned years before by the Popes and by the bishops in their pastorals. When the United States entered the war on the side of the Soviets, many American Catholics were uneasy about the alliance. When Russia did not disarm and moved into the countries of Eastern Europe, American Catholics were among the first to protest and to blame the American government officials for allowing the Russian conquests. There were many Catholic complaints against the agreements made at Yalta and Potsdam. American Catholic interest in the persecuted Catholics in Eastern Europe was intensified when the Pope sent Bishop Joseph Hurley of St. Augustine as a special nuncio to Yugoslavia to attend the trial of Archbishop Stepinac and Bishop Gerald O'Hara of Savannah as regent for the nuncio to Roumania. The Communist takeover in Czechoslovakia had resulted in further persecutions of

Catholics. The Soviet domination of Poland was complicated by the question of the problem of the Oder-Neisse Line. In China the communists under Mao-Tse-Tung, who had been treated lightly during the war with Japan, soon proclaimed themselves communists and drove Chiang-Kai-Shek off the mainland. Later North Korea with the aid of the communist Chinese attacked South Korea. The Korean war, despite the temporary victories of General MacArthur, with its stalemate was considered a communist victory by some.

In the reaction to Soviet persistence in conquest after the war, the American Government had to recognize that Russia was no longer an ally but an opponent. In World War II there had been many sympathizers with Russia in the Government, some of whom were tolerated because of the alliance with Russia. Under the Administration of President Truman, Congressional Committees began to attack the friends of Russia within the Government. The State Department, never a popular part of the American Government in rural America, became the butt of many wild charges which Truman tried to check, partly by setting up loyalty tests and partly by denials of the charges. The culmination of legal action against communists in Government was probably the conviction of Alger Hiss, a one-time member of the State Department, of perjury in connection with a charge of treason. In the welter of accusations and counteraccusations, Senator Joseph McCarthy of Wisconsin achieved great publicity by his charges against the State Department and members of other parts of the federal government. His sweeping charges and his demagogic speeches were cheered by those who felt that the federal government had not handled the Soviets properly. Senator McCarthy's wild charges of disloyalty led to Congressional investigations under his direction which were televised throughout the country. By his demagogic appeals and harsh methods, McCarthy brought upon himself contempt of people in Government, in business, and in education. He failed to prove his wild charges, and brought down a Senatorial vote of censure for his conduct. He harmed the efforts of proper government agencies to rid the government of communists. Among his supporters were many Catholics who felt that the government, especially the State Department, had betrayed to the communists the interests of the government and of the people whom Russia and China had conquered after the war.

The American bishops generally kept silent, but priests and Catholic laymen took sides in the public discussion. When Senator

McCarthy was censured by his own fellow Senators, his name and that of his friends were tainted in the minds of most Americans. He was a Catholic and was supported by many Catholics in their zeal to fight communism. But he had been elected by a Wisconsin electorate that had refused school bus transportation to Catholic children. Probably many Catholics were supporting his charges against not only government officials who had been friendly to communists but also against leftist intellectuals and especially university professors who usually espoused the cause of political liberalism. Many bishops, priests, and Catholic laymen regarded the discussion as political and kept out of it. A smaller group led by such Catholics as Professor Jerome Kerwin of Chicago, President George N. Shuster of Hunter College, the editors of *Commonweal*, and others supported those who censured McCarthy. Many of McCarthy's supporters were not Catholics, especially those in the rural areas who were traditionally isolationist and suspicious of the State Department. Certainly McCarthy's demagogic claims did not improve the reputation of American Catholicism. On the other hand in the question of the elections of Italy, the bishops were not restrained by the shouts of any doubtful demagogue and pleaded with the faithful to support the Catholic party in the Italian elections by prayers and in the case of Italian immigrants by letters and other aids. Catholics gave clothing and millions of dollars in other aid to the suffering people of Europe and Asia without question and with little fanfare.

The question of the relations between Church and State was wider than the relation between Catholics and the Government, although Catholics watched with breathless interest all cases regarding Church and State before the Supreme Court. In *Everson* v. *the Board of Education* of Ewing, New Jersey, the Court ruled that the transportation of children to and from parochial schools was a safety measure, but held that there could be no state support of religious education. In the case of *Vashti McCollum* v. *the Board of Education* of Champaign, Illinois, the Illinois law on released time for religious education was declared invalid because the teaching of religion was done on public school property. In the *Zorach* v. *Clawson* case, released time for religious education was permitted.

Among American Catholics themselves there developed at this time a conflict about the Catholic doctrine on the relations between Church and State. Father John A. Ryan had held that, if the country ever became Catholic, Catholicism would have to be the religion of the state, contrary to the first Amendment. Father John Courtney Murray advanced a theory that the real Catholic

doctrine recognized the State as a separate society and that therefore the Church did not have any power over the State in civil
matters. This was not the doctrine usually taught by Catholic theologians during recent centuries, and his theory was attacked by
Father Francis J. Connell, C.Ss.R., and by Monsignor Joseph
Fenton of the Catholic University theological faculty. Both appealed to Roman authorities. Pope Pius XII seemed to favor
Father Murray's position while the Secretary of the Holy Office,
Cardinal Ottaviani, seemed to support the claim of an indirect
power of the Church over the States taught by his student, Monsignor Fenton.

In actual politics there was no Catholic vote, even on the question of communism in government. The chief political battles of
the day were fought over the various efforts to have the government impress social and economic reforms by federal legislation.
Each Catholic, like his neighbor, decided this according to his
own interests. Catholics were predominantly urban and wage
earners and were for legislation that would increase their economic security. But some Catholics who were at least of the second
or third generations in the country were beginning to advance in
business and to have a share in ownership. These latter began to
disagree with their less favored brethren and to oppose "New
Deal Measures," which they claimed were socialistic. Some Catholics acquired wealth in new businesses. In the entertainment business Catholics also began to acquire reputations, not always the
best. Some Catholics were exemplary, like Stan Musial and Rocky
Marciano in sports or, in the movies, Bing Crosby, Ann Blythe,
and Irene Dunne, and Perry Como in radio and television. But
other Catholics seemed to forget their religious principles under
the temptations of quick riches and soft living. In politics the
tradition of the Catholic machine politician was replaced in some
communities with examples of Catholic political leaders.

There was one major point of dissatisfaction in American
Catholic life that was brought out pointedly by the comments of
Catholic refugees from Europe during the persecutions before
and during the war. Many of these refugees were learned and
scholarly and interested in cultural advancement. They came
from a higher social level than those from which the vast majority
of American Catholic immigrants had come during the nineteenth
and early twentieth centuries and therefore complained of the
low cultural levels of the older immigrants. After a generation or
two in this country, the descendants of peasants had begun to
have security, some wealth, and the beginning of an education.
But, in comparison to the cultural leaders of the non-Catholic

majority of the country, they had not reached the higher levels of education or culture. There were not enough Catholic publications of a philosophical or theological character to constitute an American Catholic opinion. Most of the journals for priests were devoted to occasional matters of liturgy or pastoral problems. There were a few Catholic devotional periodicals with some literary merit, but they were without influence in the American literary world. *Thought, The Thomist,* and *The Review of Politics* were voices of American Catholic higher culture but had meager subscription lists, and their best contributors were often refugees from Europe.

This complaint about the lack of Catholic scholarship had been raised by George Shuster in *America* in 1925 and later by Father John A. O'Brien. It was brought out again by Monsignor John Tracy Ellis[18] in 1955 and by Father Gustave Weigel, S.J., in 1957. Monsignor Ellis' essay of criticism was reprinted in many forms, and he was joined by many others so that the criticism of Catholic cultural efforts became a full chorus as the decade of the 1950s drew to a close. Most of the criticism, however, was negative, and the critics were not welcomed by those of episcopal authority. Perhaps this self criticism was a sign of growth. Some thought that this was just the result of so many Catholics who were achieving college education after the war. The criticism of Catholic cultural institutions was not new, but its volume was, and this time there was no anti-Catholic attack or overwhelming wave of new immigrants to exempt the Catholic minority from blame.

This seemed to be an American phenomenon to Americans until events in Europe directly affecting the Church in Europe widened the horizon of these critics on the mediocrity of American Catholicism. American Catholics began to hear of Teilhard de Chardin, Karl Rahner, Yves Congar, and many others. There were stories of sharp differences in the Roman Curia itself. Pope Pius XII, who had done much to bring up Catholic activities to modern times, had been very ill in 1954, and, while he rallied, he remained in fragile health. His death on October 9, 1958, was the conclusion of a life highly regarded in the United States. The election of his successor was carefully watched by the American Catholic minority because the new Pope could shape the immediate future of Catholicism in the United States in the choice of new bishops and in the enforcement of restrictive legislation.

[18] The central essay in this controversy was John T. Ellis, *American Catholics and the Intellectual Life* (Chicago, 1956). The paper was first given in St. Louis on May 14, 1955, and then published in *Thought* (1955) XII, 351–388.

CHAPTER FOURTEEN

American Catholicism
and the *Aggiornamento*

POPE PIUS XII HAD BEEN BETTER KNOWN to the people of the United States than any other pontiff.[1] He had visited the country before his election, had manifested a personal interest in the country, and had probably shaken the hands of more Americans than any previous pontiff. The image of Pope Pius XII in the American press was of an ascetical, scholarly, and noble man who had manifested an interest in almost every phase of human existence. The image of his successor, the former Cardinal Angelo Joseph Roncalli, a short squat man of peasant origins, was quite different. As Nuncio in postwar Paris he had become known to some Americans as a friendly diplomat, but he did not speak English and had never been to the United States. He was seventy-six years old and according to some had been elected by compromise between the liberals and conservatives. He quickly became famous for his smiling humility and approachableness, his readiness to go anywhere, and his manifest intention to be a very active pope. Americans soon learned of his friendliness, above all of his openness to non-Catholics and of his special desire to bring the Greek Orthodox Catholics back to union with Rome.

Americans continued to hear how the new pope broke protocol. He enlarged the College of Cardinals by his appointment of

[1] An earlier draft of this chapter appeared in *The Review of Politics* (July 1968) XXX, 275–291.

twenty-three new cardinals of whom three were of special interest to the United States: Archbishop Cushing of Boston, a man like the Pope; the ascetic Archbishop of Philadelphia, John F. O'Hara; and Archbishop Amleto Cicognani, who had been exiled from Rome for twenty-five years as Apostolic Delegate to the United States. Pope John called for a Synod of Rome—the first in centuries—and announced publicly on January 25, 1959, that there would be in the near future an ecumenical council.

The American Catholic press received the announcement of the new council with some surprise and interpreted the council as coming from the Pope's desire to welcome back into the fold the Catholics of the Greek schisms. As if he knew he had only a few years to live, the Pope quickly established the commission to prepare for the council and then the other preparatory commissions and set the date of the council for the autumn of 1962.

To say when the genial spirit of Pope John and later his council first affected American Catholics in some force is at present impossible. Future generations with diaries, letters, and other records now unattainable will have to determine when the movements already stirring in American Catholicism first joined up with the *aggiornamento*. A close scrutiny of the Catholic press in 1958 and 1959 reveals only light evidence of several movements in the United States that developed momentum within a few years and became associated in the press with the *aggiornamento* of Pope John. An exception was *Worship,* a monthly with 10,000 subscribers, published by Father Godfrey Diekmann, O.S.B., at St. John's, Collegeville, in the interests of liturgical reform. The contributors from all walks of Catholic life were agitating for reform, primarily of course in liturgy, but not exclusively. In the Middle West, besides *Worship,* there were several local publications sponsored by local Catholic Action groups, such as *Today* and *Act,* published in Chicago, and *Apostolic Perspectives,* published at Notre Dame. While they did not have large circulations, the names of the editors and contributors and the proposed reforms were to figure prominently in the movements associated with conciliar reforms and renewal.

During the decade following the end of World War II, American Catholicism had prospered both in the number of the faithful and in their fervor, particularly among the younger families. Statistically the *Official Catholic Directory*[2] in 1958 gave the Catholic population of the country, including Alaska and

[2] (New York, 1958) Statistical summary insert.

Hawaii, as 36,023,977, although some observers who based their statistics on other sources maintained the Catholic population to be over forty millions or even over fifty millions. There were two bastions of Catholic life: the Catholic family and the Sunday Mass. But, just as the religious renewal of the postwar decade was shared in many aspects with Protestants and other religious bodies, much that was prominent in the fervent Catholicism of the postwar decade was not peculiar to Catholicism.

All America had participated in the blossoming of young families among the returned veterans. Catholics had joined with non-Catholics in taking advantage of the government scholarships to complete interrupted educations. Catholics had, like others, taken advantage of government loans to move to the suburbs and build homes. It was among these younger Catholic families that there grew the elements later recognized as the "new" Catholicism. Scarcely half of these parents had been trained in the Catholic school system. Of the Catholics who had gone to college or beyond, an even smaller portion had studied in Catholic colleges and universities. This latest generation of Catholics had all come a full generation after the restoration of frequent Holy Communion as the sign of full Catholic life. Also this generation of Catholics had in large measure achieved high school education and, in a much lower percentage, collegiate training. There was with the aid of government grants a significant increase in the number of Catholic graduate students. Naturally there was among these young Catholics a sense of progress.

Again a scrutiny of Catholic publications at the end of the decade of the fifties shows that American Catholicism was prosperous but unexciting. There was practically no national Catholic movement outside of the usual fraternal and social organizations. Catholics faced the dilemma of forming their own business or educational society or of being swallowed up in a general organization. Neither choice was satisfactory. The Catholic press, meanwhile, was given over almost entirely to local news. Even the National Catholic Welfare Conference exercised little influence because of the supremacy of diocesan government and the general conservatism of the hierarchy. The efforts of Monsignor Frederick Hochwalt of the Catholic Educational Association to defend the rights of private schools to government aid attracted little attention.

Only on what might be called the lower levels of Catholic organization were there signs that the period of postwar religious fervor had brought changes. An unofficial estimate in late 1957 claimed 25,000 units were active in the Christian Family Movement and that the Movement had spread into 150 dioceses in all but six states.[3] Far less numerous were the groups fostering liturgical renaissance, seeking lay participation through dialogue in the Mass, the use of liturgical prayers, and the introduction of the vernacular in Church services. There was some agitation—chiefly from these same groups—for greater lay participation in the administration of Church affairs. In the fall of 1957 there appeared in *Commonweal* several articles on the proposed role of the layman in the Church. Actual statistics on Catholics were scarce, but practical parish priests estimated that the attendance of the faithful at Sunday Mass was approximately seventy-five percent. Most professed Catholics went to Mass at least on occasion. The greatest cause of pastoral worry was the large number of marriages with non-Catholics, nearly one fifth of all Catholic marriages. One third of the Catholics entering such marriages were said to leave the Church. In matters of social and political movement, the Catholic body was generally inert. As Catholics they were represented in the press, especially the diocesan weekly, as opposed to birth control and to communism. The myth of the Catholic vote in politics persisted, although close observers found the political bond to be rather nationalistic or social and seldom religious.

If there was a point of tension in American Catholicism, it was probably the parish school system now greatly overcrowded because of the continuing population movement to the cities and to suburbia and the impossibility of producing schools, and above all religious teachers, to accommodate the rising numbers of youngsters. Within the sisterhoods which taught most Catholic schools, there existed another movement propelled by the First Congress of Major Superiors at Notre Dame in 1952 and furthered by regional meetings in 1954, the regional conferences to plan juniorates in 1956, and the foundation of the Sister Formation Conferences at Seattle, Washington, in 1957.[4] The sisters with the approval of Catholic educators were making serious efforts to insure that the sisters who bore the brunt of the Catholic school effort received proper training before they entered the classroom, continued their training during their educational careers, and had proper living and working conditions while employed in teaching. This system of Catholic schools was the most sensitive point in

[3] *America*, September 14, 1957, p. 410.
[4] *New Catholic Encyclopedia* (New York, 1967) "Sister Formation Movement," XIII, 261–71.

the whole national Catholic organization and was probably the most misunderstood. Only the force of canon law, gradually enforced since 1918, could explain the effort to maintain the Catholic school system, which had never been able to handle even two thirds of the Catholic children of the nation and which was now called upon to embrace the postwar population explosion.

Canon law best explained how the thirty-eight millions of Catholics retained their unity despite the fact that American Catholicism included all national origins, crossed class and race barriers, and adapted itself to all languages and rites. In 1958 the lack of a national organization, except that provided by canon law (which was strictly clerical in cast and operation), hid from the public the chief dissatisfaction in American Catholicism—the lack of lay leadership and the lack of any realistic provision for lay participation in the government of the Church. There were in nearly every urban center a few Catholics who were prominent in business, such as John Coleman of New York, Ignatius A. O'Shaughnessy of St. Paul, Thomas Murray of New York. Many labor leaders, such as George Meany and Joseph Curran, were Catholics. There were Catholic governors and senators, especially two young victors in the 1958 senatorial elections, Eugene McCarthy of Minnesota and John F. Kennedy of Massachusetts, and a few Catholics prominent in the field of amusements and sports such as Bing Crosby, Loretta Young, Stan Musial. But even these Catholic laymen had little or nothing to say in the government or the management of the Church. Further, laymen had little voice in the public affairs of the Church because practically all the editors of Catholic weeklies were priests. The two chief exceptions, among the conservatives, were Patrick Scanlan, the managing editor of the Brooklyn *Tablet,* and Joseph Matt of the *Wanderer* of St. Paul. William Buckley, Jr. was a Catholic conservative but his journal was secular. The chief voice of the liberal lay Catholic was the *Commonweal,* and its editors were Edward Skillen, John Cogley, and James O'Gara, but the *Commonweal* never had a subscription list worthy of its fine effort. John G. Deedy, Jr., of the Worcester *Catholic Free Press* and John A. O'Connor of the San Francisco *Monitor* were also liberal voices among the Catholic weeklies. Catholic literary leaders such as Helen White, Edwin O'Connor, and Paul Horgan gave good examples but did not write on current religious topics.

Most Catholic journalists with a national following were priests. The two most important editors were Father Matthew Smith of the Denver *Register* chain and Father Richard Ginder of the

Sunday Visitor chain. The editor of the *Catholic World,* Father John Sheerin, C.S.P., also was influential. Many of the weekly diocesan papers were little more than diocesan chronicles and bulletins of the local chancery, and their editors were of minor importance. Exceptions were Monsignor Francis Lally of the Boston *Pilot* and Father Raymond Bosler of the *Indiana Catholic Record;* and the magazine editors, Father Thurston Davis of *America* and Father John Reedy of the *Ave Maria,* exercised independent opinions. Other exceptions to the diocesan limit of influence of priests were the two leaders of the Social Action Department of the N.C.W.C., Fathers George Higgins and John Cronin, S.S., who continued the tradition of fostering the doctrines of the social encyclicals begun under Fathers John A. Ryan and Raymond McGowan. Monsignor Frederick Hochwalt combined his position in the N.C.W.C. with the secretariat of the National Catholic Educational Association to defend the position of Catholic education.

Few indeed were the bishops of national importance. European observers were surprised to learn that the bishops numbered two hundred. Bishop Fulton Sheen was above diocesan limits as the national director of the Propagation of the Faith but, by dropping his television program, had lost much of his impact. Bishop John J. Wright of Pittsburgh was generally known and respected for his speaking ability and his ecumenical activities. Archbishops Joseph Ritter of St. Louis and Albert Meyer of Chicago had not yet become the spokesmen for Catholic liberal causes that they were to be in the Council. The great exception to the diocesan limit of episcopal power was Cardinal Francis Spellman who, despite advancing years and the death of his close personal friend, Pope Pius XII, was recognized as an undaunted defender of Catholic interests. Similarly, Cardinal Richard Cushing of Boston, a generous friend of the poor and of the missions, was respected for his humility and forthright statements and later for his defense of the religious fidelity of John F. Kennedy.

Two traditions particularly handicapped the American bishop in his dealings with the American public, aside from the limitations of his episcopal office as imposed by canon law. Nearly all Catholic bishops were very faithful in observing the tradition of separation of Church and State, seldom making any statement on public questions to which political significance might be attached. Some bishops spoke out strongly against communism and in favor of movie censorship and censorship of books and against contraceptive literature, but they maintained they were speaking of moral issues. Even here most bishops refrained from trying to influence legislatures. And, secondly, probably because of the controversies of a previous generation, they abstained generally from any ecumenical cooperation with non-Catholic churchmen and organizations. This was a serious handicap for the leader of a religious minority. It was significant that ecumenical movements among Catholics were usually led by laymen and that these same Catholics were frequently leaders in new liturgical movements and very active in promoting lay leadership.

The role of the Catholic layman was discussed, but no one offered a solution to the lack of lay leadership. There was no agitation for lay participation in the priestly ceremonies or diaconate but the liturgical movement did advocate a greater use of the vernacular and the final liturgical decrees under Pope Pius XII called for greater lay participation in the liturgy of the Mass. Lay participation in the American Catholic school system was urged. The critical essay of Father John Tracy Ellis in 1955 on the Catholic intellectual had had far wider and more lasting effect than anyone could have foreseen. Certainly his major contention could not be denied, that American Catholics lacked their share of intellectual leaders and, further, were not utilizing the lay leaders in the financial and educational projects of the Church. Efforts by some ecclesiastical writers to explain away these facts served chiefly to make them better known.

A book by a lay educator, Thomas O'Dea, *American Catholic Dilemma,*[5] seemed to presume the failure of the Catholic intellectual by giving the factors explaining the failure. When Father John Cavanaugh, C.S.C., in a Washington Communion breakfast talk on December 15, 1957, repeated Ellis' charges with the phrase, "Where are the Catholic Salks, Oppenheimers, Einsteins?" the reactions from members of the hierarchy, college presidents, and apologists were very strong in condemnation of Father Cavanaugh. Since the presumption of these criticisms was failure of those in charge of the Catholic educational system, there began to appear in some Catholic papers, notably in the correspondents' columns, letters and articles attacking the administration of Catholic schools and calling for greater sharing with lay people of the financial and administrative work of the Catholic school system. These complaints usually contained at least implicitly two errors. The first was the presumption that the Catholic school system was in charge of the education of all Catholics, instead of only about fifty percent of Catholic children.

[5] (New York, 1958) with an introduction by Gustave Weigel, S.J.

The second error presumed that, since Catholics did not achieve their share of intellectual and social leadership, Catholic schools must be responsible for the failure and were therefore inferior. The studies published subsequently found that generally Catholic schools were not inferior to the public schools. Other criticisms appeared charging misuse of funds and questioning the cost of the Catholic system. There was really no forum outside the press where these problems could be discussed, and the loyal Catholic lay people, following the tradition of a minority, did not care to air its internal problems in public. But the victory of Senator John F. Kennedy in Massachusetts in 1958 made evident that Roman Catholicism was more than a private affair in the United States. On January 2, 1960, Kennedy formally announced his candidacy for the presidency. Although the criticisms of Catholic schools and clerical administration continued, the most important fact in American Catholicism in 1960 was the Kennedy candidacy.

Many Americans, and that included most Catholics, felt after the defeat of Alfred E. Smith in 1928 that the presidency was beyond the reach of a Catholic. Yet, John Kennedy came near being nominated by the Democratic Party for Vice President in 1956; he had won with an overwhelming majority in his 1958 campaign for reelection as senator; he had the backing of a wealthy and active family. He was unwilling to believe that his religion could prevent his election as President. There were, of course, Catholics who did not agree with him in his political views. There was also a mild controversy among Catholics in 1959 over his statement in *Look* magazine that he would regard the obligations of his oath of office as superior to his religious obligations. But Catholics could not help hoping that the unwritten barrier between Catholics and the presidency be lifted. Catholic editors found it very difficult and at times impossible to stand aside quietly when others questioned the loyalty of Catholics or the ability of a Catholic to fill the office of President. Liberal Protestant clergymen and laymen, particularly Dr. John Bennett and Dr. Reinhold Niebuhr, took the Kennedy side of the argument.

The first real test of the Kennedy thesis was the Wisconsin primary, a state with a large Catholic minority, and Kennedy won handily over Hubert Humphrey.[6] The next test was the West Vir-

---

[6] Theodore C. Sorenson, *Kennedy*, Bantam Edition (New York, 1966) Chapter V, "The Primaries," pp. 138–178. Arthur M. Schlesinger, *A Thousand Days* (Cambridge, 1965) is less complete on the primaries. Lawrence H. Fuchs, *John F. Kennedy and American Catholicism* (New York, 1967) believes that Catholicism in the United States was modified by Kennedy.

ginia primary where there was a much smaller Catholic minority. Kennedy went on to win that primary and eventually the Democratic nomination in the convention on the first ballot. His opponent was Vice President Richard Nixon who did nothing to raise the religious issue. Nevertheless, the press was filled with discussions and speculations about the religious issue. Somehow most Catholics felt that their Americanism was on trial, and the relations between Catholic and non-Catholic became tense. One of the most important events of the campaign was a televised interview between Kennedy and the Greater Houston Ministerial Association in which Kennedy strongly defended his ability as a Catholic to fulfill his obligations if elected President.[7] The voting was close and there has been much speculation about the factors that determined the election. Certainly Kennedy's religion hampered him seriously in certain areas of the country but many Catholics voted for a Democratic nominee for the first time. Altogether the campaign had been a tremendous experience for American Catholicism. The American Catholic way of living had been exposed to unrelenting criticism and defended by Protestant and Jewish friends as well as by Catholics. The great achievement of the election of Kennedy was that the barrier against a Catholic's becoming President was erased, and the American Catholic was by just that much elevated socially and politically. Tension between Catholic and non-Catholic was by no means ended by the election, but the happy regime of John F. Kennedy as President helped to lessen the tension, and his death at the hands of an assassin in 1963 sealed with glory the first Catholic presidency.

The campaign and the election had not changed any Catholic belief or practice but they had improved greatly the public acceptance of Catholicism. During the election year there was less interest in the Catholic press in the controversies among Catholics. Nevertheless, the discussion about the faults of Catholic education continued. The Catholic press also participated mildly in the controversy over the U-2 air incident; it gave only some attention to the Negro sit-in strikes in the South and the discussion of the morality of our foreign policy. Questions were raised about the increasing costs of Catholic schools and about the role of the layman in the modern Church. Some laymen asked why the final liturgical document of Pius XII calling for greater lay participation in the Mass had not been put into effect in the country.

[7] Theodore H. White, *The Making of the President 1960* (New York, 1962) pp. 260–262. Kennedy's speech is given in the Appendix, pp. 391–393.

Perhaps the Kennedy campaign had a side effect in causing the Catholic layman to speak out. A few new names emerged besides those who contributed regularly to *Commonweal* and *America*. Among them were Donald McDonald, Donald Thorman, John Leo, Daniel Callahan, and Michael Novak. Under the editorship of Father John Reedy, the *Ave Maria* changed from a devotional magazine to a weekly periodical in which all topics of interest to middle-class Catholics were discussed. Certain diocesan weeklies began to open their pages to critical opinions. Notable among them were the *Catholic Messenger* of Davenport, Iowa, the Worcester *Catholic Free Press,* and the *Oklahoma Courier.* Laymen who broke into print were critical of Catholic schools, pushed for liturgical reforms, and sought for new ways of lay participation in the activities of the Church.

But there were some who sensed the change going on among American Catholics. Father Gustave Weigel, S.J., one of the most active Catholic leaders, spoke of this change to a group of Catholic laymen in July 1960.

We have, however, in our time, a special problem. The world is new. The situation of 1960 is revolutionary. It is quite unlike the world of 1900. Consequently, the relationship of the action of the laity and hierarchy must be seen in the light of the new world. . . .

We are living in a revolutionary moment. World society and our own institutions are changing. We can see the change reflected in new approaches to old problems, in our own critical evaluation of our role in the new world. We can see the change in this meeting.

One thing we have noticed in your presence today here as a group. The laity have manifested an eagerness to do something more than to assume the layman's posture of 1900. That was a simple posture as described by an English Catholic. He was to be on his knees and his hand was to hover over the collection basket.

To many of our Catholics today, that posture is too simple. Our Catholics today have been through all the forms of education which our time can offer. In most cases, as for example in our country, they're quite secure in their Catholic status; they're not on the defensive. They want now a holiness proper to their lives. They want to know theology. They want a program of responsible action. . . .[8]

In the meantime the central commission preparing for the Council and the subcommittees had drawn many American bishops and theologians to Rome to help prepare for the Council which was now set to open on October 11, 1962. In *America* and *Commonweal* and in the correspondence columns of the weekly

[8] *Act,* (January 1961) p. 3.

Catholic press there were appeals for lay participation in the Council and pleas for full coverage of its activities in the press. Meanwhile Pope John XXIII by his humble and smiling openness to all had become a symbol of a new spirit in Catholicism which through the Council promised to renew and reform the Church.

The full story of Vatican II has not been written[9] and that includes the activities of the American episcopate. Most of the American episcopate had received part of their training in Rome, although some had been to Rome only for visits. The Council, however, was a new experience since there were no American survivors of Vatican I. Nor were there survivors of the last American Plenary Council of 1884. As a matter of fact most of the hierarchy had not had the experience of even a diocesan synod. The first important fact for them was that in the Council each bishop was the equal of the others except for the Pope. The influence of older and more experienced prelates was cut sharply and the all-powerful role of the Curia was also limited by the actions of the Council itself. A second important experience of American bishops was the realization that, instead of examining and following the decrees of a central authority, the bishops themselves with the Pope were the authority. The problems they were to discuss were also universal in their application.

For Americans, one of the less fortunate aspects of the first session of the Council was the attempt made to control the published reports on the Council. The N.C.W.C. issued colorless accounts, and the American press followed the rules laid down by the Council, but the European press followed its own rules and published an almost complete account of the sessions. The first breakthrough for American readers came with the publication of "Letters from Vatican City" in *The New Yorker* under the pen name Xavier Rynne, depicting the differences among the prelates, the general division between the liberal bishops from northern Europe and the Curia and other presumably conservative prelates, and making a few observations about the activities of the prelates. The American public was impatient to learn more. *The New York Times* began to publish frequent reports and, beginning with the second session, daily reports on the events of the Council were available to the American press.

But the actions of the American bishops were seldom spectacular. The American bishops were generally classified with the mod-

[9] Vincent A. Yzermans, editor, *American Participation in the Second Vatican Council* contains the interventions of the American members of the Council with commentaries on the Council documents.

erate group of the Council. Cardinal McIntyre and Archbishop Vagnozzi were reported as conservatives. Cardinals Ritter and Meyer, who were both active, were generally classified as daring and liberal. Archbishop Paul Hallinan achieved recognition for his work on the constitution on the liturgy and, until ill health hampered him, for his activity throughout the Council. The American bishops were most active in the discussion of the documents on the Jews and on religious liberty. Cardinal Spellman spoke occasionally but was a moderate in most of his opinions. As a matter of fact the majority in the Council was liberally inclined, although the overwhelming majority votes on the final documents would indicate that the numerical divergence within the Council was less than the press claimed. That there were wide divergences in opinions among the prelates on certain subjects was manifest in the speeches and discussions, but, in general, the Council was carried on in the spirit of Pope John's *aggiornamento,* a bringing of the Church up to date. American Catholics strained their ears to learn what was going on in Rome, and the movements that had been manifest on the lower levels of American Catholicism found in the news from Rome justification for a new spirit. Pope John and his condemnation of "the prophets of doom" were stimulants to the American Catholicism that was searching for solutions to its own problems. Naturally, then, Americans shared the alarm of the Council at the illness of Pope John; and the sorrow at his death on June 3, 1963, in the American press was general and genuine. His successor, Pope Paul VI, was well received as a friend and former visitor but not with the warmth accorded Pope John.

Just as the American bishops were participating in a new experience, American Catholicism through the press watched the events of the Council for some solutions of American Catholic problems. Despite the absence of the bishops from the country, there was a continuous discussion of the role of the layman in the Church, of a proposal that the Church's rules on contraception be changed, and of proposed reforms in the rules for sisters and in the program for seminary training. A new critical spirit appeared on the campuses of several Catholic colleges. The Catholic press began to take sides in the liberal-conservative dispute going on in the Council. The whole nation seemed more alert to religious problems.

It is important to distinguish in these multiplying arguments those which arose because of the Council and those which had their origins in American postwar conditions. The lectures and arguments of certain liberal theologians, such as Hans Küng, helped to bring the two together so that the word *aggiornamento* was to be used for all reform and renewal, and there was a tendency to make all arguments for change part of the Johannine reform. The attack on the Catholic school system, however, had no real connection with the Council. The agitation for greater recognition of the laity was under way before Pope John called the Council. The argument for reform in the sisterhoods seemed to arise because of the crisis in the Catholic parochial system in the face of the population explosion. The incentive that produced the Sister Formation Conference came originally from Rome in 1950 and from the writings and speeches of Cardinal Suenens. The argument for reforming the seminary and the arguments against clerical celibacy reached the public during the Council and seemed to receive new impetus from the preliminary discussions before the Council; yet there were many criticisms of seminary training published in the United States before the Council met. The pleas for greater freedom for the clergy seemed to have risen independently of the Council, and the arguments against celibacy were attributed chiefly to clergy in the Netherlands. The attacks on clerical celibacy in certain American periodicals and the sharp criticism of the regimen of nuns appeared about the same time as the first arguments about such matters to be discussed in the Council. In some seminaries the changes in discipline were in effect before the Council met, and the spread of new ideas about Scripture study, liturgical experimentation, and the arguments about the relations between clergy and laymen and priests and bishops had spread orally without public discussion in the weekly Catholic press. Not all but most of the "new breed" of clergymen in American Catholicism were those who carried on or were involved in the changes in the seminaries.

Early in 1963, Dr. Hans Küng of the University of Tübingen, a *peritus* at the Council, gave a series of lectures on the Council and reform to Catholic and mixed audiences across the country, especially to university audiences. A speaker of ability and a strong protagonist of the liberal side of the Council, he aroused much attention by his condemnation of the conservatives and his assurance that the liberals would make great changes in the Church. He was criticized by conservatives and refused permission to speak in Los Angeles by Cardinal McIntyre and at Catholic University. The public reaction was generally favorable to Küng, and the acceptance of his ideas and those of other liberal speakers became a kind of touchstone in a sharp controversy in the American press and in lectures throughout the country. Actually the Council had issued no decrees, although it had passed the constitution on the liturgy and the declaration on the means of social communication, but the stories from Rome about the Council's division on the reform of the Curia and the division over the question of revelation, coupled with the refusal of the Catholic University of its forum to Küng, Father Godfrey Diekmann, O.S.B., Father John Courtney Murray, S.J., and Father Gustave Weigel, S.J., stimulated greatly the American interest in the Council and gave encouragement to those American Catholics who were agitating for reforms in the Church in this country. Father Murray had not been invited to the first session but was taken to the second session as a *peritus* by Cardinal Spellman. He became the architect of the document on religious liberty, wherein he included his ideas on Church and State for which he had suffered a virtual persecution in the years before the Council.

The desires of many American laymen for participation in the liturgy were soon to be answered by the formal decree on the liturgy at the end of the session in 1963 and the press began carrying stories on reform in the American seminaries, on suggestions for change in the Catholic school systems, on reform in the rules for the sisterhoods, and on proposals for new relations with non-Catholics. The tendency toward anticlericalism seemed to receive new impetus in these discussions about reform. When Father William DuBay of Los Angeles refused to obey Cardinal McIntyre in matters of public policy on housing, the liberal press rushed to his support.

The intensified argument about civil rights was an important side issue for Catholics. Although Catholic Negroes numbered only about four percent of the American Negro population, the Catholic bishops, generally, and particularly Archbishop Rummel in the South, followed the Popes' decrees which recognized no distinction of race or color. In the public actions of protest against discrimination some sisters and priests took a prominent part, notably in Selma, Alabama, and in Chicago. By presidential appointment Father Theodore Hesburgh, C.S.C., also served as a member of the very important national Civil Rights Commission. There were, however, Catholics, particularly where an area was inhabited by a national group, who resisted efforts of Negroes to move into their neighborhoods and fought efforts to secure open housing legislation.

Events in the Council were soon well known in the United States, at least to those Catholics who were interested in them. The

division into liberals and conservatives in American Catholicism
seemed approved by the division in the Council. By the end of the
second session the first important constitution, that on the liturgy,
had been officially enacted. The division between the liberals and
conservatives became apparent when the liberals hastened to make
the changes allowed by the decree while the conservatives retained
the Latin, the altar against the wall, and the old forms as long as
possible. The argument about lay participation in the Church
received a certain impetus from this constitution, but the lay participation in the Mass was limited. Nevertheless, there were manifestations of reform that did not have hierarchical approval. In
the management of Church property there have been a few efforts
to bring laymen into greater participation in trusteeships but the
most important changes of this type have been the sharing of the
ownership and administration of Catholic colleges and universities. Leading in these changes were Notre Dame, St. Louis, and
Georgetown. A source of great scandal in the Church was the
peremptory firing of many professors at St. John's University in
Brooklyn and the subsequent strike of the faculty. Despite a very
confused public discussion, the university continued to operate
but most of the defects of American Catholic education were
aired in the discussion. The discussion of the roles of the sisters
in the reformed Church had startling effects within the sisterhoods
themselves. Large numbers of sisters—some members for many
years—left their communities, sometimes in a body. Following the
enactment of the constitution for religious reform, there were
many changes in religious costume and in the restrictions about
the public conduct of sisters.

A new public discussion on celibacy and the hardships of
priestly life made the resignations of many priests and their subsequent marriages more acceptable to the American public. Estimates of the number of priests who were seeking dispensations
from their priestly vows have ranged into the thousands, and hundreds of priests have married publicly without seeking dispensations. A further change in the public life of American Catholics
was the brotherly recognition of non-Catholics. Protestants have
been embraced as "separated brethren" and allowed to speak from
Catholic pulpits and to share in officiating at marriages. In these
departures the essentials have not been changed but the variations
in acceptances and practice have been wide.

An event of spectacular importance in the history of Catholicism in the United States was the visit of Pope Paul VI to the
United Nations in New York on October 2, 1965. The Pope made

the trip by air to New York. While his visit was officially to the UN in the interests of peace, he was the guest of Cardinal Spellman, toured through Harlem, held a conference with non-Catholic clergymen, and visited President Lyndon Johnson, Vice President Hubert Humphrey, and Secretary of State Dean Rusk at the Waldorf-Astoria before addressing the United Nations Assembly. His speech to the Assembly was essentially a plea for peace. That night the Pope said Mass publicly in Yankee Stadium before returning by air to Rome. Besides the throngs that watched him in New York, millions were able to follow the ceremonies and hear his address by television.

A new element in American Catholic discussion has been the *National Catholic Reporter,* begun October 28, 1964, under the direction of Robert G. Hoyt and Michael Greene, formerly editors of the Kansas City *Catholic Reporter.* The weekly newspaper, a laymen's project, was begun with the blessing and the aid of Bishop Charles Helmsing of Kansas City, Missouri. It quickly became an organ of lay and clerical criticism of the hierarchy and the Church, especially of those in the Church who cling to old and sentimental ideas. It soon acquired tens of thousands of subscribers and became a feared source of criticism, especially that from the pen of John Leo. Under the lead of the *National Reporter,* many other Catholic newspapers and magazines became much more critical of Catholic pietism, and even the secular press felt freer to talk of Catholic problems that were formerly not discussed publicly. The American press had come to recognize a "new" Catholicism and to marvel that the Catholicism which had seemed so solid and so immovable the decade before could have changed so much.[10]

The factor that has held American Catholicism in check through these changes is that the bishops have in general remained the same. A few earned themselves the reputation as liberals, some because of their speeches in the Council and others because of the quickness with which they have been carrying out the decrees of the Council, especially those on the liturgy and on ecumenism. For the most part the bishops have had to hold in check the extremists—those who refuse to change and those whose zeal for change seems limitless. They still have the Church debts to pay,

[10] Among the articles on the new Catholicism in the American press were "Not Peace but the Sword" by Edward R. F. Sheehan in the *Saturday Evening Post,* November 28, 1964, pp. 21–42; "Catholic Revolution" by Joseph Roddy in *Look,* February 9, 1965, pp. 21–27; and "How U.S. Catholics view their Church" in *Newsweek,* March 20, 1967, pp. 68–75.

although many of them would like laymen to help them in their financial problems. They have to meet approximately the same sacramental problems with a shrinking number of priests. Some have seminaries to reform, most have schools for which they will have to secure more lay teachers. They are very happy that the great majority of their priests continue to serve, even though the priests in their senates and associations have begun to demand a greater share in governing the diocese, even in choosing the bishop. One of the major changes in the government of the Church decreed by the Council is recognition of the collegiality of the bishops; the important phase for the United States has been the formation of the Bishops' Conference. The President of the Conference is Archbishop John Dearden of Detroit, elected November 14, 1966. The decrees of the Conference were at first minor, changing the rules for fast and abstinence and setting the dates for the liturgical changes, but unlike the N.C.W.C. the new Conference has power and with papal approval can make decrees binding on the American Church. There is here the major force for interpreting the further changes decreed by the Council or demanded by the American phase of the *aggiornamento*.

The first major document to be issued by the National Council of Catholic Bishops was the collective pastoral, *The Church in Our Day,* published on January 21, 1968. Based generally on the constitution, on the Church, *Lumen Gentium,* issued by Vatican II, it outlines the nature and activity of the Church not as a formal organization as it exists in the United States but as the "Mystery of the Church" as described by Popes John XXIII and Paul VI, yet as actually constituted by laity, priests, and bishops. At their November 1967 meeting, the Council of Bishops also issued two other statements reaffirming the existing traditions of the American hierarchy on Catholic schools and on clerical celibacy.

Important changes in the hierarchy included the election of Father Harold Perry, S.V.D., a Negro, as Auxiliary Bishop in New Orleans and the transfer of Archbishop Cody of New Orleans to Chicago to replace the deceased Cardinal Meyer. Auxiliary Bishop Philip Hannon of Washington became Archbishop of New Orleans. Cardinal Ritter died on June 10, 1967, and Cardinal Spellman on December 2, 1967. Bishop John Carberry of Columbus has been named Archbishop of St. Louis and Auxiliary Bishop Terence Cook, Archbishop of New York.

During the Second Vatican Council Pope Paul VI had reserved to himself the discussion of the Church's policy on birth control and appointed his own commission to study the problem. The commission divided on the question with a majority submitting a report supporting a relaxation of the Church's laws against artificial contraception and a minority submitting a report supporting the continuance of the existing laws. Finally on July 27, 1968 Pope Paul VI issued his Encyclical, *Humanae Vitae* dated July 25 in which while admitting that he was not speaking infallibly, he condemned all artificial contraception. The reaction to the Encyclical was mixed and several national councils of bishops issued their interpretation of the papal document. Finally at their annual meeting in Washington the National Council of Catholic Bishops on November 15 issued their second pastoral letter "Human Life in Our Day" in which they upheld the papal teaching against artificial birth control in their defense of the family and human life. The document also called for a reconsideration of the military draft law, recognized the right of the individual citizen to conscientious objection to a particular war and made a general plea for the reduction of nuclear armaments and for international peace.

Looking over the two decades since World War II, we see that the major changes in American Catholicism were the liturgical reforms and the relaxing of religious discipline. Despite the fact that most of the arguments in the Catholic press have been about Catholic intellectual efforts and the participation of the layman in the government of the Church, there has been no real change in the status of either question. There is still a lack of Catholic intellectuals and no real change in the status of the Catholic layman. *Aggiornamento* has become a word to cover all changes but many of the changes in American Catholicism during the past few years were already in evidence before Pope John XXIII became Pope.

READING LIST

The student beginning a study of the history of the Catholic Church in the United States is quickly made to realize that the Roman Catholic Church was a minority institution in the English-speaking world of the seventeenth century. Only when the number of Catholics grew by the immigration of non-English people would this minority become a recognizable part of the general history. Nevertheless during all the history of the English in the New World, there were Catholics in the English-speaking world; some were English or later Anglo-American, some Irish and Scotch, and others were from nearly every land of the earth. The history of American Catholicism is a part of the general history of the Church, but this reading list will not list the general account of Catholic history for these modern periods. Neither will it list the abundance of materials on French and Spanish religious efforts in colonial North America.

The Counter-Reformation in England needs a new historian. New material for such a story is quite abundant. Besides scattered family records in England and the Archives at Westminster, the reports sent to Rome by papal agents and others in the Archives of Propaganda, the Archives of the Papal Secretary of State in the Secret Vatican Archives, and the Barberini Collections in the Vatican Library have not been exhausted in the accounts now in print.

For original sources on the Catholic Church in English America, besides the occasional data in the *Maryland Archives,* chief centers are the Archdiocesan Archives at Baltimore, and the Jesuit Archives in Woodstock, Maryland. Much material on early American Catholicism has been destroyed by fires, floods, and other accidents. Nevertheless each diocesan chancery has some records of the diocesan history. Most religious institutions have some records of their previous history.

At the University of Notre Dame, an early librarian, James F. Edwards, attempted during the latter decades of the nineteenth century to organize The Catholic Archives of America in which he hoped to gather all the records of Catholicism in America, to which he hoped to add a reference library of printed sources and a museum of relics and pictorial records. The Catholic

Archives was maintained by his successors and in recent years, under the name of The Archives of the University of Notre Dame, the Archives obtained several collections of personal papers and related items about American Catholics as well as about the University of Notre Dame. Microfilm copies have been accumulated of American letters to the mission centers of France, Germany, Austria, and Ireland and of the American letters to the Sacred Congregation of Propaganda from 1622 to 1865.

The Manuscript Collections of the Catholic University of America contain several important collections of personal papers, chiefly the personal papers of Terence Powderly, John Mitchell, Bishop Francis Haas, Philip Murray, and Monsignor John A. Ryan. Other collections exist at Georgetown University and, for Texas history, in the chancery office of the Diocese of Austin, Texas.

For the general history of the Catholic Church in the present territory of the United States, John Gilmary Shea published *The History of the Catholic Church in the United States* (New York, 1886–1892) in four volumes. His history ends with the Second Plenary Council. Although it is now outdated by the discovery of new materials and although he was handicapped by an effort to maintain the history of the chief ecclesiastical divisions intact, this history has not been replaced by any better or more complete history. Thomas O'Gorman published a one-volume condensation of Shea's study with some extensions in 1907, and John Tracy Ellis has published a brief survey based on four lectures, *American Catholicism* (Chicago, 1956). While there are some superior studies of periods, areas, or persons, the student has to form his own history, with an understanding that these materials have not been thoroughly evaluated or related and that vast source materials now available by microfilm and photostat have yet to be incorporated even in these local or personal studies. There cannot be a guide to American Catholic Church History, there can be only some suggested accounts of historical writings and sources for further reading.

To understand the position of the Catholic minority who settled in Maryland in 1634, some notion of the position of the Catholic minority in England must be had. Two books by Philip Hughes: *The Catholic Question* and *Rome and the Counter-Reformation in England* (London, 1944) are useful. For older accounts W. Mazière Brady's *Annals of the Catholic Hierarchy in England and Scotland, 1585–1871* (Rome, 1877) and Charles Dodd's *Church History of England* edited by M.A. Tierny in four volumes are enlightening. *The Memoirs of Gregorio Panzani*, edited by the Reverend Joseph Berington (Birmingham, 1793) is an important but controversial report on Roman Catholicism in England in 1634–1636. Other reports by Roman agents and representatives in Roman Archives now available in microfilm indicate the sad position of Roman Catholicism in England when Lord Baltimore applied for his charter.

CHAPTER ONE

For a brief survey of Spanish colonization in America, Edward G. Bourne's *Spain in America* (New York, 1904) is old but still useful. Good selections of contemporary accounts of the Spanish settlements are to be found in F.V. Hodge and T.H. Lewis, *Spanish Explorers in the Southern United States, 1528–1543* and Herbert E. Bolton, *Spanish Exploration in the Southwest, 1542–1706.* Herbert Bolton, *The Rim of Christendom* and Paul Horgan, *Conquistadores in North American History* are readable accounts of phases of Spanish adventure in the new world. On the French exploration and settlement, Reuben G. Thwaites, *France in America* is also old but balanced, and Francis Parkman, *The Jesuits in North America in the Seventeenth Century* is a literary classic that is somewhat sympathetic to the Catholic French but never gives up the Parkman theme of English Protestant superiority. A good collection of original accounts of the era is found in Edna Kenton's selection and edition of the Jesuit reports in *Black Gown and Redskins* (New York, 1956); first published as *Jesuit Relations and Allied Documents 1610–1791* (New York, 1926).

For the colony of Maryland, Charles Andrews, *The Colonial Period of American History,* Vol. II *The Settlements,* pp. 274–379 is a brief political and legal account. J. Thomas Scharf, *History of Maryland* (Volume I) *1600–1765* and (Volume II) *1766–1812* (Baltimore, 1879) is rich in quoted documents. Thomas Hughes, S.J., *The History of the Society of Jesus in North America, Colonial and Federal* has two volumes of text and two volumes of documents (New York, 1907–1911). Edwin Warfield Beitzell, *The Jesuit Missions of St. Mary's County, Maryland* (Abell, Maryland, 1960) is a good supplement to Scharf. The Catholic story needs retelling in the context of the other history. Thomas O'Brien Hanley, S.J., *Their Rights and Liberties* (Westminster, 1959) is an interesting effort to find an influence of St. Thomas More on Lord Baltimore.

CHAPTER TWO

Most studies of the prerevolutionary period give only brief accounts of the first Charles Carroll in Maryland. Probably the most satisfactory is found in Ellen Hart Smith, *Charles Carroll of Carrollton* (Cambridge, 1942) pp. 3–42 and Kate Mason Rowland, *The Life of Charles Carroll of Carrollton, 1737–1832,* 2 vol. (New York, 1898) I, 1–18. Scharf pays slight attention to the first Charles Carroll—J. Thomas Scharf, *History of Maryland,* 3 vol. (Baltimore, 1879).

Hughes concentrates almost entirely on the Jesuits—Thomas Hughes, S.J., *The History of the Society of Jesus in North America, Colonial and Federal* (New York, 1907–1911).

Shea, despite his limitations, has not been replaced as a balanced historian of the Church—John Gilmary Shea, *The History of the Catholic Church in the United States,* 4 vol. (New York, 1886–1892) I, 68–99, 344–453.

Much local information is found in Edwin Warfield Beitzell, *The Jesuit Missions of St. Mary's County, Maryland* (Abell, Maryland, 1960) pp. 44–69. Charles A. Barker, *The Background of the Revolution in Maryland* (New Haven, 1940) is a well balanced account of the economic, social, and political causes of the Revolution but does not pay close attention to the Catholic colonists.

CHAPTER THREE

The story of Catholics in the American Revolution has been retold in great measure by Peter Guilday in *Life and Times of John Carroll, Archbishop of Baltimore (1735–1815)* 2 vol. (New York, 1922) I, 1–368. Annabelle Melville, *John Carroll of Baltimore* (New York, 1955) is briefer. Charles Metzger, S.J., *Catholics and the American Revolution* (Chicago, 1962) gives the details of the Catholic position, with a slight tendency to argue that Catholics had a religious interest in the success of the revolt. Edwin Warfield Beitzell, *The Jesuit Missions of St. Mary's County, Maryland* (Abell, Maryland, 1960) gives the parish records for the period in Maryland. Joseph L.J. Kirlin, *Catholicity in Philadelphia* (Philadelphia, 1909) has a brief but interesting account of Catholics in Philadelphia during the Revolution. Robert H. Lord, John E. Sexton, and Edward T. Harrington, *History of the Archdiocese of Boston, 1604–1943,* 3 vol. (New York, 1944) I, 220–372 is a good account of Catholicism in the land of the Puritan during this period.

CHAPTER FOUR

For the episcopate of John Carroll, the best accounts are again: Peter Guilday, *Life and Times of John Carroll, Archbishop of Baltimore (1735–1815)* 2 vol. (New York, 1922); John Gilmary Shea, *The History of the Catholic Church in the United States,* 4 vol. (New York, 1886–1892); and Annabelle Melville, *John Carroll of Baltimore* (New York, 1955). For the history of the laity of the period, useful biographies of Charles Carroll of Carrollton are by Ellen Hart Smith (Cambridge, 1942) and Kate Mason Rowland, 2 volumes (New York, 1897).

Local accounts of value are: Joseph L.J. Kirlin, *Catholicity in Philadelphia* (Philadelphia, 1909) pp. 114–209; Robert H. Lord, John E. Sexton, and Edward T. Harrington, *History of the Archdiocese of Boston, 1604–1943,* 3 vol. (New York, 1944) I, 376–714; John Talbot Smith, *The Catholic Church in New York,* 2 vol. (New York, 1905) I, 20–34; and James R. Bayley, *A Brief Sketch of the Early History of the Catholic Church on the Island of New York,* 2d ed. (New York, 1870) pp. 50–83. Edwin Warfield Beitzell, *The Jesuit Missions of St. Mary's County, Maryland* (Abell, Maryland, 1960) pp. 68–101 gives detailed information of St. Mary's County until 1805. The following chapter extends the story to 1850.

For the Church on the frontier in what is now the Middle West, Sister Ramona Mattingly, *The Catholic Church on the Kentucky Frontier, 1785–1812* (Washington, 1936); Thomas T. McAvoy, C.S.C., *The Catholic Church in Indiana, 1780–1834* (New York, 1940) pp. 35–136; George Paré, *The Catholic Church in Detroit, 1701–1888* (Detroit, 1951) pp. 228–326; Herman J. Schauinger, *Stephen T. Badin, Priest in the Wilderness* (Milwaukee, 1956) pp. 1–184; and Roger Baudier, *The Catholic Church in Louisiana* (New Orleans, 1939) pp. 251–272. For the Kentucky frontier, Martin J. Spalding, *Sketches of the Early Catholic Missions of Kentucky from their Commencement in 1787 to the Jubilee of 1826* (Louisville, 1844) and *Sketches of the Life, Times and Character of the Rt. Rev. Benedict Joseph Flaget, First Bishop of Louisville* (Louisville, 1852) pp. 17–147 are irreplaceable because so many of the sources have been destroyed. Benjamin J. Webb, *The Centenary of Catholicity in Kentucky* (Louisville, 1884) has many interesting details, but the story is fragmented.

CHAPTER FIVE

For the brief episcopate of Archbishop Leonard Neale, there is the essay by Sister M. Bernetta Brislen, O.S.F., "The Episcopacy of Leonard Neale" in *Historical Records and Studies* of the U.S. Catholic Historical Society (New York, 1945) XXXIV, 20–111. Peter Guilday, *The Catholic Church in Virginia (1815–1822)* (New York, 1924) pp. 1–62, discusses the problems of Archbishop Neale, especially that in Norfolk. Much of this is also covered in his biography of Bishop John England, *The Life and Times of John England, First Bishop of Charleston (1786–1842)* 2 vol. (New York, 1927).

A satisfactory biography of Archbishop Ambrose Maréchal has not been written. The first account is that of John Gilmary Shea, *The History of the Catholic Church in the United States,* 4 vol. (New York, 1886–1892) III, 39–406, but it is divided into geographical areas and episcopates. Peter Guilday, *England,* see above, treats of the Maréchal episcopate in I, 124–473 and II, 68–110.

For local history during the Maréchal episcopate, one may consult for New York, John Talbot Smith, *The Catholic Church in New York* (New York, 1870), I, 55–77; for Philadelphia, Joseph L. J. Kirlin, *Catholicity in Philadelphia* (Philadelphia, 1909) pp. 214–261, and Francis E. Toursher, O.S.A., *The Hogan Schism and Trustee Troubles in St. Mary's Church, Philadelphia, 1820–29* (Philadelphia, 1930); for Boston, Robert H. Lord, John E. Sexton, and Edward T. Harrington, *History of the Archdiocese of Boston, 1604–1943,*

3 vol. (New York, 1944) I, 715–812; for Virginia, Guilday, *Virginia (1815–1822)*, see above, pp. 63–156; and for Charleston, Guilday, *England*, see above, I, 164–379.

The subject of trusteeism badly needs a revisionist historian. Patrick J. Dignan, *A History of the Legal Incorporation of Church Property in the United States, 1784–1932* (Washington, 1933) offers a brief and concise summary of the background of the problem. Peter Guilday, "Trusteeism" in *Historical Records and Studies,* U.S. Catholic Historical Society (New York, 1928) 7–73 is a brief study of the problem in Philadelphia and New York. Robert F. McNamara, "Trusteeism in the Atlantic States, 1785–1863" in the *Catholic Historical Review* (July, 1944) XXX, 135–154 and Alfred G. Stritch, "Trusteeism in the Old Northwest" in the same volume, pp. 156–164, are valuable summaries of the problem.

CHAPTER SIX

John Gilmary Shea, *The History of the Catholic Church in the United States,* 4 vol. (New York, 1886–1892) III, 407–721 and IV, 23–259, is the only comprehensive treatment of the period, but it is fragmented geographically. Archbishop James Whitfield also lacks a biography. See Father Bosco David Cestello, O.S.B., "James Whitfield, Fourth Archbishop of Baltimore: the Early Years, 1770–1828" in *Historical Records and Studies* (1957) XLV, 32–106, and Matthew Leo Panczyk, "James Whitfield, Fourth Archbishop of Baltimore, the Episcopal Years: 1828–1834," *Records of the American Catholic Historical Society,* LXXV, 222–251 and LXXVI, 21–53. The only other account is in Richard H. Clarke, *Lives of the Deceased Bishops of the Catholic Church in the United States,* 3 vol., rev. ed. (New York, 1888) I, 456–472. The first years of his archiepiscopate are treated in Guilday, *The Life and Times of John England, First Bishop of Charleston (1786–1842)* 2 vol. (New York, 1927) I, 453–596; II, 111–269.

Peter Guilday, *A History of the Councils of Baltimore (1791–1884)* (New York, 1932) treats the two Councils over which Whitfield presided, pp. 81–111. P. K. Guilday, *The National Pastorals of the American Hierarchy, 1792–1919* (Washington, 1923) gives the Pastorals published after each Council. They are important in expressing the minds of the bishops to the faithful. On Archbishop James Eccleston, the only biography is Columba E. Halsey, O.S.B., "The Life of Samuel Eccleston, Fifth Archbishop of Baltimore, 1801–1851," *Records of the American Catholic Historical Society,* LXXVI, 69–128 and LXXVII, 131–156. Clarke outlines Eccleston's career in *Deceased Bishops,* see above, I, 525–546. Guilday, *Councils,* see above, pp. 112–170 treats the five Provincial Councils held under Eccleston's direction. Guilday, *England,* see above, II, 270–554, treats of the activities of Bishop England under Eccleston until England's death in 1842.

The Church in Philadelphia is recorded by the story of Eccleston's successor in Hugh J. Nolan, *The Most Reverend Francis Patrick Kenrick, Third Bishop of Philadelphia 1830–1851* (Washington, 1948) pp. 82–434. Joseph L. J. Kirlin, *Catholicity in Philadelphia* (Philadelphia, 1909) pp. 246–351, is less technical.

On the nativistic reaction to the increase of Roman Catholicism, Ray Allen Billington, *The Protestant Crusade, 1800–1860, A Study of the Origins of American Nativism* (New York, 1938) is the best account, which can be supplemented by Nolan, above; Kirlin, above; and Robert H. Lord, John E. Sexton, and Edward T. Harrington, *History of the Archdiocese of Boston, 1604–1943,* 3 vol. (New York, 1944) II, 110–265; John Talbot Smith, *The Catholic Church in New York* (New York, 1870) I, 124–157; and John R. Hassard, *Life of the Most Reverend John Hughes, D.D., First Archbishop of New York with Extracts from His Private Correspondence* (New York, 1866) pp. 223–288.

On the West during this period Robert Trisco, *The Holy See and the Nascent Church in the Middle Western United States 1826–1850* (Rome, 1962) tries to cover too much territory but has made good use of the letters to the Sacred Congregation of Propaganda. Victor F. O'Daniel, O.P., *The Right Reverend Edward Dominic Fenwick, O.P., Founder of the Dominicans in the United States* . . . (Washington, 1920) is one of the better biographies treating of the Middle West. The biography of his successor, John Baptist Purcell, is not yet completed.

The account of the converts during the period is scattered in many accounts. Rev. Clarence E. Walworth, *The Oxford Movement in America or Glimpses of Life in an Anglican Seminary* (New York, 1893) treats an important phase. Vincent F. Holden, C.S.P., *The Yankee Paul, Isaac Thomas Hecker* (Milwaukee, 1958) pp. 1–224 is the best account of young Hecker, and Theodore Maynard, *Orestes Brownson, Yankee, Radical, Catholic* (New York, 1943) pp. 1–191, the best written account of young Brownson, the chief convert of the period.

On the American Catholics in the controversy over Negro slavery, Madeleine Hooke Rice, *American Catholic Opinion in the Slavery Controversy* (New York, 1944) examines the Catholic opinions and actions critically. The nearest to an official statement on the question appeared in *The Metropolitan* (June, 1855) III, 265–273, "The Catholic Church and the Question of Slavery." *Letters of the Late Bishop England to the Hon. John Forsyth on the Subject of Domestic Slavery* . . . (Baltimore, 1844) is an important contemporary document, although the Bishop did not live to complete the series.

CHAPTER SEVEN

John Gilmary Shea, *The History of the Catholic Church in the United States,* 4 vol. (New York, 1886–1892) IV, 359–714, treats this period in unequal detail with the usual geographical fragmentation. Ray Allen Billington, *The Protestant Crusade, 1800–1860, A Study of the Origins of American Nativism* (New York, 1938), treats of the second period of nativism after 1850, pp. 289–436, and seems to put the blame for the revival on the Catholics.

Robert H. Lord, John E. Sexton, and Edward T. Harrington, *History of the Archdiocese of Boston, 1604–1943*, 3 vol. (New York, 1944), consider this movement in New England in II, 648–703. John Talbot Smith, *The Catholic Church in New York*, 2 vol. (New York, 1870), devotes a chapter, I, 227–242, to the movement in New York. John Lancaster Spalding, *The Life of the Most Rev. M. J. Spalding, D.D., Archbishop of Baltimore* (New York, 1873) pp. 174–199, considers this movement in Kentucky.

Peter Guilday, *A History of the Councils of Baltimore (1791–1884)* (New York, 1932) pp. 167–186, sketches the activities of the First Plenary Council of Baltimore, and P. K. Guilday, *The National Pastorals of the American Hierarchy, 1792–1919* (Washington, 1923) pp. 181–196, reprints the pastoral issued at the end of the council.

James F. Connelly, *The Visit of Archbishop Gaetano Bedini to the United States of America (June, 1853–February, 1854)* (Rome, 1960) gives a good account of the Church in the United States in the beginning of the period. The Nuncio's report, pp. 190–287, is an invaluable document on the status of the Church in the country. Besides the local Catholic newspapers, there were two important magazines published by Catholics at this time. *The Metropolitan* (1853–1858) was a monthly publication in Baltimore, more or less under the supervision of Archbishop Francis P. Kenrick. *Brownson's Quarterly Review* (1844–1864) was recognized by the bishops for a while but they asked him not to publish their approval after some pungent articles in the 1850s. Thomas T. McAvoy, C.S.C., "Orestes A. Brownson and Archbishop Hughes in 1860," *Review of Politics*, XXIV, 19–47, treats of one of the stormiest periods of the difficulties between Brownson and the hierarchy. Henry Brownson treats of his father's problems at this time in the biography, Henry F. Brownson, *Orestes A. Brownson*, 3 volumes (Detroit, 1898–1900) II, 528–642 and III, 1–269.

For the story of Catholicism in the Civil War, Father Benjamin Blied, *Catholics and the Civil War* (Milwaukee, 1945) is the only book entirely devoted to this topic. Most writers have had to depend on Robert J. Murphy, "The Catholic Church in the United States During the Civil War Period 1852–1866," in *Records of the American Catholic Historical Society of Philadelphia* (1928) XXXIX, 271–346. Dom Aidan Germain, *Catholic Military and Naval Chaplains 1776–1917* (Washington, 1929) gives a brief account of the nature of their services and basic biographical data about the chaplains. Two recent studies give new information about Catholics in the South during the war: Michael V. Gannon, *Rebel Bishop, The Life and Era of Augustin Verot* (Milwaukee, 1964) pp. 31–114; and James J. Pillar, O.M.I., *The Catholic Church in Mississippi, 1837–65* (New Orleans, 1964) pp. 15–347. At the present time John R. Hassard's *Life of the Most Reverend John Hughes, D.D., First Archbishop of New York with Extracts from His Private Correspondence* (New York, 1886) pp. 356–505, has not been replaced for the role of Archbishop Hughes.

CHAPTER EIGHT

John Lancaster Spalding, *The Life of the Most Rev. M. J. Spalding, D.D., Archbishop of Baltimore* (New York, 1873) pp. 298–460, is the best account of the period at the present time, but, having been written so soon after the events, it lacks some perspective and wide sources. Peter Guilday, *A History of The Councils of Baltimore (1791–1884)* (New York, 1932) pp. 187–220, treats of the Second Plenary Council and his *The National Pastorals of the American Hierarchy, 1792–1919* (Washington, 1923) pp. 197–225, reprints the Pastoral issued from the Council, one of the best statements of the relations between the Catholic minority and the majority. S. Smith, *Notes on the Second Plenary Council of Baltimore* (New York, 1874) is less a commentary on the decrees of the Council than a summary of the canon law as known in the United States at the time.

On conditions among Catholics in the South during the Reconstruction period, Michael V. Gannon, *Rebel Bishop, The Life and Era of Augustin Verot* (Milwaukee, 1945) pp. 115–191, is very interesting and informing.

On the Catholics and labor disturbances and organizations during this period there is some uncertainty. J. Walter Coleman, *Labor Disturbances in Pennsylvania, 1850–1880* (Washington, 1936) treats of the Molly Maguires; Wayne G. Broehl, Jr., *The Molly Maguires* (Cambridge, 1964) stresses the court records and the diary of the spy; Fergus Macdonald, C.P., *The Catholic Church and the Secret Societies in the United States* (New York, 1946) pp. 1–99, treats of the secret organizations; Henry J. Browne, *The Catholic Church and the Knights of Labor* (Washington, 1949) pp. 1–33, of the union of the two factors before the Knights of Labor. Terence V. Powderly, *The Path I Trod: The Autobiography of Terence Vincent Powderly* (New York, 1940) has to be read with caution.

On American participation in Vatican Council I, James Hennesey, *The First Vatican Council, The American Experience* (New York, 1963) is the latest and best account, superseding Raymond J. Clancy, C.S.C., "American Prelates in the Vatican Council," *Historical Records and Studies* (1937) XXVIII, 7–135. Gannon, *Rebel Bishop,* see above, pp. 193–227, explains Bishop Verot's unusual conduct in Vatican Council I. John J. O'Shea, *The Two Kenricks, Most Rev. Francis Patrick, Archbishop of Baltimore, Most Rev. Peter Richard, Archbishop of St. Louis* (Philadelphia, 1904) is not scholarly but does add some information on Peter Richard Kenrick at the Council as well as in the controversy over the Drake Oath.

CHAPTER NINE

Bishop Bayley had been a successful Bishop in Newark. Sister M. Hildegarde Yeager, C.S.C., *The Life of James Roosevelt Bayley, the First Bishop of Newark and Eighth Archbishop of Baltimore 1814–1877* (Washington, 1947) indicates that Bayley was a very competent man held in check by serious illness during his years in Baltimore. There are two important Roman documents issued for the Church in the United States during this period: the Instruction of 1875 of the Sacred Congregation of Propaganda on the "Public Schools," *The Pastor* (June 1886) IV, 232–237, and the Instruction of 1878 of the same Congregation on "The Method to be Observed by the Bishops of the United States of America in Examining into and Deciding Criminal and Disciplinary Cases of Ecclesiastics," *The Pastor* (April 1883) I, 170–178.

The question of the Catholic Indian Missions and government support has been examined by Father Peter J. Rahill, *The Catholic Indian Missions and Grant's Peace Policy 1870–1884* (Washington, 1953). John Cardinal Farley, *The Life of John Cardinal McCloskey, First Prince of the Church in America 1810–1885* (New York, 1918) contains a few documents of value; John Talbot Smith, *The Catholic Church in New York* (New York, 1870) I, 276–328, and II, 329–413, has a better account of the Church in the area.

On the question of secret societies at the time Fergus Macdonald, *The Catholic Church and Secret Societies* (New York, 1946) pp. 32–149, is informative and William D'Arcy, O.F.M., *The Fenian Movement in the United States: 1858–1886* (Washington, 1947) considers one of its important phases.

John Tracy Ellis, *The Life of James Cardinal Gibbons, Archbishop of Baltimore 1834–1921,* 2 vol. (Milwaukee, 1952) I, 72–202, is informative about the Church in the Carolinas and Virginia and Gibbons' first year as Archbishop.

The *Acta et Decreta Concilii Plenarii Baltimorensis Tertii* (Baltimore, 1886), like all the decrees of the Baltimore Councils, were left in Latin except for a few passages translated on occasions. An exception was the Pastoral in that volume, pp. lxviii–ci. *The Memorial Volume, A History of the Third Plenary Council of Baltimore, November 9–December 7, 1884* (Baltimore, 1885) contains, besides the Pastoral, most of the sermons preached on the occasion of the Council. The best account of the Third Plenary Council is that by Ellis, see above, I, 203–290. Frederick J. Zwierlein, *The Life and Letters of Bishop McQuaid, Prefaced with the History of Catholic Rochester Before His Episcopate,* 3 vol. (Rochester, 1926) gives a wealth of original letters and other documents and writes of this period from the viewpoint of his hero. He treats the Third Plenary Council, II, 289–344. Zwierlein's smaller volume, *Letters of Archbishop Corrigan to Bishop McQuaid and Allied Documents* (Rochester, 1946) contains documents he did not have when he wrote the McQuaid biography.

CHAPTER TEN

The sermons of the Council are in *The Memorial Volume, A History of the Third Plenary Council of Baltimore, November 9–December 7, 1884* (Baltimore, 1885).

Colman J. Barry, O.S.B., *The Catholic Church and German Americans* (Milwaukee, 1953) is the best account of the German-American Catholics and particularly of the events related to the intervention of Peter Paul Cahensly; James Moynihan, *The Life of Archbishop John Ireland* (New York, 1953) defends the Archbishop's role in the controversy over nationalisms. William V. Shannon, *The American Irish* (New York, 1963) is laudatory and not always exact. He discusses the Irish Catholics of this era in "Chapter VIII, Cardinal Gibbons," pp. 114–130.

Aaron I. Abell, *American Catholicism and Social Action: A Search for Social Justice, 1865–1950* (New York, 1960) is a balanced story of the development of a social consciousness among American Catholics and treats this period before 1900, pp. 11–136. Aaron Abell, editor, *American Catholic Thought on Social Questions* (Indianapolis, 1968) documents his story. On the Knights of Labor and their relations with Catholicism, Henry J. Browne, *The Catholic Church and the Knights of Labor* (Washington, 1949) pp. 34–378, has the most complete documentation.

Daniel F. Reilly, O.P., *The School Controversy (1891–1893)* (Washington, 1943) is definitely on the side of Archbishop Ireland and should be read in conjunction with Frederick J. Zwierlein, *The Life and Letters of Bishop McQuaid, Prefaced with the History of Catholic Rochester before His Episcopate*, 3 vol. (Rochester, 1926) III, 160–251; Moynihan, *Ireland*, see above, pp. 79–103; and John Tracy Ellis, *The Life of James Cardinal Gibbons, Archbishop of Baltimore, 1834–1921*, 2 vol. (Milwaukee, 1952) I, 653–707. Important documents on the relations between Catholic and public schools can be found in the *Journal of Proceedings and Addresses of the National Educational Association; Session of the Year 1889 Held at Nashville, Tennessee* (Topeka, 1889) pp. 111–189, which gives the speeches and discussion of Cardinal Gibbons, Bishop John J. Keane, Edwin D. Meade and John Jay; *Session of the Year 1890 Held at St. Paul, Minnesota* (Topeka, 1890) contains the speech of Archbishop Ireland, one by Oscar Cooper, and the discussion following both papers. On the factual history of the Catholic school system, the two volumes of James A. Burns, C.S.C., *Principles, Origin and Establishment of the Catholic School System in the United States* (New York, 1908) and *Growth and Development of the Catholic School System in the United States* (New York, 1912) are old but not yet displaced. Ellis, *Gibbons*, see above, I, gives a chapter to each of these major problems: on Gibbons' reception of the Cardinal's hat, pp. 291–330, on the founding of the Catholic University, pp. 389–485, on the nationalistic controversy, pp. 331–438, on secret societies, pp. 439–485, and on the Knights of Labor, pp. 486–547.

CHAPTER ELEVEN

The chief anti-Catholic organization of the late nineteenth century in the United States was the American Protective Association, about which Donald L. Kinzer, *An Episode in Anti-Catholicism: The American Protective Association* (Seattle, 1964) has written. Kinzer has been very objective in assaying the causes of this phenomenon. William J. Lallou, *The Fifty Years of the Apostolic Delegation* (Washington, 1943) contains pertinent dates and names and a few documents. Robert Cross, *The Emergence of Liberal Catholicism in America* (Cambridge, 1958) is a sympathetic study of American Catholicism during this period.

The most complete treatment of the Parliament of Religions, including a survey of the Catholic Columbian Congress, is that edited by the Reverend John Henry Burrows, *The World's Parliament of Religions. An Illustrated and Popular History of the World's First Parliament of Religions, Held in Chicago in Connection with the Columbian Exposition of 1893*, 2 vol. For the Catholic activities, there is the badly edited *Progress of the Catholic Church in America and the Catholic Columbian Congress of 1893*, 2 vol. in 1 (4th ed., Chicago, 1897). Sister M. Sevina Pahorezki, O.S.F., *The Social and Political Activities of William James Onahan* (Washington, 1942) tells the story of the lay Congresses in the life of Onahan.

The important sermons of Archbishop John Ireland are mostly in two volumes, *The Church and Modern Society* (Chicago, 1903–1904), among them "The Church and the Age," I, 105–134.

The series of controversies more or less known as "Americanism" have been treated by Thomas T. McAvoy, C.S.C., *The Great Crisis in American Catholic History 1895–1900* (Chicago, 1957), reprinted without the first and last chapters and the appendix as *The Americanist Heresy in Roman Catholicism, 1895–1900* (Notre Dame, 1963).

James Moynihan, *The Life of Archbishop John Ireland* (New York, 1953) pp. 104–135; John Tracy Ellis, *The Life of James Cardinal Gibbons, Archbishop of Baltimore, 1834–1921*, 2 vol. (Milwaukee, 1952) II, 1–80; Frederick J. Zwierlein, *The Life and Letters of Bishop McQuaid, Prefaced with the History of Catholic Rochester before His Episcopate*, 3 vol. (Rochester, 1926) III, 160–251; and Patrick Henry Ahern, *The Life of John J. Keane, Educator and Archbishop, 1839–1918* (Milwaukee, 1955) pp. 87–290 offer other treatments of the controversies of the day.

Of the contemporary literature, Charles Maignen's book has been translated into English, *Studies in Americanism—Father Hecker, Is He a Saint?* (Paris and Rome, 1898), and the original biography of Hecker, *The Life of Father Hecker* (New York, 1891) has interest if read after a study of the controversy. For the years between the condemnation of Americanism and the condemnation of Modernism there is no special volume. Ellis, *Gibbons*, see above, II, 81–650 treats the last five decades of Gibbons sympathetically. Thomas T. McAvoy has outlined the period in "The Catholic Minority After the Americanist Controversy, 1899–1917: A Survey," *Review of Politics* (1959) XXI, 53–82. Robert North, S.J., "The American Scripture Century," *The American Ecclesiastical Review* (1964) CL, 314–345, treats of the more theological aspects of the period. On the origins of the Federation of Catholic Societies, the chief effort at united action during the period, the definitive study is the unpublished doctoral dissertation at the University of Notre Dame by Sister M. Adele Francis Gorman, O.S.F., "Federation of Catholic Societies in the United States 1870–1920" (Notre Dame, 1962). On any American beginnings or developments of Modernism there is no separate study. John A. Ryan, *Social Doctrine in Action* (New York, 1941) pp. 9–99 treats of the origins of his important apostolate in the field of social reform. Peter E. Hogan, *The Catholic University of America, 1896–1903: The Rectorship of Thomas J. Conaty* (Washington, 1949) and Colman J. Barry, *The Catholic University of America, 1903–1909: The Rectorship of Denis J. O'Connell* (Washington, 1950) give clear indications of the internal disorders that rendered the University ineffective.

CHAPTER TWELVE

Sister Adele Francis Gorman, "Federation of Catholic Societies," (unpublished doctoral dissertation, University of Notre Dame) pp. 108–319, is the basic story of this era, because the failure of the Federation is symbolic of the Catholic efforts to unite before World War I. John Philip Gleason, "The Central-Verein, 1900–1917: A Chapter in the History of the German-American Catholics" (unpublished doctoral dissertation at the University of Notre Dame, 1960), discusses the activities of one of the larger Catholic groups of the country during this time. His *The Conservative Reformers* (Notre Dame, 1968) concentrates on the German Catholic conservatives.

Aaron I. Abell, *American Catholicism and Social Action, A Search for Social Justice, 1865–1950* (New York, 1960) Chapter V, "Not Socialism but Social Reform, 1900–1917," pp. 137–188, is the best summary of this subject. Probably the most important leaders in the application to American society of the *Rerum Novarum* of Pope Leo XIII were John A. Ryan, *Social Doctrine in Action* (New York, 1941) pp. 62–142, and Peter E. Dietz, who is discussed in Mary Harrita Fox, *Peter E. Dietz, Labor Priest* (Notre Dame, 1953) pp. 22–172. They are treated also by Sister Adele Francis Gorman and Gleason, see above.

There is no satisfactory account of American Catholic activity in World War I. Michael Williams, *American Catholics in the War, National Catholic Welfare Council, 1917–1921* (New York, 1921) lists the committees and groups that participated in the formation of the National Catholic War Council, but the volume is not critically written. Maurice Francis Egan and John B. Kennedy, *The Knights of Columbus in Peace and War,* 2 vol. (New Haven, 1920) has the letter of the Archbishops in April 1917 and some useful statistics, but is not a real history. George J. Waring, *Catholic United States Chaplains in the World War* (New York, 1924) is mostly statistical with some brief biographies of the chaplains and their superiors.

The transition from a National Catholic War Council to the National Catholic Welfare Council is outlined in brief in "The September Meeting of the American Hierarchy," *American Ecclesiastical Review* (1919) LXI, 1–19, but the full story has not been told. Ryan, *Social Doctrine,* see above, pp. 143–159, gives the origin of the "Bishops' Program of Social Reconstruction," but that program must be distinguished from the "Pastoral Letter of 1919," which is a much longer document. The nearest to an official source of information concerning Catholic activities during the period between the two world wars is the *National Catholic War Council Bulletin,* later to be the *National Catholic Welfare Council Bulletin,* the *National Catholic Welfare Conference,* and *Catholic Action.*

For the story of the Eucharistic Congress in Chicago, the official record is *The Story of the Twenty-Eighth International Eucharistic Congress Held at Chicago, Illinois, United States of America from June 20 to 24, 1926,* compiled by C. F. Donovan (Chicago, 1927). The contemporary biographies of several prelates published during the prosperous years of the 1920s are uncritical and are useful chiefly for names and dates.

The Directory of Catholic Colleges and Schools, compiled by James H.

Ryan (Washington, 1921) is a very useful document on Catholic education at the beginning of the third decade of the century but needs interpretation.

A satisfactory account of the rise of Alfred E. Smith of New York and the presidential campaign of 1928 has not been written. Oscar Handlin, *Al Smith and His America* (Boston, 1958) is the most scholarly account. Ruth C. Silva, *Rum, Religion and Votes: 1928 Re-examined* (Pennsylvania State University Press, 1962) is one of the latest attempts to reassess the data.

Directory of Catholic Colleges and Schools for 1930 (Washington, 1930) is a good statistical survey of Catholic education before the depression but lacks any critical evaluation of the institutions.

Abell, *Catholicism and Social Action,* see above, pp. 188–233, surveys the Catholic social activity from World War I to the depression. Ryan, *Social Doctrine in Action* (New York, 1941) pp. 159–232, tells of his participation in the battles for social and economic reform during the twenties. Charles J. Tull, *Father Coughlin and the New Deal* (Syracuse, 1965) continues a careful analysis of available sources, but the author was not permitted to see Father Charles Coughlin's own correspondence. George Q. Flynn, *American Catholics and the Roosevelt Presidency 1932–1936* (Lexington, 1968) is written from the viewpoint of politics. David J. O'Brien, *American Catholics and Social Reform The New Deal Years* (New York, 1968) pays better attention to the religious aspects.

CHAPTER THIRTEEN

There is no adequate study of American Catholicism during the depression, World War II, and since. *Catholic Action* continued to be a source of official statements until 1953, when it ceased publication. Perhaps more official were the pastorals and statements of the bishops. Those before 1952 are in *Our Bishops Speak . . . 1919–1951* with a foreword and notes by Raphael M. Huber, O.F.M. Conv. (Milwaukee, 1952). John A. Ryan, *Social Doctrine in Action* (New York, 1941) pp. 233–290, contains his recollections of the New Deal. Charles J. Tull concentrates on Father Coughlin, *Father Coughlin and the New Deal* (Syracuse, 1965) pp. 23–238. Aaron I. Abell, *American Catholicism and Social Action, A Search for Social Justice, 1865–1950* (New York, 1960) pp. 234–285, surveys Catholic social action through the depression and World War II.

Undoubtedly the most important single volume for the period is Robert I. Gannon, *The Cardinal Spellman Story* (New York, 1962). The exchanges between the Archbishop of New York and President Roosevelt are carefully narrated, pp. 90–248. The Cardinal's postwar activities are treated, pp. 249–423.

Catholic activities have become more and more matters of general news. Encyclicals, the bishops' pastorals, and similar documents were usually printed in full and in such newspapers as *The New York Times* and discussed not only in the daily and weekly press but in magazines of public opinion. The chief Catholic magazines of opinion during the period were *America* and *Commonweal.* The local Catholic weekly newspaper usually chronicled the local news, used the releases sent from the Washington News Bureau of the National Catholic Welfare Council, and, in editorial opinion, expressed the views of the local ordinary. The Catholic newspaper was in general too costly to be conducted as a personal enterprise, and when in doubt the editors usually said nothing on controversial items.

CHAPTER FOURTEEN

The growing literature about Pope John XXIII, the *aggiornamento,* and the Second Vatican Council has not necessarily improved our understanding of the events that have been taking place since 1958. No one really knows the factors in the papal election of 1958. No one expected Pope John XXIII to conquer the world by his personality. The wisest critics still hesitate to evaluate Pope Paul VI.

In the United States there is an almost parallel story of John F. Kennedy from 1958 to 1963. There are many analyses of the election and estimates of the critical issues and events, but the tragedy of the assassination has checked critical estimates of John F. Kennedy's political victory or the real value of his unusual international triumphs. The two most important biographies are Arthur M. Schlesinger, *A Thousand Days* (Boston, 1965) and Theodore C. Sorensen, *Kennedy* (New York, 1965). On the effect his election had on American Catholicism and on the American attitude toward the Catholic Church, Lawrence H. Fuchs, *John F. Kennedy and American Catholicism* (New York, 1967) is premature.

American religious attention was drawn to the drama of the Vatican Council. The official news bulletins of the N.C.W.C. Press Bureau were not very informative. Suddenly under the pen name, "Xavier Rynne," there appeared in *The New Yorker* (Dec. 29, 1962) pp. 34–59, "Letters from Vatican City" in which the "inside" story of the Council was told and the activities of the American prelates were described with some humor and acidity. There were subsequent letters also. The four volumes, one for each session, were: Xavier Rynne, *Letters from Vatican City* (New York, 1963); *The Second Session* (New York, 1964); *The Third Session* (New York, 1965); and *The Fourth Session* (New York, 1966). There followed some guesswork about the identity of the author, but there were probably several writers.

Other critical accounts of the Council followed after the close of the First Session. The "letters" during the second session lost some of their startling nature. Some other accounts of the Council were bitter. Vincent A. Yzermans, editor, *American Participation in the Second Vatican Council* (New York, 1967) contains all the actual interventions of American members of the Council. There was genuine sympathy and grief in the United States at the sickness and death of Pope John and some measured criticism of Pope Paul VI. One effect of the critical writings about the Council in the United States seemed to be a rash of writings critical of the American Church.

Index

Abbelen, Peter, presents petition of German priests to Propaganda, 273; Denis O'Connell warns American hierarchy of his petition, 273, 274

Abolitionism opposed by Irish Catholics, 181; not supported by Catholic theology, 183, 185

Acadians, expelled from Canada, come to English colonies along the coast, 27–28; many reached Louisiana where they settled in Evangeline country, 28

Adams, John, describes a Catholic service in Philadelphia on October 9, 1774, 38–39

Agretti, Abbate Claudio, reported on the condition of Catholics in the English colonies, 14

Aid to Catholic schools opposed by state constitutions, 237; by Blaine Amendment that passed the House of Representatives, 238; Catholic attitude on, changed in 1940s, 446

Albany, New York, Scotch Catholics with their chaplain Father John McKenna settled near, in 1773, 35; retreat to Canada in the Revolution, 35

American Academy of Christian Democracy for Women formed by Father Peter E. Dietz in Hot Springs, North Carolina, 361; moved to Cincinnati in 1917, 361

American Catholicism in the late nineteenth century, 247, 248; characteristics of, in the decade after the condemnation of Americanism, 336, 337; as described by Henry D. Sedgwick in October, 1899, 337–338; after World War I, 388–391

American Party, national name for Know-Nothing Party, 169

American Protective Association arises out of traditional prejudices plus new occurrences, 314

Americanism described by Msgr. Denis O'Connell at Fribourg Scientific Congress, 327; name given to the opinions ascribed to the advocates of Father Hecker in France, 328; described as a threat to the Church in articles in *La Vérité* and book of Abbé Charles Maignen, 329–330; condemned by papal letter *Testem Benevolentiae*, 333; American Catholicism in the decade after the condemnation of, 334–341